M000233152

MOUNTAIN OF FIRE AND MIRACLES MINISTRIES

GOSPEL HYMN BOOK

Headquarters

13, Olasimbo Street, Off Olumo Road,
By University of Lagos 2nd Gate, Onike
P.O. Box 2990, Sabo, Yaba,
Lagos, Nigeria.
01-4703737, 01-47087759
08037348882

A Publication of
Mountain of Fire and Miracle Ministries

Obtainable at
MFM Bookshop
13, Olasimbo Street, Off Olumo Road,
By University of Lagos 2nd Gate, Onike
Sabo, Yaba, Lagos, Nigeria.

PREFACE AND COPYRIGHT ACKNOWLEDGMENT

"Bless the LORD, O my soul: and all that is with me, bless his holy name" (Psalm 103:1).

My heart is filled with joy as I present to you the Mountain of Fire and Miracle Ministries Hymn Book. The hymns have been selected from a wide variety of hymnbooks which have been in use by Christians from time immemorial and from some recent hymnal.

The Mountain of Fire Miracles Ministries believes in singing old and new hymn and gospel songs.

A lot of efforts have gone into the production of this hymn book. The hymns and gospel songs have been specially chosen to bring out "the best"

The production of any hymnbook is a considerable undertaking. I take this opportunity to express my thanks all who assisted in one form or the other. I knowledge with considerable gratitude the received from Brother Remi Collins.

I pray that each verse and word in these hymn and gospel songs be charged with fire of the Holy Ghost and bless the users.

Dr. D. K. Olukoya
General Overseer

TABLE OF CONTENTS

i

HOLY TRINITY

1

Wells - 7.7.7.7.7.7.

1. Father, Son, and Holy Ghost,
One in Three, and Three in One,

   As by celestial host,
   Let Thy will on earth be done;
   Praise by all to Thee be given,
   Glorious Lord of earth and heaven.

2. If a sinner such as I
May to Thy great glory live,
All my actions sanctify,
All my words and thoughts receive;
Claim me for Thy service, claim
All I have and all I am.

3. Take my soul and body's powers;
Take my memory, mind, and will,
All my goods, and all my hours,
All I know, and all I feel,
All I think, or speak, or do;
Take my heart; but make it new.

4. O my God, Thine own I am,
Let me give Thee back Thine own;
Freedom, friends, and health, and
Fame,
Consecrate to Thee alone;
Thine to live, thrice happy I;
Happier still if Thine I die.

5. Father, Son, and Holy Ghost.
One in Three, and Three in One.
As by the celestial host,
Let Thy will on earth be done;
Praise by all to Thee be given.
Glorious Lord of earth and heaven.
                    -Charles Wesley

2

Capetown 7.7:7.5.

1. Three in One, and One in Three,
Ruler of the earth and sea,
Hear us. while we lift to thee
Holy chart and psalm.

2. Light of lights! With morning shine;
Lift on us thy light divine;
And let charity begin
Breathe on us her balm.

3. Light of lights! when falls the even,
Let it close on sin forgiven;
Fold us in the peace of heaven;
Shed a holy calm.

4. Three in One and One in Three,
Dimly here we worship thee;
With the saints hereafter we
Hope to bear the palm.
                    -G Rorison

3

Crofts -6.6.6.6.8.8.

1. We give immortal praise
To God the Father's love,
For all our comforts here,
And better hopes above.
He sent His own eternal Son,
To die for sins that man had done.

2. To God the Son belongs
Immortal glory too,
Who bought us with His blood
From everlasting woe;
And now He lives, and now He
reigns,
And sees the fruit of all His pains.

3. To God the Spirits name
Immortal worship give,
Whose new-creating power
Makes the dead sinner live.
His work completes the great
design,
And fills the soul with joy divine.

4. Almighty God, to Thee
Be endless honours done,
The undivided Three.
And the mysterious One.
Where reason fails, with all her
Powers,
There faith prevails and love
Adores.
                    -Isaac Watts

HOLY TRINITY

4.

Worcester -8.7.8.7.4.

1. Glory be to God the Father
   Glory be to God the Son,
   Glory be to God the Spirit,
   Great Jehovah, Three in One:
   Glory, glory,
   While eternal ages run!

2. Glory be to Him who loved us,
   Wash'd us from each spot and
   stain;
   Glory be to Him who bought us,
   Made us kings with Him to reign:
   Glory, glory.
   To the Lamb that once was slain!;

3. Glory to the King of angels,
   Glory to the church's King,
   Glory to the King of the nations;
   Heaven and earth your praises
   bring:
   Glory, glory,
   To the King of glory bring!

4. Glory, blessing, praise eternal,
   Thus the choir of angels sings;
   Honour, riches', power, dominion
   Thus its praise creation brings:
   Glory glory
   Glory to the King of kings!
   -W. G. Whinfield

5.

Groningen.6.8.6.6.8.3.3.6.6.

1. God is in His temple
   The Almighty Father,
   Round His footstool let us gather:
   Him with adoration
   Serve, the Lord most holy,
   Who hath mercy on the lowly;
   Let us raise
   Hymns of praise
   For His great salvation:
   God is in His temple

2. Christ comes to His temple:
   We, His word receiving,
   Are made happy in believing;
   Lo! from sin delivered,
   He hath turned our sadness,
   Our deep gloom, to light and
   gladness;
   Let us raise
   Hymns of praise,
   For our bonds are severed:
   Christ comes to His temple

3. Come and claim thy temple
   Gracious Holy Spirit,
   In our hearts. Thy home inherit;
   Make in us Thy dwelling,
   Thy high work fulfilling,
   Into ours Thy will instilling;
   Till we raise
   Hymns of praise,
   Beyond mortal telling,
   In the eternal temple.
   -William Tidd Matson

6.

Dunfermline - C.M.

1. Hail! Holy, holy, holy Lord
   Whom One in Three we know;
   By all Thy heavenly host adored;
   By all Thy Church below.

2. One undivided Trinity
   With triumph we proclaim;
   Thy universe is full of Thee,
   And speaks Thy glorious name.

3. Thee, Holy Father, we confess,
   Thee, Holy Son, adore,
   Thee, Spirit of truth and holiness,
   We worship evermore.

4. Three Persons equally divine
   We magnify and love;
   And both the choirs ere tong shall
   To sing Thy praise above. , .

5. Hail holy, holy, holy Lord,
   our heavenly song shall be,
   Supreme, essential One, adored
   In co-eternal Three.   Amen.

HOLY TRINITY

7

Rivaulx - L.M.

1. Father of heaven, whose love
profound
A ransom for our souls hath
found,
Before Thy throne we sinners bend;
To us Thy pardoning love extend.

2. Almighty Son, incarnate Word,
our prophet, Priest, Redeemer,
Lord,
Before Thy throne we sinners bend;
To us Thy saving grace extend.

3. Eternal Spirit, by whose breath
The soul is raised from sin and
death,
Before Thy throne we sinners bend,
To us Thy quickening power extend.

4 Thrice holy; Father; Spirit, Son;
Mysterious Godhead, Three in One,
Before Thy throne we sinners bend;
Grace, pardon, life to us extend.

Edward Cooper

8

Italian hymn - 6.6.4.6.6.6.4.

1. Come, Thou Almighty King,
Help us Thy name to sing,
Help us to praise:
Father! all-glorious,
O'er all victorious.
Come, and reign over us,
Ancient of Days.

2. Come, Thou Incarnate
Word,
Gird on Thy mighty sword,
Our prayer attend! , ,
Come, and Thy people
bless,
And give Thy word success:
Spirit of holiness,
On us descend.

3. Come, Holy Comforter,
Thy sacred witness bear
In this glad hour!
Thou, who almighty art,
Now rule in ev'ry heart
And ne'er from us depart,
Spirit of pow'r.

4. To Thee, great One in
Three,
Eternal praises be,
Hence evermore;
Thy sov'reign majesty
May we in glory see,
And to eternity
love and adore.

Source unknown

9

EIN'FESTE BURG 878766667

1. A mighty fortress is our God,
   A bulwark never falling;
   Our helper He amid the flood
   Of mortal ills prevailing.
   For still our ancient be
   Doth seek to work us woe
   His craft and pow'r are great,
   And, armed with cruel hate,
   On earth is not his equal.

2. Did we in our own strength confide
   Our striving would be losing,
   Were not the right Man on our side,
   The Man of God's own choosing.
   Dost ask who that may be?
   Christ Jesus, it is He-
   Lord Saba-oth His name,
   From age to age the same -
   And He must win the battle.

3. And tho this world, with devil filled,
   Should threaten to undo us,
   We will not fear. for God hath willed
   His truth to triumph through us.
   The prince of darkness grim -
   We tremble not for him;
   His rage we can endure,
   For lo! his doom is sure-
   One little word shall fell him.

4. That word above all earthly pow'rs
   No thanks to them - abideth;
   The Spirit and the gifts are ours
   Through Him who with us sideth.
   Let goods and kindred go,
   This mortal life also:
   The body they may kill:
   God's truth abideth still-
   His kingdom is forever.

   -Martin Luther

10

ODE TO JOY

1. Joyful, joyful, we adore Thee,
   God of glory, Lord of love;
   Hearts unfold like flow'rs before
   Thee, Hail Thee as the sun above.

Melt the clouds of sin and
sadness;
Drive the dark of doubt away;
Giver of immortal gladness,
Fill us with the light of day!

2. All Thy works with joy surround
   Thee,
   Earth and heaven reflect Thy
   rays,
   Stars and angels sing around
   Thee,
   Centre of unbroken praise;
   Field and forest, vale and moun
   tain,
   Bioss'ming meadow, flashing
   sea,
   Chanting bird and flowing
   fountain,
   Call us to rejoice in Thee.

3. Thou art giving and forgiving,
   Ever blessing, ever blest,
   Well spring of the joy of living,
   Ocean depth of happy rest!
   Thou our Father, Christ our
   Brother
   All who live in love are Thine;
   Teach us how to love each other,
   Lift us to the Joy Divine.

4. Mortals join the mighty chorus
   Which the morning stars began;
   Father love is reigning o'er us,
   Brother love binds man to man.
   Ever singing, march we onward,
   Victors in the midst of strife;
   Joyful music lifts us sunward
   In the triumph song of life.

   Henry Van Dyke

11

All Hail, Immanuel

1. All hail to Thee. Immanuel.
   We cast our crowns before Thee;
   Let ev'ry heart obey Thy will,
   And ev'ry voice adore Thee.
   In praise to Thee, our Saviour
   King,
   The vibrant chords of Heaven ring,
   And echo back the mighty strain:
   All hail! All hail All hail! All hail
   Immanuel

WORSHIP AND ADORATION

Chorus
Hail! (Hail to the King we love so well)
Immanuel! Immanuel
Hail (Hail to the King we love so well!)
Immanuel! Immanuel!
Glory and honour and majesty,
Wisdom and power be unto Thee,
Now and ever more;
Hail! (Hail to the King we love so well!)
Immanuel! Immanuel!
Hail! (Hail to the King we love so well!)
Immanuel! Immanuel!
King of kings and Lord of Lords,
All hail, Immanuel!

2. All hail to Thee, Immanuel,
The ransomed hosts surround Thee;
And earthly monarchs?
Their Sov'reign King to crown Thee.
While those redeemed in ages gone,
Assembled round the great white throne,
Break forth into immortal song:
All hail! All hail! All hail! All hail!
Immanuel!

3. All hail to Thee, Immanuel,
Our risen King and Saviour!
Thy foes are vanquished, and
Thou art Omipotent forever.
Death, sin and hell no longer reign,
And Satan's pow'r is burst in twain:
Eternal glory to Thy Name:
All hail! All hail! All hail! All hail)
Immanuel
                        -D.R. Van Sickle

12

Old Hundredth-LM
1. All people that on earth do dwell,
Sing to the Lord-with cheerful Voice.
Him serve with fear. His praise forthtell,
Come ye before Him and rejoice.

2. Know that the Lord is God indeed:
Without our aid He did us make;
We are His folk. He doth us feed,
And for His sheep He doth us take.

3. O enter then His gates with praise,
Approach with joy His courts unto;
Praise, laud and bless His name always,
For it is seemly so to do.

4. For why? the Lord our God is good,
His mercy is forever sure;
His truth at all times firmly stood,
And shall from age to age endure.
                        -Psalm 100

13

Glorious Name - 8.7.8.7.
with Refrain

1. Blessed Saviour, we adore Thee,
We Thy love and grace proclaim;
Thou art mighty, Thou art holy,
Glorious is Thy matchless name!

Chorus
Glorious (Glorious is Thy name, O Lord!)
Glorious (Glorious is Thy name, O Lord!)
Glorious is Thy name, O Lord)
Glorious
(Glorious is Thy name, O Lord!)
Glorious (Glorious is Thy name, O Lord!)
Glorious is Thy name, O Lord!

2. Great Redeemer, Lord and Master,
Light of all eternal days;
Let the saints of ev'ry nation Sing
Thy just and endless praise!

3. From the throne of heaven's glory
To the cross of sin and shame,
Thou didst come to die a ransom,
Guilty sinners to reclaim!

WORSHIP AND ADORATION

4. Come, O come, Immortal Saviour,
Come and take Thy royal throne;
Come, and reign, and reign
forever,
Be the kingdom all Thine own!
-B. B. McKinney

14

Harts - 7.7.7.7.

1. Brethren, let us join to bless
Christ, the Lord our righteousness;
Let our praise to Him be given,
High at God's right hand in heaven.

2. Son of God. to Thee we bow;
Thou art Lord, and only Thou;
Thou the blessed virgin's seed,
Glory of Thy church, and head.

3. Thee the angels ceaseless sing;
Thee we praise, our Priest and
King;
Worthy is Thy name of praise,
Full of glory, full of grace.

4. Thou hast the glad tidings brought
Of salvation by Thee wrought:
Wrought to set Thy people free,
Wrought to bring our souls to
Thee.

5. May we follow and adore
Thee, our Saviour, more and more:
Guide and bless us with Thy love,
Till we join Thy saints above.
-J. Cennick

15

Harewood -6.6.6.6.4.4.4.4.

1. Christ is our corner-stone,
On him alone we build;
With his true saints alone
The courts of heaven are filled;
On his great love
Our hopes we place
Of present grace
And joys above.

2. O then with hymns of praise
These hallowed courts shall ring;
Our voices we will raise
The Three in One to sing;
And thus proclaim In joyful song,
Both loud and long,
That glorious name.

3. Here, gracious God, do thou
For evermore draw nigh;
Accept each faithful vow,
And mark each suppliant sigh;
In copious shower
On all who pray
Each holy day
Thy blessings pour

4. Here may we gain from heaven
The grace which we implore;
And may that grace, once given,
Be with us evermore;
Until that day
When all the blest
To endless rest
Are called away.
-Tr. John Chandler

16

Lydia-C.M.

1. Come, let us join our cheerful
songs
With angels round the throne;
Ten thousand thousand are their
tongues
But all their joys are one,

2. "Worthy the Lamb that died," they
cry.
"To be exalted thus:"
"Worthy the Lamb," our lips reply,
"For He was slain for us."

3. Jesus is worthy to receive Honour
and power divine:
And blessings more than we can
give
Be, Lord, for ever Thine.

4. Let all that dwell above the sky.
And air, and earth, and seas,
Conspire to lift Thy glories high,
And speak Thine endless praise.

5. The whole creation join in one,
To bless the sacred name
Of Him that sits upon that throne,
And to adore the Lamb.
-Isaac Watts

17

Day is Dying In the West

1. Day is dying in the west,
Heav'n is touching earth with
rest;
Wait and worship while the night
Sets her evening lamps alight
Thro' all the sky.

Chorus
Holy, Holy, Holy,
Lord God of Hosts!
Heav'n and earth are full of Thee!
Heav'n and earth are praising
Thee, O Lord Most High!

2. Lord of life, beneath the dome
Of the universe, Thy home
Gather us, who seek Thy face,
To the fold of Thy embrace,
For Thou art nigh.

3 While the deep'ning shadows fall,
Heart of Love, enfolding all,
Thro' the glory and the grace
Of the stars that veil Thy face,
Our hearts ascend.

4. When forever from our sight
Pass the star, the day, the night,
Lord of angels, on our eyes
Let eternal morning rise,
And shadows end!
-Mary A. Lathbury

18

Low Divine - 8.7.8.7.D.
1. God, our Father, we adore Thee!
We Thy children, bless Thy
name!
chosen in the Christ before Thee,
We are "holy without blame."

We adore Thee! we adore Thee!
Abba's praises we proclaim!
We adore Thee! We adore Thee!
Abba's praises we proclaim!

2. Son Eternal, we adore Thee!
Lamb upon the throne on high!
Lamb of God, we bow before Thee,
Thou hast bro't Thy people nigh!
We adore Thee! we adore Thee!
Son of God, who came to die!
We adore Thee! we adore Thee!
Son of God, who came to die!

3. Holy Spirit, we adore Thee!
Paraclete and heav'nly guest!
Sent from God and from the
Saviour,
Thou hast led us into rest.
We adore Thee! we adore Thee!
By Thy grace forever blest:
We adore Thee! we adore Thee!
Thee we bless, thro' endless days!

4. Father, Son, and Holy Spirit
Three in One! we give Thee praise!
For the riches we inherit,
Heart and voice to Thee we raise!
We adore Thee! we adore Thee!
Thee we bless, thro' endless days'
We adore Thee! we adore Thee!
Thee we bless, thro' endless days!
-George W. Frazer

19

Geneva -8.5.8.5.

1. God, who touchest earth with
beauty,
Make me lovely too;
With Thy Spirit recreate me,
Make my heart anew. .

2. Like Thy springs and running
waters,
Make me crystal pure,
Like Thy rocks of towering
grandeur
Make me strong and sure.

3 Like Thy shining waves in
sunlight, Make me glad and free;
Like the straightness of the pine
trees,
Let me upright be.

4. Like the arching of the heavens,
Lift my thoughts above;
Turn my dreams to noble action,
Ministries of love.

5. God, who touches! earth with beauty,
Make me lovely too;
Keep me ever, by Thy Spirit,
Pure and strong and true.
                    -Mary S: Edgar

20

Luckington -1.0.4.6.6.6.6.10.4.

1. Let all the world in every corner sing,
My God and King!'
The heavens are not too high, his praise may thither fly;
The earth is not too low,
his praises there may grow:
let all the world in every corner sing,
"My God and King!'

2. Let all the world in every corner sing,
My God and King!'
The church with psalms must shout no door can keep them out;
But above all, the heart
must bear the longest part:
let all the world in every corner sing,
My God and King!'
                    -G. Herbert

21

Rendez A Dieu- 9 8.9.8.D

1. New songs of celebration render
to him who has great wonders done;
Love sits enthroned in ageless splendour
come and adore the mighty one!
He has made known his great salvation
which all his friends with joy confess;
he has revealed to every nation
His everlasting righteousness.

2. Joyfully, heartily resounding,
let every instrument and voice
peal out the praise of grace abounding,
calling the whole world to rejoice.
Trumpets and organs, set in motion
such sounds as make the heavens ring;
all things that live in earth and ocean,
'make music for your mighty king.

3. Rivers and seas and torrents roaring, honour the Lord with wild acclaim;
mountains and stones look up adoring
and find a voice to praise his name.
Righteous, commanding, ever glorious,
praises be his that never cease:
just is our God, whose truth victorious
establishes the world in peace.
                    -Erik Routley

22

Blessed be the Name

1. O for a thousand tongues to sing,
Blessed be the name of the Lord!
The glories of my God and King,
Blessed be the name of the Lord!

Chorus
Blessed be the name,
Blessed be the name,
Blessed be the name of the Lord!
Blessed be the name,
Blessed be the name,
Blessed be the name of the Lord!

2. Jesus, the name that calms my fears,
Blessed be the name of the Lord!
'Tis music in the sinner's ears,
Blessed be the name of the Lord!

3. He breaks the power of canceled sin
Blessed be the name of the Lord!
His blood can make the foulest Clean,
Blessed be the name of the Lord!
                    -Charles Wesley

WORSHIP AND ADORATION

23

O Store God

1. O Lord my God, when I in
   awesome wonder
   Consider all the worlds Thy
   hands have made,
   I see the stars, I hear the rolling
   thunder,
   Thy pow'r thru-out the universe
   displayed!

   Chorus
   Then sings my soul, my Saviour
   God, to Thee;
   How great Thou art, how great
   Thou art!
   Then sings my soul, my Saviour
   God, to Thee;
   How great Thou art, how great
   Thou art!

2. When thru the woods and forest
   glades I wander
   And hear the birds sing sweetly in
   the trees.
   When I look down from lofty
   Mountain grandeur
   And hear the brook and feel
   the
   gentle breeze

3. And when I think that God, His
   Son not sparing,
   Sent Him to die, I scarce can take
   It in
   That on the cross, my burdens
   gladly bearing,
   He bled and died to take away
   my sin!

4. When Christ shall come with
   shout of acclamation
   And take me home, what joy
   shall fill my heart!
   Then I shall bow in humble
   adoration
   And there proclaim, my God,
   how great Thou art!
   -Cari Bober

24

Joyful Praise - 12.10.12.10.D.

1. Praise Him, Praise Him, Jesus our
   blessed Redeemer. Sing, O earth,
   His wonderful love proclaim.
   Hail Him! hail Him! highest
   archangels in glory,
   Strength and honour give to His
   holy name.
   Like a shepherd, Jesus will guard
   His children,
   In His arms He carries them all
   day long.
   O ye saints that dwell on the
   mountain of Zion,
   Praise Him praise Him ever in
   joyful song.

2. Praise Him, Praise Him, Jesus our
   blessed Redeemer,
   For our sins He suffer'd and bled
   and died;
   He, our rock, our hope of eternal
   Salvation,
   Hail Him Hail Him! Jesus the
   Crucified
   Loving Saviour, meekly enduring
   sorrow.
   Crown'd with thorns that cruelly
   pierc'd His brow;
   Once for us rejected, despis'd and
   forsaken.
   Prince of Glory, ever triumphant
   now.

3. Praise Him. Praise Him, Jesus our
   blessed Redeemer,
   Heav'nly portals, loud with
   hosannahs ring;
   Jesus, Saviour, reigneth forever
   and ever,
   Crown Him, crown Him, Prophet
   and Priest and King!
   Death is vanquish'd! Tell it with joy,
   ye faithful,
   Where is now thy victory, boasting
   grave?
   Jesus lives! no longer thy portals
   are cheerless,
   Jesus lives, the mighty and strong
   to save.
   -Fanny J. Crosby

WORSHIP AND ADORATION

25

Gerontius - C. M.

1. Praise to the Holiest in the height,
And in the depth be praise:
in all His words most wonderful,
Most sure in all His ways.

2. loving wisdom of our God!
When all was sin and shame,
A second Adam to the fight,
And to the rescue came,

3. O wisest love! that flesh and blood
Which did in Adam fall,
Should strive afresh against the foe,
Should strive, and should prevail.

4. And that a higher gift than grace
Should flesh and blood refine,
God's presence, and His very self
And essence all-divine.

5. O generous love! that He, who smote
In man for man the foe.
The double agony in man
For man should undergo.

6. And in the garden secretly,
And on the Cross on high,
Should teach His brethren, and Inspire
To suffer and to die.

7. Praise to the Holiest in the height,
And in the depth be praise:
In all His words most wonderful,
Most sure in all His ways.
                    -J. H. Newman

26

Laudate Dominum -10.10.11.11.

1. O praise to the Lord!
praise Him in the height;
rejoice in his word
you angels of light:
you heavens adore him
by whom you were made,
and worship before him
In brightness arrayed.

2. O praise ye the Lord!!
Praise Him upon earth
in tuneful accord,
you saints of new birth:
praise Him who has brought you
his grace from above;
praise him who has taught you
to sing of his love.

3. O priase ye the Lord!
all things that give sound,
each jubilant chord
re-echo around:
loud organs, his glory
proclaim in deep tone,
and sweet harp, the story
of what he has done.

4. O praise ye the Lord!
Thanksgiving and song
to him be outpoured
all ages along:
for love in creation,
for heaven restored,
For grace of salvation,
O praise ye the Lord!
                    -H. W Baker

27

Carlisle-S.M.

1. Stand up and bless the Lord,
Ye people of His choice:
Stand up and bless the Lord
your God
With heart and soul and voice.

2. Though high above all praise,
Above all blessing high,
Who would not fear His holy name,
And laud and magnify?

3. O for the living flame,
From His own altar brought,
To touch our lips, our minds inspire,
And wing to heaven our thought!

4. God is our strength and song,
And His salvation ours;
Then be His love in Christ -
proclaimed
With all our ransomed powers.

5. Stand up and bless the Lord.
The Lord your God adore;
Stand up and bless His glorious name,
Henceforth for evermore.
                    -J. Montgomery

28

The Spacious Firmament - L.M D

1. The Spacious firmament on high,
With all the blue, ethereal sky,
And spangled heavens, a shining frame,
Their great Original proclaim:
Th'unwearied sun, from day to day,
Does his Creator's power display;
And publishes, to every land
The work of an almighty hand.

2. Soon as the evening shades prevail,
The moon takes up the wondrous tale;
And nightly, to the listening earth,
Repeats the story of her birth;
While all the stars that round her burn,
And all the planets in their turn,
Confirm, the tidings as they roll,
And spread the truth from pole to pole

3. What though, in solemn silence,
all Move round the dark terrestrial ball?
What though no real voice nor sound
Amid their radiant: orbs be found?
In reason's ear they all rejoice,
And utter forth a glorious voice,
Forever singing as they shine,
"The hand that made us is divine."
                    -Joseph Addison

29

Quam dilecta -6.6.6.6.

1. We love the place, O God,
Where in Thine honour dwells,
The joy of Thine abode
All earthly joy excels.

2. We love the house of prayer,

Wherein Thy servants meet;
And Thou, O Lord, art there
Thy chosen flock to greet.

3. We love the sacred font,
For there the Holy Dove
Pours out, as He is wont,
His blessing from above.

4. We love the word of life.
The word that tells of peace,
Of comfort in the strife,
And joys that never cease.

5. We love our Father's board,
O what on earth so dear?
Where faithful hearts, O Lord,
Still find Thy presence near.

6. We love to sing below
for mercies freely given;
But O! we long to know
The triumph-song of heaven.

7. Lord Jesus, give us grace
On earth to love Thee more,
In heaven to see Thy face,
And with Thy saints adore.
                    -W. Bullock

30

Darwall's 148th-6.6.6.6.4.4.4.4.

1. Ye holy angels bright,
Who wait at Gods right hand.
Or through the realms of light
Fly at your Lord's command,
Assist our song,
Or else the theme
Too high doth seem
For mortal tongue.

2. Ye blessed souls at rest,
Who ran this earthly race,
And now, from sin released,
Behold the Saviour's face,
His praises sound,
As in His sight
With sweet delight
Ye do abound.

WORSHIP AND ADORATION

3. Ye saints, who toil below,
   Adore your heavenly King,
   And onward as ye go
   Some joyful anthem sing;
   Take what He gives
   And praise Him still,
   Through good and ill,
   Who ever lives!

4. My soul, bear thou thy part,
   Triumph in God above,
   And with a well-tuned heart
   Sing thou the songs of love!
   Let all thy days
   Till life shall end,
   Whate'er He send,
   Be filled with praise.

   -R. Baxter

31

Hanover-10.10.11.11.

1. Ye servants of God. Your Master proclaim,
   And publish abroad His wonderful name:
   The name all victorious of Jesus extol:
   His kingdom is glorious. And rules over all.

2. God ruleth on high, Almighty to save
   And still He is nigh, His presence we navel
   The great congregation His triumph shall sing,
   Ascribing salvation To Jesus our King.

3. Salvation to God, Who sits on the throne,
   Let all cry aloud, and honour the Son: The praises of Jesus All angels proclaim,
   Fall down on their faces. And worship the Lamb.

4. Then let us adore And give Him His right;
   All glory and power. All wisdom and might;
   All honour and blessing, With

angels above;
And thanks never-ceasing. And infinite love.

   -C. Wesley

32

Unser Herrher -8.7.8.7.8.7.

1. Alleluia! raise the anthem,
   let the skies resound with praise; .
   sing to Christ who brought salvation,
   wonderful his works and ways:
   God eternal. Word incarnate,
   whom the heaven of heavens obeys.

2. Long before he formed the mountains,   .
   Spread the seas or made the sky,
   love eternal, free and boundless,
   moved the Lord of life to die;
   fore-ordained the Prince of princes
   for the throne of Calvary.

3. There for us and our redemption
   see him all his life-blood pour,
   there he wins our full salvation,
   dies that we may die no more
   then arising lives forever,
   King of kings, whom we adore.

4. Praise and honour to the Father,
   praise and honour to the Son,
   praise and honour to the Spirit,
   ever three and ever one:
   one in grace and one in glory
   while eternal ages run!

   -J. Hupton

33

Tidings-10.10.10.14

1. Tell out, my soul, the greatness of the Lord!
   Unnumbered blessings, give my spirit voice,
   Tender to me the promise of His word;
   In God my Saviour shall my heart rejoice.

2. Tell out, my soul. the greatness of His name!

Make known his might, the deeds
His arm has done;
His mercy sure, from age to age
the same;
His holy name-the Lord, the
Mighty One.

3. Tell out, my soul, the greatness of
His Mighty!
Powers and dominions lay their
glory by.
Proud hearts and stubborn wills
are put to flight,
The hungry fed, the humble lifted
high.

4. Tell out, my soul, the glories of
His word!
Firm is His promise, and His
mercy sure.
Tell out, my soul, the greatness of
the Lord
To children's children and for
ever more!
                          -T. Dudley-Smith

34

University-C.M.

1. The God of love my shepherd is,
And he that doth me feed;
While he is mine and I am his,
What can I want or need?

2. He leads me to the tender grass,
Where I both feed and rest;
Then to the streams that gently
pass:
In both I have the best

3. Or if I stray, he doth convert,
And bring my mind in frame,
And all this not for my desert,
But for his holy name.

4. Yea. in death's shady black abode
Well may I walk, not fear,
For thou art with me, and thy rod
To guide, thy staff to bear.

5. Surely thy sweet and wondrous
love Shall measure all my days;
And, as it never shall remove,
So neither shall my praise.
                          -George Herbert

35

Ariel-8.8.6.8.8.6.6.

1. O could I speak the matchless
worth,
O could I sound the glories forth
Which in my Saviour shine, I'd
sing His glorious righteousness,
And magnify the wondrous grace
Which made salvation mine.
Which made salvation mine.

2. I'd sing the characters He bears,
And all the forms of love He
wears, Exalted on His throne:
In loftiest songs of sweetest praise,
I would to everlasting days
Make all His glories known,
Make all His glories known.

3. Soon the delightful day will come
When my dear Lord will bring me
home,
And I shall see His face;
Then with my Saviour, Brother,
Friend,
A blest eternity I'll spend,
Triumphant in His grace,
Triumphant in His grace.
                          -Samuel Medley

36

We're Marching to Zion

1. Come. Ye that love the Lord,
And let your joys be known;
Join in a song with sweet accord,
Join in a song with sweet accord,
And thus surround the throne,
And thus surround the throne.
Chorus
We're marching to Zion,
Beautiful, beautiful, Zion:
We're marching upward to Zion,
The beautiful city of God

2. Let those refuse to sing
Who never knew our God:
But children of the heav'nly King.
But children of the heav'nly King
Shall speak their joys abroad,
Shall speak their joys abroad.

3. The hill of zion yields
A thousand sacred sweets;
Before we reach the heav'nly
fields,
Before we reach the heav'nly
fields,
Or walk the golden streets,
Or walk the golden streets.

4. Then let our songs abound,
And ev'ry tear be dry;
We're marching thro' Immanuel's
ground,
We're marching thro' Immanuel's
ground
To fairer worlds on high,
To fairer worlds on high.
-Isaac Watts

37

Lasst Uns erfreuen L.M.
with Alleluias

1. All creatures of our God and King,
Lift up your voice and with us sing
Alleluia Alleluia
Thou burning sun with golden
beam,
Thou silver moon with softer
gleam,
O praise Him, O praise Him,
Alleluia, alleluia, alleluia'.

2. Thou rushing wind that art so
strong,
Ye clouds that sail in heav'n along,
O praise Him, Alleluia!
Thou rising morn in praise rejoice,
Ye lights of evening, find a voice,
O praise Him, O praise Him,
Alleluia, alleluia, alleluia!

3. Thou flowing water, pure and clear,
Make music for thy Lord to hear,
Alleluia, Alleluia!
Thou fire so masterful and bright,
That givest man both warmth and
light,
O praise Him, O praise Him,
Alleluia, alleluia, alleluia!

4. And all ye men of tender heart,
For giving others, take your part,

O sing ye, Alleluia!
Ye who long pain and sorrow bear,
Praise God and on Him cast your
care,
O praise Him, O praise Him,
Alleluia, alleluia alleluia!

5. Let all things their Creator bless,
And worship Him in humbleness,
O praise Him, Alleluia!
Praise, praise the Father, praise
the Son,
And praise the Spirit, Three in
One,
O praise Him, O praise Him,
Alleluia, alleluia, alleluia!
-St. Francis of Assist;

38

Coronation - C.M. with Repeats

1. All hail the pow'r of Jesus' name!
Let angels prostrate fall;
Bring forth the royal diadem,
And crown Him Lord of all;

2. Crown Him, ye martyrs of our God
who from His altar call;
Extol Him in whose path ye trod
And crown; Him Lord of all.

3. Ye chosen seed of Israel's race,
Ye ransomed from the fall, Hail
Him who saves you by His
Grace,
And crown Him Lord of all;

4. sinners! whose love can ne'er
forget
The wormwood and the gall;
Go spread your trophies at His feet
And crown Him Lord of all.

5. Let ev'ry kindred, ev'ry tribe,
On this terrestrial ball,
To Him all majesty ascribe,
And crown Him Lord of all;

6. O that with yonder sacred throng
We at His feet may fall.
We'll join the everlasting song,
And crown Him Lord of all;
-Edward Perronet;

39

Old 100th-L.M.

1. Before Jehovah's awful throne,
Ye nations, bow with sacred joy;
Know that the Lord is God alone: "
He can create, and he destroy.

2. His sovereign power, without our aid,
Made us of clay, and formed us men;
And, when like wandering sheep we strayed,
He brought us to his fold again.

3. We'll crowd thy gates with thankful songs,
High as the heavens our voices raise;
And earth, with her ten thousand tongues,
Shall fill thy courts with sounding praise.

4. Wide as the world is thy command
Vast as eternity thy love:
Firm as a rock thy truth shall Stand.
When rolling years shall cease to move.
-Isaac Watts

40

Dix-7.7.7.7.7.7

1. For the beauty of the earth,
For the glory of the skies
For the love which from our birth
Over and around us lies;
Lord of all, to Thee we raise
This our hymn of grateful praise.

2. For the wonder of each hour
Of the day and of the night.
Hill and vale and tree and flower.
Sun and moon and stars of light
Lord of all, to Thee we raise
This our hymn of gratefull praise.

3. For the joy of human love,
Brother, sister, parent, child;
Friends on earth and friends above;
For all gentle thoughts and mild:
Lord of all, to Thee we raise
This our hymn of grateful praise.

4. For Thy Church that evermore
Lifteth holy hands above,
Offering up on every shore
Her pure sacrifice of love:
Lord of all, to Thee we raise
This our hymn' of gratefull praise.

5. For Thyself, best gift divine,
To our race so freely given;
For that great, great love of Thine,
Peace on earth and joy in heaven:
Lord of all, to Thee we raise
This our hymn of gratefull praise
-Folliott S. Pierpoint

41

Faithfulness -11.10.11.10.
with Refrain

1. Great is Thy faithfulness, O God my Father,
There is no shadow of turning with Thee;
Thou changest not, Thy compassions they fail not;
As Thou hast been Thou forever wilt be.

Chorus
Great is Thy faithfulness!
Great is Thy faithfulness!
Morning by morning new mercies I see;
All I have needed Thy hand hath provided
Great is Thy faithfulness, Lord unto me!

2. Summer and winter, and spring time and harvest,
Sun. moon and stars in their courses above
Join with all nature in manifold witness
To Thy great faithfulness, mercy, and love.

3. Pardon for sin and peace that endureth,
Thy own dear presence to cheer
And to guide;
Strength for today and bright hope for tomorrow,
Blessings all mine, with ten thousand beside!
                    -Thomas O. Chisholm

42

Nicaea - 11.12.12.10

1. Holy, holy, holy!
Lord God Almighty!
Early in the morning
our song shalt rise to Thee:
Holy, holy, holy
merciful and mighty!
God in three Persons,
blessed Trinity!

2. Holy, holy, holy!
all the saints adore Thee,
Casting down their golden crown
around the glassy sea;
Cherubim and seraphim
Falling down before Thee,
Which wert and art and
evermore shaft be.

3. Holy. holy, holy
though the darkness hide Thee,
Though the eye of sinful man
Thy glory may not see;
Only Thou art to holy
there is none beside Thee,
Perfect in pow'r, in
love and purity. .

4. Holy, holy, holy!
Lord God Almighty!
All Thy works shall praise Thy name
in earth and sky and sea;
Holy, holy, holy!
merciful and mighty!
God in three Persons,
Blessed Trinity!
                    -Reginald Heber

43

St Denio -11.11.11.11.I

1. Immoral invisible God only wise,
In light inaccessible hid from our eyes,
Most blessed, most glorious, the Ancient of Days,
Almighty, victorious Thy great name we praise.

2. Unresting, unhasting, and silent as light,
Nor wanting, nor wasting. Thou rulest in might;
Thy justice, like mountains, high Soaring above
Thy clouds, which are fountains of goodness and love.

3. To all, life Thou givest to both great and small,
In all life Thou livest the true life of all
We blossom and flourish as leaves on the tree,
And wither and perish but naught changeth Thee.

4. Great Father of glory, pure Father Of light
Thine angels adore Thee, all veilling their sight;
All praise we would render O help us to see
Tis only the splendor of light hideth Thee!. Amen.
                    -Walter Chalmers Smith;

44

Lyons-10.10.11.11.

1. O worship the King, all glorious above,
And gratefully sing His wonderful love;
Our Shield and Defender, the Ancient of Days,
Pavillioned in splendor and girded with praise.

WORSHIP AND ADORATION

2. O tell of His might,
   O sing of His grace,
   Whose robe is the light,
   whose canopy space!
   His chariots of wrath
   the deep thunder clouds form,
   And dark is His path
   on the wings of the storm.

3. The earth with its store
   of wonders untold,
   Almighty thy pow'r
   Hath founded of old.
   Hath stablish'd it fast
   by changeless decree,
   And round it hath cast,
   Like a mantle, the sea.

4. Thy bountiful care
   what tongue can recite?
   It breathes in the air,
   it shines in the light,
   It streams from the hills,
   it descends to the plain,
   And sweetly distills
   in the dew and the rain.

5. Frail children of dust,
   and feeble as frail,
   In Thee do we trust,
   nor find Thee to frail,
   Thy mercies how tender,
   how firm to the end,
   Our Maker, Defender,
   Redeemer, and Friend.

6. O measureless Might!
   Inefable love!
   while angels delight,
   To hymn thee. Above,
   The humbler creation,
   though feeble their days.
   With true adoration,
   Shall lisp to Thy praise.
   -Robert Grant

45

Austrian Hymn - 8.7.8.7.D.

1. Praise the Lord! Ye heav'ns,
   adore Him;
   Praise Him angels in the height;
   Sun and moon, rejoice before Him;
   Praise Him, all ye stars of light.
   Praise the Lord! For He hath
   spoken;
   Worlds His mighty voice obeyed;
   Laws which never shall be broken
   For their guidance He hath made.

2. Praise the Lord! For He is
   glorious;
   Never shall His promise fail;
   God hath made His saints
   victorious;
   Sin and death shall not prevail.
   Praise the God of our salvation!
   Hosts on high, His pow'r proclaim;
   Heav'n and earth and all creation,
   Laud and magnify His name.

3. Worship, honour, glory, blessing,
   Lord, we offer unto Thee;
   Young and old, Thy praise
   expressing,
   In glad homage bend the knee.
   All the saints in heav'n adore
   Thee;
   We, would bow before Thy throne:
   As Thine angels serve before
   Thee,
   So on earth Thy will be done.
   -Foundling
   Hospital Collection

46

Laudes Domini -6.6.6.6.6.6.

1. When morning gilds the skies,
   My heart awaking cries,
   May Jesus Christ be praised!
   Alike a work and prayer
   To Jesus I repair
   May Jesus Christ be praised!

2. Does sadness fill my mind?
   A solace here I find, May
   Jesus Christ be praised!
   Or fades my earthly bliss?
   My comfort still is this,
   May Jesus Christ be praised!

3. The night becomes as day,
   When from the heart we Say,
   May Jesus Christ be praised!
   The pow'rs of darkness fear
   When this sweet chant they hear,

4. Ye nations of mankind,
In this your concord find,
May Jesus Christ be praised!
Let all the earth around,
Ring joyous with the sound,
May Jesus Christ be praised!

5. Sing, suns and stars of space,
Sing ye that see His face,
May Jesus Christ be praised!
God's whole creation o'er,
For aye and evermore
May Jesus Christ be praised!

6. Be this, while life is mine,
My canticle divine,
May Jesus Christ be praised!
Be this th'eternal song
Thro' all the ages long,
May Jesus Christ be praised!
-Katholistisches Gesangbuch,
Wuruzburg, 1828;

47

Laus Deo -6.4.6.4.

1. Father of heaven above,
Dwelling in light and love,
Ancient of days,
Light unapproachable,
Love inexpressible,
Thee, the Invisible,
Laud we and praise.

2. Christ the eternal Word,
Christ the incarnate Lord,
Saviour of all,
High throned above all height,
God of God, Light of Light,
Increate infinite
On Thee we call.

3. O God, the Holy Ghost,
Whose fires of Pentecost
Burn evermore,
In this far wilderness
Leave us not comfortless:
Thee we love, Thee we bless,
Thee we adore.

4. Strike your harps, heavenly
powers
With your glad chants shall ours
Trembling ascend.

All praise, O God, to Thee,
Three in One, One in Three,
Praise everlastingly
World without end.
                              -E. H. Thome

48

Shine Thou Upon Us, Lord - 6.6.6.6.D.

1. Shine Thou upon us, Lord,
True Light of men today,
And through the written word
Thy very self display;
That so, from-hearts which burn
With gazing on Thy face,
The little ones may learn
The wonders of Thy grace.

2. Breathe Thou upon us, Lord
Thy Spirit's living flame;
That so with one accord
Our lips may tell Thy name;
Give Thou the hearing ear,
Fix Thou the wandering thought,
That those we teach may hear
The great things Thou has wrought.

3. Speak Thou for us, O Lord,
In all we say of Thee,
According to Thy word,
Let all our teaching be
That so Thy lambs may know
Their own true Shepherd's voice,
Where'er He leads them go,
And in His love rejoice.

4. Live Thou within us. Lord;
Thy mind and will be ours;
Be Thou beloved, adored,
And served, with all our powers;
That so our lives may teach
Thy children what Thou art.
And plea, by more than speech,
For Thee with every heart.

49

We Sing A Song Of Thy Law L.M.

1. We sing a song of Thy great love
   Almighty and glorious God
   There's nought thy power cannot
   provide
   Thy goodness endureth for aye.

2. In love He created the world,
   And He made man to dwell in it
   And have dominion over all,
   Sing a song to our Creator.

3. Every day He takes care of us,
   He feeds and provides all our
   needs,
   Without asking ought of our hand,
   Praise our God the giver of all.

4. He finds us roaming in darkness,
   Nor Knowing how to worship Him
   In His love He showed us the way
   Praise His name, our benefactor.

5. In love He gave Jesus to us
   Christ, His only begotten Son
   He came to redeem us from sin
   We praise Thy great love, our
   Saviour.

6. In love He sent His word to us
   And this Thy love opened our
   ear,
   And established us in the faith
   Sing His wonderful grace to us.

7. Creation is full of Thy love Our
   God, King of the universe,
   All join the chorus of His praise
   And sing of the love of our God.

PRAISE AND THANKSGIVING

50

Monkland- 7.7.7.7.

1. Let us, with a gladsome mind,
Praise the Lord, for he is kind:
For his mercies ay endure,
Ever faithful, ever sure.

2. Let us blaze his name abroad,
For of gods he is the God:
For his mercies ay endure,
Ever faithful, ever sure.

3. He with all commanding might
Filled the new made world with
light
For his mercies ay endure,
Ever faithful, ever sure.

4. He the golden tressed sun
Caused all day his course to run:
For his mercies ay endure,
Ever faithful, ever Sure.

5. And the homed moon at night
'Mid her spangled sisters bright
For his mercies ay endure,
Ever faithful, ever sure.

6. All things living he doth feed,
His full hand supplies their need:
For his mercies ay endure,
Ever faithful, ever sure.

7. Let us, with a gladsome mind,
Praise the Lord, for he is kind:
For his mercies ay endure,
Ever faithful, ever sure.
-John Milton

51

Praxis pietatis-14.14.4.7.8.

1. Praise to the Lord, the Almighty, the
King of creation;
O my soul, praise him, for he is thy
health and salvation:
All ye who hear,
Now to his temple draw near,
Joining in glad adoration.

2. Praise to the Lord, who o'er all thing
so wondrously reigneth,
Shieldeth thee gently from harm, or
when fainting sustaineth:
Has thou not seen
How thy heart's wishes have been
Granted in what he ordaineth?

3. Praise to the Lord, who doth
prosper thy work and defend thee;
Surely his goodness and mercy
shall daily attend thee:
Ponder anew
What the Almighty can do,
If to the end he befriend thee.

4. Praise to the Lord! O let all that is
In me adore him
All that hath life and breath, come
Now with praises before him!
Let the Amen
Sound from his people again:
Gladly for ay we adore him.
J.Neander

52

Luther-8.7.8.7.8.8.7.

1. Sing praise to God who reigns above
The God of all creation,
The God of power, the God of love,
The God of our salvation;
With healing balm my soul he fills,
And every faithless murmur stills:
To God all praise and glory.

2. The Lord is never far away,
But, through all grief distressing,
An ever-present help and stay,
Our peace and Joy and blessing;
As with a mother's tender hand,
he leads his own, his chosen band;
To God all praise and glory.

3. Thus all my gladsome way along
I sing aloud thy praises,
That men may hear the grateful
song
My voice unwearied raises.
Be joyful in the Lord, my heart;
Both soul and body bear your part:
To God all praise and glory.
-J. J. Schutz

PRAISE AND THANKSGIVING

53

Northampton 7.7.7.7.

1. Songs of praise the angels sang,
   Heaven with alleluias rang,
   When creation was begun,
   When God spake and it was done.

2. Songs of praise awoke the morn,
   When the Prince of peace was
   born;
   Songs of praise arose when He
   Captive led captivity.

3. Heaven and earth must pass away:
   Songs Of praise shall crown that
   day:
   God will make new heavens and
   earth;
   Songs of praise shall hail their birth.

4. And shall man alone be dumb,
   Till that glorious kingdom come?
   No: the church delights to raise
   Psalms and hymns and songs of
   Praise

5. Saints below, with heart and voice,
   Still in songs of praise rejoice'
   Learning here, by faith and love
   Songs of praise to sing above.
   —J. Montoomery

54

Duke Street-L.M.

1. Awake, my tongue, thy tribute bring
   To Him Who gave thee pow'r to
   sing;
   Praise Him who is all praise above
   The sources of wisdom of love.

2. How vast His knowledge, how
   profound!
   A deep where all our tho'ts are
   drowned;
   The stars He numbers, and their
   names
   He gives to all those heav'nly
   Flames

3. Thro'each bright world above,
   behold

Ten thousand thousand charms
unfold;
Earth, air. and mighty seas combine
To speak His wisdom all divine.

4. But in redemption, O what grace!
   Its wonders, O what tho't can trace!
   Here, wisdom shines for ever bright;
   Praise Him, my soul, with sweet
   delight
   —John Needham

55

To God be the Glory-
11.11.t1.11. with Refrain

1. To God be the glory great things He
   hath done!
   So loved He the world that He gave
   us His Son,
   Who yielded His life an a nement
   for sin
   And opened the Life-gate that all
   may go in.

Chorus
Praise the Lord, praise the Lord,
Let the earth hear His voice!
Praise the Lord, praise the Lord,
Let the people rejoice!
O come to the Father, thro' Jesus
the Son.
And give Him the glory, great things
He hath done.

2. O perfect redemption, the purchase
   of blood
   To ev'ry believer the promise of
   God;
   The vilest offender who truly
   believes,
   That moment from Jesus a pardon
   receives.

3. Great things He hath taught us.
   great things He hath done.
   And great our rejoicing thru Jesus
   the Son:
   But purer and higher and greater
   will be
   Our wonder, our transport, when
   Jesus we see.
   —Fanny J. Crosby

PRAISE AND THANKSGIVING

56
Russian Hymn -11.10.11.9.

1. God the almighty One! Wisely or
daining
Judgements unsearch able, famine
and sword;
Over the tumult of war Thou art
reigning:
Give to us peace in our time, O
Lord

2. God the all merciful earth hath
forsaken
Thy ways of blessedness, slighted
Thy Word;
Bid not Thy wrath in its terrors
awaken:
Give to us peace in our time, O
Lord!

3. God the all righteous One! man
hath defied Thee;
Yet to eternity standeth, Thy Word;
Falsehood and wrong shall not tarry
beside Thee:
Give to us peace in our time, O
Lord!
                        -Henry F. Chortey

57
Harwell 8.7.8.7.7.7. with Alleluias
1. Hark, ten thousand harps and
voices
Sound the note of praise above;
Jesus reigns and heaven rejoices,
Jesus reigns, the God of love;
See, He sits on yonder throne,
Jesus rules the world alone;
Alleluia! alleluia! alleluia! Amen

2. Jesus, hail! whose glory brightens
All above, and gives it worth:
Lord of life, Thy smile enlightens,
Cheers and charms Thy saints on
earth;
When we think of love like Thine,
Lord, we own it love divine:
Alleluia! alleluia' alleluia! Amen

3. King of glory, reign for ever;
Thine an everlasting crown:
Nothing from Thy love shall sever
Those whom Thou hast made
Thine own;
Happy objects of Thy grace,
Destined to behold Thy face,
Alleluia! Alleluia! alleluia! Amen

4. Saviour, hasten Thine appearing;
Bring, O bring the glorious day,
When, the awful summons hearing,
Heaven and earth shall pass away;
Then with golden harps we'll sing,
"Glory, glory to our King!"
Alleluia! Alleluia! alleluia! Amen
                        -Thomas Kelly

58
Lyons -10.10.11.11.

1. Jehovah the Lord, our Saviour
and King.
Glad praises to Thee we ever shall
sing;
We come to Thine altar, the place
of retreat
Where we shall find peace at Thine
own mercy seat.

2. Thanks givings we bring in our
Songs toThee.
For bounties of earth, for fruit of
the tree,
For glorious fountains of water so
pure.
For temples of worship all time to
Endure.

3. Abundant the yield of ripe fruited
grain,
From forest and field, from valley
and plain;
The verdant green pastures, so
useful to man,
Are tokens of blessings in Thy
wondrous plan.

4. Jesus our Lord, Thou ruler of all,
Thou art ever true, what ever the
call;
Be Thou our defender in all time
of stress,
And help us live daily in true
Thankfulness

59

Kremser - Irregular

1. O God of our fathers, we praise and adore Thee
For all Thy great mercies through years that are gone;
Thy guidance and goodness through many generations
Have brought us now at last to a new day's bright dawn.

2. Help us to be faithful to Thee and Thy kingdom,
Thy church, and the work of our Christ in all lands:
May loyalty, sacrifice, courage now attend us;
And bring to fullest triumph Thy work in our hands:

3. Our task is no greater than that watch our fathers
Assumed with fidelity, courage, and pride:
We know that all mountains will vanish now before us
If Thou wilt point the way and; remain at our side.

4. We now re-affirm our undying devotion;
We pray Thou wilt fill us with all strength and grace:
Crown all high endeavors with victories for ever,
And may we run with faithfulness life's fateful race.

-Edward Hughes Pruden

60

Regent Square - 8.7.8.7.8.7.

1. Praise, my soul, the King of heaven,
To His feet thy tribute bring;
Ransomed, healed, restored, forgiven,
Who like the His praise shall sing;
Praise Him, Praise Him
Praise the everlasting King.

2. praise Him for His grace and favour
To our fathers in distress;
Praise, Him, still the same for ever
Slow to chide, and swift to bless;
Praise Him, Praise Him
Glorious in His faithfulness.

3. Father like, He tends and spare us;
Well our feeble frame He knows;
In His hands He gently bears us,
Rescues us from all our foes;
Praise Him, Praise Him
Widely as His mercy flows.

4. Angels in the height, adore Him;
Ye behold him face to face;
Sun and moon, bow down before Him,
Dwellers all in time and space;
Praise Him, Praise Him
Praise with us the God of grace.

- Henry F. Lyte

61

Dix - 7.7.7.7.7.7

1. Praise to God, immortal praise,
For the love that crowns our days;
Bounteous source of ev'ry joy,
Let Thy praise our tongue employ;
All to Thee, our God, we owe,
Source whence all our blessings flow.

2. All the plenty summer pours;
Autum's rich o'er-flowing stores;
Flocks that whiten all the plain;
Yellow sheaves of ripened grain:
Lord, for these our souls hail raise
Grateful vows and solemn praise.

3. Peace, prosperity and health,
Private bliss, and public wealth,
Knowledge with its gladd'ning Streams,
Pure religion's holier beams:
Lord, for these our souls shall raise
Grateful vows and solemn praise.

4. As Thy prosp'ring hand hath blest,
May we give Thee of our best;
For Thy mercies grateful prove;
Singing thus thro' all days,
Praise to God, immortal praise.

-Anna L. Barbauld

PRAISE AND THANKSGIVING

62

Redhead - L.M.

1. Oh render thanks to God above,
   The fountain of eternal love,
   Whose mercy firm through ages past
   Has stood, and shall for ever last.

2. Who can His mighty deeds
   express,
   Not only vast, but numberless?
   What mortal eloquence can raise
   His tribute of immortal praise?

3. Happy are they, and only they,
   Who from His judgements fear to
   stray
   Who know and love His perfect will,
   And all His righteous laws fulfil.

4. Extend to me that favour. Lord,
   Thou to Thy chosen dost afford;
   When Thou return'st to set them
   free
   Let Thy salvation visit me.

63

Neander -8.7.8.7.8.7.

1. Come, ye faithful, raise the anthem;
   Cleave the skies with shouts of
   praise;
   Sing to Him who brought salvation,
   Wondrous in His works and ways:
   God eternal, Word incarnate,
   Whom the heaven of heavens
   Obeys.

2. Ere He raised the lofty mountains.
   Form'd the sea, or spread the sky,
   Love eternal, free and boundless,
   Moved the Lord of life to die;
   Foreordain'd the Prince of princes
   For the throne of Calvary

3. Now above the sapphire pavement,
   High in unapproached light,
   Lo, He lives and reigns for ever
   Victor after hard-won fight!
   Where the song of the redeemed
   Rings unceasing day and night.

4. Yet this earth He still remembers,
   Still by Him the flock are fed:
   Yea, He gives them food immortal,
   Gives Himself, the living bread:
   Leads them where the precious
   fountain
   From the smitten Rock is shed
                         -Joachim Neander

64

St. Stephen. C.M.

1. When all Thy mercies. O my God,
   My rising soul surveys,
   Transported with the view, I'm lost
   In wonder, love, and praise.

2. Unnumbered comforts to my soul
   Thy tender care bestow'd,
   Before my infant heart conceived
   From whom these comforts flow'd.

3. When worn with sickness, oft hast
   Thou
   With health renew'd my face;
   And, when in sins and sorrows
   sunk.
   Revived my soul with grace.

4. Ten thousand thousand precious
   Gifts
   My daily thanks employ;
   Nor is the least a cheerful heart,
   That tastes those gifts with joy.

5. Through every period of my life
   Thy goodness I'll pursue;
   And after death, in distant worlds,
   The glorious theme renew.

6. Through all eternity to Thee
   A joyful song I'll raise:
   For oh! eternity's too short
   To utter all Thy praise.
                         -W. Jones

65

Angel voices -8.5.8.5.8.4.3

1, Angel voices ever singing
   Round Thy throne of light
   Angel harps for ever ringing.

PRAISE AND THANKSGIVING

Rest not day or night;
Thousands only live to bless Thee,
And confess Thee,
Lord of might.

2. Thou, who art beyond the farthest
mental eye can scan,
Can it be that Thou regardest
songs of sinful man?
Can we feel that Thou art near us
And wilt hear us?
Yea, we can.

3. Yea, We know Thy love rejoices
O'er each work of Thine;
Thou didst ears and hands and
voices
For Thy praise combine;
Craftsman's art and music's
measure
For Thy pleasure
Didst design.

4. Here, great God, today we offer
of Thine own to Thee;
And for Thine acceptance proffer,
All unworthily,
Hearts and minds, and hands, and
voices
In our choicest
Melody.

5. Honour, glory, might, and merit,
Thine shall ever be,
Father, Son, and Holy Spirit,
Blessed Trinity:
Of the best that Thou hast given,
Earth and heaven
Render Thee.

-E. G. Monk

66

Covenant - 6.6.8.4.6.6.8.4

1. The God of Abra'am praise
to reigns enthroned above:
Ancient of everlasting days,
And God of love:
Jehovah, Great I AM,
By earth and heaven confess'd
I bow and bless the sacred name
For ever bless'd.

2. The God of Abra'am praise,
At whose supreme command
From earth I rise, and seek the joys
At His right hand:
I all on earth forsake
Its wisdom, fame, and power;
And Him my only portion make,
My shield and tower.

3. He by Himself hath sworn;
I on His oath depend;
I shall, on eagle's wings upborne,
To heaven ascend;
I shall behold His face,
I shall His power adore;
And sing the wonders of His grace
for evermore.

4. Though nature's strength decay,
And earth and hell withstand.
To Canaan's bounds I urge my way.
At this command
the watery deep I pass.
With Jesus in my view;
And through the howling wilderness
My way pursue.

5. The God, who reigns on high,
The great archangels sing,
And Holy. Holy, Holy" cry
Almighty King;
Who was and is the same,
And evermore shall be:
Jehovah, Father, Great I AM,
We worship Thee.

6. The whole triumphant host
Give thanks to God on high;
Hail, Father, Son, and Holy Ghost,
They ever cry.
Hail Abra'am's God. and mine,
I join the heaven lays:
All might and majesty are Thine,
And endless praise.

-J. Stainer

67

Rustington -8.7.8.7.D.

1. God, we praise you! God, we bless
you
God, we name you sovereign Lord!
Mighty King whom angels worship,
Father, by your church adored:
all creation show your glory,

PRAISE AND THANKSGIVING

heaven and earth draw near your
Throne,
Singing Holy, holy, holy,
Lord of hosts, and God alone!'

2. True apostles, faithful prophets,
saints who set their world ablaze,
martyrs, once unknown, unheeded,
join one growing song of praise,
while your church on earth confesses
one majestic Trinity:
Father, Son, and Holy Spirit,
God, our hope eternally.

3. Jesus Christ, the king of glory,
everlasting Son of God,
humble was your virgin mother,
hard the lonely path you trod:
by your cross is sin defeated,
hell confronted face to face,
heaven opened to believers,
sinners justified by grace.

4. Christ, at God's right hand
Victorious,
you will judge the world you made;
Lord, in mercy help your servants
for whose freedom you have paid:
raise us up from dust to glory,
guard us from all sin today;
King enthroned above all praises,
save your people. God, we pray.
-Christopher Idle

68
Llanfair -7.7.7.7. And Alleluias

1. Praise the Lord, his glories show
Alleluia,
all that lives on earth below,
alleluia,
Angels round his throne above,
alleluia.
all who see and share his love.
Alleluia!

2. Earth to heaven and heaven to
earth Alleluia,
tell his wonders, sing his worth;
Alleluia,
age to age, and shore to shore,
alleluia,"
praise him, praise him evermore
alleluia!

3. Praise the Lord, his mercies trace,
Alleluia,
praise his providence and grace;
alleluia,
All that he for us has done,
alleluia,
all he give us in his son!
alleluia!
-H. F. Lyte

69
Alleluia, dulice carmen - 8.7.8.7.8.7.

1. Praise we offer, Lord of glory
for your coming to our earth;
called to be the son of Man,
taking manhood by your birth:
praise we offer, Lord of glory
for your coming to our earth.

2. Praise we offer, Lord of glory,
for your passion and your death
Called to suffer for us sinners,
Faithful till your final breath:
praise we offer, Lord of glory
for your passion and your death.

3. praise we offer. Lord of glory
for your Spirit's touch of power,
called to break the chains which
bound us,
rising, faithful souls to save:
praise we offer, Lord of glory
for your conquest of the grave.

4. Praise we offer, Lord of glory,
for your Spirit's touch of power;
called to give our lives new
radiance,
filling us from hour to hour;
praise we offer, Lord of glory
for your Spirit's touch of power.

5. Praise we offer, Lord of glory,
for the hope which all our days,
called to being by your labours,
turns our thought to endless praise:
praise we offer, Lord of glory
endless songs of joyful praise!
Micheal Saward

PRAISE AND THANKSGIVING

70

Gopsal -6.6.6.6.8.8

1. Rejoice, the Lord is king!
   Your Lord and king adore:
   mortals, give thanks and sing,
   and triumph ever more:
   Lift up your heart, lift up your voice:
   rejoice! Again I say, rejoice!

2. Jesus, the saviour, reigns,
   the God of truth and love;
   when he had purged our stains
   he took his seat above:
   Lift up your heart, lift up your voice:
   rejoice! Again I say, rejoice!

3. His kingdom cannot fail,
   he rules both earth and heaven;
   the keys of death and hell
   to Jesus now are given:
   Lift up your heart, lift up your voice:
   rejoice! Again I say, rejoice!

4. He sits at God's right hand,
   till all his foes submit
   and bow to his command
   and fall beneath his feet:
   Lift up your heart, lift up your voice:
   rejoice! Again I say, rejoice!

5. Rejoice in glorious hope!
   Jesus the judge shall come
   and take his servants up
   to their eternal home:
   We soon shall hear the archangel's voice:
   the trumpet sounds rejoice, rejoice!
   -C. Wesley

71

Hallelujah, Praise Jehovah

1. Hallelujah, praise Jehovah!
   From the heavens praise His name;
   praise Jehovah in the highest;
   All His angels praise proclaim.
   All His hosts together praise Him,
   sun and moon and stars on high;
   praise Him, O ye heav'n of heavens,
   And ye floods above the sky.

Chorus
Let them praises give Jehovah,
For His name alone is high,
And His glory is exalted,
And His glory is exalted,
And His glory is exalted
Far above the earth and sky.

2. Let them praises give Jehovah!
   They were made at His command;
   Them for ever He established:
   His decree shall ever stand.
   From the earth, O praise Jehovah,
   All ye floods, ye dragons all,
   Fire and hail and snow and vapours,
   Stormy winds that hear Him call.

3. All ye fruitful trees and cedars,
   All ye hills and mountains high,
   Creeping things and beasts and cattle,
   Birds that in the heavens fly,
   Kings of earth, and all ye people,
   Princes great, earth's judges all;
   Praise His name, young men and maidens,
   Aged men, and children small,
   -Wm.J. Kirkpatrick

72

My Redeemer -8.7.8.7. with Refrain

1. I will sing of my Redeemer
   And His wondrous love to me;
   On the cruel cross He suffered,
   From the curse to set me free.

Chorus
Sing, O sing of my Redeemer,
With His blood He purchased me;
On the cross He sealed my pardon,
Paid the debt and made me free.

2. I will tell the wondrous story,
   How, my lost estate to save,
   In His boundless love and mercy,
   he the ransom freely gave.

3. I will praise my dear Redeemer,
   His triumphant pow'r I'll tell ,

PRAISE AND THANKSGIVING

How the victory He giveth
Over sin and death and hell.

4. I will sing of my Redeemer
And His heav'nly love to me;
He from death to life hath bro't me,
Son of God with Him to be.
                              -Philip P. Bliss

73

Worthy art Thou

1. Worthy of praise is Christ our
Redeemer;
Worthy of glory, honour and pow'r!
Worthy of all our soul's adoration,
Chorus
Worthy art Thou! Worthy art Thou!
Worthy of riches, blessings and
honour,
Worthy of wisdom, glory and pow'r!
Worthy of earth and heaven's
thanksgiving,
Worthy art Thou! Worthy art Thou!

2. Lift up the voice in praise and
devotion,
Saints of all earth before Him should
bow;
Angels in heaven worship Him,
saying,

3. Lord, may we come before Thee
with singing,
Filled with Thy Spirit, wisdom and
pow'r;
May we ascribe Thee glory and
honour,
                              -Tillit S. Teddlie

74

The Blood of My Redeemer

1. I will praise the Lord for His love to
me,
I am wash'd in the blood of my
Redeemer;
In the fount that flows at the cross
so free,
I am wash'd in the blood of my

Chorus
Glory, glory, glory to the Lamb,
I am sav'd from sin and He makes
me what I am;
Oh, glory, glory, glory to the Lamb,
I am wash'd in the blood of my
Redeemer.

2. I am saved by grace and to Him
bro't near,
I am wash'd in the blood of my
Redeemer;
I would sing so loud that the world
might hear,
I am wash'd in the blood of my
Redeemer.

3. What a constant peace in my
heart I feel.
I am wash'd in the blood of my
Redeemer;
There's holy joy I can ne'er reveal,
I am wash'd in the blood of my
Redeemer.

4. I will lift my voice while on earth I
stay,
I am wash'd in the blood of my
Redeemer;
Then my soul shall sing in the
realms of day,
I am wash'd in the blood of my
Redeemer.
                              -Henrietta E. Blair

75

Regent Square - 8.7.8.7.4.7.

1. Come, my brethren, praise your
Saviour,
Let your songs with rapture swell,
Thro His grace have ye found
favour,
Who His boundless love can tell?
Sing His praises! Sing His praises,
For He hath done all things well.

2. Louder yet, yea grander, greater,
As your gladsome hearts rejoice
In your Saviour, Lord, Creator,
Swell, O swell the trembling chords;
Wake the echoes! The echoes!
Louder than the ocean a roar.

3. What! Ye tire? shame upon you!
Dare ye cease to sing His praise?
Shall the very stones provoke you?
Louder sing your wondrous lays,
Till creation, till creation
Owns His mighty power to save.

4. Blessed Lord, we will adore Thee,
Praise Thee, bless Thee, shout
and sing,
Till that day when we shall see
Thee,
Crowning Thee, all glorious King;
Hallelujah! Hallelujah!
How the courts of glory ring.
                        -E. T. Mellor

76

Rejoice In the Lord - 8.8.8.8. with Refrain

1. Be glad in the Lord, and rejoice,
All ye that are upright in heart;
And ye that have made Him your
choice,
Bid sadness and sorrow depart.

chorus
Rejoice! Rejoice!
Be glad in the Lord and rejoice!
Rejoice! Rejoice!
Be glad in the Lord and rejoice!

2. Be joyful, for He is the Lord,
On earth and in heaven supreme:
He fashions and rules by His word;
The 'Mighty' and 'Strong' to
redeem.

3. What tho'in the conflict for right
Your enemies almost prevail!
God's armies, just hid from your
sight,
Are more than the foes which
assail.

4. Tho' darkness surround you by day,
Your sky by the night be o'ercast,
Let nothing your spirit dismay,
But trust till the danger is past.

5. Be glad in the Lord, and rejoice,
His praises proclaiming in song;

With harp, and with organ, and
voice,
The loud hallelujahs prolong
                        -M. E. Servoss

77

Falcon Street - S.M. with Refrain

1. Come, sound His praise abroad,
And hymns of glory sing!
Jehovah is the soreign God,
The universal King!

Chorus
Praise ye the Lord, Hallelujah,
Praise ye the Lord, Hallelujah,
Hallelujah, Hallelujah, Hallelujah,
Praise ye the Lord.

2. He formed the deeps unknown;
He gave the seas their bound:
The watery worlds are all His own,
And all the solid ground.

3. Come, worship at His throne,
Come, bow before the Lord:
We are His work, and not our own,
He formed us by His word.

4. Today attend His voice.
Nor dare provoke His rod:
Come, like the people of His
choice,
And own your gracious God.
                        -Isaac Watts

78

Truro-LM.

1. Now in a song of grateful praise,
To Thee O Lord, my voice I'll raise;
With all Thy saints I'll joint to tell,
My Jesus hath done all things well.

2. How sov'reign, wonderful, and free
Has been Thy love to sinful me!
Thou sav'dst me from the jaws of
hell;
My Jesus hath done all things well.

3. Since e'er my soul has known His
love,
What mercies He has made me
prove!

PRAISE AND THANKSGIVING

Mercies which do all praise excell
My Jesus hath done all things well.

4. And when to that bright world I rise,
   And join the anthems of the skies,
   Above the rest, this note shall swell.
   My Jesus hath done all things well.
   -Samuel Medley

79

Bless The Lord, My Soul

1. Praise the King of Glory, He is God
   alone:
   Praise Him for the wonders He to
   us hath shown;
   For His promised presence all the
   pilgrim way,
   For the flaming pillar, and the cloud
   by day.

Chorus
Praise Him, shining angels, strike
your harps of gold;
All His hosts adore Him, who His
face behold;,
Through His great dominion, while
The ages roll,
All His works shall praise Him, all
His works shall praise Him,
All His works shall praise Him;
bless the Lord, my soul!

2. Praise Him for redemption, free to
   ev'ry soul;
   Praise Him for the Fountain that
   can make us whole;
   For His gifts of kindness and His
   loving care,
   For the blest assurance that He
   answers prayer.

3. Praise Him for the trials sent as
   Cord of love,
   Binding us more closely to the gins
   above;
   For the faith that coquers, hope
   that naught can dim,
   For the land where loved ones
   gather unto Him.
   -E. E. Hewitt

80

Lasst Uns Erfreuen-LM. with Hallelujah

1. From all that dwell below the skies
   Let the Creator's praise arise:
   Hallelujah! Hallelujah!
   Let the Redeemer's Name be sung
   Thro' ev'ry land in ev'ry tongue.
   Hallelujah! Hallelujah! Halleluiah!
   Hallelujah! Hallelujah! Hallelujah!

2. Eternal are Thy mercies. Lord;
   Eternal truth attends Thy word:
   Hallelujah! Hallelujah!
   Thy praise shall sound from shore
   to shore
   Till sun shall rise and set no more.
   Hallelujah! Hallelujah! Hallelujah!
   Hallelujah! Hallelujah! Hallelujah!
   -Isaac Watts

81

Nun Danket - 6.7.6.7.6.6.6.6.

1. Now thank we all our God
   With heart and hands and voices,
   Who wondrous things hath done,
   In whom His world rejoices;
   Who, from our mother's arms,
   Hath blest us on our way
   With countless gifts of love,
   And still is ours today.

2. O may this bounteous God
   Through all our life be near us,
   With everjoyful hearts And blessed
   peace to cheer us;
   And keep us in His grace,
   And guide us when perplexed,
   And free us from all ills
   In this world and the next.

3. All praise and thanks to God
   The Father now be given,
   The Son, and Him who reigns
   With them in highest heaven,
   The one eternal God, Whom earth
   and heav'n adore,
   For thus it was, is now,
   And shall be evermore.
   -Martin Rinkart

PRAISE AND THANKSGIVING

82

Wareham- L.M.

1. Rejoice, O land, in God thy might:
   His will obey, him serve aright;
   For thee the saints uplift their voice:
   Fear not, O land, in God rejoice.

2. Glad shalt thou be, with blessing
   crowned
   Yea, love with thee shall make his
   home
   Until thou see God's Kingdom come

3. He shall forgive thy sins untold:
   Remember thou his love of old;
   Walk in his way, his word adore,
   And keep His truth for evermore.
   -R Bridges

83

Azmon-C.M.

1. O for a thousand tongues to sing
   My great Redeemer's praise,
   The glories of my God and King,
   The triumphs of His grace.

2. Jesus! the name that Charms our
   fears,
   That bids our sorrows cease,
   " Tis music in the sinner's ears,
   "Tis life and health and peace.

3. He breaks the power of cancelled
   sin
   He sets the prisoner free;
   His blood can make the foulest
   clean;
   His blood availed for me.

4. He speaks and listening to His voice
   New life the dead receive
   the mournful broken hearts rejoice
   the humble poor believe.

5. Hear Him, ye deaf-. His praise, ye
   dumb,
   your loosened tongues employ;
   ye blind, behold your Saviour
   come;
   and leap, ye lame, for joy.

6. My gracious Master and my
   God, Assist me to proclaim,
   To spread thro' all the earth
   abroad,
   The honors of Thy name.
   -Charles Wesley

84

Blessed be the name - L.M.
with Refrain

1. All praise to Him who reigns above
   In majesty supreme.
   Who gave His Son for man to die,
   That He might man redeem!

   Chorus
   Blessed be the name, blessed be
   the name,
   Blessed be the name of the Lord;
   Blessed be the name, blessed be
   the name.
   Blessed be the name of the Lord.

2. His name above all names shall
   stand
   Exalted more and more,
   At God the Father's own right hand,
   where angel hosts adore.

3. His name shall be the Counsellor,
   the mighty Prince of Peace,
   Of all earth's kingdoms Conqruor,
   whose reign shall never cease.
   -William H. Clark

85

Marion -S. M. with Refrain

1. Rejoice, ye pure in heart,
   Rejoice, give thanks and sing,
   Your festival banner wave on high,
   the cross of Christ your King

   chorus
   Rejoice, rejoice, Rejoice,
   Give thanks, and sing!

2. With all the angel choirs,
   With all the saints on earth,
   Pour out the Strains of Joy and bliss.
   True scripture, no blest mirth.

3. Yes, on through life's long path,
Still chanting as we go;
From youth to age. by night and day,
In gladness and in woe.

4. Still lift your standard high,
Still march in firm array;
As warriors through the darkness toil
Till dawns the golden day.
-Edward H. Plumptre

86

Holy-L. M.

1. We thank Thee, Lord, for this fair earth,
The glittering sky, the silver sea;
For all their beauty, all their worth,
Their light and glory, come from Thee.

2. Thanks for the flowers that clothe the ground,
The trees that wave their arms above.
The hills that gird our dwellings round,
As Thou dost gird Thine own with love.

3. Yet teach us stilt how far more fair
More glorious, Father, in Thy sight,
Is one pure deed, one holy prayer,
One heart that owns Thy Spirits might.

4. So. while we gaze with thoughtful eye
On all the gifts Thy love has given
Help us in Thee to live and die,
By Thee to rise from earth to heaven.
-George Edward, Lynch Cotton

87

Nttleton -8.7.8.7.D.
1. Come, Thou Fount of every blessing,
Tune my heart to sing Thy grace;
Streams of mercy, never ceasing.
Call for songs of loudest praise.

Teach me some melodious sonnet,
Sung by flaming tongues above;
Praise His name I'm fixed upon it
Name of God's redeeming love.

2. Hither to Thy love has blest me;
Thou hast bro't me to this place;
And I know Thy hand will bring me
Safely home by Thy good grace.
Jesus sought me when a stranger,
Wandering from the fold of God;
He, to rescue me from danger,
Bought me with His precious blood.

3. O to grace how great a debtor
Daily I'm constrained to be!
Let Thy goodness, like a fetter,
Bind my wandering heart to Thee:
Prcne to wander. Lord, I feit it,
Prone to leave the God I love;
Here's my heart, O take and seal it;
Seal it for Thy courts above.
-Robert Robinson

88

St. George's (Windsor)

1. Come, ye thankful people come,
Raise the song of harvest home:
All is safely gathered in,
Ere the winter storms begin,
God, our maker, doth provide
For our wants to be supplied:
Come to God's own temple, come,
Raise the song of harvest home!

2. All the world is God's own field,
Fruit unto His praise to yield:
Wheat and tares together sown,
Unto joy or sorrow grown.
First the blade, and then the ear,
Then the full corn shall appear
Lord of harvest, grant that we
Whole-some grain and pure may be.

3. For the Lord our God shall come,
And shall take His harvest home;
From His field shall in that day
All offenses purge away;
Give His angels charge at last
In the fire the tares to cast,

PRAISE AND THANKSGIVING

But the fruitful ears to store
In His garner evermore.

4. Even so, Lord, quickly come
To Thy final harvest home:
Gather Thou Thy people in,
Free from sorrow, free from sin;
There, for ever purified,
In Thy presence to abide:
Come, with all Thine angels, come,
raise the glorious harvest home
-Henry Alford

89

Let All the people praise Thee
1. O magnify the Lord with me,
Ye people of His choice,
Let all to whom He lendeth breath
Now in His name rejoice;
For love's blest revelation,
For rest from condemnation,
For uttermost salvation
To Him give thanks.

Chorus
Let all the people praise Thee,
Let all the people praise Thee!
Let all the people praise Thy name
Forever and forever more,
(for evermore, O Lord!)
Let all the people praise Thee,
Let all the people praise Thee!
Let all the people praise Thy name
Forever and forever more.

2. O praise Him for His holiness,
His wisdom and His grace,
Sing praises for the precious blood
Which ransomed all our race
In tenderness He sought us,
From depths of sin He brought us,
The way of life then taught us,
To Him give thanks.

3. Had I a thousand tongues to sing,
The half could ne'er be told
Of love so rich, so full-and free,
Of blessings manifold;
Of grace that faileth never,
Peace flowing like a river,
from God the glorious Giver,
To Him give thanks.

90

Glory to God, Hallelujah

1. We are never, never weary of the
grand old song:
Glory to God, Hallelujah
We can sing it loud as ever with our
faith more strong;
Glory to God, Hallelujah!

Chorus
O the children of the Lord
have a right to shout and sing!
For the way is growing bright,
and our souls are on the wing;
We are going by and bye
to the palace of a King
Glory to God, Hallelujah!

2. We are lost amid the rapture of
redeeming love;
Glory to God, Hallelujah!
We are rising on its pinons to the
hills above;
Glory to God, Hallelujah!

3. We are going to a palace that is
built of gold;
Glory to God, Hallelujah!
Where the King in all His splendour
we shall soon behold;
Glory to God, Hallelujah!

4. There we'll shout redeeming mercy
in a glad new song;
Glory to God, Hallelujah!
There we'll sing the praise of Jesus
with the blood wash'd throng;
Glory to God, Hallelujah!
-Fanny J. Crosby

91

St. Aubin -8.5.8.5.

1. Praise the Saviour, ye who
Know Him;
Who can tell how much we
owe Him?
Gladly let us render to Him
All we have and are.

PRAISE AND THANKSGIVING

2. Jesus" is the name that charms us;
He for conflicts fits and arms us;
Nothing move and nothing harm us,
When we trust Him.

3. Trust in Him, ye saints for ever;
He is faithful, changing never;
Neither force nor guile can sever
Those He love from Him.

4. Keep us, Lord, oh, keep us cleaving
To Thyself and still believing,
Till the hour of our receiving
Promised joys in heaven.

5. Then we shall be where would be:
Then we shall be what we should be;
Things which are not now, nor could be,
Then shall be our own.

-T. Kelly

92

Christ Is My Portion For Ever- . 8.7.8.7. with Ref

1. Christ is my portion for ever,
He is my Saviour from sin;
He is my blessed salvation
I have the witness within

Chorus
I have the witness within
Jesus now saves me from sin
In His heart I've place,
I am saved by His grace
And I have the witness within.

2. He is my fortress and tower,
He is my guide and my King;
He is my Shepherd, my Keeper,
Joyfully now I can sing.

3. Praise to the One who redeems me,
Praise to my Crucified Lord,
Now I am saved, Hallelujah,
Praise for the wonderful word.

93

Name Of Jesus! Highest Name- 7.7.7.7.

1. Name of Jesus! Highest Name!
Name that earth and heaven adore!
From the heart of God it came,
Leads me to God's heart once more.

2. Name of Jesus! living tide!
Days of drought for me are past;
How much more than satisfied
Are the thirsty lips at last!

3. Name of Jesus Dearest Name!
Bread of heaven, and balm of love
Oil of gladness, surest claim
To the treasures stored above.

4. Jesus gives forgiveness free,
Jesus cleanses all my stains;
Jesus gives His life to me, Jesus
always He remains

5. Only Jesus! Fairest Name!
Life, and rest, and peace, and
bliss Jesus, evermore the same,
He is mine, and I am His.

94

O Christ, Whose Glory Fills Our Days L. M.

1. O Christ, whose glory fills our days,
Whose beauty shines from shore to shore.
Our gladdest songs on high we raise
To Thee whom earth and heav'n adore.

2. The glory Thou to us hast shown.
Thy name proclaimed by Thy word;
Thy majesty is surely known,
Thy praise among all people

PRAISE AND THANKSGIVING

The drooping spirit lives again,
The fainting heart regains its
power,
The sick and lame. Thy promise
claim
In this Thy great appointed hour,

4. With what a wealth of faith and
hope
Thy word is grasped, the weak
Made strong;
We stretch our hands to touch Thy
robe
And healed and blessed Thy praise
Prolong.

95

Praise, O Praise Our God
And King-7.7.7.7.

1. Praise, O praise our God and King;
Hymns of adoration sing;
For His mercies still endure
Ever faithful, ever sure.

2. Praise Him that He made the sun
Day by day his course to run;
For His mercies, still endure
Ever faithful, ever sure.

3. And the silver moon by night,
Shining with her gentle light;
For His mercies, still endure
Ever faithful, ever sure.

4. Praise Him that He gave the rain
To mature the swelling grain;
For His mercies, still endure
Ever faithful, ever sure.

5. And hath bid the fruitful field,
Crops of precious increase yield;
For His mercies, still endure
Ever faithful, ever sure.

6. Praise Him for our harvest-store;
He hath filled the garner floor:
For His mercies, still endure
Ever faithful, ever sure.

7. And for richer food than this,
Pledge of everlasting bliss,
For His mercies still endure
Ever faithful, ever sure.

8. Glory to our bounteous King;
Glory let creation sing;
Glory to the Father, Son,
And blest Spirit, Three in One.

96

What Shall 1 Render To My
God -C.M.

1. What shall 1 render to my God
For all His mercy's store?
I'll take gifts He hath bestowed,
And humbly ask for more.

2. The sacred cup of saving grace
I will with thanks receive,
And all his promises embrace,
And to His glory live.

3. My vows I will to his great name
Before His people pay.
And all i have and all I am
Upon His altar lay.

4. Thy lawful servant Lord, I owe
To Thee whate'er is mine,
Born in Thy family below
And by redemption Thine.

5. Thy hands created me, thy hands
From sin have set me free,
Offer the sacrifice of praise
And call upon His name.

6. Praise Him, ye saints, the God
of love,
Who hath my sins forgiven,
Till, gathered to the church above.
We sing the songs of heaven.

MORNING

97

Gerran -6.6.8.6.11.11.

1. Awaked from steep we fall
Before thee, God of love.
And chant the praise the angels
raise.
O God of might, above:
Holy, Holy, Holy! Thou art God
adored!
In thy pitying mercy show us mercy.
Lord.

2. As at thy call I rise,
Shine on this mind and heart,
And touch my tongue, that I among
Thy choir may take my part:
Holy. Holy, Holy! Trinity adored!
In thy pitying mercy show us mercy,
Lord.

3. The Judge will come with speed,
And each man's deeds be known;
Our trembling cry shall rise on high
At midnight to thy throne:
Holy, Holy, Holy! King of Saints
adored!
In the hour of judgement show us
mercy, Lord.

-R. M. Moorsom

98

Arfon -7.7.7.7.7.7.

1. At thy feet, O Christ we lay
Thine own gift of this new day;
Doubt of what it holds in store"
Makes us crave Thine aid the more;
Lest it love a time of loss,
Mark it, Saviour, with Thy cross.

2. If it flow on calm and bright,
Be Thyself our chief delight;
If it bring unknown distress,
Good is all that Thou canst bless;
Only, while its hours begin,

Pray we, keep them dear of sin.

3. We in part our weakness know,
And in part discern our foe;
Well for us, before Thine eyes
All our danger open lies;
Turn not from us, while we plead
Thy compassion and our need.

4. Fain would we Thy word embrace,
Live each moment on Thy grace,
All our selves to Thee consign,
Fold up all our wills in Thine,
Think, and speak, and do, and be
Simply that which pleases Thee.

5. Hear us, Lord, and that right soon;
Hear, and grant the choicest boon
That Thy love can e'er impart,
Loyal singleness of heart;
So shall this and all our days,
Christ our God, show forth Thy
praise.

-William Bright

99

Ratisbon-7.7.7.7.7.7.

1. Christ, whose glory fills the skies,
Christ, the true, the only Light,
Sun of Righteousness, arise,
Triumph o'er the shades of night;
Dayspring from on high, be near.
Daystar, in my heart appear.

2. Dark and cheerless is the morn
Unaccompanied by thee;
Joyless is the day's return,
Till thy mercy's beams I see,
Till they inward light impart, Glad
my eyes, and warm my heart.

3. Visit then this soul of mine,
Pierce the gloom of sin and grief;
fill me, radiancy divine,
Scatter all my unbelief;
More and more thyself display,
Shining to the perfect day

-C. Wesley

MORNING

100

Melcombe - L. M.

1. New every morning is the love
   Our wakening and uprising prove;
   Through sleep and darkness safely
   Brought,
   Restored to life and power and
   Thought

2. New mercies, each returning day,
   Hover around us while we pray;
   New perils past, new sins forgiven,
   New thoughts of God, new hopes
   of heaven.

3. If on our daily course our mind
   Be set to hallow all we find,
   New treasures still, of countless
   Price,
   God will provide for sacrifice.

4. The trivial round, the common task,
   we furnish all we need to ask.
   Room to deny ourselves, a road
   To bring us daily nearer God!

5. Only, O Lord, in thy dear love
   Fit us for perfect rest above;
   And help us, this and every day.
   To live more nearly as we pray.
   —J. Keble

101

Keine Schonheit hat die
Welt 7.7.7.7.

1. Through the night thy angels kept
   Watch beside me while I slept;
   Now the dark has passed away,
   Thank thee, Lord, for this new day.

2. North and south and east and west
   May thy holy name be blest;
   Everywhere beneath the sun,
   As in heaven, thy will be done.

3. Give me food that I may live;
   Every naughtiness forgive;
   Keep all evil things away
   From thy little child this day.
   —W. Canton

102

Tallis Canon-L.M.

1. Glory to Thee, who safe hast kept
   And hast refreshed me whilst I
   slept;
   Grant, Lord, when I from death shall
   wake
   I may of endless life partake.

2. Lord, I my vows to Thee renew;
   Disperse my sins as morning dew;
   Guard my first springs of thought
   and will, And with Thyself my
   spirit fill.

3. Direct, control, suggest, this day
   All I design or do or say;
   That all my powers, with all their
   mighty
   In Thy sole glory may unite.

4. Praise God, from whom all bless
   ings flow,
   Praise Him, all creatures here
   below,
   Praise Him above, ye heavenly host,
   Praise Father, Son, and Holy Ghost
   —T. Ken

103

Truro-LM.

1. God of the morning, at whose voice
   The cheerful sun makes haste to rise,
   And like a giant doth rejoice
   To run his journey through the
   skies;

2. O, like the sun, may I fulfil
   The appointed duties of the day,
   With ready mind and active will
   March on and keep my heavenly
   way.

3. Give me Thy counsel for my guide,
   And then receive me to Thy bliss:
   All my desires and hopes beside
   Are saint and cold, compared with
   this.

   -Isaac. Watts

104

Wareham -L. M.

1. My God, how endless is Thy love;
   Thy gifts are every evening new;
   And morning mercies from above
   Gently distil, like early dew.

2. Thou spreads! the curtains of the
   night.
   Great Guardian of my steeping
   hours:
   Thy sovereign word restores the
   light,
   And quickens all my slumbering
   Powers.

3. I yield my life to Thy command,
   To Thee I consecrate my days:
   Perpetual blessings from Thine
   hand
   Demand perpetual songs of praise.
   -Isaac. Watts

105

Gott des Himmels - 8.7.8.7.7.7.

1. Now the morn new light is pouring:
   Lord, may we our spirits raise,
   Through Thy grace our souls
   restoring,
   So, on Thy great day of days,
   We with joy its dawn may meet
   Fearless at the mercy-seat.

2. Jesus, who our steps art guiding
   By Thy word's celestial light,
   Now and evermore abiding,
   Our defence, our rock of might:
   Nowhere, save alone in Thee,
   Can we rest from danger free.

3. Lo! we yield to Thy direction Soul
   and body, heart and mind:
   Keep Thou all by Thy protection
   To Thy mighty hand resigned,
   Thee our glorious God we own;
   let us, Lord, be Thine alone.
   -H. Albert

106

Awake, and Sing the
Song - 6.6.8.6

1. Awake, and sing the song Of
   Moses and the Lamb;
   Wake, ev'ry heart arid ev'ry
   tongue, To praise the Savior's
   name.

2. Sing of His dying love; Sing of His
   rising pow'r,
   Sing how He intercedes above
   For those whose sins He bore,

3. Sing on your heav'nly way, Ye
   ransomed sinners, sing;
   Sing on, rejoicing ev'ry day In
   Christ, the glorious King

4. Soon shall you hear Him say, "Ye
   blessed children, come!
   Soon will He call you hence away,
   And take His pilgrims home.
   -Wm. Hammond

107

WARRINGTON-L.M.

1. Forth in Thy Name, O Lord, I go,
   My daily labour to pursue,
   Thee, only Thee, resolved to know
   in all I think, or speak, or do.

2. The task Thy wisdom hath assigned
O let me cheerfully fulfill,
In all my works Thy presence find,
And prove Thy good and perfect
Will.

3. Thee may I set at my right hand.
Whose eyes mine inmost substance
see,
And labour on at Thy command,
And offer all my works to Thee.

4. Give me to bear Thy easy yoke,
And every moment watch and pray,
And still to things eternal look.
And hasten to Thy glorious day;

5. For Thee delightfully employ
Whate'er Thy bounteous grace hath
given,
And run my course with even joy,
And closely walk with Thee to
heaven

-Charles Wesley

108
Gounod - 8.7.8.7.7.7.

1. Morning comes with light all
cheering,
Shades of night have fled apace;
Source of light, by Thine appearing,
From our minds all darkness chase:
Thou hast blest us in our sleep;
Through the day direct and keep.

2. Earth refreshed Thy praise is
sounding,
All Thy works Thy glory sing;
May our hearts, with love abound
Ing,
Gratefully their tribute bring:
Thou hast taught the birds their
lays
Teach our hearts to sing Thy praise

3. All day long to praise Thee help us,
And to strive against all sin;
Finding all our help in Jesus,
Who for us the fight did win:
He was tempted here below.
And doth all our weakness know.

4. Man goes to his work till evening
Brings again the needed rest;
Grant that we, Thy grace receiving,
May in all we do be blest:
And wherever we may be
Find our joy in pleasing Thee.

-James Englebert Vanner

109
There is Sunshine

1. There is sunshine in the valley
there is sunshine on the hill Jesus
brought it of this darken'd
world below,
There is sunshine in the flowers,
Blooming by the rippling rill,
There is blessed sunshine ev'ry
where I go

Chorus
Sunshine, sunshine of His love
divine
Sunshine, sunshine beams so
brightly shine
sunshine, sunshine, in this world
below,
Sunshine, sunshine ev'rywhere I go

2. There is sunshine on the meadow,
And upon the mossy lane,
Where the birds are warbling notes
of joy and praise
there is sunshine on the mountain
Let all nature now the happy
chorus Praise.

3. Tho' the world is full of sunshine
   Brightly beaming everyday
   There are souls who live in
   darkness all the while
   They have never heard of Jesus
   Nor His tender, loving care,
   Let us help and cheer them with a
   sunny smile

110

Moseley - 6.6.8.4.

1. The star of morn has risen:
   O Lord, to Thee we pray
   O uncreated Light of Light.
   Guide Thou our way.

2. Sinless be tongue and hand,
   And innocent the mind;
   Let simple truth be on our lips.
   Our hearts be kind.

3. As the swift day rolls on,
   Still. Lord, our guardian be;
   And keep the portals of our hearts
   from evil free.

4. Grant that our daily toil
   May to Thy glory tend;
   And as our hours begin with
   Thee, So may they end.
   -Greville Phillimore

111

Child's Morning Hymn - 8.8.8.8

1. Father, we thank Thee for the
   night,
   And for the pleasant morning light;
   For rest and food and loving care,
   And all that makes the world so
   fair.

2. Help us to do the things we
   should,
   To be to others kind and good;
   In all we do, in work or play,
   To love Thee better day by day.
   -Rebecca J. Weston

112

The Morning Bright with rosy with Light

1. The Morning bright with rosy
   light
   Has waked me from my sleep;
   Father, I own Thy love alone
   Thy little one doth keep.

2. All through the day, I humbly
   pray,
   Be Thou my guard and guide;
   My sins forgive, and let me live,
   Lord Jesus, near Thy side.

3. Oh, make Thy rest within my
   breast,
   Great Spirit of all grace;
   Make me like Thee, then shall I
   be
   Prepared to see Thy face.

113

Lux Prima

1. Jesus, sun of righteousness,
   Brightest beam of love divine,
   With the early morning rays,
   Do Thou on our darkness shine,
   And dispel with purest light
   All our night.

2. As on drooping herb and flower
   Falls the soft refreshing dew.
   Let Thy Spirit's grace and power
   All our weary souls renew;
   Showers of blessing over all
   Softly fall:

3. Like the sun's reviving ray,
   May Thy love with tender glow
   All our coldness melt away,
   Warm and cheer us forth to go,
   Gladly serve Thee and obey
   All the day.

4. Oh, our only Hope and Guide,
   Never leave us nor forsake;
   Keep us ever at Thy side
   Till the eternal morning break
   Moving on to Zion's hill,
   Homeward still.

5. Lead us all our days and years
   In Thy strait and narrow way,
   Lead us through the vale of
   tears
   To the land of perfect day.
   Where Thy people, fully blest,
   Safely rest.
   -G. A. Macfarren

114

Awake, My Soul, and With The Sun

1. Awake, my soul, and with the sun
   Thy daily stage of duty run;
   Shake off dull sloth, and Joyful rise,
   To pay thy morning sacrifice.

2. All praise to Thee, who safe has
   kept,
   And hast refreshed me whilst I
   slept.
   Grant, Lord, when I from death shall
   wake,
   I may of endless life partake

3. Lord, I my vows to Thee renew;
   Disperse my sins as morning dew;
   Guard my first springs of thought
   and will,
   And with Thyself my spirit fill.

4. Direct, control, suggest this day.
   All I design, or do. or say,
   That all my powers, with all their
   might,
   In Thy sole glory may unite.

5. Redeem Thy misspent moments
   past, And live this day as if thy
   last;
   Thy talents to improve take care;
   Far the great day thyself
   prepare.

6. Let all thy, converse be sincere,
   Thy conscience as the noonday
   dear:
   For God's all-seeing eye surveys
   Thy secret thoughts, thy words
   and ways.

7. By influence of the fight Divine
   Let thy own light to others shine;
   Reflect all Heaven's propitious rays
   In ardent love and cheerful praise.

115

Come To The Morning. Prayer S.M.

1. Come to the morning prayer.
   Come, let us kneel and pray;
   Prayer is the Christian pilgrim's
   staff,
   To walk with God all day.

2. At noon beneath the Rock
   Of Ages rest and pray:
   Sweet is the shadow from the heat,
   When the sun smites by day.

3. At eve shut to the door,
   Round the home-altar pray.
   And finding there the house of
   God,
   At heaven's gate closed the day.

4. When midnight seals our eyes,
   Let each in spirit say,
   I sleep, but my heart waketh, Lord.
   With Thee to watch and
   pray.

EVENING

116

Canon-L.M.

1. Glory to thee, my God, this night
For all the blessings of the light;
Keep me, 0 keep me. King of kings,
Beneath thy own almighty wings.

2. Forgive me. Lord. for thy dear Son,
The ill that I this day have done,
That with the world, myself, and
Thee,
I ere I sleep, at peace may be.

3. Teach me to live, that I may dread
The grave as little as my bed;
Teach me to die, that so I may
Rise glorious at the awful day.

4. 0 may my soul on thee repose,
And may sweet sleep mine eyelids
close,
Sleep that may me more vigorous
make
To serve my God when I awake.

5. When in the night I sleepless lie,
My soul with heavenly thoughts
supply;
Let no ill dreams disturb my rest
No powers of darkness me molest.

6. Praise God, from whom all blessing
flow.
Praise him, all creatures here below,
Praise him above, angelic host,
Praise Father, Son, and Holy Ghost.
Bishop T. Ken

117

St. Timothy-C.M.

1. My Father, for another night
Of quiet sleep and rest,
For all the joy of morning light,
Thy holy name be blest.

2. Now with the new-born day I give
Myself anew to thee,
That as thou willest I may live,
And what thou willest be.

3. Whate'er I do, things great or small,
Whate'er I speak or frame.
Thy glory may I seek in all
Do all in Jesus' name.

4. My Father, for his sake, I pray,
Thy child accept and bless;
And lead me by thy grace today
In paths of righteousness.
-Sir H.W. Bater

118

Thuringia - 5.5.8.8.5.5.

1. Round me falls the night;
saviour, be my light:
Through the hours in darkness
shrouded
Let me see thy face unclouded;
Let thy glory shine
In this heart of mine.

2. Earthly work is done,
Earthly sounds are none;
Rest in sleep and silence
seeking,
Let me hear thee softly speaking;
In my spirit's ear
Whisper, 'I am near.'

3. Blessed, heavenly Light,
Shining through earth's night;
Voice, that oft of love hast told
me;
Arms, so strong to clasp and
hold me;
Thou thy watch wilt keep,
Saviour, o'er my sleep.

-W. Romanis

EVENING

119

Ellen 10.10.10.10.

1. Saviour, again to Thy dear Name we
raise With one accord
our parting hymn of praise; We
stand to bless Thee
ere our worship cease. Then, lowly
kneeling, wait Thy word of peace.

2. Grant us Thy peace upon our homeward way; With Thee began,
with Thee shall end the day; Guard
Thou the lips from
sin, the hearts from shame. That in
this house have called upon Thy
Name.

3. Grant us Thy peace. Lord, thro' the
coming night. Turn Thou for us
its darkness into light; From harm
and danger
Keep Thy children free. For dark and
light are both alike to Thee.

4. Giant us Thy peace through - out
our earthly life. Our balm in
Sorrow and our stay in strife; Then,
when thy voice shall
Bid our conflict cease, call us, O
Lord, to Thine eternal peace.
                        -John Ellerton

120

Hursely-L.M.

1. Sun of my soul, Thou saviour dear,
It is not night if Thou be near,
O may no earth-born cloud arise
To hide Thee from Thy servant's
eyes!

2. When the soft dews of kindly sleep
My weary eyelids gently sleep,
Be my last thought, how sweet to
rest
Forever on my Saviour's breast!

3. Abide with me from morn till eve,
For without Thee I cannot live;
Abide with me when night is nigh,
For without Thee I dare not die.

4. Be near to bless me when I wake,
Ere thru the world my way I take;
Abide with me till in Thy love
I lose myself in heav'n above.
                        -John Keble

121

St Matthias-8.8.8.8.8.8.

1. Sweet Saviour, bless us ere we go;
Thy word into our minds instil,
And make our lukewarm hearts to
glow
With lowly love and fervent will.
Through life's long day and death's
dark night,
O gentle Jesus, be our Light.

2. The day is done. Its hours have run,
And thou hast taken count of all,
The scanty triumphs grace hath
won,
The broken vow, the frequent fall.
Through life's long day and death's
death night,
O gentle Jesus, be our Light.

3. Grant us, dear Lord, from evil ways
True absolution and release;
And bless us, more than in past
days,
With purity and inward peace.
Through life's long day and death's
dark night,
O gentle Jesus, be our Light.

4. Do more than pardon; give us joy,
Sweet fear, and sober liberty,
And loving hearts without alloy
That only tong to be tike thee.
Through life's long day and death's
dark night,
O gentle Jesus; be our Light.

5. For all we Love, the poor, the sad,
The sinful, unto thee we call;
O let thy mercy make us glad:
Thou art our Jesus, and our all
Through life's long day and death's
dark night,
O gentle Jesus, be our Light.
                        -F. W. Fabe

EVENING

122

St Anatotius -7.6.7.6.8.8.

1. The day is past and over;
   All thanks, O Lord, to thee;
   I pray thee now that sinless
   The hours of dark may be:
   O Jesus. keep me in thy sight,
   And guard me through the coming
   night

2. The joys of day are over.
   I lift my heart to thee,
   And ask thee that offenceless
   The hours of dark may be:
   O Jesus, keep me in thy sight,
   And guard me through the coming
   night

3. The toils of day are over;
   I raise the hymn to thee,
   And ask that free from peril
   The hours of dark may be:
   O Jesus. keep in thy sight,
   And guard me through the coming
   night.

4. Be thou my soul's preserver,
   For thou alone dost know
   How many are the perils
   Through which I have to go:
   O loving Jesus, hear my call,
   And guard and save me from them
   all.

   -J. M. Neale

123

Ardgowan 9.8.9.8.

1. The day thou gavest, Lord, is
   ended,
   The darkness falls at thy behest;
   To thee our morning hymns
   ascended,
   Thy praise shall sanctify our rest

2. We thank thee that thy Church
   unsleeping,
   While earth rods onward into light.
   Through all the world her watch is
   keeping,
   And rests not now by day or night.

3. As o'er each continent and island
   The dawn leads on another day,
   The voice of prayer is never silent.
   Nor dies the strain of praise away.

4. The sun that bids us rest is waking
   Our brethren' neath the western sky,
   And hour by hour fresh lips are
   making
   Thy wondrous doings heard on high

5. So be it. Lord; thy throne shall
   never,
   Like earth's proud empires, pass
   away;
   Thy Kingdom stands, and grows for
   ever
   Till all thy creatures own thy sway.

   J. Ellerto

124

Innsbruck -7.7.6.7.7.8.

1. The duteous day now closeth,
   Each flower and tree reposeth,
   Shade creeps o'er wild and wood:
   Let us, as night is falling,
   On God our Maker calling,
   Give thanks to him, the giver of
   good.

2. Now all the heavenly splendour
   Breaks forth in starlight tender
   From myriad worlds unknown:
   And man, the marvel seeing,
   Forgets his selfish being.
   For joy of beauty not his own.

3. His care he drowneth yonder,
   Lost in the abyss of wonder:
   To heaven his soul doth steal:
   This life he disesteemeth.
   The day it is that dreameth,
   That doth from truth his vision seal

4. Awhile his mortal blindness
   May miss God's loving-kindness,
   And grope in faithless strife:
   But when life's day is over
   Shall death's fair night discover
   The fields of everlasting life.

   -P. Gerhaa

EVENING

125

St. Columba -6.4.6.6

1. The sun is sinking fast,
The daylight dies;
Let love awake, and pay
Her evening sacrifice.

2. As Christ upon the Cross
His head inclined,
And to his Father's hands
His parting soul resigned,

3. So now herself my soul
Would wholly give
Into his sacred charge,
In whom all spirits live;

4. So now beneath his eye
Would calmly rest,
Without a wish or thought
Abiding in the breast,

5. Save that this will be done,
Whate'er betide,
Dead to herself, and dead
In him to all beside.

6. Thus would I live; yet now
Not I but he,
In all is power and love
Henceforth alive in me.

7. Once sacred Trinity!
One Lord divine!
May I be ever his.
And he forever mine.
                    -E. Caswall

126

Dretzel- 8.7.8.7.7.7

1. Through the day Thy love has
spread us;
Now we lay us down to rest;
Through the silent watches
Guard us,

Let no foe our peace molest
Jesus, thou our guardian be;
Sweet it is to trust in thee.

2. Pilgrims here on earth and
strangers,
Dwelling in the midst of foes,
Us and ours preserve from
dangers;
In thine arms may we repose,
And, when life's sad day is past,
Rest with thee in heaven at last.
                    -T. Kelly

127

Thanet -8.3.3.6

1. Ere I sleep, for every favour
This day showed
By my God,
I will bless my Saviour.

2. O my Lord, what shall I render
To Thy name, Still the same,
Gracious, good and tender?

3. Thou hast ordered all my goings
In Thy way,
Heard me pray,
Sanctified my doings.

4. Leave me not, but ever love me;
Let Thy peace
Be my bliss,
Till Thou hence remove me.

5. Thou my Rock, my Guard, my
tower
Safely keep.
While I sleep,
Me, with all Thy power.

6. So, whene'er in death I slumber,
Let me rise
With the wise,
Counted in thieir number.
                    -J. I Sennick

EVENING

128

Quern Pastores Laudavere - 8.8.8.7

1. Light of gladness. Lord of glory,
Jesus Christ our king most holy,
shine among us in your mercy:
earth and heaven join their hymn.

2. Let us sing at sun's descending as
we see the lights of evening.
Father, Son, and Spirit praising
with the holy seraphim.

3. Son of God, through all the ages
worthy of our holiest praises.
yours the life that never ceases,
light which never shall grow dim.
                    -Christopher Idle

129

Christy Sanctorum-11.11.11.5

1. Lighten our darkness now the day
is ended:
Father in mercy, guard your
children sleeping;
From every evil, every harm
defended,
safe in your keeping.

2. To the last hour, when heaven's
day
is dawning, far spent the night that
knows no earthly waking;
keep us as watchmen, longing for
the morning.
Till that day's breaking.
                    -Timothy Dudley-Smith

130

**Saviour, Breathe An Evening
Blessing -8.7.8.7**

1. Saviour, breathe an evening
blessing.
Ere repose our spirits seal;
Sin and want we come confessing;
Thou canst save, and Thou canst
heel.

2. Though the night be dark and
dreary
Darkness cannot hide from Thee:
Thou art He who, never weary,
Watchest where Thy people be.

3. Though destruction walk around us,
Though the arrow past us fly,
Angels guard from Thee surround us
We are safe if Thou art nigh.

4. Blessed Spirit, brooding o'er us,
Chase the darkness of our night;
Till the Defect day before us
Breaks in everlasting light.
                    -James Edmeston

131

Eventide-10.10.10.10.

1. Abide with me - fast falls the
eventide,
The darkness deepens-Lord, with
me abide:
When other helpers fail and
comforts flee,
Help of the helpless, O abide
with me!

2. Swift to its close ebbs out life's tittle
day,
Earth's joys grow dim, its glories
pass away:
Change and decay in all around I
see
O Thou who changes! not. abide ;
with me'

3. I need Thy presence ev'ry passing
hour -
What but Thy grace can foil the
tempter s powr?
Who like Thy-self my guide and
stay can be?
Thru cloud and sunshine, O abide
with me!

4. Hold Thou Thy word before my
closing eyes.
Shine thru the gloom and point me
to the skies;
Heaven's morning breaks and
earth's vain shadows flee -
In life, in death, O Lord, abide with
me!

-Henry F.Lyte

132

EUDOXIA - 6.5.6.5

1. Now the day is over,
Night is drawing nigh;
Shadows of the evening
Steal across the sky.

2. Jesus, give the weary
Calm and sweet repose;
With Thy tend'rest blessing
May our eyelids close.

3. Grant to little children
Visions bright of Thee;
Guard the sailors tossing
On the deep blue sea.

4. Thru the long night watches
May Thine angels spread
Their white wings above me,
Watching round my bed.

5. When the morning wakens,
Then may I arise
Pure and fresh and sinless
In Thy holy eyes.

-Sabine Baring-Gould

133

Alberta -10.4.10.4.10.10.

1. Lead, kindly Light, amid the
encircling gloom,
Lead thou me on;
The night is dark, and I am far from
home;

Lead thou me on.
Keep thou my feet; I do not ask to
see
The distant scene; one step enough
for me

2. I was not ever thus, nor prayed that
thou
Shouldst lead me on;
I loved to choose and see my path;
but now
Lead thou me on.
I loved the garish day and spite of
fears,
Pride ruled my will: remember not
past years

3. So long thy power hath blest me,
sure it still
Will lead me on,
o'er moor and fen, o'er crag and
torrent, till
The night is gone,
And with the morn those angel faces
smile,
Which I have loved long since, and
lost a while.

-Cardinal J. H. Newman

134

St. Gabriel 8.8-8.4

1. The radiant morn hath pass'd away,
And spent too soon her golden store;
The shadows of departing day,
Creep on once more.

2. Our life is but an autumn day,
Its glorious noon how quickly past;
Lead us o Christ, Thou living way,
Safe home at last.

3. O by Thy soul-inspiring grace
Uplift our hearts to realms on high;
Help us to look to that bright place
Beyond the sky.

4. where light, and life, and joy, and peace
In undivided empire reign
And thronging angels never cease their deathless strain;

5. Where saints are cloth'd in spotless white
and ev'ning shadows never fall;
Where Thou, eternal Light of Light,
Art Lord of all.

135

Lord, His Eventide

1. Lord. it is eventide: the light of day is waning;
Far o'er the golden land earth's voices faint and fall;
Lowly we pray to Thee for strength and love sustaining,
Lowly we ask of Thee Thy peace upon us all.
Oh, grant unto our souls.

Chorus
Light that groweth not pale
Love that never can fail till life shall cease;
Joy no trial shall mar,
Hope that shineth afar,
Faith serene as a star,
And Christ's own peace.

2. Lord, it is eventide we turn to Thee for healing
Like those of Galilee who came at close of day;
Speak to our waiting souls their hidden founts unsealing;
Touch us with hands divine that take our sin away.
Oh, grant unto our souls

3. Saviour, Thou knowest all the trial and temptation,
Knowest the wilfulness and way-wardness of youth:
Help us to cling to Thee, our Strength and our salvation,
Help us to find in Thee one eternal Truth.
Oh, grant unto our souls.

4. Lord it is eventide: our hearts await thy giving,
Wait for that peace divine that none can take away,
Peace that shall lift our souls to loftier heights of living,
Till we abide with Thee in ever lasting day.
Oh, grant unto our souls.

136

We lift Up Our Eyes To Thee - 7.7.7.7.

1. We lift up our eyes to Thee
And our hands and all our hearts,
Lord accept the prayer we make,
Though unworthy, weak and faint.

2. Lord grant that we may know Thee,
May we all know Thy name,
Help us here to do Thy will,
As is done up there in heaven.

3. When we sleep, at dead of night,
Guard us, keep and stand by us.
And when breaks forth morning light,
Let us wake. and praise Thy name.

THE LORD'S DAY

137
Church Triumphant-LM.

1. Again the Lord's own day is here,
   The day to Christian people dear,
   As week by week it bids them tell
   How Jesus rose from death and
   hell.

2. For by His flock their Lord declared
   His resurrection should be shared;
   And we who trust in Him to save
   With Him are risen from the grave.

3. We, one and all, of Him possessed,
   Are with exceeding treasures blest;
   For all He did and all He bare
   He gives us as our own to share.

4. Eternal glory, rest on high,
   A blessed immortality,
   True peace and gladness, and a
   throne,
   Are all His gifts and all our own.

5. And therefore unto Thee we sing.
   O Lord of peace, eternal King;
   Thy love we praise. Thy name
   adore,
   Both on this day and evermore.
   -Jame W. Eliott

138
Tarra Beata - S.M.D

1. This is my Father's world,
   And to my listening ears
   All nature sings, and round me rings
   The music of the spheres.
   This is my Father's world:
   I rest me in the thought
   Of rocks and trees, of skies and
   seas
   His hand the wonders wrought.

2. This is my Father's world,
   The birds their carols raise,
   The morning light, the lily white,
   Declare their Makers praise.
   This is my Father's world:

He shine in all that's fair.
In the rustings grass f hear Him
pass.
He speaks to me everywhere.

3. This is my Father's world.,
   O let me ne'er forget
   That though the wrong seems oft so
   strong.
   God is the Ruler yet.
   This is my Father's world:
   The battle is not done;
   Jesus who died shall be satisfied.
   And earth and heav'n be one.
   -Maltbte D. Babcock

139

St Hugh- C.M.

1. Behold, we come, dear Lord, to
   Thee.
   And bow before Thy throne;
   We come to offer on our knee
   Our vows to Thee alone.

2. Whate'er we have whate'er we are,
   Thy bounty freely gave;
   Thou dost us here in mercy spare,
   And wilt hereafter save.

3. Come then, my soul, bring all thy
   powers,
   And grieve thou hast no more;
   Bring every day thy choicest hours,
   And thy great God adore.

4. But, above all, prepare thine heart
   On this, His own blest day,
   in its sweet task to bear thy part,
   And sing and love and pray.
   -J. Austin

140

St Monica - C.M,

1. Blest day of God, most calm, most
   bright,
   A day of joy and praise;
   The labourer's rest, the saint's
   delight,
   The first and best of days.

2. This day the Lord our Saviour rose
Victorious from the dead;
And, as a conqueror. His foes
In glorious triumph led.

3. This day of days doth saints enrich
And smiles upon them all:
It is their Pentecost, on which
The Holy Ghost doth fall.

4. As the first fruits an earnest prove
Of all the sheaves behind,
So they who do the Sabbath love
A happy week shall find.

-M. Rock

141

Madrid - 8.8.8.8.8.8.

1. Come let us with our Lord arise!
our Lord who made both earth and
skies.
who died to save the world he made
and rose triumphant from the dead:
he rose, the prince of life and peace
and stamped the day for ever his.

2. This is the day the Lord has made
that all may see his love displayed,
may feel his resurrection's power
and rise again to fall no more,
In perfect righteousness renewed
and filled with all the life of God.

3. Then let us render him his own
with solemn prayer approach the
Throne,
with meekness hear the gospel
word,
with thanks his dying love record,
our joyful hearts and voices raise
and fill his courts with songs of
praise

-C. Wesley

142

Farley Castle -10.10.10.10.

1. Most glorious Lord of life, that on
this day
Didst make Thy triumph over death
and sin,
And having harrowed hell, didst
bring away
Captivity thence captive, us to win:
love, dear Love, like as we ought;
Love is the lesson which the Lord us
taught

2. This joyous day, dear Lord, with
joy begin
And grant that we for whom Thou
diddest die,
Being with Thy dear blood clean
washed from sin,
May live for ever in felicity:
love, dear Love, like as we ought;
Love is the lesson which the Lord us
taught

3. And that Thy love we weighing
worthily,
May likewise love Thee for the same
again;
And for Thy sake, who dost all
grace supply,
With love may one another
entertain;
love, dear Love, like as we ought;
Love is the lesson which the Lord
us taught.

-Edround Spenser

143

Mendebras - 7.6.76.D

1. O day of rest and gladness,
O day of joy and light,
O balm of care and sadness,
Most beautiful, most bright:
On thee, the high and lowly,
Through ages joined in tune,
Sing"hloly, holy, holy;
To the great God Triune.

THE LORD'S DAY

2. On thee at the creation
   The right first had its birth;
   On thee for our salvation,
   Christ rose from depths of earth;
   On thee, our Lord, victorious,
   The Spirit sent from heaven,
   And thus on thee, most glorious,
   A triple light was given.

3. Today on weary nations
   The heavenly manna fall;
   To holy convocation
   The silver trumpet, calls,
   Where gospel is glowing
   With pure and radiant beams,
   And living water, flowing,
   With soul refreshing streams.

4. New graces ever gaining
   From this our day of rest,
   We reach the rest remaining;
   To spirits of the blest.
   To Holy Ghost be praises.
   To Father and to Son;
   The church her voice upraises
   To Thee, blest Three in One.
   -Christopher Wordsworth

144
Lubeck-7.7.7.7.

1. On this day, the first of days,
   God the Father's name we praise;
   Who, creation's Lord and spring,
   Did the world from darkness bring.

2. On this day the eternal Son
   Over death His triumph won;
   On this day the Spirit came
   with His gifts of loving flame.

3. O that fervent love today
   May in every heart have sway,
   Teaching us to praise aright God
   the source of life and light

4. Father, who didst fashion me
   Image of Thyself to be.
   Fill me with Thy love divine.
   Let my every thought be Thine.

And, by love inflamed, arise
Unto Thee a sacrifice.

6. Thou who dost all gifts impart,
   Shine, blest Spirit, in my heart;
   Best of gifts, Thyself bestow;
   Make me burn Thy love to know,

7. God, eternal Three in One,
   Dwell within my heart alone;
   Thou dost give Thyself to me,
   May I give myself to Thee,
   -Carcassonne Breviary

145
SWABIA -S. M.

1. Our day of praise is done;
   The evening shadows fall;
   But pass not from us with the sun,
   True Light that lightenest all.

2. Around the throne on high,
   Where night can never be,
   The white-robed harpers of the sky
   Bring ceaseless hymns to Thee.

3. Too faint our anthems here;
   Too soon of praise we tire:
   But oh, the strains how full and clear
   Of that eternal choir!

4. Yet, Lord, to Thy dear will
   If Thou attune the heart
   We in Thine angels music still
   May bear our lower part

5. Tis Thine each soul to calm,
   Each wayward thought reclaim,
   And make our life a daily psalm
   Of glory to Thy name.

6. A little while, and then
   Shall come the glorious end;
   And songs of angels and of men
   In perfect praise shall blend
   -Unknown

THE LORD'S DAY

146

Sabbath - 7.7.7.7.D.

1. Safely through another week
God has brought us on our way;
Let us now a blessing seek,
Waiting in His courts today:
Day of all the week the best,
Emblem of eternal rest:
Day of all the week the best,
Emblem of eternal rest

2. While we pray for pardoning grace,
Thro' the dear Redeemer's name,
Show Thy reconciled face.
Take away our sin and shame:
From our worldly cares set free.
May we rest this day in Thee:
From our worldly cares set free,
May we rest this day in Thee.

3. Here we come Thy name to praise;
Let us feel Thy presence near
May Thy glory meet our eyes.
While we in Thy house appear;
Here afford us, Lord, a taste
Of our everlasting feast.

4. May Thy Gospel's joyful sound
Conquer sinners, comfort saints;
May the fruits of grace abound.
Bring relief for all complaints:
Thus may all our Sabbaths prove,
Till we join the church above:
Thus may all our Sabbaths prove.
Till we know the church above.
                                    -John Newton

147

Galilee - 8.8.8.8.

1. Sweet is the work, my God, my King,
to praise your name, give thanks and sing,
to show your love by morning light.
and talk of all your truth at night.

2. Sweet is the day, the first and best,
on which I share your sacred rest
so let my heart in tune be found,
like David's harp of joyful sound

3. My heart shall triumph in the Lord
and bless his works, and bless
his word:
God's works of grace, how bright
they shine
how deep his counsels; how divine!

4. Soon I shall see and hear and know
all I desired on earth below,
and an my powers for God employ
in that eternal world of joy.
                                    -Isaac. watts

148

St George (Gauntlett)-S.M.

1. This is the day of light:
Let there be light today;
O Day spring rise upon our night,
And chase its gloom away.

2. This is the day of rest
Our failing strength renew,
On weary brain and troubled breast
Shed Thou Thy freshening dew,

3. This is the day of peace:
Thy peace our spirits fill:
Bid Thou the blasts of discord:
Cease;
The waves of strife be still.

4. This is the day of prayer:
Let earth to heaven draw near,
Lift up our hearts to seek Thee there:
Come down to meet us here.

5. This is the first of days:
Send forth Thy quickening breath
And wake dead souls to love and praise.
O Vanquisher or death. "
                                    -H. J. Gauntlett

THE LORD'S DAY

149
Bishopthorpe C.M

1. This is the day the Lord has made,
   he calls the hours his own:
   let heaven rejoice, let earth be glad,
   and praise surround the throne.

2. Today he rose and left the dead,
   and Satan's empire fell;
   today the saints his triumphs
   spread,
   and all his wonders tell.

3. Hosanna to the anointed king,
   to David's holy Son!
   help us, O Lord; descend and bring
   salvation from your throne,

4. Blessed be the Lord, who freely came
   to save our Sinful race;
   he comes, in God his Father's
   name.
   with words of truth and grace.

5. Hosanna in the highest strains the
   church on earth can raise
   the highest heaven in which he reigns
   shall give him noble praise.
   -Isaac Watts

150
Moravia -S. M.

1. Welcome, sweat day of rest,
   That saw the Lord arise,
   Welcome to this reviving breast,
   And these rejoicing eyes.

2. The King Himself comes near,
   And feasts His saints today;
   Here we may seek and see Him
   here,
   And love, and praise, and pray.

3. One day of prayer and praise
   His sacred courts within,
   Is sweeter than ten thousand days
   Of pleasurable sin.

My willing soul would stay
In such a frame as this;
And wait to hail the brighter day
Of everlasting bliss.
                    -L. R. West

151
O quanta qualia - 10.10

1. What are those Sabbaths of joy
   without end,
   Angels in light and the glorified
   spend:
   Rest for the weary, for victors
   reward:
   There God Himself all and in all
   adored?

2. Who is the Monarch? who
   circle His throne?
   What is the calm restful bliss of
   His own?
   Tell us, ye blessed ones
   worshiping there,
   rapture declare.

3. Oh true Jerusalem, city most
   bright,
   Whose perfect peace is eternal
   delight
   Longings in thee are fulfill'd, ere
   express'd;
   More than was long'd for
   embrace and possess

4. Troubles all past, in the courts of
   our King
   We without fear Zion's anthems
   Shall sing,
   Off'rring Thee, Lord, in Thy
   presence above
   Love's pure responses for gifts
   Of Thy love.

5. There never Sabbath to Sabbath
   gives place!
   One is their Sabbath who gaze
   on Thy face
   There never cease heaven's
   jubilee songs.
   Chanted by saints and by sweet
   angel tongues.

THE LORD'S DAY

6. Meantime in heart and with faith-
winged prayers
Seek we our Fatherland yonder
and theirs;
While to Jerusalem bounden we
roam,
Exiles returning from Babylon
home:

7. Now before Him we adoringly
fail,
Of whom and through whom
and in whom are all;
Of whom the Father, and
through whom the Son,
In whom the Spirit of Both, ever
One.

-From la Feuillee

152

Brown C.M.

1. With joy we hail the sacred day
Which God has called His own;
With joy the summons we obey
To worship at His throne.

2. Spirit of grace, O deign to dwell
Within Thy church below!
Make her in holiness excel,
With pure devotion glow.

3. Let peace within her walls be found;
Let all her sons unite,
To spread with grateful zeal around
Her clear and shining light.

4. Great God, we hail the sacred day
Which Thou hast called Thine own;
Which joy the summons we obey
To worship at Thy throne.

-Harriet Auber

153

Weber-7.7.

1. Ere another Sabbath's close,
Ere again we seek repose,
Lord, our song ascends to Thee,
At Thy feet we bow the knee.

2. For the mercies of the day.
For this rest upon our way,
Thanks to Thee alone be given,
Lord of earth, and King of heaven.

3. Cold our services have been,
Mingled every prayer with sin;
But Thou canst and wilt forgive,
By Thy grace alone we live.

4. Whilst this thorny path we tread
May Thy love our footsteps lead;
When our journey here is past,
May we rest with Thee at last.

5. Let these earthly Sabbaths prove
Foretastes of our joys above;
While their steps Thy pilgrims bend
To the rest which knows no end.

-Weber

154

Aurelia-7.6.D.

1. O God, the Rock of Ages,
Who evermore hast been,
What time the tempest rages,
Our dwelling place serene:
Before Thy first creations,
O Lord, the same as now,
To endless generations
The Everlasting Thou!

2. Our years are like the shadows
On sunny hills that lie,
Or grasses in the meadows
That blossom but to die;
A sleep, a dream, a story
By strangers quickly told.
An unremaining glory
Of things that soon are old.

3. O Thou, who canst not slumber,
Whose light grows never pale,
Teach us aright to number
Our years before they fail,
On us Thy mercy lighten,
On us Thy goodness rest,
And let Thy Spirit brighten
The hearts Thyself hast bless'd.

4. Lord, crown our faiths endeavour
   With beauty and with grace.
   Till clothed in light for ever,
   We see Thee face to face:
   A fountain brimming o'er,
   An endless flow of pleasures;
   An ocean without shore.
   -S. S. Wesley

155

St. Silvester-P.M.

1. Days and moments quickly flying
   Speed us onward to the dead:
   Oh, how soon shall we be lying
   Each within his narrow bed!

2. Jesus, merciful Redeemer,
   Rouse dead souls to hear Thy
   voice;
   Wake, oh wake each idle dreamer
   Now to make the eternal choice.

3. Mark we wither we are wending;
   Ponder how we soon must go
   To inherit bliss unending,
   Or eternity of woe.

4. As a shadow life is fleeting;
   As a vapour so it flies;
   For the bygone years retreating
   Pardon grant, and make us wise.

5. Wise that we our days may number
   Strive and wrestle with our sin,
   Stay not in our work nor slumber
   Till Thy holy rest we win.

6. Soon before the Judge all glorious
   We with all the dead shall stand;
   Saviour, over death victorious,
   Place us then on Thy right hand.
   J. B. Dykes

156

Lord Of The Sabbath! Hear Our vows - L.M.

1. Lord of the Sabbath! Hear our vows
   On this Thy day, in this Thy
   house;
   And own, as grateful sacrifice,
   The songs which from the
   desert rise.

2. Thine earthly Sabbaths, Lord.
   we love
   But there's a nobler rest above:
   To that our labouring soul aspire.
   With ardent pangs of strong
   desire.

3. No more fatigue, no more distress.
   Nor sin, nor hell, shall reach the
   place:
   No groans to mingle with the
   songs
   Which warble from immortal
   tongues.

4. No rude alarms of raging foes,
   No cares to break the long repose:
   No midnight shade, no clouded
   Sun,
   But sacred, high, eternal noon.

5. O long-expected day, begin!
   Dawn on these realms of woe
   and sin;
   Fain would we leave this weary
   road,
   And sleep in death to rest with
   God.

THE WORD OF GOD

157

Spanish Chant -7.7.7.7.7.7.

1. Come, divine Interpreter,
   Bring us eyes Thy Book to read.
   Ears the mystic words to hear.
   Words which did from Thee
   proceed,
   Words that endless bliss impart,
   Kept in an obedient heart.

2. All who read, or hear, are blessed.
   If Thy plain commands we do;
   Of Thy kingdom here possessed,
   Thee we shall in glory view:
   When Thou com'st on earth to
   abide.
   Reign triumphant at Thy side
   　　　　　　　-Charles Wesley

158

Bread of life-6.4.6.4.D.

1. Break Thou the bread of life.
   Dear Lord, to me,
   Thou didst break the loaves
   Beside the sea;
   Beyond the sacred page
   I seek Thee, Lord.
   My spirit pants for Thee,
   O living Word.

2. Bless Thou the truth, dear Lord.
   To me .to me,
   As Thou didst bless the bread
   By Galileo,
   Then shall all bondage cease.
   All fetters fall;
   And I shall find my peace,
   My All in all.

3, Thou art the bread of life.
   O Lord, to me,
   Thy holy Word the truth

That saveth me;
Give me to eat and live
With Thee above;
Teach me to love Thy truth,
For Thou art love.

4. O send Thy Spirit. Lord,
   Now unto me,
   That He may touch my eyes
   And make me see:
   Show me the truth concealed
   Within Thy Word,
   And in Thy Book revealed
   I see the Lord.
   　　　　　　　-Mary A. Lathbury,

159

Munich-7.6.7.6.D.

1. O Word of God incarnate,
   O Wisdom from on high,
   O Truth unchanged, unchanging,
   O Light of our dark sky;
   We praise Thee for the radiance
   That from the hallowed page,
   A lantern to our foot steps,
   Shines on from age to age.

2. The Church from her dear Master
   Received the gift divine,
   And still that light she lifteth
   O'er all the earth to shine.
   It is the golden casket
   Where gems of truth are stored;
   It is the heav'n drawn picture
   Of Christ, the living Word.

3. It floateth like a banner
   Before God's host unfurled;
   It shineth like a beacon
   Above the darkling world.
   It is the chart and compass
   That o'er life's surging sea,
   'Mid mists and rocks and quick
   sands,
   Still guides,O Christ, to Thee.

THE WORD OF GOD

4. O make Thy Church, dear Saviour,
A lamp of purest gold.
To bear before the nations
Thy true light as of old.
O teach Thy wand'ring pilgrims
By this their path to trace,
Till. clouds and darkness ended.
They see Thee face to face.
-William W. How

160

Ottawa- 8.7.8.7.7.7.

1. Master, speak! Thy servant hereth,
Waiting for Thy gracious word,
Longing for Thy voice that cheereth,
Master, let it now be heard.
I am list'ning. Lord. for Thee:
What hast Thou to say to me?

2. Speak to me by name,O Master.
Let me know it is to me;
Speak, that I may follow faster,
With a step more firm and free,
Where the Shepherd leads the flock
In the shadow of the Rock.

3. Master, speak! though least and lowest,
Let me not unheard depart;
Master, speak! for oh. Thou knowest
All the yearning of my heart,
Knowest all its truest need;
Speak! And make me blest indeed-

4. Master, speak! and make me ready,
When Thy voice is truly heard,
With obedience glad and steady,
Still to follow every word.
I am listening. Lord, for Thee:
Master, speak, oh. speak to me!
-F. R. Havergal

161

Angmering - C. M.

1. Father of mercies, in thy word
What endless glory shines
Forever be thy name adored
For these celestial lines.

2. Here may the blind and hungry come,
And light and food receive;
Here shall the lowliest guest have room,
And taste and see and live.

3. Here springs of consolation rise
To cheer the fainting mind,
And thirsting souls receive supplies,
And sweet refreshment find.

4. Here the Redeemer's welcome voice
Spread heavenly peace around,
And life and everlasting joys
Attend the blissful sound.

5. O may these heavenly pages be
My ever dear delight,
And still new beauties may I see.

6. And still increasing light.
Divine instructor, gracious Lord.
Be thou for ever near;
Teach me to love thy sacred word,
And view my Saviour here.
-Anne Steele

162

All saints- 8. 7. 8. 7.D.

1. God hath spoken by His prophets.
Spoken His unchanging word.
Each from age to age proclaiming

THE WORD OF GOD

God the One, the righteous Lord:
Mind the world's despair and turmoil
One firm anchor holden fast.
God is King, His throne eternal,
God the first and God the last.

2. God hath spoken by Christ Jesus,
Christ, the everlasting Son,
Brightness of the Father's glory,
With the Father ever one;
Spoken by the Word Incarnate,
God of God, ere time began,
Light of Light, to earth descending,
Man, revealing God to man.

3. God yet speaketh by his Spirit
Speaketh to the hearts of men,
In the age-long word expounding
God's own message, now as then;
Through the rise and fall of nations
One sure faith yet standing fast,
God abides, His word unchanging,
God the first and God the last.
-G. W. Briggs

163

Sandys- 6.6.8.6. (S. M.)

1. Help us, O Lord, to learn
the truths your word imparts,
to study that your laws may be
inscribed upon our hearts.

2. Help us. O Lord, to live
the faith which we proclaim,
that all our thoughts and words and
deeds
may glorify your name.

3. Help us Lord, to teach
the beauty of your ways,
that yearning souls may find the
Christ
and sing aloud his praise.
-W. W. Reid.junior

164

Croft's-6.6.6.6.4.4.4.4.

1. How, sure the Scriptures are!
God's vital, urgent word,
as true as steel, and far
more sharp than any sword:
So deep and fine.
at his control
they pierce where soul
and spirit join.

2. They test each human thought,
refining like a fire;
they measure what we ought
to do and to desire;
For God knows all
exposed it lies
before his eyes
to whom we call.

3. Let those who hear his voice
confronting them today,
reject the tempting choice of
doubting or delay:
For God speaks still
his word is clear,
so let us hear
and do his will!
-Christopher Idle

165

Dunfermline - C.M.

1. Lamp of our feet, whereby we
trace
Our path when wont to stray;
Stream from the fount of heavenly
grace;
Brook by the traveller's way:

REDEMPTION WORK

2. Bread of our souls, whereon
we feed,
True manna from on high;
Our guide and chart, wherein
we read
Of realm beyond the sky:

3. Pillars of fire through watches dark,
Or radiant cloud by day;
When waves would whelm our
tossing
Our anchor and our stay:

4. Word of the ever-living God,
Will of His glorious Son,
Without thee how could earth be
trod,
Or heaven itself be won?

5. Lord, grant that we aright may
learn.
The wisdom it imparts,
And to its heavenly teaching turn
With simple, childlike hearts.
                        -Bernard Barton

166

Dunfermline - C. M.

1. Lord, I have made Thy word my
choice,
My lasting heritage,
There shall my noblest engage
rejoice
My warmest thoughts engage.

2. I'll read the histories of Thy love,
And keep Thy laws in sight:
While though Thy promises I rove,
With ever fresh delight.

3. 'Tis a broad land of wealth
unknown
Where springs of life arise
Seeds of immortal bliss are sown,
And hidden glory lies.

4. The best relief that mourners have;
It makes our sorrow blest;
Our fairest hope beyond the grave,
And our eternal rest.
                        -Isaac Watts

167

Ibstone - 6.6.6.6.

1. Lord, make your word my rule,
In it may I rejoice;
Your glory be my aim,
Your holy will, my choice:

2. Your promises my hope,
Your providence my guard;
Your arm my strong support,
Yourself my great reward.
                        -C. Wordsworth

168

Fiat lux - 6.6.4.4.

1. 'Lord of all power and might,
Father of love and light,
Speed on Thy word:
Oh let the Gospel sound,
All the wide world around,
Wherever man is found;
God speed His word.

2. Hail, blessed Jubilee:
Thine, Lord, the glory be;
Hallelujah!
Thine was the mighty plan
From Thee the work began;
Away with praise of man,
Glory to God!

3. Lo, what embattled foes,
Stern in their hate, oppose
God's holy word:
One for His truth we stand,
Strong in His own right hand,
Firm as a martyr bank;
God shield His word.

4. Onward shall be our course,
Despite of fraud or force;
God is before;
His word ere long shall run
Free as the noon day sun;
His purpose must be done:
God bless His word.

-S. Barkworth

169

Ravenshaw - 6.6.6.6.

1. Lord your word shall guide us
and with truth provide us:
teach us to receive it
and with joy believe it.

2. When our foes are near us,
Then your word shall cheer us
word of consolation,
message of salvation.

3. When the storm distress us
and dark cloud oppress us
then your word protects us
and its light direct us.

4. Who can tell the pleasure,
who recount the treasure
By your word imparted
to the simple hearted?

5. Word of mercy, giving
courage to the living;
word of life, supplying
comfort to the dying.

6. O that we discerning
its most holy learning,
Lord, may love and fear you
evermore be near you!

-H. W. Baker

170

Prims - L. M.

1. My lord, who in the desert fed
On soul-sustaning heavenly
bread,
Words that were meat and drink
to Thee
O let them daily nourish me!

2. And since the sword that
served Thee well
In battling with the powers of hell
Is even now at hand for me,
Help me to wield it manually.

3. But first, O holy, gracious Lord,
I pray Thee, let Thy Spirit's
Sword
Pierce heart and conscience, till i
see
Both what I am and ought to be.

4. Thy word my rule and my delight,
My strength for service and for
fight!
For this exhaustless treasure
store
My Lord, I praise Thee and adore!

-F. Houghton

171

Living Word -11.10.11.10.

1. Powerful in making us wise to
salvation
Witness to faith in Christ Jesus the
word
breathed out to men by the life
giving Father
These are the scriptures, and thus
speaks the Lord.

THE WORD OF GOD

2. Tool for employment and
compass for travel,
map in the desert and lamp in the
dark;
teaching, rebuking, correcting and
training
these are the scriptures, and
this is their work.

3. History, prophecy, song and
commandment.
Gospel and letter and dream
From on high;
written by men borne along by
the Spirit
these are the scriptures; on
them we rely.

4. Gift for God's servants to fit
them completely.
fully equipping to walk in his
ways;
guide to good work and
effective believing
these are the scriptures, for
these we give praise!,
                    -Christopher Idle

172

Quietude- 6.5.6.5.

1. Speak, Lord, in the stillness
While I wait on Thee;
Hushed my heart to listen
In expectancy.

2. Speak, O blessed Master,
In this quiet hour;
Let me see Thy face. Lord,
Feel Thy touch of power.

3. For the words Thou speakest,
They are life indeed;
Living Bread from heaven.
Now my spirit feed.

4. Speak, Thy servant heareth!
Be not silent. Lord;
Waits my soul upon Thee
For the quickening word.

5. Fill me with the knowledge
Of Thy glorious will
All Thine own good pleasure
In Thy child fulfil.
                    -Emily M Crawford

173

Church Triumphant - L.M.

1. The heavens declare Thy glory,
Lord;
In every star Thy wisdom shines;
But when our eyes behold Thy
word.
We read Thy name in fairer lines.

2. Sun. moon, and star convey Thy
praise
Round the whole earth, and never
stand;
So, when Thy truth began its race,
It touched and glanced on every
land.

3. Nor shall Thy spreading gospel rest
Till through the world Thy truth has
run;
Till Christ has all the nations blest,
That see the light or feel the sun.

4. Great Sun of righteousness, arise;
Bless the dark world with heavenly
light;
Thy gospel makes the simple wise,
Thy laws are pure, thy judgements
right.

5. Thy noblest wonders here we view,
In souls renewed and sins forgiven:
Lord, cleanse my sins, my soul
renew,
And make Thy word my guide to
heaven.
                    -Isaac Watts

THE WORD OF GOD

174

West Burn-C.M.

1. The Spirit breathes upon the word,
   And brings the truth to sight;
   Precepts and promises afford
   A sanctifying light.

2. A glory gilds the sacred page,
   Majestic like the sun:
   It gives a light to every age,
   It gives, but borrows none.

3. The hand that gave it still supplies
   The gracious light and heat:
   His truths upon the nations rise,
   They rise but never set.

4. Lord, everlasting thanks be Thine
   For such a bright display,
   As makes a world of darkness
   Shine
   With beams of heavenly day.

5. My soul rejoices to pursue
   The steps of Him I love,
   Till glory breaks upon my view
   In brighter worlds above.
                    -William Cowper

175

Clonmel- C.M.D.

1. Thy word is like a garden. Lord,
   With flowers bright and fair;
   And ev'ry one who seeks may pluck
   A lovely cluster there.
   Thy Word is like a deep, deep mine,
   And jewels rich and rare
   Are hidden in its mighty depths
   For ev'ry searcher there.

2. Thy Word is like a starry host;
   A thousand rays of light
   Are seen to guide the traveller
   And make his path way bright.

O may I love Thy precious Word,
May I explore the mine,
May I the fragrant flowers glean,
May light upon me shine.
                    -Edwin Hodder

176

Ellacombe - D.C.M.

1. We limit not the truth of God
   To our poor reach of mind,
   By notions of our day and sect,
   Crude, partial, and confined:
   No, let a new and better hope
   Within our hearts be stirred
   The Lord hath yet more light and
   truth
   To break forth from His word.

2. Darkling our great forefathers went
   The first steps of the way;
   'Twas but the dawning, yet to grow
   Into the perfect day.
   And grow it shall, our glorious sun
   More fervid rays afford:

3. The valleys past, ascending still,
   Our souls would higher climb,
   And look down from supernal
   heights
   On all the bygone time.
   Upward we press, the air is clear:
   And the sphere music heard;

4. O Father. Son. and Spirit, send
   Us increase from above;
   Enlarge, expand all Christian souls
   To comprehend Thy love;
   And make us all go on to know,
   With nobler powers conferred,
   The Lord hath yet more light and
   truth
   To break forth from His word.
                    -George Rawson

THE WORD OF GOD

177

Wonderful Words of life
8.6.8.6.6.6. with Refrain

1. Sing them over again to me,
   Wonderful words of Life;
   Let me more of their beauty see,
   Wonderful words of Life.
   Words of life and beauty,
   Teach me faith and duty;

   Chorus
   Beautiful words, wonderful words,
   Wonderful words of Life.
   Beautiful words, wonderful words,
   Wonderful words Of Life;

2. Christ; the blessed One, gives to all
   Wonderful words of Life;
   Sinner, list to the loving call,
   Wonderful words of Life.
   All so freely given,
   Wooing us to Heaven:

3. Sweetly echo the gospel call,
   Wonderful words of Life;
   Offer pardon and peace to all,
   Wonderful words of Life.
   Jesus, only Saviour.
   Sanctify forever
   -Philip P. Bliss

178

Ravenshaw- 6.6.6.6.

1. Lord, Thy word abideth,
   And our footsteps guideth,
   Who its truth believeth,
   Light and joy receiveth.

2. When our foes are near us,
   Then Thy word-doth cheer us,
   Word of consolation,
   Message of salvation.

3. When the storms are o'er us,
   And dark clouds before us.
   Then its light directeth,
   And our way protecteth.

4. Who can tell the pleasure,
   Who recount the treasure,
   By Thy word imparted
   To the simple hearted? -

5. Word of mercy,
   giving Succour to the living;
   Word of life, supplying
   Comfort to the dying!

6. O that we. Discerning
   Its most holy learning,
   Lord. may love and fear Thee,
   Evermore be near Thee!
   -H. W. Baker

179

St Flavian- C.M.

1. There is a book. who runs may
   read.
   Which heavenly truth imparts;
   And all the lore its scholars need,
   Pure eyes and Christian hearts.

2. The works of God above, below,
   Within us and around,
   Are pages in that book to show
   How God Himself is found.

3. The glorious sky embracing all
   Is like the Maker's love;
   Wherewith encompass'd, great and
   Small
   In peace and order move.

4. The moon above, the church below,
   A wondrous race they run;
   But all their radiance. all their glow,
   Each borrows of its sun.

5. The Saviour tends the light and heat
   That crown His holy hill;
   The saints. like stars, around His
   seat
   Perform their courses still.

6. The dew of heaven is like Thy
   grace,
   It steals in silence down;
   But where it lights, the favour'd
   Place.
   By richest fruits is known.

THE WORD OF GOD

7. One name above all glorious names
With its ten thousand tongues,
The everlasting sea proclaims,
Echoing angelic songs.

8. Thou, who hast given me eye to see
And love this sight so fair,
Give me a heart to find out Thee,
And read Thee everywhere.

-T. Ravenscroft

180

Oh, Wonderful, Wonderful Word Of The Lord

1. Oh, wonderful, wonderful Word
of the Lord! True wisdom its pages
unfold:
And though we may read them a
thousand time o'er.
They never, no, never grow old,
Each fine hath a treasure, each
promise a pearl
That all if they will may secure;
And we know that when time and
the world pass away, God's Word
shall for ever endure.

2. Oh, wonderful, wonderful Word of
the Lord!
The lamp that our Father above
So kindly has lighted to teach us
the way
That leads to the arms of His love!
Its warnings, its counsels, are
faithful and just;
Its judgements are perfect and
pure;
And we know that when time and
the world pass away;
God's Word shall for ever endure.

3. Oh, wonderful, wonderful Word
of the Lord!
Our only salvation is there;
It carries conviction down deep
In the heart,
And shows us ourselves as we
are
It tells of a Saviour, and points to
the cross,

Where pardon we now may
secure;
For we know that when time
and the world pass away;
God's Word shall for ever
Endure.

4. Oh, wonderful, wonderful Word
of the Lord!
The hope of our friends in the
Its truth here so firmly they
anchored their truth,
Through ages eternal shall last,
Oh, wonderful, wonderful Word
of the Lord!
Unchanging, abiding, and sure;
For we know that when time and
the world pass away;
God's Word shall for ever
endure.

181

Once Again The Gospel Message 8.7.8.7.

1. Once again the Gospel message
From the Saviour you have
heard;
Will you heed the invitation?
Will you turn and seek the Lord?

Chorus
Come believing! Come believing!
Come to Jesus! Look and live!
Come believing! Come believing!
Come to Jesus! Look and live!

2. Many summers you have
wasted,
Ripened harvests you have
seen;
Winter snows by spring have
melted,
Yet you linger in your sin.

3. Jesus for your choice is waiting;
Tarry not: at once decided!
While the Spirit now is striving,
Yield, and seek the Saviour's
side.

THE WORD OF GOD

4. Cease of fitness to be thinking;
   Do no longer fry to feel;
   it is trusting, and not feeling,
   That will give the Spirit's seal.

5. Let your will to God be given,
   Trust in Christ's atoning blood;
   Look to Jesus now in heaven,
   Rest to His unchanging word.

182

Thou Bible everlasting book? -C.M.

1. Thou Bible everlasting book!
   Who knows thy deep secrets?
   Your beginning on earth who
   knows?
   And who can know thy end?

2. The secrets of the God of heaven;
   Ambassador from heaven;
   The sword that killed the sting of
   death,
   God's own image divine.

3. A book indeed among thousands
   A book of ancient days;
   Thou made salvation way so
   plain
   To all mankind on earth.

4. The treasure of the Three-in-one
   The blessed Trinity
   Do, interpret Thyself to me
   And all my doubts dispel.

5. Thy pages Il'l open with prayer
   To learn Thy doctrines Lord:
   The everlasting Book divine
   Show me the saviour's love

183

**Thy Word Is A Lamp To My Feet -
8.7.8.7. with Ref.**

1. Thy word is a lamp to my feet
   A light to my path always
   To guide and to save me from sin
   And show me the heav'nly way.

   Chorus
   Thy word have I hid in my heart
   That f might not sin against Thee
   That I might not sin
   That I might not sin
   Thy word have I hid in my heart.

2. Forever O Lord Thy word
   Established and fixed on high
   Thy faithfulness unto all men
   Abideth forever nigh.

3. At morning, at noon and at night
   I ever will give Thee praise
   For Thou art my portion, O Lord
   And shall be thro' all my days

4. Thro' Him whom Thy word hath
   foretold
   The saviour and morning star
   Salvation and peace have been
   bro't
   To those who have strayed afar.

THE BIRTH OF JESUS CHRIST

184

Es istein' Ros'entsprungen
- 7.6.7:6.6.7.6.

1. A great and mighty wonder,
A full and holy cure?
The virgin bears the infant
With virgin honour pure:
Repeat the hymn again!
To God on high be glory,
And peace on earth to men.

2. The Word becomes incarnate,
And yet remains on high;
And cherubim sing anthems
To Shepherds from the sky:
Repeat the hymn again! etc.

3. While thus they sing your Monarch.
Those bright angelic bands,
Rejoice, ye vales and mountains,
Ye oceans, clap your hands:
Repeat the hymn again! Etc.

4. Since all He comes to ransom,
By all be He adored,
The infant born in Bethlem,
The Saviour and the Lord;
Repeat the hymn again! Etc.

-St Germanu

185

God rest you merry. Gentlemen
8.6.8.6.8.6. with Refrain

1. God rest you merry, gentlemen,
Let nothing you dismay,
For Jesus Christ our Saviour
Was born upon this day;
To save us all from Satan's
power
When we were gone astray.

Chorus
O tidings of comfort and joy!
Comfort and joy!
O tidings of Comfort and joy!

2. In Bethlehem in Jewry
This blessed babe was born;
And laid within a manger
Upon this blessed morn;
The which His mother Mary
Did nothing take in scorn.

3. From God our heavenly Father
A blessed angel came,
And unto certain shepherds
Brought tidings of the same,
How that in Bethlehem was born
The Son of God by name.

4. 'Fear not,' then said the angel.
'Let nothing you affright,
This day is born a Saviour
Of a pure virgin bright,
To free all those who trust in Him
From Satan's power and might.

5. The shepherds at those tidings
Rejoiced much in mind,
And left their flocks a feeding
In tempest, storm and wind,
And went to Bethlehem
Straightway,
This blessed babe to find.

6. And when to Bethlehem they
came.
Whereat this infant lay,
They found Him in a manger
Where oxen feed on hay;
His mother Mary kneeling
Unto the Lord did pray.

7. Now to the Lord sing praises,
All you within this place,
And with true love and
brotherhood
Each other now embrace;
This holy tide of Christmas
All anger should efface.

-Traditional

THE BIRTH OF JESUS CHRIST

186

Iris - 8.7.8.7. With Refrain

1. Angels, from the realms of glory,
   Wing your flight o'er all the earth;
   Ye who sang creation's story,
   Now proclaim Messiah's birth:

   Chorus
   Come and worship,
   Christ, the new born king,
   Come and worship,
   Worship Christ, the new born king.

2. Shepherds, in the fields abiding,
   Watching o'er your flocks by night,
   God with man is now residing,
   Yonder shines the infant light:

3. Sages, leave your contemplations,
   Brighter visions beam afar,
   Seek the great Desire of nations,
   Ye have seen His natal star.

4. Saints before the altar bending,
   Watching long in hope and fear,
   Suddenly the Lord, descending,
   In His temple shall appear.
   —James Montgomery

187

Yorkshire-10.10.10.10.10.10.

1. Christians, awake, salute the happy
   Morn
   Whereon the Saviour of the world
   was born:
   Rise to adore my mystery of love
   Which hosts of angels chanted from
   above;
   With them the joyful tiding first
   begun
   Of God incarnate and the virgin's
   Son.

2. Then to the watchful shepherds it
   was told,
   Who heard the angelic herald's
   voice: 'Behold,
   I bring good tidings of a Saviour's
   birth

   To you and all the nations upon
   earth:
   This day hath God fulfilled His
   promised word,
   This day is born a Saviour, Christ
   the Lord.

3. He spake; and straightway the
   celestial choir
   In hymns of joy, unknown before,
   conspire:
   The praises of redeeming love
   they sang,
   And heaven's whole orb with
   alleluias still,
   Peace upon earth, and unto men
   goodwill,

4. To Bethlehem straight the enlight
   ened shepherds ran,
   To see the wonder God had
   wrought for man:
   And found, with Joseph and the
   blessed maid,
   Her Son, the Saviour, in a
   manger laid;
   Amazed, the wondrous story they
   proclaim,
   The first apostles of His infant fame.

5. Let us, like these good shepherds,
   then employ
   Our grateful voice to proclaim the joy;
   Trace we the babe, who hath
   retrieved our loss
   From His poor manger to His bitter
   cross;
   Treading His steps, assisted by His
   grace,
   Till man's first heavenly state again
   takes place.

6. Then may we hope, the angelic
   hosts among,
   To sing redeemed a glad triumphal
   song:
   He that was born upon this joyful
   day
   Around us all His glory shall display;
   Saved by His love, incessant we
   shall sing
   Eternal praise to heaven's almighty
   King.   —J. Byrom

THE BIRTH OF JESUS CHRIST

188

Vom Himmel hoch -L. M.

1. Give heed, my heart, lift up thine
   eyes;
   Who is it in yon manger lies?
   Who is this child so young and fair?
   The blessed Christ child lieth there.

2. Ah, dearest Jesus, holy child,
   Make Thee a bed, soft, undefiled,
   Within my heart, that it may be
   A quiet chamber kept for Thee.

3. My heart for very joy doth leap,
   My lips no more can silence keep;
   I too must sing with joyful tongue.
   That sweetest ancient cradle song:

4. Glory to God in highest heaven,
   Who unto men His Son hath given;
   While angels sing with pious mirth,
   A glad new year to all the earth.
                              -Martin Luther

189

In dulci jubilo Irregular meter

1. Good Christian men, rejoice
   With heart and soul and voice;
   Give ye heed to what we say:
   Jesus Christ is born today;
   Ox and ass before Him bow,
    And He is in the manger now:
   Christ is born today.
   Christ is born today.

2. Good Christian men, rejoice
   With heart and soul and voice;
   Now ye hear of endless bliss:
   Jesus Christ was born for this;
   He has opened heaven's door,
   And man is blessed evermore:
   Christ was born for this,
   Christ was born for this.

3. Good Christian men, rejoice
   With heart and soul and voice:
   Now ye need not fear the grave:
   Jesus Christ was born to save;
   Calls you one and call you all
   To gain His everlasting hall:
   Christ was born for this.
   Christ was born for this.
                              -John M. Neate

190

Fragrance - 9.8.9.8.9.8.

1. Thou who was rich beyond all
   splendor.
   All for love's sake becamest poor;
   Thrones for a manger didst
   surrender,
   Sapphire paved courts for stable
   floor.
   Thou who was rich beyond all
   splendour.
   All for love's sake becamest poor.

2. Thou who art God beyond all
   praising,
   All for love's sake becamest man;
   Stooping so low, but sinners raising
   Heavenwards by Thine eternal plan,
   Thou who art God beyond all
   praising,
   All for love's sake becamest man.

3. Thou who art love beyond all telling,
   Saviour and King, we worship
   Thee
   Emmanuel, within us dwelling,
   Make us what Thou wouldst have
   us be:
   Thou who art love, beyond all telling,
   Saviour and King, we worship
   Thee.
                              -F. Houghton

THE BIRTH OF JESUS CHRIST

191

Cordo natus ex parentis-
8.7.8.7.8.7.7.

1. Of the Father's love begotten,
   Ere the worlds began to be,
   He, the Alpha and Omega,
   he the source, the ending
   He Of the things that are, that
   have been,
   And that future years shall see.
   Evermore and evermore.

2. He is here, whom seers aforetime
   Chanted white the ages ran,
   Whom the faithful word of prophets
   Promised since the world began;
   Long foretold, at length appearing,
   Praise Him every child of man,
   Evermore and evermore.

3. Blessed was the day for ever.
   When by God the Spirit's grace
   From the womb of virgin mother
   Came the Saviour of our race,
   When the child, the world's
   Redeemer,
   First displayed His sacred face.
   Evermore and evermore.

4. Praise Him, O ye heaven of
   heavens;
   Praise Him, angels in the height;
   All dominions bow before him,
   And exalt His wondrous might;
   Let no tongue of man be silent;
   Let each voice and heart unite,
   Evermore and evermore.

5. Christ, to Thee, with God the Father
   And, O Holy Ghost to Thee,
   Hymn and chant and high thanks
   giving,
   And unwearied praises be,
   Honour, glory and dominion,
   And eternal victory,
   Evermore and evermore.
                    -Aurelius C. Prudentius

192

Mendelssohn .7.7.7.7.0. with
Refrain

1. Hark! The herald angels sing
   Glory to the new born King.
   Peace on earth and mercy mild.
   God and sinners reconciled!
   Joyful all ye nations rise,
   Join the triumph of the skies;
   With the angelic host proclaim.
   'Christ is born in Bethlehem.'

Chorus
Hank! The herald angels sing
Glory to the new born King.

2. Christ by highest heaven adored;
   Christ, the everlasting Lord;
   Late in time behold Him come,
   Offspring of a virgin's womb:
   Veiled in flesh the God head see;
   Hail the incarnate Deity,
   Pleased as Man with man to dwell,
   Jesus our Emmanuel!

3. Hail the heaven born Prince of
   peace.
   Hail the Sun of righteousness;
   light and life to all He brings,
   Risen with healing in His wings,
   Mild. He lays His glory by,
   Born that man no more may die,
   Born to raise the sons of earth,
   Born to give them second birth.

4. Come, Desire of nations, come.
   Fix in us Thy humble home;
   Rise, the woman's conquering
   seed,
   Bruise in us the serpent's head.
   Adam's likeness, Lord, efface;
   Stamp Thy image in its place;
   O, to all Thyself impart,
   Formed in each believing heart.
                    -Charles Wesley

193

Infant holy - 4.4.7.4.4.7.4.4.4.4.7.

1. Infant holy, Infant lowly,
   For His bed a cattle stall;
   Oxen lowing,
   Little knowing
   Christ the babe is Lord of all.
   Swift are winging
   Angels singing,
   Nowells ringing,
   Tidings bringing,
   Christ the babe is Lord of all.

2. Flocks were sleeping,
   Shepherds keeping
   Vigil till the morning new
   Saw the glory,
   Heard the story,
   Tidings of a gospel true.
   Thus rejoicing.
   Free from sorrow,
   Praises voicing
   Greet the morrow,
   Christ the babe was born for you!
   —Edith M. G. Reed

194

Noel - D. C. M.

1. It came upon the midnight clear,
   That glorious song of old.
   From angels bending near the earth
   To touch their harps of gold:
   Peace on the earth, good will to
   men,
   From heav'n s all gracious King!'
   The world in solemn stillness lay
   To hear the angels sing.

2. Still thru the cloven skies they come
   With peaceful wings unfurled,
   And still their heav'nly music floats
   O'er all the weary world:
   Above its sad and lowly plains.

They bend on hov'ring wing,
And ever o'er its Babel sounds
The blessed angels sing.

3. And ye, beneath life's crushing
   load,
   Whose forms are bending low,
   Who toil along the climbing way
   With painful steps and slow,
   Look now! For glad and golden
   hours
   Come swiftly on the wing:
   O rest beside the weary road
   And hear the angels Sing.

4. For lo, the days are hast'ning on,
   By prophet bards fore - told,
   When with the ever circling years
   Shall come the time foretold,
   When the new heaven and earth
   shall own
   The Prince of peace their King,
   And the whole world send back the
   song Which now the angels sing.
   —Edmund H. Sears

195

Adeste Fideles - Irregular

1. O come, all ye faithful, joyful and
   triumphant,
   O come ye, O come ye to
   Bethlehem,
   Come and behold Him, born the
   King of angels:

Chorus
O come, let us adore Him,
O come, let us adore Him,
O come, let us adore Him,
Christ the Lord.

2. God of God, and Light of light
   begotten,
   Lo, He abhors not the virgin's
   womb;
   Very God, begotten not created;

THE BIRTH OF JESUS CHRIST

3. Sing Choirs of angels, sing in
exultation,
Sing, all ye citizens of heaven
abov'em, Glory to God, all glory in
the highest;

3 Yea, Lord, we greet Thee, born
this happy morning, Jesus, to
Thee be glory given;
Word of the Father, now in flesh
appearing'
-J. F. Wade

196
England's Lane-7.7.7.7.7.7.

1. Sing, O sing. this blessed morn!
Unto us a child is born.
Unto us a son is given.
God Himself comes down from
heaven;

Chorus
Sing, O sing, this blessed morn,
Jesus Christ today is born!

2. God of God and Light of Light
Comes with mercies infinite.
Joining in a wondrous plan
Heaven to earth, and God to man:

3. God with us, Emmanuel.
Deigns for ever now to dwell;
He on Adam's fallen race
Sheds the fulness of His grace:

4. God comes down that man may
rise,
Lifted by Him to the skies,
Christ is Son of Man. that we
Sons of God in Him may be:

5. O renew us, Lord, we pray,
With Thy Spirit day by day,
That we ever one may be,
With the Father and win Thee:
-C. Wordsworth

197

The first Nowell - Irregular

1. The first Noel, the angel did say,
Was to certain poor shepherds in
fields as they lay;
In fields where they lay keeping
their sheep,
On a cold winter's night that was so
Deep.

Chorus
Nowell, Nowell, Nowell, Nowell,
Born is the King of Israel!

2. They looked up and saw a star
Shining in the east. beyond them
far;
And to the earth it gave great light,
And so it continued both day and
night

3. And by the light of that same star.
Three wise men came from country
far;
To seek for a king was their intent,
And to follow the star wherever it
went.

4. This star drew nigh to the northwest;
O'er Bethlehem it took its rest,
And there it did both stop and stay.
Right over the place where Jesus
lay.

5. Then entered in those wise men
three
Full rev'rently upon their knee,
And offered there in His presence
Both gold and myrrh and frankin
cense.

6. Then let us all with one accord
Sing praises to our heavenly Lord,
That hath made heav'n and earth of
naught,
And with His blood mankind hath
bought.
-Traditional English carol

THE BIRTH OF JESUS CHRIST

198

Winchester Old-CM

1. While shepherds wateh'd their
flocks by night.
All seated on the ground,
The angel of the Lord came down,
And glory shone around,

2. "Fear not!" said he, (for mighty
dread
Had seized their troubled mind);
Glad tidings of great joy I bring
To you and all mankind.

3. 'To you in David's town this day
is born, of David's line,
The Saviour who is Christ the
Lord, And this shall be the sign;

4. The heavenly babe you there
shall find
To human view displayed,
All meanly wrapped in swathing
bands, And in a manger laid.'

5. Thus spake the seraph; and
forthwith
Appeared a shining throng
Of angels praising God, who thus
Addressed their joyful song;

6. 'All glory be to God on high,
And to the earth be peace;
Good-will henceforth from heaven
to men
Begin and never cease.'
-Fanny J. Crosby

199

In excelsis gloria - Irregular

1. When Christ was born of Mary free,
In Bethlehem that fair city,
Angels sang there with mirth and
glee,

Chorus
'In excelsis gloria. In excelsis gloria,
In excelsis gloria. In excelsis gloria,
In excelsis gloria, In excelsis gloria.'

2. Herdsmen beheld these angels
bright,
To them appearing with great light,
Who said 'God's Son is born to
night:'

3. The King is come to save mankind,
As in scripture truths we find,
Therefore this song we have in
mind;

4. Then, dear Lord, for Thy great
grace,
Grant us in bliss to see Thy face,
That we may sing to Thy solace:
-Traditional 15th century

200

Otannenbaum -8.8.8.8.8.8.8.7.

1. A messenger named Gabriel
came to the land of Israel;
and he proclaimed that Mary's son
was God's messiah, holy One.
O Jesus Christ, strong Son of God,
once born for us at Bethlehem:
we listen to the angel's song and
worship you for ever.

2. Angelic hosts of God most high with
radiant glory fill the sky;
enraptured voices joyful sing
to welcome Christ, the new born
King.
O Jesus Christ...

3. In awesome fear and bitter cold the
sepherds huddle in their fold;
then since the message is for them
they make their way to Bethlehem.
O Jesus Christ.

THE BIRTH OF JESUS CHRIST

4. Within the sacred stable shrine
they see the holy child divine;
the manger stands amidst the
straw and humble fold their God
adore. O Jesus Christ...

5. Since then have passed two
thousand years
of human misery and tears;
yet Christ alone can bring release:
he loves us still - the prince of
peace.
O Jesus Christ...
                              -M. J. Walker

201

Quem Pastores Laudavere - 8.8.8.6.

1. Shepherds came, their praises
bringing,
who had heard the angels singing:
'Far from you be fear unruly,
Christ is king of glory born.

2. Wise men whom a star had guided
incense, gold, and myrrh provided,
made their sacrifices truly
to the King of glory born.

3. Jesus born the King of heaven,
Christ to us through Mary given,
to your praise and honour duly
be resounding glory done.
                              -G. B. Caird

202

Mabledon - 8.7.8.7.3.3.7.

1. Christmas for God's holy people
is a time of joy and peace:
so, all Christian men and women,
hymns and carols let us raise
to our God
come to earth,
Son of Man, by human birth.

2. Child of Mary, virgin mother,
peasant baby, yet our King.
cradled there among the oxen:
joyful carols now we sing
to our God
come to earth,
Son of Man, by human birth.

3. Angel armies sang in chorus to our
Christ's nativity;
he who came to share our nature:
so we sing with gaiety
come to earth,
Son of Man, by human birth.

4. Shepherds hurried to the manger,
saw the babe of Bethlehem,
glorified the God in heaven:
now we join to sing with them
To our God
come to earth,
Son of Man. by human birth.

5. Infant lowly born in squalor,
prophet king and great high priest,
Word of God to man descending:
still we sing, both great and least,
to our God
Come to earth,
Son of Man, by human birth.
                              -Michael Saward

203

Gallery carol-11.11.11.11.

1. Come all you good people and burst
into song!
be joyful and happy, your praises
prolong;
remember the birthday of Jesus our
King,
who bring us salvation: his glory we
Sing.

2. His mother, a virgin so gentle and
pure,
Was told of God's promise,

unchanging and sure,
foretelling the birthday of Jesus our
King,
who brings us salvation: his glory
we sing.

3. To Bethlehem hurried the shepherds
amazed,
with stories of angels and heavens
that blazed,
proclaiming the birthday of Jesus
our King,
who brings us salvation: his glory
we sing.

4. So come let us honour the babe in
the hay
and give him our homage and
worship today,
recalling the birthday of Jesus our
King,
who brings us salvation: his glory
we sing.

-Michael Saward

204

Owalywaly- 8.8.8.8. (L. M.)

1. Glad music fills the Christmas sky
a hymn of praise, a song of love;
the angels worship high above and
Mary sings her lollaby.

2. Her costly love foreshadows pain
this gentle girl has much to bear;
the fingers twining in her hair will
grasp the hideous and profane.

3. The angel armies of the skies who
tell God's glory and his grace
have yet to know his human face,
to watch him die, to see him rise.

4. Let praise be true and love sincere,
rejoice to greet the Saviour's birth,
let peace and honour fill the earth
and mercy reign for God is here!

5. Then lift your hearts and voices
high,
sing once again the Christmas
song:
for love and praise to Christ belong
in shouts of Joy, and lullaby.

-Michael Perry

205

**All through the night -
8.4.8.4.8.8.8.4.**

1. Come and sing the Christmas story
this holy night!
Christ is born: the hope of glory
dawns on our sight.
Alleluia! earth is ringing
with a thousand angels singing
hear the message they are bringing
this holy night.

2. Jesus. Saviour, child of Mary this
holy night,
in a world confused and weary
you are our light
God is in a manger lying,
manhood taking, self denying,
life embracing, death defying
this holy night.

3. Lord of all! Let us acclaim him
this holy night;
king of our salvation name him,
throned in the height.
Son of Man let us adore him,
all the earth is waiting for him;
Son of God we bow before him
this holy night.

-Michael Perry

206

O Little Town of Bethlehem

1. O little town of Bethlehem,
How still we see thee lie!
Above thy deep and dreamless
sleep

THE BIRTH OF JESUS CHRIST

The silent stars go by;
Yet in thy dark streets shineth
The everlasting Light;
The hopes and fears of all the years
Are met in thee tonight.

2. For Christ is born of Mary;
   And gathered all above,
   While mortals sleep, the angels
   keep
   Their watch of wond'ring love,
   O morning stars, together
   Proclaim the holy birth,
   And praise sing to God the King.
   And peace to men on earth.

3. How silently how silently
   The wondrous gift is giv'n!
   So God imparts to human hearts
   The blessings of His heav'n.
   No ear may hear His coming;
   But in this world of sin,
   Where meek souls will receive Him
   still,
   The dear Christ enters in.

4. O holy Child of Bethlehem,
   Descend to us. we pray;
   Cast out our sin and enter in,
   Be born in us today.
   We hear the Christmas angels
   The great glad tidings tell.
   O come to us, abide with us,
   Our Lord Emmanuel!
   -Phillips Brooks

207

Antioch - C. M.

1. Joy to the world! The Lord is come:
   Let earth receive her King;
   Let ev'ry heart prepare Him room,
   And heav'n and nature sing,
   And heav'n and nature sing.
   And heav'n and heav'n and nature
   sing.

2. Joy to the world! The Saviour
   reigns:
   Let men their songs employ;
   While fields and floods, rocks, hills
   and plains
   Repeat the sounding joy,
   Repeat the sounding joy,
   Repeat, repeat the sounding joy.

3. No more let sins and sorrows grow,
   Nor thorns infest the ground;
   He comes to make His blessings
   flow
   Far as the curse is found,
   Far as the curse is found.
   Far as. far as the curse is found.

4. He rules the world with truth and
   grace:
   And makes the nations prove
   The glories of His righteousness,
   And wonders of His love,
   And wonders of His love,
   And wonders and wonders of His
   love.
   -Isaac Watts

208

Quem Pastores Laudavere
-8.8.8.7.

1. Jesus, good above all other,
   Gentle child of gentle mother,
   In a stable born our brother,
   Give us grace to persevere.

2. Jesus, cradled in a manger,
   For us facing every danger,
   Living as a homeless stranger,
   Make we thee our King most dear.

3. Jesus, for thy people dying,
   Risen Master, death defying,
   Lord in heaven, thy grace supplying,
   Keep us to thy presence near.

Jesus, who our sorrows bearest,
All our thoughts and hopes thou shares!,
Thou to man the truth declares!;
Help us all thy truth to hear.

5. Lord, in all our doings guide us;
Pride and hate shall ne'er divide us
We'll go on with thee beside us.
And with joy we'll persevere!
— P. Dearmer

209

Ellacombe - C. M. D.

1. Hail to the Lords Anointed,
Great David's greater Son;
Hail in the time appointed,
His reign on earth begun!
He comes to break oppression,
To set the captive free;
To take away transgression,
And rule in equity.

2. He shall come down like showers
Upon the fruitful earth:
And love, joy, hope, like flowers,
Spring in His path to birth.
Before Him on the mountains
Shall Peace, the herald, go;
And righteousness in fountains
From hill to valley flow.

3. Kings shall fall down before Him,
And gold and incense bring;
All nations shall adore Him,
His praise all people sing.
For He shall have dominion
O'er river, sea. and shore,
Far as the eagle's pinion
Or dove's light wing can soar.

4. For Him shall prayer unceasing,
And daily vows ascend;
His kingdom still increasing.
A kingdom without end.
The tide of time shall never
His covenant remove;

His name shall stand forever
That name to us is Love!
— James Montgomery

210

I Heard the Bells on Christmas Day

1. I heard the bells on Christmas day
Their old familiar carols play,
And wild and sweet the words
repeat Of peace on earth, good-will
to men.

2. I thought how, as the day had come.
The belfries of aft Christendom
Had rolled along th' unbroken song
Of peace on earth, good-will to men.

3. And in despair I bowed my head.
"There is no peace on earth," I said,
"For hate is strong, and mocks the
song
Of peace on earth, good-will to
men."

4. Then pealed the bells more loud and
Deep.
"God is not dead, not doth He sleep;
The wrong shall fail, the right
prevail,
With peace on earth, good-will to
men:"

5. Till, ringing, singing on its way,
The world revolved from night to day,
A voice, a chime, a chant sublime,
Of peace on earth, good-will to men!
— Henry W. Longfellow

211

Gloria.- 7.7.7.7. with Refrain

1. Angels we have heard on high,
Sweetly singing o'er the plains,
And the mountains in reply
Echo back their joyous strains.

THE BIRTH OF JESUS CHRIST

Chorus
Gloria in excelesis Deo
Gloria in excelsis Deo

2. Shepherds, why this jubilee?
Why your joyous strains prolong?
Say what may the tidings be,
Which inspire your heav'nly song?

3. Come to Bethlehem, and see
Him whose birth the angels sing;
Come, adore on bended knee
Christ the Lord, the new born King.

4. See within a manger laid
Jesus, Lord of heav'n and earth!
Mary, Joseph, lend your aid,
With us sing our Savior's birth.
      -Traditional French carol

212

Caudate - 8.6.8.6.4.

1. Joy fills our inmost heart today:
The royal Child is born:
And angel hosts in glad array
His Advent keep this morn

Chorus
Rejoice, rejoice! The incarnate word
Has come on earth to dwell;
No sweeter sound than this is
heard Emmanuel.

2. Low at the cradle throne we bend,
We wonder and adore;
And feel no bliss can our transcend,
No joy was sweet before.

3. For us the world must lose its charms
Before the manger shrine,
When, folded in Thy mother's arms
We see Thee, Babe divine.

4. Thou Light of uncreated Light,
Shine on us, Holy Child;
That we may keep Thy birthday bright,
With service undefiled.
      -S. Smith

213

**As With Gladness Men of Old -
7.7.7.7.7.7.**

1. As with gladness men of old
Did the guiding star behold,
As with joy they hailed its light,
Leading onward, beaming bright;
So, most gracious Lord, may we
Evermore be led to Thee.

2. As with joyful steps they sped,
Saviour, to Thy lowly bed,
There to bend the knee before
Thee, whom heaven and earth adore;
So may we with willing feet
Ever seek the mercy-seat.

3. As they offered gifts most rare
At Thy cradle rude and bare;
So may we with holy joy,
Pure, and free from sin's alloy,
All our costliest treasures bring,
Christ, to Thee, our heavenly King:

4. Holy Jesus, every day
Keep us in the narrow way;
And, when earthly things are -past,
Bring our ransomed souls at last
Where they need no star to guide.
Where no clouds Thy glory hide.

5. In the heavenly country bright
   Need they no created light
   Thou its light, its joy, its crown;
   There for ever may we sing
   Hallelujah to our King.
                    -William Chatterton Dix

214

Silent Night, Holy Night-
6.6.8.8.6.6.

1. Silent night, holy night,
   All is calm, all is bright
   Round you Virgin Mother and
   Child
   Holy infant so tender and mild,
   Sleep in heavenly peace,
   Sleep in heavenly peace.

2. Silent night, holy night,
   Darkness flies all is night,
   Shepherds hear the angels sing,
   "Hallelujah hail the king!
   Christ the Saviour is born,
   Christ the Saviour is born.

3. Silent night, holy night,
   Guarding Star, lend Thy light;
   See the eastern wise men bring,
   Gifts and homage to our king!
   Christ the Saviour is born
   Christ the Saviour is born

4. Silent night, holy night,
   wondrous Star, lend thy light;
   With the angels let us sing,
   Hallelujah to our King!
   Christ the Saviour is born,
   Christ the Saviour is born.

THE GOSPEL CALL

215

Grafton-8.7.8.7.8.7.

1. Come, ye souls by sin afflicted,
   Bowed with fruitless sorrow down.
   By the broken law convicted.
   Through the cross behold the
   crown;
   Look to Jesus; took to Jesus;
   Mercy flows through Him alone.

2. Blessed are the eyes that see Him,
   Blest the ears that hear His voice;
   Blessed are the souls that trust Him
   And in Him alone rejoice;
   His commandments, His command
   ments.
   Then become their happy choice.

3. Take His easy yoke and wear it;
   Love will make obedience sweet;
   Christ will give you strength to bear it.
   While His wisdom guides your feet
   Safe to glory, safe to glory.
   Where His ransomed captives meet.

4. Sweet as home to pilgrims weary,
   Light to newly opened eyes,
   Or full springs in deserts dreary,
   Is the rest the cross supplies;
   All who taste it, all who taste it
   Shall to rest immortal rise.
   -J. Swain

216

Stephanos - 8.5.8.3.

1. Art thou weary, heavy laden,
   Art thou sore distrest?
   "Come to Me." saith One, "and, oming,
   Be at rest."

2. Hath he marks to lead me to Him,
   If He be my guide?
   "In His feet and hands are wound
   prints,
   And His side."

3. If I still hold closely to Him,
   What hath He at last?
   "Sorrow vanquished, labour
   ended, Jordan passed."

4. If I ask Him to receive me,
   Will He say me nay?
   "Not till earth and not till heaven
   Pass away."
   -Greek. English Century

217

Thompson -11.7.11.7. with Refrain

1. Softly and tenderly Jesus is calling,
   Calling for you and for me;
   See on the portals He's waiting
   and watching,
   Watching for you and for me.

Chorus
   Come home. come home,
   Ye who are weary, come home;
   Earnestly, tenderly, Jesus is calling,
   Calling, O sinner, come home!

2. Why should we tarry when Jesus
   is pleading,
   Pleading for you and for me?
   Why should we linger and heed not
   His mercies,
   Mercies for you and for me?

3. Time is now fleeting, the moments
   are passing,
   Passing from you and from me.
   Shadows are gathering, death's
   night is coming,
   coming for you and for me.

4. O for the wonderful love He has
   promised,
   Promised for you and for me!
   Though we have sinned, He has
   mercy and pardon,
   Pardon for you and for me,
   -Will L Thompson

THE GOSPEL CALL

218

Sheffield-Irregular with Refrain

1. Why do you wait. deal-brother.
   Oh, why do you tarry so long?
   Your Saviour is waiting to give you
   A place in His sanctified throng.

   Chorus
   Why not? why not?
   Why not come to Him now?
   Why not? why not?
   Why not come to Him now?

2. What do you hope, dear brother,
   To gain by a further delay?
   There's no one to save you but
   Jesus.
   There's no other way but His way.

3. Do you not feet, dear brother.
   His Spirit now striving within?
   Oh, why not accept His salvation
   And throw off your burden of sin?

4. Why do you wait, dear brother?
   The harvest is passing away;
   Your Saviour is longing to bless you,
   There's danger and death in delay.
   　　　　　　　　　-George F. Root

219

Invitation-6.6.6.6. D.

1. Come to the Saviour now,
   He gently calleth thee;
   In true repentance bow,
   Before Him bend the knee;
   He waiteth to bestow
   Salvation, peace, and love,
   True joy on earth below,
   A home in heaven above.

2. Come to the Saviour now,
   Ye who have wandered far;
   Renew your solemn vow,
   For His by right you are;

Come, like poor wandering sheep
Returning to His fold:
His arm will safely keep.
His love will ne'er grow cold.

3. Come to the Saviour, all,
   Whate'er your burdens be;
   Hear now His loving call,
   "Cast all your care on Me."
   Come, and tor every grief
   In Jesus you will find
   A sure and safe relief,
   A loving mend and king.
   　　　　　　　　　-John M. Wigner

220

Crimson - Irregular

1. "Tho" your sins be as scarlet,
   They shall be as white as snow;
   Tho' your sins be as scarlet,
   They shall be as white as snow:
   Tho' they be red like crimson.
   They shall be as wool!"
   Tho' your sins be as scarlet,
   Tho' your sins be as scarlet,
   They shall be as white as snow,
   They shall be as white as snow."

2. Hear the voice that entreats you,
   O return ye unto God!
   Hear the voice that entreats you,
   O return ye unto God! He is of
   great compassion,
   And of wondrous love;
   Hear the voice that entreats you,
   Hear the voice that entreats you.
   O return ye unto God
   O return ye unto God!

3. He'll forgive your transgressions,
   And remember them no more;
   He'll forgive your transgressions.
   And remember them no more;
   "Look unto Me. ye people,
   "Saith the Lord your God!
   He'll forgive your transgressions,
   Hell forgive your transgressions.
   And remember them no more,
   And remember them no more.
   　　　　　　　　　-Fanny J. Crpsby

THE GOSPEL CALL

221

Lura -10.7.10.7. with Refrain

1. When the sun shines bright and
   your heart is light,
   Jesus is the friend you need;
   When the clouds hang tow in this
   world of woe,
   Jesus is the friend you need.

Chorus
Jesus is the friend you need,
Such a friend is He indeed
He who noteth ev'ry tear,
He will banish ev'ry fear,
Jesus is the friend you need.

2. If you're lost in sin, all is dark within,
   Jesus is the friend you need;
   God alone can save thro' the Son
   He gave,
   Jesus is the friend you need,

3. When in that sad hour, when in
   death's grim pow'r,
   Jesus is the friend you need;
   If you would prepare "gainst the
   tempter's snare,
   Jesus is the friend you need.

4. When the cares of life alt around
   are rife
   Jesus is the friend you need,
   Glory to His name, always He's the
   same,
   Jesus is the friend you need.
   - Isham E. Reynolds

222

Surrey-8.8.8.8.8.8.

1 Behold, the Lamb of God, who
  bears
  The sins of all the world away!
  A servant's form He meekly wears,
  He sojourns in a house of clay;
  His glory is no longer seen,
  But God with God is man with men.

2. See where the God incarnate stands
   And calls His wandering creatures
   home!
   He all day long spreads out His
   hands,
   come, weary souls, to Jesus come!
   Ye all may hide you in My breast;
   Believe, and I will give you rest.

3. Sinners, believe the gospel word,
   Jesus is come your souls to save!
   Jesus is come, your common Lord;
   Pardon ye all through Him may have
   This man receiveth sinners still.
   -Charles Wesley

223

What love

1. There's a love beyond all human
   comprehension,
   There's a love that satisfies the
   yearning heart;
   And to share this love with us was
   God's intention
   When He made this world
   and formed us at the start.

Chorus
What love, what matchless grace,
What love, He took my place;
For a world so full of sin He died on
calv'ry,
paid a price of blood for me and now
I'm free.

2. Jesus gave a call that all will have to
   reckon.
   He has opened wide His arms to all
   who will;
   If we choose His love alone tho'
   Satan beckon.
   Then the promise of His love He will
   Fulfill.

3. When the Bridegroom comes I'm
   going to a wedding,
   That will make us one with Christ,
   God's only Son;

All the angels will be there and they'll be singing
Songs of love that made God gave His only Son.

4. They will come from ev'ry tribe and ev'ry nation,
For the love of God has placed no boundary;
We will be made one in final consumation,
Chosen for His bride to be eternally
                                    -Lois Rowe

224

Won't you let Him be your Saviour too

1. I have a precious Saviour, He came from heav'n above,
And died for me on Calvary, To prove his matchless love.
The love so freely given. He offers now to you;
Won't you let my Saviour Be your Saviour too?

Chorus
Won't you let him be your Saviour too?
He would prove a faithful' friend to you;
He would purify your soul, keep you ever pure and whole;
Won't you let my Saviour Be your Saviuor too?

2. I have a loving Saviour, He hears me when I call;
He helps to bear each load of care, And lift me when I fall;
So kind is he, so tender, Compas sionate and true;
Won't you let my Saviour Be your Saviour too?

3. I have a faithful Saviour; With me he will abide;
And hold my hand until I land upon the other side,
Someday in all his glory, My Saviour shall view
Brother, won't you let him Be your Saviour too?
                                    -James Rowe

225

That means you

1. Blessed invitation from the King of heav'n,
Blessed invitation by the spirit giv'n
Falling on the weary like refreshing dew,
"Whosoe'er believeth that means You

Chorus
That means you, brother, that means you,
Trust the Saviour's promise tried and true;
That means you, brother, that means you;
"Whosoe'er believeth that you.

2. Reconciliation thro' his precious blood,
He hath wrought salvation Blessed Son of God!
All the work is finished, there is naught to do.
But to claim the blessing; that means you.

3. Saving all who trust him to the uttermost,
Boasting is excluded, yet in him we Boast;
Soul, receive the message wonderful and true,
"Whosoe'er believeth' that means you.

4. Doubt His word no longer come to
him today,
Turning from your sins forevermore
away:
Thro' his boundless mercy all shall
beforgiv'n;
He will safely guide you home to
heav'n.

5. There in realms of glory we will sin
his praise,
With the shout of triumph, Thro
eternal days
For the invitation old yet ever new:
Glory hallelujah' that means you
-Thoro Harris

226
The way, the truth, the life.

1. "I am the Way," the Saviour said,
And I would follow on,
Content to know that after night
Shall break a glorious dawn.

Chorus
I am the way, the Truth, and the
Life,
No man cometh unto the Father but
by Me.
No man cometh unto the Father but
by Me

2. "I am the Truth." then Truth shall be
A beacon light to guide
My bark across the stormy sea
To where still waters glide.

3. "I am the Life," there is no death
For me to fear, nor dread,
Since by His all atoning blood
My life to His is wed.
-C. Austin Miles

227
Come and see

1. 'Tis the gospel invitation,
Come and see, come and see,
Unto ev'ry tribe and nation.
Come and see, come and see,
Jesus offers free salvation, come
and see,

Chorus
What the Lord hath done for me.
Come and see, come and see
What the Lord hath done for me,
For He found my soul in sin, and
He washed me pure and clean,
This the Lord hath done for me.

2. Oh, He never will deceive you,
Come and see, come and see,
Of your burden He'll relieve you,
Come and see, come and see,
He is waiting to receive you, come
and see,

3. Come, to Jesus now confiding,
Come and see, come and see,
In His shadow quickly hiding,
Come and see, come and see,
In His mercy there abiding come
and see.
-W. A. Ogden

228
Jesus Came To Save

1. Jesus came from heav'n above,
Sinners to save with His own
blood;
Gave His life upon the cross,
Suffered there in agony for the
lost!

Chorus
Yes, Jesus came to save the lost;
Came to save us with His blood
on he cross;
O, sinner friend, no longer roam;
March with us a happy band to
our home.

THE GOSPEL CALL

2. How could Jesus love me so
That he should save me from such
woe?
He in heav'n and earth now reigns!
I shall serve Him while on earth I
Remain.

3. Sinner now obey His call;
Jesus will save you from the fall
In this life you'll happy be
And in heaven His glories rare you
shall see.

-Holland L.

229
They crucified Him

1. Come, sinner, behold what Jesus
hath done,
Behold how He suffer'd for thee:
They crucified Him, God's innocent
Son,
Forsaken, He died on the tree!

Chorus
They crucified Him, they crucified
Him.
They nail'd Him to the tree,
And so there He died, a King
crucified
To save a poor sinner like me, like
Me.

2. From heaven He came, He loved
you He died,
Such love as His never was known;
Behold, on the cross your King
crucified,
To make you an heir to His throne!

3. No pitying eye, a saving arm, none,
He saw us, and pitied us then;
Alone in the fight, the vict'ry he won;
O praise Him, ye children of men.

4. They crucified Him, and yet He
forgave.

"My Father, forgive them, "He cried,
What must He have borne the
sinner to save, When under the
burden He died!

5. So what will you do with Jesus
your King?
Say, how will you meet Him at last?
What plea in the day of wrath will
you bring,
When offers of mercy are past?

-J. M. Whyte

230
When the door is shut

1. When the door is shut it will be too :
Late;
Enter while you may, enter in today;
Why live on in sin? why in danger
wait?

Chorus
Enter while you may, while you may'
Oh, enter, enter in today?
Oh, enter, enter while you may;
Do the Saviour's bidding, lest you
hear him say,
The door is shut, Too late! too late!

2. When the door is shut all your
hopes will die;
Enter while you may, enter in today;
Vainly then to heav'n you for help
will cry;

3. When the door is shut mercy's calls
will cease;
Enter while you may, enter in today;
Hasten, needy one, with thy God
Make peace;

4. When the door is shut count the
dreadful cost;
Enter while you may, enter in today;
Oh, the shut out soul all's for ever
lost;

-T. C. Neal

THE GOSPEL CALL

231

Come Unto Me

1. O heart bow'd down with sorrow!
   O eyes that long for sight!
   There's gladness in believing;
   In Jesus there is light.

Chorus
"Come unto Me, all ye that labour
and are heavy laden, and I will give
you rest
Take My yoke upon you, and learn
of Me;
for I am meek and lowly in heart:
and ye shall find rest unto your
souls."

2. Earth's fleeting gain and pleasure
   Can never satisfy:
   Tis love our joy doth measure,
   For love can never die.

3. Divinest consolation
   Doth Christ the Healer give;
   Art thou in condemnation?
   Believe, repent, and live.

4. His peace is like a river,
   His love is like a song;
   His yoke's a burden never;
   Tis easy all day long.
                          -F. E. Belde

232

Oh, it is glory

1. Oh, if you could know my Saviour.
   If you could but taste and see,
   If you knew your sins forgiven.
   Heav'n on earth it then would be.

Chorus
Oh, it is glory! Oh, it is glory!
Oh, it is glory in my soul.
Jesus hath saved me, He has
redeem'd me,
Oh, it is glory in my soul.

2. I will tell you why the glory
   Streams so freely in my soul;
   I have been receiv'd by Jesus.
   He has made my spirt whole.

3. He has stoop'd low down from
   heaven,
   Stoop'd so low my soul to win;
   And I know and feel He pardons,
   Now I know He takes me in.

4. This is why the heav'nly glory
   Now comes streaming thro' my
   soul;
   Glory, glory be to Jesus,
   For His blood has made me
   whole.
                          -J. J. Sims

233

Decide Now

1. O wand'rer, come. this hour decide
   The path thy heart will choose!
   Say, wilt thou live for Christ alone
   Oh, canst thou still refuse?

Chorus
Decide now. decide now!
The Saviour is tenderly calling thee;
Decide now, decide now!
Tomorrow may never be.

2. Behold, He stands with open arms
   To give thee life and light;
   His word believe. His grace
   receive:
   Oh. come, be saved tonight!

3. Decide tor Him, thy dearest Friend
   Why wilt thou yet delay?
   What tho' thy sins are crimson red,
   He'll wash them all away.

4. No other name but His can save;
   Then haste His love to share:
   Throw open wide thy yielding
   heart.
   And He will enter there.
                          -Anon.

THE GOSPEL CALL

234
Why do you linger

1. O why do you linger, my brother?
   O why do you still stay away?
   For you a dear Saviour is waiting
   To give you salvation today.

Chorus
Why do you linger? Why do you linger?
The Saviour is calling today;
O come and believe, Free pardon receive,
And have all your sins wash'd away.

2. To save your poor soul he is
   yearning, O come to Him now
   while you may:
   His hand, pierced for you, holds
   out mercy,
   O why not receive it today?

3. O careless one, great is your
   danger,
   Around you are fetters of sin;
   Escape to the only safe refuge,
   And Jesus will welcome you in.

4. O wait not for further conviction,
   But come to Him Just as you are;
   Look up thro' the gloom and the
   darkness,
   To Jesus, the bright Morning Star.
   -Mrs W. J. Kennedy

235
Why not say yes tonight

1. Oh, why not say Yes to the Saviour
   tonight?
   He's tenderly pleading with thee,
   To come to Him now with thy sin
   burden'd heart
   For pardon so full and so free, so
   free,

Chorus
Why not say Yes tonight?
Why not? Why not?
While He so gently, so tenderly
pleads:
Oh, accept Him tonight!

2. For with you the Spirit will not
   always plead
   Oh, do not reject Him tonight!
   Tomorrow may bring you the
   darkness of death.
   Unbroken by heavenly, heav'nly
   light.

3. Take Christ as your Saviour, then
   all shall be well,
   The morrow let bring what it may;
   His love shall protect you, His
   Spirit guide,
   And safely keep you in His way.
   His way.
   -Effie Wells Loucks

236
Where will you spend eternity

1. Where will you spend eternity?
   This question comes to you and me!
   Tell me, what shall your answer be?
   Where will you spend eternity?
   Eternity, eternity!
   Where will you spend eternity?

2. Many are choosing Christ today,
   Turning from all their sins away,
   Heav'n shall their happy portion be,
   Where will you spend eternity?
   Eternity, eternity!
   Where will you spend eternity?

3. Leaving the straight and narrow
   Way,
   Going the downward road today,
   Sad will their final ending be,
   Lost thro' a long eternity!
   Eternity, eternity! Lost thro' a long
   eternity!

THE GOSPEL CALL

4. Repent, believe, this very hour.
   Trust in the Saviour's grace and pow'r,
   Then will your Joyous answer be,
   Saved thro' a long eternity
   Eternity, eternity!
   Saved thro' a long eternity
                              -E. A. Hoffman

237
You mean to be saved - but when

1. You mean to be saved but when?
   No longer the blessing delay;
   Now, now. is the time accepted,
   O come and be saved today!

Chorus
You mean to be saved but when?
You mean to be saved but when?
He loves you. He calls you,
He's waiting just now,
You mean to be saved but when?

2. You mean to be saved but when?
   The way is provided and free:
   He will not compel, O choose Him,
   Your Saviour and Friend to be!

3. You wish to be saved but when?
   No longer a wanderer roam;
   Believe and receive full pardon,
   You mean to be saved come home!

4. You hope to be saved you say,
   You've said it again and again;
   You may not behold tomorrow,
   You mean to be saved but when
                              -Mrs. Frank A. Breck

238
Just obey

1. Just as God who reign on high
   Spake to men in days gone,
   So the Lord is calling men today;
   And, my brother this is true,

Whatsoe'er he says to you,
There is but one thing to do just obey.

Chorus
Just obey, just obey Is the way,
God's way;
When his message comes to you,
There is but one thing to do,' Just obey, just obey.

2. If you're in the Saviour's hands,
   You must do as he commands,
   For there is no other gospel way:
   Never put the message by,
   Never stop to reason "why,"
   When the Saviour speaks to you just obey.

3. If for mansions fair you sigh
   In that land beyond the sky,
   After time with you has pass'd away;
   Tho' the way you may not see.
   Christ is calling. "follow me,"
   Faith and duty still will cry just obey.
                              - Rev- Johnson Oatman, Jr.

239
Regeneration

1. A ruler once came to Jesus by night.
   To ask Him the way of salvation and light;
   The Master made answer in words true and plain,
   Ye must be born again.

Chorus
"Ye must be born again, again!"
Ye must be born again!"
I verily, verily say unto you
"Ye must be born again!"

2. Ye children of men! attend to the word
   So solemnly uttered by Jesus, the Lord,

And tet not his message to you
be in vain,
"Ye must be born again!"

3. O ye who would enter the glorious
rest,
And sing with the ransomed the
song of the blest;
The life everlasting if ye would
obtain.
"Ye must be born again!"

4. A dear one in heaven thy heart
yearn to see,
At the beautiful gate may be
watching for thee;
Then list to the note of this solemn
refrain,
"Ye must be born again!"
-W. T. Sleeper

240

I've a Message from the Lord, Hallelujah!

1. I've a Message from the Lord,
Hallelujah!
The message unto you I'll give,
Tis recorded in His world,
Hallelujah,
It is only that you "look and live."

Chorus
"Look and live," my brother, live;
Look to Jesus now and live;
Tis recorded in His world,
Hallelujah,
It is only that you "look and live."

2. I've a Message full of Love,
Hallelujah!
A message, O my friend, for you.
Tis a message from above,
Hallelujah!
Jesus said it, and I know 'tis true.

3. Life is offer'd unto you,
Hallelujah!
Eternal life your soul shall have,
If you only look to Him,
Hallelujah!
Look to Jesus who alone can save.
-W. A Ogden

241

Wells-7.7.7.7.7.7.

1. Weary souls, that wander wide,
From the central point of bliss,
Turn to Jesus crucified,
Fly to those dear wounds of His;
Sink into the cleansing flood;
Rise in to the life of God!

2. Find in Christ the way of peace,
Peace unspeakable, unknown.
By His pain expiring ease,
Life by His exalted groan;
Rise, exalted by His fall,
Find in Christ your all in all.

3. Oh believe the record true.
God to you His Son hath given!
Ye may now be happy too,
Find on earth the life of heaven,
Live the life of heaven above,
All the life of glorious love.

4. This the universal bliss,
Bliss for every soul designed;
God's divinest promise this,
God's great gift to all mankind:
Blest in Christ this moment be!
Blest to all eternity!
-C. Wesley

242

Calcutta-8.7.8.7.4.7,

1. Come, ye sinners, poor and needy,
Weak and wounded, sick and sore;
Jesus ready stands to save you.
Full of pity, love and power:
He is able,
He is willing, doubt no more,

THE GOSPEL CALL

2. Now, ye needy, come and welcome
   God's free bounty glorify:
   True belief and true repentance
   Every grace that brings you nigh
   Without money,
   Come to Jesus Christ and buy.

3. Let nol conscience make
   you linger,
   Nor of fitness fondly dream;
   All the fitness He requireth
   Is to feel your need of Him:
   This He gives you
   Tis the Spirit's rising beam.

4. Come, ye weary heavy laden,
   Bruised and ruined by the Fall;
   If you tarry till you're better
   You will never come at all:
   Not the righteous
   Sinners, Jesus came to call.

5. View Him, prostrate in the garden,
   On the, ground your Maker lies!
   On the awful tree behold Him,
   Hear Him cry before He dies,
   "It is finished!"
   Sinner, will not this suffice?

6. Lo, the incarnate God ascended.
   Pleads the merit of His blood;
   Venture on Him, venture wholly,
   Let no other trust intrude:
   None but Jesus
   Can do helpless sinners good.
   　　　　　　　　　　　-J. Hart

243

Yes, I know

1. Come, ye sinners, lost and
   hopeless,
   Jesus' blood can make you free,
   For He saved the worst among you,
   When He saved a wretch like me

Chorus
And I know, yes, I know, Jesus"
blood can make the vilest
sinner clean,

And I know. yes, I know, Jesus'
blood can make the vilest
Sinner clean;

2. To the faint He giveth power,
   Through the mountains makes a
   way;
   Findeth water in the desert.
   Turns the night to golden day.

3. In temptation He is near thee.
   Holds the pow'rs of hell at bay;
   Guides you to the path of safety.
   Gives you grace for ev'ry day.

4. He will keep thee while the ages
   Roll thro' out eternity;
   Tho' earth hinders and hell rages,
   All must work for good to thee.
   　　　　　　-Mrs. Anna W. Waterman

244

Wonderful story of love

1. Wonderful story of love;
   Tell it to me again;
   Wonderful story of love;
   Wake the immortal strain!
   Angels with rapture announce it.
   Shepherds with wonder receive it;
   Sinner, O won't you believe it?
   Wonderful story of love.

Chorus
Wonderful! Wonderful! Wonderful!
Wonderful story of love'

2. Wonderful story of love;
   Tho' you are far away;
   Wonderful story of love;
   Still He doth call today;
   Calling from Calvary's mountain,
   Down from the crystal bright
   Fountain.
   E'en from the dawn of creation.
   Wonderful story of love.

THE GOSPEL CALL

3. Wonderful story of love'
   Jesus provides a rest;
   Wonderful story of love;
   For all the pure and blest,
   Rest in those mansions above us,
   With these who've gone on before
   Us.
   Singing the rapturous chorus
   Wonderful story of love'
        -J. M. Driver

245

Regent square - 8.7 8.74.7.

1. Hark! the gospel news is sounding,
   Christians suffered on the tree;
   Streams of mercy are abounding,
   Grace for all is rich and free,
   Now, poor sinner,
   Now, poor sinner,
   Come to Him who died for thee.

2. Oh! escape to yonder mountain,
   Refuge find in Him today;
   Christ invites you to the fountain,
   Come and wash your sins away;
   Do not tarry, Do not tarry, Come to
   Jesus while you may.

3. Grace is flowing like a river,
   Millions there have been supplied
   still it flows as fresh as ever
   From the Saviour's wounded side;
   None need perish,
   All may live, for Christ hath died.

4. Christ alone shall be our portion;
   Soon we hope to meet above;
   Then we'll bathe in the full ocean
   Of the great Redeemer's love;
   All His fulness
   We shall then forever prove.
       -H. Bourne and W. Sanders

246

Dearer than all

1. Ye who the love of a mother
   have known
   There is a love sweeter far you
   may own,
   Love all sufficient for sin to atone;
   Jesus is dearer than all.

Chorus
Dearer than all yes, dearer than all
 He is my King, before Him I fall;
No friend like Jesus my soul can
enthral,
Jesus is dearer far dearer than all.

2. Jesus entreats you in Him to
   confide,
   Make Him your constant companion
   and guard;
   He can do more than the whole
   world beside;
   Jesus is dearer than all.

3. Heaven, with all of its beauty so
   rare,
   With my Redeemer can never
   Compare;
   He is the glory transcendent up
   there;
   Jesus is dearer than all.
        -H. Ackley

247

The gospel bells

1. The gospel bells are ringing,
   Over land, from sea to seas;
   Blessed news of free salvation
   Do they offer you and me.
   "For God so loved the world,
   That His only Son He gave!
   Whosoe'er believeth in Him
   Everlasting life shall have."

THE GOSPEL CALL

Chorus
Gospel bells! how they ring,
Over land from sea to sea;
Gospel bells freely bring
Blessed news to you and me.

2. The gospel bells invite us
To a feast prepared for all;
Do not slight the invitation,
Nor reject the gracious call.
"I am the Bread of life;
Eat of me, thou hungry soul;
Though your sins be red as
crimson.
They shall be as white as wool."

3. The gospel bells give warning,
As they sound from day to day,
Of the fate which doth await them
Who for ever will delay.
"Escape thou for thy life!
Tarry not in all the plain;
Nor behind thee lock, oh, never,
Lest thou be consumed in the
plain."

4. The gospel bells are joyful
As they echo far and wide,
Bearing notes of perfect pardon,
Through a Saviour crucified:
"Good tidings of great joy
To all people do I bring;
Unto you is born a Saviour.
Which is Christ, the Lord and King."
                        -S. Wesley Martin

248
Life for a look

1. There is life for a look at the
Crucified One,
There is life at this moment for thee.
Then look, sinner, look unto Him and
be saved,
Unto Him who was nailed to the
tree

Chorus
Look, look, look and live.
There is life for a look at the
Crucified One.
There is life at this moment for
Thee.

2. Oh, why was He there as a
Bearer of sin,
If on Jesus thy sins were not
laid?
Oh, why from His side flowed the
sin cleansing blood.
If His dying thy debt has not paid?

3. It is not thy tears of repentance;
nor prayers,
But the blood that atones for the
soul;
On Him then believe, and a
pardon receive,
For His blood can now make thee
quite whole

4. We are healed by His stripes;
wouldst thou add to the word? ;
And He is our righteousness
made;
The best robe of heaven He bids
thee to wear.
Oh, couldst thou be better
arrayed?

5. The doubt not thy welcome,
since God has declared
There remaineth no more to be
done;
That once in the end of the world
He appeared,
And completed the work He begun.

6. But take, with rejoicing, from Jesus
at once.
The life everlasting He gives;
And know with assurance thou
never canst die,
Since Jesus thy righteousness lives.
                        -Asa M. Hull

THE GOSPEL CALL

249

Pow'r in the blood - 10,9.10.8.
with Refrain

1. Would you the free from the burden
   of sin?
   There's pow'r in the blood, pow'r in
   the blood;
   Would you o'er evil a victory win'?
   There's wonderful pow'r in the
   blood.'

Chorus
There is pow'r, pow'r wonder
working pow'r
In the blood of the Lamb;
There is pow'r, pow'r, wonder
working pow'r in the precious blood
of the Lamb.

Would you be free from your
passion and pride?
There's pow'r in the blood, pow'r in
The blood;
Come for a cleansing to Calvary's
tide?
There's wonderful pow'r in the
Blood.

3. Would you be whiter, much whiter
   than snow?
   There's pow'r in the blood, pow'r in
   the blood;
   Sin stains are lost in its life giving
   flow;
   There's wonderful pow'r in the
   blood.

4. Would you do service for Jesus
   Your King?
   There's pow'r in the blood, pow'r in
   the blood;
   Would you live daily His praises to
   sing?
   There's wonderful pow'r in the
   Blood.

250

Him that Is Thirsty

1. Ho! ev'ry one that is thirsty in
   spirit,
   Ho! ev'ry one that is weary and
   sad;
   " Come to the fountain, there's
   fulness in Jesus,
   All that you're longing for, come
   and be glad,

Chorus
I will pour water on him that is
thirsty,
I will pour flood upon the dry
ground;
Open your heart for the gift I am
bringing;
While ye are seeking Me,
I will be found.

2. Child of the world, are you
   tir'd of your bondage?
   Weary of earth joys, so false, so
   untrue?
   Thirsting for God and His
   fulness of blessing?
   List to the promise, a message
   for you!

3. Child of the Kingdom, he fili'd
   with the Spirit
   Nothing but fulness thy longing
   can meet
   Tis the endurement for life and
   for service;
   Thine is the promise, so certain,
   so sweet.
   			-Lucy J. Rider

251

Are you Coming home Tonight?

1. Are you coming Home,
   ye wand'rers Whom Jesus died
   to win,
   All footsore, lame, and weary,

your garments stain'd with sin?
Will you seek the blood of Jesus
To wash your garments white?
Will you trust His precious promise
Are you coming Home tonight?

Chorus
Are you coming Home tonight?
Are you coming Home tonight?
Are you coming Home to Jesus,
Out of darkness into light?
Are you coming Home tonight?
Are you coming Home tonight?
To your loving heavenly Father
Are you coming Home tonight?

2. Are you coming Home,
ye lost ones? Behold, your Lord
doth wait;
Come then! no longer linger,
Come ere it be too late'
Will you come, and let Him save
you?
Oh, trust His love and mighty
Will you, come while He is calling?
Are you coming Home tonight?

3. Are you coming Home, ye guilty,
Who bear and load of sin?
Outside you've long been
standing, Come now and venture in!
Will you heed the Saviour's
promise,
And dare trust Him quite?
"Come unto Me!" saith Jesus:
Are you coming Home tonight?
                                    -Anon

252
Christ Receiveth Sinful Men -
7.7.7.71

1. Sinners Jesus will receive;
Sound this word of grace to all
Who the heavenly pathway leave,
All who linger, all who fall

chorus
Sing it o'er and o'er again;
Christ receiveth sinful men:
make the message dear and plain:
Christ receiveth sinful men

2. Come, and He will give you rest;
Trust Him, for His word is plain;
He will take the sinfulest;
Christ receiveth sinful men.

3. Now my heart condemns me not,
pure before the law I stand;
He who cleansed me from all spot,
satisfied its last demand.

4. Christ receiveth sinful men
even me with all my sin;
purge from every spot and stain.
Heaven with Him I enter in;
                                    -Mrs. Bevan

253
Mercy is boundless and free

1. Praise be to Jesus, His mercy is
free:
Mercy is free, mercy is free
Sinner, that mercy is flowing for
thee
Mercy is boundless and free!
If thou art willing on Him to
believe:
Mercy is free, mercy is free!
Life everlasting thou mayest
receive:
Mercy is boundless and free!

Chorus
Jesus, the Saviour, is seeking for
thee,
seeking for thee, seeking for thee,
Lovingly, tenderly calling for thee;
Calling and seeking for thee!

2. Why on the mountains of sin will'
thou roam?
Mercy is free, mercy is free!
Gently the Spirit is calling thee;
Home:

THE GOSPEL CALL

Mercy is boundless and free!
Art thou in darkness? Oh, come to
the light '
Mercy is free, Mercy is free,
Jesus is waiting, He'll save you
tonight
Mercy is boundless and free!

3. Think of His goodness, His
Patience, and love
Mercy is free, mercy is free!
Pleading thy cause with His father
above
Mercy is boundless and free!
Come and repenting, oh, give Him
thy heart:
Mercy is free, mercy is free!
Grieve Him no longer, but come as
they art
Mercy is boundless and free!

4. Yes; there is pardon for all who
believe:
Mercy is free, mercy is free!
Come and this moment a blessing
receive:
Mercy is boundless and free!
Jesus is waiting, oh, hear Him
proclaim:
Mercy free! Mercy is free!
Cling to His promise believe of His
name
Mercy is boundless and free!
-Hanrietta E. Blair

254
Come, for all things are ready
- P M

1. Come, for all things are ready!
Tis a banquet of love;
Here's a free invitation
From the Master above:
It is written in crimson,
Drawn from Calvary's flood,
From the wonderful fountain
Of the soul cleansing blood.

Chorus
Oh, what fulness in Jesus!
Oh; what gladness to know,
Tho' our sins be as scarlet.
He'll make them as snow.

2. Come for all things are ready!
Heaven's bounty is spread;
Take; the cup of salvation,
Take the life giving bread:
Come, and unworthy;
Come, tho' sinful and weak
Tis the hungry and thirsty
Whom the Master doth seek.

3. Come, for all things are ready!
Here's a robe, snowy white,
Fairer far than the raiment
Of the angels of light:
For the beauty of Jesus
Will thy covering be
Only ask for this garment,
'Twill be given to thee.
-L. H. Edmunds

255
Oh, what a saviour - P.M.

1. Come to the Saviour, hear His
loving voice!
Never will you find a Friend so true;
Now He is waiting, trust Him and
rejoice,
Tenderly He calleth you!

Chorus
Oh, what a Saviour standing at the
door!
Haste while He lingers; pardon now
implore!
Still He is waiting, grieve His love
no more
Tenderly He calleth you.

2. Blest words of comfort, gently now
they fall
Jesus is the Life, the Truth the Way;

THE GOSPEL CALL

Come to the fountain, there is room
for all.
Jesus bids you come today.

3. Softly the Spirit whispers to thy
Heart
Do not slight the Saviours offer'd
grace;
Gladly receive Him, let Him not
depart
Happy they who seek His face!

J. Sterling

256

Look unto Me, and be ye Saved - C. M.

I. "Look unto Me, and be ye saved"
Oh, hear the blest command!
Salvation full salvation free.
Proclaim o'er ev'ry land!

Chorus
Look unto Me, and be ye saved!
all ye ends of the earth!
for I am God, there is none else:
Look unto Me, and be ye saved.

2. "Look unto Me," upon the cross,
O weary ..burdened soul;
Twas there on Me thy sins were laid
Believe, and be made whole!

3. Look unto me "thy risen Lord,
In dark temptation's hour
The needful grace I'll freely give,
To keep from Satan's power.

4. Look unto Me" and not within,
No help is there for thee:
For pardon, peace, and all thy need.
Look only" unto Me!

-EL. Nathan

257

Jesus will hot Cast you Out

1. Tho' your sin? are manifold
Jesus will not cast you out!
He's a friend of love untold
Jesus will not cast you out!
God, to save us ev'ry one,
Freely gave His only Son;
Come, whate'er you may have
done
Jesus will not c-ast you out!

2. Tho' you spum'd Him day by day
Jesus will not cast you out!
Come to Him - the Light, the Way
Jesus win not cast you out! .
He will cleanse and make you
whole;
Waves of sin may o'er you roll
He will save your deathless soul
Jesus will not cast you out!

3. Grace is freely offer'd now
Jesus will not cast you out!;
At the cross; O wand'rer, bow
Jesus will not cast you out!
Come, nor turn again to sin!
Come, He bid you enter in!
Come, and life eternal win!
Jesus will not cast you out!

- Geo. Cooper

258

Jesus is passing by - C. M.

1. Come, weary one, and find sweet
rest:
Jesus is passing by!
Come where the longing heart is
Blest;
And on His word rely.

Chorus
Passing by! Passing by!
Hasten to meet Him on the way,
Jesus is passing by today!
Passing by! Passing by!

2. Come, burden'd one, bring all your,
- care:
   Jesus is passing by!
   The love that listens to your pray'r
   Will "no good thing" deny.

3. Come, hungry one, and tell your
   need:
   Jesus is passing by!
   The Bread of life your soul Will feed,
   And fully satisfy.

4. Come, contrite one, and seek His
   grace;
   Jesus re passing by!
   See in His reconciled face
   The sunshine of the sky.
   —E. E. Hewitt

259

Over the Threshold

1. Step over the threshold, and
   wander no more
   Oppress'd by the burden of sin;
   Step over the threshold: why stand
   at the door?
   The Healer is waiting within.

Chorus
Then come as thou art: thy poor
broken heart
Renew'd by His Spirit shall be:
Step over the threshold: why stand
at the door?
Come in, there is mercy for thee.

2. Step over the threshold: let faith be ,
   thy guide
   To Him, thy Physician so kind;
   Go wash in the fountain that flews
   from His side,
   And health to thy soul thou shall
   find.

3. Step over the threshold, repent and
   believe,
   And quickly thy burdens will fail..

Oh, touch but His garment, and
thou shalt receive
The pardon He offers to all.

4. Step over the threshold, no
   shelter hast thou;
   Thy refuge He offers to be:
   Step over the threshold, and
   come to Him now;
   O lost one. He tarries for thee!
   —Frank Gould

260

Life at best is very brief

1. Life at best is very brief,
   Like the falling of a leaf,
   Like the binding of a sheaf:
   Be in time!
   Fleeting days are telling fast
   That the die will soon be cast,
   And the fatal line be pass'd:
   Be in time!

Chorus
Be in time! Be in time!
While the voice of Jesus calls you,
Be in time! If in sin you longer wait,
You may find no open gate,
And your cry be just too late:
Be in time!

2. Fairest flowers soon decay,
   Youth and beauty pass away;
   Oh, you have not long to stay:
   Be in time!
   While God's Spirit bids you come.
   Sinner, do not longer roam.
   Lest you seal your hopeless doom
   Be in time!

3. Time is gliding swiftly by,
   Death and Judgement draweth nigh
   To the-arms of Jesus fly:
   Be in time!

THE GOSPEL CALL

Oh, I pray you count the cost,
Ere the fatal line be crossed,
And your soul in hell be long:
Be in time!

4. Sinner, heed the warning voice,
Make the Lord your final choice,
Then all heaven will rejoice:
Be in time!
Come from darkness into light;
Come; let Jesus make you right;
Come, and start for heaven tonight:
Be in time!

-W m. J. Kirkpatrick

261

Look not behind thee

1. Look not behind thee; O Sinner
beware!
Haste to the mountain, Thy refuge is
there;
Trust not the voices That lure thee
to stay:
Jesus is calling thee then why still
delay?

Chorus
List to the warning' no longer
Remain!
Fly from the valley escape from the
plain!
Turn from the voices that lure thee
to stay:
Angels are calling thee then why still
delay?

2. Look not behind thee; O lost one,
beware!
Why dost thou linger Twixt hope
and despair?
Danger and darkness Encompass
thy way:
Jesus is calling thee Then why still
delay?

5. Look not behind thee, The tempter
is near;
Speed to the mountain, Thy

pathway is dear:
Jesus who loves thee is calling
today:
Come to thy Father's house Oh
why still delay?

-F. J. Crosby

262

Oh, come to me - L M

1. Wouldst thou, O weary soul, be
blest?
In Christ the Lord thy Saviour see;
His grace alone can give thee rest,
And lo! He calleth, "Come to Me!

Chorus
Oh, come to Me! Oh, come to Me!
The Saviour calleth, "Come to Me,
Ye heavy laden, Come to Me,
And I will give, will give you rest."

2. He does not wait for greater worth,
Or more of holiness in thee;
He brings good news to all the
earth
And still He calleth, "Come to Me!"

3. Hast thou not sinned ten thousand
times?
His pardoning grace will set thee
free;
Count unbelief the worst of crimes,
And trust thy Saviour's "Come to me!

4. Eternal life is in His Word,
He asks thee now His child to be;
No sweeter sound was ever heard
Than His most gracious
"Come to Me!

5. Be this thine answer now, and here:
"Since Thou hast kindly called for
me,'
Thy tender love dispels my fear,
I come, I come, O Lord, to Thee!
-Rev. J. Clark

THE GOSPEL CALL

263
Look, and Thou Shalt Live

1. Look to the Saviour on Calvary's
   tree
   See how He suffer'd for you and
   me;
   Hark, while He lovingly calls to thee,
   "look, and thou Shall live

Chorus
Look, and thou shall live
Look, and thou shall live!
Look to the cross where He died for
thee:
Look, and thou shall live!

2. Hast thou a sin burden'd soul to
   save?
   Life everlasting wouldst thou have?
   Jesus Himself a ransom gave:
   Look, and thou shall live!

3. Look to the Saviour who rose from
   the tomb
   Haste now to Him, while there yet is
   room
   His shining face will dispel thy
   gloom
   Look, and thou shall live!

4. Jesus on high lives to intercede,
   He knows the weary sinner's need
   surely thy footstep he will lead:'
   Look, and thou shall live!
   -F. T. W.

264
Whoever Will - L. M.

1. O wand'ring souls, why will roam
   Away from God, away from House?
   The Saviour calls, oh, hear Him say
   "Whoever will" may come today!

Chorus
"Whoever will "who ever will"
"whoever will" may come today

"Whoever will" may come today,
And drink of the water of life.

2. Behold His hands extended now,
   The dews of night are on His brow;
   He knocks, He calls, He waiteth still
   Oh, come to Him, "whoever will"

3. In simple faith His word believe,
   And life abundant grace receive,
   No love like His the heart can fill;
   Oh, come to Him, " whoever will"

4. The "Spirit and the bride say,
   Come!"
   And find in Him sweet rest, and
   home;
   Let him that heareth echo still
   The blessèd "whosoever will!"
   -Monteith

265
The habour bells - D.L.M.

1. Our life is like a stormy sea
   Swept by the gales of sin and grief:
   While on the windward and the lee
   Hang heavy clouds of unbelief
   But o'er the deep a call we hear,
   Like habour bell's inviting voice;
   It tells the lost that hope is near
   And bids the trembling soul rejoice

Chorus
"This way this way, O heart opprest,
So long by storm and tempest
driv'n;
This way, this way lo! Here is rest,
"Rings out the harbour bell of
heaven.

2. Oh, let us now the call obey,
   And steer our bark for yonder shore
   Where still that voice directs the
   Way,
   In pleading tones for ever more.
   A thousand life wrecks strew the
   sea;

They're going down at ev'ry swell:
Come unto Me! Come unto Me!
"Rings out th' assuring harbour bell.

3. O tempted one, look up, be strong!
The promise of the Lord is sure.
That they shall sing the victor's
song.
Who faithful to the end endure.
God's Holy Spirit comes to thee,
Of His abiding love to tell,
To blissful port, o'er stormy sea,
Calls heaven's inviting harbour bell.

4. Come, gracious Lord. and in Thy
love
Conduct us o'er life's stormy wave;
Oh, guide, us ,to the home above,
The blissful home beyond the
grave;
There, safe from rock, and storm,
and flood,
Our song of praise shall never
cease,
To Him who bought us with His
blood,
And brought us to the port of peace.
　　　　　　　　　　-John H. Yates

266
Abundantly able to save -P. M.

1. Whoever receiveth the Crucified
One,
Whoever believeth on God's only
Son.
A free and a perfect salvation shall
have:
For He is abundantly able to save.

Chorus
My brother, the Master is calling for
thee;
His grace and His mercy are
wondrously free!
His blood as a ransom for sinners
He gave,
And He is abundantly able to save.

2. Whoever receiveth the message of
God,
And trusts in the power of the soul
cleansing blood,

A full and eternal redemption
shall have:
For He is both able and willing to
save.

3. Whoever repents and forsakes
ev'ry sin.
And open his heart for the Lord
to come in,
A present and perfect salvation
shall have:
For Jesus is ready this moment
to save.
　　　　　　　　　　-E. A. Hoffman

267
Believe and obey -11.8.

1. Press onward, press onward, and
trusting the Lord,
Remember the promise proclaim
His word;
He guideth the footsteps, directeth
the way.
Of all who confess Him: believe
and obey!

Chorus
Believe and obey, believe and obey!
The Master is calling no longer
delay
The light of His mercy shines bright
on the way
Of all who confess Him: believe and
Obey!

2. Press onward,, press onward, if you
would secure
The rest of the faithful, abiding and
sure;
The gift of salvation is offer'd today
To all who confess Him believe and
obey!

3. Press onward, press onward, your
courage renew;
The prize is before you. the crown is
in view;

His love is so boundless, He'll never say Nay
To those who confess Him: believe and obey!

-Julia Sterling

268

Weary Wanderer- 8.78.7.

1. Weary Wand'er, stop and listen,
Happy news we bring to thee;
Jesus has prepared banquet;
Come, and welcome thou shall be.

Chorus
Make no longer vain excusses,
Jesus calls, and calls thee now;
Come, for ev'rything is ready:
Weary soul, why waitest thou?

2. Are thy sins a heavy burden
Come to God, confess them now
He is willing to forgive thee;
Ask, receive, why waitest thou?

3. On the loving arm of Jesus
Wouldst thou lean, and trust Him now?
Let Him cleanse thee at the fountain;
Come at once Why waitest thou?

4. See the beauteous wedding garment;
In his hands He holds It now:
Haste, oh haste, there to the banquet
Enter in! Why waitest thou?

-Grace J. France!

269

Let Him In

1. There's a Stranger at the door, let Him in:
He has been there oft before, Let Him in;
let Him in, ere He is gone, Let Him In the Holy One
Jesus Christ, the Father's Son, Let Him in.

2. Open now to Him your heart, Let Him in;
If you wait He will depart, Let Him in:
Let Him in, He is your Friend, He' your soul will sure defend,
He will keep you to the end, Let Him in.

3. Hear you now His loving voice? Let him in;
Now, oh, now make Him your choice, Let Him in;
He to standing at your door, Joy to you He will restore,
And His name you will adore, Let Him in.

4. Now admit the heavenly Guest, Let Him in;
He will make for you a feast, Let Him in;
He will speak your sin forgiven,
And when earth ties all are riven,
He will take you home to heaven,
Let Him in.

-J. B. Atchinson

270

Room at the Cross for You

1. The cross upon which Jesus died is a shelter in which we can hide;
And its grace so free is sufficient for me
And deep is its fountain as wide as the sea.

Chorus
There's room at the cross for you,
There's room at the cross for you,
Tho' millions have come, There's Still room for one,
Yea, there's room at the cross for You.

THE GOSPEL CALL

2. Tho' millions have found Him a friend
And have turned from the sins they have sinned,
The Saviour still waits to open the gates
And welcome a sinner before it's too late.

3. The hand of my Saviour is strong,
And the love of my Saviour is long;
Through sunshine or rain, through loss or in gain.
The blood flows from Calv'ry to cleanse ev'ry stain
            -Ira F. Stanphill,

271

Washed in the blood-11.9.11.9. With Refrain

1. Have you been to Jesus for the cleansing power?
Are you washed in the blood of the Lamb?
Are you fully trusting in His grace this hour?
Are you washed in the blood of the lamb?

Chorus
Are you washed in the blood,
In the soul-cleansing blood of the Lamb?
Are your garments spotless?
Are they white as snow?
Are you washed in the blood of the Lamb?

2. Are you walking daily by the Savior's side?
Are you washed in the blood of the Lamb?
Do you rest each moment in the Crucified?
And be washed in the blood of the Lamb?

3. When the Bride-groom cometh will your robes be white?
Are you washed in the blood of the Lamb?
Will your soul be ready for the mansions bright,
Are you washed in the blood of the Lamb?

4. Lay aside the garments that are stained with sin.
And be washed in the blood of the Lamb?
There's a fountain flowing for the soul unclean,
O be washed in the blood of the Lamb?
            -Elisha A. Hoffmann

272

Bourne

1. "Give Me thy heart," says the Father above,
No gift so precious to Him as our love;
Softly He whispers, wherever thou art
"Gratefully trust Me, and give Me thy heart"

Chorus
Give Me thy heart', give Me thy heart."
Hear the soft whisper, wherever ' thou art:
From this dark world He would draw thee apart;
Speaking so tenderly, -Give Me thy heart.

2. "Give Me thy heart." says the Saviour of men,
Calling in mercy again and again;
Turn now from sin. and from evil depart,
Have I not died for thee? Give Me thy heart."

THE GOSPEL CALL

3. "Give Me thy heart, "say the spirit divine,
"All that thou hast, to My keeping resign;
Grace more abounding is Mine to thy to impart,
Make full surrender and give Me thy heart."

-Eliza E. Hewitt

273

He Brought Me Out

1. My heart was distressed neath Jehovah's dread frown,
And low in the pit where my sins dragged me down;
I cried to the Lord from the deep miry clay,
Who tenderly brought me out to golden day.

Chorus
He bro't me out of the miry clay,
He set my feet on the Rock to stay;
He puts a song in my soul today,
A song of praise, hallelujah!

2. He placed me upon the strong Rock by His side,
My steps were established and here II'l abide;
No danger of falling while here I remain,
But stand by His grace until the crown I gain

3. He gave me a song, twas a new song of praise;
By day and by night its sweet notes I will raise;
My heart's over flowing, I'm happy and free,
I'll praise my Redeemer, who has rescued me.

4. I'll sing of His wonderful mercy to me,
I'll praise Him till all men His goodness shall see;
I'll sing of salvation at home and abroad,
Till many shall hear the truth and trust in God.

5. I'll tell of the pit, with its gloom and despair,
I'll praise the dear Father, who answered my prayer;
I'll sing my new song, the glad story of love,
Then join in the chorus with the saints above.

-Henry J. Zalley,
Chorus by H.L.G.

274

Whosoever Will

1. Whosoever heareth shout, shout the sound!
Spread the blessed tidings all the world around!
Tell the joyful news whenever man is found:
"Whosoever will" may come!

Chorus
Whosoever will! whosoever will!
Send the proclamation over vale and hill:
Tis the loving Father calls the wand'rer home;
Whosoever will may come!

2 Whosoever cometh need not delay;
Now the door is open, enter while you may;
Jesus is the true and only Living Way.
Whosoever will may come!

THE GOSPEL CALL

3. Whosoever will! the promise is
   secure;
   Whosoever will! for'ver shall
   endure;
   Whosoever will! 'Tis life for
   evermore!
   Whosoever will may come!

   -Philip P. Bliss

275

What will you do with Jesus

1. Jesus is standing in Pilate's hall
   Friendless, forsaken, betrayed by all!
   Hearken! What meaneth the sudden
   Call:
   What will you do with Jesus?

Chorus
1. What will you do with Jesus?
   Neutral you cannot be,
   Some day your heart will be asking,
   "What will He do with me?"

2. Jesus is standing on trial still,
   You can be false to him if you will,
   You can be faithful through good or
   ill:
   What will you do with Jesus?

3. Will you evade Him as Pilate tried?
   Or will you choose Him, whate'er
   betide?
   Vainly you struggle from Him to
   hide;
   What will you do with Jesus?

4. Will you, like Peter, your Lord deny?
   Or will you scorn from His foes to fly
   Daring for Jesus to live or die? What
   will you do with Jesus?

5. "Jesus I give Thee my heart today?
   Jesus, I'll follow Thee all the way.
   Gladly obeying Thee!" will you say:
   "This will I do with Jesus!"

   -Albert B. Simpson

276

Fill my cup, Lord

1. Like the woman at the well I was
   seeking
   For thing that could rot satisfy;
   And then I heard my Saviour
   Speaking
   "Draw from My well that never shall
   run dry."

Chorus
Fit! my cup. Lord, I lift it up, Lord!
Come and quench this thirsting of
my soul;
Bread of Heaven, feed me till ,I
want no more,
Fill my cup, fill it up and make me
Whole!

2. There are millions in this world who
   are craving
   The pleasure earthly things afford;
   But none can match the wondrous
   treasure
   That I find in Jesus Christ my Lord.

3. So. my brother, if the things this
   world gave you
   Leave hungers that won't pass
   away,
   My blessed Lord will come and
   save you.
   If you kneel to Him and humbly
   pray:

   -Richard Blanchard

277

The Saviour Is Waiting

1. The Saviour is waiting to enter your
   heart;
   Why don't you let Him come in?
   There's nothing in this world to
   keep you apart,
   What is your answer to Him?

THE GOSPEL CALL

Chorus
Time after time, He has waited before,
And now He is waiting again.
To see if you;re willing to open the door,
Oh, now He want to come in.

2. If you'll take one step t'ward the Saviour; my friend;
You'll find His arms open wide.
Receive Him and all of your darkness will end,
Within your heart He'll abide.
-R. Carmichael!

278

Why not now

1. While we pray and while we plead,
While you see your soul's deep need,
While our Father calls you home,
Will you not, my brother, come?

Chorus
Why not now? Why not now?
Why not come to Jesus now?
Why not now? Why not now?
Why not come to Jesus now?

2 You have wandered far away,
Do not risk another day;
Do not turn from God thy face,
But today accept His grace.

3. In the world you've failed to find
Aught of peace for troubled mind;
Come to Christ on Him believe,
Peace and joy you shall receive.

4. Come to Christ, confession make;
Come to Christ, and pardon take;
Trust in Him from day today,
He will keep you all the way
-El Nathan

279

You Must Open the Door

1. There's a Saviour who stands at the door of your heart,
He is longing to enter, why let Him depart?
He has patiently called you so often before.
But you must open the door.

Chorus
You must open the door,
You must open the door,
When Jesus comes in,
He will save you from sin,
But you must open the door.

2. He has come from the Father salvation to bring
And His name is called Jesus, Redeemer and King;
To save you and keep you He pleads evermore,
But you must open the door.

3. He is loving and kind, full of infinite grace,
In your heart, in your life, will you give Him a place?
He is waiting to bless you. your soul to restore,
But you must open the door.

4. He will lead you at last to that blessed abode
To the city of God, at the end of the road.
Where the night never fails, when life's journey is o'er,
But you must open the door.
- Ina Duley Ogdon

THE GOSPEL CALL

280

Only Trust Him

1. Come, ev'ry soul by sin oppressed
   There's mercy with the Lord,
   And He will surely give you rest
   By trusting in His word.

Chorus
Only trust Him, only trust Him;
Only trust Him now;
He will save you, He will save you,
He will save you now.

2. For Jesus shed His precious blood
   Rich blessing to bestow
   plunge now into the crimson flood
   That washes white as snow.

3. Yes, Jesus is the truth, the Way,
   That leads you into rest.,
   Believe in Him without delay
   And you are fully blest.
   -John H. Steatton

281

Let Jesus Come into Your Heart

1. If you are tired of the load of your sin.
   Let Jesus come into your heart;
   If you desire a new life to begin,
   Let Jesus come into your heart.

Chorus
Just now your doubting give! O'er,
Just now reject Him no more;
Just now throw open the door
Let Jesus come into your heart.

2. If 'tis for purity now that you Sigh,
   Let Jesus come into your heart:
   Fountains for cleansing are flowing
   near by,
   Let Jesus come into your heart

3. If there's a tempest your voice
   cannot still,
   Let Jesus come into your heart.

If there's a void this world never
can fill
Let Jesus come into your heart.

4. If you would Join the glad songs
   of the blest.
   Let Jesus come into your heart.
   If you would enter the mansions
   of rest
   Let Jesus come into your heart.
   -Lelia Moris

282

Come Just As You Are

1. Ye who are troubled and
   burdened by sin,
   Come just as you are!
   Come to the Saviour, a new life.
   Begin.
   Oh, come just as you are!

Chorus
Come just as you are
Oh, come just as you are!
Turn from your sin, let the saviour
come in
And come just as you are.

2. Deep in your heart sin has written
   its scar,
   Come Just as you are.
   Tho from your Father you've
   wandered afar,
   Oh, come just as you are.

3. Sinful and guilty, heart broken
   and lost.
   Come just as you are.
   Think what your ransom on
   Calvary cost!
   Oh, come just as you are!

4. Naught of your goodness for sin
   can atone;,
   Come just as you are.
   Trust in the merit of Jesus alone,
   And come just as you are!.

THE GOSPEL CALL

5. Come with your heart ache, your
   sorrow and pain;
   Come just as you are!
   No one has come to the Saviour in
   vain.
   Oh, come just as you are!

   -Haldor Lillenas"

283

Oh, why not tonight

1. Oh, do not let the word depart,
   And close thine eyes against the
   light;
   Poor sinner, harden not your heart.
   Be saved oh, tonight.

Chorus
Oh, why not tonight!
Oh, why not tonight?
Wilt thou be saved?
Then why not tonight?

2. Tomorrow's sun may never rise,
   To bless thy long deluded sight;
   This is the time, oh, then be wise,
   Be saved oh, tonight.

3. Our Lord in pity lingers still,
   And wilt thou thus His love requite?
   Renounce at once thy stubborn will.
   Be saved oh, tor-right

4. Our blessed Lord refuses none
   Who would to Him their souls unite;
   Believe, obey, the work is done.
   Be saved oh, tonight.

   -Elizabeth Reed

284

Jesus is calling

1. Jesus is tenderly calling thee home
   Calling today, calling today;
   Why from the sunshine of love wilt
   thou roam
   Farther and farther away?

Chorus
Calling day, Calling today.
Jesus is calling,
Is tenderly catling today.

2. Jesus is calling the weary to rest -
   Calling today, calling today;
   Bring Him thy burden and thou
   shaft be blest
   He will not turn thee away.

3. Jesus is waiting, O come to Him
   now
   Waiting today, waiting today;
   Come with thy sins, at His feet
   lowly bow
   Come, and no longer delay.

4. Jesus is pleading, O list to His
   Hear Him today, hear Him today;
   They who believe on His name
   shall rejoice
   Quickly arise and away.

   -Fanny J. Crosby

285

St. Mark - 7.7.0.

1. Sinners, turn: why will ye die?
   God, your Maker, asks you why
   God, who did your being give,
   Made you with Himself to live
   He the fatal cause demands.
   Asks the work of His own hands;
   Why, ye thankless creatures, why
   Will you cross His love, and die'?

2. Sinners. turn: why will ye die?
   God, your Saviour, asks you why
   God, who did your souls retrieve.
   Died Himself that ye might live.
   Will you tet Him die in vain,
   Crucify the Lord again?
   Why, ye ransom'd sinners, why
   Will you slight His grace, and die?

THE GOSPEL CALL

3. Sinners, turn: why will ye die?
   God, the Spirit, asks you why.,
   He who all your lives hath striven,
   Urged you to contend for heaven;
   Will you not His grace receive?
   Will you still refuse to live? ,
   Why, ye long-sought sinners, why
   Will you grieve your God, and die.

4. Can you doubt if God is love,
   If to all His yearnings move?
   Will you not His word receive?
   Will you not His oath believe?
   See, your dying Lord appears!
   Jesus weeps: believe His tears!
   Mingled with His Mood they cry,
   "Why will you resolve to die?"
   —Berthold Tours

286

Midian- 8.6.8.6.4.

1. Return, O wanderer, to thy home.
   Thy father calls for thee:
   No longer now an exile roam
   In guilt and misery: Return, return;

2. Return, O wanderer, to thy home,
   'Tis Jesus calls for thee;
   The Spirit and the bride say, Come,
   Oh, now for refuge flee: Return,
   return.

3. Return, O wanderer, to thy home,
   'Tis madness to delay:
   There are no pardons in the tomb.
   And brief is mercy's day: Return,
   return.
   —W. H. Havergal

287

Come - 7.G.

1. O word, of words the sweetest,
   O word, in which there lie
   All promise, all fulfilment,
   And end of mystery!

Lamenting, or rejoicing,
With doubt or terror nigh,
I hear the "Come!" of Jesus,
And to His cross I fly.

Chorus
"Come! oh, come to Me!
Come! oh, come to Me!"
"Weary, heavy laden,
Come! oh come to Me!"
"Come! oh, come to Me!
Come, oh, come to Me!"
"Weary heavy laden,
come, oh. come to Me!"

2. O soul! why shouldst thou wander
   from such a loving Friend?
   Cling closer, closer to Him,
   Stay with Him to the end:
   Alas! I am so helpless.
   So very full of sin,
   For I am ever wand'ring,
   And coming back again:

3. Oh, each time draw me nearer,
   That soon the "Come" may be,
   Naught but a gentle whisper,
   To one close, close to Thee:
   Then over sea and mountain
   Far from, or near my home.
   L'll lake Thy, hand and follow,
   At that sweet whisper, "Come!"
   —J. McGranahan

288

Come, O Come, When Christ is Calling-8.7.8.7. with Ref

1. Come, O come, When Christ is
   calling,
   Linger not in paths of sin;
   Sever ev'ry tie that binds you.
   And the Heav'nly race begin.

THE GOSPEL CALL

Chorus
Calling now, calling now;
Hear the Saviour calling now;
Calling now, calling now.
Hear the Saviour calling now.

2. Come, oh come, while Christ is
pleading;
Oh, what love His tones convey!
Will you slight His proffer'd mercy,
Will you longer from Him stray!

3. Come, oh come, delay no longer,
For th' accepted time is now;
Yield, oh yield yourself to Jesus,
And before His sceptre bow.

289

Come To The Saviour, Make No Delay -P. M.

1. Come to the Saviour, make no
delay;
Here in His world He has shown us
the way;
Here in our midst He's standing
today,
Tenderly saying, "Come"

Chorus
Joyful, joyful, will the meeting be,
When from sin our hearts are
pure and free,
And we shall gather, Saviour, with
Thee, In our eternal home.

2. "Suffer the children!" Oh, hear
His voice
Let ev'ry heart leap forth and
rejoice;
And let us freely make Him our
choice;
Do not delay, but come.

3. Think once again. He's with us
today;
Heed now His blest command
and obey;
Hear now His accents tenderly
say,
"Will you, my children, come?"

290

Once My Eyes Were Blind - 12.12.12.13. with Ref

1. Once my eyes-were blind to the
beauty of the Lord
Once my ears were closed to the
pleading of His word;
Once these hands of mine
pressed the thorn-crown on His
brow;
But all this He has forgiven, and
it's alright now

Chorus
Yes, it's alright now. Yes, it's
alright now
He has heard my prayer and its
alright now:
Yes, it's alright now, yes. it's
alright now
All my sins are covered and it's
alright now.

2. Once I loved the world with its
glitter and its now;
I was captive held with the
pleasures here below,
But one day He came, though I
cannot tell you how,
With His blood my sins He
covered, and it's alright now.

THE GOSPEL CALL

3. Oh it is so precious to be alone
with Him,
When the shadows fall and my
eyes with tears are dim,
Just to feel His hand rest in love
upon my brow,
And to hear Him gently whisper,
"It is alright now."

291

Sinner. How Thy Heart Is Troubled - 8.7.8.7.

1 Sinner, how thy heart is
troubled!
God is coming very near;
Do not hide thy deep emotion.
Do not check that falling tear.

Chorus
Oh, be saved, His grace free!;
Oh, be saved, He died for thee!
Oh, be saved, He died for thee!

2. Jesus now is bending o'er thee,
Jesus lowly, meek, and mild;
To the Friend who died to save
Thee.
Wilt thou not be reconciled?

3. Art thou waiting till the morrow?'
Thou may'st never see its light:
Come at once! Accept His mercy;
He is waiting - come tonight!

4. With a lowly, contrite spirit,
Upward to the courts of heaven!
Let them sing, with holy rapture,
O'er another soul forgiven!

292

Today The Saviour Calls - 6.4.6,4

1. Today the saviour call
Ye wand'rer, come
Oh, ye benighted souls
Why longer roam?

2. Today the Saviour call
Oh, listed now!
Within these sacred walls
To Jesus bow

3. Today the Saviour call
For refuge fly;
The storm of justice falls
And death is nigh.

4. The Spirit calls today;
Yield to His power;
Oh, grieve Him not away!
Tis mercy hour.

ACCEPTANCE AND REPENTANCE

293

Franconia - S. M.

1. I give myself to Thee,
   My Saviour and my God,
   To be Thine own for evermore,
   The purchase of Thy blood.

2. I give myself to Thee,
   My Father and my Friend.
   To walk in all Thy perfect way
   Until my life shall end.

3. O help me to renounce
   The hateful works of sin,
   The empty vanities of life,
   The flesh that strives within.

4. O help me to believe
   Thy living word of truth,
   And take it as the perfect guide
   Of my imperfect youth.

5. O help me to obey
   The law which Thou hast given,
   And daily by Thy grace to tread
   The path that leads to heaven.

6. And ever more and more,
   Lord. let Thy servant prove
   The riches of redeeming grace,
   The wonder of Thy love.   \

7. Thus rooted in Thy love.
   And steadfast in Thy faith.
   Joyful through hope may I remain
   Still faithful unto death.

8. So having passed the waves
   Of this world's troubled sea,
   May I within Thy kingdom reign,
   My Saviour God. with Thee.
                    -Emay Symons

294

Saffron Walden - 8.8.8.6.

1. Just as I am, Thine own to be,
   Friend of the young, who lovest me,
   To consecrete myself to Thee,
   O Jesus Christ -I come.

2. In the glad morning of my day,
   My life to give my vows to pay;
   With no reserve and no delay,
   With all my heart I come.

3. I would live ever in the light,
   I would work ever for the right,
   I would serve Thee with all my
   might.
   Therefore to Thee I come.

4. Just as I am, young, strong and
   free,
   To be the best that I can be;
   For truth and righteousness and
   Thee,
   Lord of my life I come,

5. And for Thy sake to win renown,
   And then to take the victor's crown,
   And at Thy feet to lay it down,
   O Master, Lord -I come.
                    -Marianne Heam

295

Auretta -7.6.7.6.D.

1. I need Thee, precious Jesus,
   For I am full of sin;
   My soul is dark and guilty,
   My heart is dead within:
   I need the cleansing fountain
   Where I can always flee,
   The blood of Christ most precious.
   The sinner's perfect plea.

2. I need Thee, blessed Jesus,
   For I am very poor,

A stranger and a pilgrim, I have no
earthly store:
I need the love of Jesus
To cheer me on my way,
To guide my doubting footsteps,
To be my strength and stay.

3. I need Thee, blessed Jesus,
I need a friend like Thee,
A friend to soothe and pity,
A friend to care for me:
I need the heart of Jesus
To feel each anxious care,
To tell my ev'ry trial,
And all my sorrows share.
-Frederick Whitfield

296
Old, Old Story - 7.6.7.5.D. with Refrain

1. Tell me the old, old story
Of unseen things above,
Of Jesus and His glory,
Of Jesus and His love:
Tell me the story simply,
As to a little child.
For I am weak and weary,
And helpless and defiled.

Chorus
Tell me the old, old story,
Tell me the old, old story,
Tell me the old, old story
Of Jesus and His love.

2. Tell me the story slowly,
That I may take it in,
That wonderful redemption,
God's remedy for sin!
Tell me the story often,
For I forget so soon.
The early dew of morning
Has passed away at noon!

3. Tell me the story softly,
With earnest tones, and grave,
Remember! I'm the sinner

Whom Jesus came to save:
Tell me that story always,
If you would really be.
In any time of trouble,
A comforter to me.

4. Tell me the same old story.
When you have cause to fear
That this world's empty glory
Is costing me too dear.
Yes, and when that world's glory
Is dawning on my soul,
Ted me the old, old story:
"Christ Jesus makes thee whole."
-Katherine Hankey

297
Story of Jesus-8.7.8.7.D. with Refrain

1. Tell me the story of Jesus.
Write on my heart every word;
Tell me the story most precious,
Sweetest that ever was heard.
Tell how the angel in chorus
Sang as they welcomed His birth,
"Glory to God in the highest
Peace and good tidings to earth."

Chorus
Tell me the story of Jesus,
Write on my heart every word;
Tell me the story most precious
Sweetest that ever was heard

2. Fasting alone in the desert,
Tell of the day that are past,
How for our sins He was tempted,
Yet was triumphant at last.
Tell of the years of His labour,
Tell of the sorrow He bore,
He was despised and afflicted,
Homeless, rejected and poor.

3. Tell of the cross where they nailed Him,
Writhing in anguish and pain;

ACCEPTANCE AND REPENTANCE

Tell of the grave where they laid
Him
Tell how He liveth again.
Love in that story so tender,
Clearer than ever I see:
Stay, let me weep while you this
whisper.
Love paid the ransom for me.
-Fanny J. Crosby

298

Walls- 7.7.7.7.8.8.

1. From the deeps of grief and fear,
Lord, to Thee my soul repairs:
From Thy heaven bow down Thine
ear;
Let Thy mercy meet my prayers.
O if Thou mark'st what's done
amiss,
What soul so pure, can see Thy
Bliss?

2. But with Thee sweet mercy stands,
Sealing pardons, working fear:
Wait, my soul, wait on His hands;
Wait, mine eye, O wait, mine ear:
" If He His eye or tongue affords.
Watch all His looks, catch all His
words.

3. As a watchman waits for day, Looks
for light, and looks again;
When the night grows old and grey,
For relief he calls again:
So look, so wait, so long mine eyes,
To see my Lord, my Sun, arise.

4. Wait, ye saints, wait on our Lord
From His tongue sweet mercy flows:
Trust His cross, wait on His word;
On that tree redemption grows.
He will redeem His Israel
From sin and wrath, from death and
hell.
-Phineas Fletcher

299

Since Jesus passed by

1. Like the blind man I wandered.
So lost and undone,
A beggar so helpless, Without
God or His Son;
Then my Saviour in mercy,
heard and answered my cry arid
Oh,
what a difference since Jesus
passed by!

Chorus
Since Jesus passed by, Since
Jesus passed by,
Oh, what a difference since
Jesus passed by!
Well, I can't explain it, and I
cannot tell you why,
but Oh, what a difference, since
Jesus passed by!

2. All my yesterdays are buried in
the deepest of the sea;
That old load of guilt I carried, is
all gone, Praise God. I'm free!
Looking for that bright tomorrow,
where no tears will dim the eye
Well, Oh,
what a difference since Jesus
passed by!
-William J. Gaither

300

I'm Living in Canaan

1. All that drew me I have left behind,
Here in Canaan better joys I find;
Peace abiding, blessings
unconfined, For I'm living in Canaan
now.

Chorus
I am living in Canaan now,
Where the showers of blessing
abound;

Where the riches of grace in plenty
are found,
I am living in Canaan now.

2. Safe abiding I will never fear,
For my Saviour ever will be near
When I call Him He will always
bear, For I'm living in Canaan now.

3. I am drinking from a ceaseless
well.
Here in Canaan where I love to
dwell.
So to others I am glad to tell,
That I'm living in Canaan.

4. Praises ever I am glad to bring
Unto Jesus, my Redeemer, King;
For His mercies I will shout and sing.
For I'm living in Canaan now.
-C. Austin Miles

301
Come not to tarry, but stay

1. My heart is open to thee. dear Lord,
Come in, come in;
My faith is clinging to thy dear word,
Come in come in.

Chorus
Come not to tarry, but stay, dear
Lord.
All shall be thine love can afford,
Here in my heart ever make thine
abode
Come in come in.

2. Yes, there is room in my heart, dear
Lord,
Come in, come in;
Thy presence makes heaven real to
me,
Come in, come in.

3. I kept thee standing outside so long.
Come in, come in;
I pray thee pardon this shameful
Wrong,
Come in, come in.

4. I hear thee knocking at my heart's
door,
Come in, come in.
I'll keep thee waiting outside no
more,
Come in, come in.
-Arthur Willis Spooner

302
St Agnes C. M.

1. Approach, my soul, the mercy-seat,
Where Jesus answers prayer;
There humbly fall before His feet,
For none can perish there.

2. Thy promise is my only plea,
With this I venture nigh:
Thou callest burden'd souls to
Thee,
And such, O Lord, am I.

3. Bow'd down beneath a load of sin,
By Satan sorely press'd,
By war without, and fears within,
I come to Thee for rest

4. Be Thou my should and hiding-
place.
That, shelter'd near Thy side, I may
my fierce accuser face.
And tell him, Thou hast died.

5. Oh, wondrous love, to bleed and
die.
To bear the cross and shame.
That guilty sinners, such as I,
Might plead Thy gracious name.
-J. B. Dykes

ACCEPTANCE AND REPENTANCE

303

Barnby - 8.8.8.8.8.8.

1. Weary of wandering from my God
And now made willing to return,
I hear and bow me to the rod;
For Thee, not without hope, I mourn:
I have an Advocate above,
A Friend before the throne of love.

2. O Jesus, full of truth and grace.
More full of grace than I of sin,
Yet once again I seek Thy face.
Open Thine arms and take me in;
And freely my backslidings heal.
And love the faithless sinner still.

3. Thou know'st the way to bring me back.
My fallen spirit to restore:
Oh, for Thy truth and mercy's sake,
Forgive, and bid me sin no more:
The ruins of my soul repair,
And make my heart a house of prayer.

4. Ah! give me. Lord, the tender heart
That trembles at the approach of sin;
A godly fear of sin impart,
Implant, and root it deep within;
That I may dread Thy gracious power
And never dare offend Thee more.
-J. Barnby

304

I am Coming Home

1. Jesus, I am coming home today,
For I have found there's joy in Thee alone;
From the path of sin I turn away,
Now
I am coming home.

Chorus
Jesus, I am coming home today,
Never, never more from Thee to stray;
Lord, I now accept Thy precious promise,
I am coming home.

2. Many years my heart has strayed from Thee,
And now repentant to Thy throne I come,
Jesus opened up the way for me,
Now I am coming home.

3. Oh, the misery my sin has caused me,
Naught but pain and sorrow I have known;
Now I seek Thy saving grace and many.
I am coming home,

4. Fully trusting in Thy precious promise,
With no righteousness to call my own,
Pleading nothing but the blood of Jesus, I am coming home.

5. Now I seek the cross where Jesus died!
For all my sins His blood will still atone,
Flowing o'er till ev'ry stain is covered, I am coming home.
-A. H. Ackley

305

His Grace Aboundeth More

1. O what a wonderful Saviour,
In Jesus my Lord I have found,
Tho' I had sins without number,
His grace unto me did abound.

Chorus
His grace aboundeth more.
His grace aboundeth more,
Tho' sin abounded in my heart.
His grace aboundeth more.

2. When a poor sinner He found me,
No goodness to offer had I;
Often His law I had broken,
And merited naught but to die.

3. Nothing of merit possessing,
All helpless before him I lay.
But in the precious blood flowing
He wash'd all my sin stain away.

4. In Him my precious Redeemer,
My Prophet, my Priest and my
king;
Mercy I find and forgiveness,
My all to His keeping I bring.

5. How can I keep from rejoicing?
I'll sing of the Joy in my soul;
Praising the love of my Saviour,
While years of eternity roll.
                              -Kate Ulmer

306

I hear Thy Welcome Voice - S.M.
with Refrain

1. I hear Thy welcome voice,
That calls me. Lord, to Thee,
For cleansing in Thy precious blood
That flowed on Calvary.

Chorus
I am coming, Lord'
Coming now to thee!
Trusting only in the blood
That flowed on Calvary.

2. Tho' coming weak and vile,
Thou dost my strength assure;

Thou dost my vileness fully
cleanse.
Till spotless all and pure.

3. 'Tis Jesus calls me on
To perfect faith and love, .
To perfect hope, and peace, and
trust,
For earth and heavens above

4. Tis Jesus who confirms The
blessed work within,
By adding grace to welcomed
grace,
Where reigned the power of sin.

5. And He the witness gives
To loyal hearts and free,
That every promise is fulfilled;
If faith but brings the plea.

6. All hail, atoning blood!
All hail, redeeming grace;
All hail, the gift of Christ, our Lord,
Our strength and righteousness!
                              -L. Hartsough

307

Pelan -7.6.7.6.D.

1. Today Thy mercy calls me.
To wash away my sin;
However great my trespass,
Whate'er I may have been.
However long from mercy I may
Have turn'd away
Thy blood, O Christ can cleanse
me,
And make me white today.

2. Today Thy gate is open,
And all who enter in,
Shall find a Father's welcome. And
pardon for their sin;
The past shall be forgotten,
A present joy be given;
A future grace be promised
A glorious crown in heaven.

3. O all embracing mercy, Thou ever
Open door.
What should I do without Thee.
When heart and eyes run o'er?
When all things seem against me,
To drive me to despair,
I know one gate is open, One ear
Will hear my prayer.

-Oswald Alien

308

Love Lifted Me

1. I was sinking deep in sin.
Sinking to rise no more.
Over whelm'd by guilt within,
Mercy I did implore.
Then the Master of the sea
Heard my despairing cry,
Christ my Saviour lifted me,
Now safe am I.

Chorus
Love lifted me! Love lifted me!
When no one but Christ could help,
Love lifted me!
Love lifted me! Love lifted me!
When no one but Christ could help,
Love lifted me.

2. Souls in danger, look above,
Jesus completely saves;
He will lift you by His love
Out of the angry waves.
He's the Master of the sea,
billows His will obey;
He your Saviour wants to be,
Be saved today!

3. When the waves of sorrow roll,
When Iam in distress,
Jesus takes my hand in His,
Ever He loves to bless,
He will every fear dispel,
Satisfy every need;
All who heed His loving call
Find rest indeed.

309

Coming Home

1. Like a wayward child I wandered
From my Father's house away,
But I hear His voice entreating,
And I'm coming home today,

Chorus
Coming home, Coming home,
For I can no longer roam;
I am sad and broken hearted,
And I'm coming, coming home!

2. I have wandered in the darkness.
And my path was lone and drear,
But my Father did not leave me,
He was watching ever near.

3. O the rapture that awaits me
When I reach my Father's door!
Once within its blest enclosure,
I am safe forever more.

4. I will ask Him to forgive me
For the wrong that I have done.
To receive, accept, and bless me,
Thro" His well beloved Son.

-Fanny J. Crosby

310

Trust -L. M.

1. He tells me to trust and not fear.
He bids me each promise believe:
His presence and glory seems near.
I open my heart to receive:
I am ransom'd, t know, For His Word
Tell me so.
So I trust, trust, trust!
I am ransom'd, I know For His
Word tells me so.
So I trust, trust, trust! .

2. My need He is pledged to supply
I trust for each breath that I
breathe:
And since I take life at His hands.
Why not all He wishes to give?
Lord, I yield evermore, For Thy
promise is sure
So I trust, trust, trust!
Lord, I yield evermore, For Thy
promise is sure
So I trust, trust, trust!

3. He offers me pardon and peace,
He offers me cleansing from sin;
The fountain once open'd I see,
Dear Jesus, I dare to plunge in:
Now I know I am free, for Thy
blood cleanseth me,
While I trust, trust, trust!
Now I know I am free, for Thy
blood cleanseth me,
While I trust, trust, trust!

4. Praise God, it is done I am His
The blood covers body and soul;
I am pandon'd and cleans'd, I am
heal'd
All glory, I'm ev'ry whit whole!
Praise His name, I believe. And
this moment receive,
While trust, trust, trust!
Praise His name, I believe, And
this moment receive,
While I trust, trust, trust!
-Mrs S. R. G. Cark:

311

Rawlins -7.7.7.5.D.

1. I will go, I cannot stay
From the arms of love away;
O for strength of faith to say,
Jesus died for me,

Chorus
Can it be, O can it be,
There is hope for one like me?

I will go with this my plea.
Jesus died for me.

2. Tho' I long have tried in vain,
Tried to break the tempter's chain,
Yet today Il'l try again,
Jesus, help Thou me.

3. Iam lost, and yet I know
Earth can never heal my woe;
I will rise at once and go.
Jesus died for me.

4. Something whispers in my soul,
Tho' my sins like mountains roll,
Jesus' blood will make me whole,
Jesus died for me.
-Martha J. Lankton

312

Say Me at the Cross

1. Loving Saviour, Hear my cry,
Hear my cry, hear my cry;
Trembling to Thine arms I fly
O save me at the Cross!
I have sinn'd, but Thou hast died,
Thou hast died. Thou hast died;
In Thy mercy let me hide:
O save me at the Cross!

Chorus
Lord Jesus, receive me,
No more would I grieve Thee,
Now, blessed Redeemer,
O save me at the Cross!

2. Tho' I perish I will pray,
I will pray, I will pray;
Thou of life the Living Way;
O save me at the Cross!
Thou hast said Thy grace is free,
Grace is free, grace is free:
Have compassion, Lord, on me:
O save me at the Cross!

3. Wash me in Thy cleansing blood,
Cleansing blood, cleansing blood;

Plunge me now beneath the flood:
O save me at the Cross!
Only faith will pardon bring,
Pardon bring, pardon bring:
In that faith to Thee cling:
O save me at the Cross!

-Fanny J. Crosby

313

Now I am Coming Home

1. Long I have wander'd afar from my
   Lord,
   Now am coming home;
   Longing to be to His favour restor'd,
   Now I am coming home.

Chorus
Yes, I am coming, Dear Lord, I'm
coming,
Just now I'm coming home.
Yes, I am coming, Dear Lord, I'm
coming,
Just now I'm coming home

2. Tired of the world with its folly and
   sin,
   Now I am coming home;
   Believing the Saviour will welcome
   men,
   Now I am coming home.

3. Knowing my Saviour can give me
   His rest,
   Now I am coming home;
   Longing to anchor my soul on His.
   breast,
   Now I am coming home.

4. Humbly I crave but a poor servant's
   place,
   Now I am coming home.
   Only desiring to taste of His grace,
   Now I am coming home.

5. O bless the Lord, my dear Saviour I
   see,
   Now I am coming home.

Waiting to welcome a sinner like me,
Now I am coming home.

-Johnson Oatman

314

I Do Believe-C.M.

1. Father, I stretch my hands to Thee;
   No other help I know:
   If Thou withdraw Thyself from me,
   Ah, whither shall I go?

Chorus
I do believe, I do believe
That Jesus died for me;
And through His blood, His precious
blood.
I shall from sin be free.

2. What did Thine only Son endure,
   Before I drew my breath;
   What pain, what labour, to secure,
   My soul from endless death!

3. O Jesus, could I this believe,
   I now should feel Thy power;
   And, all my wants Thou wouldst
   relieve
   In this accepted hour.

4. Author of faith, to Thee I lift
   My weary, longing eyes:
   Oh, let me now receive that gift:
   My soul without it dies.

-Charles Wesley

315

O Blessed Lord, I Come -8.8.8.6.

1. O Jesus, Saviour, hear my call
   While at Thy feet I humbly fall:
   To Thee my Hope, my Life, my all,
   O blessed Lord, I come!

Chorus
I come and this my only plea,
That Thou didst give Thyself for me;

And casting all my care on Thee,
O blessed Lord, I come!

2. I have no merit of my own.
Thou only canst for sin atone;
And looking up to Thee alone,
O blessed Lord, I come!

3. Thy precious name salvation brings.
To Thee my weary spirit clings;
And now, to rest beneath Thy wings,
O blessed Lord, I come!

4. Oh, take this wandering heart of mine
And seal it, Lord, for ever Thine;
That I may know Thy love Divine,
O blessed Lord, I come!
-F. J. Crosby

316

Take Me, O my father" 8.7.8.7.

1. Take me, O my Father, take me!
Take me, save me, thro' Thy Son;
That which Thou wouldest have me, make me,
Let Thy will in me be done.
Long from Thee my footsteps straying,
Thorny proved the way I trod;
Weary come I now, and praying,
Take me to Thy love, my God'

2. Fruitless years with grief recalling,
Humbly I confess my sin;
At Thy feet, O Father, falling,
To Thy household take me in.
Freely now to Thee I proffer
This repenting heart of mine;
Freely life and soul I offer,
Gift unworthy of love like Thine.

3. Once the world's Redeemer or Dying
Bare our sins upon the tree;

On what Sacrifice relying,
Now I look in hope to Thee:
Father, take me I all forgiving,
Fold me to Thy loving breast;
In Thy for ever living,
I must be forever blest!
-Ray Palmer, D. D.

317

Take Me as I am - 8.8.8.6.

1. Jesus, my Lord, to Thee I cry;
Unless Thou help me, I must die:
Oh, bring Thy free salvation nigh,
And take me as I am.

Chorus
And take me as I am!
And take me as I am!
My only plea Christ died for me!
Oh, take me as I am!

2. Helpless Iam, and full of guilt;
But yet for me Thy blood was spilt,
And Thou canst make me what Thou wilt,
And take me as I am:

3. No preparation can I make,
My best resolves I only break,
Yet save me for Thine own name's sake,
And take me as I am!

4. Behold me, Saviour, at Thy feet.
Deal with me as Thou seest meet;
Thy work begin, Thy work com plete.
But take me as I am!
-Eliza H. Hamilton

318

I am Coming to the Cross - 7.7.

1. I am coming to the cross;
I am poor, and weak, and blind;
I am counting all but dross;
I shall full salvation find.

ACCEPTANCE AND REPENTANCE

Chorus
I am trusting, Lord, in Thee,
Blessed Lamb of Calvary;
Humbly at Thy cross I bow;
Save me, Jesus, save me now.

2. Long my heart has sigh'd for
Thee, Long has evil reign'd within;
Jesus sweetly speaks to me "I will
cleanse you from all sin."

3. Here I give my all to Thee.
Friends, and time, and earthly
store,
Soul and body Thine to be
Wholly Thine for evermore.

4. Jesus comes! He fills my soul!
Perfected in Him I am;
I am every whit made whole;
Glory, glory to the Lamb!

Chorus Ver.4
Still I'm trusting, Lord, in Thee,
Blessed Lamb of Calvary;
Humbly at Thy cross I bow;
Jesus saves me, saves me now!
                              -W. McDonald

319
The Mistakes of my Life

1. The mistakes of my life have been
many,
The sins of my heart have been
more,
And I scarce can see for weeping.
But I knock at the open door.

Chorus
I know I am weak and sinful,
It comes to me more and more;
But when the dear Saviour shall bid
Me come in,
I'll enter the open door.

2. I am lowest of those who love Him,
I am weakest of those who pray;
But I come as He has bidden,
And He will not say me nay.

3. My mistakes His free grace will
cover,
My sins He will wash away;
And the feet that shrink and falter
Shall walk through the gates of day.

4. The mistakes of my life have been
many,
And my spirit is sick with sin,
And I scarce can see for weeping,
But the Saviour will let me in.
                              -U. L Bailey

320
My Burdens Rolled Away

1. I remember when my burdens
rolled away,
I had carried them for years, night
and day;
When I sought the blessed Lord,
and I took Him at His word,
Then at once all my burdens rolled
away,

Chorus
Rolled away, rolled away
I am happy since my burdens rolled
away:
Rolled away, rolled away,
I am happy since my burdens rolled
away.

2. I remember when my burdens
rolled away,
That I feared would never leave
night or day;
Jesus showed to me the loss, so I
left them at the cross;
I was glad when my burdens rolled
away.

I remember when my burdens rolled away,
That had hindered me for years,
night and day;
As I sought the throne of grace, just a glimpse of Jesus' face,
And I knew that my burdens could not stay.

4. I am singing since my burdens rolled away,
There's a song within my heart night and day;
I am living for my King, and with joy
I shout and sing Hallelujah! all my burdens rolled away.

-M. A. Steele

321

Only a Sinner

1 Naught have I gotten but what I received;
Grace hath bestowed it since I have believed;
Boasting excluded, pride I abase;
I'm only a sinner saved by grace!

Chorus
Only a sinner saved by grace!
Only a sinner saved by grace!
This is my story, to God be the glory,
I'm only a sinner saved by grace!

2 Once I was foolish, and sin ruled my heart,
Causing my footsteps from God to depart;
Jesus hath found me, happy my case;
I now am a sinner saved by grace!

3. Tears unavailing, no merit had I;
Mercy had saved me, or else I must die;

Sin had alarmed me, fearing God's face;
But now I'm a sinner saved by grace!

4. Suffer a sinner whose heart overflows,
Loving his Saviour to tell what he knows;
Once more to tell it, would I embrace
I'm only a sinner saved by grace!

-James M. Gray

322

Old Things Have Passed Away

1. Jesus on Calvary Died in my place,
Saved to the uttermost. Wonderful grace.
I saw him lifted up, My heart He drew,
Old things have passed away, All things are new.

Chorus
Old things have passed away, All things are new,
Old things have passed away, All things are new,
Jesus my Saviour, Saves me thro' and thro',
Old things have passed away, All things are new.

2. Tho' I was far away, He saw my need,
His Spirit touched my heart, Caused me to plead,
His Name above all names, His work so true,
Old things have passed away, All things are new.

3. My heart in tune with His, Fellowship
His joy He gives to me, My joy Complete.

Thro' all eternity, His face I'll view,
Old things have passed away, All
things are new.

-S. Cox

323

I Am Resolved

1. I am resolved no longer to linger,
   Charmed by the world's delight;
   Things that are higher, things that
   are nobler,
   These have allured my sight

Chorus
I will hasten to Him,
Hasten so glad and free,
Jesus, greatest, highest,
I will come to Thee.

2. I am resolved to go to the Saviour,
   Leaving my sin and strife;
   He is the true one, He is the just
   one,
   He hath the words of life.

3. I am resolved to follow the Saviour,
   Faithful and true each day;
   Heed what He sayeth, do what He
   willeth,
   He is the living way.

4. I am resolved to enter the Kingdom,
   Leaving the paths of sin;
   Friend may oppose me, foes may
   beset me,
   Still will I enter in.

5. I am resolved, and who will go with
   me?
   Come, friends, without delay;
   Taught by the Bible, led by the Spirit,
   We'll walk the heavenly way.

-Palmer Hartsough

324

Amazing Grace

1. Amazing grace! How sweet the
   sound,
   That saved a wretch like me!
   I once was lost, but now am found,
   Was blind, but now I see.

2. T was grace that taught my heart to
   fear,
   And grace my fears relieved;
   How precious did that grace appear
   The hour I first believed!

3. Thro' many dangers, toils and
   snares,
   I have already come:
   'Tis grace hath bro't me safe thus
   far,
   And grace will lead me home.

4. When we've been there ten
   thousand years,
   Bright shining as the sun,
   We've no less days to sing God's
   praise
   Than when we first begun.

-John Newton

325

Aberystwyth-7.7.7.7.D.

1. Saviour, when in dust to thee
   Low we bow the adoring knee;
   When repentant, to the skies Scarce
   we lift our weeping eyes:
   O, by all thy pains and woe,
   Suffered once for man below,
   Bending from thy throne on high,
   Hear our solemn Litany.

2. By thy helpless infant years,
   By thy life of want and tears,
   By thy days of sore distress
   In the savage wilderness,

ACCEPTANCE AND REPENTANCE

By the dread mysterious hour
Of the insulting tempter's power
Turn, O turn a favouring eye,
Hear our solemn Litany.

3. By the sacred griefs that wept
O'er the grave where Lazarus slept;
By the boding tears that flowed
Over Salem's loved abode;
By the anguished sigh that told
Treachery lurked within thy fold:
From thy seat above the sky
Hear solemn Litany.

4. By Thine hour of dire despair,
By tune agony of prayer.
By the Cross, the nail, the thorn,
Piercing spear and torturing scorn;
By the gloom that veiled the skies
O'er the dreadful Sacrifice:
Listen to our humble cry,
Hear our solemn Litany.

5. By thy deep expiring groan,
By the sad sepulchral stone,
By the vault whose dark abode
Held in vain the rising God;
O! from earth to heaven restored,
Mighty reascended Lord,
Listen, listen to the cry
Of our solemn Litany.
-Sir R. Grant

326
Without Him -8.7.8.7. with Refrain

1. Without Him I could do nothing.
Without Him I'd surely fail;
Without Him I would be drifting
Like a ship without a sail.

Chorus
Jesus, O Jesus! Do you know Him today?
Do not turn Him away.
O Jesus O Jesus.
Without Him, how lost I would be.

2. Without Him I would be dying,
Without Him I'd be enslaved
Without Him life I'd be would be hopeless,
But with Jesus, thank God. I'm saved.
-Mylon R. Lefevre

327
Othello -C.M. With Refrian

1. I have a song I love to sing,
Since I have been redeemed,
Of my Redeemer, Saviour, King,
Since I have been redeemed.

Chorus
Since I have been redeemed,
Since I have been redeemed,
I will glory in His name;
Since I have been redeemed,
I will glory in my Saviour's name.

2. I have a Christ who satisfies,
Since I have been redeemed,
To do His will my highest prize,
Since I have been redeemed.

3. I have a witness bright and clear,
Since I have been redeemed,
Dispelling every doubt and fear.
Since I have been redeemed.

4. I have a home prepared for me,
Since I have been redeemed,
Where I shall dwell eternally,
Since I have been redeemed.
-Edwin O. Excell

328
Coming Home - 8.5.8.5. with Refrain

1. I've wandered far away from God
Now I'm coming home;
The paths of sin too tong I've trod
Lord, I'm coming home.

Chorus
Coming home, coming home,
Never more to roam;
Open now Thine arms of love
Lord, I'm coming home.

2. I've wasted many precious years
Now I'm Coming home;
I now repent with bitter tears
Lord, I'm coming home.

'3. I've tired of sin and straying, Lord
Now I'm coming home;
I'll trust Thy love, believe thy word
Lord,
I'm coming home.

4. My soul is sick, my heart is sore
Now I'm coming home;
My strength renew, my hope restore
Lord, I'm coming home.
                    -William J. Kinpatrick

329

Jena - L.M.

1. Wherewith, O God, shall I draw
near.
And bow myself before Thy face?
How in Thy purer eyes appear?
What shall I bring to gain Thy grace?

2. Who'er to Thee themselves approve
Must take the path Thy word hath
showed.
Justice pursue, and mercy love,
And humbly walk by faith with God.

3. But though my life henceforth be
Thine.
Present for past can ne'er atone;
Though I to Thee the whole resign.
I only give Thee back Thine own.

4. What have I that wherein to trust?
I nothing have, I nothing am;
Excluded is my every boast,
My glory swallowed up in shame.

5. Guilty I stand before Thy face,
On me I feel Thy wrath abide;
Tis just the sentence should take
place;
Tis Just but O Thy Son hath died.

5. Jesus, the Lamb of God, hath bled.
He bore our sins upon the tree;
Beneath our curse He bowed His
head;
Tis finished! He hath died for me!

6. See where before the throne He
stands,
And pours the all prevailing prayer.
Points to His side, and lifts His
hands,
And shows that I am graven there.

7. He ever lives for me to pray;
He prays that I with Him may reign:
Amen to what my Lord doth say!
Jesus, Thou canst not pray in vain.
                    -Charles Wesley

330

Marlenbourn - 8.8.8.8.8-8.

1. Jesus, in whom the weary find
Their late, but permanent repose,
Physician of the sin sick mind,
Relieve my wants, assuage my
woes,
And let my soul on Thee be cast
Till life's fierce tyranny be past.

2. Loosed from my God, and far
removed,
Long have I wandered to and fro,
O'er earth in endless circles roved,

Nor found whereon to rest below:
Back to my God at last I fly.
For O the waters still are high.

3. Selfish pursuits, and nature's maze,
The things of earth, for Thee I
Leave;
put forth Thy hand, Thy hand of
grace.
into the ark of love receive,
Take this poor fluttering soul to rest,
And lodge it, Saviour, in Thy breast.

4. Fill with inviolable peace.
Stablish and keep my settled heart;
In Thee may all my wanderings
cease.
From Thee no more may I depart;
Thy utmost goodness called to
prove
Loved with an everlasting love
-Charles Wesley

I build not there, but on His word
And in His goodness trust
Up to His care myself I yield
He is my tower, my rock. my shield
And for His help I tarry.

4. And though it linger till the night,
And round again till mom,
My heart shall ne'er mistrust Thy
might.
Nor count itself forlorn.
Do thus, O ye of Israel's seed,
Ye of the Spirit born indeed,
Wait for your God's appearing.

5. Though great our sins and sore our
wounds,
And deep and dark our fall,
His helping mercy hath no bounds,
His love surpasseth all.
Our trusty loving Shepherd, He
Who shall at last set Israel free
From all their sin and sorrow.
-Martin Luthe

331

St. Martin-8.6.8.6.8.8.7.

1. Out of the depths I cry to Thee.
Lord God, O hear my prayer!
Incline a gracious ear to me,
And bid me not despair
If Thou rememberest each
misdeed,
If each should have its rightful
meed,
Lord, who shall stand before Thee?

2. "Tis through Thy love atone we gain
The pardon of our sin;
The strictest life is but in vain
Our works can nothing win;
That none should boast himself of
aught,
But own in fear Thy grace hath
wrought
What in him seemeth righteous.

3. Wherefore my hope is in the Lord.
My works I count but dust,

332

St Christopher

1. Beneath the cross of Jesus
I fain would take my stand,
The shadow of a mighty Rock
Within a weary land;
A home within the wilderness,
A rest upon the way,
From the burning of the noontide
heart,
And the burden of the day.

2. Upon that cross of Jesus
Mine eye at times can see
The very dying form of One
Who suffered, there for me;
And from my smitten heart with
tears
Two wonders I confess,
The wonders of redeeming love
And my unworthiness.

3. I take, O cross, thy shadow for
My abiding place;
I ask no other sunshine than
The sunshine of His face;
Content to let the world go by,
To know no gain nor loss,
My sinful self my only shame,
My glory all the cross.
                    -Elizabeth C. Clephane

333

Jesus Paid It All

1. I hear the Saviour say,
Thy strength indeed is small!
Child of weakness, watch and pray
Find in Me thine alt in all."

Chorus
Jesus paid it all,
All to Him I owe;
Sin had left a Crimson stain
He washed it white as snow.

2. Lord, now indeed I find Thy pow'r,
and Thine alone,
Can change the leper's spots
And melt the heart of stone.

3. For nothing good have I
Whereby Thy grace to claim
I'll wash my garments white
In the blood of Calv'ry's Lamb.

4. And when before the throne
I stand in Him complete.
"Jesus died my soul to save,"
My lips shall still repeat.
                    -Elvina M. Hall

334

He Took My Sins Away

1. I came to Jesus, weary, worn, and
sad
He took my sins away, He took my
sins away,

And now His love has made my
heart, so glad.
He took my sins away.

Chorus
He took my sins away. He took my
sins away,
And keeps me singing ev'ry day.'
I'm so glad He took my sins away,
He took my sins away

2. The load of sin was more than I
could bear,
He took my sins away, He took my
sins away,
And now on Him I roll ev'ry care,
He took my sins away.

3. No condemnation have I in my
heart,
He took my sins away, He took my
sins away,
His perfect peace He did to me
impart,
He took my sins away.

4. If you will come to Jesus Christ
today,
He took my sins away, He took my
sins away,
And keep you happy in His love
each day, He took my sins away.
                    -Margaret J. Hams

335

Victory In Jesus

1. I heard an old, old story,
How a Saviour came from glory,
How He gave His life on Calvary
To save a wretch like me;
I heard about His groaning,
Of His precious blood's atoning,
Then I repented of my sins
And won the victory.

Chorus
O victory in Jesus,
My Saviour, for ever,
He sought me and bought me
With His redeeming blood;
He loved me ere I knew Him
And all my love is due Him,
He plunged me to victory.
Beneath the cleansing flood.

2. I heard about His healing,
Of His cleansing pow'r revealing.
How He made the lame to walk again
And caused the blind to see;
Come and heal my broken spirit,"
And somehow Jesus came an bro't
To me the victory.

3. I heard about a mansion
He has built for, me in glory,
And I heard about the streets of gold
Beyond the crystal sea;
About the angels singing.
And the old redemption story,
And some sweet day I'll sing up there
The song of victory.
-Eugene M. Bartlett

336
Springs Of Living Water

1. I thirsted in the barren land of sin
and shame,
And nothing satisfying there I
found;
But to the blessed cross of Christ
one day I came,
Where springs of living water did
abound.
Chorus
Drinking at the springs of living
water,
Happy now am I, My soul they
satisfy;
Drinking at the springs of living
water.
O wonderful and bountiful supply.

2. How sweet the living water from
the hills of God,
It makes me glad and happy all
the way;
Now glory, grace and blessing mark
the path I've trod,
I'm shouting "Hallelujay" ev'ry day.

3. O sinner, won't you come today to
Calvary,
A fountain there is flowing deep and
wide;
The Saviour now invites you to the
water free.
Where thirsting spirits can be
satisfied.
-J. W. Peterson

337
He' A Wonderful Saviour To Me

1. I was lost in sin but Jesus rescued
me.
He's a wonderful Saviour to me;
I was bound by fear but Jesus set
me free,
He's a wonderful Saviour to me.

Chorus
For He's a wonderful Saviour to
me,
He's a wonderful Saviour to me;
I was lost in sin, but Jesus took me
in.
He's a wonderful Saviour to me.

2. He's a Friend so true so patient
and so kind,
He's a wonderful Saviour to me;
Ev'rything I need in Him always
Find,.
He's a wonderful Saviour to me!

3. He is always near to comfort and to
I cheer,
He's a wonderful Saviour to me;
He forgives my sins. He dries my
ev'ry tear,
He's a wonderful Saviour to me;

4. Dearer grows the love of Jesus day
by day,
He's a wonderful Saviour to me;
Sweeter is His grace while pressing
on my way,
He's wonderful, saviour to me.
-Virgil P. Brock

338

A New Name In Glory

1. I was once a sinner, but I came
Pardon to receive from my Lord:
This was freely given and found
That He always kept His wad.

Chorus
There's a new name written down in
glory,
And it's, mine, O yes, it's mine!
And the white-robed angel sing the
story.
"A sinner has come home."
For there's a new name written in
glory,
And it's mine O yes it's mine
With my sins forgiven I am bound
for heaven,
Never more to roam,

2. I was humbly Kneeling at the cross
Fearing naught but God's angry
Frown;
When the heavens opened and I
saw
That my name was written down.

3. In the Book 'tis written "Saved by
Grace,"
O the Joy that came to my soul!
Now I am forgiven and I know'
By the blood I am made whole.
-C. Austin Miles

339

Since The Fullness Of His Low Came In

1. Once my way was dark and dreary,
For my heart was full of sin;
But the sky is bright and cheery.
Since the fullness of His love came
in.

Chorus
I can never tell how much I love Him;
I can never fell His love for me.
For it passeth human measure,
Like a deep, unfathomed sea.
Tis redeeming love in Christ, my
Saviour;
In my soul the heav'nly joys begin;
And I live for Jesus only,
Since the fullness of His love
Came in.

2. There is grace for all the lowly,
Grace to keep the trusting soul;
Pow'r to cleanse and make me holy.
Jesus shall my yielded life control.

3. Let me spread abroad the story,
Other souls to Jesus win;
For the Cross is now my glory,
Since the fullness of His love came
in
-Eliza E. Hewitt

340

Toplady

1. Rock of Ages, cleft for me
Let hide myself in Thee;
Let the water and the blood,
From Thy riven side which flowed
Be of sin the double cure,
cleanse me from its guilt and pow'r.

2. Not the labours of my hands
   Can fulfill Thy law's demands;
   Could my zeal no respite know,
   Could my tears forever flow,
   All for sin could not atone;
   Thou must save and Thou alone.

3. Nothing in my hand I bring,
   Simply to Thy cross I cling;
   Naked, come to Thee for dress.
   Helpless, look to Thee for grace;
   Foul, I to the fountain fly.
   Wash me. Saviour or I die;

4 While I draw this fleeting breath.
   When my eyes shall close in death,
   When I rise to worlds unknown
   See Thee on Thy judgement throne,
   Rock of Ages, cleft for me,
   Let me hide myself in Thee.
   —Augustus M. Toplady

3. The song of my soul, since the
   Lord made me whole,
   Has been the old story so blest
   Of Jesus who'll save whosoever
   will have A home in the "Haven of
   Rest."

4. How precious the thought that we
   all may recline,
   Like John the beloved and blest,
   On Jesus' strong arm, where no
   tempest can harm, Secure in the
   "Haven of Rest."

5. Oh, come to the Saviour, He
   patiently waits
   To save by His power divine;
   Come, anchor your soul in the
   "Haven of Rest," And say, "My
   Beloved is mine."
   —H. L. Gilmour

341

The Haven of Rest

1. My soul in sad exile was out on
   life's sea,
   So burdened with sin and distress,
   Till I heard a sweet voice saying
   "Make Me your choice;"
   And I entered the "Haven of Rest!"

Chorus
I've anchored my soul in the "Haven
of Rest,"
I'll sail the wide seas no more;
The tempest may sweep o'er the
wild, stormy deep.
In Jesus I'm safe ever more.

2. I yielded myself to His tender embrace,
   And faith taking hold of the word,
   My fetters fell off, and I anchored my
   soul:
   The "Haven of Rest" is my Lord.

342

Nothing But The Blood

1. What can wash away my sin?
   Nothing but the blood of Jesus;
   What can make me whole again?
   Nothing but the blood of Jesus.

Chorus
Oh! Precious is the flow
That makes me white as snow;
No other fount I know,
Nothing but the blood of Jesus.

2. For my pardon this I see
   Nothing but the blood of Jesus;
   For my cleansing, this my plea
   Nothing but the blood of Jesus.

3. Nothing can for sin atone
   Nothing but the blood of Jesus;
   Naught of good that I have done
   Nothing but the blood of Jesus.

4. This is all my hope and peace
   Nothing but the blood of Jesus;
   This is all my righteousness
   Nothing but the blood of Jesus.
                              -Robert Low

343

SB. Philip-7.7.7.

1. Lord, in this thy mercy's day,
   Ere it pass for ay away,
   On our knees we fall and pray.

2. Holy Jesus, grant us tears,
   Fill us with heart-searching fears,
   Ere that awful doom appears.

3. Lord, on us thy Spirit pour
   Kneeling lowly at the door,
   Ere it dose for evermore.

4. By the night of agony,
   By the supplicating cry.
   By thy willingness to die;

5. By thy tears of bitter woe
   For Jerusalem below,
   Let us not thy love forgo.

6. Grant us neath thy wings a place,
   Lest we lose this day of grace
   Ere we shall behold thy face.
                              -I. Williams

344

St. Bees - 7.7.

1. Sinful signing to be blest;
   Bound, and longing to be free;
   Weary, waiting for my rest;
   God be merciful to me.

2. Goodness I have none to plead,
   Sinfulness in all I see,
   I can only bring my need:
   God be merciful to me.

3. Broken heart and downcast eyes
   Dare not lift themselves to Thee;
   Yet Thou canst interpret sighs:
   God be merciful to me.

4. From this sinful heart of mine
   To Thy bosom I would flee;
   I am not my own but Thine:
   God be merciful to me.

5. There is One beside the Throne
   And my only hope and plea
   Are in Him, and Him alone:
   God be merciful to me.

6. He my cause will undertake,
   My Interpreter will be;
   He's my all; and for His sake God
   be merciful to me.
                              -J. B. Dykes

345

Andenken -S. M.

1. Lord Jesus, think on me,
   And purge away my sin:
   From earthborn passions set me
   free,
   And make me pure within.

2. Lord Jesus, think on me
   With many a care oppress'd;
   Let me Thy loving servant be,
   And taste Thy promised rest.

3 Lord Jesus, think on me,
   Nor let me go astray;
   Through darkness and perplexity
   Point Thou the heavenly way.

4. Lord Jesus, think on me,
   That, when the flood is past,
   I may the eternal brightness see,
   And share Thy joy at last.

5. Lord Jesus, think on me,
   That I may sing above
   To Father, Holy Ghost, and Thee
   The songs of praise and love.
                                    -J. Bamby

346

St. Mary -C. M.

1. O Lord, turn not Thy face from me,
   Who lie in woeful state,
   Lamenting all my sinful life
   Before Thy mercy-gate-

2. A gate which opens wide to those
   That do lament their sin.
   Shut not that gate against me. Lord,
   But let me enter in;

3. I need not to confess my life
   To Thee, who best can tell
   What I have been; and what I am,
   I know Thou know'st it well.

4. So come I to Thy mercy-gate,
   Where mercy doth abound,
   Imploring pardon for my sin,
   To heal my deadly wound.

5. O Lord, I need not to repeat
   The comfort I would have:
   Thou know'st, O Lord, before I ask
   The blessing I do crave.

6. Mercy, good Lord, mercy I ask;
   This is the total sum;
   For mercy, Lord. is all my suit,
   Lord, let Thy mercy come.
                                    -J. Marckant

347

Silchester - S. M.

1. Not all the blood of beasts,
   On Jewish altars slain.

Could give the guilty conscience
peace.
Or wash away the stain.

2. But Christ the heavenly Lamb,
   Takes all our sins away;
   A sacrifice of nobler name
   And richer blood than they.

3. My faith would lay her hand
   On that dear head of Thine,
   While like a penitent I stand,
   And there confess my sin.

4. My soul looks back to see
   The burdens Thou didst bear,
   When banging on the cursed tree,
   And knows her guilt was there.

5. Believing, we rejoice
   To see the curse remove:
   We bless the Lamb with cheerful
   voice
   And sing His bleeding love?
                                    -Isaac Watts

348

St. Ambrose -L. M.

1. And dost Thou say. Ask what Thou
   wilt?
   Lord, I would seize the golden hour;
   I pray to be released from guilt
   And freed from sin and Satan's
   power.

2. More of Thy presence, Lord, impart,
   More of Thine image let Me bear,
   Erect Thy throne within my heart,
   And reign without a rival there.

3. Give me to read my pardon seal'd,
   And from Thy joy to draw my
   strength,
   To have Thy boundless love
   reveal'd,
   Its height, and depth, its breath
   and length.

4. Grant these requests, I ask no
more,
But to Thy care the rest resign;
Living or dying, rich or poor,
All shall be well if Thou art mine.
-Isaac Watts

349

I am Happy in Him

1. My soul is so happy in Jesus
For He is so precious to me:
His voice it is music to hear it,
His face it is heaven to see.

Chorus
I am happy in Him, I am happy in
Him,
My soul with delight He fills day
and night,
For I am happy in Him.

2. He sought me so long ere I knew
Him
When wand'ring afar from the fold;
Safe home in His arms He hath
bro't me.
To where there are pleasures
Untold.

3. His tow and His mercy surround
Me
His grace tike a river doth flow;
His Spirit, to guide and to comfort
Is with me wherever I go.

4. They say I shall some day be like
Him
My cross and my burdens lay
down;
Till then I will ever be faithful.
In gathering gems for His crown.
-E. O. Excell

350

I Strive To Walk The Narrow Way
8.8.8.6. with Ref.

1. I strive to walk the narrow way;
To live near Jesus every day;
To Him each trying, hour I pray
For saving keeping grace;

Chorus
O what wonderful grace,
O what wonderful grace.
For my every need, see.
There's grace enough for me.

2. His voice recalls my erring soul.
And yielding all to His control, '
I feel His glory, o'er me for The
glory of is grace.

3. I seek my Lord on bended knee;
His saving grace my only plea,
And then through tear-dimmed
yes
I see,
The glory of His face.

351

Just As I Am, Without One Plea

1. Just as I am, without one plea
But that Thy blood was shed for
me,
And that Thou bidd'st me come
to Thee,
O Lamb of God, I come!

2. Just as I am, and waiting not
To rid my soul of one dark blot,
To Thee, whose blood can
cleanse each spot.
O Lamb of God, I come?

3. Just as I am, though tossed about
   With many a conflict, many a doubt,
   Fighting and fears within, without,
   O Lamb of God, I come!

4. Just as I am, poor, wretched, blind;
   Sight, riches, healing of the mind,
   Yea, all I need, in Thee fo find,
   O Lamb of God. I come!

5. Just as I am. Thou wilt receive,
   Wilt welcome, pardon, cleanse, relieve;
   Because Thy promise I believe,
   O lamb of God, I come!

6. Just as I am - Thy love unknown
   Has broken every barrier down
   Now to be Thine, yea Thine alone
   O Lamb of God. I come!.

352

No, Not Despairingly-
6.4.6.4.6.6.4.

1. No, not despairingly
   Come I to Thee;
   No, not distrustingly
   Bend I the knee:
   Sin hath gone over me,
   Yet is this still my plea:
   Yet is this still my plea:
   Jesus hath died.

2. Ah! Mine iniquity
   Crimson has been
   Infinite, infinite,
   Sin upon sin;
   Sin of not loving Thee,
   Sin of not trusting Thee,
   Sin of not trusting Thee,
   Infinite sin.

3. Lord, I confess to Thee
   Sadly my sin;
   All I am tell I Thee,

All I have been:
Purge Thou my sin away,
Wash Thou my soul this day:
Wash Thou my soul this day;
Lord, make me clean.

4. Faithful and just art Thou,
   Forgiving all;
   Loving and kind art Thou
   When poor ones call;
   Lord, let the cleansing Blood,
   Blood of the Lamb of God,
   Blood of the Lamb of God,
   Pass o'er my soul.

5. Then all is peace and light
   This soul within;
   Thus shall walk with Thee,
   The loved Unseen;
   Leaning on Thee, my God,
   Guided along the road,
   Guided along the road,
   Nothing between.

353

O Thou, From Whom All Goodness
Flows-C.M.

1. O Thou, from whom all goodness flows,
   I lift my heart to Thee;
   In all my sorrows, conflicts, woes,
   Good Lord, remember me.

2. When on my aching burdened heart
   My sins lie heavily.
   Thy pardon grant. Thy peace Impart
   Good Lord, remember me.

3. When trials sore obstruct my way,
   And ills I cannot flee,
   Then let my strength be as my day:
   Good Lord, remember me.

4. If worn with pain, disease, and grief,
This feeble spirit be,
Grant patience, rest, and kind relief:
Good Lord. remember me.

5. And O, when in the hour of death
I bow to thy decree,
Jesus, receive my parting breath
Good Lord, remember me.

354

Running Over

1. Since the Saviour to this
heart to mine,
My cup's fill'd and running over,
filling my poor soul with His joy
divine,
My cup's fill' d and running over.

Chorus

Running over, Running over,
My cup's fill'd and running over,
Since the Lord saved me. I'm as
happy as can be,
My cup's fill'd and running over.

2. With the Lord so dear, I have
naught to fear,
My cup's fill'd and running over,
Thou' my way be dear He is ever
near,
My cup's fill'd and running over.

3. Even tho' I walk thro' death's
darksome vale,
My cup's fill'd and running over,
Christ my Lord shall be my comfort
still,
My cup's fill'd and running over.

4. Sinner, seek the lord, trust His
precious word,
While the angels round you hover,
Heaven's bells will ring, and you
then will sing,
My cup's fill'd and running over.

DECISION AND DEVOTION

355

Ibstone - 6.6.6.6.

1. Thy way, not mine. O Lord,
   However dark it be!
   Lead me by Thine own hand,
   Choose out the path for me.

2. Smooth let it be or rough,
   It will be still the best;
   Winding or straight, it leads,
   Right onward to Thy rest.

3. I dare not choose my lot;
   I would not if I might;
   Choose Thou for me, my God,
   So shall I walk aright

4. Take Thou me cup, and it
   With joy or sorrow fill
   As best to Thee may seem;
   Choose Thou my good or ill:

5. Choose Thou for me my friends,
   My sickness or my health;
   Choose Thou my cares for me,
   My poverty or wealth.

6. Not mine, not mine the choice,
   In things or great or small;
   Be Thou my guide and strength
   My wisdom and my all
   　　　　　　　-Horatius Bonar

356

I'm a Millionaire

1. I am now a child of God.
   I've been washed in Jesus' blood
   Making me an heir to wealth beyond
   compare;
   So while here I press along,
   daily, this shall be my song,
   I'm a happy millionaire.

Chorus
I'm a millionaire, I'm a millionaire
My Father is rich in houses and
lands and I'm His heir,
I'm a millionaire I'm a millionaire,
I'm a happy millionaire.

2. I had rather serve my Lord, feast
   upon His holy word,
   Than to own the world with all its
   jewels rare;
   By His Spirit I am led,
   and on milk and honey fed,
   I'm a happy millionaire.

3. Lord I'd rather worship Thee
   with the people who are free,
   Than the pleasures of this world a
   season share;
   For my Father is the King,
   and His praise I'll ever sing,
   I'm a happy millionaire.

4. Since salvation now is mine, for the
   Lord I'll shout and shine,
   Tho' I have to go 'thru life on :
   meager fare;
   Rich in grace beyond recall, for my
   Father owns it all,
   I'm a happy millionaire,
   　　　　　　　-Adger M. Pace

357

Maryton-L.M.

1. O Master, let me walk with Thee .
   In lowly paths of service free;
   Tell me Thy secret; help me bear
   The strain of toil, the fret of care.

2. Help me to slow the heart to move
   By some clear, winning word of
   love;
   Teach me the way-ward feet to stay,
   And guide them in the home-ward
   way.

3. Teach me Thy patience! still with Thee
In closer, dearer company,
In work that keeps faith sweet and strong,
In trust that triumphs over wrong;

4. In hope that sends a shining ray
Far down the future's broadening way,
In peace that only Thou canst give
with Thee, O Master. let me live.
-Washington Gladden

358

Heaven Came Down - Irregular

1. O what a wonderful, wonderful day
Day I will never forget;
After I'd wandered in darkness away,
Jesus my Saviour I met.
O what a tender compassionate friend
He met the need of my heart;
Shadows dispelling, With joy I am telling.
He made all the darkness depart!

Chorus
Heaven came down and glory filled; My soul,
When at the cross the Saviour made me whole;
My sins were washed away
And my night was turned to day
Heaven came down and glory filled my soul!

2. Born of the Spirit with life from above
Into God's family divine,
Justified fully thro' Calvary's love,
O what a standing is mine!
And the transaction so quickly was made

When as a sinner I came,
Took of the offer Of grace He did proffer
He saved me, O praise His dear name!

3. Now I've a hope that will surely endure
Alter the passing of time;
I have a future in heaven for sure,
There in those mansions sub-lime.
And it's because of that wonderful day
When at the cross I believed;
Riches eternal And blessings Supernal
From His precious hand I received.
-John W. Peterson

359

Isn't the Love of Jesus Something Wonderful

1. There will never be a sweeter story
Story of the Saviour's love divine
Love that bro't Him from the realms of glory,
Just to save a sinful soul like mine.

Chorus
Isn't the love of Jesus something wonderful, wonderful, wonderful;
O isn't the love of Jesus something 'wonderful! Wonderful it is to me.

2. Boundless as the universe around me.
Reaching to the farthest soul away
Saving, keeping love it was that found me,
That is why my heart can .truly say:

3. Love beyond all human comprehending.
Love of God in Christ, how can it be!
This will be my theme and never ending,
Grace redeeming love of Calvary.
-J. W. Peterson

DECISION AND DEVOTION

360

The Blood Will Never Loss its Power

1. The blood that Jesus shed for me
   way back on calvary;
   The blood that gives me strength
   from day to day.
   It will never lose its power

Chorus
It reaches to the highest mountain
It flows to the lowest valley
the blood that gives me strength
from day to day
It will never lose its power.

2. It soothes my doubts and calm my fears,
   and it dries all my tears;
   the blood that gives me strength
   from day to day,
   It will never lose its power.
   - Andre crouch

361

Herongate- 8.8.8.8. (L.M.)

1. Lord Jesus, let these eyes of mine ,
   reflect your beauty and your grace;
   so joyful and so tender shine
   that other eyes shall seek your face.

2. Lord, use my ears, for I rejoice
   to hear the word of life with awe
   I listen for the whispering voice that
   calls beyond the thunder's roar.

3. And holy Jesus, set my mind
   to search for truth and find your Way
   to think upon the good I find,
   to spurn the night and love the day,

4. And may my hands, which I learned their skill
   at your direction, by your love,
   now deftly moving at your will
   console, encourage and improve.

5. So to your throne, O Christ, again
   my sense of sight and sound I bring;
   and in my mind I let you reign,
   and with my hands serve you, my king.

6. Speak through this voice that you have given,
   your love and mercy to proclaim,
   until we worship you in heaven
   and sing the glory of your name!
   -Michael Perry

362

The Great Redeemer

1. How I love the great Redeemer
   Who is doing so much for me;
   With what joy I tell story
   Of the love that makes men free.
   Till my earthly life is ended.
   I will send songs above,
   Then beside the crystal sea
   More and more my soul shall be
   Praising Jesus and His love.

Chorus

He is ev'rything to me. to me,
He is He is ev'rything to me,
And ev'rything shall always be;
I will never cease to raise
A song of gladness in His praise;
Here. and In the world above,
My soul shall sing of saving love;
Life and light and joy is He,
The precious Friend who died for me.

2. He has purchased my redemption,
   Rolled my burden of sin away,
   And is walking on beside me,
   Growing dearer day by day.
   That is why I sing His praises,
    That is why joy is mine.
   That Is why forever more
   On the everlasting shore
   I shall sing of love divine.

3. Glory be to Him forever!
   Endless praises to Christ the Lamb!
   He has filled my life with sunshine.
   He has made me what I am.
   O that ev'ry one would know Him,
   O that all would adore!
   O that all would trust the love
   Of the mighty Friend above
   And be His forever more.
                    -Francis Foster

363

Sitting At the Feet of Jesus

1. Sitting at the feet of Jesus.
   O what words I hear Him say!
   Happy place! so near, so precious!
   May it find me there each day!
   Sitting at the feet of Jesus,
    I would look upon the past;
   For His love has been so gracious,
   It has won my heart at last.

2. Sitting at the feet of Jesus.
   Where can mortal be more blest?
   There I lay my sins and sorrows,
   And when weary, find sweet rest;
   Sitting at the feet of Jesus,
    There I love to weep and pray.
   While I from His fullness gather
   Grace and comfort ev'ry day.

3. Bless me, O my Saviour, bless me,
   As I sit low at Thy feet;
   O look down in love upon me,
   Let me see Thy face so sweet;
   Give me. Lord, the mind of Jesus,

Make me holy as He is;
May I prove I've been with Jesus,
Who is all my righteousness.
                         -Anon

364

He is So Precious To Me

1. So precious is Jesus, my Saviour,
   my king,
   His praise all the day long with
   rapture I sing;
   To Him in my weakness for strength
   I can cling,
   For He is so precious to me.

Chorus
For He is so precious to me.
For He is so precious to me,
'Tis heaven below my Redeemer to
know,
For He is so precious to me-

2. He stood at my heart's door mid
   sunshine and rain,
   And patiently waited an entrance to
   gain;
   What shame that so long
   He entreated in vain,
   For he is so precious to Me

3. I stand on the mountain of blessing
   at last.
   No cloud in the heavens a shadow
   To cast;
   His smile is upon me, the valley is
   past.
   For He is so precious to Me

4. I praise Him because He appointed
   a place
   Where some day, thru faith in His
   wonderful grace,
   I know I shall see Him shall took on
   His face,
   For He is so precious to Me
                    -Charles H.Gabriel

DECISION AND DEVOTION

365
Where He Leads I'll Follow

1. Sweet are the promises, Kind is the word,
   Dearer far than any message man ever heard;
   Pure was the mind of Christ, Sinless I see;
   He the great example is, and Pattern for me.

   Chorus
   Where He leads I'll follow,
   Follow all the way
   Where He leads I'll follow,
   Follow Jesus ev'ry day.

2. Sweet is the tender love Jesus hath shown,
   Sweeter far than any love that mortals have known;
   Kind to the erring one. Faithful is He;
   He the great example is, and pattern for me.

3. List to His loving words, "Come unto Me;"
   Weary, heavy laden, there is sweet rest for thee;
   Trust in His promises, Faithful and sure;
   Lean upon the Saviour, and thy soul is secure.
   -W.A Ogden

366

The Mercies of God

1. The mercies of God! what a theme For my song.
   Oh! I never could number them o'er,
   They're more than the stars in the heavenly dome,
   Or the sands of the wave beaten shore.

   Chorus
   For mercies so great, what return Can I make?
   For mercies so constant and sure?
   I'll love Him, I'll serve Him with all that I have
   As long as my life shall endure.

2. They greet me at morn when I waken from sleep,
   And they gladden my heart at the noon,
   They follow me on into shades of the night When the day with its labour is done.

3. His angels of mercy encompass me 'round.
   Wheresoever my pathway lead;
   Each turn of the road some new token reveals
   Oh! for me life is blessed Indeed.

4. His goodness and mercy will follow me still,
   Even on to the end of the way,
   I have His sure promise and that cannot fail,
   That His mercy endureth for aye.
   -T. O. Chisholm

367

My Saviour

1. I am not skill'd to understand
   What God hath will'd, what God hath plann'd;
   I only know at His right hand
   Stands One who is my Saviour!

2. I take Him at His word indeed:
   "Christ died for sinners," this I read;
   For in my heart I find a need
   Of Him to be my Saviour!

3. That He should leave His place on high,
   And come for sinful man to die,
   You count it strange? so Once did,
   Before I knew my saviour

4. And oh, that He fulfilled may see
   The travail of His soul in me,
   And with His work contented be,
   As I with my dear Saviour

5. Yea, living, dying, let me bring
   My strength, my solace from this spring,
   That He who lives to be my King
   Once died to be my Saviour
   -Dora Greenwell

368

I will

1. Once more, my soul, thy Saviour, thro' the Word.
   Is offered full and free;
   And now, O Lord, I must, I must decide:
   Shall I accept of Thee?

Chorus
I will! I will! I will!
God helping me, I will. O Lord, be Thine!
Thy precious blood was shed to purchase me
I will be wholly Thine!

2. By grace I will Thy mercy now receive,
   Thy love my heart hath won:
   On Thee, O Christ, I will, I will believe,
   And trust in Thee alone!

3. Thou knowest, Lord, how very weak I am,
   And how I fear to stray;

For strength to serve I look to Thee alone
The strength Thou must supply!

4. And now, O Lord, give all with us today
   The grace to join our song;
   And from the heart to gladly with us say:
   "I will to Christ belong!"

5 To all who came when Thou wast here below
   And said, "O Lord, will Thou?
   To them, "I will!" was ever Thy reply:
   We rest upon it now.
   -El Nathan

369

Toiling for Jesus

1. Gladly, gladly toiling for the Master,
   Go we forth with willing hands to do,
   Whatsoe'er to us He hath appointed,
   Faithfully our mission we'll pursue

Chorus
Toiling for Jesus, Joyfully we go.
Joyful we go;
Toiling for Jesus, In His vineyard here below.

2. Sweetly, sweetly we will tell the Story
   Of His love to mortals here below;
   Christ, the brightness of the Father's glory,
   Freely here His blessing will bestow.

3. Meekly, meekly toiling for the Master,
   Walking, faithfully the path He trod;

DECISION AND DEVOTION

Leading wand'rers to the dear
Redeemer,
Pointing sinners to the Lamb of
God.

-W. A. Ogden

370

Surrender - 8.7.8.7. with Refrain

1. All to Jesus I surrender,
   All to Him I freely give;
   I will ever love and trust Him,
   In His presence daily live.

   Chorus
   I surrender all, I surrender
   All to Thee, my blessed Saviour,
   I surrender all.

2. All to Jesus I surrender,
   Humbly at his feet I bow
   Wordly pleasures all forsaken,
   Take me, Jesus, take me now.

3. All to Jesus I surrender, Lord,
   I give myself to Thee;
   Fill me with Thy love and power,
   Let Thy blessing fall on me;

4. All to Jesus I surrender,
   Now I feel the sacred flame;
   O the joy of full salvation!
   Glory, glory to His Name.
   -Judson W. Van De Venter

371

The way of the cross leads home

1. I must needs go home by the way of
   the cross,
   There's no other way but this;
   I shall ne'er get sight of the Gates
   of Light.
   If the way of the cross I miss.

   Chorus
   The way of the cross leads home;

The way of the cross leads home,
It is sweet to know, as I onward go,
The way of the cross leads home.

2. I must needs go on in the blood
   sprinkled way.
   The path that the Saviour trod,
   If I ever climb to the heights sublime,
   Where the soul te at home with God.

3. Then I bid farewell to the way of the
   world;
   To walk in it never more;
   For my Lord says "Come," and I
   seek my home,
   Where He waits at the open door.
   -J.B. Pounds

372

I Need Thee every Hour - 6.4.6.4. With Refrain

1. I need Thee ev'ry hour,
   Most gracious Lord;
   No tender voice like Thine
   Can peace afford.

2. I need Thee every hour,
   Stay Thou nearby;
   Temptations lose their power
   When Thou art nigh.

3. I need Thee every hour,
   In Joy or pain;
   Come quickly and abide,
   Or life is vain.

4. I need Thee every hour,
   Teach me Thy will;
   And Thy rich promises
   In me fulfill.

5. I need Thee every hour,
   Most Holy one;
   Oh, make me Thine indeed,
   Thou blessed Son!
   -Annie Hawkes

DECISION AND DEVOTION

373

Newington- 7.7.7.7.

1. Thine forever! Lord of love,
Hear us from Thy throne above;
Thine forever may we be.
Here and in eternity.

2. Thine for ever! Lord of life,
Shield us through our earthly strife;
Thou the Life, the Truth, the Way.
Guide us to the realms of day.

3. Thine for ever! O how blest
They who find in Thee their rest!
Saviour, Guardian, Heavenly Friend,
O defend us to the end!

4. Thine for ever! Shepherd, keep
These Thy frail and trembling sheep;
Safe alone beneath Thy care,
Let us all Thy goodness share.

5. Thine for ever! Thou our guide,
All our wants by Thee supplied,
All our sins by Thee forgiven,
Lead us. Lord, from earth to heaven.

-Mary Fowler Maude

374

Serving Him truly

1. It pays to serve Jesus, I speak from my heart;
He'll always be with us if we do our part;
There's naught in this wide world can pleasure afford,
There's peace and contentment 'in serving the Lord.'

2. And oft when I'm tempted to turn from the track.'
I think of my Saviour, my mind wanders back
To the place where they nail'd Him on.
Calvary's tree I hear a voice saying:
Suffer'd for thee.

3. A place I remember where I was set free,
'Twas where I found pardon, a heaven to me;
There Jesus spoke sweetly to my weary soul,
My sins were forgiven, He made my heart whole.

4. How rich is the blessing the world cannot give,
I'm satisfied fully for Jesus to live,
Tho' friends may forsake me and trials arise,
I'm trusting in Jesus, His love never dies.

5. There's no one like Jesus can cheer me today,
His love and His kindness can ne'er fade away;
In winter, in summer, in sunshine and rain,
His love and affection are always the same.

6. Will you have this blessing that Jesus bestows?
A free, full salvation for sin's bitter throes,
O come to the Saviour, to Calvary's tree!
The fountain is open'd, is flowing for thee.

-Eli G. Christy

DECISION AND DEVOTION

375

Oaksville- C.M.

1. Jesus, Thine all victorious love
   Shed in my heart abroad;
   Then shall my feet no longer rove,
   Rooted and fixed in God.

2. O that in me the sacred fire
   Might now begin to glow!
   Burn up the dross of base desire,
   And make the mountains flow,

3. Thou who at Pentecost didst fall,
   And at all sin consume!
   Come, Holy Ghost, for Thee I call
   Spirit of burning, come!

4. Refining fire, go through my heart,
   Illuminate my soul;
   Scatter Thy life thro' ev'ry part
   And sanctify the whole.

5. My steadfast soul, from falling free,
   Shall then no longer move;
   While Christ is all the world to me,
   And all my heart is love.
   -Charles Wesley

376

Jesus, I will Trust Thee -6.5.

1. Jesus, I will trust Thee,
   Trust Thee with my soul:
   Guilty, lost, and helpless,
   Thou canst make whole.
   There is none in heaven
   Or on earth like Thee:
   Thou hast died for sinners
   Therefore, Lord, for me;

Chorus
In Thy love confiding,
I will seek Thy face,
Worship and adore Thee,

For Thy wondrous grace.
Jesus, I will trust Thee,
Trust Thee with my soul!
Guilty, lost, and helpless,
Thou canst make me whole.

2. Jesus, I can trust Thee,
   Trust Thy written Word;
   Since Thy voice of mercy
   I have often heard.
   When Thy Spirit reacheth,
   To my taste how sweet!
   Only may I hearken,
   Sitting at Thy feet.

3. Jesus do trust Thee,
   Trust thee Without doubt;
   "Whosoever cometh,"
   Thou"wilt not cast our:
   Faithful is Thy promise,
   Precious is Thy blood
   These my souls salvation.
   Thou my Saviour God!
   -Mary Walker

377

The Saviour with me - 8.7.

1. I would have the Saviour with me,
   For I dare not walk alone;
   I would feel His presence near me,
   And His arm around me thrown.

Chorus
Then my soul shalt fear no ill,
While He leads me where He will;
I will go without a murmur,
And His footsteps follow still.

2. I would have the Saviour with me,
   For my faith, at best, is weak;
   He can whisper words of comfort
   That no other voice can speak.

3. I would have the Saviour with me,
   In the onward march of life,

Thro, the tempest and the sun shine,
Thro' the battle and the strife.

4. I would have the Saviour with me,
That His eye the way may guide,
Till I reach the vale of Jordan,
Till I cross the rolling tide.

-L Edwards

378

Hendson-7.7.7.7. with Refrain

1. Take my life and let it be
Consecrated, Lord, to Thee;
Take my moments and my days,
Let them flow In ceaseless praise.

2. Take my hands and let them move
At the impulse of Thy love;
Take my feet and let them be
Swift and beautiful for Thee.

3. Take my voice and let me sing
Always, only, for my King;
Take my lips and let them be
Filled with messages from Thee.

4. Take my silver and my gold
Not a mite would I with-hold;
Take my intellect and use
Ev'ry pow'r as Thou shalt choose.

5. Take my will and make it Thine
It shall be no longer mine;
Take my heart it is Thine own,
It shall be Thy royal throne.

6. Take my love my Lord, I pour
At Thy feet its treasure store;
Take myself and I will be
Ever, only, all for Thee.

-Frances Ridley Havergal

379

Whosoever Meaneth Me

1. I am happy today and the sun shines bright,
The clouds have been rolled away;
For the Saviour said, Whosoever will
May come with Him to stay.

Chorus
"Whosoever," surely meaneth me,
Surely meaneth me, O surely
Meaneth me;
"Whosoever," surely meaneth me
"Whosoever," meaneth me.

2. All my hopes have been raised, O His name be praised,
His glory has filled my soul:
I've been lifted up, and from sin set free,
His blood has made me whole.

3. O what wonderful love,
O what grace divine,
That Jesus should die for me;
I was lost in sin, for the world I pined,
But now I am set free.

-J. Edwin McConnell

380

Belgrave-C.M.

1. My God, accept my heart this day
and make it yours alone;
no longer let my footsteps stray
from your beloved Son.

2. Before the cross of him who died
in awe and shame I fall:
let every sin be crucified
and Christ be all in all.

3. Anoint me with your heavenly grace
and seal me as your own,
that I may see your glorious face
and worship at your throne.

4. Let every thought and work and word
to you be ever given;
then life shall be your service, Lord,
and death the gate of heaven.

5. All glory to the Father be,
the Spirit and the Son;
all love and praise eternally
to God the Three-in- One.
                              -M. Bridges

381

Lundie

1. Fade, fade, each earthly joy; Jesus is mine
Break every tender tie; Jesus is mine.
Dark is the wilderness, Earth has no resting place,
Jesus alone can bless; Jesus is mine.

2. Tempt not my soul away; Jesus is mine.
Here would I ever stay; Jesus is mine.
Perishing things of clay, Born but for one brief day,
Pass from my heart away, Jesus is mine.

3. Farewell, ye dreams of night; Jesus is mine.
Lost in this dawning bright, Jesus is mine.
All that my soul has tried Left but a dismal void;
Jesus has satisfied; Jesus is mine.

Farewell, mortality, Jesus is mine.
Welcome, eternity; Jesus is mine.
Welcome, O loved and blest,
Welcome, sweet scenes of rest,
Welcome, my Saviour's breast;
Jesus is mine.
                              -Jane C. Bonar

382

Peek

1. I would be true, for there are those that trust me;
I would be pure, for there are those who care;
I would be strong, for there is much to suffer;
I would be brave, for there is much To dare,
I would be brave for there is much to dare

2. I would be friend of all the foe, the friendless.
I would be giving, and forget the gift;
I would be humble, for I know my weakness;
I would look up, and laugh, and love; and lift,
I would look up, and laugh, and love, and lift.

3. I would be prayerful thro' each busy moment;
I would be constantly in touch with God;
I would be tuned to hear the Slightest whisper;
I would have faith to keep the path Christ trod,
I would have faith to keep the path Christ trod.
                              -Howard Arnold Walter

DECISION AND DEVOTION

383

Dare to Be a Daniel

1. Standing by a purpose true,
   Heeding God's command,
   Honour them, the faithful few!
   All hail to Daniel's Band!

   Chorus
   Dare to be a Daniel,
   Dare to stand alone,
   Dare to have a purpose firm!
   Dare to make it known!

2. Many mighty men are lost,
   Daring not to stand,
   Who for God had been a host,
   By joining Daniel's Band!

3. Many giants, great and tall,
   Stalking through the land,
   Head long to the earth would fall,
   If met by Daniel's Band!

4. Hold the Gospel banner high?
   On the victory grand!
   Satan and his host defy,
   And shout for Daniel's Band!

   -P. P. Bliss

384

Rathbun- 8.7.8.7.

1. In the cross of Christ I glory,
   Tow'ring o'er the wrecks of time;
   All the light of sacred story
   Gathers round its head sublime.

2. When the woes of life o'ertake me,
   Hopes deceive, and fears annoy,
   Never shall the cross forsake me:
   Lo! it glows with peace and joy.

3. When the sun of bliss in beaming
   Light and love upon my way,

From the cross the radiance streaming
Adds more luster to the day.

4. Bane and blessing, pain and pleasure,
   By the cross are sanctified;
   Peace is there that knows no measure,
   Joys that thro' all time abide.

   -John Bowring

385

Hamburg

1. When I survey the wondrous cross,
   On which the Prince of glory died,
   My richest gain I count but loss,
   And pour contempt on all my pride

2. Forbid it, Lord! that I should boast.
   Save in the death of Christ my God
   All the vain things that charm me most,
   I sacrifice them to His blood.

3. See, from His hands, His feet,
   Sorrow and love flow mingled down
   Did e'er such love and sorrow meet
   Or thorns compose so rich a crown?

4. Were the whole realm of nature mine,
   That were a present far too small;
   Love so amazing, so divine.
   Demands my soul, my life. my all.

   - Isaac Watts

386

Martyn

1. Jesus, Lover of my soul,
   Let me to Thy bosom fly.
   While the nearer waters roll,
   While the tempest still is high!
   Hide me, O my Saviour, hide,

DECISION AND DEVOTION

Till the storm of life is past;
Safe into the haven guide,
O receive my soul at last!

2. Other refuge have I none;
Hangs my helpless soul on Thee;
Leave, ah, leave me not alone,
Still support and comfort me!
All my trust on Thee is stayed,
All my help from Thee I bring;
Cover my defenseless head
With shadow of Thy wing.

3. Thou, O Christ art all I want
More than all in Thee I find;
Raise the fallen, cheers the faint,
Heal the sick and lead the blind.
Just and holy is Thy name,
I am all unrighteousness;
False and full of sin I am,
Thou art full of truth and grace.

4. Plenteous grace with Thee is found
Grace to cover all my sin;
Let the healing streams abound,
Make and keep me pure within
Thou of life the Fountain art,
Freely let me take of Thee;
Spring Thou up within my heart,
Rise to all eternity.
                              -Charles Wesley

387

Something For Jesus

1. Saviour, Thy dying love
Thou gavest me,
Nor should I aught with-hold,
Dear Lord from Thee;
In love my soul would bow,
My heart fulfill its vow,
Some off'ring bring Thee now,
Something for Thee

2. At the blest mercy seat,
Pleading for me,
My feeble faith looks up,

Jesus, to Thee:
Help me the cross to bear,
Thy wondrous love declare,
Some song to raise, or prayer.
Something for Thee

3. Give me a faithful heart,
Likeness to Thee,
That each departing day
Hence forth may see
Some work of love begun,
Some deed of kindness done,
Some wand'rer sought and won,
Something for Thee.

4. All that I am and have,
Thy gift to free.
In joy, in grief, thro' life,
Dear Lord, for Thee!
And when Thy face I see,
My ransomed soul shall be,
Thro' all eternity,
Something for Thee.
                              -S. D. Phelps

388

Falls Creek - 8.6.8.7. with Refrain

1. "Take up thy cross and follow Me,"
I heard my Master say;
"I gave My life to ransom thee,
Surrender your all today."

Chorus
Wherever He leads I'll go,
Wherever He toads I'll go,
I'll follow my Christ who loves me so,
Wherever He leads I'll go.

2. He drew me closer to His side,
I sought His will to know,
And in that will I now abide,
Wherever He leads I'll go.

3. It may be through the shadows dim,
Or o'er the stormy sea,

DECISION AND DEVOTION

I take my cross and follow Him,
Wherever He leadeth me.

4. My heart, my life, my all I bring
To Christ who loves me so;
He is my Master, Lord, and King,
Wherever He leads I'll go.
-B. B. McKinney

389

Constancy - 8.7.8.7. with Refrain

1. All for Jesus, all for Jesus!
All my being's ransomed pow'rs:
All my tho'ts and words and doings,
All my days and all my hours.
All for Jesus! all for Jesus!
All my days and all my hours;
All for Jesus! all for Jesus!
All my days and all my hours.

2. Let my hands perform His bidding,
Let my feet run in His ways;
Let my eyes see Jesus only,
Let my lips speak forth His praise.
All for Jesus! all for Jesus!
Let my lips speak forth His praise;
All for Jesus! all for Jesus!
Let my lips speak forth His praise.

3. Since my eyes were fixed on Jesus,
I've lost sight of all beside;
So enchained my spirit's vision.
Looking at the Crucified.
All for Jesus! all for Jesus!
Looking at the Crucified;
All for Jesus! all for Jesus!
Looking at the Crucified.

4. Oh, what wonder! How amazing!
Jesus glorious King of kings,
Deigns to call me His beloved,
Lets me rest beneath His wings.
All for Jesus! all for Jesus!

Resting now beneath His wings;
All for Jesus! all for Jesus!
Resting now beneath His wings.
-Mary D. James

390

Ellesdie- 8.7.8.7.D.

1. Jesus, I my cross have taken,
All to. leave and follow Thee;
Destitute, despised, forsaken,
Thou from hence my all shalt be:
Perish every fond ambition,
All I've sought, and hoped and known;
Yet how rich is my condition,
God and heav'n are still my own!

2. Let the world despise and leave me,:
They have left my Saviour too;
Human hearts and looks deceive me;
Thou art not, like man,untrue;
And, while Thou shalt smile upon me,
God of wisdom, love, and might,
Foes may hate and friends may Shun me;
Show Thy face, and all is bright.

3. Man may trouble and distress me.
'Twill but drive me to Thy breast;
Life with trials hard may press me,
Heav'n will bring me sweeter rest
O tis not in grief to harm me, While
Thy love is left to me;
O 'twere not in joy to charm me,
Were that joy unmixed with Thee.

4. Hasten on from grace to glory,
Armed by faith and winged by prayer;
Heav'n's eternal days before me,
God's own hand shall guide me there.
Soon shall dose my earthly Mission,

DECISION AND DEVOTION

Swift shall pass my pilgrim days,
Hope shall change to glad fruition,
Faith to sight, and prayer to praise.

Henry F. Lyte

391

Ives- 8.7.8.7.8.8.8.7

1. I have one deep, supreme desire,
That I may be like Jesus.
To this I fervently aspire,
That I may be like Jesus.
I want my heart His throne to 'be,
So that a watching world may see
His likeness shining forth in me.
I want to be like Jesus.

2. He spent His life In doing good;
I want to be like Jesus.
In lowly paths of service trod;
I want to be like Jesus.
He sympathized with hearts
distressed;
He spoke the words that cheered
and blessed;
He welcomed sinners to His breast.
I want to be like Jesus.

3. A holy, harmless life He led;
I want to be like Jesus.
The Father's will, His drink and
bread;
I want to be like Jesus
And when at last He comes to die,
"Forgive them, Father,"hear Him
For those who taunt and crucify.
I want to be like Jesus.

4. Oh, perfect life of Christ, my Lord!
I want to be like Jesus.
My recompense and my reward,
That I may be like Jesus.
His spirit fill my hung'ring soul,
His power all my life control;
My deepest pray'r, my highest goal,
That I may be like Jesus.

-Thomas O. Chisholm

392

I'd rather have Jesus - Irregular

1. I'd rather have Jesus than silver or
gold;
I'd rather be His than have riches
untold;
I'd rather have Jesus than houses
or lands.
I'd rather be led by His nail-pierced
hand

Chorus
Than to be the king of a vast domain
Or be held in sin's dread sway.
I'd rather have Jesus than anything
This world affords today.

2. I'd rather have Jesus than men's
applause;
I'd rather be faithful to His dear
cause;
I'd rather have Jesus than world-
wide fame.
I'd rather be true to His holy name

3. He's fairer than lilies of rarest
Bloom;
He's sweeter than honey from out
the comb;
He's all that my hungering spirit
needs.
I'd rather have Jesus and let Him
lead

-Rhea F. Miler

393

Near the cross - 7.6.7.6.
with Refrain

1. Jesus, keep me near the cross
There a precious fountain,
Free to all, a healing stream,
Flows from Calv'ry mountain.

Chorus
In the cross, in the cross
Be my glory ever.
Till my raptured soul shall find
Rest, beyond the river.

2. Near the cross, a trembling soul,
Love and mercy found me;
There the Bright and Morning Star
Sheds its beams around me.

3. Near the cross! O Lamb of God,
Bring its scenes before me;
Help my walk from day to day
With its shadows o'er me.

4. Near the cross I'll watch and wait,
Hoping trusting ever,
Till I reach the golden strand
Just beyond the river.
                    -Fanny J. Crosby

394

Living

1. Living for Jesus a life that is true,
Striving to please Him in all that I do;
Yielding allegiance, glad hearted
and free,
This is the pathway of blessing for
me.

Chorus
O Jesus, Lord and Saviour,
I give myself to Thee;
For Thou, in Thy atonement.
Didst give Thy self for me.
I own no other Master,
My heart shall be Thy throne.
My life I give. henceforth to live,
O Christ for Thee alone.

2. Living for Jesus who died in my
place,
Bearing on Calv'ry my sin and

disgrace;
Such love constrains me to answer
His call,
Follow His leading and give Him my
all.

3. Living for Jesus wherever I am,
Doing each duty in His holy name;
Willing to suffer affliction and loss
Deeming each trial a part of my
cross.   '

4. Living for Jesus through earth little
while,
My dearest treasure, the light of His
smile;
Seeking the lost ones He died to
redeem,
Bringing the weary to find rest in
Him.
                    -Thomas O.Chisholm

395

Angel's Story - 7.6.7.6.D.

1. O Jesus, I have promised
To serve Thee to the end;
Be Thou forever near me,
My Master and. My Friend:
I shall not fear the battle
If Thou art by my side,
Nor wander from the pathway
If Thou wilt be my guide.

2. O let me feel Thee near me.
The world is ever near;
I see the sights that dazzle,
The tempting sounds I hear:
My foes are ever near me,
Around me and within;
But, Jesus, draw Thou nearer,
And shield my soul from sin.

3. O Jesus, Thou hast promised
To all who follow Thee,
That where Thou art in glory,
There shall Thy servant be;

DECISION AND DEVOTION

And. Jesus, I have promised
To serve Thee to the end;
O give me give me grace to follow,
My Master and my Friend.

-John E. Bode

396

Dunbar - 8.8.8.6. with Refrain

1. My life, my love I give to Thee,
Thou Lamb of God who died for
Me;
O may I ever faithful be,
My Saviour and my God!

Chorus
I'll live for Him who died for me,
How happy then my life shall be!
I'll live for Him who died for me,
My Saviour and my God!

2. I now believe Thou dost receive.
For Thou hast died that I might live;
And now hence-forth I'll trust in
Thee,
My Saviour and my God!

3. O Thou who died on Calvary,
To save my Soul and make me free,
I'll consecrate my life to Thee,
My Saviour and my God!

-Ralph E. Hudson

397

St. Margaret 8.8.8.8.6.

1. O Love that will not let me go",
I rest my weary soul in Thee
I give Thee back the life I owe,
That in Thine ocean depths its flow
May richer fuller be.

2. O Light that followest all my way,
I yield my flick'ring torch to Thee;
My heart restores its borrowed ray,
That in Thy sunshine's blaze its day
May brighter, fairer be.

3. O Joy that seekest me thru pain,
I cannot close my heart to Thee;
I trace the rainbow thru the rain,
And feel the promise is not vain
That morn shall tearless be.

4. O Cross that liftest up my head,
I dare not ask to fly from Thee;
I lay in dust life's glory dead,
And from the ground there blossoms
red
Life that shalt endless be.

George Matheson

398

Give me Jesus 8.7.8.7. With Refrain

1. Take the world, but give me Jesus,
All its joys are but a name;
But His love abideth ever.
Thru eternal years the same.

Chorus
O the height and depth of mercy!
O the length and breadth of love!
O the fullness of redemption,
Pledge of endless life above!

2. Take the world, but give me Jesus,
Sweetest comfort of my soul;
With my Saviour watching o'er me,
I can sing tho billows roll.

3. Take the world, but give me Jesus,
Let me view His constant smile;
Then thru out my pilgrim Journey
Light will cheer me all the while.

4. Take the world, but give me Jesus.
In His cross my trust shall be;
Till, with clearer, brighter vision.
Face to face my Lord I see.

-Fanny J. Crosby

DECISION AND DEVOTION

399

I Will praise Him - 8.7.8.7. with Refrain

1. When I saw the cleansing fountain,
   Open wide for all my sin,
   I obeyed the Spirit's wooing
   When He said,"Wilt thou be
   clean?"

Chorus
I will praise Him! I will praise Him!
Praise the Lamb for sinners slain;
Give Him glory,.all ye people,
For His blood can wash away each
stain.

2. Tho' the way seems straight and
   narrow,
   All I claimed was swept away;
   My ambitions, plans & and wishes
   At my feet in ashes lay.

3. Blessed be the name of Jesus!
   I'm so glad He took me in;
   He's forgiven my transgressions,
   He has cleansed my heart from sin.

4. Glory, glory to the Father!
   Glory, glory to the Son!
   Glory, glory to the spirit
   Glory to the Three in One! -
   -Margaret J. Harris

400

Draw Me Nearer

1. I am Thine, O Lord, I have heard
   Thy voice,
   And it told Thy love to me;
   But I long to rise in the arms of
   Faith,
   And be closer drawn to Thee.

Chorus
Draw me nearer, nearer, blessed
Lord
To the cross where thou hast died;
Draw me nearer, nearer, nearer
blessed Lord.
To thy precious, bleeding side.

2. Consecrate me now to thy
   service, Lord,
   By the power of grace divine;
   Let my soul look up with a
   steadfast hope,
   And my will be lost in thine.

3. O, the pure delight of a single hour
   That before Thy throne I spend,
   When I kneel in prayer, and with
   Thee, my God,
   I commune as friend with friend!

4. There are depths of love that I
   cannot not know
   Till I cross the narrow sea;
   There are heights of joy that I may
   not reach
   Till I rest in peace with Thee.
   -Fanny J. Crosby

401

Blessed Assurance

1. Blessed assurance, Jesus is mine!
   O what a foretaste of glory divine!
   Heir of salvation, purchase of God
   Born of His Spirit, washed in His
   blood.

Chorus
This is my story, this is song,
Praising my Saviour all the day
long;
This is my story, this is my song,
Praising my Saviour all the day long

2. Perfect submission, perfect delight
   Visions of rapture now burst on my
   Sight;

DECISION AND DEVOTION

Angels descending, bring from above
Echoes of mercy, whispers of love.

3 perfect submission, all is at rest,
I in my saviour am happy and blest;
Watching and waiting, looking above,
Filled with His goodness, lost in His love.

-Fanny J. Crosby

402

Wonderful Peace

1. Coming to Jesus, my saviour, I found
Wonderful peace, wonderful peace,
Storms in their fury may rage all around
I have peace, sweet peace.

Chorus
Peace, peace, wonderful peace;
Peace, peace, glorious peace;
Since my Redeemer has ransomed my soul.
I have peace, sweet peace.

2. Peace like a river, so deep and so broad,
Wonderful peace, wonderful peace,
Resting my soul on the bosom of God
I have peace, sweet peace.

3. Peace like a holy and infinite calm,
Wonderful peace, wonderful peace,
Like to the strains of an evening psalm.
I have peace, sweet peace.

4. Gone is the battle that once raged within,
Wonderful peace, wonderful peace,
Jesus has saved me and cleansed

Me from sin,
I have peace, sweet peace.

-H. Lilenas

403

Deeper, Deeper

1. Deeper, deeper in the love of Jesus
Daily let me go;
Higher, higher in the school of wisdom
More of grace to know

Chorus
O deeper yet, I pray
And higher ev'ry day,
And wiser, blessed Lord
In Thy precious holy word.

2. Deeper, deeper, blessed Holy Spirit
Take me deeper still,
Till my life is wholly lost in Jesus
And His perfect will

3. Deeper, deeper, thro' it cost hard trials
Deeper let me go!
Rooted in the holy love of Jesus.
Let me fruitful grow.

4. Deeper, higher ev'ry day in Jesus
Till all conflict past,
Finds me conqu'or and in His image
Perfected at last

-C. P. Jones

404

Wonderful Peace

1. Far away in the depths of my spirit tonight
Rolls a melody sweeter than psalm;
In celestial like strains it unceasingly falls
O'er my soul like an infinite calm

DECISION AND DEVOTION

Chorus
Peace! Peace! Wonderful peace,
Coming down from the Father
above;
Sweep over my spirit forever, I
Pray,
In fathomless billows of love.

2. What a treasure I have in this
wonderful peace,
Buried deep in the heart of my soul;
So secure that no power can mine
it away,
White the years of eternity roll

3. I am resting tonight in this wonder
ful peace,
Resting sweetly in Jesus' control;
For I'm kept from all danger by
night and by day,
And His glory is flooding my soul.

4. And I think when I rise to that City of
peace,
Where the Author of peace I shall
see,
That one strain of the song which
the ransomed will sing,
In that heavenly kingdom shall be:

5. Ah! soul, are you here without
comfort or rest.
Marching down the rough pathway
of time?
Make Jesus your friend ere the
shadows grow dark;
Oh, accept this sweet peace so
sublime.
                    -W. D. Cornell,alt,

405

Bernard

1. Give of your best to the Master,
Give of the strength of your youth;

Throw your soul's fresh, glowing
ardor
Into the battle for truth.
Jesus has set the example;
Dauntless was He, young and
Brave;
Give Him your loyal devotion,
Give Him the best that you have

Chorus
Give of your best to the Master,
Give of the strength of your youth
Clad in salvation's full armor.
Join in the battle for truth.

2. Give of your best to the Master.
Give Him first place in your heart
Give Him first place in your service
Consecrate ev'ry part.
Give and to you shall be given
God His beloved Son gave;
Gratefully seeking to serve Him.
Give Him the best that you have.

3. Give of your best to the Master,
Nought else is worthy of His love;
He gave Himself for your ransom,
Gave up His glory above:
Laid down His life without murmur
You from sin's ruin to save;
Give Him your heart's adoration
Give Him the best that you have.
                    -Howard B. Grose

406

Higher Ground

1. I'm pressing on the upward way,
New heights I'm gaining ev'ry day;
Still praying as I'm onward, bound.
"Lord, plant my feet on higher
ground.

Chorus
Lord, lift me up and let me stand,
By faith, on Heaven's table land,
A higher plane than I have found;
Lord, plant my feet on higher
ground.

DECISION AND DEVOTION

2. My heart has no desire to stay
Where doubts arise and fears
dismay;
Tho' some may dwell where these
abound,
My prayer, my-aim is higher
ground."

3. I want to five above the world,
Tho' Satan's darts at me are hurled;
For faith has caught the joyful
sound,
The song of saints oh higher
ground."

4. I want to scale the utmost height
And catch a gleam of glory bright;
But still I'll pray till Heav'n I've
Found,
"Lord, lead me on to higher
ground."
-Johnson Oatman, Jr.

407

O To Be Like Thee

1. O to be like Thee! Blessed
Redeemer,
This is my constant longing and
prayer;
Gladly I'll forfeit all of earth's
treasures,
Jesus Thy perfect likeness to wear.

Chorus
O to be like Thee' O to be like
Thee,
Blessed Redeemer, pure as Thou
art!
Come in Thy sweetness, come in
Thy fullness;
Stamp Thine own image deep on
my heart.

2. O to be like Thee! Full of compassion,
Loving, forgiving, tender and kind;
Helping the helpless, cheering the
fainting,
Seeking the wand'ring sinner to find.

3. O to be like Thee! lowly in spirit,
Holy and harmless, patient and brave;
Meekly enduring cruel reproaches,
Willing to suffer others to save.

4. O to be like Thee! Lord ,I am coming
Now to receive th" anointing divine;
All that I am and have I am bringing,
Lord, from this moment all shall be
Thine.

5. O to be like Thee! While I am pleading,
Pour out Thy Spirit, fill with Thy love;
Make me a temple meet for Thy
dwelling,
Fit me for life and heaven above.
-Thomas O. Chisholm

408

More Love To Thee

1. More love to Thee, O Christ,
More love to Thee!
Hear Thou the pray'r I make
On bended knee;
This is my earnest plea;
More love. O Christ, to Thee,
More love to Thee,
More love to Thee!

2. Once earthly joy I craved,
Sought peace and rest;
Now Thee alone I seek,
Give what is best;
This all my pray'r shall be:
More love, O Christ, to Thee,
More love to Thee,
More love to Thee!'

3. Then shalt my latest breath
Whisper Thy praise:
This be the parting cry
My heart shalt raise;
This still its pray'r shall be:
More love, O Christ, to Thee,
More love to Thee,
More love to Thee!

-Elizabeth Prentiss

409

I Am Praying For You

1. I have a Saviour, He's pleading in glory.
A dear, loving Saviour, though earth friends be few;
And now He is watching in tender ness o'er me,
And, oh, that my Saviour were your Saviour, too.

Chorus
For you I am praying, For you I am praying,
For you I am praying, I'm praying for you.

2. I have a Father; to me He has given
A hope for eternity, blessed and true;
And soon will He call me to meet . Him in heaven,
But, oh, that He'd let me bring you With me, too!

3. I have a robe: tis resplendent in whiteness,
Awaiting in glory my wondering view,
Oh, when I receive it all shining in brightness,
Dear friend, could I see you receiving one, too!

4. When Jesus has found you, tell others the story,
That my loving Saviour is your Saviour, too;
Then pray that your Saviour may bring them to glory,
And prayer will be answered twas answered for you!

-S O malley Cluff

410

Jesus, I Come

1. Out of my bondage, sorrow and , night,
Jesus, I come, Jesus, I come;
Into Thy freedom, gladness and light,
Jesus I come to Thee.
Out of my sickness into Thy health,
Out of my want and into Thy Wealth,
Out of my sin and into Thyself,
Jesus, I come to Thee.

2. Out of my shameful failure and loss,
Jesus, I come, Jesus, I come;
Into the glorious gain of Thy cross,
Jesus, I come to Thee.
Out of earth's sorrows into Thy balm,
Out of life's storm and into Thy Calm,
Out of distress to jubilant psalm,
Jesus, I come to Thee.

3. Out of unrest and arrogant pride,
Jesus, I come, Jesus, I come;
Into Thy blessed will to abide,
Jesus, I come to Thee
Out of my self to dwell Thy love,
Out of despair into raptures above,
Upward for aye on wings like a dove
Jesus, I come to Thee.

4. Out of the fear and dread of the tomb
Jesus, I come, Jesus, I come;
into the joy and light of Thy home,
Jesus, I come to Thee.
Out of the depths of ruin untold,
into the peace of Thy sheltering fold
Ever Thy glorious face to behold,
Jesus, I come to Thee.
-William T. Sleeper

411

I 'll go - 9.7.9.7.9.8. with Refrain

1. it may not be on the mountain's Height
Or over the stormy sea,
it may not be at the battle's front
My Lord will have need of me;
But if by a still, small voice
He calls To paths I do not know,
I'll answer, dear Lord, with my hand in Thine,
I' ll go where You want me to go.

Chorus
' I'll go where You want me to go, dear Lord,
O'er mountain or plain or sea;
I' ll say what you want me to say, dear Lord,
I' ll be what You want me to be.

2. perhaps today there are loving Words.
Which Jesus would have, me Speak,
There may be now, in the paths of Sin.
Some wand' r er whom I should Seek;
O Saviour, if Thou wilt be my Guide.
Tho' dark and rugged the way.
My' voice shall echo the message sweet,
I'll say what You want me to say.

3. There's surety somewhere a lowly place
In earth's harvest fields so wide,
Where I may labour thru life's short day
For Jesus the Crucified;
So, trusting my all unto Thy care I know Thou lovest me
I'll do Thy will with a heart sincere,
I'll be what You want me to be.
-Mary Brown,

412

Follow, I Will Follow Thee

1. Jesus call me, I must follow,
Follow Him to day;
When His tender voice is pleading
How can I delay?

Chorus
Follow, I will follow Thee, my Lord,
Follow ev' ry passing day;
My tomorrow are all known to Thee,
Thou wilt lead me all the way.

2. Jesus calls me, I must follow,
Follow ev'ry hour,
Know the blessing of His presence,
Fullness of His pow'r.

3. Jesus calls me, I must follow,
Follow Him always;
When my Saviour goes before me
I can never stray.
-Howard L. Brown
& Margaret Brown

413

St. Agnes

1. Jesus, the very thought of Thee
With sweetness fills my breast;
But sweeter far Thy face to see,
And in Thy presence rest.

2. No voice can sing, no heart can
frame,
Nor can the memory find
A sweeter sound than Thy blest
name
O Saviour of mankind!

3. O Hope of ev'ry contrite heart.
O Joy of all the meek,
To those who ask, how kind Thou
art!
How good to those who seek!

4. But what to those who Find? Ah!
this
Nor tongue nor pen can show,
The of Jesus, what it is
None but His loved ones know.
-Attr. to Bernard
of Clairvaux

414

Morris-9.10.9.10.

1. Nearer, still nearer, close to Thy
heart,
Draw me, my Saviour, so precious
Thou art;
Fold me, O fold me close to Thy
breast,
Shelter me safe in that "Haven-of
Rest,"
Shelter me safe in that "Haven of
Rest."

2, Nearer, stilt nearer, nothing I bring,
Naught as an offering to Jesus my
King;
Only my sinful, now contrite heart,
Grant me the cleansing Thy blood
doth impart,
Grant me the cleansing Thy blood
doth impart.

3. Nearer, still nearer, Lord. to be
Thine,
· Sin. with its follies, gladly resign;

All of its pleasures, pomp and its
pride,
Give me but Jesus, my Lord
crucified,
. Give me but Jesus, my Lord
Crucified.

4. Nearer, still nearer, while life shall
last,
Till safe in glory my anchor is
cast;
Through endless ages, ever to be,
Nearer, my Saviour, still nearer to
Thee,
Nearer, my Saviour, still nearer to
Thee.
-Letia N. Morris

415

Old rugged cross - Irregular

1. On a hill far away stood an old
rugged cross,
The emblem of suff'ring and shame;
And I love that old cross where the
dearest and best
For a world of lost sinners was
Slain.

Chorus
So I'll cherish the old rugged cross',
Till my trophies at last I lay down;
I will cling to the old rugged cross,
And exchange it some day for a
crown.

2. Oh that old-rugged cross, so
despised by the world,
Has a wondrous attraction for me;
For the dear Lamb of God left His
glory above
To bear it to dark Calvary.

3. In the old rugged cross, stained
with blood so divine,
A wondrous beauty I see;
For 'twas on that old cross Jesus
suffered and died
To pardon and sanctify me.

DECISION AND DEVOTION

4. To the old rugged cross I will ever
be true,
Its shame and reproach gladly bear;
Then he'll call me some day to my
Home far away.
Where his glory for ever I 'll share.
-George Bennard

416

Revive us again -11.11. With Refrain

1. We praise Thee, O God
For the son of Thy love
For Jesus who died and
is now gone above.

Chorus
Hallelujah, Thine the glory!
Hallelujah, Amen!
Hallelujah, Thine the glory!
Revive us again.

2. We praise Thee, O God,
For Thy spirit of light,
Who has shown us our saviour
and scattered our night.

3. All glory and praise
to the lamb that was slain,
Who has borne all our sins and
Has cleansed ev'ry stain.

4. Revive us again;
Fill each heart with Thy love;
May each soul be rekindled
With fire from above.
-William P. Mackay

417

It Is Mine

1. God 's abiding peace is in my soul
Today,
Yes, I feel it now, yes I feel it now;

He has taken all my doubts and
fears away,
Tho' I cannot tell you how.

Chorus
It is mine, mine, blessed be His
name!
It is mine mine, He has given
peace, perfect peace
To me;
It is mine, mine, Blessed be His
name!
Mine for all eternity!

2. He has wrought in me a sweet and
perfect rest.
In my raptured heart I can feel it
now;
He each passing moment keeps
me
saved and blest.
Floos with light my heart and brow.

3. He has given me a never failing joy,
Oh, I have it now! Oh, I have it now!
To His praise I will my ransomed
pow'rs employ,
And renew my grateful vow.

4. Oh, the love of God is comforting
my soul,
For His love is mine. yes, His love
is mine!
Waves of joy and gladness o'er my
spirit roll,
Thrilling me with divine.
-Elisha A. Hoffman

418

His Way with Thee

1. Would you live for Jesus, and be
always pure and good?
Would you walk with Him within the
narrow road?
Would you have Him hear your
burden, carry all your load?
Let Him have His way with thee.

DECISION AND DEVOTION

His pow'r can make you what you
ought to be;
His blood can cleanse your heart
and make you free;
His love can fill your soul; and you
will see
T'was best for Him to have His way
with thee.

2. Would you have him make you free
and follow at His call?
Would you know the peace that
comes by giving all?
Would you, have Him save you, so
that you need never fall?
Let Him have His way with thee.

3. Would you in His Kingdom find a
place of constant rest? Would you
prove Him true in providential test?
Would you in His service labour
always at your best?
Let Him have his way with thee
                    -Cyrus S. Nusbaum

419

Susquehanna

1. Near to Thy heart, O Christ divine,
Leaning like John on Thy breast
Till with Thy glory I will shine,
Near to Thy heart I'd rest.

2. Near to Thy heart O may I be.
Hearing Thy sweet words of love,
Learning Thy precious will for me,
Seeking those things above.

3. Near to Thy heart where all is peace.
Lost in the light of Thy face, There
will my faith and trust increase,
There will I grow in grace.
                    -John W. Peterson

420

Stepping in the light

1. Trying to walk in the steps of the,
Saviour
Trying to follow our Saviour and king,
Shaping our lives by His blessed
example,
Happy, how happy, the songs that
we bring.

Chorus
How beautiful to walk in the steps of
saviour,
Stepping in the light. Stepping in
the light;
How beautiful to walk in the steps of
the Saviour,
Led in paths of tight.

2. Pressing more closely to Him who
is leading
When we are tempted to turn from
the way,
Trusting the arm that is strong to
defend us,
Happy, how happy, our praises
each day.

3. Walking in footsteps of gentle
forbearance,
Footsteps of faithfulness mercy and
love,
Looking to Him for the grace freely
promised,
Happy, how happy, our journey
above.

4. Trying to walk in the steps of the
Saviour,
Upward, still upward we'll follow
Guide;

DECISION AND DEVOTION

When we shall see Him, the King in
His beauty,
happy, how happy, our place at His
Side.

-Eliza E - Hewitt

421

Not My Own

1. Not my own, but saved by Jesus,
   Who redeemed me by His Blood;
   Gladly I accept the message,
   I belong to Christ the Lord'

   Chorus
   Not my own, Not my own,
   saviour belong to Thee, belong to
   Thee;
   All I have and all I hope for,
   Thine for all eternity.

2. Not my own! To Christ, my Saviour,
   I, believing, trust my soul.
   Every thing to Him committed,
   While eternal ages roll.

3. Not my own! My time, my talents,
   freely all to Christ I bring,
   To be used in joyful service
   For the glory of my King.

4. Not my own! The Lord accepts me,
   One among the ransomed throng,
   Who in Heaven shall see His glory,
   And to Jesus Christ belong.

422

Open and let the Master In

Once I heard a sound at my heart's
dark door
And was roused from the slumber
of sin:

It was Jesus knocked, He had
knocked before:
Now I said, Blessed Master, come
in!

Chorus
Then open, open, Open, and let the
Master in!
For your heart will be bright with the
heavenly light
If you 'only let the Master in.

2. Then He spread a feast of redeem
   ing love,
   And He made me His own happy
   guest;
   In my joy I thought that the saints
   above
   Could be hardly more favoured or
   Blest.

3. In the holy war with the foes of
   truth,
   He's my Shield; He my table
   Prepares,
   He restores my soul, He renews my
   youth,
   And gives triumph in answer to
   Prayers.

4. He will feast me still with His
   presence dear,
   And the love He so freely hath
   given;
   While His promise tells, as I serve
   Him here,
   Of the banquet of glory in Heaven.

423

Where do you journey?

1. Oh, where do you journey, my
   brother?
   Oh, where do you journey, I pray?
   Oh. where do you journey, my
   Sister,

DECISION AND DEVOTION

And when we get safely to Glory,
Oh, say, shall we meet you all
there?

Chorus
Oh, say, shall we meet you all
there?
Oh, say, shall we meet you all
there?
And when we get safely to Glory,
Oh, say, shall we meet you all
There?

2. Oh, what is your mission, my
brother?
Oh, what is your mission below?
Oh, what is your mission, my sister,
As journeying onward you go?
Our mission is practising mercy,
Sweet charity, patience, and love,
And following the footsteps of Jesus
That lead to the mansions above.

3. Oh, yes, you will meet us. my
brother.
God helping our weakness and sin
And bearing the Cross, we, my
sister.
The crown will endeavour to win,
We'll walk through the vale and the
shadow.
Through sufferings and trials and
care,
And when you get safely to Glory,
You'll meet us. you'll meet us all
there.

HOSANNA SONGS

424

St. Theodulph -7.6.7.6.D.

1. All glory, lund and honour
   To Thee, Redeemer, King,
   To whom the lips of children
   Made sweet hosannas ring:

2. Thou art the King of Israel.
   Thou David's royal Son.
   Who in the Lord's name comest,
   The King and blessed One!
   All glory, etc.

3. The company of angels
   Are praising Thee on high.
   And mortal men and all things
   created make reply:
   All glory, etc.

4. The people of the Hebrews
   With palms before Thee went:
   Our praise and prayer and
   anthems
   Before Thee we present.
   All glory, etc.

5. To Thee, before Thy passion,
   They sang their hymns of praise;
   To Thee, now high exalted,
   Our melody we raise:
   All glory, etc,

6. Thou didst accept their praises
   Accept the praise we bring,
   who in all good delightest,
   Thou good and gracious King!
   All glory, etc.
   -St. Theodulph of Orleans

425

St. Drostane - L.M.

1. Ride on! ride on in majesty!
   Hark all the tribes Hosanna cry!
   O Saviour meek, pursue thy road
   With palms and scattered gar
   ments strowed.

2. Ride on! ride on in majesty!
   In lowly pomp ride on to die:
   O Christ, thy triumphs now begin
   O'er captive death and conquered
   sin.

3. Ride on! ride on in majesty!
   The winged squadrons of the sky
   Look down with sad and wondering
   eyes
   To see the approaching Sacrifice.

4. Ride on! Ride on in majesty!
   The last and fiercest strife is nigh:
   The Father on his sapphire throne
   Awaits his own anointed Son.

5. Ride on! ride on in majesty!
   In lowly pomp ride on to die;
   Bow thy meek head to mortal pain,
   Then take, O God, thy power, and
   reign.
   -H. H. Milman

426

St. Cecilia -L .M.

1. The royal banners forward go,
   The cross shines forth in mystic
   glow;
   Where, he in flesh, our flesh who
   Our sentence bore, our ransom
   paid.

2. There whilst he hung. his sacred
   side.
   By soldier's spear was opened
   wide,
   To cleanse us in the precious flood
   Of water mingled with his blood.

3. Fulfilled is now; what David told
   In true prophetic song of old,

How God the hearthen's king
Should be;
For God is reigning from the Tree.

4. O Tree of glory, Tree most fair,
Ordained those holy limbs to bear;
how bright in purples robe it stood,
The purple of a savior's blood!

5. Upon its arms like balance true,
He weighed the price for sinners due,
The price which none but he could Pay,
And spoiled the spoiler of his prey.

6. To thee, eternal Three in One,
Let homage meet by all be done:
As by the Cross thou dost restore,
So rule and guide us evermore.
                -Bishop Venantius Fortunatus

427

St Mary-C.M.

1. Weep not for Him who onward bears
His Cross to Calvary;
He does not ask man's pitying tears,
Who wills for man to die.

2. The awful sorrow of His face,
The bowing of His frame,
Come not from torture nor disgrace:
He fears not Cross nor shame.

3. There is a deeper pang of grief,
An agony unknown,
In which His love finds no relief
He bears it all alone.

4. He sees the souls for whom
   He dies
Yet clinging to their sin,

And heirs of mansions in the skies
who will not enter in.

5. O may I in Thy sorrow share,
And mourn that sins of mine
Should ever wound with grief or care
That loving heart of Thine.
                -Thomas Benson Pollock

428

Infant Praise -7.7.7.7.and Refrain

1. Children of Jerusalem
Sang the praise of Jesus's name:
Children, too. of modern days.
Join to sing the Saviour's praise.

   Chorus
Hark, hark, hark! while infant voices sing,
Hark, hark, hark! While infant voices sing
Loud hosannas, loud hosannas
loud hosannas to our King.

2. We are taught to love the Lord,
We are taught to read His Word,
We are taught the way to heaven;
Praise for all to God be given.

3. Parents, teachers, old and young,
All unite to swell the song;
Higher and yet higher rise,
Till hosannas reach the skies.
                -John Henley

REDEMPTION WORK

429

St. Prisca -7.7.7.7.

1. In the Lord's atoning grief
   Be our rest and sweet ,relief,
   Store we deep in heart's reccess
   All the same and bitterness;

2. Thorn and cross and nail and
   lance,
   : wounds, our rich inheritance,
   Vinegar and gall and reed,
   And the cry his soul that freed.

.3.May these all our sprits fill,
   And with love's devotion thrill;
   In our souls plant virtue's root'
   And mature its glorious fruit

4. Crucified, we the adore,
   Thee with all heart implore,
   Us with all thy saints unite
   In the realms of heavenly light.

5. Christ, by coward hands betrayed,
   Christ, for us a captive made,
   Christ, upon the bitter Tree
   Slain for man, be praise to thee.
                        -St. Bonaventura

430

Love Unknown-6.6.6.6.4.4.4.4.

1. My song is love unknown,,
   Saviour's love to me,
   Love to the loveless shown,
   That they might lovely be.
   O who am I,
   That for my sake
   My lord should take
   Frail flesh, and die?

2. He came from his blest throne,
   Salvation to bestow;
   But men made strange, and none
   The longed for Christ would know.
   But O, my friend,

My Friend indeed,
Who at my need
His life did spend!

3. Sometimes they strew his way,
   And his sweet praises sing;
   Resounding all the day
   Hosannas to their king.
   Then crucify!
   Is all their breath,
   And for his death
   Thy thirst and cry.

4. Wh, what hath my lord done?
   What makes this rage and spite?
   He made the lame to run,
   He gave the blind their sight.
   Sweet injuries!
   Yet they at these
   Themselves displease,
   And 'gainst him rise.

6. In life, no house, no home
   My Lord on earth might have;
   In death, no friendly tomb
   But what a stranger gave.
   What may I say?
   Heaven was his home;
   But mind the tomb
   Wherein he lay.

7. Here might I stay and sing,
   No story so divine;
   Never was love, dear King.
   Never was grief like thine!
   This is my Friend,
   In whose sweet praise
   In all my days
   Could gladly spend
                        -S. Crossman

REDEMPTION WORK

431

Ten Thousand Angels

1. They bound the hands of Jesus
in the garden where He prayed;
They led Him thro the streets in
shame.
They spat upon the Saviour,
so pure and free from sin;
They said "Crucify Him; He's to
blame."

Chorus
He could have called ten thousand
angels
To destroy the world and set Him
free.
He could have called ten thousand
angels,
But He died alone, for you and me.

2. Upon His precious head
they placed a crown of thorns;
They laughed and said, "Behold
the King."
They struck Him and they cursed
Him
and mocked His holy name.
All alone He suffered ev'rything.

3. When they nailed Him to the
cross,
His mother stood nearby;
He said, "Woman, behold thy
son!"
He cried, "I thirst for water,"
but they gave Him none to drink.
Then the sinful work of man was
done.

4. To the howling mob He yielded;
He did not for mercy cry.
The Cross of shame He took alone.
And when He cried, 'it's finished,"
He gave Himself to die;

Salvation's wondrous plan was
done.

-Ray Overhlole

432

A Wonderful Saviour -11.8.11.8.
with Refrain

1. A wonderful Saviour is Jesus my
Lord
A wonderful Saviour to me;
He hideth my soul in the cleft of the
Rock,
Where rivers of pleasure I see.

Chorus
He hideth my soul in the cleft of
rock
That shadows a dry, thirsty land;
He hideth my life in the depths of
His love,
And covers me there with His
hand.
And covers'me there with His hand.

2. A wonderful Saviour is Jesus my
Lord.
He taketh my burden away;
He holdeth me up and I shall not
be moved,
He giveth me strength as my day.

3. With numberless blessings each
moment He crowns,
And, filled with His fullness divine,
I sing in my rapture, "O glory to
God
For such a Redeemer as mine!"

4 When clothed in His brightness
transported I rise,
To meet Him in clouds of the sky,
His perfect salvation His
wonderful love,
I'll shout with the millions on high.
-Fanny J. Crosby

REDEMPTION WORK

433

Redeemed

1 Sweet is the song I am singing today;
I'm redeemed! I'm redeemed
Trouble and
Sorrow have vanished away;
I have been redeemed!

Chorus
I'm redeemed by love divine,
Glory, glory, Christ is mine,
Christ is mine, All to him
I now resign, I have been
Redeemed.

2. Great is my joy now as onward I go;
I'm redeemed! I'm redeemed! All the way
homeward my praises shall flow;
I have been redeemed!

3. precious indeed is my Saviour to me;
I' m redeemed! I'm redeemed!
Happy in
glory some day I shall be;
I have been redeemed.

-James Rowe

434

Benton Harbor - 8.7.8.7. With Refrain

1. Christ has for sin atonement made
what a wonderful Saviour!
We are redeemed, the price is Paid
what a wonderful Saviour!

Chorus
What a wonderful
Saviour is Jesus, my Jesus,
What a wonderful
saviour is Jesus, my Lord!

2. I praise Him for the cleansing blood
What a wonderful Saviour!
That reconciled my soul to God
What a wonderful Saviour!

3. He cleansed my heart from all its sin
What a wonderful Saviour!
And now He reigns and rules therein
What a wonderful Saviour!

4. He gives me over coming pow'r
What a wonderful Saviour!
And triumph in each trying hour
What a wonderful Saviour!
-Elisha A. Hoffman

435

Moody 9.9.9.9. with Refrain

1. Marvelous grace of our loving Lord,
Grace that exceeds our sin and our guilt!
Yonder on Calvary's mount outpoured,
There where the blood of the Lamb was spilt.

Chorus
Grace, grace, God's grace, Grace
that will pardon and cleanse within,
Grace, grace. God's grace,
Grace that is greater than all our sin!

2. Sin and despair, like the sea waves cold, Threaten the soul with infinite loss;
Grace that is greater yes, grace untold
Points to the refuge, the mighty Cross.

3. Dark is the stain that we cannot hide
What can avail to wash it away?

REDEMPTION WORK

Look! There is flowing a crimson
tide
Whiter than snow you may be
today.

4. Marvelous. infinite, matchless
grace,
Freely bestowed on all who believe!
You that are longing to see His
face,
Will you this moment His grace
receive?

-Julia H. Johnson

436

The Wonderful Story

1. O sweet is the story of Jesus,
The wonderful Saviour of men,
Who suffered and died for the
sinner,
I'll tell it again and again!

Chorus
O wonderful, wonderful, story,
The dearest that ever was told;
I'll repeat it in glory, The wonderful
story,
Where I shall His beauty behold.

2. He came from the brightest of
glory;
His blood as a ransom He gave,
To purchase eternal redemption;
And O, He is mighty to save!

3. His mercy flows on like a river;
His love is unmeasured free;
His grace is forever sufficient, It
reached and purifies me.

-Chas. H. Gabriel

437

He loved Me So

1. By faith the Lamb of God I see
Expiring on the cross for me;
He paid the mighty debt I owe;

He died because He loved me so.

Chorus
He loved me so. He loved me so,
He died because he loved me so.

2. For me the Father sent His Son,
For me the victory He won;
To save my soul from endless woe,
He died because He loved me.

3. So glad I am that He is mine,
So glad that I with Him shall shine;
I'll trust in Him, for this I know.
He died because He loved me so.

-E. O. Excell

438

Sagina - 8.8.8.8.8.8. with Refrain

1. And can it be that I should gain
An interest in the Savior's blood?
Died He for me. who caused His
pain?
For me, who Him to death
pursued?
Amazing love! how can it be That
Thou, my God shouldst die for
Me?

Chorus
Amazing love! how can it be That
Thou. my God, shouldst die
for me!

2. 'Tis mystery all! The Immortal dies!
Who can explore His strange
design?
In vain the first born seraph tries
To sound the depth of love divine!
Tis mercy all! let earth adore,
Let angel minds inquire no more.

3. He left His Father's throne above.
So free, so infinite His grace!
Emptied Himself of all but love.

REDEMPTION WORK

And bled for Adam's helpless
race!
Tis mercy all, immense and free.
For, O my God, it found out me.

4. Long my imprisoned spirit lay
Fast bound in sin and nature's
Thine eye diffused a quick'ning
ray:
I woke the dungeon flamed with
light!
My chains fell off, my heart was
free,
I rose, went forth, and followed
Thee.

5. No condemnation now I dread;
Jesus, and all in Him, is mine!
Alive in Him, my living Head,
divine,
And clothed in righteousness
divine,
bold I approach the eternal throne,
and claim the crown, thru Christ
my own.

-Charles Wesley

439

Grace! 'tis a Charming Sound -
S. M. And Refrain

1. Grace! 'tis a charming sound,
harmonious to the ear,
Heav' n with the echo shall
resound,
And all the earth shall hear.

Chorus
Saved by grace alone!
This is my plea:
Jesus died for all mankind,
And Jesus died for me.

2. 'Twas grace that wrote my name
In life's eternal book;
'T was grace that gave me to the
Lamb,
Who all my sorrows took.

3. Grace taught my wand 'ring feet
To tread the heavenly road,
And new supplies each hour I
meet,
While pressing up to God.

4. Grace taught my soul to pray,
And made mine eyes o' erflow;
'Tis grace has kept me to this day,
And will not let me go.

5. Oh, let Thy grace inspire
My soul with strength divine!
May all my powers to Thee aspire,
And all my days be Thine.

-P. Doddridge

440

Blessed Be The Fountain

1. Blessed be the Fountain of blood,
To a world of sinners reveal' d;
Blessed be the dear Son of God.
Only by His stripes are we heal' d:
Tho' I've wander' d far from His
fold,
Bringing to my heart pain and woe,
Wash me in the blood of the
Lamb.
And I shall be whiter than snow.

Chorus
Whiter than the snow
Whiter than the snow,
Wash me in the blood of the
Lamb.
And I shall be whiter than snow.

2. Thorny was the crown that He
wore,
And the cross His body o'er came;
Grievous were the sorrows He
Bore,
But He suffer 'd thus not in vain:
May I to that Fountain be led,
Made to cleanse my sins here
below;

REDEMPTION WORK

Wash me in the blood that He
shed,
And I shall be whiter than snow.

3. Father, I have wander'd from
Thee,
Often has my heart gone astray;
Crimson do my sins seem to me:
Water can not wash them away;
Jesus, to that Fountain of Thine,
Leaning on Thy promise I go,
Cleanse me by Thy washing
divine.
And I shall be whiter than snow.
-E. R. Latta

441

The Blood will never lose its Power

I. In the misty days of yore,
Jesus' precious blood had pow'r
E'en the thief upon the Cross to save;
Like a bird his spirit flies
to its home in Paradise,
Thro' the pow'r of Calv'ry 's
crimson wave.

Chorus
And the blood has never lost its
pow'r,
No, never; no, never;
Jesus' blood avail's for sin ever.
And will never lose its pow'r.

2. I was lost and steep'd in guilt;
but the blood for sinners spilt
Wash'd away my sins and set me
free;
Now and evermore the same,
praise, O praise His holy name!
Will the cleansing stream availing be.

3. God in mercy asks you why,
brother sinner, will you die,
When such full redemption He
provides?
You have but to look and live,

life eternal He Will give,
For the pow'r of Calv'ry still abides

4. Bring your burdens, come today,
turn from all your sins away,
He can fully save and sanctify,
From the wrath to come now flee
let your name recorded be
With the blood wash'd, and
redeem'd on high.
-Mrs. C.H. Morris

442

Grace of God the Father

1. Grace of God the Father, Grace of
God the Son,
Grace of God the Spirit, blessed
Three in One.
Came in all its beauty light and life
to bring,
Chase away the shadows, make
sad hearts to sing.

Chorus
Grace, grace, wonrous gift of God
to all the human race;
Grace, grace, bountiful and free,
found in ev'ry place;
Grace, grace, beautiful and sweet
would all mankind embrace;
Grace, grace, ev'ry one may taste
God's great gift of grace

2. Where sin is abounding. Grace
abundeth more;
Precious is the message,
boundless is the store;
Never be discouraged, Grace is
flowing free,
Higher than the heavens, deeper
than the sea.

3. Now this grace is kindly Offered
ev'ry soul,
Come with all your burdens, Grace
will make you whole:

REDEMPTION WORK

"Him that cometh to Me I will not cast out,
But will love Him freely,
Come and do not doubt."
-Tom Jones

443

Attainment - 8.7.8.7.D.

1. Oh, this uttermost salvation!
'Tis a fountain full and free,
Pure, exhaustless, ever flowing,
Wondrous grace! It reaches me!

Chorus
It reaches me! it reaches me!
Wondrous grace! it reaches me!
Pure, exhaustless, ever flowing,
Wondrous grace! it reaches me!

2. How amazing God's compassion,
That so vile a worm should prove
This stuppendous bliss of heaven,
This unmeasured wealth of love!

3. Jesus, Saviour, I adore Thee!
Now Thy love I will proclaim;
I will tell the blessed story,
I will magnify Thy name!
-Mary D. James

444

Redeemed

1. Redeem'd how I love to proclaim it,
Redeem'd by the blood of the Lamb;
Redeem'd thro His infinite mercy,
His child and forever I am.

Chorus
Redeem'd, Redeem'd,
Redeem'd by the blood of the Lamb,
Redeem'd, Redeem'd,
His child and forever I am.

2. Redeem'd and so happy In Jesus,
No language my rapture can tell;
I know that the light of His presence
With me doth continually dwell.

3. I think of my blessed Redeemer,
I think of Him all the day long;
I sing, for I cannot be silent,
His love is the theme of my song.

4. I know I shall see in His beauty,
The King in whose law I delight;
Who lovingly guardeth my footsteps,
And giveth me songs in the night.

5. I know there's crown that is waiting
In yonder bright mansion tor me.
And soon with the spirits made perfect,
At home with the Lord 1 shall be.
-Fanny J. Crosby

445

Calvary - 9.9.9.4. with Refrain

1. Years I spent in vanity and pride,
Caring not my Lord was crucified,
Knowing not it was for me He died
On Calvary.

Chorus
Mercy there was great and grace was free,
Pardon there was multiplied to me,
There my burdened soul found liberty
At Calvary.

2. By God's Word at last my sin I learned
Then I trembled at the law I'd spurned,
Till my guilty soul imploring turned
To Calvary.

3. Now I've giv'n to Jesus ev'ry thing,
Now I gladly own Him as my King,
Now my raptured soul can only
Sing
Of Calvary.

4. O the love that drew salvation's
plan!
Oh! the grace that bro't it down to
man!
O the mighty gulf that God did
Span
At Calvary.

-William R.Newell

446

Cleansing fountain - C.M.D.

1. There is a fountain filled with blood
Drawn from Immanuel's veins,
And sinners plunged beneath that
flood
Loose all their guilty stains:
Lose all their guilty stains,
Lose all their guilty stains;
And sinners plunged beneath that
flood
Lose all their guilty stains.

2. The dying thief rejoiced to see
That fountain in his day,
And there may I, though vile as he,
Wash all my sins away:
Wash all my sins away,
Wash all my sins away;
And there may I, though vile as he,
Wash all my sins away.

3 Dear dying Lamb, Thy precious
blood
Shall never lose its pow'r,
Till all the ransomed Church of God
Be saved to sin no more:
Be saved to sin no more,
Be saved to sin no more;
Till all the ransomed Church of God
Be saved to sin no more.

4. E'er since by faith I saw the stream
Thy flowing wounds supply,
Redeeming love has been my
theme
And shall be till I die:
And shall be till I die,
And shall be till I die;
Redeeming love has been my
theme
And shall be till I die.

5. I do believe, I will believe,
That Jesus died for me!
That on the cross He shed His
blood,
From sin to set me free
From sin to set me free
From sin to set me free
That on the cross He shed His
blood,
From sin to set me free.

-William Cowper

447

He died of a broken heart

1. Have you read the story of the
Cross.
Where Jesus bled and died;
Where your debt was paid by
precious blood
That flowed from His wounded
side?

Chorus
He died of a broken heart for you
He died of a broken heart;
Upon a tree, for you, for me,
He died of a broken heart.

2. Have you read how they placed
the crown of thorns
Upon His brow for you,
When He prayed, "Forgive them,
oh, forgive;
They know not what they do?"

REDEMPTION WORK

3. Have you read how He saved the
   dying thief,
   When hanging on the tree.
   When He looked with pleading
   eyes and said,
   "Dear Lord, remember Me?"

4. Have you read that He looked to
   heaven and said,
   "Tis finished?" Twas for thee!
   Have you ever said, "I thank
   Theee, Lord,
   For giving Thy life for me?"
   -T. Dennis

448

The unveiled Christ -8.7.8.7, will Refrain

1. Once our blessed Christ of beauty
   Was veiled off from human view;
   But thro' suff'ring, death and
   sorrow
   He has rent the veil in two.

   Chorus
   O behold the Man of Sorrows,
   O behold Him in plain view;
   Lo! He is the mighty conqu'ror,
   Since He rent the veil in two.
   Lo! He is the mighty conqu'ror,
   Since He rent the veil in two.

2. Now He is with God the Father,
   Interceding there for you;
   For He is the mighty conqu'ror
   Since He rent the veil in two.

3. Holy angels bow before Him;
   Men of earth give praises due, For
   He is the well beloved
   Since He rent the veil in two.

4. Thro'- out time and endless ages,
   Heights and depths of love so
   true;

He alone can be the giver
Since He rent the veil in two.
-N.B. Herrell

449

Harwich- 5.5.11.D.

1. O God of all grace,
   Thy goodness we praise,
   Thy Son Thou hast given to die in
   our place.
   He came' from above
   Our curse to remove;
   He hath loved. He hath loved us.
   because He would love.

2. Love had moved Him to die,
   And on this we rely.
   He hath loved. He hath loved us:
   we cannot tell why;
   But this we can tell,
   He hath loved us so well
   As to lay down His life to redeem
   us from hell.

3. He hath ransomed our race;
   O how shall we praise
   Or worthly sing Thy unspeakable
   grace?
   Nothing else will we know
   In our journey below,
   But singing Thy grace to Thy
   paradise go.

4. Nay, and when we remove
   To Thy presence above,
   Our heaven shall be still to sing of
   Thy love.
   We all shall commend
   The love of our Friend,
   For ever beginning what never
   shall end.
   -Charles Wesley

REDEMPTION WORK

450

Shirland- S.M.

1. When shall Thy love constrain,
   And force me to Thy breast?
   When shall my soul return again
   To her eternal rest?

2. Thy condescending grace
   To me did freely move;
   It calls me still to seek Thy face,
   And stoops to ask my love.

3. Lord, at Thy feet I fall!
   I long to be set free;
   I fain would now obey the call.
   And give up all for Thee.

4. To rescue me from woe,
   Thou didst with all things part:
   Didst lead a suffering life below,
   To gain my worthless heart.

5. My worthless heart to gain,
   The God of all that breathe
   Was found in fashion as a man,
   And died a cursed death.

6. And can I yet delay
   My little all to give?
   To tear my soul from earth away,
   For Jesus to receive?

7. Nay, but I yield!
   I can hold out no more,
   I sink, by dying love compelled,
   And own Thee conqueror.
   -Charles Wesley

451

When I see the blood

1. Christ our Redeemer died on the
   cross,
   Died for the sinner, paid all his
   due;
   Sprinkle your soul with the blood
   of the Lamb,
   And I will pass, will pass over

Chorus
When I see the blood,
When I see the blood,
When I see the blood,
I will pass, I will pass over you.

2. Chiefest of sinners, Jesus will
   save;
   All He has promised, that He will
   do;
   Wash in the fountain opened for
   sin,
   And I will pass, will pass over you

3. Judgement is coming, all will be
   there,
   Each one receiving, justly his due
   Hide in the saving sin cleansing
   blood,
   And I will pass. will pass over you

4. O great compassion! O boundless
   love!
   O loving kindness, faithfull and
   true!
   O boundless love! under the
   blood,
   And I will pass, will pass over you
   J.F.G. and E.A.H.

452

Saved By The Blood

1. Saved by the blood of the
   Crucified One!
   Now ransomed from sin and a
   new work begun,
   Sing praise to the Father and
   praise to the Son,
   Saved by the blood of the
   Crucified One!

REDEMPTION WORK

Chorus
Saved! Saved!
My sins are all pardoned, my guilt
is all gone!
Saved! Saved'
I am saved by the blood of the
Crucified One!

2. Saved by the blood of the
   Crucified One!
   The angels rejoicing because it is
   done;
   A child of the Father, joint her with
   the Son,
   Saved by the blood of the
   Crucified One!

3. Saved by the blood of the
   Crucified One!
   The Father He spake, and His will
   it was done;
   Great price of my pardon, His own
   precious Son;
   Saved by the blood of the Crucified
   One!

4. Saved by the blood of the
   Crucified One!
   All hail to the Father, all hail to the
   Son.
   All hail to the Spirit, the great
   Three in One!
   Saved by the blood of the
   Crucified One!
                               -S. J. Henderson

453

**Glory to His name - 9.9.9.5.
with Refrain.**

1. Down at the cross where my
   Saviour died,
   Down where for cleansing from sin
   I cried.
   There to my heart was the blood
   applied;
   Glory to His name!

Chorus
Glory to His name,
Glory to His name;
There to my heart was the blood
applied;
Glory to His name!

2. I am so wondrously saved from
   Sin,
   Jesus so sweetly abides within,
   There at the cross where He took
   me in;
   Glory to His name!

3. O precious fountain that saves from
   sin,
   I am so glad I have entered in;
   There Jesus saves me and keeps
   me clean;
   Glory to His name!

4. Come to this fountain so rich and
   sweet;
   Cast your poor soul at the savior's
   feet;
   Plunge in today and be made
   complete;
   Glory to His name!
                               -Elisha A. Hoffman

454

I believe Jesus saves

1. I am coming to Jesus for rest,
   Rest, such as the purified know;
   My soul is athirst to be blest,
   To be washed and made whiter
   than snow.

Chorus
I believe Jesus saves,
And His blood washes whiter than
snow;
I believe Jesus saves,
And His blood washes whiter than
Snow,

REDEMPTION WORK

2. In coming, my sin I deplore,
My weakness and poverty show;
I long to be saved evermore,
To be washed and made whiter
than snow.

3. To Jesus I give up my all,
Ev'ry Measure and idol I know;
For His fullness of blessing I call,
Till His blood washes whiter than
snow.

4. I am trusting in Jesus alone,
Trusting now His salvation to know;
And His blood doth so folly atone,
I am washed and made whiter than
snow.

5. My heart is in raptures of love,
Love, such as the ransomed ones
know;
I am strengthened with might from .
above,
I am washed and made whiter
than snow.
                    -Wm. McDonald

455

Once For All

1. Free from the law, O happy
Condition!
Jesus hath bled, and there is
remission;
Cursed by the law and bruised by
the fall,
Grace hath redeemed us once for all

Chorus
Once for all, O sinner, receive it!
Once for all, O brother, believe it!
Cling to the cross, the burden will
fall;
Christ hath redeemed us once for all!

2. Now are we free, there's no
condemnation!

Jesus provides a perfect salvation;
"Come unto Me"O hear His
sweet call!
Come and He saves us once for all.

3. Children of God, O glorious calling!
Surely His grace win keep us from
falling;
Passing from death to life at His call,
Blessed salvation once for all.
                    -Phlip P. Bliss

456

The Nail Scarred Hand

1. Have you failed in your plan of your
storm tossed life?
Place your hand in the nail scarred
hand;
Are you weary and worn from Its
toil arid strife?
Place your hand in the hail scarred
hand.

Chorus
Place your hand in the nail scarred
hand,
Place your hand in the nail
scarred hand;'
He will keep to the end,
He's your dearest friend.
Place your hand in the nail scarred
hand.

2. Are you walking alone through the
shadows dim?
Place your hand in the nail scarred
hand:
Christ will comfort your heart, put
your trust in Him,
Place your hand in the nail scarred
hand.

3. Would you follow the will of the
Risen lord?
Place your hand in the nail scarred
hand;

REDEMPTION WORK

Would you live in the light of His blessed Word?
Place your hand in the nail scarred hand

4. Is your soul burdened down with its load of sin?
Race you hand in th nail scarred hand,
Throw your heart open wide, let the Saviour in,
Place your hand in the nail scarred hand.

-B. B. McKinney

457
Verily, I Say Unto You

1. Oh, what a Saviour that He died for me
From condemnation He hath made me free;
"He that believeth on the Son," said He,
"Hath everlasting life."

Chorus
'Verily, verily, I say unto you;
verily, verily," message ever new!
"He that believeth on the Son" tis true! .
"Hath everlasting life!"

2. All my iniquities on Him were laid,
All my indebtedness by Him was paid;
All who believe on Him, the Lord hath said,
"Hath everlasting life."

3 Though poor and needy. I can trust my Lord;
Though weak and sinful, I believe His Word;
O glad message! Ev'ry child of God
hath everlasting life.

4. Though all unworthy, yet I will not doubt;.
For him that cometh He will not cast out:
"He that believeth," oh, the good news shout!
"Hath everlasting life.'

-James McGranahan

458
My Hope Is In The Lord

I. My hope is in the Lord Who gave Himself for me.
And paid the price of all my sin at Calvary.

Chorus
For me He died, For me He lives,
And everlasting life and light He Freely gives.

2. No merit of my own His anger to suppress.
My only hope is found in Jesus' righteousness.

3. And now for me He stands Before the Father's throne.
He shows His wounded hands, and names me as His own.

4. His grace has planned it all, Tis mine but to believe.
And recognize His work of love ' and Christ receive.

-Norman J. Clayton

459
Look To, The Lamb Of God

1. If you from sin are longing, to be free, Look to the Lamb of God;
He, to redeem you, died on Calvary.
Look to the Lamb of God.

REDEMPTION WORK

Chorus
Look to the Lamb of God,
Look to the Lamb of God,
For He alone is able to save you,
Look to the Lamb of God.

2. When Satan tempts, and doubts.
and fears assail,
Look to the Lamb of God;
You in His strength shall over all
prevail,
Look to the Lamb of God.

3. Are you aweary, does the way
seem long?
Look to the Lamb of God;
His love will cheer and fill your
heart with song,
Look to the Lamb of God.

4. Fear not when shadows on your
path way fall,
Look to the Lamb of God;
In joy or sorrow Christ all in all,
Look to the Lamb of God.
　　　　　　　　　　-KG. Jackson

460

Wounded For Me

1. Wounded for me, wounded for me,
There on the cross He was
wounded for me;
Gone my transgressions, and now I
am free.
All because Jesus was wounded for
me.

2. Dying for me. dying for me,
There on the cross He was dying for
me;
Now in His death my redemption I see,
All because Jesus was dying for me.

3. Risen for me. risen for me.
Up from the grave He has risen for
Me;

Now evermore from death's sting I
am free,
All because Jesus has risen for me

4. Living for me. living for me,
Up in the skies He is living for me;
Daily He's pleading and praying for me
All because Jesus is living for me

5. Coming for me, coming for me,
One day to earth He is coming for
Then with what joy His dear face I
shall see.
Oh, how I praise Him, He's coming
for me.
　　　　　　　　　　-W. G. Oven:
　　　　　　　　& Gladys Watkin Roberts

461

You Can Touch Him

1. The God that made the world out
yonder
and others yet unknown, Reached
out His hand
in mighty power and spoke from
heaven's throne.
"Let there be earth, Let there be
Man,
And give Him all therein." But all
too soon
man chose the path way that leads
to death and sin.

Chorus
The mighty God of all creation
is the loving God of our salvation.
And you can touch His hand of
healing,
You can .ouch Him now, if you'll
only try.

2. He reached again, this time in
mercy
with gentle hand so kind, To heal
the man
of sin and sickness to soothe his
angry mind.

REDEMPTION WORK

And still today with hands now reaching
The Saviour stands near by, And you can touch
His hand of healing if you will only try.

-Ralph Carmichael

462

Tell It, Sing It, Shout It

1. There's a blessed story of redeeming love,
How it keeps us thinking of the joys above,
How lightens sorrow, trouble. grief and care
Let us, tell it, sing it, shout it ev'ry where.

Chorus
O tell it o'er and o'er,
Yes tell it more and more,
Till no soul can doubt it. fill the air,
Oh, tell it, sing it, shout it,
ev'ry where.

2. Many long to hear it. for they need its cheer,
Need its light to guide, them when the way is drear;
Many need its comfort in the hour of woe;
Tell it, sing it, shout it, as along we go.

3. It Has blessed the ages with its golden light;
Guided countless pligrims thro' the dreary night;
That we may adore Him on His throne above.
Tell and sing and shout the story of His love.

-James Rowe

463

Redemption! O Wonderful Story
9.8.9.8.D

1. Redemption! oh, wonderful story
Glad message for you and for me:
That Jesus has purchased our pardon,
And paid all the debt on the tree.

Chorus
Believe it, O sinner, believe it;
Receive the glad message tis true;
Trust now in the crucified Saviour,
Salvation He, offers to you.

2. From death unto life He hath brought us,
And made us by grace sons of God;
A Fountain is opened for sinners:
Oh, wash and be cleansed in the blood!

3. No longer shall sin have dominion,
Though present to tempt and annoy,
For Christ in his blessed redemption.
The power of sin shall destroy.

4. Accept now God's offer of mercy;
To Jesus, oh, hasten today.
For He will receive him that cometh,
And never will turn him away.

-P. Bilhorn

464

Chorale -8.7.8.7.D.

1. Great high Priest, we see Thee stooping,
With our names upon Thy breast;
In the garden groaning, drooping,
To the ground with horrors priest:
Wondering angels stood con founded,

To behold their Maker thus:
And can we remain unwounded;
When we know 'twas all for us?

2. Nothing but Thy blood, O Jesus,
   Can our wayward souls convert;
   Nothing else from guilt release us,
   Nothing else can melt the heart:
   Law and terrors do but harden,
   All the while they work alone:
   But the sense of blood bought
   pardon
   Can dissolve a heart of stone.

3. Jesus, all our consolations
   Flow from Thee, the sovereign
   good;
   Love, and faith, and hope, and
   patience :
   All are purchased by Thy blood:
   From Thy fulness we receive them;
   We have nothing of our own:
   Freely Thou delight'st to give them
   To the needy who have none.

465

St. Cross - L. M.

1. Oh come and mourn with me
   awhile;
   Oh come ye to the Saviour's side;
   Oh come, together let us mourn;
   Jesus, our Lord, is Crucified

2. Have we no tears to shed for Him,
   While soldiers scoff and Jews
   deride?
   Ah! look patiently He hangs;
   Jesus, our Lord. is crucified.

3. Seven times He spake, seven
   words of love:
   And all three hours His silence cried
   For mercy on the souls of men;
   Jesus, our Lord, is crucified,

4. Oh break, oh break, hard heart of
   mine!
   Thy weak self-love and guilty pride
   Betray'd condemn'd, and scourged
   Thy Lord;
   Jesus, our Lord, is crucified.

5. A broken heart, a fount of tears,.
   Ask, and they will not be denied:
   Lord Jesus, may we love and
   weep:
   Since Thou for us art crucified.

6. O love of God, O sin of man,
   In this dread act your strength is
   tried;
   And victory remains with love;
   For love Himself was crucified-
   -J. B. Dykes

466

Caswall - 6.5.6.5.

1. Glory be to Jesus,
   Who, in bitter pains,
   Pour'd for me the life blood
   From His sacred veins.

2. Grace and life eternal
   In that blood I find;
   Blest be His compassion Infinitely
   kind.

3. Blest through endless ages
   Be the precious stream.
   Which from endless torments
   Did the world redeem.

4. Abel's blood for vengeance
   Pleaded to the skies;
   But the blood of Jesus
   For our pardon cries.

5 Oft as it is sprinkled
   On our guilty hearts,
   Satan in confusion
   Terror-struck departs;

REDEMPTION WORK

6. Oft as earth exalting
   Wafts its praise oh high,
   Angel hosts rejoicing
   Make their glad reply.

7. Lift ye then your voices;
   Swell the mighty flood;
   Louder still and louder
   Praise the Lamb of God.
   -Filitz

467

Calvary - 8.7.8.7.4.

1. Hark! the voice of love and mercy
   sounds aloud from calvary.
   See it rends the rocks asunder
   Shakes the earth, and veils the sky:
   "Its is finish'd."
   Hear the dying Saviour cry.

2 "H s finish'd." Oh what pleasure
   Do the wondrous words afford!
   Heavenly blessings without measure
   Flow to us from Christ the Lord.
   "It is finish'd," Saints the dying words
   record.

3. Finish'd all the types and shadows
   Of the ceremonial law,
   Finish'd all that God had promised:
   Death and hell no more shall awe.
   "It is finish'd,"
   Saints from hence your comfort
   Draw.

4 Tune your harps anew, ye seraphs;
   Strike them to Emmanuel's name.
   All on earth, and all in heaven,
   Join the triumph to proclaim.
   Hallelujah!
   Glory to the bleeding Lamb!
   -J. Stanley

468

Baca 6.6.6.6.6.6.

1. Thy life was giv'n for me!
   Thy blood, O Lord, was shed
   That I might ransomed be.
   And quickened from the dead.
   Thy life was giv'n for me:
   What have I giv'n for Thee?

2. Long years were spent for me
   In weariness and woe,
   That thro' eternity
   Thy glory I might know,
   Long years were spent for me:
   Have I spent one for Thee?

3. Thy Father home of light.
   Thy rainbow circle throne.
   Were left for earthly night
   For wanderings sad and lone.
   Yea, all was left for me:
   Have I left aught for Thee?

4. Thou, Lord, hast borne for me
   More than my tongue can tell
   Of bitterest agony,
   To rescue me from hell. "
   Thou suff'redst all for me;
   What have I borne for Thee?

5. And Thou hast brought to me,
   Down from Thy home above,
   Salvation full and free,
   Thy pardon and Thy love.
   Great gifts Thou broughtest me:
   What have I brought to Thee?

6. Oh, let my life be given,
   My years for Thee be spent;
   World-fetters alt be riven.
   And joy with suffering blent;
   To Thee my alt t bring.
   My Saviour and my King!
   -W. H. Havergal

REDEMPTION WORK

469

Batty-8.7.8.7.

1. Sweet the moments, rich in
   blessing,
   Which before the cross I spend;
   Life, and health, and peace
   possessing,
   From the sinner's dying Friend.

2. Here I'll sit for ever viewing
   Mercy's streams in streams of
   blood;
   Precious drops, my soul bedwing,
   Plead, and claim my peace with
   God.

3. Truly blessed is this station,
   Low before His cross to lie;
   While I see divine compassion
   Beaming in His languid eye.

4. Love and grief my heart dividing,
   With my tears His feet I'll bathe;
   Constant stilt in faith abiding.
   Life deriving from His death.

5. Lord, in ceaseless contemplation
   Fix my thankful heart on Thee;
   Till I taste Thy full salvation,
   And Thine unveil'd glory see.

470

Southwell -S. M.

1. Oh perfect life of love!
   All, all, is finish'd now;
   All that He left His throne above
   To do for us below.

2. No work is left undone
   Of all the father will'd;
   His toil. He sorrows, one by one,
   The Scripture have fulfil'd

3. No pain that we can share
   But He has felt its smart,
   All forms of human grief and care
   Have pierced that tender heart.

4. And on His thorn crown'd head,
   And on His sinless soul,
   Our sins in all their guilt were laid,
   That He might make us whole.

5. In perfect love He dies:
   For me He dies, for me:
   Call atoning Sacrifice.
   I cling by faith to Thee.

6. In every time of need.
   Before the judgement throne,
   Thy work, O Lamb of God.
   I'll plead, Thy merits, not my own.

7. Yet work, O Lord, in me
   As Thou for me hast wrought;
   And let my love the answer be
   To grace Thy love has brought.

471

**Alas, and did my Saviour bleed -
PM**

1. Alas, and did my Saviour bleed?
   And did my Sovereign die?
   Would He devote that sacred head
   For such a worm as I?

Chorus
   At the cross, at the cross where I
   first saw the light
   And the burden of my heart rolled
   away
   It was there by faith I received my
   sight.
   And now I am happy all the day!

2. Was it for crimes that I have done.
   He groened upon the tree?

REDEMPTION WORK

Amazing pity! Grace unknown!
And love beyond degree!

3. Well might the sun in darkness hide,
And shut his glories in,
When Christ, the mighty Maker,
Died
For man the creature's sin

4. Thus might I hide my blushing face
Whilst His dear cross appears.
Dissolve my heart in thankfulness,
And melt mine eyes to tears.

5. But drops of grief can ne'er repay
The debt of love I owe:
Here, Lord, I give myself away,
Tis all that I can do!

472
Hark! Hark! The Song The Ransomed Sing

1. Hark! hark! the song the ransomed sing.
A new-made song of praise
The Lord the lamb they glorify,
And these the strains they raise;

Chorus
"Glory to Him who loved us,
And washed us in His blood;
Who cleansed our souls from guilt
and sin,
By that pure living flood!

2. Made white by His redeeming blood.
Our heavenly garments shine;
Our minds, by Him enlightened
prove.
The power of truth divine.

3 By Jesus' blood we overcame
When Satan's host assailed;

"Twas by the power of truth divine
Our feeble arms prevailed.

4. Then be the lamb of God adorned
The Lord of Life and light!
To Him be glory, honour, power,
And majesty and might!"

473
Man Of Sorrows, What A Name
7.7.7.8.

1. "Man of sorrows," what a name
For the Son of God who came
Ruined sinners to reclaim!
Hallelujah! what a Saviour!

2. Bearing shame and scoffing rude,
In my place condemned He stood:
Sealed my pardon with His blood:
Hallelujah! What a Saviour!

3. Guilty, vile, and hepless we,
Spotless Lamb of God was He;
"Full atonement "can it be?
Hallelujah! what a Saviour!

4. Lifted up was me to die,
"It is finished was His cry;
Now in heaven exalted high;
Hallelujah! what a Saviour!

5. When He comes our glorious King,
All His ransomed home to bring
Then anew this song we'll sing:
Hallelujah! What a Saviour!

RESURRECTION

474

When Tempted To Wander Away From The Lord -11.8.11.9. with Ref.

1. When tempted to wander away
form the Lord
I think of the Calvary tree;
Where Jesus once suffered my
soul to redeem
And the heart that was broken for
me.

Chorus
For me, a sinner like me like me,
His heart was broken for me,
By faith I can see on Calvary,
The heart that was broken for me.

2. When friends are unfaithful I know
He is true, No love is so full and so
free;
My eyes fill with tears as I think of
my sins,
And the heart that was broken for
Me.

3. Atonement divine He has made by
His blood,
For ever my story shall be
Of Jesus this loving Redeemer of
mine,
And the heart that was broken for
me,

475

Wonderful Saviour

1. There is a story covered with glory
That I would tell to you,
Song of the angels, heav'ns angels
To the believers true.
Jesus was given, coming from
Heaven,
Message of love divine;
He, the oblation, offers salvation
Unto your soul and mine.

Chorus
Wonderful, beautiful, merciful,
bountiful
Is the friend divine,
Tenderly, lovingly, wondrously,
masterly,
Saves this soul of mine;
Have no fear.,He is near, all the
way, night and day,
Caring for His own;
Hear the call, unto all, turn from
wrong, join the song
That redemption makes known.

2. Unto each nation all of creation,
Let us toll this great news,
Sounding His glory, echo the story
So that none need refuse,
Trusting in Jesus, quickly He frees
us,
Healing our souls from sin;
With Him abiding, in Him
confiding,
Glorious life we win.

3. Jesus the Saviour, grants us His
favour;
Gift of God's love divine;
With past hidden, sin is forbidden,
If we on Him recline.
Living the story; giving Him glory,
Rapture brings on the way;
Hear and believe it, truly receive
it,
Make Him your Lord today.

RESURRECTION

476

St. Albinus -7.8.7.8.4.

1. Jesus lives! thy terrors now
Can no more, O death, appal us.
Jesus lives! by this we know Thou,
O rave, canst not enthrall us
Alleluia!

2. Jesus lives! henceforth is death
But the gate of life immortal
This shall calm our trembling
breath
When we pass its gloomy portal.
Alleluia!

3. Jesus lives for us to died
Then, alone to Jesus living pure in
heart may we abide, glory to our
saviour giving.
Alleluia!

4. Jesus live! Our heart know well
Naught from us his love shall sever;
Life nor death nor power of hell
Tear us from his keeping ever.
Alleluia!

5. Jesus lives! to him the throne
Over all the world is given:
May we go where he is gone,
Rest and reign with him in heaven.
Alleluia!
                    -C.F. Gellert

477

Hermas - 6.5.6.5.D. and Refrain

1. "Welcome, happy morning," Age to
age shall say;
Hell today is vanquished, Heaven is
won today!
Lo! the dead is living: God forever
more,

Chorus
"Welcome, happy morning,"
Age to age shall say;
Hell today is vanquish'd.
Heav'n is won today

2. Earth her joy confesses, Clothing
her for spring.
All, good gifts returned with Her
returning, King,
Bloom in every meadow, Leaves on
every bough
Speak His sorrows ended. Hail His
triumphant now.

3. Come then, true and faithful. Now
fulfill Thy word.
'Tis Thine own third morning. Rise,
O buried Lord!
Show Thy face in brightness: Bid
the nations see,
Bring again our daylight; Day returns
with Thee!
                    -Venantius Fortunatus

478

Ellacombe-7.6.7.6.D.

1. The day of resurrection'.
Earth, tell it out abroad;
The pass over of gladness.
The pass over of God!
From death to life eternal,
From earth unto the sky,
Our Christ hath brought us over
With hymns of victory.

2. Our hearts be pure from evil,
That we may see aright
The Lord in rays eternal
Of resurrection light,
And, listening to His accents,
May hear, so calm and plain,
His own All hail and hearing,
May raise the victor strain.

RESURRECTION

3. Now let the heavens be joyful;
   Let earth her song begin;
   The round world keep high triumph,
   And all that is therein;
   Let all things seen and unseen,
   Their notes of gladness blend:
   For Christ the Lord hath risen.
   Our joy that hath no end.
                    –John, of Damascus

479

Nonington - 8.7.8.3.

1. On the resurrection morning
   Soul and body meet again;
   No more sorrow, no more weeping
   No more pain.

2. Here awhile they must be parted;
   And the flash its sabbath keep.
   Waiting in a holy stillness
   Wrapt in sleep.

3. Soul and body reunited
   Thenceforth nothing shall divide,
   Waking up in Christ's own likeness
   Satisfied.

4. O the beauty, O the gladness
   Of that resurrection day,
   Which shall not through endless
   ages Pass away!

5. To that brightest of all meetings
   Bring us, Jesus Christ, at last;
   To Thy cross, through death and
   judgement,
   Holding fast.
                    –S. Baring Gould

480

Maccabaeus -10.11.11.11..and Refrain

1. Thine be the glory, risen, conque ·
   ing Son

Endless is the victory Thou o'er
death has won;
Angels in bright raiment rolled the
stone away,
Kept the folded grave-clothes,
where Thy body lay.

Chorus
Thine be the glory. risen conquering
Son,
Endless is the victory Thou o'er
death has won.

2. Lo! Jesus meets us, risen from the
   tomb;
   Lovingly He greets us, scatters fear
   and gloom;
   Let the Church with gladness,
   hymns of triumph sing,
   For her Lord now liveth, death hast ·
   lost its sting.

3. No more we doubt Thee, glorious
   Prince of life;
   Life is naught without Thee: aid us
   in our strife;
   Make us more than conquerors,
   through Thy deathless love;
   Bring us safe through Jordan to
   Thy home above.
                    –Edmond Louis Budry

481

Orientis Partibus - 7.7.7.7.4.

1. Love's redeeming work is done;
   Fought the fight, the battle won:
   Lo, our Sun's eclipse is o'er!
   Lo, He sets in blood no more!
   Hallelujah!

2. Vain the stone, the watch, the seal!
   Christ has burst the gates of hell;
   Death in vain forbid His rise;
   Christ has opened Paradise.
   Hallelujah!

REDEMPTION WORK

3. Lives again our glorious King;
   Where, O death, is now thy sting?
   Dying once, He all doth save;
   Where thy victory, O grave?
   Hallelujah!

4. Soar we now where Christ has led
   Following our exalted Head
   Made like Him, like Him we rise
   Ours the cross, the grave, the skies.
   Hallelujah!

5. Hail the Lord of earth and heaven!
   Praise to Thee by both be given:
   Thee we great triumphant now;
   Hail, the Resurrection Thou!
   Hallelujah!

   -Charles Wesley

482
Ascension - 7.7.7.7. and Hallelujah

1. Hail the day that sees Him rise,
   Hallelujah
   To His throne above the skies;
   Hallelujah
   Christ, awhile to mortals given,
   Hallelujah;
   Enters now the highest heaven:
   Hallelujah;

2. There for Him high triumph waits:
   Hallelujah;
   Lift your heads, eternal gates;
   Hallelujah;
   Christ hath conquered death and sin;
   Hallelujah;
   Take the King of glory in:
   Hallelujah

3. Lo, the heaven its Lord receives,
   Hallelujah
   Yet He loves the earth He leaves;
   Hallelujah
   Though returning to His throne,

Hallelujah
Still He calls mankind His own:
Hallelujah

4. See, He lifts His hands above;
   Hallelujah
   See, He shows the prints of love;
   Hallelujah
   Hark, His gracious lips bestow
   Hallelujah
   Blessings on His Church below:
   Hallelujah

5. Still for us He intercedes.
   Hallelujah
   His prevailing death He pleads,
   Hallelujah
   Near Himself prepares our place,
   Hallelujah
   He the first-fruits of our race:
   Hallelujah

6. Lord, though parted from our sight,
   Hallelujah
   Far above the starry height,
   Hallelujah
   Grant our hearts may thither rise,
   Hallelujah
   Seeking Thee above the skies:
   Hallelujah

   -Charles Wesley

483
Victory - B.8.8. with Refrain

1. Alleluia! Alleluia! Alleluia!
   The strife is o'er. the battle done;
   Now is the Victor's triumph won;
   O let the song of praise be sung;
   Alleluia!

2. Death's mightiest powers have
   done their worst,
   And Jesus hath His foes dispersed;
   Let shouts of praise and joy
   Outburst

3. On the third morn He rose again
   Glorious in majesty to reign;
   O let us swell the joyful strain:

4. He brake the age bound chains of
   hell;
   The bare from heaven's high
   portals fell;
   Let hymns of praise His triumph

5. Lord, by the stripes which
   wounded Thee,
   From death's dread sting Thy
   servants free,
   That we may live. and sing to Thee.
   Alleluia!

   -Latin, 17th cent.

484

Vulpius -8.8.8.4.

1. Good Christian all, rejoice and sing!
   Now is the triumph of our king;
   to all the world glad news we bring:
   Alleluia, alleluia, alleluia!

2. The Lord of life risen today;
   death's mighty stone is rolled away;
   let all mankind rejoice and say.
   Alleluia, alleluia, alleluia!

3. We praise in songs of victory
   that love, that life, which cannot die.
   and sing with hearts uplifted high,
   Alleluia, alleluia, alleluia!

4. Your name we bless, O risen Lord,
   and sing today with one accord the
   life laid down, the life restored:
   Alleluia, alleluia, alleluia!

   -C. A. Alington

485

Wurttemberg - 7.7.7.7.4.

1. All creation join to say:
   Christ the Lord is risen today'.
   Raise your joys and triumphs high;
   Sing, you heavens, and earth reply;
   Alleluia!

2. Love's redeeming work is done;
   fought the fight, the battle won:
   see, our
   Sun's eclipse has passed; see, the
   dawn has come at last!
   Alleluia!

3. Vain the stone, the watch, the seal:
   Christ has burst the gates of hell;
   death in vain forbids his rise
   Christ has opened paradise:
   Alleluia!

4. Now he lives, our glorious king;
   Now,
   O death, where is your sting?
   Once he died, our souls to save
   where's your victory, boasting grave?
   Alleluia!

5. So we rise where Christ had led,
   following our exalted head;
   made like him, like him we rise ours
   the cross, the grave, the skies:
   Alleluia!

6. Hail the Lord of earth and heaven' ,
   praise to you by both be given;
   every knee to you shall bow, risen
   Christ, triumphant now:
   Alleluia!

   -C. Wesley

RESURRECTION

486

Diademata -6.8.6.8.D. (D.S.M.)

1. Crown him with many crowns;
   the Lamb upon his throne,
   while heaven's eternal anthem
   drowns
   all music but its own!
   Awake, my soul, and sing
   of him who died to be
   your saviour and your matchless
   king
   through all eternity.

2. Crown him with the Lord of life
   triumphant from the grave, who
   rose victorious from the strife
   for those he came to save:
   his glories now we sing who died
   and reigns on high;
   he died eternal life to bring and lives
   that death may die.

3. Crown him the Lord of love, who
   shows his hands and side those
   wounds yet visible above in beauty
   glorified.
   No angel in the sky can fully bear
   that sight, but downward bends his
   burning eye at mysteries so bright.

4 Crown him the Lord of peace his
   kingdom is at hand;
   from pole to pole let warfare cease
   and Christ rule every land!
   A city stands on high,
   his glory it displays,
   and there the nations Holy' cry
   in joyful hymns of praise.

5. Crown him the Lord of years, the
   potentate of time, creator of the
   rolling spheres

in majesty sublime:
all hail, Redeemer, hail,
for you have died for me;
your praise shall never, never fail
through all eternity!

   -M Bridges

487

Hallelujay! We Shall Rise

1. In the resurrection morning,
   When the trump of God shall
   sound,
   We shall rise, (Hallelujah) we shall
   rise!.
   Then the saints will come rejoicing.
   And no tears will e'er be found
   We shall rise, (Hallelujah) we shall
   rise!

Chorus
(We shall rise.) Hallelujah (we shall
rise!)
Amen! We shall rise, (Hallelujah!)
In the resurrection morning.
When death's prison bars are
broken,
We shall rise, (Hallelujah in the
morning)we shad rise!

2. In the resurrection morning,
   What a meeting it will be,
   We shall rise, (Hallelujah)we shall
   rise!
   When our fathers and our mothers.
   And our loved ones we shall see.
   We shall rise, (Hallelujah! we shall
   rise!

3. In the resurrection morning,
   Blessed thought It is to me,
   We shall rise. (Hallelujah)we shall
   rise!
   I shall see my blessed Saviour,
   Who so freely died for me,
   We shall rise, (Hallelujah)we shall
   rise!

RESURRECTION

4. In the resurrection morning
   We shall meet Him in the air,
   We shall rise, (Hallelujah)we shall
   rise!
   And be carried up to glory,
   To our home so bright and fair.
   We shall rise, (Hallelujah)we shall
   rise!

   -J. E. Thomas

488

He Lives! He Lives!

1. I serve a risen Saviour,
   He's in the world today;
   I know that He is living,
   whatever men may say;
   I see His hand of mercy,
   I hear His voice of cheer,
   And just the time I need
   Him He's always near.

   Chorus
   He lives, He lives,
   Christ Jesus lives today!
   He walks with me and talks with me
   along life's narrow way.
   He lives, He lives,
   salvation to impart!
   You ask me how I know He lives?
   He lives within my heart.

2. In all the world around me
   I see His loving care,
   And tho my heart grows weary
   I never will despair;
   I know that He is leading,
   thro" all the stormy blast,
   The day of His appearing
   will come at last.

3. Rejoice, rejoice, O Christian.
   lift up your voice and sing
   Eternal hallelujahs
   to Jesus Christ the King!
   The hope of all who seek Him,

The help of all who find,
None other is so loving,
so good and kind.

   -Alfred H. Ackley

489

Crown the Saviour - 8.7.8.7.4.7.

1. Lord, enthron'd in heav'nly
   splendour,
   First begotten from the dead,
   Thou alone, our strong Defender,
   Liftest up Thy people's head.
   Alleluia, Alleluia, Jesus, True and
   living Bread!
   Alleluluia, Alleluia, Jesus, True
   and living Bread!

2. Here our humblest homage pay we;
   Here in loving reverence bow;
   Here, for faith's discernment pray
   we,
   Lest we fail to know Thee now.
   Alleluia.
   Thou art here, we ask not how.

3. Though the lowliest form doth veil
   Thee
   As of old in Bethlehem, Here as
   there Thine angels hail Thee,
   Branch and Flower of Jesus's stem.
   Alleluia.
   We In worship join with them.

4. Paschal Lamb, Thine Offering,
   finished
   Once for all when Thou wast slain,
   In its fulness undiminished Shall for
   evermore remain,
   Alleluia.
   Cleansing souls from every stain.

5. Life imparting Heavenly Manna,
   Stricken Rock with streaming Side,
   Heav'n and earth with loud Hosan
   nas,

RESURRECTION

Worship Thee, the Lamb who died
Alleluia.
Risen, ascended, glorified!
-Geo C. Stebbins

490

Ascalon -6.6.8.6.6.8,

1. My heart and voice raise.
To spread Messiah's praise.
Messiah's praise let all repeat;
The universal Lord,
By whose almighty word
Creation rose in form complete

2. A servant's form He wore,
And in His body bore
Our dreadful curse on Calvary:
His life a victim stood,
And pour'd His sacred blood,
To set the guilty captives free.

3. But soon the Victor rose
Triumphant o'er His foes,
And led the vanquish'd host in
chains:
He threw their empire down,
His foes compeli'd to own,
O'er all the great messiah reigns.

4. With mercy's mildest grace,
He governs all our race
In wisdom, righteousness, and low
Who to Messiah fly
Shall find redemption nigh,
And all His great salvation prove.

5. Hail, Saviour, Prince of Peace'.
Thy kingdom shall increase.
Till all the world Thy glory see,
And righteousness around,
As the great deep profound,
And fill the earth with purity!
-B. Rhodes

491

The Whole Bright World Rejoices

1. The whole bright world rejoices
now,
Alleluia, Alleluia!
The birds do sing on every bough,
Alleluia, Alleluia!

2. Then shout beneath the racing
skies,
Alleluia, Alleluia!
To Him that rose that we might
rise,
Alleluia, Alleluia!

3. And all you living things, make
praise,
Alleluia, Alleluia!
He guideth you in all your ways,
Alleluia, Alleluia!

4. He. Father. Son, and Holy Ghost,
Alleluia, Alleluia!
Our God most high, our Joy and
Boast,
Alleluia, Alleluia!
-Oxford Book of Carols

492

In The Great Triumphant Morning

1. In the great triumphant morning.
when we hear the Bridegroom cry.
And the dead in Christ shall rise,
We'll be changed to life immortal,
in the twinkling of an eye,
And meet Jesus in the skies.

Chorus
We shall all rise to meet Him,
we shall all go to greet Him,
In the morning when the dead in
Christ shall rise.
We shall all rise to meet Him,
we shall all go to greet Him.
And shall have the marriage
supper in the skies.

2. In the great triumphant morning,
   what a happy time will be,
   When the dead in Christ shall rise,
   When the Lord descends in glory,
   Sets His waiting children free,
   And we meet Him in the skies.

3. In the great triumphant morning,
   when the harvest is complete,
   And the dead in Christ shall rise,
   We'll be crowned with life immortal,
   Christ and all the loved ones meet,
   In the rapture in the skies.

4. In the great triumphant morning, all
   the kingdom we'll possess,
   Then the dead in Christ shall rise,
   Reign as kings and priests eternal,
   Under Christ for ever blest,
   After meeting in the skies.
   —R-. E. Winsett

493

Mead House-8.7.8.7.D.

1. Alleluia, Alleluia!
   Hearts to heaven and voices raise;
   Sing to God a hymn of gladness
   Sing to God a hymn of praise:
   He who on the cross a victim
   For the world's salvation bled,
   Jesus Christ, the King of glory,
   Now is risen from the dead.

2. Now the iron bars are broken,
   Christ from death to life is born,
   Glorious life, and life immortal,
   On this holy Easter morn.
   Christ has triumphed, and we
   conquer
   By his mighty enterprise,
   We with him to life eternal
   By his resurrection rise.

3. Christ is risen, Christ the first-fruits
   Of the holy harvest field.
   Which will all its full abundance
   At his second coming yield;
   Then the golden ears of harvest
   Will their heads before him wave,
   Ripened by his glorious sunshine,
   From the furrows of the grave.

4. Christ is risen, we are risen;
   Shed upon us heavenly grace,
   Rain and dew and gleams of glory
   From the brightness of thy face;
   That, with hearts in heaven
   dwelling,
   We on earth may fruitful be,
   And by angel hands be gathered,
   And be ever, Lord, with thee.
   —Christopher Wordsworth

494

Llanfair

1. Jesus Christ is risen today, Alleluia!
   Our triumphant holy day. Alleluia!
   Who did once, upon the cross,
   Alleluia!
   Suffer to redeem our loss, Alleluia!

2. Hymns of praise then let us sing,
   Alleluia!
   Unto Christ, our heavenly King,
   Alleluia!
   Who endured the cross and grave,
   Alleluia!
   Sinners to redeem and save.
   Alleluia!

3. But the pains which He endured,
   Alleluia!
   Our salvation have procured;
   Alleluia!
   Now above the sky He's King,
   Alleluia!
   Where the angels ever sing:
   Alleluia!

4. Sing we to our God above. Alleluia!
   Praise eternal as His love; Alleluia!
   Praise Him, all ye heavenly host.
   Alleluia!
   Father, Son, and Holy Ghost.
   Alleluia!

   -14th Century Latin Hymn

495

Roll Call

1. When the trumpet of the Lord shall
   sound
   and time shall be no more
   And the morning breaks eternal,
   bright and fair
   When the saved of earth shall
   gather
   over on the other shore
   And the roll is called up yonder, I'll
   be there!

   Chorus
   When the roll is called up yonder,
   when the roll is called up yonder.
   when the roll is called up yonder,
   When the roll is called up yonder,
   I'll be there.

2. On that bright and cloudless
   morning when
   the dead in Christ shall rise
   And the glory of His resurrection
   share
   When His chosen ones shall gather
   to their home beyond the skies
   And the roll is called up yonder, I'll
   be there!

3. Let us labour for the Master from the
   dawn till setting sun,
   Let us talk of all His wondrous love
   and care;
   Then when all of life is over and our
   work on earth is done
   And the roll is called up yonder, I'll
   be there!

   -James M. Black

496

Belgrave -C. M.

1. Awake, glad soul, awake, awake!
   Thy Lord hath risen long;
   Go to His grave, and with thee
   take Both tuneful heart and song.

2. Where life is waking all around,
   Where love's sweet voices sing,
   The first bright blossom may be
   found Of an eternal spring.

3. The shade and gloom of life are
   fled This resurrection day;
   Henceforth in Christ are no more
   dead,
   The grave hath no more prey.

4. In Christ we live, in Christ we sleep,
   In Christ we wake and rise;
   And the sad tears death makes us
   weep,
   He wipes from all our eyes.

5. Then wake. glad heart, awake.
   awake! And seek thy risen Lord;
   Joy in His resurrection take,
   And comfort in His word.

6. And let thy life through all its ways
   One long thanksgiving be;
   Its theme of joy, its song of praise
   Christ died and rose for me.
   -John Samuel Bewley

497

Gratitude-6.6.6.6.8.8.

1. On wings of living light,
   At earliest dawn of day,

4. Came down the angel bright.
   And rolled the stone away.

Chorus
Your voices raise with one accord,
To bless and praise your risen Lord.

2. The keepers, watching near.
   At that dread sight and sound
   Fell down with sudden fear
   Like all dead men to the ground:

3. Then rose from death's dark gloom,
   Unseen by mortal eye,
   Triumphant o'er the tomb.
   The Lord of earth and sky'.

4. Ye children of the light,
   Arise with Him, arise
   See how the Daystar bright
   Is burning in the skies'.

5. Leave in the grave beneath
   The old things passed away,
   Buried with Him in death.
   O live with Him today

6. We sing Thee, Lord to divine,
   With all our hearts and powers,
   For we are ever Thine.
   And Thou art ever ours.
                    -William Walsham How

498

Festus -L. M.

Ye faithful souls who Jesus know,
If risen indeed with Him ye are,
Superior to the joys below.
His resurrection's power declare.

2. Your faith by holy tempers prove,
   By actions show your sins forgiven ,
   And seek the glorious things above,
   And follow Christ your Head, to
   Heaven.

3. There your exalted Saviour see,
   Seated at God's right hand again,
   In all His Father's majesty,
   In everlasting pomp to reign.

4. To Him continually aspire,
   Contending for your native place:
   And emulate the angel choir,
   And only live to love and praise.

5. For who by faith your Lord receive,
   Ye nothing seek or want beside;
   Dead to the world and sin ye live,
   Your creature love is crucified.

6. Your real life, with Christ concealed,
   Deep in the Father's bosom lies;
   And, glorious as your Head
   revealed,
   Ye soon shall meet Him in the skies.
                    -Charles Wesley

499

Rejoice And be Glad - Irregular

1. Rejoice and be glad! the Redeemer
   hath come:
   Go, look on His cradle, His cross.
   and His tomb.

Chorus
Sound His praises, tell the story of
Him who was slain:
Sound His praises, tell with gladness
He liveth again.

2. Rejoice and be glad! it is sunshine at
   last;
   The clouds have departed, the
   shadows are past.

3. Rejoice and be glad'. For the blood
   hath been shed;
   Redemption is finished, the price
   hath been paid.

RESURRECTION

4. Rejoice and be glad! Now the
   pardon is free;
   The just for the unjust hath died on
   the tree.

5. Rejoice and be glad! for the Lamb
   that was slain.
   O;er death is triumphant, and liveth
   again.

6. Rejoice and be glad! for the King is
   He pleadeth for us on His throne
   in the sky.

7. Rejoice and be glad! for the cometh
   again
   He cometh in glory, the Lamb that
   as slain.

   -Horatius Bonar

500
Hermann - L. M. and Hallelujah

1. Our Lord is risen from the dead!
   Our Jesus is gone up on high
   The powers of hell are captive led,
   Dragged to the portals of the sky.

2. There His triumphant chariot waits,
   And angels chant the solemn lay:
   Lift up your heads, ye heavenly
   gates;
   Ye everlasting doors, give way;
   Hallelujah.

3. Loose all your bars of massy light.
   And wide unfold the ethereal
   Scene:
   He claims these mansions as His
   right;
   Receive the King of Glory in!
   Hallelujah.

4. Who is the King of Glory? Who?
   The Lord that all our foes o'er
   Came,
   The wood. sin, death, and hell o'er
   threw;
   And Jesus is the Conqueror's
   Name.
   Hallelujah.

5. There His triumphant chariot waits,
   And angels chant the solemn lay:
   Let up your heads, ye heavenly
   gales
   Ye everlasting doors, give way;
   Hallelujah.

6. Who is this King of Glory? Who?
   The Lord, of glorious power
   possest;
   The King of saints, and angels too,
   God over all, for ever blest! Hallelu
   jah.

   -Charles Wesley

501
Christ arose 6.5.6.4. with Refrain

1. Low in the grave He lay, Jesus my
   Saviour!
   Waiting the coming day. Jesus my
   Lord!

Chorus
Up from the grave He arose,
With a mighty triumph o'er His foes;
He arose a victor from the dark
domain,
And He lives forever with His saints
to reign,
He arose! He arose! Hallelujah.
Christ arose!

2. Vainly they watch His bed. Jesus
   my Saviour!
   Vain they seal the dead, Jesus my
   Lord!

RESURRECTION

3. Death cannot keep his prey, Jesus
   my Saviour!
   He tore the bars away, Jesus my
   Lord!

-Robert Lowry

502

Easter Hymn

1. Christ the Lord is ris'n to day,
   Sons of men and angels say,
   Alleluia!
   Raise your joys and triumphant sigh,
   Alleluia!
   Sing, ye heavens, and earth, reply,
   Alleluia!

2. Lives again our glorious King,
   Alleluia!
   Where, O death, is now thy sting?
   Alleluia!
   Where thy victory, O grave?
   Alleluia!

3. Love's redeeming work is done,
   Alleluia!
   Fought the fight, the battle won
   Alleluia!
   Death in vain forbids Him rise,
   Alleluia!
   Christ has opened paradise,
   Alleluia!

4. Soar we now where Christ has led,
   Alleluia!
   Foll'wing our exalted Hear,
   Alleluia!
   Made like Him, like we rise,
   Alleluia!
   Ours the cross, the grave, the skies
   Alleluia!

-Charles Wesley

503

He Arose

Chorus
He 'rose, He, 'rose He 'rose from the
dead,
He 'rose, He, 'rose He 'rose from the
dead,

1. They crucified my saviour and nailed
   Him to the cross,
   They crucified my saviour and nailed
   Him to the cross,
   They crucified my saviour and nailed
   Him to the cross,
   And the lord shall bear my spirit
   home.

2. And Joseph begged His body and
   laid in it the tomb,
   And Joseph begged His body and
   laid in it the tomb,
   And Joseph begged His body and
   laid in it the tomb,
   And the lord shall bear my spirit
   home.

3. Sister Mary, she came running a
   looking for my Lord
   Sister Mary, she came running a
   looking for my Lord
   Sister Mary, she came running a
   looking for my Lord
   And the lord shall bear my spirit
   home.

4. Angels came from heaven and rolled
   the stone away,
   Angels came from heaven and rolled
   the stone away,
   Angels came from heaven and rolled
   the stone away,
   And the lord shall bear my spirit
   home.

-Phil. V. S. Lindsley

RESURRECTION

504

Because He Lives

1. God sent His Son, they called Him
   Jesus
   He came to love, heal and forgive;
   He lived and died to buy my pardon.
   An empty grave is there to prove
   my saviour lives.

Chorus
   Because He lives I can face
   tomorrow
   Because He lives all fear is gone;
   Because I know He holds the future,
   And life is worth the living just
   because He lives

2. How sweet to hold a new born baby,
   And feel the pride and joy he gives;
   But greater still the calm assurance,
   This child can face uncertain days
   because He lives.

3. And then one I'll cross the river;
   I'll fight life's final war with pain;
   And then as death gives way to
   vict'ry
   I'll see the lights of glory and I'll
   know He lives.

   -Gloria Gaither

505

Maidstone - 6.8.6.8.

1. The happy morn is come:
   Triumphant o'er the grave.
   The saviour leaves the tomb;
   Omnipotent to save.
   Captivity is captive led;
   For Jesus liveth, that was dead

2. Who now accuses them
   For whom their Surety died?
   Who now shall those condemn
   Whom God hath justified?
   Captivity is captive led;
   Foe Jesus liveth, that was dead.

2. Christ hath the ransom paid;
   The glorious work done;
   On Him our help is laid;
   By Him our victory won.
   Captivity is captive led;
   Foe Jesus liveth, that was dead

   -Charles Steggall

506

Maidstone - 7.7.7.7.D.

1. Pleasant are Thy courts above,
   In the land of light and love;
   Pleasant are Thy courts below,
   In this land of sin and woe.
   O! My spirit longs and faints
   For the converse of Thy saints,
   For the brightness of Thy face,
   For Thy fulness, God of grace!

2. Happy birds that sing and fly
   Round Thy altar, O most high!
   Happier souls that find a rest
   In a heavenly father's breast!
   Like the wandering dove that found
   No repose on earth around
   They can to their ark, repair,
   And enjoy it ever there.

3. Happy souls! there praise flow
   Even in this vale of woe;
   Waters in the desert rise,
   Manna feeds them from the skies,
   On they go from strength to strength,
   Till they reach Thy throne at length;
   At Thy feet adoring fall,
   Who hast led them safe through all.

ASCENSION

4. Lord. be mine this prize to win;
   Guide me through a world of sin;
   Keep me by Thy saving grace;
   Give me at Thy side a place.
   Sun and shield alike Thou art;
   Guide and guard my erring heart:
   Grace and glory flow from Thee;
   Shower, O shower them. Lord, on me!

   -W. B. Gilbert

507

Leigh - .M.

1. I know that my Redeemer lives;
   Oh the sweet joy this sentence gives!
   He lives, He lives, who once was dead;
   He lives, my everlasting Head.

2. He lives to bless me with His love,
   And still He pleads for me above;
   He lives to raise me from the grave, And me eternally to save.

3. He lives, my kind, wise, constant Friend;
   'Who still will keep me to the end;
   He lives, and while He lives I'll sing,
   Jesus, my Prophet, Priest, and King.

4. He lives my mansion to prepare,
   And He will bring me safely there;
   He lives, all glory to His name.
   Jesus, unchangeably the same.
   -A. R. Retnagle

ASCENSION

508

St. Patrick-7.7.0.

1. He is gone, (or) A cloud of light
Has received Him from our sight,
High in heaven, where eye of men
Follows not, nor angers ken,
Through the veils of time and space,
Pass'd into the holiest place.
All the toil, the sorrow done,
All the battle fought and won.

2. He is gone, And we remain
In this world of sin and pain:
In the void which He has left
On earth, of Him bereft,
We have still His work to do.
We can still His path pursue;
Seek Hun both in friend and foe,
In ourselves His image show.

3. He is gone (or) We heard Him say,
"Good that I should go away."
Gone is that dear form and face.
But not gone His present grace;
Though Himself no more we see,
Comfortless we cannot be:
No, His Spirit still is ours,
Quickening, freshing all our powers.

4. He is gone. (or) Towards the goal
World and church must onward roll:
Far behind we leave the past;
Forward are our glances cast:
Still His words before us range
Through the ages, as they change:
Wheresoe'er the truth stall lead.
He will give whate'er we need.

5. He is gone. (or) But we once more
Shall behold Him as before;
In the heaven of heavens the same
As on earth He went and came.
In the many mansions there,

Place for us He will prepare:
In that world unseen, unknown,
He and we may yet be one.

6. He is gone. (or) But not in vain,
Wait until He comes again:
He is risen. He is not here,
Far above this earthly sphere;
Evermore in heart and mind
Where our peace in Him we find,
To our own eternal Friend,
Thitherward let us ascend.
                              -Arthur Sullivan

509

Paulinzell8-8.7.8.7.D.

1. Glory to the King of Glory!
Thou has raised Thine only Son
With creation's Hallelujahs
To Thy bosom and Thy Throne;
And the echo of that triumph
Through the centuries oif years,
Gathering strength with lapse of
ages,
Falls today upon our ears.

2. Lo, the Lamb of God, for sinners
On the attar sacrificed,
In the brightness of Thy presence
Lives for ever Lord and Christ.
Lo, our great High Priest is pleading
At the blood-stain'd mercy seat
All the love of His atonement,
Fragrance infinitely sweet.

3. Jesus, Heir of all things, enters
On His heritage of bliss;
His the glory and the blessing,
His the power, the wisdom His:
Jesus reigns, and warrior angels
Strike their harps and sheathe their
swords,
Crowning Him the mighty Victor,
King of kings, and Lord of lords.

4. Who shall fix decline or limit,
   To His government's increase,
   Father of the age of ages,
   Prince omnipotent of peace?
   Who the infinite horizon
   Of His royalty shall span,
   On the throne of all dominion.
   Son of God and Son of Man?

5. Yea, amen, Thy church triumphant
   And Thy pilgrim church on earth
   Hail this day of Thine espousals
   Through the firmament of glory
   Ring their everlasting songs;
   Ours are from the desert rising
   Feeble voice, faltering tongues.

6. God, our God, Thou will not leave
   us
   In his far off wilderness,
   Lonely mourners for the Bride
   groom,
   Orphan children comfortless:
   Send Thy comforter, the Spirit,
   Till our frail hearts heavenward rise,
   And we dwell where our Redeemer
   Dwells with Thee beyond the skies.
   　　　　　　　　　-John Hopkins

510

St. Basil The Great - 7.6.7.6.D

1. O Christ, Thou hast ascended
   Triumphantly on high,
   By cherub guards attend
   And armies of the sky:
   Let earth tell forth the story,
   Our very flesh and bone,
   Emmanuel in glory,
   Ascends His Father's throne.

2. Heaven's gate unfold above Thee;
   But canst Thou forget
   The little band who love Thee
   And gaze from Olivet?
   Nay, on Thy breast engraven

Tho bearest every name,
Our priest in earth and heaven
Eternally the same.

3. There, there Thou standast pleading
   The virtue of Thy blood
   For sinners interceeding,
   Our Advocate with God;
   And every changeful fashion
   Of Thy brief joys and cares
   Finds thought in Thy compassion
   And echo in Thy prayers.

4. Oh, for the priceless merit
   Of Thy redeeming cross,
   Vouchsafe Thy sevenfold Spirit
   And turn to gain our loss;
   Till we by strong endeavour
   In heart and mind ascend
   And dwell with Thee for ever
   In glories without end.
   　　　　　　　　　-C. V. Standford

511

Ein'Faste Bung - P. M.

1. Lift up your heads, eternal gates;
   Ye everlasting doors, give way.
   The king, the king of glory comes.
   Ascending to His throne today!
   Who is the king of glory?
   Who is the king of glory?
   It is the Lord of mighty
   The Victor in the fight
   Triumphant o'er the powers of night.

2. Lift up your heard, eternal gates
   Ye gates of pearl, and streets of gold;
   The king, the king of glory comes;
   Before His chariot wheels unfold!
   Who is the king of glory?
   Who is the king of glory?
   The Lord of hosts is He,
   The God of Majesty,
   He is the king eternally.

Now with the Father, God most High,
And with the Spirit, ever one,
The angels own the Christ, the king,
And bow before His shining throne.
He is the King of glory!
He is the King of glory!
Him let all earth adore;
To Him our praises pour
For ever and for evermore.

- German Chorals

512

Olivet - D. S. M.

1. Thou art gone up on high
To mansions in th skies,
And round Thy throne unceasingly
The songs of praise arise
But we are lingering here,
With sin and care oppress'd;
Lord, send Thy promised Com
forter,
And lead us to Thy rest.

2. Thou art gone up high:
But Thou didst first come down,
Through earth's most bitter agony
To pass unto Thy crown:
And girt with griefs and fears
Our onward course must be,
But only let that path of tears
Lead us at last to Thee.

3. Thou art gone up high,
But Thou first come again,
With all the bright one of the sky
Attendenth in Thy train
Oh by Thy saving power
So make us live and die,
That we may stand in that dread
hour,
At Thy right hand on high.

-J. B. Dyskes

513

Crucified And Crowned - 7.7.

1. Wearied in the strife of sin,
Foes without and fears within,
Listen, look, I hear, I see
Jesus, crucified for me

2. Listen, how He pleads "forgive",
Look, my soul, on Him and live:
All my guilt on Jesus laid,
Perfect reconcilement made.

3. Counting all the world but loss,
Let me clasp the blood stain'd cross;
What can sinners crave beside
Jesus only, crucified?

4. Resting in His love, forgiven,
Thoughs will come of home and
heaven
Listen, look, I hear, I see
Jesus crown'd, and crown'd for me

5. Listen to His might prayer;
He would have me with Him there
With the saints before His throne,
Clothed in glory like His own:

6. Look, He reigns for ever now:
Many crowns are on His brow:
By His father's side adored
Priest and King and God and Lord

7. Yea, amen, Thy will be done,
All my prayers are breathed in one:
Jesus, let me rest in Thee,
Crucified and crowned for me.

-Charles Vincent

514

Hyfrydol - 8.7.8.7.D

1. Alleluia, sing to Jesus!
his the sceptre, his the throne
Alleluia! His the triumph

his the victory alone.
Hear the songs of holy Zion thunder
like a mighty flood:
Jesus out of every nation has
redeemed is by his blood!'

2. Alleluia! not as orphans are we left
in sorrow now:
Alleluia! he is near us,
faith believes, nor questions how.
Though the cloud from sight
received Him
whom the angels now adore,
shall our hearts forget his promise,
'I am with you evermore'?

3. Alleluia! bread of heaven, here on
earth our food, our stay:
Alleluia! here the sinful
come to you from day to day.
Intercessor, friend of sinners,
earth's redeemer, plead for me.
where the songs of all the sinless
sweep across the crystal sea.

4. Alleluia, sing to Jesus!
his the sceptre, his the throne:
Alleluia! his the triumph,
his the victory alone.
Hear the songs of holy Zion
thunder like a mighty flood:
'Jesus out of every nation has
redeemed us by his blood!
                        -W. C. DiX

515

Darwalls 148th - 6.6.6.6.4.4.4.4.

1. Ascended Christ, who gained
the glory that we sing.
anointed and ordained,
our prophet, priest, and King:
by many tongues
the church displays
your power and praise
in all her songs.

2. No titles, thrones, or powers can
ever rival yours;
no passing mood of ours can turn
aside your laws:
you reign above
each other name
of worth or fame,
the Lord of love.

3. Now from the Father's side
you make your people new;
since for our sins you died our
lives belong to you:
from our distress
you set us free
for purity
and holiness.

4. You call us to belong
within one body here;
in weakness we are strong
and all your gifts we share:
in you alone
we are complete
and at your feet
with joy bow down.

5. All strength is in your hand,
all power to you is given:
all wisdom to command
in earth and hell and heaven:
beyond all words
creation sings
the King of kings
and Lord of lords.
                        -Christopher Idle

516

Ebenezer-8.7.8.7.D.

1. Hail, our once rejected Jesus!
Hail, our Galilean king!
You have suffered to release us,
hope and joy and peace to bring.
Patient friend and holy saviour,
bearer of our sin and shame;
by your merits we find favour,
life is given through your name.

ASCENSION

2. Paschal Lamb, by God appointed,
   all our sins on you were laid;
   by almighty love anointed.
   full atonement you have made.
   All your people are forgiven through
   the virtue of your blood:
   opened is the gate of heaven,
   man is reconciled to God

3 Jesus! Heavenly hosts adore you
   seated at your father's side.
   Crucified, this world once saw you,
   Now in glory you abide
   There for sinners you are pleading,
   and our place you now prepare,
   always far us interceding,
   till glory we appear.

4. Worship, honour, power and
   blessing
   you are worthy to receive;
   loudest praises, without cleasing,
   right it is for us to give.
   Help us, bright angelic spirits joined
   with ours, your voices raise;
   help to show our saviour's merits,
   help to sing Emmanuel's praise.

   -J. Bakewell

517

Metzler -8.6.8.6. C. M.

1. Jesus our hope, our heart's desire,
   your work of grace we sing:
   you are the saviour of the world,
   its maker and its king.

2. How vast the mercy and the grace,
   how great the love must be,
   which led you to a cruel death
   to set your people free!

3. But now the chains of death are
   burst,
   the ransom has been paid,

and you are at your Father's side
in glorious robes arrayed.

4. All praise to you, triumphant Lord
   ascended high in heaven
   to God, the Father. Spirit. Son,
   be praise and glory given!

   -J. Chandler

518

St Magnus - 8.6.8.6.C.M.

1. The head that once was crowned
   with thorns
   is crowned with glory now;
   a royal diadem adorns the mighty
   victor's brow.

2. The highest place that heaven
   affords
   is his, is his by right;
   the King of kings and Lord of lords
   and heaven's eternal light.

3. The joy of all who dwell above, the
   joy of all below;
   to whom he demonstrated his love
   and grants his name to know.

4. To them the cross with all its shame.
   with all its grace is given;
   their name, an everlasting name,
   their joy, the joy of heaven.

5. They suffer with their Lord below,
   they reign with him above;
   their profit and their joy to know the
   mystery of his love.

6. The cross he bore is life and health,
   though shame and death to him;
   his people's hope, his people's
   wealth, their everlasting theme.

   -T. Kelly

519

Church Triumphant-8.8.8.8. (L.M.)

1. The Lord is king! Lift up your voice,
O earth, and all you heavens,
rejoice;
from world to world the song shall
sing:
The Lord omnipotent is king!'

2. The Lord is king! Who then shall
dare
resist his will, distrust his care or
quarrel with his wise decrees, or
doubt his royal promise?

3. The Lord is king! Child of the dust,
the judge of all the earth is just;
holy and true are all his ways let
every creature sing his praise!

4. God reigns! He reigns with glory
crowned:
let Christians make a joyful sound!
And Christ is seated at his side:
the man of love, the crucified.

5. Come, make your needs, your
burdens known:
he will present them at the throne;
and angel hosts are waiting there his
messages of love to bear.

6. One Lord one kingdom all secures:
he reigns, and life and death are
yours;
through earth and heaven one song
shall ring:
The Lord omnipotent is king!'
                                    -J. Conder

520

Warrington 8.8.8.8. (L.M.

1. Where high the heavenly temple
stands,
the house of God not made with
hands,
a great high priest our nature wears
the guardian of mankind appears

2. He who for us as surety stood
and poured on earth his precious
blood,
pursues in heaven his mighty plan,
the saviour and the friend of man.

3. Though now ascended up on high
he sees us with a brother's eye
he shares with us the human name
and knows the frailty of our frame

4. Our fellow sufferer yet retains
a fellow feeling of our pains,
he still remembers in the skies
his tears, his agonies and cries.

5. With boldness therefore at his throne
let us make all our sorrows known:
to help us in the darkest hour,
we ask for Christ the saviour's power.
                                    -M. Bruce

521

Ephraim -7.7.7.7.

1. Clap your hands, ye people all
Praise the God on whom ye call
Lift your voice, and shout His praise
Triumph is His sov'reign grace!

2. Glorious is the Lord most High
Terrible in majesty;
He His sovereign sway maintains,
King o'er all the earth He reigns.

ASCENSION

3. Jesus is gone up on high,
   Takes His seat above the sky:
   Shout the angel-choirs aloud,
   Echoing to the trump of God.

4. Sons of earth, the triumph join,
   Praise Him with the host divine;
   Emulate the heavenly powers,
   Their victorious Lord is ours.

5. Shout the God enthroned above,
   Trumpet forth His conquering love;
   Praises to our Jesus sing,
   Praises to our glorious King!

6. Power is all to Jesus given,
   Power o'er bell, and earth, and
   heaven!
   Power He now to us imparts;
   Praise Him with believing hearts.

7. Wonderful in saving power,
   Him let all our hearts adore;
   Earth and heaven repeat the cry
   "Glory be to God most High!"
                              -C. Wesley

522
St. Stephen - C.M.

1. The golden gates are lifted up,
   The doors are opened wide,
   The King of Glory is gone in
   Unto His Father's side.

2. Thou art gone up before us, Lord,
   To make for us a place,
   That we may be where now Thou
   art,
   And look upon God's face.

3. And ever on our earthly path
   A gleam of glory lies,
   A light still breaks behind the cloud
   That veiled Thee from our eyes.

4. Lift up our hearts, lift up our minds;
   Let Thy dear grace be given,
   That while we wander here below,
   Our treasure be in heaven;

5. That where Thou art, at God's right
   Our hope, our love, may be:
   Dwell Thou in us, that we may dwell
   For evermore in Thee!.
                              -Mrs C. F. Alexander

523
Rachie -6.5.

1. Golden harps are sounding,
   Angel voices ring
   Pearly gates are open'd
   Open'd for the King;
   Jesus, King of glory,
   Jesus, King of love,
   Is gone up in triumph to
   His throne above.

Chorus
All His work is ended,
Joyfully we sing,
Jesus hath ascended;
Glory to our King.

2. He who came to save us,
   He who bled and died
   Now is crowned with glory
   At His Father's side.
   Nevermore to suffer,
   Nevermore to die;
   Jesus, King of glory,
   Is gone up on high.

3. Praying for His children
   In that blessed place;
   Calling them to glory,
   Sending them His grace;
   His bright home preparing,
   Faithful ones for you;
   Jesus ever liveth,
   Ever loveth too.
                              -F. R. Havergal

ASCENSION

524

Hennas-6.5.6.5.D.

1. In the Name of Jesus
Ev'ry knee shall bow,
Ev'ry tongue confess Him
King of glory now:
Tis the Father's pleasure
We should call Him Lord,
Who from the beginning
Was the Mighty Word.

2. At His voice, creation
prang at once to sight,
All the angels faces,
irones and Dominations,
tars upon their way,
All the heavenly Orders,
In their great array.

3. Humbled for a season,
To receive a Name
From the lips of sinner
unto whom He came;
Faithfully He bore it,'
Spotless to the last,
Brought it back victorious,
When from death He passed.

4. Bore it up triumphant,
With its human light,
Through all ranks of creatures,
To the central height;
To the Throne of Godhead,
To the Father's breast,
Filled it with the glory
Of that perfect rest

5. In your hearts enthrone Him;
There let Him subdue
All that is not holy,
All that is not true;
Crown Him as your Captain
In temptation's hour,
Let His Will enfold you
In its light and power.

6. Brothers, this Lord Jesus
Shall return again
With His Father's glory,
With His angel train;
For ail wreaths of empire
Meet upon His brow,
And our hearts confess Him
King of glory now.

-C. M. Noel

525

Warrington -L.M.

1. Jesus shall reign where'er the sun
Does his successive journeys run;
His kingdom spread from shore to
shore,
Tin moons shall wax and wane no
More.

2. For Him shall endless prayer be
made.
And praises throng to crown His
head;
His name like sweet perfume shall
rise
With every morning sacrifice.

3. People and realms of ev'ry tongue
Dwell on His love with sweetest
song,
And infant voices shall proclaim
Their early blessings on His name.

4. Blessings abound where'er He
reigns;
The prisoner leaps to lose his
chains;
The weary find eternal rest;
And alt the sons of want are blest

5. Where He displays His healing
Power,
Death and the curse are known no
more;
In Him the tribes of Adam boast
More blessings than their father
lost.

6. Let every creature rise and bring,
Its grateful honours to our King;
Angels descend with songs aga' ı,
And earth prolong the joyful strain.
-Isaac Watts

ASCENSION

526

Martyrdom -C. M.

1. Majestic sweetness sits enthron'd
Upon the Saviour's brow;
His Head with radiant glories
crown'd,
His tips with grace o'er flow.

2. No mortal can with Him compare,
Among the sons of men;
Fairer is He than all the fair
That fill the heavenly train.

3. He saw me plunged in deep
distress,
He flew to my relief;
For me He bore the shameful
cross,
And carried all my grief.

4. To Him I owe my life and breathe,
And all the joys I have;
He makes me triumph over death,
He saves me from the grave.

5. To heaven, the peace of His abode,
He brings my weary feet, Shows
me the glories of my God,
And makes my joy complete.

6. Since from His bounty I receive
Such proofs of love divine:
Had I a thousand hearts to give,
Lord, they should aft be Thine!
-Samuel Stennett

5 7

Rex Gloriae -8.7.8,7.D.

1. See the Conqueror mounts in
triumph,
See the King in royal state
Riding on the clouds his chariot
To his heavenly palace gate;
Hark, the choirs of angel voices
Joyful alleluias sing,
And the portals high are lifted
To receive their heavenly King.

2. Who is this that comes in glory,
With the trump of jubilee?
Lord of battles, God of armies,
he has gained the victory;
He who on the cross did suffer,
He who from the grave arose,
He has vanquished sin and Satan,
He by death has spoiled he foes.

3. He has raised our human nature
In the clouds to God's right hand;
There will sit in heavenly places,
There with him in glory stand;
Jesus reigns, adored by angels;
Man with God is on the throne;
Mighty Lord, in thine ascension
We by faith behold our own.

4. Glory be to God the Father, Glory
be to God the Son,
Dying, risen, ascending for us,
Who the heavenly realm has won;
Glory to the Holy Spirit;
To One God in: Persons Three;
Glory both in earth and heaven,
Glory, endless glory, be.
-Christopher Wordsworth

528

Dulcina -8.7.8.7.

1. Christ, above all glory seated!
King triumphant, strong to save!
Dying, Thou hast death defeated;
Buried, Thou hast spoiled the
grave.

2. Thou art gone where now is given,
What no mortal might could gain,
On the eternal throne of heaven.
In Thy Father's power to reign.

3. There Thy kingdoms all adore
Thee,
Heaven above and earth below;
While the depths of hell before
Thee
Trembling and defeated bow.

4. We, O Lord, with heart's adoring.
Follow Thee above the sky;

ASCENSION

Hear our prayers Thy grace
imploring,
Lift our souls to Thee on high.

5. So when Thou again in glory
On the clouds of heaven shalt
shine,
We Thy flock may stand before
Thee,
Owned for evermore as Thine.

6. Hail! at hail In Thee confiding,
Jesus, Thee shall I adore.
In Thy Father's might abiding
With one Spirit evermore!
-Anonymous

529
Salzburg -8.7.8.7.7.7.7.7.

1. Conquering Prince and Lord of glory,
Majesty enthroned in light;
All the heavens are bowed before
Thee,   .
Far beyond them spreads Thy
might
Shall not I fall at Thy feet,
And my heart with rapture beat,
Now Thy glory is displayed,
Thine ere yet the worlds were
Made?

2. As Swatch Thee far ascending
To the right hand of the throne,
See the host before Thee bending,
Praising Thee in sweetest tone;
Shall not I too at Thy feet
Here the angel's strain repeat,
And rejoice that heaven doth ring
With the triumph of my King?.

3. Power and Spirit are o'er flowing,
On me also be they poured;
Every hinderance overthrowing,
Make Thy foes Thy footstool. Lord!
Yea, let earth's remotest end
To Thy righteous sceptre bend,
Make Thy way before Thee plain,
O'er all hearts and spirits reign.

4. Lo! Thy presence now is filling
All Thy Church in every place;
Fill my heart too; make me willing

In this season of Thy grace;
Come, Thou King of glory, come,
Deign to make my heart Thy home.
There abide and rule alone.
As' upon Thy heavenly throne!
-Gerhard Tersteegen

530
Austria-8.7.8.7.D.

1. Hail, thou once despised Jesus!
Hail, Thou Galilean King!
Thou didst suffer to release us;
Thou didst free salvation bring.
Hail, Thou agonizing Saviour,
Bearer of our sin and shame!
By Thy merits we find favour;
Life is given through Thy name.

2. Paschal Lamb by God appointed,
All our sins on Thee were laid;
By almighty love anointed,
Thou hast full atonement made:
All Thy people are forgiven
Through the virtue of Thy blood;
Opened is the gate of heaven;
Peace is made 'twixt man and God.

3. Jesus, hail! enthroned in glory,
There for ever to abide;
All the heavenly host adore Thee,
Seated at Thy Father's side:
There for sinners Thou art pleading,
There Thou dost our place prepare.
Ever for us interceding,
Till in glory we appear.

4. Worship, honour, power, and
blessing.
Thou art worthy to receive;
Loudest praises without ceasing,
Meet it is for us to give.
Help, ye bright, angelic spirits!
Bring your sweetest, noblest lays;
Help to sing our Saviour's merits,
Help to chant immanuel's praise!
-John Bakewell

THE BAPTISM IN THE HOLY SPIRIT

531

Christ lag in todesbandon-
8.7.8.7.7.8.7.4.

1. Christ Jesus lay in death's strong
   bands
   For our offe nces given;
   But now at God's right hand He
   stands,
   And brings us life from heaven:
   Wherefore let us joyful be,
   And sing to God right thankfully
   Loud songs of Hallelujah! Hallelujah!

2. It was a strange and dreadful strife,
   When Life and Death contended;
   The victory remained with Life,
   The reign of Death was ended:
   Stript of power, no more he reigns;
   An empty form alone remains:
   His sting is lost for ever. Hallelujah!

3. So let us keep the festival .
   Whereto the Lord invites us;
   Christ is Himself the joy of all.
   The Sun that warms and lights us;
   By His grace He doth impart
   Eternal sunshine to the heart;
   The night of sin is ended. Hallelu
   jah!

4. Then let us feast this Easter day
   On the true Bread of heaven.
   The word of grace hath purged
   away
   The old and wicked leaven;
   Christ alone our souls will feed,
   He is our meat and drink indeed,
   Faith lives upon no other. Hallelu
   jah!

   -Martin Luther

532

Victory-8.8.8.4.

1. The strife is o'er, the battle done;
   Now is the Victor's triumph won;
   Now be the song of praise begun;
   Alleluia!

2. The powers of death have done
   their worst,
   But Christ their legions hath
   dispersed;
   Let shouts of holy joy outburst:
   Alleluia!

3. The three sad days have quickly
   sped;
   He rises glorious from the dead:
   All glory to our risen Head:
   Alleluia!

4. Lord, by the stripes which wounded
   Thee
   From death's dreed sting Thy
   servants free,
   That we may live and sing to Thee:
   Alleluia!

   -Anonymous

533

God Is Gone Up On High - 6.6.8.8.

1. God is gone up of high.
   With a triumphant noise;
   The clarions of the sky
   Proclaim the angelic joys!

   Chorus
   Join all on earth, rejoice and sing;
   Glory ascribe to glory's King.

2. God in the flesh below,
   For us He reigns above:
   Let all the nations know
   Our Jesus conquering love

3. All power to our great Lord
   Is by the Father given;
   By angel hosts adored.
   He reigns supreme in heaven:

4. High on His holy seat
   He bears the righteous sway:
   His foes beneath His feet
   Shall sink and die away:

5. His foes and ours are one,
   Satan, the world, and sin;
   But He shall tread them down,
   And bring His kingdom in:

THE BAPTISM IN THE HOLY SPIRIT

534

Kybald Twychen - 7.7.7.7.5.7.7.7

1. Holy Spirit, gently come,
   Raise us from our fallen state,
   Fix thy everlasting home
   In the hearts thou didst create,
   Gift of God most high!
   Visit every troubled breast,
   Light and life and love supply,
   Give our spirits perfect rest.

2. Heavenly unction from above.
   Comforter of hearts that faint,
   Fountain, life, and fire of love,
   Hear and answer our complaint:
   Thee we humbly pray,
   Finger of the living God,
   Now thy sevenfold gift display,
   Shed our Saviour's love abroad.

3. Now thy quickening influence bring.
   On our spirits' sweetly move,
   Open every mouth to sing
   Jesus' everlasting love:
   Lighten every heart;
   Drive our enemies away, Joy and
   peace to us impart, ·
   Lead us in the heavenly way

4. Take the things of Christ and show
   What our Lord for us hath done;
   May we God the Father know
   Only in and through the Son:
   Nothing will we fear,
   Thought to wilds and deserts
   driven,
   White we feel thy presence near,
   Witnessing our sins forgiven.

5. Glory be to God alone, God whose
   hand created all!
   Glory, be to God the Son,
   Who redeemed us from our fall!
   To the Holy Ghost

Equal praise and glory be,
When the course of time is lost,
Lost in wide eternity!
                    -W. Hammord

535

Venice. S. M.

1. Lord God the Holy Ghost,
   In this accepted hour,
   As on the day of Pentecost,
   Descend in all thy power

2. The young, the old, inspire
   With wisdom from above;
   And give us hearts and tongues of
   fire.
   To pray and praise and love.

3. Spirit of truth, be thou In life and
   death our guide;
   O Spirit of adoption, now
   May we be sanctified.
                    -J. Montgomery

536

Angels' Song - L. M.

1. O Breath of God, breathe on us
   now,
   And move within us while we pray
   The spring of our new life art Thou
   The very light of our new day.

2. O strangely art Thou with us,
   Lord Neither in height nor depth to
   seek:
   In nearness shall Thy voice be
   heard:
   Spirit to spirit Thou dost speak.

3. Christ is our advocate on high;
   Thou art our advocate within:
   O plead the truth, and make reply
   To every argument of sin.

4. But ah, this faithless heart of mine!
The way I know; I know my guide:
Forgive me, O my Friend divine,
That I so often turn aside.

5. Be with me when no other friend
The mystery of my heart can share;
And be Thou known, when fears transcend,
By Thy best name of Comforter.
-A. H. Vine

537
St. Michael-S. M.

1. Come, Holy Spirit, come;
Let Thy bright beams arise;
Dispel the sorrow from our minds,
The darkness from our eyes.

2. Cheer our desponding hearts,
Thou heavenly Paraclete;
Give us to lie with humble hope
At our Redeemer's feet.

3. Revive our drooping faith.
Our doubts and fears remove;
And kindle in our breasts the flame
Of never-dying love.

4. Convince us all of sin,
Then lead to Jesus blood:
And to our wondering view reveal
The secret love of God.

5. Tis Thine to cleanse the heart,
To sanctify the soul,
To pour fresh life in every part,
And new create the whole.

6. Dwell therefore in our hearts,
Our minds from bondage free;
Then we shall know and praise and love
The Father, Son, and Thee.
-J. Hart

538
Trentham S. M.

1. Breathe on me, Breath of God,
fill me with life -new,
That I may love what Thou dost love,
And do what Thou wouldst do

2. Breathe on me, Breath of God.
Until my heart is pure,
Until my will is one with Thine,
To do and to endure.

3. Breathe on me, Breath of God.
Till I am wholly Thine,
Till all this earthly part of me
Glows with Thy fire divine.

4. Breathe on me. Breath of God,
So shall I never die,
But live with Thee the perfect life of
Thine eternity.
-Edwin Hatch

539
Boylston -S. M.

1. The Holy Ghost is here.
Where saints in prayer agree,
As Jesus' parting Gift is near
Each pleading company.

2. Not far away is He,
To be by prayer bro't nigh,
But herein present majesty,
As in His courts on high.

3. He dwells within our soul.
An ever welcome guest;
He reigns with absolute control,
As monarch in the breast

4. Obedient to Thy will,
We wait to feel Thy pow'r;
O Lord of life, our hopes fulfill,
And bless this hallowed hour.
-Charles H. Spurgeon

THE BAPTISM IN THE HOLY SPIRIT

540

Seymour -7.7.7.7.

1. Holy Spirit, from on high,
Bend o'er us a pitying eye;
Now refresh the drooping heart:
Bid the pow'r of sin depart.

2. Light up ev'ry dark recess
Of our heart's ungodliness;
Show us ev'ry devious way
Where our steps have gone astray.

3. Teach us, with repentant grief,
Humbly to implore relief
Then the Saviour's blood reveal,
And our broken spirits heal.

4. May we daily grow in grace,
And with patience run the race
Trained wisdom, led by love.
Till we reach our home above
-William H. Bathur

541

Brecon -C. M.

1. Spirit divine, attend our pray'r,
And make our heart Thy home;
Descend with all Thy gracious
pow'r;
Come, Holy Spirit, come.

2. Come as the light! to us reveal
The truth we long to know;
Reveal the narrow path of right,
The way of duty show.

3. Come as the fire and purge our
hearts
Like sacrificial flame,
Till our whole souls an off'ring be
In love's redeeming name.

4. Come as the wind, O Breath of God
O Pentecostal grace!
Come, make Thy great salvation
known,
Wide as the human race.
-Adrew Reed

542

Carson '.7.7.8.7. and Refrain

1. Seal us, O Holy Spirit,
Grant us Thine impress, we pray.
We would be more like the Saviour,
Stamped with His image today.

Chorus
Seal us, seal us,
Seal us just now, we pray,
Seal us, O Holy Spirit,
Seal us for service today.

2. Seal us, O Holy Spirit,
Help us Thy likeness to show;
Then from our life unto others
Streams of rich blessing shall flow.

3. Seal us, O Holy Spirit,
Make us Thine own from this hour;
Let us be useful, dear Master,
Seal us with witnessing power.
-Isaac H. Meredth

543

O Lord, Send the Power

1. When the pow'r of God descended
On the day of Pentecost
All the days of waiting ended
They received the Holy Ghost.

Chorus
O Lord. send the pow'r just now;
O Lord, send the pow'r just now;
O Lord, send the pow'r just now:
And baptize ev'ry one

REDEMPTION WORK

2. Tongues of flame, came down upon them,
And they preach'd the word with Pow'r.
List ning multitudes awakened
Turn'd to God that very hour.

3. We are waiting Holy Spirit
We all of one accord
Lord fulfill just now the promise
that is given in thy word

4. Fill and thrill us with thy, presence,
Grant the blessing that we need
Flood our souls with, wondrous glory,
While the pray'r of faith we plead.
                    -Mary Hudbert Munford

544

Revive the hearts of all

1. God is here, and that to bless us
With the Spirit's quick'ning pow'r!
see, the cloud, already bending,
waits to drop the grateful show'r.

Chorus
Let it come, O Lord, we pray Thee,
Let the show'r of blessing fall;
We are waiting, We are waiting
Oh, revive the hearts of all.

2. God is here! we feel His presence ;
In this consecrated place;
But we need the soul refreshing
Of His free, unbounded grace.

3. God is here! oh, then; believing,
Bring to Him our one desire,
That His love may now be kindled.
Till its flame each heart inspire:

4. Saviour, grant the pray'r we offer,
While in simple faith we bow;
From the windows of Thy mercy
Pour us out a blessing now.
                    -James L. Black

545

Begin In Me

1. O Lord, in me Thy work revive,
Begin this very hour,
Oh, may my eye in rapture see?
Thy Spirit mighty power!

Chorus
Begin in me, begin in me
Thy work of love and power
O Spirit of the living God,
Begin this very hour.

2. Thy weary church has waited long
May it not wait in vain;
Break thro' the darksome clouds we dread,
And send refreshing rain

3. Might but a shower of grac⌣ descend,
Our hearts would lose their gloom;
The barren hills would all rejoice,
The wilderness would bloom.
                    -T. M. Eastwood

546

Normandy -8.7;8.7.D.

1. Come, Thou everlasting Spirit,
Bring to ev'ry thankful mind,
All the Saviour's dying merit
All His suff'rings for mankind:
True Recorder of His passion,
Now the living faith impart:
Now reveal His great salvation
Unto ev'ry faithful heart.

'2. Come, Thou witness of His dying;
Come, Remembrancer divine;
Let us feel Thy power applying
Christ to every soul, and mine,
Yes, in me, in me He dwelleth;

I in Him, and He in me!
And my empty soul He filleth,
Here and through eternity.

-C. Wesley

547

Bring Your Vessels, Not A Few

1. Are you looking for the fulness
of the blessing of the Lord
In your heart and We today?
Claim the promise of your Father,
comes according to His word,
In the blessed old time way.

Chorus
He will fill your heart today to over
flowing,
As the Lord commandeth you,
'Bring your vessels, not a few;
'He will fill your heart today to
overflowing
With the Holy Ghost and pow'r

2. Bring your empty earthen vessels,
clean thro' Jesus' precious blood,
Come, ye needy, one and all:
And in human consecration wait
before the throne of God.
Till the Holy Ghost shall fall.

3. Like the cruse of oil, unfailing is
His grace for evermore,
And His love unchanging still;
And according to His promise with the
Holy Ghost and pow'r. He will ev-ry
vessel fill.

-Mrs. C. H. Morris

548

Let the Fire fall

1. They were gather'd in an upper
chamber,
As commanded by the risen Lord.
And the promise of the Father

There they sought with one accord
When the Holy Ghost from heav'n
descend
Like a rushing wind and tongues of
fire:
So dear Lord, we seek Thy blessing
Come with glory now our hearts
inspire.

Chorus
Let the fire fall, let the fire fall,
Let the fire from heaven fall;
We are waiting and expecting,
Now in faith, dear Lord. we call;
Let the fire fall, let the fire fall,
On Thy promise we depend;
From the glory of Thy presence
Let the Pentecostal fire descend.

2. As Elijah we would raise the altar
For our testimony clear and true,
Christ the Saviour, loving Healer,
Coming Lord, Baptizer too.
Ever flowing grace and full
salvation,
For a ruined race Thy love has
plann'd;
For this blessed revelation,
For Thy written word we dare to
stand.

3. 'Tis the convenanted promise given,
To as many as the Lord shall call,
To the fathers and their children,
To Thy people, one and all;
So, rejoicing in Thy word unfailing
We draw nigh in faith Thy power to
know
Come, O come, Thou burning
Spirit.
Set our hearts with heav'nly fire
Aglow.

4. With a living coal from off Thy altar
Touch our tips to swell Thy
wondrous praise,
To extol Thee, bless, adore Thee

THE BAPTISM IN THE HOLY SPIRIT

And our songs of worship raise;
Let the cloud of glory now descending
Fill our hearts with holy ecstacy,
come in all Thy glorious fulness,
Blessed Holy Spirit, have Thy way.
-H. Tee

549

When the Tithes are gatherd in

1. There'll be show'rs of blessing from
   Our Father's hand,
   His word of promise we may
   firmly stand;
   There'll be rains refreshing on the
   thirsty land
   When the tithes are gather'd in.

   Chorus
   Tithes of love and willing service,
   Tithes of silver and of gold;
   When the tithes are gather'd in,
   When the tithes are gather'd in
   There'll be blessings more than we
   can contain,
   When the tithes are gather'd in.

2. There'll be shouts of triumph from
   the conq'ring host,
   There'll be perfect freedom in the
   Holy Ghost;
   Ev'ry one empower'd as at Pente
   cost,
   When the tithes are gather'd in.

3. Then will come the dawning of the
   Reign of peace,
   When the wars and conflicts shall
   forever cease,
   And for struggling saints shall come
   a sweet release,
   When the tithes are gathered in.

4. We will rob no longer, then, our
   Lord and King,
   What to Him belongeth we will
   gladly bring.

And we'll shout hosanna, while the
glad harps ring,
When the tithes are gathered in.
-Mrs. C. H. Morris

550

Cambridge-S.M.

1. Blow, pentecostal breeze,
   Breathe apostolic blast,
   Stir pentecostal hearts at ease,
   And sinners slumb'ring fast!

2. Breathe, Holy Ghost today,
   Dispel the ancient sloth;
   The guilty deadness sweep away
   In resurrection growth.

3. Make sweeter graces bloom,
   And lovelier virtues shine.
   And mightier influences perfume
   A world by purchase thine.

4. Revive the ancient glow,
   The fierce prophetic fire,
   The ancient miracle bestow,
   The former power inspire.

5. Breathe on this soul of ours.
   On branch and stem and root,
   Till Christ shall smell His fragrant
   flowers
   And taste His ripened fruit

6. Breathe on us, Mighty Breath,
   On leaf and naked God.
   Breathe o'er the church's creeping
   death
   The pulsing life of God.

7. Breathe till the perfume flows
   O'er wastes where sins abound,
   Till Calvary's gospel incense blows
   The stricken world around.
   -Harold Norton

THE BAPTISM IN THE HOLY SPIRIT

551

A World Wide Revival

1. For a world wide revival,
Blessed Master we pray,
Let the pow'r of the highest,
Be upon us today;
For this world dearly purchased,
By the blood of God's Son,
Back from Satan's dominion,
And from sin must be won.

Chorus
Send the pow'r, Oh, Lord,
Send the pow'r, Oh Lord,
Send the Holy Ghost power,
let it now be out poured,
Send it surging and sweeping
like the waves of the sea,
Send a world wide revival,
and begin it in me.

2 Send the showers of blessing,
As declared in Thy Word,
Let the Spirit of promise
On all flesh be outpoured;
Send the latter rain on us,
Till the land overflows,
Till the desert rejoicing.
Blossoms forth as the rose.

3. There's a sound of a going
In the mulberry trees,
News of nations awaking,
Borne upon ev'ry breeze;
For the prayers of His children,
God in mercy doth own,
The revival's beginning,
And the power's coming down.
                    -Mrs. C. H. Morris

552

Send the Fire - 8.3.8.3.8.8.8.3.

1. Thou Christ of burning, cleansing flame,
Send the fire! Send the fire!
Thy blood bought gift today we claim,
Send the fire! Send the fire!
Look down and see this waiting host,
Give us the promis'd Holy Ghost,
We want another Pentecost,
Send the fire! Send the fire!

2. God of Elijah, hear our cry!
Send the fire! Send the fire!
Oh, make us fit to live or die!
Send the fire! Send the fire!
To burn up every trace of sin,
To bring the fight and glory in,
The revolution now begin,
Send the fire! Send the fire!

3. 'Tis fire we want, for fire we plead,
Send the fire! Send the fire!
The fire will meet our every need.
Send the fire! Send the fire!
For strength to ever do the right,
For grace to conquer in the light,
For power to walk the world in white,
Send the fire! Send the fire!

4. To make our weak heart strong and brave,
Send the fire! Send the fire!
To live a dying world to save,
Send the fire! Send the fire!
Oh, see us on Thy altar lay
Our lives, our all, this very day;
To crown the offering now, we pray
Send the fire! Send the fire!
                    -William Booth

553

Showers of Blessing 8.7.8.7. and Refrain

1. Here in Thy name we are gathered Come and revive us, O Lord;
"There shall be showers of blessing,"
Thou hast declar'd in Thy word.

THE BAPTISM IN THE HOLY SPIRIT

Chorus
Oh, graciously hear us,
Graciously hear us we pray:
pour from Thy windows upon us
Showers of blessing today

2. Oh! that the showers of blessing
Now on our souls may descend,
While at the footstool of mercy
Pleading Thy promise we bend!

3. "There shall be showers of
Blessing,"
Promise that never can fail;
Thou wilt regard our petition;
Surely our faith will prevail.

4. Showers of blessing, we need
them,
Showers of blessing from Thee;
Showers of blessing, oh, grant
them,
Thine all the glory shall be.
                            -Jennie Garnett

554

He Abides

1. I'm rejoicing night and day,
As I walk the pilgrim way,
For the hand of God in all my life I
see,
And the reason of my bliss,
Yes, the secret all is this
That the Comforter abides with me

Chorus
He abides, He abides,
Hallelujah, He abides with me!
I'm rejoicing night and day,
As I walk the narrow way.
For the Comforter abides with me.

2. Once my heart was full of sin,
Once I had no peace within,
Till I heard how Jesus died upon the
tree;

Then I fell down at His feet,
And there came a peace so sweet,
Now the Comforter abides with me.

3. He is with me ev'ry where,
And He knows my ev'ry care,
I'm as happy as a bird and just as
free;
For the Spirit has control,
Jesus satisfies my soul,
Since the Comforter abides with me.

4 There's no thirsting for the things
Of the world they've taken wings;
Long ago I gave them up. and
instantly
All my night was turn'd to day,
All my burdens roll'd away,
Now the Comforter abides with me.
                            -Herbert Buffum

555

The Power that fell at Pentecost

1. The pow'r that fell at Pentecost,
When in the upper room,
Upon the watching, waiting ones,
The Holy Ghost had come,
Remaineth evermore the same;
Unchanging still, O praise His
name.

Chorus
The pow'r, the pow'r, the Pentecos
tal pow'r
Is just the same today,
Is just the same today,
The pow'r. the pow'r, The Pente
costal pow'r.
Is just the same today.

2. "Ye shall have power (said Jesus)
when
The Holy Ghost is come;"
Your loosened tongues shall speak
His praise,

THE BAPTISM IN THE HOLY SPIRIT

Your lips no more be dumb:
The timid, shrinking ones be brave,
To reach a hand the lost to save.

3. The wav'ring shall steadfast
become,
The weak in faith be strong,
With holy boldness going forth,
Denouncing sin and wrong;
With burning zeal each heart
aflame,
A whole salvation to proclaim.

4. Breathe on us now the Holy Ghost
The young and old inspire;
Let each receive his Pentecost,
Set hearts and tongues a fire!
Thou wonderful transforming power,
Come now in this accepted hour.
-Mrs. C. H. Morris

556

Rachie -6.5.

1. Tarry for the Spirit,
He shall come in show'rs,
Energising wholly
All your ransom'd pow'rs;
Signs shall follow service
In the Holy Ghost,
Then the Church of Jesus
Prove a mighty host.

Chorus
On then Church of Jesus,
Claim your Pentecost;
God shall now baptize thee
In the Holy Ghost.

2. "Rivers" is Try promise,
This shall be our plea,
Less than this can never
Meet our cry for Thee;
Tired of lukewarm service,
And the loss it brings;
We would live entirely
For eternal things.

3. When the Spirit cometh.
Loosened lips shall tell,
Of the wondrous blessing
Which upon them fell;
Life of Jesus springing,
Like a well within,
Hearts with loud hosannas,
Constantly shall ring.

4. When with joy we follow In
Christ's triumph train,
And our lives are flooded
With the Latter Rain;
Then the world around us
Shall the impact feel,
Of a Church with vision,
Fired with holy zeal.

.5. Then the Lord of glory
Shall be magnified,
He who trod the wine-press,
Fully satisfied;
Walking in the Spirit,
Condemnation o'er,
Blessed life of worship,
Now and evermore.
-E. C. W. Boulton

557

Pentecostal Power

1. Lord, as of the old at Pentecost
Thou didst Thy pow'r display,
With cleansing, purifying flame
Descend on us today.

Chorus
Lord, send the oldtime pow'r, the
Pentecostal pow'r!
Thy flood gates of blessing
on us throw open wide!
Lord, send the old time pow'r, the
Pentecostal pow'r,
That sinners be converted and
Thy name glorified!

2. for mighty works for Thee prepare,
And strengthen ev'ry heart;
Each waiting heart to work for
Thee;
Lord, our faith renew!

3. All self consume, all sin destroy!
with earnest zeal endue
Each waiting heart to work for
Thee;
O Lord, our faith renew!

4. Speak, Lord' before Thy throne we
wait,
Thy promise we believe,
And will not let Thee go until
The blessing we receive!
                    -Charlotte G. Homer

558

Winchester Old-C.M.

1. Come, Holy Ghost, our hearts
inspire,
Let us Thine influ'nce prove;
Source of the old prophetic fire,
Fountain of light and love.

2. Come, Holy Ghost, for, mov'd by
Thee,
The prophets wrote and spoke;
Unlock the truth, Thy-setf the Key.
Unseal the sacred book.

3. Expand Thy wings, celestial Dove,
Brood o'er our nature's night;
On our disorder'd spirits move
And let there now be light,

4. God; thro' Himself, we then shall
Know.
If Thou within us shine;
And sound, with all Thy saints
below,
The depths of love divine.
                    -Charles Wesley

559

Mercy -7.7.7.7.

1. Holy Ghost with light divine.
Shine upon this heart of mine;
Chase the shades of night away,
Turn my darkness into day.

2. Holy Ghost, with pow'r divine,
Cleanse this guilty heart of mine;
Long hath sin without control
Held dominion O'er my soul.

3. Holy Ghost, with joy divine,
Cleanse this sadened heart of mine;
Bid my many woes depart.
Heal my wounded, bleeding heart.

4. Holy Spirit, all divine,
Dwell within this heart of mine;
Cast down ev'ry idol throne,
Reign supreme and reign alone
                    -Andrew Reed

560

Maryton -L. M.

1. Come, Holy Spirit, heavenly Dove,
With all thy quickening powers,
Kindle a flame of sacred love
In these cold hearts of ours;

2. Look! how we grovel here below,
Fond of these earthly toys;
Our souls can neither fly nor go
To reach eternal joys.

3. Dear Lord, and shall we ever live
At this poor dying rate,
Our love so faint, so cold to Thee,
And Thine to us so great?

4. Come, Holy Spirit, heavenly Dove,
With all thy quickening powers;
Come, shed abroad a Saviour's
love
And that Shall kindle ours
                    -Isaac Watts

THE BAPTISM IN THE HOLY SPIRIT

561

The Comforter Has Come

1. O Spread the tidings 'round,
   Wherever man is found,
   Wherever human hearts and
   human woes abound;
   Let ev'ry Christian tongue
   proclaim the joyful sound;
   The Comfoter has come!

Chorus
The Comforter has come,
The Comforter has come!
The Holy Ghost from Heav'n,
The Father's promise giv'n;
O spread the tidings 'round,
wherever man is found
The Comforter has come!

2. The long, long night is past,
   The morning breaks at last,
   And hushed the dreadful wail and
   fury of the blast.
   As o'er the golden hills
   the day advances fast!
   The Comforter has borne!

3. Lo, the great King of kings,
   with healing in His wings.
   To ev'ry captive soul
   a full deliv'rance brings;
   And thro' the vacant cells
   the song of triumph rings;
   The Comforter has come!

4. O boundless love divine!
   How shall this tongue of mine
   To wond'ring mortals tell the
   matchless grace divine
   That I, a child of hell,
   should in His image shine!
   The Comforter has come!
           -F. Bottome.

562

Fill me now - 8.7.8.7. with Refrain

I. Hover o'er me. Holy Spirit.
   Bathe my trembling heart and brow;
   Fill me with Thy hallow'd presence,
   Come, O come and fill me now.

Chorus
Fill me now, fill me now,
Jesus, come and fill me now;
Fill me with Thy hallowed presence
Come, O come and fill me now.

2. Thou canst fill me, gracious Spirit,
   Though I cannot tell Thee how;
   But I need Thee, greatly need Thee,
   Come, O come and fill me now.

3. I am weakness, full of weakness,
   At Thy sacred feet I bow;
   Blest, divine, eternal Spirit,
   Fill with pow'r, and fill me now.
   Cleanse and comfort, bless and
   save me,
   Bathe, O bathe my heart and brow;
   Thou art comforting and saving,
   Thou art sweetly filling now.
           -Elwood H. Stokes

563

Tarsus - 8.8.8.0.

1. Come, Holy Ghost, all quickening
   fire!
   Come, and my hallowed heart
   inspire,
   Sprinkle with the atoning blood:
   Now to my soul Thyself reveal,
   Thy mighty working let me feel,
   And know that I am born of God.
2. Humble, and teachable, and mild,
   O may I, as a little child,

THE BAPTISM IN THE HOLY SPIRIT

My lowly Master's steps pursue!
Be anger to my soul unknown,
Hate, envy, jealousy, be gone,
In love create Thou all things new.

3. Let earth no more my heart divide.
With Christ may I be crucified,
To Thee with my whole soul aspire:
Dead to the world and all its toys,
Is idle pomp, and fading joys,
Be Thou alone my one desire.

4. My will be swallowed up in Thee;
Light in Thy light still may I see,
Beholding Thee with open face;
Called the full power of faith to
prove
Let all my hallowed heart be love,
And all my spotless life be praise.
-Charles Wesley

564

Blessed Quietness

1. Joys are flowing like a river.
Since the Comforter has come;
He abides with us for ever,
Makes the trusting heart His home.

Chorus
Blessed quietness, holy quietness,
What assurance in my soul!
On the stormy sea He speaks
Peace to me,
And the billows cease to roll!

2. Like the rain that falls from heaven.
Like the sunlight from the sky
So the Holy Ghost is given,
Coming on us from on high.

3. What a wonderful salvation'
Where we always see His face;
What a perfect habitation!
What a quiet resting place!
-Manie Payne Feroguson

565

Iverson - Irregular

1. Spirit of the Living God, afresh on me,
Spirit of the living God, afresh on me,
Melt me, mould me, fill me. use me,
Spirit of the living God, afresh on me.
-Daniel Iverson

566

Morecambe -10.10.10.10.

1. Spirit of God, descend upon my
heart;
Wean it from earth, thro' all its pulses
move.
Stoop to my weakness, mighty as
Thou art.
And make me love Thee as I ought
to love.

2. Hast Thou not bid us love Thee,
God and King?
All, all Thine own soul, heart and
strength and mind.
I see Thy cross there teach my
Heart to cling;
O let me seek Thee, and O let me find.

3. Teach me to feel that Thou art always
nigh;
Teach me the struggles of the soul
to bear .
To check the rising doubt, the rebel
sigh:
Teach me the patience of unanswered
prayer.

4. Teach me to love Thee as Thine
Angels love.
One holy passion filling all my
frame:
The baptism of the heav'n de
scended Dove,
My heart an altar and Thy love the
flame.
-Geocge Croly

THE BAPTISM IN THE HOLY SPIRIT

567

Cuthbet -8.6.8.4.1.

1. Our bless'd Redeemer, ere He
   breathed
   His fender last farewell,
   A Guide, a comfonter, bequeath'd
   With us to dwell.

2. He came in semblance of a dove,
   with sheltering wings outspread,
   The holy balm of peace and love
   on earth to shed.

3 He came sweet influence to impart.
   A gracious, willing Guest.
   While He can find one humble heart
   Wherein to rest

4. And His that gentle voice we hear
   Soft as the breath of even,
   That checks each fault, that calms
   each fear,
   And speaks of heaven.

5. And every virtue we possess,
   And every victory won,
   And every thought of holiness,
   Are His alone.

6. Spirit or purity and grace,
   Our weakness, pitying, see.
   Oh make our hearts Thy dwelling
   place.
   And meet for Thee.
   -J. B. Dykes

568

Mulcombe - L. M.

1. Come. gracious Spirit, heavenly
   dove.
   Without and comfort from above:
   Be Thou our Guardian, Thou our
   Guide;
   O'er every thought and step

2. The light or truth to us display,
   And make us know and love Thy
   way:

plant holy fear in every been,
That we from God may ne'er ,
depart.

3. Lead us to Christ, the living way;
   Nor let us from His pastures stray:
   Lead us to holiness, the mad
   Which we must take to dwell with
   God.

4. Lead us to heaven, its bliss to
   share.
   Fulness of joy for ever there:
   Lead us to God, our final rest,
   To be with Him forever bless'd
   -S. Wobbe

569

Gracious Spirit, dwell with me - 7.7.7.7.7.7.

1. Gracious Spirit, dwell with me!
   I myself would gracious be
   And with words that help and heal
   Would Thy life in mine reveal,
   And with actions bold and meek
   Would for Christ my Saviour
   speak.

2. Truthful Spirit, dwell with me!
   I myself would truthful be,
   And with wisdom kind and dear
   Let Thy life in mine appear,
   And with actions brotherly
   Speak my Lord's sincerity

3. Tender Spirit, dwell with me!
   I myself would tender be;
   Shut my heart up like a flower,
   At temptation's darksome hour,
   Open it when shines the sun,
   And His love by fragrance own

4. Mighty Spirit, dwell with me!
   I myself would mighty be.
   Mighty so as to prevail
   Where unaided man must fall,
   Ever by a mighty hope '
   Pressing on and bearing up.

THE BAPTISM IN THE HOLY SPIRIT

5. Holy Spirit, dwell with me!
   I myself would holy be,
   Separate from sin, I would
   Choose and cherish alt things good,
   And whatever I can be,
   Give to Him who gave me Thee.
   -C. Kocher

570

Come, Holy spirit

1. The Holy spirit came at Pentecost
   He came in mighty fullness then;
   His witness thru believers won the lost,
   and multitudes wore born again,
   The early Christians, scattered o'er the world
   They preached the gospel fearlessly;
   Tho some were martyred and to lions hurled,
   They marched along in victory!

Chorus
Come, Holy spirit, dark is the hour,
We need Your filling,
Your love and Your mighty pow'r
Move now among us,
Stir us, we pray,
Come, Holy spirit,
Revive the Church tody!

2. Then in an age when darkness gripped the earth,
   The just shall we by faith" was earned;
   The Holy spirit gave the Church new birth
   As reformation fires burned.
   In later years the great revivals came
   When saints would seek the Lord and pray;
   O once again we need that holy came
   To meet the challenge of today!
   -John w. Peterson

571

Come Down, O Love Divine - 6.6.11.D.

1. Come down, O Love divine,
   Seek Thou this soul of mine,
   And visit it with Thine own ardour glowing;
   O Comforter, draw near,
   Within my heart appear,
   And kindle it, Thy holy flame bestowing.

2. O let it freely burn,
   Till earthly passions turn
   To dust and ashes, in its heat consuming;
   And let Thy round, mine inner
   Shine ever on my sight,
   And clothe me round, the white my path illuming.

3. Let holy charity,
   Mine outward vesture be,
   And lowliness becomes mine inner doming
   True lowliness of heart
   Which takes the humbler part,
   And o'er its own shortcomings weeps with loathing.

4. And so the yearning strong,
   With which the soul will tong,
   Shall far outpass the power of human telling;
   For none can guess its grace,
   Till he become the place
   Wherein the Holy Spirit makes His dwelling.

572

O Breath Of Life, Come Sweeping Through Us -9.9.8.6.

1. O Breath of Life, come sweeping through us
   Revive Thy Church with life and

THE BAPTISM IN THE HOLY SPIRIT

Breath of Life, come cleanse, renew us,
And ft Thy Church to meet this Hour.

2. O wind of God, come bend us, break us,
Till humbly we confess our need;
Then in Thy tenderness remake us.
Revive, restore, for this we plead.

3. O Breath of Love, come breathe within us,
Renewing thought and will and heart:
Come, Love of Christ, afresh to win us,
Revive Thy Church in every part.

4. O heart of Christ, once broken for us,
Tis there we find our strength and rest;
Our broken contrite hearts now solace,
And let Thy waiting Church be Blest.

5. Revive us. Lord! Is zeal abating
While harvest fields are vast and white?
Revive us. Lord. the world is waiting,
Equip Thy Church to spread the light

.

573

O Holy Spirit, Come - S. N.

1. O Holy Spirit, come,
Anoint us one and all,
And tet some mighty deed be done,
While at Thy feet we fall.

2. Thy Presence now we feel,
To Thee our all we give,

Oh, let Thy love our spirits seal
Henceforth for Thee to live

3. The glow of love divine
Refines us, at Thy feet;
For this our souls will always pine
And yearn to be complete.

4. O unction from on high,
Come, permeate within,
Then I shall bear Thy searching
Without a trace of sin.

574

Our Heav'nly Father, We Come Nigh-8.7.8.7.D.

1. Our heav'nly Father, we come nigh
We Thy children weak and faint
Fill us withy Thy Holy Spirit .
Grant that we be all renewed;
Come, Thou Holy Spirit do, come
Speak through us in a new tongue
For Thy great gift we are pleading
Thy great gift of Pentecost.

2. Lord. remember Thou Thy promise
Poor Thy Spirit on all flesh
Give us of Thy peace, we pray Thee
Peace, the world cannot afford,
Come Thou Holy Spirit, do come
Sin destroy Thou in our hearts
For Thy great gift we are pleading
Thy great gift of Pentecost

3. Heav'nly Dove, descend upon us
Fill us with Thy power divine,
That the nations all may worship
To our Saviour yielded be.
Let us hear of Thy great power through
This dark continent of ours
For Thy great gift we are pleading
Thy great gift of Pentecost.

THE BAPTISM IN THE HOLY SPIRIT

575

Spirit Of Wisdom, Turn Our Eyes - 8.8.6.D.

1. Spirit of wisdom, turn our eyes
From earth and earthly vanities
To heavenly truth and love;
Spirit of understanding Sure,
Our souls with heavenly light
endue
To seek the things above.

2. Spirit of counsel, be our guide;
Teach us, by earthly struggles tried,
Our heavenly crown to win:
Spirit of fortitude, Thy power
Be with us in temptation's hour,
To keep us pure from sin.

3. Spirit of knowledge, lead our feet
In Thine own paths, safe and sweet,
By angel footsteps trod;
Where Thou our guardian true shall
be,
Spirit of gentle piety,
To keep us dose to God.

4. A Through all our life be ever near,
Spirit of God's most holy fear,
In our heart's inmost shrine,
Our souls with awful reverence fill,
To worship His most holy will,
All-righteous and divine.

5. So lead us, Lord, through peace or
strife.
Onward to everlasting life.
To win our high reward:
So may we fight our lifelong fight.
Strong in Thine own unearthly
might,
And reign with Christ our Lord.

576

The Holy Ghost To Me Is Given

1. The Holy Ghost to me is given
An earnest of my home in heaven;
Since He has taken full control,
I've Pentecost in my soul.

Chorus
I've Pentecost in my soul
I've Pentecost in my soul
The Spirit has come for ever to
abide;
I've Pentecost in my soul.

2. He deigns to dwell my heart within,
And quell the power of pardoned
sin,
Though o'ar my head dark clouds
may roll,
I've Pentecost in my soul.

3. I shout aloud with sacred joy.
His praise shall my powers
employ;
His blessed name my tongue extol,
For Pentecost in my soul.

4. And when I reach your world of
bless
A land more glorious far than this
I'll sing while countless ages roll,
For Pentecost in my soul.

5. Then seek this gift without delay,
Receive the royal Guest today;
Yield all to His benign control.
Let Pentecost fill your soul.

577

When First The Risen Lord Of Power.
8.6.8.6.8.8.8.6.

1. When first the risen Lord of Power
His chosen one sent forth,
A charge He gave, that solemn hour,
To preach His saving worth.
"Go ye' said He, "to all mankind;
Declare My word, and ye shall find:
The signs shaft surely follow them
Who on Mv name believe

2. "No demons shall stand before them
No poison do them harm:
Nor subtle serpent in their hand
Cause pain or dread alarm."
For satan's kingdom He o'er came.
To give His people right to dim;
These signs shall surely follow them;
Who on My name believe.

3. 'They shall with other tongues declare
The wonders of their God;
The sick beneath their heads, by prayer,
Shall rise, to prove My Word"
So let it be! Firm as His Throne
Stands this dear promise to His own:
These sign shall surely follow them
Who on My name believe.

4. Crowned with the flame of Pentecost,
A faithful, fearless band
Proclaimed His Name: a ransomed host
Arose from every land.
The Lord worked with them from on High.

His proven Word could none deny:
These signs shall surely follow them
Who on My name believe.

5. No word of Thine is void of power;
No promise, Lord, is vain,
Be this a Pentecostal hour
Confirm Thy Word again!
Nor Canst Thou fall! Thou art the same
As when of old Thou didst proclaim:
These signs shall surely follow them
Who on My name believe

SECOND COMING OF CHRIST

578

Bristol -C. M

1. Hark the glad sound the Saviour come,
   The Saviour promised long:
   Let every heart prepare a throne,
   And every voice a song.

2. He comes, the prisoners to release
   In Satan's bondage held;
   The gates of brass before him burst,
   The iron fetter yield.

2. He comes, the broken heart to bind,
   The bleeding soul to cure,
   And with the treasures of his grace ;
   To bless the humble poor.

3. Our glad Hosannas, Prince of Peace,
   Thy welcome shall proclaim;
   And heaven's eternal arches ring
   With thy beloved name.
   -P. Doddridge

579

Hyfrydol -7.8.7.D.

1. Come, Thou long expected Jesus,
   Born to set Thy people free;
   From our fears and sins release us;
   Let us find our rest in Thee

2. Israel's strength and consolation.
   Hope of all the earth Thou art
   Dear Desire of ev'ry nation,
   Joy of ev'ry longing heart

3. Born Thy people to deliver,
   Born a Child, and yet a King.
   Born to reign in us forever,
   Now Thy gracious kingdom bring.

4. By Thine own eternal Spirit
   Rule in all our hearts alone;
   By Thine all sufficient merit,
   Raise us to Thy glorious throne.
   -Charles Wesley

580

Old 112th-8.8.8.8-8.8.

1. O quickly come dread Judge of all;
   For, aweful though thine advent be,
   All shadows from the truth will fall.
   and falsehood die; in sight of thee:
   O quickly come! for doubt and fear
   Like clouds dissolve when thou art near.

2. O quickly come. great King of all;
   Reign all around us, and within:
   Let sin no more our souls enthral.
   Let pain and sorrow die with sin:
   O quickly come! For thou alone
   Canst make thy scattered people One

3. O quickly come, true life of all:
   For death is mighty all around,
   On every home his shadows fall,
   On very heart his mark is found:
   O quickly come! for grief and pain
   Can never cloud thy glorious reign.

4. O quickly come, sure Light of all,
   For gloomy night broods o'er our way
   And weakly souls begin to fall
   With weary watching for the day:
   O quickly come! for round thy Throne
   No eye is blind, no night is known.
   -L. Tuttiett

581

Babylon's streams LM

1. That day of wrath, that dreadful day
   When heaven and earth shall pass away,
   What power shall be the sinner's stay?,
   How shall he meet that dreadful Day?

2. When, shrivelling like a perched Scroll,
The flaming heavens together roll;
When louder yet, and yet more Dread,
Swells the high trump that wakes the dead:

3. O on that day wrathful day,
When man to judgement wakes from clay.
Be Thou O Christ, the sinner's stay,
Though heaven and earth shall pass away
-Sir Walter Scott

582

When He Cometh .8.6.8.5. with Refrain

1. When He cometh, when He cometh,
To make up His Jewels,
All His Jewels, precious jewels,
His loved and His own

Chorus
Like the stars of the morning
His bright crown adorning,
They shall shine in their beauty
Bright gems for His own

2 He will gather, He will gather,
The gems for His kingdom
All the pure ones, all the bright ones
his loved and His own.

3. Little children, little children,
Who love their redeemer,
Are His jewels, precious jewels,
His loved and His own.
-W. O. Cushing

583

Regent Square -8,7.8.7.8.7.

1. Lo, He comes with clouds descend
ing
Once for favored sinners again
Thousand thousand saint attending,
Swell the triumph of His train,
alleluia! Alleluia!
God appears on earth to reign

2. Every eye shall now behold Him,
Robed in dreadful majesty;
Those who set at naught and sold Him
Pierced and nailed Him to the tree,
Deeply wailing, deeply wailing,
Shall the true Messiah see.

3. Now redemption, long expected,
See in solemn pomp appear.
All His saints, by men rejected,
Now shall meet Him in the air
alleluia! Alleluia.
See the day of God appear

4. Yea, Amen! let all adore Thee
High on Thine eternal throne
Saviour, take the pow'r and glory,
Claim the kingdom to Thine own:
O, come quickly, O, come quickly'
Everlasting God, come down.
-Charles Wesley

584

Autumn - 8.7.8.7.D.

1. There's a light upon the mountains,
And the day is at the spring,
When our eyes shall see the beauty
And the glory of the King;
Weary was our heart with waiting,
And the night watch seemed to Long,
But His triumph day is breaking,
And we hail it with a song.

2. In the fading of the star-light
   We may see the coming morn
   And the light of men is paling
   In the splendors of the dawn;
   For the eastern sky are glowing
   As with light of hidden fire
   And the hearts of men are stiring
   With the throbs of deep desire

3. There's a hush of expectation
   And a quite in the air,
   And the breath of God is moving
   In the fervent breath of prayer;
   For the suffering, dying Jesus
   Is the Christ upon the throne
   And the travail of our spirit
   Is the travail of His own

4. Hark! We hear a distant music,
   And it comes with fuller swell?
   'Tis the triumph song of Jesus,
   Of our King immanuel!
   Go ye forth with Joy to meet Him!
   And, my soul be swift to bring
   All thy sweetest and thy dearest
   For the triumph of our King!
   —Herry Burton

585

St. Magnus - C. M.

1 The Lord will come and not be slow,
   His foolsteps cannot err
   Before Him righteousness shall go,
   His royal harbinger.

2. Truth from the earth, like to a flower,
   Shall bud and blossom then;
   And justice, from her heavenly bower
   Look down on mortal men.

3. Rise, God, judge Thou the earth in might .
   The wicked earth redress

For Thou art He who shall by right
The nations all possess.

4. For great Thou art, and wonders great
   By Thy strong hand are done
   Thou in Thy everlasting seat
   Remainest God alone.
   —John Milton

586

When He comes in glory by and by

1. O how sweet 'twill be to meet the Lord,
   When He comes in glory, by and by
   What a song of praise will be outpoured,
   When He comes in glory, by and by.

   Chorus
   How sweet, how sweet!
   When He comes in the sky
   What joy! What joy!
   When He comes in glory, by and by

2. We will have our robes all white as snow,
   When He comes in glory,
   by and by; O be ready, with the Lord to go,
   When He comes in glory, by and by

3. I am longing for that happy day
   When He comes in glory,
   by and by, for with Him I hope to soar away,
   When He comes in glory, by and by
   —A. A. Westbrook

587

Bringing back the King

1. Why say ye not a word
   Of bringing back, the king
   Why speak ye not of Jesus and His reign?
   Why tell ye of His kingdom.

SECOND COMING OF CHRIST

And of its glories sing,
But nothing of His coming back
Again?

Chorus
Bringing back the King,
Oh, bringing back the King!
The angel choirs of heav'n their
hallelujahs sing, (Hosanna!)
Bringing back the King,
Oh, bringing back the King!
Ye ransomed, let your joyous
welcome ring!

2. Dost thou not want to look
   Upon His loving face?
   Dost thou not want to see Him
   glorified?
   Would's thou not hear His
   welcome,
   And in that very place,
   Where years ago we saw Him
   Crucified?

3. O hark! creation's groans,
   How can they be assuaged?
   How can our bodies know redemp
   live joy?
   How can the war be ended
   In which we are engaged,
   Until He come the lawless to
   destroy?

4. Come quickly, blessed Lord,
   Our hearts a welcome hold!
   We long to see creation's second
   birth;
   The promises of Thy coming
   To some is growing cold,
   O hasten Thy returning back to
   earth.
                    -James M. Gray

588

Happy day

1. Jesus is coming with joy to the sky;
   Oh, happy day! oh, happy day!
   Then all who love Him shall
   heavenward fly;
   Oh, happy day! happy day!
   Upward shall fly to the Lord in the air

Together with Jesus we all shall be
there,
Far from the earth, and from sorrow
and care
Oh, happy day! happy day!

2. Parents and children shall then
   again meet
   Oh, happy day! oh, happy day!
   Sisters and brother oh it will be
   sweet!
   Oh, happy day! happy day!
   We miss'd them on earth, to Jesus
   they went;
   We love them as ever, their
   absence lament
   Soon we shall meet them, and
   then, be contented
   Oh, happy day! happy day!

3. Are we all ready, should Jesus now
   call?
   Oh, happy day! oh, happy day!
   Would each one answer, the great
   and the small?
   Oh, happy day! happy day!
   We long to rise up and with Thee
   to be,
   Thy face, blessed Jesus our
   Saviour to see.
   Would you then dear children, sing
   sweetly with me
   Oh, happy day! happy day!

4. Some will stay weeping, unable to
   sing,
   Oh, happy day oh, happy day!
   "Yet all may rejoice and their glad
   praises bring"
   Oh, happy day! happy day!
   For Jesus still waits. He tarries
   that we
   May trust in His name, and thus
   ready may be.
   When, brightly beaming, His glory
   we see:
   Oh happy day! happy day!
                    -H. F. Witherby

SECOND COMING OF CHRIST

589

Watching for the dawning

1. We are watching, we are waiting till
the mists shall clear away,
And our Lord shall come in glory
with His saints in bright array;
When the trump of God resounding
shall be heard on ev'ry shore,
And the dead in Christ shall waken
to be with Him evermore.

Chorus
We are watching, We are waiting.
For the dawning of that glorious
day;
For the coming of our Saviour,
With His saints in bright array.

2. We are looking, for the coming of
our great and glorious King.
Who shall banish from His presence
every dark and evil thing:
When His justice and His mercy
shall prevail in all the world,
And o'er ev'ry tribe and nation shall
His banner be unfurl'd.

3. Now by faith we catch a vision of
that glad millenial reign,
And be the ransom'd millions who
shall follow in His train;
And our hearts cry out, "Come
quickly!" that His beauty we may
see,
And be with our Lord in glory
through a blest eternity.
                                    -R. L. Filtcher

590

The Coming of the Kingdom

1. There's a glorious Kingdom waiting
in the rand beyond the sky,
Where the saints have been
gath'ring year by year;
And the days are swiftly passing
that will have
bring the Kingdom nigh:
For the coming of the Kingdom
draweth near!

Chorus
Oh, the coming of the Kingdom
draweth near!
Oh, the coming of the Kingdom
draweth near!
Be thou ready, O my soul, for the
trumpet soon may roll,
And the King in His glory shall
Appear!

2. Tis the hope of yonder Kingdom,
and the glory there prepared,
And the looking for the Saviour to
appear,
That delivers us from bondage to
the world that once ensnared:
For the coming of the Kingdom
draweth near!

3. With the coming of the Kingdom
we shall see our blessed Lord,
For the King ere the Kingdom
must appear,
Hallelujah to His name,
who redeem'd us by His blood!
Oh, the coming of the Kingdom
draweth near!

4. Oh, the world is growing weary, it
has waited now so long,
And the hearts of men are failing
them for fear;
Let us tell them of the Kingdom, let
us cheer them with the song,
That the coming of the Kingdom
draweth near!
                                    -El Nathan

591

A Better Day is Dawning

1. A better day is coming,
A morning promised long,
When girded Right, with holy
Might, Will overthrow the Wrong;
When God the Lord will listen
To ev'ry plaintive sigh,
And stretch His hand o'er ev'ry
land,
With justice by and by.

SECOND COMING OF CHRIST

Chorus
Coming by and by, coming by and
by!
The better day is coming.
The morning draweth nigh!
Coming by and by, coming by and
by
The welcome dawn will hasten on,
'Tis coming by and by.

2. The boast of haughty Error
No more will the air,
But Age and Youth will love the
Truth
And spread it ev'ry where;
No more from Want and sorrow
Will come the hopeless cry;
For strife will cease, and perfect
Peace
Will flourish by and by.

3. Oh, for that holy dawning
We watch and wait, and pray,
Till o'er the height the rooming light
Shall drive the gloom away;
And when the heav'nly glory
Shall flood the earth and sky,
We'll bless the Lord for all His word,
And praise Him by and by.
-Rev. R. Lowry

592
Waiting for thy Coming - 8.7.

1. We are waiting, blessed Saviour,
We are watching for the hour
When in majesty descending.
Thou shalt come to might power;
Then the shadows will be lifted,
And the darkness roll'd away,
And our eyes behold the splerdour
Of the glorious crowning day,

2. We are waiting; blessed bright to
We are watching not in vain
For the cloud that bore Thee upward,
And will bring Thee back again,

Then, among Thy ransom'd people
We shall tread the shining way
And our eyes behold the splendour
Of the glorious crowning day.

3. We are waiting; blessed Saviour
For a union, heart to heart,
With our dear ones o'er the river
Where we nevermore shall part
Then our sorrows, in a moment
Like a dream will pass way
When our eyes behold the
splendour
Of the glorious crown day.
-F. J. Crosby

593
The Hope of the Coming of Lord

1. A lamp in the night, a song in time
of sorrow.
A great glad hope which faith can
ever borrow,
To gild the passing day with the
glory of the morrow
is the hope of the coming of the Lord

Chorus
Blessed hope, blessed hope,
Blessed hope of the coming of the
coming of the Lord
How the aching heart it cheers:
How it glistens thro our tears
Blessed hope of the coming of the
Lord

2. A star in the sky, a beacon bright to
guild us;
An anchor sure to hold when
storms betide us
A refuge for the soul, where in quiet
we may hide us
Is the hope of coming of the
Lord

SECOND COMING OF CHRIST

3. A call of command, like trumpet
   clearly sounding,
   To make us hold when evil is
   surrounding;
   To stir the sluggish heart, and to
   keep in good bounding
   Is the hope of the coming of the
   Lord
4. A word from the One to all our
   hearts the dearest
   A parting word to make Him aye the
   nearest;
   O all His precious words the
   sweetest, brightest, clearest
   Is the hope of the coming of the
   Lord
   - D. W. Whittle

594
Coming - C. M.

1. O watchman on the mountain
   Height,
   Proclaim the coming day;
   Behold the spires of golden fires
   Point upward far away.
   Chorus
   Coming, yes, He's coming,
   The Day spring from on high;
   Coming, yes, He's coming
   The promised hour is nigh;
   Coming, yes, He's, coming
   Let all the ransom'd sing
   The hills are bright with shining light;
   All hail the coming King!

2. O watchman, bid the sleeping
   Church
   Awake, arise
   The heav'nly Bridegroom will come
   And now is on His way

3. All hail to zion's glorious King,
   By prophets long foretold;
   Praise Him in song, ye angel throng,
   Strike all your harps of gold
   -Rev W. O Cushing

595
Come on the Wings of the Morning

1. Come on the wing of the morning;
   Come, Thou Redeemer and King;
   Hail to the day that is dawning,
   Hail to the joy it will bring.

   Chorus
   Oh, come on the wings of the
   Morning!
   Oh, come on our hearts as we sing!
   Come as, we sing in the day that is
   dawning;
   Oh, come Thou Redeemer and
   King!

2. Come on wings of the morning;
   Come with thy glory and grace,
   All of Thy promise performing
   Showing the light of Thy face

3. Come on the wings of the morning;
   Come with a joyful surprise,
   Lifting the sad and the morning
   Wiping the tears from their eyes.

4. Come on the wings of the morning;
   Come as the King to Thy throne;
   Have we not sounded Thy warning;
   Now let Thy glory be known.
   -D. W. Whittle

596
Watch ye, Therefore

1. Watch, earnestly watch,
   The Lord's approach is nearing
   Pray, fervently pray,
   No man can know the hour
   like as a thief at night is His
   appearing;
   He cometh to judge the world in
   truth and power;

SECOND COMING OF CHRIST

Chorus
Watch ye, pray ye; soldiers of the
Lord;
Work ye, wait ye, trusting in His
word;
Keep His commandments, and His
law obey;
And He with reward you in the last
great day.

2. Work, joyfully
All ye who know His chast'ning:
Wait, patiently wait,
For your reward is high
Lift up your heads, the day of rest is
hast'ning;
Rest, glorious rest, with Jesus by
and by.

3. Trust, loyally trust,
And as to Him thou'rt clinging,
Keep, faithful keep
The Saviour's blest commands;
Then in thy heart the blest assur
ance ringing,
Know surely thy name is written in
He hands.
                              -Dr. G. L. Micheal

597

The Lord is Coming

1. The Lord is coming by and by:
Be ready when He comes!
He comes from His fair home on
high
Be ready when He comes!
He is the Lord our Righteousness
And comes His chosen ones to
bless
And at His Father's throne confess:
Be ready when He comes!

Chorus
Will you be ready when the
Bridegroom comes

Will you be ready when the ,
Bridegroom comes?
Will your lamps be trimm'd and
bright.
Be it morning, noon or night?
Will you be ready when the the
Bridegroom comes?

2. He soon will come to earth again
Be ready when He comes! ,
Begin His universal reign:
Be ready when He comes!
With Hallelujah heaven will ring,
When Jesus doth redemption
bring;
Oh, trim your lamps to meet your
your King
Be ready when He comes!

3. Behold! He comes to comes!
Be ready when He comes!
And soon we'll hear the trumpet
call:
Be ready when He comes!
To Judgement called at
His command.
From every clime, from every land,
Before His throne we all must
stand:
Be ready when He comes!
                              -E. A. Hoffman

598

Impatient heart, be still

1. Impatient heart, be still
What though He tarries long?
What tho' the triumph
song is still delay'd?
Thou hast His promises sure,
And that is all secure:
Be not afraid! be not afraid
Be still! be still!
Impatient heart be still!

2. My eager heart, be still!
Thy Lord will surely come,
And take thee to His home,
With Him to dwell:

SECOND COMING OF CHRIST

It may not be today;
And yet, my soul, it may
I cannot tell!
Be still! be still!
my eager heart, be still!

2. My anxious heart, be still!
Watch, work, and pray; and then
it will not matter when,
Thy Lord shall come.
At midnight or at noon;
He cannot come too soon;
To take thee home.
Be still! be still!
My anxious heart, be still!
-Geo. A. Warburton

599

He is Coming

1. He is coming, the "Man of Sor
rows,
Now exalted on high;
He is coming with loud hosanas,
In the clouds of the sky.

Chorus
Hallelujah! Hallelujah!
He is coming again;
And with joy we will gather round
Him, At His coming to reign!

2. He is coming, our loving Saviour,
Blessed Lamb that was stain!
In the glory of God the Father,
On the earth He shall reign.

3. He is coming, our Lord and Master,
Our Redeemer and King;
We shall see Him in all His beauty,
And His praise we shall sing.

4. He shall gather His chosen people,
Who are called by His name:
And the ransomed of every nation,
For His own He shall claim.
-Alice Monteith

600

We'll Watch and Wait

1. There's a light that is shining in
darkness,
While we wait for the dawning of
day;
And it cheers us along on our
journey,
Till the shadows shall vanish away'

Chorus
So we'll wait and watch for the
dawning,
The day of eternity blest;
Then take the wings of the morning.
And fly away to our rest.

2. From the sure word the prophets
have spoken,
There is light flashing forth thro' the
gloom;
For the Scripture can never be
broken.
And the King in His glory will come.

3. Now we sing 'mid the darkness and
shadows.
And we pray and we watch for the
dawn;
Till the Daystar, in glory arising,
Shall be token the coming of morn.

4. We are not of the night nor of
darkness.
Let us walk, then, as children of
day;
Our weeping shall be for a moment,
And our Joy shall ne'er vanish away!
-H. L. Hastings

601

When the King shall Come

1. Oh, the weary night is waning,
And the clouds are rolling by;

SECOND COMING OF CHRIST

See, the long expected morning ;
Now is dawning in the sky,
When from Zion's loft mountain
We shall hear the watchmen cry,
And rejoicing we shall gather
When the King shall come.

Chorus
O Zion! O Zion! Great will be thy
triumph
When the King shall come; O Zion!
O Zion! Thou shall be exalted
When the King shall come,

2. When the ransom'd of Jehovah,
From the East and from the West,
Shall return with joy and gladness,
To receive the promised rest
Then shall ev'ry tribe and nation
Out of ev'ry land be bless'd,
And rejoicing they shall gather
When the King shall come.

3. May He find us, when He cometh,
Faithful watchers, day and night,
At our royal post of duty,
With our armour shining bright;
May our tamps be trimm'd and
burning
With a dear and steady light,
That rejoicing we may gather
When the King shall come.
                        -F. J. Crosby

Jesus is coming again!
My heart is so happy, my soul is so
glad,
For Jesus is coining again!

2. The angels, rejoicing and singing
His praise
To Bethlehem shepherds of earlier
days,
Will come in the glory, attending His
train.
When Jesus, my Saviour, is
Coming again!

3. The saints will be with Him, O
happy bliss!
How tearful the parting from faces
we miss!
But clouds are descending, and we
who remain
Are caught up to meet them with
Jesus againt

4. O hearts that are weary, and sinful.
and sad,
We carry the tidings that make us
so glad:
We publish the Saviour o'er
mountain and plain;
The Lord who redeemed us is
coming again!
                        -James M. Gray

602

Jesus is coming

1. The Saviour who loves me and
suffered the loss
Of heavenly glory to die on the
cross,
The Babe of the manger, though
born without stain,
This Jesus is coming, is coming

Chorus
Jesus is coming, is corning, is
Coming!

603

That will be Heaven for me

1. I know not the hour when my Lord
will come
To take me away to His own dear
home,
But I know that His presence will
tighten the gloom,
And that will be glory for me.
And that will be glory for me;
Oh, that will be glory for me;
But I know that His presence will
lighten the gloom,
And that will be glory for me.

SECOND COMING OF CHRIST

know not the song that the angels
sing,
know not the sound of the harps'
glad ring;
But I know there'll be mention of
Jesus our King,
And that will be music for me;
And that will be music for me,
Oh, that will be music for me;
But I know there'll be mention of
Jesus our King.
And that will be music for me.

3. I know not the form of my mansion
fair,
I know not the name that I then
shall bear,
But I know that my Saviour will
welcome me there,
And that will be heaven for me.
And that will be heaven for me;
Oh, that will be heaven for me;
But I know that my Saviour will
welcome me, there,
And that will be heaven for me.
-P. P. Bliss

604

Christ Returneth

1. It may be at mom. when the day is
awaking,
When sunlight thro' darkness and
shadow is breaking,
That Jesus will come in the fullness
of glory,
To receive from the world "His own.

Chorus
O Lord Jesus, how long, how long
Ere we shout the glad song,
Christ returneth! Hallelujah!
hallelujah! Amen,
'Hallelujah! Amen.

2. It may be at mid-day, it may be at
twilight,
It may be. perchance, that the
blackness of mid-night
Will burst into light in the blaze of
His glory.
When Jesus receives "His own,"

3. While its host cry Hasanna, from
heaven descending,
With glorified saints and the
angels attending,
With grace on His brow, like a halo
of glory,
Will Jesus receive "His own."

4. Oh, Joy! Oh, delight! Should we go
without dying,
No sickness, no sadness, no
dread and no crying.
Caught up thro' the clouds with our
Lord into glory,
When Jesus receives "His own."
-H. L. Turner

605

The King is Coming

1. Rejoice! Rejoice! our King is
coming!
And the time will not be long,
Until we hail the radiant dawning,
And lift up the glad new song

Chorus
Oh, wondrous! Oh, glorious king,
When the Son of Man shall come!
May we with temps all trimm'd and
Burning
Gladly welcome His return!
Rejoice! Rejoice! our King is coming!
And the time will not belong,
Until we hail the radiant dawning,
And lift up the glad new song.

2. With joy we wait our King's returning
From His heav'nly mansions fair,
And with ten thousand saints
appearing We shall meet Him in the
air.

3. Oh, may we never weary, watching,
Never lay our armour down,
Until He come, and with rejoicing
Give to each the promised crown.

-Rian A. Dykes

606

Behold, the Bridegroom Cometh - 7.6.D.

1. Our lamps are trimm'd and burning,
Our robes are white and clean,
We've tarried for the Bridegroom,
Oh, may we enter in?
We know we've nothing worthy
That we can call our own:
The light, the oil, the robes we
wear,
All come from Him atone.

Chorus
Behold, the Bridegroom cometh,
And all may enter in
Whose lamps are trimm'd and
burning,
Whose robes are white and clean.

2. Go forth, go forth to meet Him!
The way is open now,
All lighted with the glory
That's streaming from His brow;
Accept the invitation,
Beyond deserving kind;
Make no delay, but take your lamps,
And joy eternal find.

3. We seethe marriage splendour
Within the open door;
We know that those who enter,
Are blest for evermore.

We see He is more lovely
Than all the sons of men,
But still we know the door once
shut,
Will never open again.

-G. F. Rock

607

He will Gather the Wheat

1. When Jesus shall gather the
nations
Before Him at last to appear,
Oh, how shall we stand in the
Judgement,
When summon'd our sentence to
hear?

Chorus
He will gather the wheat in His
garner,
But the chaff will He scatter away:
Then how shall we stand in the
Judgement
Oh, how shall we stand in that
day?

2. Shall we hear from the lips of the
Saviour
The words, "Faithful servant, well
done!"
Or, trembling with fear and with
anguish,
Be banish'd away from His throne?

3. Then let us be watching and
waiting
Our lamps burning steady and bright
That when we are call'd by the
Bridegroom,
We'll answer the call with delight.

4. Thus living with hearts fixed on
Jesus,
In patience we wait for the time
When, the days of our pilgrimage
ended,
Well rest in His presence Divine.

-H. B. M'Keever

SECOND COMING OF CHRIST

608

Jesus to Coming

1. Jesus is coming sing the glad word!
Coming for those He redeem'd by
His blood
Coming to reign as the glorified
Lord!
Jesus is coming again!

Chorus
Jesus is coming, to coming again!
Jesus is coming again! shout the
glad tiding
o'er mountain and plaint Jesus is
Coming again!

2. Jesus is coming and dead shall
arise,
Loved ones shall meet in a joyful
surprise
Caught up together to Him in the
skies
Jesus is coming again!

3. Jesus is coming! His saints to
release;
Coming to give to the warring earth
peace:
Sinning, and sighing, and sorrow,
shall cease,
Jesus is coming!

4. Jesus is coming! the promise is
true;
Who are the chosen, the faithful,
the few,
Waiting and watching, prepared for
review?
Jesus is coming!
-El Nathan

609

Surely I come Quickly - 8.7.

1. In the crimson blush of morning,
In the glitter of the noon,
In the midnight's gloomy darkness,
Or the gleaming of the moon;
In the stillness of the twilight
As it shimmers in the sky
We are watching, we are waiting,
For the end that draweth high.

2. We shall see our Lord in splendour,
And amid a countless throng,
On the clouds to earth descending,
With a movement swift and strong;
And the angels round about Him,
In they dazzling white array,
White before Him sounds the
summons
For the final Judgement day.

3. He with welcome all His people,
He will diadem His own;
He will show to them His glory,
And will share with them His throne;
And forever in His presence
They shall see Him face to face,
While they chant His matchless
wisdom,
And extol His wondrous grace.

4. He is coming, surely coming,
For His promise cannot fail,
And the scoffers shall behold Him,
And before Him they shall quail!
He is coming, quickly coming!
But His coming we shall greet;
We have waited for His evident,
And have listened for His feet.
-W. S. McKenzie

610

What a Gathering

1. On that bright and golden morning
when the Son of Man shall come,
And the radiance of His glory we
shall see;
When from ev'ry clime and nation
He shall call His people home
What a gath'ring of the ransomed
that will be!

Chorus
What a gath'ring! What a gath'ring!
What a gath'ring of the ransomed

SECOND COMING OF CHRIST

In the summer land of love!
What a gath'ring! What a gatn'ring!
Of the ransomed in that happy
home above!

2. When the blest who sleep in Jesus
at His bidding shall arise
From the silence of the grave, and
from the sea;
And with bodies all celestial
they shall meet Him in the skies
What a gath'ring and rejoicing there
will be!

3. When our eyes behold me City,
with its "many mansions' bright
And its river calm and restful,
flowing free
When the friends that death has
parted
shall in bliss again unite
What a gath'ring and a greeting
there will be!

4. Oh, the King is surety coming, and
the time is drawing nigh,
When the blessed day of promise
we shall see;
Then the changing In a moment,"
"in the twinkling of an eye,"
And for ever in His presence we
shall be!

-F. J. Crosby

611

When the King Comes!

1. They come and go, the season fair,
And bring their spoil to vale and hills.
But oh, there is waiting in the air,
And a passionate hope the spirit
Why doth He tarry, the absent Lord?
When shall the Kingdom be restored.
And earth arid heav'n, with one
accord,
Ring out the cry that the King
Comes?

Chorus
What win it be when the King comes!
What will it be when the King comes!
What will ft be when the King comes!
What will it be when the King comes!

2. The floods have lifted upon the voice
The King hath come to His own His
own!
The little hills and vales rejoice,
His right is to take the crown.
Sleepers, awake, and meet Him first
Now let the marriage hymn out burst!
And powers of darkness flee,
disperst
What will it be when the King comes!

3. A ransomed earth breaks forth in
song,
Her sin stained ages over past;
Her yearning, "Lord. How long,?
"Exchanged for Joy at last at test!
Angels, carry the royal commands;
Peace beams forth thro' out all the
lands:
The trees of the field shall clap their
hands
What will it be when the King comes!

4. Now Zion's hill, with glory crowned
Uplifts her head with joy once mom
And Zion's King, once scorned,
disowned,
Extends her rule from shore to shot
Sing, for the land her Lord regain
Sing, for the Son or David reign!
And living streams overflow her
plains
What will it be when the King
comes!

5. O brothers, stand as men that wait
The dawn is purpling in the east
And banners wave from heaven
high gate:

SECOND COMING OF CHRIST

The conflict now but soon the feast
Mercy and truth shall meet again;
Worthy the Lamb that once was
stain;
We can suffer now He will know us
then
What will it be when the King comes!
-E. S. Elliott

612

He lives on high

1. Christine Saviour came from
   heaven's glory,
   To redeem the lost from sin and
   shame;
   On His brow He wore the thorn
   crown glory,
   And upon Calvary He took my
   Blame.

   Chorus
   He lives on high, He lives on high,
   Triumphant over sin and all its stain;
   He lives on high. He lives on high,
   Some day He's coming again.

2. He arose from death and all its
   sorrow,
   To dwell in that land of joy and love;
   He is coming back some glad
   tomorrow,
   And He'll take all His children home
   Above.

3. Weary soul, to Jesus come
   confessing,
   Redemption from sin He offers thee;
   Look to Jesus and receive a
   blessing,
   There is life. there is Joy and victory.
   -B. B. McKinney

613

We'll work till Jesus comes

1. O land of rest, for thee I sight
   When will the moment come
   When I shall lay my armor by.
   And dwell in peace at home?

   Chorus
   We'll work till Jesus comes,
   We'll work till Jesus comes;
   We'll work till Jesus comes,
   And we'll be gathered home.

2. To Jesus Christ I fled for rest;
   He bade me cease to roam,
   And lean for succor on His breast
   Till He conduct me home.

3. I sought at once my Saviour's
   side,
   No more, my steps shall roam;
   With Him I'll brave death's chilling
   tide,
   And reach my heavenly home.
   -Elizabeth Mills

614

Will Jesus find us watching

1. When Jesus comes to reward His
   servants,
   Whether it be noon or night,
   Faithful to Him will He find us
   watching,
   With our lamps an trimmed and
   bright?

   Chorus
   O can we say we are ready,
   brother?
   Ready for the soul's bright home?
   Say, will He find you and me still
   watching,
   Waiting, waiting when the Lord shall
   Come?

2. If, at the dawn of the early morning,
He shall call us one by one,
When to the Lord we restore our
talents.
Will He answer thee Well done?

3. Have we been true to the trust He
left us?
Do we seek to do our best?
If in our hearts there is naught
condemns us,
We shad have a glorious rest

4. Blessed are those whom the Lord
finds watching,
In His glory they shall share;
If He shall come at the dawn or
midnight,
Will He find us watching there?
-Fanny J. Crosby

615

Second coming - Irregular

1. Jesus is coming to earth again
What if it were today?
Coming in power and love to reign
What if it were today?
Coming to claim His chosen Bride.
All the redeemed and purified, .
Over this whole earth scattered wide
What if it were today?

Chorus
Glory, glory! Joy to my heart 'twill
bring:
Glory, glory! When we shall crown
Him King;
Glory, glory! Haste to prepare the
way;
Glory, glory! Jesus Will come
someday.

2. Satan's dominion will then be o'er
O that it were today!
Sorrow and sighing shal be no more
O that it were today!
Then shall the dead in Christ arise,

Caught up to meet Him in
When shall these glories
eyes?
What if it were today?

3. Faithful and true would He find us
here
If He shouldcome today?
Watching in gladness and not
fear,
If He should come today?
Signs of His coming multiply,
Morning light breaks in easter sky
Watch, for the time is drawing high
What if it were today?
-Lella N.Morris

616

Ivory Palaces

1. My Lord has garment; so wondrous
fine,
And myrrh their texture fills;
Its fragrance reached to this heart
of mine,
With joy my being thrills.

Chorus
Out of the ivory palaces,
Into a world of woe,
Only His great, eternal love
Made my Saviour go.

2. His life had also its sorrows sore,
For aloes had a part;
And when I think of the cross He
bore.
My eyes with tear-drops start.

3. His garments too were in cassia
dipped,
With healing in a touch;
Each time my feet in some ah have
sapped.
He took me from its clutch.

SECOND COMING OF CHRIST

4. In garments glorious He will come
To open wide the door,
And shall enter my heav'nly home
To dwell for ever more.
-Henry Barraclough

617

Crowning Day - Irregular

1. Jesus may come-today, Glad day!
Glad day!
And t would see my Friend;
Dangers and troubles would end
If Jesus should come today:

Chorus
Glad day! Glad day! Is it the
crowning day?
I'll live for today, nor anxious be,
Jesus, my Lord, I soon shall see;
Glad day! Glad day! Is it the
crowning day?

2. I may go home today! Glad day!
Glad day! Seemeth I hear their song;
Hail to the radiant throng!
If I should go home today.

3. Why should I anxious be?
Glad day! Glad day!
Lights appear on the shore
Storms will affright never more,
For he is at hand today.

4. Faithful I'll be today, Glad day! Glad
day!
And I will freely tell
Why I should love him so well,
For he is my all today.
-George Walker Whitcomb

618

King is coming - Irregular meter

1. O the King is coming, the King is
coming!
I just heard the trumpets sounding,
And now His face I see;

O the King is coming, the King is
coming!
Praise God, He's coming for met
-Gloria Garther,
Willam J. Gaither
and Charles Millhuff

619

I will sing of the mercies of the Lord

1. I will sing of the mercies of the
Lord forever,
I will sing, I will sing,
I will sing of the mercies of the
Lord forever,
I will sing of the mercies of the Lord.
With my mouth will make known
Thy faithfulness Thy faithfulness.
With my mouth will I make known
Thy faithfulness to all generations.
-J. H. Fillmore

620

He is coming again

1. Lift up your head, pilgrims a weary!
See day's approach now crimson
the sky;
Night shadows flee, and your Beloved,
Awaited with longing, at fast
draweth nigh.

Chorus
He is coming again, He is coming
again
The very same Jesus rejected of men;
He is coming again. He is coming
again,
With pow'r and great glory, He is
coming again!

2. Dark was the night sin warred
against us!
Heavy the toad of sorrow we bore;
But now we see signs of His
coming
Our hearts glow within us, joy's cup
runneth o'er!

SECOND COMING OF CHRIST

3. O blessed hope! O blissful promise!
   Filling our hearts with Capture
   divine;
   O day of days! Hail Thy appearing!
   Thy transcendent glory for ever shall
   shine!

4. Even so, come, precious Lord
   Jesus!
   Creation waits redemption to see;
   Caught in clouds, soon we shall
   meet Thee
   O blessed assurance, for ever with
   Thee!

   -Mabel J. Camp

621

There's A Great Day Coming

1. There's a great day coming, A great
   day coming,
   There's a great day coming by and
   by;
   There's the saints and the sinners
   shall
   be parted right and left.
   are you ready for that day to come?

   Chorus
   Are you ready? Are you ready?
   Are you ready for the judgement
   day?
   Are you ready? Are you ready
   for that judgement day?

2. There's a bright day coming, A
   bright day coming,
   There's a bright day coming by and
   By;
   But it's brightness shall only come
   to them that love the Lord.
   Are you ready for that day to come?

3. There's a sad day coming, A sad
   day coming,
   There's a sad day coming by and by;
   When the sinner shalt hear his
   doom,

"Depart I know ye not,"
Are you ready for that day to coma?

-Will L. Thompsa

622

Southwick -P. M.

1. Thou art coming, O my Saviour,
   Thou art coming, O my King,
   In Thy beauty all-resplendent,
   In Thy glory all-transcendent;
   Well may we rejoice and sing;
   Coming: O the opening east
   Herald brightness slowly swells;
   Coming: O my glorious Priest,
   Hear we not Thy golden bells?

2. Thou art coming, Thou art coming;
   We shall meet Thee on Thy way,
   We shall see Thee, we shall know
   Thee
   We shall bless Thee, we shall shoe
   Thee
   All our hearts could never say;
   What an anthem that will be,
   Music rapturously sweet,
   Pouring out our love to Thee
   At Thine own all-glorious feet.

3. Thou art coming; at Thy table
   We are witnesses for this;
   While remembering hearts Thou
   meetest
   In communion, clearest, sweetest,
   Earnest of our coming bliss,
   Showing not Thy death alone,
   And Thy love exceeding great.
   But Thy coming, and Thy throne,
   All for which we long and wait.

4. Oh the joy to see Thee reigning,
   Thee my own beloved Lord;
   Every tongue Thy name confessing;
   Worship, honour, glory, blessing
   Ought to Thee with one accord,

Thee, my Master and my Friend,
Vindicated and enthroned,
Unto earth's remotest end
Glorified, adored, and own'd.

-Charles Vincent

623

Brant Tor- P. M.

1. The Church has waited long
   Her absent Lord to see;
   And still in loneliness she waits,
   A friendless stranger she.
   Age after age has gone,
   Sun after sun has set;
   And still, other dear Lord benefit,
   Come then, Lord Jesus come.

2. Saint after saint on earth
   Has lived, and loved, and died;
   And as they left us one by one,
   We laid them side by side.
   We laid them down to sleep,
   But not in hope forlorn:
   We laid them but to slumber there
   Till the last glorious morn,
   Come then, Lord Jesus, come.

3. The serpent's brood increase,
   The powers of he grow bold;
   The conflict thickens, faith is low,
   And love is waxing cold.
   How long, O Lord our God.
   Holy, and true, and good,
   Wilt Thou not judge Thy suffering
   church,
   Her sighs, and tears, and blood?
   Come then, Lord Jesus, come.

4. We long to hear Thy voice,
   To see Thee face to face,
   To share Thy crown and glory then
   As now we share Thy grace, Come,
   Lord, and wipe away The curse, the
   sin. the strain;
   And make this blighted world of our
   Thine own fair world again;
   Come then, Lord Jesus, come.

624

Sinai -P. M.

1. The Lord of might from Sinai's brow
   Gave forth His voice of thunder;
   And Isreal lay on earth below
   Out stretch'd in fear and wonder
   Beneath His feet wag pitchy night
   And at His left hand and His right
   The rocks were rent asunder.

2. The Lord of love on Calvary.
   A meek and suffering stranger,
   Upraised to heaven His languid eye
   In nature's hour of danger;
   For us He bore the weight of woe,
   For us He gave His blood to flow.
   And met His Father's anç . ⁻

3. The Lord of love and of might,
   The King of all created,
   Shall back return to claim His right,
   On clouds of glory seated;
   With trumpet-sound, and angel-
   song
   And Hallelujahs loud and long,
   O'er death and hell defeated.

-O'Brien

625

Light- 7.7.8.4.

1. Light, that from the dark abyss
   Madest alt things, none amiss,
   To share Thy beauty, share Thy
   bliss,
   Come to us: come.

2. Light, that dost o'er all things reign,
   Light that dost all life maintain;
   O Light, that dost create again,
   Come to us: come.

3. Light of men, that left the skies,
   Light that look'd through human
   eyes.
   And died in darkness as man dies,

SECOND COMING OF CHRIST

4. Light that stoop'd to rise and raise,
Soar'd to God above our gaze,
And still art with us all the days,
Come to us: come.

5. Light that makest manifest,
Beautifiest, hallowest,
Light in Thy joyous strength at rest,
Come to us: come.

6. Leave us not to say we see,
While we shut our eyes to Thee,
Who knockest very patiently;
Enter to us: come.

7. All our good is Thine alone;
All our evil is our own;
Oh drive it from before Thy throne,
Come to us: come.

8. Works of darkness put away;
With Thy harness us array
To walk in light and wait for day,
And Thee to come.

9. We have done great wrong to Thee,
Yet we do belong to Thee;
Oh make our life one song to Thee.
Come to us: come.

10. Come in all the majesty
Of Thy great humility;
Come, the whole world cries out to
Thee, Come to us: come.
-Charles Vincent

626

Winchester New-LM.

1. On Jordan's bank the Baptist's cry
Announces that the Lord is nigh;
Awake, and hearken, for he brings
Glad tidings of the King of Kings.

2. Then cleansed be every breast from
sin;
Make straight the way for God
within;
Prepare we in our hearts a home,
Where such a mighty guest may
come.

3. For thou art our salvation, Lord.
Our refuge, and our great reward
Without thy grace we waste away
Like flowers that wither and decay

4. To heal the sick stretch out thine
Hand.
And bid the fallen sinner stand;
Shine forth, and let thy light restore
Earth's own true loveliness once
more.

5. All praise, eternal Son, to thee
Whose advent doth thy people free
Whom with the Father we adore
And Holy Ghost for evermore:
-C. Coffin

627

Luther's Hymn-P.M.

1. Great God, what do I see and head
The end of things created!
The Judge of mankind doth
appear,!
On clouds of glory seated.
The trumpet sounds, the graves
restore
The dead which they contain'd
before:
Prepare, my soul. to meet Him.

2. The dead in Christ shall first arise,
At the last trumpet's sounding,
Caught up to meet Him in the skies.
With joy their Lord surrounding:
No gloomy fears their souls dismay;
His presence sheds eternal day
On those prepared to meet Him.

3. But sinners, fill'd with guilty fears.
Behold His wrath prevailing;
For they shall rise, and find their
tears
And sighs are unavailing:
The day of grace is past and gone
Trembling they stand before the
throne
All unprepared to meet Him

SECOND COMING OF CHRIST

4. Grant God, What do I see and hear
The end of things created!
The Judge of mankind doth appear,
On clouds of glory seated.
Low at His cross I view the day
When heaven and earth shall pass away.
And thus prepared to meet Him.

628

O Shout Aloud The Tidings

1. O shout aloud the tidings,
repeat the joyful strain;
Let all the waning nations
This message hear again:
The spotless Lamb of glory
Who once for man was stain,
Soon o'er all the earth shall reign.

Chorus
Looking for that blessed hope,
Looking for that blessed hope;
We know the hour is Hearing,
The hour of His appealing:
We're looking for that blessed hope.

2. Signs in the heav'n above us,
In sun and moon and sky,
Proclaim to all the faithful
Redemption draweth nigh;
The heart of men are quaking
And failing them for fear:
Jesus coming draweth near.

3. We'll watch for His returning
With lamps well trimmed and bright;
He cometh to the careless
As thieves break through at night;
"Well done. thou good and faithful"
O may we hear the word.
"Share the joy of Christ thy Lord."

629

Rejoice, All Ye Believers - 7.6.7.6.D.

1. Rejoice, all ye believers,
And let your lights appear;
The evening is advancing.
And darter night is near,
The Bridegroom is arising,
And soon He draweth nigh;
Up, pray, and watch, and wrestle,
At midnight comes the cry.

2. See that your lamps are burning,
Replenish them with oil, And wait
for your salvation,
The end of earthly toil.
The watches on the mount in
proclaim the Bridegroom near.
Go, meet Him as He comem
With Hallelujah clear.

3. Ye wise and holy virgins,
Now raise your voices higher,
Until in songs triumphant
They meet the Angel choir,
The marriage-feast is waiting,
The gates wide open stand:
Up! up! ye heirs of glory,
The Bridegroom is at hand!

4. Ye saints, who here in patience
Your cross and suffering bore,
Shall live and reign for ever,
When sorrow is no more,
Around the Throne of glory,
The Lamb ye shall behold.
In triumph cast before Him
Your diadems of gold.

SECOND COMING OF CHRIST

630

Rejoice, Ye Saints, The Time Draw Near

1. Rejoice, ye saints, the time draws
near
When Christ will in the cloud appear,
And for His people call,

Chorus
Trim your lamps and be ready.
Trim your lamps and be ready.
Trim your tamps, and be ready for
the midnight cry,
For the midnight cry, for the
midnight cry
Trim your lamps and be ready lord
the midnight cry.

2. The Trumpet sounds, the thunder
roll;
The heavens passing as a scroll.
The earth will bum with fire.

3. Poor sinners then on earth will cry.
White lightnings flash from the sky,
"O mountains, on us fall!"

4. Come brethren all, and let us try
To warn poor sinner, and to cry.
'Behold, the Bridegroom come!

631

Saviour, Long Thy Saints Have Waited-8.7.8.7.D.

1. Saviour, long Thy saints have
Waited
Centuries have passed away
Since the promise first was
given
Of a glorious Advent day
Grey and old the world is
growing.
Loud the scoffer's boast is heard:
But our hearts are peaceful.
Knowing
We may rest upon Thy word.

Chorus
Surely I come quickly! Surely
Surely I come quickly! Surely
Surely I come quickly! Surely
Amen, Lord Jesus, come

2. Lo; the fig-tree buds and
blossoms;
Lo! the shadows flee away;
Glad we lift our heads expectant
Brief will now be Thy delay.
Thou to raise the dead art able,
O'er the grave Thou didst prevail
Heav'n and earth may prove
unstable.
But Thy word can never fail.

3. Precious, precious parting
promise!
Sweetly linger in our ears;
Brightly gleam amid our darkness.
Gently soothe away our fears:
Ever nerve us for the conflict.
Ever fill our souls with joy;
Christ will come and will not tarry
Nothing can our hope destroy.

632

Soon Will Our Saviour From Heaven Appear - 10.10.10.10.with Ref.

1. Soon will our Saviour from heaven
appear.
Sweet is the hope and His power
to cheer;
All will be changed by a glimpse of
His face
This is the goal at the end of our
race.

SECOND COMING OF CHRIST

Chorus
Oh, what a change Oh, what a change
When I shall see His wonderful face
Oh, what a change! Oh, what a change
When I shall see His face!

2. Loneliness changed to reunion complete.
Absence exchanged for a place at His feet,
Sleeping ones raised in a moment of time.
Living one Changed to His image subtime

3. Sunrise we chase att the darkness away.
Night will be changed to the brightness of day
Tempests will be changed to ineffable calm.
Weeping will change to a jubilant psalm.

4. Weakness Will change to magnificent strength.
Failure will change to perfection at length.
Sorrow Will be change to unending delight.
Walking by faith change to walking by sight

633

The Lord Coming The World Will Quake -L. M.

1. The Lord is coming the world will quake.
And every mountain shall be moved,
And all the stars of heaven too.
Shall cease to shine nor give their light

2. The Lord is coming unlike before
When He come in humility
When He was stain as Lamb of God.
Our suffering Saviour who has died.

3. The Lord is coming, doth come in fear.
In flaming fire and in great wrath;
Coming, on cherub wings doth fly,
Coming the Great Judge of the earth.

4. Is this the one who walked on earth,
Just like s pilgrim on life's road
Was persecuted and oppressed.
Is this the one. He that was slain.

5. The wicked hid themselves in vain.
Hid in the rocks and in the dens:
But faith that has the victory.
Shall sing at last, the Lord has come."

634

We Are Just Upon The Dawning

1. We are just upon the dawning
Of that bright and glorious morning,
When the Bridegroom comes to can away His bride;
We'll be then caught up to meet Him.
Allalelujah, what a greeting,
When the Bridegroom comes, and we'll with Him abide.

Chorus
Then wen shout Hallelujah and sing allalujah.
Glory, Hallelujah to our Lord.
We will bow down before Him,
worship and adore Him.
King of kings and Lord of lords.

FAITH

2. Get your lamps all trimmed and
burning.
For the Bridegroom is returning.
And the cry, go forth to meet Him,
soon will come
Be ye wise, make haste to meet Him
With your lamps lit, soon to greet Him,
As He comes in clouds descending
for His own.

3. At the mill two will be grinding,
In field, two binding,
When the bridegroom comes to catch
away
Only one then will betaken.
And the other one forsaken,
Watch, ye know not what the hour
your Lord comes.

635
When The Trump Of the Great Archangel

1, When the trump of the great
archangel
It mighty tones shall sound
And, the end of the world
Proclaiming,
Shall pierce the depths profound;
When the Son of Man shall come in
His glory.
With all the saints on high.
What a shouting in the skies from
the multitudes that rise
Changed in the twinkling of an eye.

Chorus
Changed in the twinkling of an eye,
Changed in the twinkling of an eye;
The trumpet shall sound, the dead
shall be raised,
Changed in the twinkling of an eye.

2. When He come in the clouds
descending,
And they who loved Him here
From their graves shall awake and
praise Him
With Joy and not with fear;
When the body and the soul are
united,
And clothed no more to die,
What a shouting there will be
When each other's face we see.
Changed in the twinkling of an eye

2. Oh the seed that was sown in
weakness
Shall then be raised in power,
And the songs of the blood-bought
Millions
Shall hail that blissful hour;
When we gather safely home in the
morning,
And night's dark shadows fly.
What a shouting on the shore
When we meet to part no more.

FAITH

636

Venting -11.11.11.10. With Refrain

1. Like radiant sunshine that comes
   after rain,
   Like beautiful rest after sorrow and
   pain,
   Like hope that is kindled returning
   again
   Is the wonderful peace of my
   Saviour.

Chorus
Wonderful peace, beautiful peace,
Wonderful peace of my Saviour;
There's nothing on earth can such
gladness impart
As this wonderful peace of my
Saviour.

2. So soft and refreshing, as sweet as
   the dew,
   A promise that cannot be broken to
   you;
   A light that will shine all the long
   Journey thro
   Is the wonderful peace of my
   Saviour.

3. It brightens earth's darkness and
   banishes care
   And helps you to carry the burdens
   you bear;
   A refuge in trouble, your sorrows to
   share.
   Is the wonderful peace of my
   Saviour.

4. A guardian in danger where evil is
   rife,
   A mighty defender in conflict and
   strife,
   A beautiful guide to that heavenly
   life
   Is the wonderful peace of my
   Saviour.

   -Alfred Barratt

637

Ombersley- L.M.

1. O walk with Jesus, would'st thou
   know
   How deep, how wide His taw can
   flow
   They only fad His love to prove
   Who in the ways of sinners rove.

2. Walk thou with Him; that way is light,
   All other pathways end in night:
   Walk thou with Him, that way is rest.
   All other pathways are unblest.

3. O walk with Jesus! to thy view
   He will make all things sweet and
   new;
   Will bring new fragrance from each
   flower,
   And hallow every passing hour.

4. Jesus, a great desire have we
   To walk life's troubled path with
   Thee:
   Come to us now, in converse stay;
   And O! walk with us day by day.
   -Edwin Paxton Hood

638

Shipston -8.7.8.7.

1. God the Father of creation,
   master of the realms sublime,
   Lord of light and life's foundation:
   we believe and trust in him.

2. Christ who came from highest
   heaven,
   God from God before all time,
   Son for our redemption given:
   we believe and trust in him.

3. Spirit, God in us residing,
   power of life and love supreme,
   Intercessor pleading, guiding:
   We believe and trust in him.

FAITH

4. Trinity of adoration!
earth responds to heaven's theme;
one the church's acclamation:
we believe and trust in him!
Michael Perry

639

Halton Holgate 8.7.8.7.

1. Firmly I believe and truly
God is Three and God is One;
And I next acknowledge duly
manhood taken by the Son.

2. And I trust and hope most fully
in that manhood crucified;
and each thought and deed unruly
do to death, for he has died.

3. Simply to his grace and wholly
light and life and strength belong;
and I love supremely, solely,
Christ the holy, Christ the strong.

4. And I make this affirmation for
the love of Christ alone:
holy Church is his creation
and his teachings are her own.

5. Honour, glory, power, and merit
to the God of earth and heaven,
Father, Son, and Holy Spirit
praise for evermore be given!
-Shipston

640

St Ethelwald -6.6.8.6.S.M.

1. Have faith in God, my heart,
trust and be un afraid;
God will fulfil in everypart
each promise he has made.

2. Have faith in God, my mind,
although your light bums low;
God's mercy holds a wiser plan
than you can fully know.

3. Have faith in God, my soul,
his cross for ever stands;
and neither life nor death can pluck
his children from his hands.

4. Lord Jesus, make me whole;
grant me no resting place,
until I rest, heart, mind, and soul
the captive of your grace.
-Bryn Rees

641

All for Jesus 8.7.8.7.

1. I believe in God the Father
who created heaven and earth,
holding all things in his power,
bringing light and life to birth.

2. I believe in God the Saviour,
Son of Man and Lord most high,
crucified to be redeemer.
raised to life that death may die.

3. I believe in God the Spirit,
wind of heaven and flame of fire
pledge of all that we inherit,
sent to comfort and inspire.

4. Honour, glory, might and merit
be to God, and God alone!
Father, Son and Holy Spirit,
One-in-Three.
-Michael

642

Creator God 8.6.8.6 (CM.)

1. Safe in the shadow of the Lord,
beneath his hand and power,
I trust in him, I trust in him,
my fortress and my tower.

2. My hope is set on God alone
though Satan spreads his snare
I trust in him, I trust in him,
to keep me in his care.

3 From fears and phantoms of the night,
from foes about my way,
I trust in him, I trust in him,
By darkness as by day.

4. His holy angels keep my feet
secure from every stone;

FAITH

I trust in him, I trust in him,
unafraid go on.

5. Strong in the everlasting name,
and in my Father's care,
trust in him, t trust in him,
who hears and answer prayer.

6. Safe in the shadow of the Lord,
possessed by love divine,
I trust in him, I trust in him,
and meet his love with mine.
                    -Timothy Dudley- Smith.

643

O For A Faith That Will Not Shrink

1. O for a faith that will not shrink,
Tho 'pressed by ev'ry foe,
That will not tremble on the brink
Of any earthly woe.

2. That will not murmur or complain
Beneath the chast'ning rod,
But in the hour of grief or pain,
Will lean upon its God,

3. A faith that shines more bright and
clear .
When tempests rage without;
That when in danger knows no fear,
In darkness feels no doubt!

4. Lord, give us such a faith as this;
And then, whate'er may come,
We'll taste e'en here the hallowed
bliss
Of an eternal home.
                    -W. H. Bathurst

644

Living By Faith

1. care not today what the morrow
may bring,
If shadow or sunshine or rain,
The Lord I know ruleth o'er every
thing,
And all of my worry is vain.

Chorus
Living by faith, in Jesus above,
Trusting, confiding in His great love;
From all harm safe in His sheltering
arm
I'm living by faith aid feel no alarm.

2. Tho' tempests may blow and the
storm clouds arise,
Obscuring the brightness of life,
I'm never alarmed at the overcast
skies,
The Master looks on at the Strife.

3. I know that He safety will carry me
thru,
No matter what evils betide,
Why should I then care tho" the
tempest may blow,
If Jesus walks close to my side.

4. Our Lord will return in the clouds
some sweet day,
Our troubles will then all be o'er.
The Master so gently will lead us
away,
Beyond the blest heavenly shore.
                    -James Wells

645

I'll Live On

1. 'Tis a sweet and glorious tho't that
comes to me, I'll live on;
yes. I'll live on;
Jesus saved my soul from death
and now I'm free,
I'll live on, yes, I'll live on.

Chorus
I'll live on, yes,I 'll will live on,
Thro eternity I'll live on,
I'll live on
Thru eternity I'll live on.

2. When my body's lying in the cold,
cold clay,
I'll live on, yes, I'll live on;
I will meet my Jesus in the
judgement day,
I'll live on, yes, I'll live on.

FAITH

3. When the world's on fire and
darkness veils the sun,
I'll live on , yes, I'll live on;
Men will cry and to the rocks and
mountains run,
I'll live on, yes, I'll live on.

4. In the glory land, with God upon the
throne,
I'll live on, yes, I'll live on;
Thru eternal ages singing, home,
sweet home,
I'll live on, yes, I'll live on.
                                    -Thos. J.Laney

646

Hold To God's Unchanging Hand

1. Time is filled with swift transition,
Naught of earth unmoved can stand
Build your hopes on things eternal,
Hold to God's unchanging hand.

Chorus
Hold to God's unchanging hand!
Hold to God's unchanging hand!
Build your hopes on things eternal,
Hold to God's unchanging hand.

2. Trust in Him who will not leave you,
Whatsoever years may bring,
If earthly friends forsaken,
Still more closely to Him cling.

3. When your journey is completed,
If to God you have been true,
Fair and bright the home in glory
Your enraptured soul will view.
                                    -Jennie Wilson

647

He Knoweth The Way That I Take

1. I have a friend who is ever nigh,
Whether I sleep or wake;
Ever he guards with a watchful eye,
He knoweth the way that I take.

Chorus
He knoweth the way that I take,
And keeps me when asleep or
awake;
And leads me in his own name's
sake,
He knoweth the way that I take.

2. I have a friend who is always near
One who will ne'er forsake;
What tho' my pathway be dark and
drear,
He knoweth the way that I take.

3. I have a friend who will guide me
Until the shadows break;
Leading me in, till my crown is won;
He knoweth the way that I take.
                                    -Mrs Maud Hulit

648

Onward GO

1. Trusting in the Lord thy God.
Onward go!
Holding fast His promised word,
Onward go!
Ne'ver deny His worthy name,
Tho' it bring reproach and shame,
Spreading still His wondrous fame
Onward go!

2. Has He call 'd thee to the plough?
Onward go!
Night is coming, serve Him now
Onward go!
Faith and love in service blend
On His mighty arm depend:
Standing fast until the end.
Onward go!

3. Has He given thee; golden grain?
Onward go!
Sow, and thou shall reap again;
Onward go!
To thy Master's gate repair,

O

FAITH

Watching be and waiting there:
He will hear and answer prayer;
Onward go!

4. Has He said the end is near?
Onward go'
Serving Him with holy fear,
Onward got
Christ thy patron, Christ thy stay,
Heavenly bread upon the way;
Onward got

5. In this little moment then.
Onward go!
In thy ways acknowledge Him;
Onward go?
Let His mind be found in thee;
Let His will thy pleasure be;
Thus in life and liberty, Onward go!
—James McGranaha

649

Abiding

1. Abiding, oh, so wondrous sweet!
I'm resting at the Saviour's feet,
I trust in Him, I'm satisfied,, I'm
resting in the Crucified!

Chorus
Abiding, abiding,
Oh, so wondrous sweet!
I'm resting, resting
At the Saviour's feet.

2. He speaks, and by His word is giv'n
His peace, a rich foretaste of
heav'n!
Not as the world He peace doth
give,
"Tis thro' this hope my soul shall
live.

3. I live; not I; through Him alone
By Whom the mighty work is done,
Dead to myself, alive to Him,
I count all loss His rest to gain.

4. Now rest, my heart, the work is
done,
I'm saved through the Eternal Son!
Let all my powers my soul employ,
To tell the world my peace and joy.
—Chas. B. J. Root

650

Lowry

1. Down in the valley with my saviour
I would go,
Where the flowers are blooming
and the sweet waters flow;
Everywhere He leads me I would
follow, follow on,
Walking in His footsteps till the
crown be won.

Chorus
Follow! follow! I would follow Jesus!
Anywhere, everywhere, I would
follow on!
Follow! follow! I would follow Jesus!
Everywhere He leads me I would
follow on!

2. Down in the valley with my Saviour
I would go,
Where the storms are Sweeping
and the dark waters flow;
With His hand to lead me I will
never, never fear,
Danger cannot fright me if my Lord
is near.

3. Down in the valley, or upon the
mountain steep,
Close beside my Saviour would my
soul ever keep:
He will lead me safely, in the Path
that He has trod,
Up to where they gather on the hills
of God.
—W.O. Gushing

FAITH

651

Stella-8.8.8.8.8.8.

1. All things are possible to him
That can in Jesu's name believe;
Lord, I no more Thy name blas
pheme,
Thy truth I loving receive.
I can, I do believe in Thee;
All things are possible to me.

2. Twas most impossible of all
That here sin's reign in me should
cease;
Yet shall it be, I know it shall;
Jesus I trust Thy faithfulness!
If nothing is too hard for Thee,
All things are possible to me.

3. Though earth and hell the Word
gainsay,
The Word of God shall never fail;
The Lord can break sin's iron sway;
'Tis certain, though impossible.
The thing impossible shall be,
All things are possible to me.

4. All things are possible to God;
To Christ, the power of God in man
To me when I am all renewed,
In Christ am fully formed again.
And from the reign of sin set free,
All things are possible to me.

5. All things are possible to God;
To Christ, the power of God in me;
Now shed Thy mighty Self abroad,
Let me no longer live. but Thee;
Give me this hour in Thee to prove
The sweet omnipotence of love.
                              -C. Wesley

652

More Abundantly

1. Are you trusting Jesus, All along
the way?
Does He grow nore precious To
your heart each day?
Are you His disciple? Test His word
And see,

He will give the Spirit More abun
dantly.

Chorus
More abundantly, more abundantly
That they might have life,
abundantly,"
More abundantly, more abundantly
That they might have life, and more
abundantly"

2. For His matchless favour Magnify
the name
Of our gracious Saviour glory
came;
Let the saints adore Him wondrous
word,
Sealing our redemption thro' the
crimson flood.

3. Come to Him believing, Hark to His
call'
All from Him receiving, Yield to Him
your all;
Jesus will accept you When you
flee;
He will grant His blessing more
abundantly.
                              -Thoro Harris

653

Woolwich -S. M.

1. Away, my needless fear
And doubts no longer mine;
A ray of heav'nly light appears,
A messenger divine.

2. Thrice comfortable hope
That calms my troubled breast
My Father's hand prepares the cup;
And what He wills is best.

3. If what I wish is good,
And suits the will divine
By earth and hell in vain
I know it shall be mine

4. Still let them counsel take
To frustrate His decree
They cannot keep a blessing back
By heaven designed for

5. Here then I doubt no more,
But in His pleasure rest,
Whose wisdom, love, and truth.
and power
Engage to mate me blest .

6. To accomplish His design
The creatures all agree;
And all the attributes divine
Are now at work for me.
-C. Wesley

654
Montgomery -10.10.11.11.

1. Begone, unbelief; My Saviour is
near,
And for my relief will surely appear:
By prayer let me wrestle, and He
will perform;
With Christ in the vessel, I smile at
the storm.

2. Though dark be my way, since He
is my Guide,
Tis mine to obey, 'tis His to provide;
Though cisterns be broken and
creatures all fail,
The word He hath spoken shall
surely prevail.

3. His love in time past forbids me to
Think
He'll leave me at last in trouble to
sink;
While each Ebenezer I have in
Review
Confirms His good pleasure to help
me quite through.

4. Why should I complain of want or
Distress.
Temptation or pain? He told me no
less;
The heirs of salvation, I know from
His word.
Through much tribulation must
follow their Lord.

5. Since all that I meet shall work for
My good,
The bitter is sweet, the medicine
Food;

Though painful at present, 'twill
cease before long;
And then, O how pleasant the
conqueror's song!
-John Newton

655
Melita-8.8.8.8.8.8.

1. Eternal Father, strong to save,
Whose arm hath bound the
restless wave,
Who bidd'st the might ocean deep
Its own appointed limits keep;
O hear is when we cry to Thee
For those in peril on the sea.

2. O Christ, Whose voice the waters
heard,
And hushed their raging at Thy
word,
Who walkedst on the foaming
deep.
And calm amid the storm didst
sleep;
O hear us when we cry to Thee
For those in peril on the sea.

3. O Holy Spirit, Who did'st brood
Upon the waters dark and rude,
And bid their angry tumult cease,
And give, for wild confusion,
peace;
O hear us when we cry to Thee
For those in peril on the sea.

4. O Trinity of love and power.
Our brethren shield in danger's
hour;
From rock and tempest, fire and
foe,
Protect them, wheresoe'er they
go;
Thus evermore shall rise to Thee
Glad hymns of praise from land and
-William Whiting

656
Only in Thee
1. Only in Thee, O Saviour mine.
Dwelleth my soul m peace divine
Peace that the world, thro' all
Combine,
Never can take from me!

FAITH

Pleasures of earth, so seemingly
sweet,
Fait at the last my longings to meet;
Only in Thee my bliss is complete,
Only, dear Lord, in Thee!

2. Only in Thee a radiance bright
Shines like a beacon in the night,
Guiding my pilgrim barque aright
Over life's trackles sea!
Only in Thee, when troubles molest,
When with temptation I am op
pressed,
There is a sweet pavilion of rest,
Only, dear Lord, in Thee!

3. Only in Thee, when days are drear,
When neither sun nor stars appear
Still I can trust and feel no fear,
Sing when I cannot see!
Only in Thee, whatever betide,
All of my need Is freely supplied:
There is no hope or helper beside,
Only, dear Lord, in Thee!

4. Only in Thee. dear Saviour slain.
Losing Thy life my own to gain;
Trusting I'm cleansed from every
stain
Thou art my only plea!
Only in Thee my heart will delight.
Till in that land where cometh no
night,
Faith will be lost in heavenly sight
Only, dear Lord, in Thee!
-T. O. Chisholm

657

Nativity -C. M.

1. Father of Jesus Christ, my Lord,
My Saviour, and my Head,
I trust in Thee, whose pow'r word
hath rais'd Him from the dead.

2. Eternal life to all mankind
Thou hast in Jesus given;
And all who seek, in Him shall find
The happiness of heaven,

3. Faith in Thy power Thou seest I
have
For Thou this faith hast wrought;

Dead souls Thou callest from their
grave,
And seekest worlds from nought.

4. In hope, against all human hope,
Self-desperate, I believe;
Thy quickening word shall raise me
Up Thou shall Thy Spirit give.

5. The thing surpasses all my thought,
But faithful is my Lord;
Through unbel'ef I stagger hot
For God hath spoke the word.

6. Faith, mighty faith, the promise
sees,
And looks to that alone;
Laughs at impossibilities,
And cries: It shall be done!
-C. Wesley

658

Lloyd-C.M.

1. I worship Thee, sweet Will of God!
And all Thy ways adore;
And every day I live, I long To love
Thee more and more.

2. I have no cares, O blessed Will!
For all my cares are Thine;
I live in triumph, Lord! for Thou
Hast made Thy triumphs mine.

3. Ride on, ride on triumphantly,
Thou glorious Will, ride on!
Faith's pilgrim sons behind Thee
take
The road that Thou hast gone.

4. He always wins who sides with
God,
To him no chance is lost;
God's Will is sweetest to him when
It triumphs at his cost.

5. Ill that He blesses is our good;
And unblest good is ill;
And all is right that seems most
wrong,
If it be His sweet Will!
-F. W. Faber

FAITH

659

Firm are the Promises Standing

1. Firm are the promises standing,
   can they ever fail.
   Sealed with the blood of our Jesus
   They must, they shall avail!

   chorus
   Heaven and earth may perish,
   Mountain and hill may vanish;
   A stands the Word we cherish,
   Ever to faith made sure.

2. Follow in Abraham's footsteps,
   Turn to the heav'ns your eyes;
   Counting the stars without number,
   Your faith, your hope will rise.

3. Trust, though the darkness be
   Falling
   Soon will the sun arise,
   Shedding bright beams in the
   morning
   O'er earth and sea and skies.

4. Trust, though the world may beset
   you;
   Faith has no dread or fear
   Lo in the fiery furnace
   The Son of God draws near!

5. Trust, though your friends disap
   Joint you,
   Leaving you one by one;
   Jesus, true Friend, will stand by
   you
   Till pilgrim days are done.

6. Trust Him, whatever betide you;
   Soon in the mansions bright
   All will be clear as the noonday:
   Faith turned to glorious sight!
                        -Lewi Pethrus

660

God holds the Key - 8.4.8.8.4.

1. God holds the key of all unknown,
   And I am glad:
   If other hands should hold the key,

Or if He trusted it to me,
I might be sad,

2. What if tomorrow's cares were here
   Without its rest?
   I'd rather He unlocked the day,
   And, as the hours swing open. say,
   "My will is best."

3. The very dimness of my sight
   Makes me secure:
   For, groping in my misty way,
   I feel His hand; I hear Him say,
   "My help is sure."

4. I cannot read His future plans;
   But this I know:
   I have the smiling of His face,
   And all the refuge of His grace,
   While here below.

5. Enough, this covers all my wants;
   And so I rest!
   For what I cannot, He can see.
   And in His care I saved shall be,
   For ever blest.
                        -J. Parker

661

I've Anchored In Jesus

1. Upon life's boundless ocean where
   mighty billows roll,
   I've fixed my hope in Jesus, blest
   anchor of my soul;
   When trials fierce assail me as
   storms are gath'ring o'er,
   I rest upon His mercy and trust Him
   More.

   Chorus
   I've anchored in Jesus, the storms
   of life I'll brave,
   I've anchor'd in Jesus, Hear no
   wind or wave,
   I've anchored in Jesus for He hath
   Pow'r to save,
   I've anchored to the Rock of Ages.

FAITH

2. He keeps my soul from evil and
gives me blessed peace, His voice
hath stilled the waters and bid their
tumult cease;
My Pilot and Deliverer, to Him I all
confide,
For always when I need Him, He's
at my side.

3. He is my Friend and Saviour, in Him
my anchor's cast,
He drives away my sorrows and
shields me from the blast;
By faith I'm looking upward beyond
life's troubled sea,
There I behold a haven prepared
for me.

-L. E. Jones

662

Yesterday, Today, Forever

1. O, how sweet the glorious
message, Simple faith may claim;
Yesterday, today, forever,
Jesus is the same.
Still He loves to save the sinful,
Heal the sick and lame;
Cheer the mourner, still the
tempest,
Glory to His name!

Chorus
Yesterday, today, forever, Jesus is
the same.
All may change, but Jesus never!
Glory to His name,
Glory to His name. Glory to His
Name,
All may change, but Jesus never!
Glory to His name.

2. He who was the Friend of Sinners,
Seeks thee, lost one, now;
Sinner, come, and at
His footstool. Penitently bow.
He who said, I'll not condemn thee,
Go, and sin no more,"

Speaks to thee that word of
pardon
As in days of yore.

3. Him who pardoned erring Peter,
Never need's thou fear;
He that came to faithless Thomas,
All thy doubt will dear.
He who let the loved disciple
On His bosom rest,
Bids thee still, with love as tender.
Lean upon His breast.

4. He who 'mid the raging billows,
Walk'd upon the sea;
Still can hush our wildest tempest.
As on Galilee.
He who wept and prayed
In anguish in Gethsemane,
Drinks with us each cup of trem
bling,
In our agony.

5. As of old He walk'd to Emmaus,
With them to abide, So thro' all
life's way He walketh,
Ever near our side.
Soon again shall we behold Him,
Hasten, Lord, the day!
But twill still be "this same Jesus,'
As He went away.

-A. B. Simpson

663

Hymn us Eucharisticus - L.M.

1. O love of God, how strong and
true Eternal, and yet ever new,
Uncomprehended and unbought,
Beyond all knowledge and all
thought!

2. O heavenly love, how precious still
In days of weariness and ill,
nights of pain and helplessness,
To heal, to comfort, and to bless!

3. O wide embracing, wondrous love
We read thee in the sky above;

FAITH

We read thee in the earth below,
In seas that swell and streams that
Flow.

4. We read thee in the flowers, the
trees,
The freshness of the fragrant
breeze,
The songs of birds upon the wing,
The joy of summer and of spring.
We read thee best in him who
came
And bore for us the cross of
shame.
Sent by the Father from on high,
Our life to live, our death to die.

5. O love of God, our shield and stay
Through all the perils of our way;
Eternal love. in thee we rest,
For ever safe. for ever blest.
                                    -H .Bonar

664
It's Just Like His Great Love

1. A Friend I have called Jesus.
Whose love is strong and true,
And never fails howe'er 'tis tried,
No matter what I do;
I've sinned against this love of His,
But when I knelt to pray,
Confessing all my guilt to Him.
The sin clouds rolled away.

Chorus
it's Just like Jesus to roll the clouds
away,
It's Just like Jesus to keep me day
by day,
it's just like Jesus all long the way,
Il's just like His great love.
Sometimes the clouds of trouble
Be dim the sky above,

I doubt His wondrous love.,
But He, from Heaven's mercyseat,
Beholding my despair,
In pity bursts the clouds between,
And shows me He is there.

3. When sorrow's clouds o'er take me,
And break upon my head,
When life seems worse than
useless,
And I were better dead;
I take my grief to Jesus then,
Nor do I go in vain,
For heav'nly hope He gives that
cheers
Like sunshine after rain.
                            -Edna R. Worrell

665
S. Petersburg - L. M.

1. Awake, our souls, away, our fears!
Let every trembling thought be
gone!
Awake, and run the heavenly
race,
And put a cheerful courage on.

2. True, 'tis a strait and thorny road,
And mortal spirits tire and faint;
But they forget the mighty God
That feeds the strength of every
saint.

3. O mighty God, thy matchless
power
Is ever new and ever young,
And firm endures, while endless
years
Their everlasting circles run.

4. From thee. the ever-flowing spring,
Our souls shall drink a fresh supply;
While such as trust their native
strength
Shall melt away and droop and die

FAITH

Swift as the eagle cuts the air,
We'll mount aloft to thine abode;
On wings of love our souls shall fly.
Nor tire along the heavenly road
-Isaac Watts

666

I Am Determined To Hold Out

1. When I first found Jesus something
o'er me stole,
Like lighting it went through me,
and glory fitted my soul;
Salvation made me happy and took
my fears away,
And when I meet old Satan to him
I always say;

Chorus
"I am determined to hold out to the
end,
Jesus is with me, on 'Him I can
depend,
And I know I have' salvation,
for I feel it in my soul,
I am determined to hold out to the
end."

2. Satan, He was angry, said he'd
soon be back.
Just let the path get narrow, and He
will lose the track;
But I'm so full of glory, my Lord I
always find,
And I just say to Satan. "Old man,
get thee behind."

3. This old time religion makes me
sometimes shout,
I don't have time to gossip nor any
time to pout;
They say that I'm too noisy, but
when these blessings flow,
I shout, O hallelujah, I want the
world to know,

4. When I hear the trumpet sounding
in the sky,
And see the mountain trembling,
to heaven
I will fly
For Jesus will be calling, there'll
be no time to mend,
With joy I'll go up singing, "I've held
out to the end."
-C. S. And T. P. Hamilton

667

Crowle -C. M.

1. O thou in all thy might so far,
In all thy love so near,
Beyond the range of sun and star
And yet beside us here:

2. What heart can comprehend thy
name,
Or searching find thee out?
Who art within, a quickening flame,
A presence round about.

3. More dear than all the things I
know
Is childlike faith to me,
That makes the darkest way I go
And open path to thee.

4. Yet though I know thee but in part, I
ask not, Lord, for more;
Enough for me to know thou art,
To love thee, and adore.
-Frederick Lucian Hosmer

668

I Know That My Redeemer Liveth

1. I know that my Redeemer liveth,
And on the earth again shall stand;
I know eternal life He giveth,
That grace and power are in His
hand.

Chorus
I know, I know that Jesus liveth,
And on the earth again shad stand:

FAITH

I Know, I knew that life He giveth,
that grace and power are in His
Hand.

2. I know His promise never faileth,
he word He speaks, it cannot die;
Thro' cruel death my flesh as saiteth,
yet I shall see Him by and by.

3. I know my mansion He prepareth.
That where He is there I may be;
wondrous tho't, for me He careth.
And He at last will come for me.
-Jessie Brown Pounds

669
Our times are in Thy hand

1. Our times are in Thy hand:"
Father, we wish them there;
Our life, our soul, our all,
We leave entirely to Thy care.

2. Our times are in Thy hand."
Whatever they may be;
Pleasing or painful, dark or bright,
As best may seem to Thee.

3. Our times are in Thy hand;"
Why should we doubt or fear?
Our Father's hand will never cause
His child a needless tear.

4. "Our times are in Thy hand,"
Jesus, the crucified!
The hand our cruel sins had
pierced.
Is now our guard and guide.
-W. F. Floyd

670
Safe in the arms of Jesus

1. Safe in the arms of Jesus,
Safe on His gentle breast, "here by
His love O'er shaded.

Sweetly my soul shall rest.
Hark! tis the voice of angels.
Borne m a song to me,
Over the fields of glory,
Over tie jasper sea.

Chorus
Safe in the arms of Jesus,
Safe on His gentle breast.
There by His love o'er shaded.
Sweetly my soul shall rest.

2. Safe in the arms of Jesus.
Safe from corroding care,
Safe from the world's temptations,
Sin cannot hamune there.'
Free from the Might of sorrow,
Free from my doubts and fears;
Only a few more trials,
Only a few more tears!

3. Jesus, my heart's dear refuge,
Jesus has died for me;
Firm on the Rock of Ages.
Ever my trust shall be.
Here let me wait with patience,
Wait till the night is o'er,
Wait till I see the morning
Break on the golden shore.
-Fanny J. Crosby

671
Sturges -C. M.

1. Christ leads me through no darker
rooms
Than he went through before;
And he that to God's kingdom
comes
Must enter by this door.

2. Come, Lord, when grace hath made
me meet
Thy blessed face to see:
For if thy work on earth be sweet,
What will thy glory be?

FAITH

3. My knowledge of that life is small.
   The eye of faith is dim;
   But 'tis enough that Christ knows all,
   And I shall be with him.
   -Richard Baxter

672

Passion Chorale - 7.6.7.6.D.

1. Commit thou all that grieves thee
   And fills thy heart with care
   To him whose faithful mercy
   The skies above declare,
   Who gives the winds their course!
   Who points the clouds their way;
   Tis he will guide thy footsteps
   And be thy staff and stay.

2. O trust the Lord then wholly,
   If thou' would'st be secure;
   His work must thou consider
   For thy work to endure.
   What profit doth it bring there
   To pine in grief and care?
   God only ends his blessing
   In answer to thy prayer.

3. Thy lasting truth and mercy.
   O Father, see aright
   The needs of all thy children,
   Their anguish or delight:
   What loving wisdom chooseth.
   Redeeming might will do,
   And bring to sure fulfilment
   Thy counsel good and true.

4. Hope on, then broken spirit.
   Hope on, be no afraid:
   Fear not the griefs that plague thee
   And keep thy heart dismayed
   Thy God, on his great mercy
   Will save thee. hold thee fast.
   And in his own time grant thee
   The sun of joy at last.
   -Arthur W. Farlander

673

St Christopher- 7.6.7.6.D.

1. O Lamb of God, still keep me
   Near to thy wounded side;
   Tis only there in safety
   And peace I can abide.
   What foes and snares surround
   What lusts and fears within!
   The grace that sought and found
   Alone can keep me clean

2. Tis only in thee hiding, I feel my
   life secure;
   In thee alone abiding, The conflict
   can endure:
   Thine arm the victory gaineth
   O'er ev'ry hurtful foe;
   Thy love my heart sustaineth
   In all its care and woe.

3. Soon shall my eyes behold thee
   With rapture, face to face;
   One half hath not been told me
   Of all thy power and grace;
   Thy beauty, Lord, and glory,
   The wonders of thy love,
   Shall be the endless story
   Of all thy saints above.
   -James George Deck

674

Landas C. M. with Refrain

1. My faith has found a resting place
   Not in device or creed:
   I trust the Everliving One
   His wounds for me shall plead.

   Chorus
   I need no other argument,
   I need no other plea;
   It is enough that Jesus died.
   And that He died for me.

2. Enough for me that Jesus saves
   This ends my fear and doubt;
   A sinful soul I come to Him
   He'll never cast me out.

FAITH

3. My heart is leaning on the Word
   The written Wand of God:
   Salvation by my Savior's name
   Salvation thru His blood.

4. My great Physician heals the sick
   The lost He came to save;
   For me His precious blood He shed
   For me His life He gave.
       -Lidie H. Edmunds

675

Whittle -10.10.10.10. with Refrain

1. Dying with Jesus, by death
   reckoned mine;
   Living with Jesus a new life divine;
   Looking to Jesus till glory doth
   shine.
   Moment by moment, O Lord, I am
   Thine.

Chorus
Moment by moment! I'm kept in His
love;
Moment by moment I've life from
above;
Looking to Jesus till glory doth
shine;
Moment by moment, O Lord, I am
Thine.

2. Never a trial that He is not there,
   Never a burden that He doth not
   bear,
   Never a sorrow that He doth not
   share,
   Moment by moment, I'm under His
   care.

3. Never a weakness that He doth not
   feel,
   Never a sickness that He cannot
   heal;
   Moment by moment, in woe or in
   well,
   Jesus my Saviour abides with me
   still.
       Daniel W. Whittle

676

Binghamton -10.11.11.11. with Refrain

1. My Father is rich in houses and
   lands,
   He holdeth the wealth of the world
   in His hands!
   Of rubies and diamonds, of silver
   and gold,
   His coffers are full, He has riches
   untold.

Chorus
I'm a child of the King, A child of the
King:
With Jesus my Saviour, I'm a child of
the King.

2. My Father's own Son, the Saviour of
   men,
   Once wandered on earth as the
   poorest of them;
   But now He is reigning forever on
   high.
   And will give me a home in heav'n
   by and by.

3. I once was an outcast stranger on
   earth,
   A sinner by choice, and an alien by
   birth;
   But I've been adopted, my name's
   Written down.
   An heir to a mansion, a robe, and a
   crown.

4. A tent or a cottage, why should I
   care?
   They're building a palace for me
   over there;
   Though exiled from home, yet still I
   may sing;
   All glory to God, I'm a child of the
   King.
       -Harriet E. Buell

FAITH

677

Mainzer- L.M.

1. Author of faith, eternal Word,
   Whose Spirit breathes the active flame;
   Faith, like its Finisher and Lord,
   Today as yesterday the same:

2. To Thee our humble hearts aspire,
   And ask the gift unspeakable;
   Increase in us the kindled fire,
   In us the work of faith fulfil.

3. By faith we know Thee strong to save;
   Save us, a present Saviour Thou!
   Whate'er we hope, by faith we Have,
   Future and past subsisting now.

4. To him that in Thy name believes
   Eternal life with Thee is given;
   Into himself he all receives,
   Pardon, and holiness, and heaven.

5. The things unknown to feeble sense,
   Unseen by reason's glimmering ray,
   With strong, commanding evidence
   Their heavenly origin display.

6. Faith leads its realizing light,
   The clouds disperse, the shadows fly;
   The Invisible appears in sight,
   And God is seen by mortal eye.
   　　　　　　　-Charles Wesley

678

Ich Halte Treulich Still - D.S.M.

1. Spirit of faith, come down,
   Reveal the things of God;
   And make to us the Godhead known,
   And witness with the blood.
   'Tis thine the blood to apply
   And give us eyes to see
   Who did for every sinner die
   Hath surely died for me.

2. No man can truly say
   That Jesus is the lord,
   'Unless Thou take the veil away,
   And breathe the living word;
   Then, only then, we feel
   Our interest in His blood,
   And cry, with joy unspeakable:
   Thou art my Lord, my God!

3. O that the world might know
   The all atoning Lamb!
   Spirit of faith, descend, and show
   The virtue of His name;
   The grace which all may find,
   The saving power impart;
   And testify to all mankind,
   And speak in every heart.

4. Inspire the living faith,
   Which whosoe'er receives,
   The witness in himself he hath,
   And consciously believes;
   That faith that conquers all,
   And doth the mountain move,
   And saves whoe'er on Jesus call
   And perfects them in love.
   　　　　　　　-Charles Wesley

679

Wirksworth - S.M.

1. Ah! Whither should I go,
   Burdened, and sick. and faint?
   To whom should I my troubles show,
   And pour out my complaint?
   My Saviour bids me come;
   Ah! why do I delay?
   He carts the weary sinner home.
   And yet from Him I stay.

FAITH

3. What is it keeps me back,
from which I cannot part,
which will not let my Saviour take
possession of my heart?

4. Some cursed thing unknown
Must surely lurk within,
Some idol, which I will not own,
Some secret bosom sin.

5. Jesus, the hindrance show,
Which I have feared to see;
Yet let me now consent to know
What keeps me out of Thee.

6. Searcher of hearts, in mine
Thy trying power display;
Into its darkest corners shine,
And take the veil away.

7. I now believe in Thee
Compassion reigns alone,
According to my faith to me
O let it, Lord, be done!
-Charles Wesley

680

Hiding In Thee- 11.11.11.11.with Refrain

1. O safe to the Rock that is higher
than I,
My soul in its conflicts and sorrows
would fly;
So sinful so weary, Thine, Thine
would I be;
Thou blest Rock of Ages, I'm hiding
in Thee.

Chorus
Hiding in Thee, Hiding in Thee,
Thou blest Rock of Ages,
I'm hiding in Thee,   .

2. In the calm of the noon-tide,
In sorrow's lone hour,
In times when temptation casts o'er
me its power;
In the tempests of life, on its wide,
heaving sea,
Thou blest Rock of Ages, I'm hiding
in Thee.

3. How oft in the conflict, when
pressed by the foe,
I have fled to my Refuge and
breathed out my woe;
How often, when trials like sea
billows roll,
Have I hidden in Thee, O Thou
Rock of my soul.
-William O. Cushing

681

Showalter- 10.9.10.9. with Refrain

1. What a fellowship, what a joy divine,
Leaning on the everlasting arms;
What a blessedness, what a peace
In mine,
Leaning on the everlasting arms.

Chorus
Leaning, leaning. Safe and secure
from alt alarms;
Leaning, leaning, Leaning on the
everlasting arms.

2. O how sweet to walk in this pilgrim
way,
Leaning, leaning, Leaning on the
everlasting arms;
O, how bright the path grows from
day to day.
Leaning, leaning. Leaning on the
everlasting arms

3. What have I to dread, what have I
to fear,
Leaning, leaning, Leaning on the
everlasting arms?
I have blessed peace with my Lord
so near,
Leaning, leaning, Leaning on the
everlasting arms.
-Elisha A. Hoffman

FAITH

682

Trusting Jesus

1. Simply trusting every day,
   Trusting through a stormy way;
   Even when my faith is small,
   Trusting Jesus that is all.

Chorus
Trusting as the moments fly,
Trusting as the days go by,
Trusting Him whate'er befall,
Trusting Jesus that is all.

2. Brightly doth His Spirit shine
   Into this poor heart of mine.
   While He leads I cannot fall.
   Trusting Jesus that is all.

3. Singing if my way is dear,
   Praying if the path be drear;
   If in danger, for Him call,
   Trusting Jesus that is all.

4. Trusting Him white life shall last,
   Trusting Him till earth be past;
   Till within the jasper wall,
   Trusting Jesus that is all.
   —Edgar P. Stites

683

Hingham

1. Under His wings I am safely abiding,
   Tho the night deepens and
   tempests are wild;
   Still I can trust Him, I know He will
   Keep me,
   He has redeemed me and I am His
   child.

Chorus
Under His wings, under His wings,
Who from His love can sever?
Under His wings my soul shall abide,
Safely abide forever.

2. Under His wings, what a refuge in
   sorrow!
   How the heart yearningly turns to
   His rest!
   Often when earth has no balm for
   my healing,
   There I find comfort and there I am
   blest.

3. Under His wings, O what precious
   enjoyment!
   There will I hide till life's trials are
   o'er,
   Sheltered, protected, no evil can
   harm me,
   Resting in Jesus I'm safe evermore.
   —William O. Cushing

684

Crimond-C.M.

1. The Lord's is my shepherd, I'll not
   want,
   He makes me down to lie In pastures
   green: He
   leadeth me The quiet waters by.

2. My soul He doth restore again; And
   me to walk doth make Within the
   paths of
   righteousness, Ev'n for His own
   name's sake.

3. Yea, though I walk in death's dark
   vale, Yet
   will I fear none ill: For Thou art with
   me;
   and Thy rod And staff me comfort
   still.

4. My table Thou hast furnished In
   presence of my foes; My head Thou
   dost with
   oil anoint, And my cup over flows

5. Goodness and mercy all my life
   Shall

FAITH

surely follow me: And in God's house for
evermore My dwelling place shall be.

-William Whittingham

685

Promises -11.11.11.9. With Refrain

1. Standing on the promises of Christ our King,
Thro' eternal ages let His praises ring;
Glory in the highest, I will shout and Sing.
Standing on the promises of God.

Chorus
Standing, standing,
Standing on the promises of God my Saviour,
Standing, standing.
I'm standing on the promises of God.

2. Standing on the promises that cannot fail,
When the howling storms of doubt and fear assail,
By the living Word of God I shall prevail,
Standing on the promises of God.

3. Standing on the promises of Christ the Lord,
Bound to Him eternally by love's strong cord,
Overcoming daily with the Spirits sword,
Standing on the promises of God.

4. Standing on the promises I cannot fall,
List'ning every moment to the Spirit Call.

Resting in my Saviour as my all in all,
Standing on the promises of God.

-R. Kelso Carter

686

Trust and obey - 6.6.9.D. With Refrain

1. When we walk with the Lord in the light of His Word,
What a glory He sheds on our way!
While we do His good will He abides with us still,
And with all who will trust and obey.

Chorus
Trust and obey, for there's no other way
To be nappy in Jesus, But to trust and obey.

2. Not a shadow can rise, not a cloud in the skies,
But His smile quickly drives it away,
Not a doubt nor a fear, not a sigh nor a tear,
Can abide while we trust and obey.

3. Not a burden we bear, not a sorrow we share.
But our toil He doth richly repay;
Not a grief nor a loss, not a frown nor a cross,
But is blest if we trust and obey.

4. But we never can prove the delights of His love
Until all on the altar we lay:
For the favour He shows and the joy He bestows
Are for them who will trust and obey.

5. Then in fellowship sweet we will sit at His feet,
Or we'll walk by His side in the way;
What He says we will do, where He sends we will go
Never fear, only trust and obey.

-John H. Sammis

FAITH

687

Trust In Jesus - 8.7.8.7. And Refrain

1. 'Tis so sweet to trust in Jesus,
   Just to take Him at His word,
   Just to rest upon His promise,
   Just to know "Thus saith the Lord."

Chorus
Jesus, Jesus, how I trust Him!
How I've proved Him o'er and o'er!
Jesus, Jesus, precious Jesus!
O for grace to trust Him more!

2. O how sweet to trust in Jesus,
   Just to trust His cleansing blood!
   Just in simple faith plunge me
   Neath the healing, cleansing flood!

3. Yes, 'tis sweet to trust in Jesus,
   Just from sin and self to cease,
   Just from Jesus simply taking
   Life and rest and joy and peace.

4. I'm so glad I learned to trust Him,
   Precious Jesus, Saviour, Friend;
   And I know that He is with me,
   Will be with me to the end.
   -Louisa M.R. Stead

688

Lincoln- C.M.

1. Day after day I sought the Lord,
   And waited patiently;
   Until He bent down from His throne,
   And hearkened to my cry.

2. He drew me from the fearful pit,
   And from the miry day;
   He placed my feet upon a rock,
   And led me in His way.

3. He taught my soul a new made song,

A song of holy praise;
All they who see these things, fear
Their hopes to God shall raise.

4. Most blessed is the man whose. Hope
   Upon the Lord relies;
   Who follows not the proud, nor those
   That turn aside to lies.

5. O Lord. what wonders hast Thou
   All number far above;
   Thy thoughts to us ward overflow
   With mercy, grace, and love.
   -Julius Charles Hare

689

Sankey -C.M.D. with Refrain

1. Encamped along the hills of light,
   Ye Christian soldiers, rise,
   And press the battle ere the night
   Shall veil the glowing skies.
   Against the foe in vales below
   Let all our strength be hurled;
   Faith is the victory, we know,
   That overcomes frieworid.

Chorus
Faith is the victory!
Faith is the victory!
O glorious victory,
That overcomes the world.

2. His banner over us is love,
   Our sword the Word of God;
   We tread the road the saints above
   With shouts of triumph trod.
   By faith they, like a whirl-wind's breath,
   Swept on o'er ev'ry field;
   The faith by which they conquered death
   Is still our shining shield.

FAITH

3. on every hand the foe we find
Drawn up in dread array;
Let tents of ease be left behind,
and onward to the fray;
salvation's helmet on each head,
with truth all girt about,
The earth shall tremble 'neath our tread,
And echo with our shout.

4. To him that overcomes the foe,
White raiment shall be giv'n;
Before the angels he shall know
His name confessed in heav'n,
Then onward from the hills of light,
Our hearts with love aflame,
We'll vanquish all the hosts of night,
In Jesus' conquering name.
                              -John H. Yates

690

Singing I Go

1. The trusting heart to Jesus clings,
Nor any ill forbides.
But at the cross of Calv'ry sings,
Praise God for lifted loads!

Chorus
Singing, I go along life's road,
Praising the Lord; praising the Lord;
Singing, I go along life's road,
For Jesus has lifted my load.

2. The passing days bring many cares,
"Fear not, I hear Him say,
And when my fears are turned to pray'rs,
The burdens slip away.

3. He tells me of my Father's love
And never slumb'ring eye;
My everlasting King above
Will all my needs supply.

4. When to the throne of grace I flee,
I find the promise true,
The mighty arms upholding me
Will bear my burdens too.
                              -Eliza E. Hewitt

691

Wetherby- C.M.

1. Ye humble souls that seek the Lord,
Chase all your fears away;
And bow with rapture down to see
The place where Jesus lay.

2. Thus low the Lord of Life was brought,
Such wonders love can do;
Thus cold in death that bosom lay,
Which throbbed and bled for you.

3. But raise your eyes and tune your songs;
The Saviour lives again:
Not all the bolts and bars of death
The Conqueror could detain.

4. High o'er the angelic bands He rears
His once dishonoured head;
And through unnumbered years He reigns,
Who dwelt among the dead.

5. With joy like His shall every saint -
His vacant tomb survey;
Then rise with his ascending Lord
To realms of endless day.
                              Philip Doddridge

692

Only Believe

1. Fear not, little flock, from the cross
To the throne,
From death into life He went for His own;
All power in earth, all power above,
Is given to Him for the flock of His love.

FAITH

Chorus
Only believe, only believe;
All things are possible, only believe,
Only believe, only believe;
All things are possible, only believe.

2. Fear not, little flock, He goeth
ahead,
Your Shepherd selecteth the path
you must tread;
The waters of Marah He'll sweeten
for thee,
He drank all the bitter in
Gethsemane.

3. Fear not, little flock, whatever your
lot;
He enters all rooms, "the doors
being shut."
He never forsakes. He never is
gone,
So count on His presence in
darkness and dawn.
                                    -Paul Rader

693

Foundation-11.11.41.11.

1. How firm a foundation, ye saints of
the lord,
Is laid for your faith in His excellent
Word!
What more can He say than to you
He hath said,
To you who for refuge to Jesus
have fled?

2. "Fear not. I am with thee; O be not
dismayed,
For I am thy God, and will still give
the aid;
I'll strengthen thee, help thee, and
cause thee to stand,
Upheld by My righteous, omnipotent hand.

3. "When through fiery trials thy path
way shall lie.
My grace, all sufficient, shall be thy
supply:
The flame shall not hurt thee; I only
design
Thy dross to consume and thy gold
to refine.

4. The soul that on Jesus hath
leaned for repose
I will not, I will not desert to its foes;
That soul, though all hell should
endeavor to shake,
I'll never, no, never, no, never
forsake!"
                                    -Rippon's Selection
                                         of Hymns

694

My Anchor Holds

1. Tho' the angry surges roll
O'er my tempest driven soul,
I am peaceful, for I know,
Wildly thought the winds may blow
I've an anchor safe and sure,
That shall evermore endure.

Chorus
And it holds, my anchor holds;
Blow your wildest then, O gale,
On my bark so small and frail,
By His grace I shall not fail,
For my anchor holds, my anchor
holds.

2. Mighty tides about me sweep,
Perils lurk within the deep,
Angry clouds o'er shade the sky
And the tempest rises high;
Still I stand the tempest's shock,
For my anchor grips the Rock.

3. I can feel the anchor fast
   As I meet each sudden blast,
   And the cable, though unseen,
   Bears the heavy strain between;
   Thro' the storm I safely ride,
   Till the turning of the tide.

4. Troubles almost whelm the soul;
   Griefs like billows o'er me roll;
   Tempters seek to lure astray,
   Storms obscure the light of day;
   But in Christ I can be bold,
   I've an anchor that shall hold.
                      -W.C. Martin

695

Jesus Never Fails

1. Earthly friends may prove untrue,
   Doubts and fears assail;
   One still loves and cares for you,
   One who will not fail

Chorus
Jesus never fails, Jesus never fails;
Heav'n and earth may pass away,
But Jesus never fails.

2. Tho the sky be dark and drear,
   Fierce and strong the gale,
   Just remember He is near,
   And He will not fail

3. In life's dark and bitter hour
   Love wilt still prevail;
   Trust His everlasting pow'r
   Jesus will not fail.
                      -Arthur A. Luther

696

My Father Watches Over Me

1. I trust in God wherever I may be,
   Upon the land or on the rolling sea,
   For, come what may, From day to day,
   My heav'nly Father watches overme.

Chorus
I trust in God, I know He cares for me,
On mountain bleak or on the stormy
sea;
Tho' billows roll, He keeps my soul.
My heav'nly Father watches over me.

2. He mates the rose an object of His
   care,
   He guides the eagle thru the pathless
   air,
   And surely He Remembers me,
   My heav'nly Father watches over me.

3. I trust in God, for, in the lion's den,
   On battle field, or in the prison pen,
   Thru praise or blame. Thru flood or
   flame,
   My heav'nly Father watches over me.

4. The valley may be dark, the
   shadows deep,
   But O, the Shepherd guards His
   lonely sheep;
   And thru the gloom He 'll lead me
   home,
   My heav'nly Father watches over me.
                      Rev. W.C. Martin

697

God is The Answer

1. One day I was burdened,
   my mind was ill at ease,
   I was searching for an answer,
   I heard it in the trees. And they
   whispered to me:
   "God is the answer. God is the
   answer,
   God is the answer in the time of
   need."

Chorus
God is the answer, God is the
answer,
God is the answer in the time of
Need.

FAITH

God is the answer, God is the answer,
God is the answer in the time of need.

2. He prospers and protects me ev'ry where I go,
Just when I need Him most,
He makes the blessings flow, I'm so glad I know that:
"God is the answer. God is the answer,
God is the answer in the time of need."

-R. H. Goodrastfur

698

Have Faith In God

1. Have faith in God when your pathway is lonely,
He sees and knows all the way you have trod;
Never alone are the least of His children;
Have faith in God, have faith in God.

Chorus
Have faith in God, He's on His throne;
Have faith in God, He watcheth o'er His own;
He cannot fail. He must prevail;
Have faith in God, have faith in God.

2. Have faith in God when your prayers are unanswered,
Your earnest plea He will never forget;
Wait on the Lord, trust His Word and be patient;
Have faith in God, He'll answer yet.

3. Have faith in God in your pain and your sorrow,
His heart is touched with your grief and despair;
cast all your cares and your burdens upon Him,

3. And leave them there, oh, leave them there.

4. Have faith in God though all else about you;
Have faith in God, He provides for His own;
He cannot fail though an kingdom shad perish,
He rules. He reigns upon His throne.

-B.B. McKinney

699

I Know Who Holds Tomorrow

1. I don't know about tomorrow,
I just live from day to day;
I don't borrow from its sunshine,
For its skies may turn to gray. I don't worry o'er the future,
For I know what Jesus said,
And today I'll walk beside Him,
For He knows what is ahead.

Chorus
Many things about tomorrow,
I don't seem to understand:
But I know who holds tomorrow.
And I know who holds my hand.

2. Ev'ry step is getting brighter,
As the golden stairs I climb;
Ev'ry burden's getting lighter;
Ev-ry doubts silver lined.
There the sun is always shining,
There no tear will dim the eye,
At the ending of the rainbow,
Where the mountains touch the sky.

3. I don't know about tomorrow,
It may bring me poverty,
But the one who feeds the sparrow,
Is the one who stands by me.

FAITH

And the path that be my portion,
May be through the flame or flood,
But His presence goes before me,
And I'm covered with His blood.
-Ira F. Stanphill

700

Olivet-6.6.4.6.6.6.4.

1. My faith looks up to Thee,
Thou Lamb of Calvary,
Saviour divine'
Now hear me while I pray,
Take all my guilt away,
O let me from this day Be wholly
Thine!

2. May Thy rich grace impart
Strength to my fainting heart,
My zeal inspire;
As Thou hast died for me,
O may my love to Thee
Pure, warm, and changeless be,
A living fire!

3. While life's dark maze I tread
And griefs around me spread.
Be Thou my guide;
Bid darkness turn to day,
Wipe sorrow's tears away,
Nor let me ever stray From Thee
aside.

4. When ends life's passing dream,
When death's cold, threatening
stream
Shall o'er me roll,
Blest Saviour, then, in love,
Fear and distrust remove;
O lift me safe above, A ransomed
soul!
-Ray Palmer

701

Weeping Will not Save Me

1. Weeping will not save me
Tho' my face were bathed in
tears,
That could not allay my fears,
Could not wash the sins of
years!
Weeping will not save me.

Chorus
Jesus wept and died for me;
Jesus suffered on the tree;
Jesus waits to make me free;
He alone can save me!

2. Working will not save me!
Purest deeds that I can do.
Holiest thoughts and feelings
too,
Cannot form my soul anew!
Working will not save me

3. Waiting will not save me!
Helpless, guilty lost I lie;
In my ear is Mercy's cry,
if I wait I can but die:
Waiting will not save me.

4. Faith in Christ will save me!
Let me trust Thy weeping Son,
Trust the work that He has done;
To His arms. Lord, help me run;
Faith in Christ will save me.
-Rev. R. Lowry

702

Ephraim 7.7.7.7.

1. He will answer every pray'r
This, His promise and His will
He has never chang'd nor fall'd
Glory to His name.

2. He will answer every pray'r
To His promise I will cling
I know He'll ne'er deceive me.
Glory to His name.

3. He will answer every pray 'r
   Let us ask from Him in faith
   With is Holy Spirit's help
   Glory to His name.

4. He will answer every pray 'r
   Come thou to the mercy seat
   Blest assurance you'll receive
   Glory to His name.

703

Give Me The Faith Which Can
Remove - 8.8.8.D.

1. Give me the faith which can remove
   And sink the mountain to a plain;
   Give me the child-like praying love.
   Which longs to build Thy house
   again;
   Thy love let it my heart o'er-power,
   And alt my simple soul devour.

2. I want an even strong desire,
   I want a calmly fervent zeal,
   To save poor souls out of the fire,
   To snatch them from the verge of
   hell.
   And turn them to a pardoning God,
   And quench the brands in Jesus's
   blood.,

3. I would the precious time redeem,
   And longer five for this alone.
   To spend, and to be spent, for them
   Who have not yet my Saviour
   known;
   Fully on these my mission prove.
   And only breathe to Thy
   Love.

4. My talents gifts, and graces, Lord
   Into Thy blessed hands receive
   And let me live to preach Thy word
   And let me to Thy glory live;
   My every sacred moment spend
   In publishing the sinner's Friend.

5. Enlarge, inflame, and fill my heart
   With boundless charity divine!
   So shall I all my strength exert,
   And love them with a zeal like
   Thine;
   And lead them to Thy open side'
   The sheep for whom their shepherd
   died.

PRAYER

704

St Hugh-C.M.

1. Lord, teach us how to pray aright,
   With reverence and with fear;
   Though dust and ashes in Thy sight,
   We may, we must, draw near.

2. We perish if we cease from prayer;
   O grant us power to pray!
   And when to meet Thee we prepare,
   Lord, meet us by the way.

3. God of all grace, we come to Thee,
   With broken, contrite heart
   Give what Thine eye delights to See,
   Truth in the inward part;

4. Faith in the only sacrifice
   That can sin atone;
   To cast our hopes; to fix Our eyes
   On Christ, on Christ alone;

5. Patience to watch and wait and weep,
   Though mercy long delay;
   Courage our fainting soul to keep.
   And trust thee thought thou slay.

6. Give these, and then Thy will be done;
   Thus strengthened with all might,
   We through Thy Spirit and Thy Son
   shall pray, and pray aright
   　　　　　　　　　　-J. Montgomery

705

Arden-C.M.

1. Our Father hears us when we pray;
   A whisper He can hear;
   He knows not only what we say.
   But what we wish or fear.

2. 'Tis not enough And words of prayer to say ;
   The heart roust with the lips agree.
   Or else we do not pray.

3. Teach us, O Lold. to pray aright;
   Thy grace to us impart, That we in
   prayer may take delight, And serve
   Thee with the heart.
   　　　　　　　　　　-J. Burton jun

706

St. Bernard-C.M.

1. There is no sorrow. Lord, too light
   To bring in prayer to There
   There is no anxious care too slight
   To wake Thy sympathy.

2. Thou who hast trod the thorny road
   Wilt share each small distress;
   The love which bore the greater load
   Will not refuse the less.

3. There is no secret sigh we breathe
   But meets Thine ear divine'
   And every cross grows light beneath
   The shadow, Lord, of Thine.
   Life's ills without, sin's strife within,
   The heart would overflow,
   But for that Love which died for sin.
   That Love which wept for woe.
   　　　　　　　　　　-Jane Crewd son

707

Campmeeting - C. M.

1. Prayer is the soul's sincere desire,
   Unuttered or expressed;
   The motion of a hidden fire
   That trembles in the breast.

2. Prayer is the simplest form of speech
   That infant tips can try;
   Prayer, the sublimest strains that reach
   The Majesty on high.

3. Prayer is the contrite sinner's voice,
   Returning from his ways;
   While angels sin their songs rejoice
   And cry, "Behold, he prays!

4. O Thou by whom we come to God,
   The life, the truth. the way,
   The path of prayer Thy Self hast trod
   Lord, teach us how to pray!
   —James Montgomery

708

Cannock L. M.

1. O Thou who dost direct my feet
   To right or left where pathways part,
   Wilt Thou not, faithful Paraclete,
   Direct the journeyng of my heart?

2. Into the love of God, I pray.
   Deeper and deeper let me press,
   Exploring all along the way
   Its secret strength and tenderness.

3. Into the steadfastness of One
   Who patiently endured the cross,
   Of Him who. though He were a Son.
   Came to His crown through bitter Loss.

4. This is the road of my desire
   Learning to love God love me,
   Ready to pass through flood or fire
   With Christ's unwearying con stancy.
   —Frank Houghton

709

Chichester -C. M.

1. Talk with us. Lord, Thyself
   While here o'er earth we row
   Speak to our heats, and let us
   The kindling of Thy love.

2. With Thee conversing we forget
   All time and toil and care;
   Labour is rest and pain is Sweet
   If Thou. my God, art here,

3. Here then, my God, vouchsafe to stay,
   And bid my heart rejoice:
   My bounding heart shall own Thy sway,
   And echo to Thy voice.

4. Let this mine every hour employ,
   Till I Thy glory see,
   Enter into my Master's joy,
   And find my heaven in Thee.
   —Charles wesley

710

Mannheim - 8.7.8.7.8:7.

1. In Thy name, O Lord, assembling,
   We Thy people now draw near
   Teach us to rejoice with trembling,
   Speak, and let Thy servants
   Hear fear with meekness.
   Hear Thy word with godly fear.

2. While our days on earth are lengthened
   May we give them. Lord to thee:
   cheered by hope and daily strengthened
   Way we run nor weary be,
   Till Thy glory
   with out cloud in heaven we see.

3. There in worship purer, sweeter,
Thee Thy people shall adore:
Tasting of enjoyment greater
Far than thought conceived before;
Full enjoyment,
Full, unmixed, and evermore.
                    -Thomas Kelly

711

Whitehall-L.M.

Jesus, our best beloved friend,
Draw out our souls in pure desire;
Jesus, in love to us descen'd,
Baptize us with Thy Spirit's fire.

2. On Thy redeeming name we call.
Poor and unworthy though we be:
Pardon and sanctify us all.
Let each Thy full salvation see.

Our souls and bodies we resign
To fear and follow Thy commands:
O take our hearts. Our hearts are
Thine,
Accept the service of our hands.

4. Firm, faithful, watching unto prayer,
May we Thy blessed will obey,
Toil in Thy vineyard here, and bear
The heart and burden of the day.

5. Yet, Lord, for us a resting place
I n heaven at Thy right hand
prepare:
And till we see Thee face to face;
Be all our conversation there.

                    -James Montgomery

712

Neander-8.7.8.7.7.7.

1. Open now thy gates of beauty,
Zion. let me enter there,
Where my soul in joyful duty

Waits for His answers prayer
O how blessed b this place.
Filled with solace, light and grace!

2. Yes, my God, I come before Thee.
Come Thou also down to me:
Where we find Thee and adoreThee
There a heaven on earth must be:
To my heart, O enter Thou,
Let be Thy temple now.

3. Here Thy praise is gladly chanted.
Here Thy seed is duly sown,
Let my soul where it is planted,
Bring forth precious sheaves atone,
So that all I hear may be
Fruitful unto life in me.

4. Thou my faith increase and quicken.
Let me keep Thy gift divine:
Howsoe 'er temptations thicken.
May Thy word still o'er me shine,
As my polestar through my life,
As my comort in my strife.

5. Speak O God, and I will hear Thee,
Let Thy will be done, indeed:
May I undisturbed draw near Thee,
While Thou dost Thy people feed:
Here of life the fountain flows,
Here is balm for all our woes.
                    -Benjamin Schmolck

713

Blest Be The tie

1. Blest be the tie that binds
Our hearts in Christian love!
The fellowship of kindred minds Is
like to that above.

2. Before our Father s throne
We pour our ardent prayers;
Our fears, our hopes, bur aims are
one,
Our comforts and our cares.

PRAYER

3. We share our mutual woes,
Our mutual burdens bear,
And often for each other flows
The sympathizing tear.

4. When we asunder part
It gives us inward pain;
But we shall stiff be Joined in heart.
And hope to meet again.
-John Fawcett

714

Just A Closer Walk With Thee

1. I am weak but Thou art strong,
Jesus keep me from an wrong;
I'll be satisfied as long
As I walk close to Thee.

Chorus
Just a doser walk with Thee.
Grant it, Jesus, this my plea;
Daily let it ever be
Just a closer walk with Thee.

2. Thru this world of toils and snares.
if I falter Lord, who cares?
Who with me my burden shares?
Let me walk close to thee.
-Anon

3. When my feeble life is o'er,
Time for me will be no more.
Guide me to that peaceful shore,
Let me walk close to thee.
-Anon

715

Spend a Moment with Jesus
1. Spend a moment in pray' r with the Sawour.
When the pathway is lonely and long;
He wD turn al the shadows to sunshine,
And your sorrow and sighing to song.

Chorus
Moment praying to the saviour,
Burden is so hear;
The your burdens of care will be Lifted,
Spend a moment with Jesus a
Moment in pray' r

2. Spend a moment in pray' r with the Saviour.
When the tempter is linger near;
He will give you His strength in your weakness,
And His love light will fill you with Cheer.

3. Spend a moment in pray'r with the Saviour'
When your spirit is sad and Oppressed;
O what! comfort to near His soft whisper,
"Come to Me' weary one. and find rest.

4. Spend a moment in pray' r with Saviour,
It will keep you from doubt and despair;
Ev' ry morning and noontide and Evening'
Spend a moment with Jesus in Pray' r
-Rev. Alfred Barratt

716

Sarah Rachel -8.8.8.8

1. Eternal light, shine in my heart.
eternal hope' life up my eyes:
eternal power, be my support,
eternal wisdom, make me wise.

2. Eternal life, raise me from death
eternal brightness, help me see;
eternal Spirit, give me breath,

PRAYER

3. Until by your most costly grace,
   invited by your holy word,
   at last I come before your face
   to know you. my eternal God.
                    -Christopher idle

717

Gott Will's Machen -8.7.8.7

1. Father, hear the prayer we offer
   not for ease our prayer shall be,
   but for strength that we may ever
   live our lives courageously.

2. Not for ever in green pastures
   do we ask our way to be;
   but the steep and rugged pathway
   may we tread rejoicingly.

3. Not for ever by still waters
   would we idly rest and stay;
   but would strike the living fountain
   from the rocks along our way.

4. Be our strength in hours of
   weakness.
   in our wanderings be our guide;
   through endeavour, failure, danger,
   Father, be there at our side.
                    -Love M. Wills

718

Abridge -8.6.8.8.

1. Great Shepherd of your people,
   hear!
   your presence now display;
   as you have given a place for
   prayer,
   so give us hearts to pray.

2. Within these walls let holy peace
   and love and friendship dwell:
   here give the troubled conscience
   ease,
   the wounded spirit heal.

3. May we in faith receive your word,
   in faith present our prayers;
   and in the presence of our Lord
   unburden all our cares.

4. The hearing ear, the seeing eye,
   the contrite heart bestow;
   and shine upon us from on high.
   That we in grace may grow.
                    -J. Newton

719

Caswall -6.5.6.5.

1. Jesus, stand among us
   in your risen power;
   let this time of worship
   be a hallowed hour.

2. Breathe the Holy Sptit
   into every heart
   bid the fears and sorrows
   From each soul depart.

3. Thus with quickened footsteps
   well pursue our way
   watching for the dawning
   of the eternal day.
                    -W. Pennefather

720

Yanworth - 10. 10. 10. 10.

1. Life up your hearts!' We lift them to
   The Lord.
   and give to God our thanks with one
   accord;
   it is our joy and duty. all our days
   to lift our hearts in grateful thanks
   and praise.

2. Above the level of the former years,
   the mire of sin. the slough of guilty
   fears,
   the mist of doubt, the blight of love's
   Decay
   O Lord of light, lift all our hearts
   Today!

PRAYER

3. Above the swamps of subterfuge
and shame,
the deeds, the thoughts, that
honour may not name,
the halting tongue that dares not tell
the whole
O Lord of truth, lift every Christian
soul!

4. Above the storms that darken
human Be .
Pride, jealousy and envy, rage and
strife;
where cold mistrust holds friend
and friend apart
O Lord of love, lift every Christian
Heart!

5. Then, with the trumpet call as Christ
appears,
Lift up your hearts!' rings, pealing
in our ears;
still shall our hearts respond with
full accord
'We lift them up, we lift them to the
Lord!'

-H. M. Butler

721

God Be With You

1. God be with you till we meet again!
By His counsels guide, uphold you.
With His sheep securely fold you;
God be with you till we meet again!

Chorus
Till we meet! Till we meet!
Till we meet at Jesus' feet;
Till we meet! Till we meet
God be with you till we meet again!

2. God be with you till we meet again!
'Neath Mis wings securely hide you,
Daily manna st8l provide you:
God be with you till we meet again!

3. God be with you till we meet again!
When life's perils thick confound
you'
Put His loving arms around you;
God be with you till we me

4. God be with you till we me again!
Keep love's banner floating found
You,
smite death's threat' ning wave
before you;
God be with you till we meet again!

-J. E. Rankin, D. D

722

Cairn brook - 8.5.8.

1. Holy Fattier, in Thy mercy,
Hear our anxious prayer;
Keep our loved ones, now far
distant,
'Neath Thy care.

2. Jesus, Saviour, let Thy presence
Be their light and guide;
Keep, oh, keep them, in their
weakness,
At Thy side.

3. When in sorrow, when in danger
When in loneliness,
In Thy love look down and comfort
Their distress.

4. May the joy of Thy salvation
Be their strength and stay,
May they love and may they
Thee
Day by day.

5. Holy Spirit, let Thy teaching
Sanctify their life;
Send Thy grace, that they may
conquer
In the strife.

PRAYER

6. Father, son, and holy spirt,
   God the One in Three,
   Bless them, guide them, save them,
   keep them Near to Thee.
   -I. S. Stevenson

723

Dismissal-8.7.8.7.4.7.

1. Lord. dismiss us with Thy blessing,
   Fill our hearts with joy and peace;
   Let us each. Thy love possessing,
   Triumph in redeeming grace;
   O refresh us,
   Traveling through this wilderness.

2. Thanks we give, and adoration,
   For Thy gospel's joyful sound;
   May the fruits of Thy salvation
   In our hearts and fives abound;
   May Thy presence
   With us evermore be found.
   -John Fawcett

724

Converse - 8.7.8.7.D.

1. What a friend we have in Jesus,
   All our sins and griefs to bear;
   What a privilege to carry
   Ev'ry thing to God in prayer.
   Oh, what peace we often forfeit.
   Oh, what needless pain we bear
   All because we do not carry
   Ev'ry thing to God in prayer.

2. Have we trials and temptations?
   Is there trouble any where?
   We should never be discouraged,
   Take it to the Lord in prayer.
   Can we find a Friend so faithful,
   Who will all our sorrows share?
   Jesus knows our every weakness.
   Take it to the Lord in prayer.

3. Are we weak and heavy laden,
   Cumbered with a load of care?

Precious Saviour, still our refuge.
Take it to the Lord in prayer,
Do thy friends despise, forsake
thee?
Take it to the Lord in prayer,
In His arms Hell take and shield
thee,
Thou wilt find a solace there.
   -Joseph Scriven

725

Hall -10.10.10.10.

1. Take Thou our minds, dear Lord, we
   humbly pray;
   Give us the mind of Christ each
   passing day;
   Teach us to know the truth that sets
   us free;
   Grant us in all our thoughts to
   honour Thee.

2. Take Thou our hearts, O Christ,they
   are Thine own;
   Come Thou within our sods and
   claim Thy throne;
   Help us to shed abroad Thy
   deathless love;
   Use us to make the earth like
   heaven above.

3. Take Thou our wills, Most High!
   Hold Thou full sway;
   Have in our inmost souls Thy perfect
   way;
   Guard Thou each sacred hour from
   selfish ease;
   Guide Thou our ordered lives as
   Thou dost please.

4. Take Thou ourselves. O Lord, heart,
   mind, and will;
   Through surrendered souls Thy
   plans fulfill.
   We yield our staves to Thee time.
   talents all;
   We hear, and henceforth heed, Thy
   sovereign call.
   -William H. Foulkes

726

St. John-6.6.6.6.8.8.

1. O Thou that hearest prayer! Attend
   our humble cry;
   And let Thy servants share
   Thy blessing from on high:
   We plead the promise of Thy Word;
   Grant us Thy Holy Spirit. Lord.

2. If earthly parents hear
   Their children when the cry;
   If they, with love sincere,
   Their children's wants supply:
   Much more wilt Thou Thy love
   display,
   And answer when Thy children
   Pray.

3. Our heavenly Father Thou;
   We children of Thy grace;
   Oh, let Thy Spirit now
   Descend and fill the place;
   That all may feel the heavenly
   flame,
   And all unite to praise Thy name.
   -J. Burton

727

Hart's -7.7.

1. Jesus, we Thy premise claim,
   We are gather'd in Thy name;
   In the midst do Thou appear
   Manifest Thy presence here.

2. Sanctify all in Thee complete,
   Make us all for glory meet
   Come and dwell within each heart;
   Light, and life, and joy impart.

3. Make us al in Thee complete,
   Make us all for glory meet
   Meet appear before Thy sight;
   Partners with the saints in light!
   -C. Wesley

728

Leave Your Burdens At The place Of Prayer

1. When the clouds', are hanging low,
   When the raging tempests blow,
   When your soul is burdened With
   weight of care;
   There's a place of perfect rest,
   Where no evil can molest;
   Leave your burden at the place of
   prayer.

Chorus
Leave you burden at the place of
Prayer.
Take to Jesus all your want and
care;
For He is a Friend indeed.
And supplieth every need;
Leave your burden at the placed
Prayer.

2. There is rest for you today,
   Tho' you walk life's busy way
   There is One who waits your heavy
   load to bear.
   Jesus understands your need Your
   petition He will heed;
   Leave your burden at the place d
   prayer.

3. Bring your load of doubts and fears
   All the burdens of the years,
   You may meet your Saviour and
   blessings share;
   Bring your troubles not a few. ,
   Jesus will your strength renew,
   Leave your burden at the placed
   prayer.

4. We shall soon from care be free.
   With our eyes His glory see,
   O the blessedness of peace
   awaiting there;

PRAYER

Till your race on earth is done,
Leave your burden at the place of
prayer.

-Bertha Mae Lillenas

729

Did You Think To Pray

1. Ere you left your room this morning
   Did you think to pray?
   In the name of Christ, our Saviour,
   Did you sue for loving favor,
   As a shield today?

   Chorus
   O how praying rests the weary?
   Prayer will change the today;
   So, when life seems dark and
   dreary,
   don't forget to pray.

2. When you met with great temptation
   Did you think to pray?
   By His dying love and merit
   Did you claim the Holy Spirit
   As your guide and stay?

3. When your heart was filled with
   anger
   Did you think to pray?
   Did you plead for grace, my brother,
   That you might forgive another
   Who had crossed your way?

4. When sore trials came upon you
   Did you think to pray?
   When your soul was bowed in
   sorrow,
   Balm of Gilead did you borrow
   At the gates today?

   -Mrs. M. A. kidder

730

Sweet hour-L.M.D.

1. Sweet hour of prayer, sweet hour of
   prayer,
   That calls me from a world of care,
   And bids me at my Father's throne
   Make all my wants and wishes '
   known:
   In seasons of distress and grief,
   My soul has often found-relief,
   And oft escaped the temter 's snare
   By thy return, sweet hour of prayer.

2. Sweet hour of prayer, sweet hour of
   Prayer.
   Thy wings shall my petition bear
   To Him whose truth and faithfulness
   Engage the waiting soul to bless:
   And since He bids me seek his face,
   Believe His Word. and trust His
   grace.
   I'll cast on Him my ev'ry care,
   And wait for thee, sweet hour of
   prayer.

   -William W. Walford

731

Retreat L. M.

1. From ev' ry stormy wind that blows,
   From ev' ry swelling tide of woes,
   There is a calm, a sure retreat:
   Tis found beneath the mercy seat.

2. There is a scene where spirits
   Mend.
   Where friend holds fellowship with
   friend;
   Though sundered far by faith they
   meet
   Around one common mercy seat

3. Ah! Whither could we flee for aid,
   When tempted, desolated dismayed
   Or how the hosts of hell defeat,
   Had suff'ring saints no mercy seat.

4. Ah! there on eagle wings we soar,
   And sin and sense molest no more:
   And heav'n comes down our souls
   to greet,
   While glory crowns the mercy seat.
   -Hugh Stowell

732

Rest- 8.6.8.8.6.

1. Dear Lord and Father of mankind,
   Forgive our foolish ways!
   Reclothe us in our rightful mind;
   In purer lives Thy service find,
   In deeper rev'rence, praise.

2. In simple trust like their who
   heard.
   Beside the Syrian Sea,
   The gracious calling of the Lord,
   Let us, like them, without a word.
   Rise up and follow Thee.

3. Drop Thy still dews of quietness,
   Till an our strivings cease;
   Take from our souls the strain and
   stress,
   And let our ordered fives confess
   The beauty of Thy peace.

4. Breathe through the heats of our
   desire
   Thy coolness and thy balm;
   Let sense be dumb, let flesh retire;
   Speak through the earth-quake,
   wind, and fire,
   O still small voice of calm
   -John G. Whittier

733

Garden- Irregular

1. I come to the garden alone,
   While the dew is still on the roses;
   And the voice I hear, falling on my
   ear,
   The Son of God discloses.

Chorus
And He walks with me, and He talks
with me,
And He tete me I am His own;
And the joy we share as we tarry
there
None other has ever known.

2. He speaks, and the sound of His voice
   Is so sweet the birds hush their
   singing;
   And the melody that He gave to me
   Within my heart is ringing.

3. I'd stay in the garden with Him
   Tho the night around me be falling;
   But He bids me go thru the voice of
   woe,
   His voice to me is calling.
   -C. Austin Miles

734

Schuler -10.7.10.7. with Refrain

1. Out in the highways and by ways of
   life,
   Many are weary and sad;
   Carry the sunshine where darkness
   is rife,
   Making the sorrowing glad.

Chorus
Make me a blessing, make me a
blessing.
Out of my life may Jesus shine;
Make me a blessing. O Saviour,
I pray Thee my saviour,
Make me a blessing to someone
today.

2. Tell the sweet of Christ and
   His love,
   Tell of His pow'r to forgive;
   Others will trust Him if only you
   Prove
   True, every moment you live.

PRAYER

Give as 'twas given to you in your need,
Love as the Master loved you;
Be to the helpless a helper indeed,
Unto your mission be true.

-Ira B. Wilson

735

Scott - Irregular meter

1. Open my eyes, that I may see
   Glimpses of truth Thou hast for me;
   Place in my hands the wonderful key,
   That shall unclasp and set me free.
   Silently now I wait for Thee,
   Ready, my God, Thy will to see;
   Open my eyes, illumine me, Spirit divine!

2. Open my ears, that I may hear
   Voices of truth Thou sendest clear;
   And while the wavenotes fall on my ear,
   Ev'rything false wilt disappear.
   Silently now 1 wait for Thee,
   Ready, my God, Thy will to see;
   Open my eyes, illumine me, Spirit divine!

3. Open my mouth, and let it bear
   Gladly the warm truth ev'rywhere;
   Open my heart, and let me prepare
   Love with Thy children thus to share
   Silently now I wait for Thee,
   Ready, my God, Thy will to see;
   Open my eyes, illumine me. Spirit divine!
   Silently now I wait for Thee,
   Ready, my God, Thy will to see;
   Open my eyes, illumine me. Spirit divine!

-Clara H. Scott

736

Christ chapel-7.7.7.7.

1. Come, my soul, thy suit prepare,
   Jesus loves to answer prayer, He
   Himself has bid thee pray,
   Therefore will not say thee nay.

2. Thou art coming to a King;
   Large petitions with thee bring;
   For His grace and power are such,
   None can ever ask too much.

3. With my burden I begin:
   Lord, remove this load of sin,
   Let Thy blood, for sinners spilt,
   Set my conscience free from guilt.

4. Lord, I come to Thee for rest;
   Take possession of my breast;
   There Thy blood bought right maintain
   And without a rival reign.

5. White I am a pilgrim here,
   Let Thy love my spirit cheer:
   As my Guide, my Guard, my Friend,
   Lead me to my journey's end.

-John Newton

737

McAfee - C.M. with Refrain

1. There is a place of quiet rest
   Near to the heart of God,
   A place where sin cannot molest,
   Near to the heart of God.

Chorus
O Jesus, blest Redeemer,
Sent from me heart of God,
Hold us who wait before Thee
Near to the heart of God.

2. There is a place of comfort sweet
   Near to the heart of God,
   A place where we our Saviour meet,
   Near to the heart of God.

3. There is a place of full release
   Near to the heart of God,
   A place where all is joy and peace,
   Near to the heart of God.

-Cleland B. McAfee

PREVIEW

738

Teach me to Pray

1. Teach me to pray; Lord teach me to pray;
This is my heart cry day unto day;
I long to know Thy will and Thy way;
Teach me to pray, Lord, teach me to Pray.

Chorus
Living in Thee, Lord, and Thou in me,
Constant abiding, this is my plea;
Grant me Thy power, boundless and free,
Power with men and power with Thee.

2. Power in prayer, Lord, power in prayer!
Here 'mid earth's sin and sorrow and care,
Men lost and dying, souls in despair,
O give me power, power in prayer!

3. My weakened win. Lord, Thou canst renew;
My sinful nature Thou canst subdue;
Fill me Just now with power a new;
Power to pray and power to do!

4. Teach me to pray, Lord, teach me to pray;
Thou art my pattern day unto day;
Thou art my surety now and for aye;
Teach me to pray. Lord, teach me to pray.

-Albert S. Reitz

739

I Found the Answer

1. I was weak and weary, I had gone astray,
Walking In the darkness, I couldn't find my way;
Than a fight came shining to lead me from despair,
All my sins forgiven, and I was free

Chorus
I found the answer, I learned to pray!
With faith to guide me, I found the way;
The sun is shining for me each day,
found the answer, I learned to pray!

2. I was sad and lonely, all my hope were gone,
Days were long and dreary, I couldn't carry on;
Then I found the courage to keep my head up High,
Once again I'm happy and here's the reason why:

3. Keep your Bible with you, read it ev'ryday,
Always count your blessings and always stop to pray;
Learn to keep believing and faith will see you through,
Seek to know contentment and it will come to you.

-Johnny Lange

740

'Tis the Blessed Hour of Prayer

1. 'Tis the blessed hour of prayer,
when our hearts lowly bend,
And we gather to Jesus,
Our Saviour and Friend;

PRAYER

If we come to Him in faith,
Hi's protection to share,
What a balm for the weary!
Oh, how sweet to be there!

Chorus
Blessed hour of pray,
Blessed hour of pray,
What a balm for the weary!
Oh, how sweet to be there!

2 Tis the blessed hour of prayer,
when the Saviour draw nears
With a tender compassion,
His children to hear
When He tells us we may cast
at His feet every care;
What a balm for the weary!
Oh, how sweet to be there!

3. Tis the blessed hour of prayer,
when the tempted and tried
To the Saviour who loves them
their sorrow confide;
With a sympathizing heart
He removes every care,
What a balm for the weary!
Oh, how sweet to be there!

4. At the blessed hour of prayer,
trusting Him we believe
That the blessings we're needing
we'll surely receive;
In the fulness of this trust
we shall lose ev'ry care;
What a balm for the weary!
Oh, how sweet to be there!
-Fanny J. Crosby

741
O for a closer walk with God

1. O for a closer walk with God
A calm and heav'nly frame:
A light to shine upon the road
That leads me to the Lamb!

2. Where is the blessedness I knew
When first I saw the Lord?
Where is the soul refreshing view
Of Jesus and His word?

3. What peaceful hours I then enjoyed!
How sweet their mem'ry still
But they have left an aching void
The world can never fill.

4. Return, O Holy Dove, return,
Sweet Messenger of rest;
I hate the sins that made Thee
mourn,
And drove Thee from my breast.
-William Cowper

742

Dunelm- LM.

1. Jesus, where'er Thy people meet,
There they behold Thy mercy seat;
Where'er they seek Thee, Thou art
found,
And every place is hallow'd ground.

2. For Thou within no wails confined,
Inhabitest the humble mind;
Such ever bring Thee where they
come,
And going take Thee to their home.

3. Dear Shepherd of Thy chosen few,
Thy former mercies here renew;
Here to our wailing hearts proclaim
The sweetness of Thy saving name.

4. Here may we prove the power of
prayer
To strengthen faith and sweeten
care;
To teach our faint desires to rise,
And bring all heaven before our

PRAYER

5. Lord, we are few, Thou art near;
   Nor short Thine arm, nor deaf Thine
   ear;
   Oh rend the heavens, come quickly
   down,
   And make all hearts, O Lord, Thine
   own.

           -Charles Vincent

743

Even Me

1. Lord, I hear of showers of blessing
   Thou art scattering full and free;
   Showers the thirsty land refreshing;
   Let some drops now fall on me.
   Even me, Even me,
   Let some drops now fall on me.

2. Pass me not, O gracious Father,
   Sinful though my heart may be;
   Thou might'st leave me, but the
   rather
   Let Thy mercy light on me,
   Even me, Even me,
   Let Thy mercy light on me.

3. Pass me not, O tender Saviour,
   Let me love and cling to Thee;
   I am longing for Thy favour;
   Whilst Thou'rt calling, O call me,
   Even me, Even me,
   Whilst Thou'rt calling, O call me.

4. Love of God, so pure and change
   less,
   Blood of Christ, so rich, so free,
   Grace of God, so strong and
   boundless,
   Magnify them all in me,
   Even me, Even me,
   Magnify them all in me.

           -Elizabeth Codner

744

My Prayer

1. More holiness give me,
   More striving within;
   More patience in suffering,
   More sorrow for sin;
   More faith in my Saviour,
   More sense of His care;
   More Joy in His service,
   More purpose in prayer.

2. More gratitude give me,
   More trust in the Lord;
   More pride in His glory,
   More hope in His Word;
   More tears for His sorrows,
   More pain at His grief;
   More meekness in trial,
   More praise for relief.

3. More purity give me,
   More strength to o'er come;
   More freedom from earth stains,
   More longings for home;
   More fit for the kingdom,
   More used would! be;
   More blessed and holy,
   More, Saviour, like Thee.

           -P. P. Bliss

745

Oremus- 10.10.

1. Pray, always pray; the Holy Spirit
   pleads
   Within thee all thy daily, hourly
   needs.
   Pray, always pray; beneath sin's
   heaviest load
   Prayer sees the blood from Jesus
   side that flow'd.

PRAYER

3. Pray, always pray; though weary,
   faint, and lone,
   Prayer nestles by the Father's
   sheltering throne.

4. Pray, always pray; amid the world's
   turmoil
   Prayer keeps the heart at rest, and
   nerves for toil.

5. Pray, always pray; if joys thy
   pathway throng,
   Prayer drinks with them of springs
   that cannot fail.

6. Pray, always pray; if loved ones
   pass the veil,
   Prayer drinks with them of springs
   that cannot fail.

7. All earthly things with earth shall
   fade away;
   Prayer grasps eternity: pray, always
   pray.
   -Charles Vincent

746

Cornhill -8.8.8.4.

1. My God, is any hour so sweet,
   From blush of morn to evening star,
   As that which calls me to Thy feet,
   The hour of prayer?

2. Blest be that tranquil hour of morn,
   And blest that hour of solemn eve,
   When, on the wings of prayer
   up borne,
   The world I leave,

3. For then a day-spring shines on me
   Brighter than morn's ethereal glow;
   And richer dews descend from Thee
   Than earth can know.

4. Then is my strength by Thee
   renew'd;
   Then are my sins by Thee forgiven;

Then dost Thou cheer my solitude
With hopes of heaven.

5. No words can tell what blest relief,
   There for my every want I find;
   What strength for warfare, balm for
   grief;
   What peace of mind.

6. Hush'd is each doubt; gone every
   fear,
   My spirit seems in heaven to stay;
   And even the penitential tear
   Is wiped away.

7. Lord, till I reach your blissful shore,
   No privilege so dear shall be,
   As thus my inmost soul to pour
   In prayer to Thee
   -E. H. Thome

747

St Alkmund-LM.

1. Command Thy blessing from above,
   O God, on all assembled here;
   Behold us with a Father's love,
   While we look up with filial fear.

2. Command Thy blessing, Jesus,
   Lord.
   May we Thy true disciples be;
   Speak to each heart the mighty
   word;
   Say to the weakest, Follow Me.

3. Command Thy blessing, in this hour,
   Spirit of truth, and fill this place
   With humbling and with healing
   power,
   With quickening and confirming
   grace.

4. O Thou, our Maker, Saviour Guide,
   One true Eternal God confess'd,
   May nought in life or death divide
   The saints in Thy communion
   bless'd.

PRAYER

748

Jesus My Strength My Hope-
D.S.M.

1. Jesus, my strength, my hope,
   On Thee I cast my care,
   With humble confidence look up,
   And know Thou hear'st my prayer.
   Give me on Thee to wait,
   Till I can all things do,
   On Thee, Almighty to create,
   Almighty to renew,

2. I want a godly fear,
   A quick-discerning eye,
   That look to Thee When sin is near,
   And sees the tempter fly;
   As spirit still prepared.
   And armed with jealous care,
   For ever standing on its guard,
   And watching unto prayer.

3. I want a true regard,
   A single, steady aim,
   Unmoved by threatening or reward,
   To Thee and Thy great name;
   A jealous, Just concern
   For Thine immortal praise;
   A pure desire that all may learn
   And glorify Thy grace.

4. I rest upon Thy word;
   The promise is for me;
   My soccour and salvation, Lord
   Shall surely come from Thee:
   But let me still abide,
   Nor from my hope remove,
   Till Thou my patient spirit guide
   Into Thy perfect love.

749

O Loving Shepherd, Care For Us-
C.M.

1. O loving Shepherd, care for us
   In these precious time
   Give unto all Thy disciple,
   The power to watch and pray.

2. When our trials persist, O Lord
   And afflictions increase,
   Grant that our hearts rely on thee,
   In long prevailing prayers.

3. The spirit of supplication
   In faith, give Thou to us
   Until we shall behold Thy face,
   And know Thy mighty name.

4. Until we are in communication,
   And sweetest fellowship,
   Let this be the heart's cry of all,
   We will not let Thee go.

5. I will not let Thee go except
   Thou tells thy name to me,
   Oh, bless me with thy salvation
   And let me be like Thee.

6. O, let me clearly see Thy face
   Up there in heaven above,
   Where faith will be transformed to
   sight,
   And prayer becomes our praise.

750

Pray, Without Ceasing Pray-
D.S.M.

1 Pray, without ceasing pray,
   Your captain give the word;
   His summons cheerfully obey,
   And call upon the Lord:
   To God your every want
   In instant prayer display:
   Pray always: pray, and never faint:
   Pray, without ceasing pray!

2. In fellowship, alone,
   To God with faith draw near,
   Approach His course, besiege his
   throne
   With all the powers of prayer:
   Go to His temple, go
   Nor from His altar move:
   Let every house His worship know,
   And every heart His love.

PRAYER

3. Pour out your souls to God,
And bow them with your knees,
And spread your hearts and hands abroad
And pray for Zion's peace;
Your guides and brethren bear
For ever on your mind;
Extend the arms of mighty prayer,
In grasping all mankind.

4 From strength to strength go on,
Wrestle; and fight, and pray,
Tread all the powers of darkness down,
And win the well-fought day;
Still let the Spirit cry
In all his soldiers: Come!
Till Christ the Lord descend from on high,
And take the conquerors home.

751

Tell It To Jesus, All Of Thy Sorrow
- P.M.,

1. Tell It to Jesus, all of thy sorrow,
All of thy cares whate'er they be;
Surely and sweetly, He will deliver
He will sustain and comfort thee.

Chorus
Tell it to Jesus, tell it to Jesus
Tell it to Jesus, He will hear,
Only believe, Him trust and receive Him,
He will sustain and comfort thee.

2. Tell it to Jesus, He is thy Saviour,
Tell it, and His salvation see;
Do not deny Him, do not defy Him
He will sustain and comfort thee.

3. Tell It to Jesus, He is a refuge,
Into His arms for mercy flee,
Tell It believing, tell It receiving
Grace to sustain and comfort thee.

752

There to An Eye That Never Sleeps
- C.M.

1. There is an eye that never sleeps
Beneath the wing of night;
There is an ear that never shuts,
When sinks the beams of light

2. There is an arm that never tires,
When human strength gives way;
There is a love that never fails,
When earthly loves decay.

3. That eye is fix'd on Seraph throngs;
That arm upholds the sky;
That ear is fill'd with angel songs;
That love is throned on high.

4. But there's a power, which man can wield,
When mortal aid is vain,
That eye, that arm, that love to reach,
That listening ear to gain.

5. That power is prayer, which soars on high
Through Jesus to the throne,
And moves the hand, which moves the world,
To bring salvation down.

6. Oh, Thou whose mercy knows no end.
Whose love can never cease,
Grant that we have both faith and love,
So, we may always pray.

753

What Various Hindrances We Meet
- L.M.

1. What various hindrance we meet.
Incoming to the mercy-seat!
Yet who that knows the worth of prayer
But wishes to be often there?

PRAYER

2. Prayer makes the darken'd cloud
withdraw;
Prayer climbs the ladder Jacob
saw,
Gives exercise to faith and love,
Brings every blessing from above.

3. Restraining prayer we cease to fight;
Prayer makes the Christian's
armour bright;
And satan trembles when he sees
The weakest saint upon his knees.

4. Have we no words? ah! Think
again:
Words flow apace when we
complain,
And fill our fellow creature's ear
With the sad tale of all our care.

5. Were half the breath thus vainly
spent
To heaven in supplication sent,
Our cheerful song would oftener be
Hear what the Lord hath done for
Me.

754

Who'll Be The Next To Follow Jesus

1. Who'll be the next to follow Jesus?
Who'll be the next His cross to
bear?
Someone is ready, someone is
waiting,
Who'll be the next a crown to wear?

Chorus
Who'll be the next, who'll be the
next,
Who'll be the next to follow Jesus?
Who'll be the next to follow Jesus
now?
Follow Jesus now?

2. Who'll be the next to follow Jesus?
Come and bow at His precious feet.
Who'll be the next to lay every
burden
Down at The Father's Mercy-seat?

3. Who'll be the next to follow Jesus?
Who'll be the next to praise His
name?
Who'll swell the chorus of free
Redemption,
Sing, Hallelujah! Praise the Lamb?

HOLINESS

755

Was Lebet -13.10.13.10

1. O worship the Lord in the beauty of
   holiness!
   Bow down before him, his glory
   proclaim;
   With gold of obedience, and
   Incense of lowliness.
   Kneel and adore him: the Lord is his
   name.

2. Low at his feet lay thy burden of
   carefulness:
   High on his heart he will bear it for
   thee,
   Comfort thy sorrows, and answer
   thy prayerfulness,
   Guiding thy steps as may best for
   thee be.

3. Fear not to enter his courts in the
   slenderness
   Of the poor wealth thou wouldst
   reckon as thine:
   Truth in its beauty, and love in its
   tenderness,
   These are the offerings to lay on his
   shrine.

4. These, though we bring them in
   trembling and fearfulness,
   He will accept for the name that is
   dear,
   Mornings of joy give for evenings of
   tearfulness,
   Trust for our trembling and hope for
   our fear.

   -J. S. B. Monsell

756

St Magnus - C.M.

1. Strong Captain, in thy holy ranks
   We take our places now:

Give us the mood befitting those
Who make so great a vow.

2. For foolishness it were to come
   In hardihood of pride,
   And cowardice it were to come
   And wish to be untried.

3. We'll not mistrust our want of
   strength
   Nor trust our strength of will;
   Our only confidence, that thou
   Believest in us still.

4. Make, then, our task to match our
   strength
   Our strength to match our task,
   And make us unafraid to do
   Whatever thou wilt ask.

   -J.M.C. Crum

757

Tallis - C.M.

1. The highest and the holiest place
   Guards not the heart from sin:
   The Church that safest seems
   Without
   May habour foes within.

2. Thus in the small and chosen band
   Beloved above the rest,
   One fell from his apostleship,
   A traitor soul unblest

3. But not the great designs of God
   Man's sins shall overthrow;
   Another witness to the truth
   Forth to the lands shall go.

4. The soul that sinneth, it shall die;
   Thy purpose shall not fail:
   The word of grace no less shall
   sound.
   The truth no less prevail.

HOLINESS

5. Righteous, O Lord, are all thy ways:
Long as the worlds endure,
From foes without and foes within
Thy Church shall stand secure.

-H. Alford

758

West Burn- C.M.

1. Walk in the light so shalt thou
know
That fellowship of love
His Spirit only can bestow,
Who reigns in light above.

2. Walk in the light: and sin, abhorred,
Shall ne'er defile again;
The blood of Jesus Christ thy Lord
Shall cleanse from every stain.

3. Walk in the light: and thou shalt find
Thy heart made truly His,
Who dwells in cloudless light
enshrined,
In whom no darkness is.

4. Walk in the light: and thou shalt
own
Thy darkness passed away,
Because that light hath on thee
Shone.
In which is perfect day.

5. Walk in the light: and e'en the tomb
No fearful shade shall wear;
Glory shall chase away its gloom,
For Christ hath conquered there.

6. Walk in the light and thine shall be
A path, though thorny, bright;
For God, by grace, shall dwell in
thee.
And God Himself is Light.

-Bernard Barton

759

Hanford-10.10.11.11. with Refrain

1. More like the Master I would ever be,
More of His meekness, more
humility;
More zeal to labour, more courage to
be true,
More consecration for work He bids
me do.

Chorus
Take Thou my heart, I would be
Thine alone;
Take Thou my heart and make it all
Thine own;
Purge me from sin, O Lord. I now
implore,
Wash me and keep me Thine
forever more.

2. More like the Master is my daily
prayer;
More strength to carry crosses I
Must bear;
More earnest effort to bring His
kingdom in;
More of His Spirit, the wanderer to
Win.

3. More like the Master I would live and
grow;
More of His love to others I would
show;
More self denial, like His in Galilee
More like the Master I long to ever
be.

-Charles H. Gabriel

760

Every day And Hour - 7.9.7.9. And Refrain

l. Saviour, more, than life to me,
I am clinging, clinging close to
Thee;
Let Thy precious blood applied,
Keep me ever, ever near Thy side

HOLINESS

Chorus
Ev'ry day; ev'ry hour, Let me feel Thy
cleansing pow'r;
May Thy tender love to me
Bind me closer, closer, Lord, to
Thee.

2. Thro' this changing world below,
Lead me gently, gently as I go;.
Trusting Thee. I cannot stray,
I can never, never lose my way.

3. Let me love Thee more and more,
Till this fleeting, fleeting life is o'er.
Till my soul is lost in love,
In a brighter, brighter world above.
-Fanny J. Crosby

761

Sweney - L.M. with Refrain

1. More about Jesus would I know,
More of His grace to others show.
More of His saving fullness see,
More of His love who died for me.

Chorus
More, more about Jesus,
More, more about Jesus;
More of His saving fullness see,
More of His love who died for me!
O to be like Thee, Blessed
Redeemer,
I want to be like Jesus, my Lord

2. More about Jesus let me learn,
More of His holy will discern;
Spirit of God, my teacher be,
Showing the things of Christ to me.

3. More about Jesus; in His Word.
Holding communion with my Lord,
Hearing His voice in ev'ry line,
Making each faithful saying mine.

4. More about Jesus on His throne.
Riches in glory all His own.

More of His kingdom's sure
increase,
More of His coming Prince of Peace.
-Eliza E, Hewitt

762

Hoffman -12.9.12.9. with Refrain

I. You have longed for sweet peace
and for faith to increase,
And have earnestly, fervently
prayed;
But you cannot have rest or be
perfectly blest
Until all on the altar is laid.

Chorus
Is your all on the altar of sacrifice
laid
Your heart does the Spirit control?
You can only be blest and have
peace and sweet rest.
As you yield Him your body and
Soul.

2. Would you walk with the Lord in the
light of His word
And have peace and contentment
always?
You must do His sweet will to be free
from all ill
On the altar your all you must lay.

3. O we never can know what the Lord
will be stow
Of the blessings for which we have
prayed.
Till our body and soul He doth fully
control,
And our all on the altar is laid.

4. Who can tell all the love He will
send from above,
And how happy our hearts will be
made,
Of the fellowship sweet we shall
share at His feet
When our all on the altar is laid!
-Elisha A. Hoffman

HOLINESS

763

Purer in Heart - 6.4.6.4.6.6.4.4.

1. Purer in heart, O God, Help me to be
May I devote my life Wholly to Thee:
Watch Thou my wayward feet,
Guide me with counsel sweet;
Purer in heart Help me to be,

2. Purer in heart. O God, Help me to be
Teach me to do Thy Win Most
lovingly:
Be Thou my friend and guide,
Let me with Thee abide;
Purer in heart Help me to be;

3. Purer in heart, O God, Help me to be
Until Thy holy face One day I see:
Keep me from secret sin,
Reign Thou my soul within;
Purer in heart Help me to be:
 -Mrs. A. L. Davison

764

Coleman - 8.7.8.8. and Refrain

1. While passing thro' this world of sin.
And others your life shall view,
Be clean and pure without, within,.
Let others see Jesus in you.

Chorus
Let others see Jesus in you,
Let others see Jesus in you;
Keep telling the story, be faithful
and true,
Let others see Jesus in you.

2. Your life's a book before their eyes,
They're reading in thro' and thro':
Say, does it point them to the skies.
Do others see Jesus in you.

3. What joy 'twill be at set of sun.
In mansions beyond the blue,

To find some souls that you have
won; .
Let others see Jesus in you.

4. Then live for Christ both day and
night.
Be faithful, be brave and true.
And lead the lost to life and light;
Let others see Jesus in you.
 -B. B McKinney

765

St. Fulbert -C. M.

1. O Jesus Christ, grow Thou in me,
And all things else recede,
My heart be daily nearer Thee,
From sin be daily freed.

2. Each day let Thy supporting might
My weakness still embrace;
My darkness vanish in Thy light,
Thy life my death efface.

3. In Thy bright beams which on me
fall,
Fade every evil thought;
That I am nothing, Thou art all,
I would be daily taught.

4. More of Thy glory let me see,
Thou Holy, Wise, and True!
I would Thy living image be.
In joy and sorrow too.

5. Fill me with gladness from above,
Hold me by strength divine!
Lord, let the glow of Thy great
love Through my whole being
shine.

6. Make this poor self grow less and
less.
Be Thou my life and aim;
O make me daily, through Thy
grace,
More meet to bear Thy name!
 -Johann Caspar Lavater

HOLINESS

766

Franconia -S. M.

1. Blest are the pure in heart,
For thy shall see our God:
The secret of the Lord is theirs;
Their soul is Christ's abode.

2. The Lord. who left the heavens
Our life and peace to bring,
To dwell in lowliness with men,
Their pattern and their King,

3. Still to the lowly soul He doth
Himself impart,
And for His dwelling and His
throne Chooseth the pure in heart.

4. Lord, we Thy presence seek;
May ours this blessing be;
Give us a pure and lowly heart,
A temple meet for Thee.
　　　　　　　-John Keble

767

Caithness -C. M.

1. Search me, O God! my actions try,
And let my life appear
As seen by Thine all searching eye;
To mine my ways make dear.

2. Search all my sense, and know my
heart.
Who only canst make known,
And tell the deep, the hidden part
To me be fully shown.

3. Throw light into the darkened cells,
Where passion reigns within;
Quicken my conscience till it feels
The loathsomeness of sin.

4. Search, till Thy fiery glance has
cast
Its holy light through all

And I by grace am brought at last
Before Thy face to fall.

5. Thus prostrate I shall learn of Thee,
What now I feebly prove.
That God alone in Christ can be
Unutterable love!
　　　　　　　-Francis Bottome

768

Is Thy Heart Right

1. Have thy affections been nail'd to the
Cross?
is thy heart right with God?
Dost thou count all things for Jesus
but loss?
Is thy heart right with God?

Chorus
Is thy heart right with God.
Wash'd in the crimson flood,
Cleans'd and made holy, humble
And lowly.
Right in the Sight of God? (of God?)

2. Hast thou dominion o'er self and
o'er sin?
Is thy heart right with God?
Over all evil without and within?
Is thy heart right with God?

3. Is there no more condemnation for
sin?
Is thy heart right with God?
Does Jesus rule in the temple within?
Is thy heart right with God?

4. Are ail thy pow'r under Jesus'
control?
Is thy heart right with God?
Does He each moment abide in thy
soul?
Is thy heart right with God?

5. Art thou now walking in heaven's
pure light?
Is thy heart right with God?

HOLINESS

Is thy soul wearing the garment of white?
Is thy heart right with God?
-Elisha A. Hoffman

769

Christ the Fountain

1. Fountain of purity open'd for sin,
   Here may the penitent wash and
   be clean;
   Jesus, Thou blessed Redeemer
   from woe.
   Wash me, and I shall be whiter
   than snow.

   Chorus
   Whiter than snow,
   whiter than snow;
   Wash me, Redeemer, and I shall
   be whiter than snow.

2. Tho' I have labour'd again and
   again,
   All my self cleansing is utterly
   wain;
   Jesus, Redeemer from sorrow
   and woe,
   Wash me, and I shall be whiter
   than snow.

3. Cleanse Thou the thoughts of my
   heart, I Implore;
   Help me Thy light to reflect more
   and more:
   Daily in loving obedience to grow,
   Wash me, and I shall be whiter than
   snow.

4. Whiter than snow I nothing farther
   need;
   Christ is the Fountain: this only I
   Plead;
   Jesus, my Saviour, to Thee will I go
   Wash me, and I shall be whither
   than snow.
   -Rev. Newman Hall .D. D.

770

Bethany - 6.4.6.4.6.6.6.4

1. Nearer, my God, to Thee,
   Nearer to Thee!
   E'en though it be a cross
   That raiseth me;
   Still all my song shall be,
   Nearer, my God to Thee,
   Nearer to Thee.

2. Though like the wanderer,
   The sun gone down,
   Darkness be over me.
   My rest a stone;
   Yet in my dreams I'd be
   Nearer, my God, to Thee,
   Nearer to Thee,

3. There let the way appear
   Steps unto heav'n;
   All that Thou sendest me
   In mercy giv'n;
   Angels to beckon me
   Nearer, my God, to Thee.
   Nearer to Thee.

4. Then, with my waking thoughts
   Bright with Thy praise,
   Out of my stony griefs,
   Bethel I'll raise;
   So by my woes to be
   Nearer, my God, to Thee,
   Nearer to Thee.

5. Or if on joyful wing,
   Cleaving the sky,
   Sun, moon, and stars forgot.
   Upward I fly,
   Still all my song shall be
   Nearer, my God, to Thee.
   Nearer to Thee.
   -Sarah F. Adams

HOLINESS

771

Abridge -C. M.

1. Oh for a closer walk with God,
   A calm and heav'nly frame;
   A light to shine upon the road
   That leads me to the Lamb!

2. Where is the blessedness I knew
   When first I saw the Lord?
   Where is the soul refreshing view
   Of Jesus and His word?

3. What peaceful hours I once enjoyed
   How sweet their memory still!
   But they have left an aching void
   The world can never fill.

4. The dearest idol I have known,
   Whate'er that idol be,
   Help me rear if from Thy throne,
   And worship only Thee.

5. So shall my walk be close with God,
   Calm and serene my frame
   So purer light shall mark the road
   That leads me to the Lamb.
   -W. Cowper

772

Rockingham Old -L M.

1. Teach me; O Lord, Thy holy way,
   And give me an obedient mind,
   That in Thy service I may find
   My soul's delight from day to day.

2 Help me, O Saviour, here to trace
   The sacred footsteps Thou hast trod;
   And, meekly walking with my God,
   To grow in goodness, truth, and
   grace.

3 Guard me, O Lord, that I may ne'er

Forsake the right, or do the wrong;
Against temptation make me strong,
And round me spread Thy sheltering
Care.

4. Bless me in every task, O Lord.
   Begun, continued, done for Thee;
   Fulfill Thy perfect work in me.
   And Thine abounding grace afford.
   -Willams Matson

773

Leominster - D.S.M.

1. Make me a captive Lord,
   And then I shall be free;
   Force me to render up my sword,
   And I shall conqueror be.
   I sink in life's alarms
   When by myself I stand;
   Imprison me within Thine arms.
   And strong shall be my hand.

2. My heart is weak and poor
   Until it master find;
   It has no spring of action sure
   It varies with the wind.
   It cannot freely move.
   Till Thou hast wrought its chain;
   Enslave it with Thy matchless love,
   And deathless it shall reign.

3. My power is faint and low
   Till I have learned to serve;
   It wants the needed fire to glow,
   It wants the breeze to nerve;
   It cannot drive the world,
   Until itself be driven;
   Its flag can only be unfuried
   When Thou shalt breathe from
   heaven.

4. My will is not my own
   Till Thou hast made it Thine;
   If it would reach a monarch's throne
   It must its crown resign;

HOLINESS

It only stands unbent,
Amid the dashing strife.
When on Thy bosom it has leant
And found in Thee its life.
                    -George Matheson

774

O grant us light-L.M.

1. O, grant us light, that we may know
The wisdom Thou alone canst give:
That truth may guide where'er we go,
And virtue bless where'er we live!

2. O grant us light, that we may see
Where error lurks in human lore,
And turn our doubting minds to Thee.
And love Thy simple word the more.

3. O grant us light, that we may see
How dead is life from Thee apart;
How sure is joy for all who turn
To Thee an undivided heart.

4. O grant us light, in grief and pain,
To lift our burdened hearts above,
And count the very cross as gain.
And bless our Father's hidden love.

5. O grant us light, when, soon or late,
All earthly scenes shall pass away,
In Thee to find the open gate
To deathless home and endless day.
                    -Lawrence Tuttiett

775

Abbey-C.M.

1. O help us, Lord; each hour of need
Thy heavenly sucour give;
Help us in thought, and word, and deed,
Each hour on earth we live.

2. O help us when our spirits bleed
With contrite anguish sore;
And, when our hearts are cold and Dead.
O help us. Lord, the more.

3. O help us, through the prayer of faith.
More firmly to believe;
For still the more the servant hath
The more shall he receive.

4. If, strangers to Thy fold, we call
Imploring at Thy feet
The crumbs that from Thy table fall
Tis all we dare entreat.

5. But be it, Lord of mercy, all,
So Thou wilt grant but this;
The crumbs that from Thy table fall
Are light and life and bliss.

6. O help us, Saviour, from on high
We know no help but Thee:
O help us so to live and die
As Thine in heaven to be.
                    -Scottish Psalter

776

Affection -L.M.

1. O Thou who camest from above,
The pure celestial fire to impart,
Kindle a flame of sacred love
On the mean attar of my heart.

2. There let it for Thy glory burn
With inextinguishable blaze,
And trembling to its source return,
In humble prayer and fervent praise.

3. Jesus, confirm my heart's desire
To work, and speak, and think for Thee;
Still let me guard the holy fire.
And still stir up Thy gift in me;

HOLINESS

4 Ready for all Thy perfect will.
My acts of faith and love repeat,
Till death Thy endless mercies
seal
And make the sacrifice complete.
-Charles Wesley

777

Anima Christi - 7.7.7.7.D.

1. Soul of Jesus, make me whole,
Meek and contrite make my soul;
Thou most stainless Soul Divine,
Cleanse this sordid soul of mine,
Hallow this my contrite heart,
Purify my every part;
Soul of Jesus hallow me,

2. Save me. Body of my Lord,
Save a sinner, vile, abhorred;
Sacred Body, wane and worn,
Bruised and mangled, scourged
and torn,
Pierced hands, and feet, and
side,
Rent. insulted, crucified:
Save me to the Cross I flee,

3. Blood of Jesus, stream of life,
Sacred stream with blessings rife,
From thy broken Body shed
On the Cross, that altar dread;
Given to be our drink Divine,
Fill my heart and make it thine;
Blood of Christ, my succour be,

4. Holy Water, stream that poured
From thy riven side, O Lord,
Wash thou me without, within,
Cleanse me from the taint of sin,
Till my soul is clean and white,
Bathed, and purified, and bright
As a ransomed soul should be,

5. Jesus, by the wondrous power
Of thine awful Passion hour,
By the unimagined woe Mortal
man may never know;

By the curse upon thee laid,
By the ransom thou hast paid,
By thy Passion comfort me,

6. Jesus, by thy bitter Death,
By thy last expiring breath,
Give me the eternal life,
Purchased by that mortal strife;
Thou didst suffer death that
I Might not die eternally;
By thy dying quicken me,

7. Let me be
Never parted Lord, from thee:
Guard me from my ruthless foe,
Save me from eternal woe;
When the hour of death is near,
And my spirit faints for fear,
Call me with thy voice of love,
Place me near to thee above,
With thine Angel host to raise
An undying song of praise,
-Anon

778

Kildrostan -8.8.8.4.

1. One thing I of the Lord desire,
For all my way hath miry been
Be it by water or by fire,
O make me clean!

2. If clearer vision Thou impart,
Grateful and glad my soul shall be;
But yet to have a purer heart
Is more to me.

3. Yea, only as the heart is clean
May larger vision yet be mine,
For mirrored in its depths are seen
The things divine.

4. I watch to shun the miry way,
And stanch the spring of guilty
thought;
But, watch and wrestle as I may,
Pure I am not

HOLINESS

5. So wash Thou me without, within,
Or purge with fire. if that must be,
No matter how, if only sin
Die out in me.
-Walter Chalmers Smith

779

Fisher -11.11.11.11. with Refrain

1. Lord Jesus, I long to be perfectly
whole;
I want Thee forever to live in my
soul.
Break down every idol, cast out
every foe
Now wash me and I shall be
whiter than snow.

Chorus
Whiter than snow, yes, whiter than
snow
Now wash me and I shall be whiter
than snow.

2. Lord Jesus, look down from
Your throne in the skies
And help me to make a complete
sacrifice.
I give up my self and whatever I
know
Now wash me and I shall be whiter
than snow.

3. Lord Jesus, for this I most humbly
entreat.
I wait, blessed Lord, at Thy
crucified feet.
By faith, for my cleansing I see
Your blood flow
Now wash me and I shall be whiter
than snow.

4. Lord Jesus, before You I patiently
wait;
Come now and within me a new
heart create.
To those who have sought You,
You never said, "No"
Now wash me and I shall be whiter
than snow.
-James Nicholson

780

Pure and Holy -7.7.7.7, and Refrain

1. Pure and holy I would be,
worthy of Your love for me.
Teach me while Your light is clear,
change me while my heart is near.

Chorus
Holy, holy, holy Lord.
Holy, holy, holy Lord.

2. You are great and I am small,
You are King and God of all.
You are wise in all You do,
Lord I put my trust in You.
-Mike Hudson

781

Ellers -10.10.10.10.

1. Search me, O God, and know my
heart today;
Try me, O Saviour, know my
thoughts, I pray.
See if there be some wicked way in
me;
Cleanse me from ev'ry sin and set
me free.

2. I praise Thee, Lord, for cleansing
me from sin;
Fulfill Thy Word and make me pure
within.
Fill me with fire where once I
burned with shame;
Grant my desire to magnify Thy
name.

3. Lord, take my life and make it
wholly Thine;
Fill my poor heart with Thy great
love divine.
Take all my will, my passion, self.
and pride;
I now surrender; Lord.
In me abide.

HOLINESS

4. O holy Ghost, revival comes from
"Thee;
Send a revival; start the work in me.
Thy word declares Thou wilt supply
our need;
For blessings now,
O Lord, humbly plead.
-J. Edwin Orr

782

Azmon -C.M.

1. O for a heart to praise my God,
A heart from sin set free,
A heart that always feels Thy blood
So freely shed for me!

2. A heart in every thought renewed.
And full of love divine;
Perfect and right and pure and good
A copy, Lord, of Thine!

3. Thy nature, gracious Lord, Impart;
Come quickly from above,
Write Thy new name upon my heart,
Thy new, best name of Love.
-Charles Wesley

783

Holiness -6.5.6.5.D.

1. Take time to be holy.
Speak oft with thy Lord;
Abide in Him always,
And feed on His Word.
Make friends of God's children.
Help those who are weak;
Forgetting in nothing
His blessing to seek.

2. Take time to be holy,
The world rushes on;
Much time spend in secret
With Jesus alone;

By looking to Jesus,
like Him thou shalt be;
Thy friends in thy conduct
His likeness shall see.

3. Take time to be holy, .
Let Him be thy guide,
And run not before Him
Whatever betide;
In joy or in sorrow
Still follow thy Jesus
And, looking to Jesus,
Still trust His Word,

4. Take time to be holy,
Be calm in thy soul;
Each thought and each motive
Beneath His control;
Thus led by his Spirit
To fountains of love,
Thou soon shalt be fitted
For service above
-William D. Longstaff

784

Uffingham -L. M.

1. Holy, and true, and righteous Lord, .
I wait to prove Thy perfect will;
Be mindful of Thy gracious word,
And stamp me with Thy Spirit's
Seal

2. Confound o'er power me by Thy
grace,
I would be by myself abhorred;
All might, all majesty, all praise,
All glory, be to Christ my Lord.

3. Now tet me gain perfection's height,
Now let me into nothing fall,
Be less than nothing in Thy sight,
And feel that Christ is all in all.
-Charles Wesley

HOLINESS

785

Aynhoe-S.M.

1. The thing my God doth hate
That I no more may do,
Thy creatures, Lord, again create,
And all my soul renew.

2. My soul shall then, like Thine.
Abhor the thing unclean,
And, sanctified by love divine,
For ever cease from sin.

3. That blessed law of Thine,
Jesus, to me impart;
The Spirit's law of life divine,
O write it in my heart!

4. Implant it deep within,
Whence it may ne'er remove,
The law of liberty from sin,
The perfect law of love.

5. Thy nature be my law,
Thy spotless sanctity,
And sweetly every moment draw
My happy soul to Thee.

6. Soul of my soul remain!
Who didst for all fulfil.
In me, O Lord, fulfil again
Thy heavenly Father's will!
                    -Charles Wesley

786

Channels Only

1. How I praise Thee, precious
Saviour, That Thy love laid hold of
me;
Thou hast saved and cleansed and
Filled me
That I might Thy channel be.

Chorus
Channels only, blessed Master
But with all Thy wondrous pow'r
Flowing thro' us, Thou canst use us
Ev'ry day and ev'ry hour.

2. Emptied that Thou shouldest fill me
A clean vessel in Thy hand;
With no pow'r but as Thou givest
Graciously with each command

3. Witnessing Thy pow'r to save me
Setting free from self and sin;
Thou who boughtest to possess;
Me,
In Thy fullness. Lord come in.

4. Jesus, fill now with Thy Spirit
Hearts that full surrender know
That the streams of living water
From our inner man may flow.
                    -Mary E. Maxwell

787

Christian Walk carefully - 10.10.10.10.

1, Christian, walk carefully: danger is
near!
On in thy journey with trembling and
fear;
Snares from without, and
temptations within,
Seek to entice thee once more into
Sin.

Chorus
Christian, walk carefully: Christen
walk carefully,
Christian, walk carefully: danger is
Near!

2. Christian, walk cheerfully through
the fierce storm,
Dark though the sky with its threats
of alarm;

HOLINESS

Soon will the clouds and the trees be o'er,
Then with thy Saviour thou'll rest evermore.
Christian, walk prayerfully: oft wilt thou fall,
If thou forget on thy Saviour to call.
Safe thou shalt walk through trial and care,
If thou art clad in the armour of Prayer.

788
Give Me A Gentle Heart - 6.4.6.4.6.6.6.4;

1. Give me a gentle heart
   Filled with meekness,.
   Diligent heart like Thine
   Jesus, my Lord
   Humbleness and patience
   A heart of compassion
   In every small detail
   To be like Him.

2. Give me contentment in
   All conditions
   Be it e'en humbler than
   His lowly birth
   Give me Thou Thy comfort
   Give me also thy help
   In every small detail
   To be like Him.

3. Give me enthusiasm
   In things of Thine
   Earnestness and more love
   For things of heav'n
   Give me hatred for sin
   Give me also Thy help
   In every small detail
   To be like Him.

4. Give me a heart of faith
   A hope in Thee give joy of salvation

In Jesus Christ
Give me a living soul
Give me a crown of glory
And when I shall awake
To be like Him.

789
I Want Dear Lord, A Heart

1. I want, dear Lord, a heart
   That's true and clean
   A sunlit heart with not a cloud between.
   A heart like Thine, a heart divine.
   A heart as white as snow;
   On me, dear Lord. a heart like this Bestow.

2. I want dear Lord, a love that feels for all;
   A deep strong love that answers every call,
   A love like Thine, a love divine,
   A love for high and low,
   On me, dear Lord, a love like this bestow.

3. I want, dear Lord, a soul on fire for Thee;
   A soul baptized with heav'nly energy.
   A willing mind, a ready hand
   To do whate'er I know
   To spread Thy light wherever I may go.

790
Lord, I Desire A Sinless Heart -C.M.

1. Lord, I desire a sinless heart
   With which to praise my God
   A heart that knows Thy cleansing blood
   That was shed free for me.

2. A heart of patience and meekness
My dear Redeemer's throne
Where Christ is in perfect control
And absolutely reigns.

3. A humble heart that flees from sin
Full of faith and is clean
That life nor death can separate
From Christ who dwells within.

4. A heart that's entirely holy
That's full of divine love
Perfect, honest, holy and good,
An image. Lord, of Thee.

5. Lord I desire a life like Thine
Come quickly down I pray,
And write a new name in my heart
Thy name, O love divine.

791

O God, I Know That Thou Art Mine
-C.M.

1. O God I know that Thou art mine
And I will not leave Thee,
Till all I have become Thine own
And I shall be renewed.

2. I hold to thee with trembling hands
And I will not leave Thee;
Till in the faith, I'm established
And Thy goodness I know.

3. When will the moment come,
O Lord
When Thou Will dwell in me;
Spirit of life and pow'r and might
And of perfect wisdom.

4. Lord let the triumph of Thy love
Be shed abroad within
That my feet may ne'er go astray
But, be grounded in Thee.

5. Thy Holy flame, grant that it may
Light up within my heart;
To burn the dross of wicked lust
And melt the heart of stone.

6. Let Thy fire come down from above
And consume all my sins
Come, Holy Spirit, hear my cry
Come, Thou Spirit of fire.

7. Refining fire, come to my heart,
Shed Thou Thy light abroad
Fill me within with Thy Spirit
Consecrated to Thee.

792

O Saviour, May We Never Rest -C.M.

1. O Saviour, may we never rest
Till Thou art formed within,
Till Thou hast calmed our troubled
breast,
And crushed the power of sin.

2. O may we gaze upon Thy Cross;
Until the wondrous sight
Makes earthly treasures seem but
dross,
And earthly sorrows light.

3. Until, released from carnal ties,
Our Spirit upward springs.
And sees true peace above the
skies,
True joy in heavenly things.

4. There as we gaze, may we become
United, Lord, to Thee,
And, in a fairer, happier home,
Thy perfect beauty see.

HOLINESS

793

What Is Our Calling's Glorious Hope -C M.

1. What is our calling's glorious hope
But inward holiness?
For this to Jesus I look up,
I calmly wait for this.

2. I wait, till He shall touch me clean.
Shall life and power Impart,
Give me the faith that casts out sin
And purifies the heart.

3. This is the dear redeeming grace,
For every sinner free:
Surely it shall on me take place,
The chief of sinners, me.

4. From all iniquity, from all,
He shall my soul redeem:
In Jesus I believe and shall
Believe myself to Him.

5. When Jesus makes my heart His Home,
My sin shall all depart;
And lo, He saith; I quickly come.
To fill and rule Thy heart.

6. Be it according to Thy word!
Redeem me from all sin:
My heart would now receive Thee,
Lord
Come in, my Lord, come in!

794

What Is The Thing That I Long For L.M.

1. What Is the thing that I long for!
What is my hope or my desire?
How I crave to follow the Lamb
And I His image to adopt.

2. All my hope, Lord on Thee is stayed
I long to be the one you love
I want to be saved here on earth
And fellowship with Thee above.

3. I hunger for the Lord of life
Who died for me on Calvary
For the source of water and blood
That from Thy wounded side which flowed.

4. I desire Thy water of love Spirit of
joy that's yet unknown
Grant that I may yet drink above
As it does stream forth from Thy
throne

LOVE SHARING AND CARING

795

Charity-7.7.7.5.

1. Gracious Spirit, Holy Ghost,
Taught by Thee, we covet most,
Of Thy gifts at Pentecost, Holy,
heavenly love.

2. Love is kind and suffers long,
Love is meek and thinks no wrong,
Love than death itself more strong;
Therefore give us love.

3. Prophecy will fade away,
Melting in the light of day;
Love will ever with us stay;
Therefore give us love.

4. Faith will vanish into sight;
Hope be emptied in delight;
Love in heaven will shine more
bright;
Therefore give us love.

5. Faith and hope and love we see,
Joining hand in hand, agree;
But the greatest of the three,
And the best, is love.
                        -C. Word sworth

796

Binchester - C.M.

1. Happy are they, they that love God,
Whose hearts have Christ confest,
Who by His cross have found their
life.
. And 'neath His yoke their rest.

2. Glad the praise, sweet are the
songs, When they together sing;
And strong the prayers that bow
the ear
Of heaven's eternal King.

3. Christ to their homes giveth his
peace,
And makes their loves His own:
But ah, what tares the evil one
Hath in His garden sown!

4. Sad were our lot, evil this earth
Did not its sorrows prove
The path whereby the sheep may
find
The fold of Jesus' love.

5. Then shall they know, they that love
Him, How all their pain is good;
And death itself cannot unbind
Their happy brotherhood-
                        -Robert S. Bridges

797

Albano - C. M.

1. Immortal Love, forever full,
For ever flowing free,
For ever shared, for ever whole
A never ebbing seal

2. We may not climb the heavenly
steeps
To bring the Lord Christ down
In vain-we search the lowest deeps,
For Him no depths can drown.

3. But warm, sweet, tender even yet
A present help is He;
And faith has still its Olivet,
And love its Galilee.

4. The healing of His seamless dress
Is by our beds of pain;
We touch Him in life's throng and
Press,
And we are whole again.

5. O Lord and Master of us all,
Whate'er our name or sign,
We own Thy sway, we hear Thy
Call,
We test our lives by Thine.
                        -J. G. Whittier

LOVE SHARING AND CARING

798

St. Leonard-C.M.

1. Lord, I would own Thy tender care,
   And all Thy love to me;
   The food I eat, the clothes I wear,
   Are all bestowed by Thee.

2. Tis Thou preservest! me from death
   And dangers every hour:
   I cannot draw another breath
   Unless Thou give me power.

3. My health and friends and parents dear
   To me by God are given;
   I have not any blessing here
   But what is sent from heaven.

4. Kind angels guard me every night,
   As round my bed they stay;
   Nor am I absent from Thy sight in
   darkness or by day.

5 Such goodness, Lord, and constant
   care, I never can repay:
   But may it be my daily prayer,
   To love Thee and obey.
        -Jane Taylor

799

Gwalchmai -7.4.7.4.D.

1. King of glory, King of peace,
   I will love Thee;
   And that love may never cease,
   I will move Thee.
   Thou hast granted my request,
   Thou hast heard me;
   Thou didst note my working breast.
   Thou hast spare me.

2. Wherefore with my utmost art
   I will sing Thee,
   And the cream of all my heart

I will bring Thee.
Though my sins against me cried,
Thou didst clear me,
And alone, when they replied,
Thou didst hear me.

3. Seven whole days. not one in
   seven.
   I will praise Thee;
   In my heart, though not in heaven,
   I can raise Thee.
   Small it is, in this poor sort
   To enrol Thee;
   E'en eternity's too short
   To extol Thee.
        -George Herbert

800

Do You Really Care

1. I look around in the place that I live;
   I see people with so much to give;
   Yet are those who are dying to
   know
   Just that somebody cares.
   Do you realty care? Do you know
   how to share
   With people ev'ry where? Do you
   really care?

   Chorus
   People grope in darkness.
   Searching for away,
   Don't you know of someone You
   Can help today?

2. I see people just longing to know
   What they can live for and where
   they can go;
   We have the hope and the purpose
   to share,
   But, do we really care? Will you take
   the dare? Spread
   Good News ev'rywhere? The cross
   of Christ to bear? Do you
   really care?
        -Bill Cates

LOVE SHARING AND CARING

801

O, how I love Jesus C. M. with Refrain

1. There is a name I love to hear,
   I love to sing its worth;
   It sounds like music; in my ear,
   The sweetest name on earth.

   Chorus
   O, how I love Jesus.
   O, how I love Jesus
   O, how I love Jesus
   Because He first loved me!

2. It tells me of a Savior's love,
   who died to set me free;
   It tells me of His precious blood,
   The sinner's perfect plea.

3. It tells me what my Father hath
   In store for ev'ry day,
   And, tho I tread a dark- some path,
   Yields sunshine all the way.

4. It tells of One whose loving heart
   Can feel my deepest woe,
   Who in each sorrow bears a part
   That none can bear below.
   -Frederick Whitfield

802

Stuttgart-8.7.8.7.

1: God is love; His mercy brightens
   All the path in which we rove;
   Bliss He wakes and woe He lightens:
   God is wisdom. God is love.

2. Chance and change are busy ever,
   Man decays and ages move;
   But His mercy waneth never.
   God is wisdom. God is love.

3. E'en the hour that darkest seemeth
   Will His changeless goodness prove;

Thro' the gloom His brightness streameth;
God is wisdom, God is love.

4. He with earthly cares entwineth
   Hope and comfort from above
   Everywhere His glory shineth
   God is wisdom, God is love.
   -Johns Bowring

803

Trentham -S. M.

1. O Love of God most full,
   O Love of God most free,
   Come, warm my heart, come fill my soul.
   Come, lead me unto Thee!

2. Warm as the glowing sun,
   So shines Thy love on me;
   It wraps me 'round with kindly care
   It draws me unto Thee!

3. The wildest sea is calm,
   The tempest brings no fear,
   The darkest night is full of light
   Because Thy love is near.

4. O Love of God most full
   O Love of God most free,
   Thou warm'st my heart, Tho fill'st My soul,
   With might Thou strength 'nest me
   -Oscar Clute

804

Somebody Loves Me

1. I'm in love with my Saviour and He's in love with me,
   He is with me from day to day
   What a friend is He;
   Watches over me while I sleep
   Hears me when I pray,
   I am happy as I can be, And I now Can say:

LOVE SHARING AND CARING

Chorus
Somebody loves me, answers my prayer,
I love somebody, I know He cares;
Somebody tells me not to repine,
That Somebody is Jesus, and I
know He's mine.

2. You'll be happy if you will let Jesus have His way.
He has work for us all to do
Ev'ry passing day;
Feed the hungry and cheer the sad,
For the sinner, pray.
You'll have joy that you never had,
And you then can say:

3. Then at last when our work is done,
He will call us home
To a mansion He has prepared
Never more to roam,
We'll sit down by the riverside,
Cares all passed away,
And with never a pain to bear.
What a happy day.

-W. F. Crumley

805

Barnstaple -10.10.10.10.

1. It passeth knowledge, that dear love of Thine,
My Saviour, Jesus: yet this soul of mine
Would of Thy love. in all its breadth and length,
Its height and depth, its everlasting strength,
Know more and more.

2. It passeth telling, that dear love of Thine,
My Saviour, Jesus: yet these lips of mine
Would fain proclaim to all men, far and near,
A love which can cast out all faithless fear, And waken love:

3. It passeth praises, that dear love of Thine,
My Saviour, Jesus: yet this heart of mine
Would sing that love, so full. so rich, so free.
Which draws a guilty fugitive like me
Nigh unto God:

4. But tho I cannot sing, or tell, or know
The fulness of Thy love,
while here below
My empty vessel I may freely bring;
O Thou, who art of love the living spring,
My vessel fill.

5. And when Thee. Saviour, face to face I see,
When at Thy glorious throne I bow the knee,
Then of Thy love, in all its breadth and length,
Its height and depth, its everlasting strength.
My soul shall sing.

-Henry J. Edwards

806

St. David-C.M.

1. My blessed Saviour, is Thy love
So great, so full, so free?',
Behold, I give my love. my heart.
My life, my all, to Thee.

2. I love Thee for the glorious worth
Which in Thyself I see;
I love Thee for that shameful cross
Thou hast endured for me.

3. Though in the very form of God,
With heavenly glory crown'd,
Thou wouldst partake of human flesh
Beset with troubles round.

LOVE SHARING AND CARING

4. Thou wouldst like wretched man
be made,
In every thing but sin,
That we as like Thee might become
As we unlike had been.

5. Like Thee in faith, in meekness,
love,
In every beauteous grace;
From glory thus to glory changed,
As we behold Thy face.
-Ravenscroft

807

St Mary Tavy - 8.8.8.8,8.8.

1. O Thou whose wondrous love had
given
Thine own and only Son for man,
Ere shone the earliest star in
heaven
Or earth was framed or time began,
And chosen us in Him to be His
bride for all eternity.

2. Thou, who hast deign'd for us to
build
The mansions of Jerusalem.
With all Thy gifts of goodness fill'd
And rich with crystal gold and gem,
Whose gates and walls and streets
declare
One glorious name. "The Lord is
there;

3. Now in this little space between
Two vast eternites of love,
This narrow is themus of things
seen
Thy children cross to rest above.
Wilt Thou refuse to be our guide
And all our daily needs provide?

4. Oh shame upon the faithless heart
Which harbours such a thought of
Thee
My God, that Thou art what Thou
art

Is promise, aye and proof to me
While passing through this shadowy
vale
The cruse of oil shall never fail.

5. From everlasting I am Thine ,
In Thy free covenant of grace
To everlasting Thou art mine
In faith's response and love's
embrace
The life our Father gave and plann'd
Is safe in His Almighty hand.
-Joseph Barby!

808

Westminster - C. M.

1. My God, how wonderful Thou art,
Thy majesty how bright,
How beautiful Thy mercy seat.
In depths of burning light!

2. How dread are Thine eternal years
O everlasting Lord,
By prostrate spirits day and night
Incessantly adored!

3. How wonderful, how beautiful
The sight of Thee must be,
Thine endless wisdom, boundless
power,
And awful purity!

4. Oh, how I fear Thee, living God
With deepest, tenderest fears
And worship Thee with trembling
hope
And penitential tears!

5. Yet I may love Thee too. O Lord
Almighty as Thou art,
For Thou hast stoop'd to ask of me
The love of my poor heart.

6. No earthly father loves like thee
No mother, half so mild,
Bears and forbears as Thou has
done
With me Thy sinful child.

LOVE SHARING AND CARING

7. Father of Jesus, love's reward,
   What rapture will it be,
   Prostrate before Thy Throne to lie.
   And gaze and gaze on Thee.
                              -J. Turie

809

Martydom -C. M.

1. With joy we meditate the grace
   Of our High Priest above;
   His heart is made of tenderness,
   And yearns with faithful love.

2. Touch'd with a sympathy within,
   He knows our feeble frame:
   He knows what sore temptations
   mean,
   For He has felt the same.

3. He, in the days of feeble flesh,
   Pour'd out His cries and tears
   And in His measure feels afresh
   What every member bears.

4. He'll never quench the smoking
   flax,
   But raise it to a flame:
   The bruised reed He never
   breaks.
   Nor scorns the meanest name.

5. Then let our humble faith address
   His mercy and His power,
   We shall obtain delivering grace
   In every needful hour.
                              -Hugh Wilson

810

It's Just Like Him

1, Oh, I love to read of Jesus and His
   love,
   How He left His Father's mansion
   far above;
   How He came on earth to live,

How He came His life to give
Oh, I love to read of Jesus and His
love!

Chorus
It's Just like Him" to take my sins
away.
To make me glad and free, to keep
me day by day;
"It's just like Him" to give His life for
me,
That I might go to heaven, and ever
With Him be.

2. Oh, I love to read of Jesus as He
   went
   Ev'rywhere, to do His Father's will
   intent;
   How He gave the blind their sight,
   How He gave the wrong'd ones
   right.
   How He swift deliv'rance to the
   captive sent.

3. Oh, I love to read of Jesus on the
   tree,
   For it shows how great the love that
   died for me;
   And the blood that from His side
   Flow'd.
   when on the cross He died,
   Paid my debt, and evermore doth
   make me free.

4. Oh, my dear and precious Saviour,
   at Thy feet
   Here I give my self and all I have
   complete;
   I will serve Thee all my days
   With a heart all fill'd with praise.
   And I'll thank Thee face to face
   when we shall meet
                              -W. L Stone

811

The Love Of Jesus

1. Tis the love of Jesus
   Cheers our hearts today.
   Makes our earth an Eden,
   Drives the clouds away.

LOVE SHARING AND CARING

Chorus
Love of Jesus, love unbounded,
love so free
Sweetest story ever told to me!

2. Tis the love of Jesus
Lightens ev'ry task,
Gives us strength and comfort,
More than we can ask.

3. Tis the love of Jesus .
Makes our pathway bright,
Fills our hearts with singing,
And our lives with tight.

4. Blessed love of Jesus,
Freely to us giv'n
Theme of all the ages.
Sweetest song of heav'n.
-L B. Mitchell

812

Jesus Is Best to All

1. My happy heart is singing
My heav'nly Father's love;
He sends so many blessings
Like sunbeams from above,

Chorus
But Jesus is the best of all,
Yes, Jesus is the best of all.
Of all the joys that may surround
me,
The best of all is Jesus.

2. Tho' other joys may fail me.
And sorrows may befall,
My saviour will be with me,
And he is best of all.

3. O let me tell to others
The story of his grace,
Rejoicing in his service
Until I see his face.

4. And when I view the glories
Within the jasper wall,

I'll sing, with all the ransomed,
My saviour's best of all
-E. E. Hewitt

813

Affection-11.11.11.11.

1. My Jesus, I love Thee, I know
Thou art mine;
For Thee ail the follies of sin
I resign;
My gracious Redeemer, my Saviour
art Thou;
If ever I loved Thee, my Jesus, 'its
now.

2. I love Thee. because Thou hast first
loved me,
And purchased my pardon on
Calvary's tree;
I love Thee for wearing the thorns
on Thy brow;
If ever I loved Thee, my Jesus, 'tis
now.

3. I'll love Thee in life, t will love Thee
in death,
And praise Thee as long as Thou
lendest me breath;
And say when the death dew lies
cold on my brow;
If ever I loved Thee, my Jesus, 'tis
now

4. In mansions of glory and endless
delight.
I'll ever adore Thee in heaven so
bright;
I'll sing with the glittering crown on
my brow;
If ever I loved Thee, my Jesus, tis
now.
-William R. featherstone

LOVE SHARING AND CARING

814

None but Christ can Satisfy -
C. M. with Refrain

1. O Christ, in Thee my soul hath
   found,
   And found in Thee alone,
   The peace, the joy
   I sought so long,
   The bliss till now unknown.

Chorus
Now none but Christ can satisfy,
None other name for me.
There's love and life and lasting
joy,
Lord Jesus found in Thee.

2. I sighed for rest and happiness,
   I yearn'd for them, not Thee;
   But while I passed my Saviour by,
   His love laid hold on me.

3. I tried the broken cisterns. Lord,
   But, ah! the waters failed!
   E'en as I stooped to drink they fled.
   And mocked me as I wailed.

4. The pleasures lost I sadly
   mourned, But never wept for Thee;
   Till grace my sightless eyes
   received,
   Thy loveliness to see.
   -J. McGranahan

815

Where Jesus Is, 'tis heaven there
-L.M. with Refrain

1. Since Christ my soul from sin set
   free,
   This world has been a heav'n to
   me;
   And 'mid earth's sorrows and its
   woe,
   Tis heav'n my Jesus here to know.

Chorus
O hallelujah, yes, 'tis heav'n,
'Tis heav'n to know my sins forgiv'n;
On land or sea, what matters
where,
Where Jesus is,'tis heaven there.

2. Once heaven seemed afar off
   Place
   Till Jesus showed His smiling face;
   Now its begun within my soul,
   Twill last while endless ages roll.

3. What matters where on earth we
   dwell?
   On mountain top, or in the dell?
   in cottage, or in mansion fair,
   Where Jesus is, 'tis heaven there.
   -C. F. Butter

816

Dominus Regit me -8.7.8.7.

1. The King of love my Shepherd is,
   Whose goodness faileth never;
   I nothing lack if I am His
   And He is mine forever.

2. Where streams of living water flow
   My ransomed soul He leadeth.
   And where the verdant pastures
   grow
   With food celestial feedeth.

3. Perverse and foolish oft I strayed,
   But yet in love He sought me,
   And on His shoulder gently laid.
   And home rejoicing bro't me.

4. In death's dark vale I fear no ill
   With Thee. dear Lord, beside me;
   Thy rod and staff my comfort still,
   Thy cross before to guide me.

5. Thou spread'stl a table in my sight;
   Thy unction grace bestoweth:
   And O what transport of delight
   From thy pure chalice floweth!

LOVE SHARING AND CARING

6. And so thru all the length of days
Thy goodness faileth never:
Good Shepherd, may I sing Thy praise
Within Thy house forever.
-Henry W. Baker

817

St Aidan-7.5.7.5.

1. Thine are all the gifts, O God,
Thine the broken bread;
Let the naked feet be shod.
And the starving fed.

2. Let thy children, by thy grace,
Give as they abound,
Till the poor have breathing space
And the lost are found.

3. Wiser than the miser's hoards
Is the giver's choice;
Sweeter than the song of birds
Is the thankful voice.

4. Welcome smiles on faces sad
As the flowers of spring;
Let the tender hearts of spring;
Let the tender hearts be glad
With the joy they bring.
-A. G.Whittier

818

Cheerful Giving

1. Give as the Lord hath prospered thee.
Give, give to the Lord;
Give, with a willing mind and free,
Give, give to the Lord;
He hath supplied thee o'er and o'er,
Blessed thee in basket and in store.
Promised to fill thee more and more,
Thy gracious Lord.

Chorus
Give, give with a willing hand,
Give, give with a lib'ral hand,
Give at His blest command,
Who propered thee,
Give at His best command,
Who prospered thee.

2. Give, to the poor along the way,
Give, give to the Lord;
Give to the heathen far away,
Give, give to the Lord;
Give to His Needy as they cry,
Give to His people ere they die,
Give to His gospel that it fly,
O give, give. Give.

3. Give, tho' so poor thy gift may seem,,
Give, give to the Lord;
Give but the cup in Jesus' name,
Give, give to the Lord;
Cheerful then give the good thou hast,
Fearless thy bread on waters cast
It will return to thee at last
In harvests great.
-P. H

819

Es Ist Kein Tag-8.8.8.4.

1. O Lord of heaven, and earth, and sea,
To thee all praise and glory be;
How shall we show our love to thee
Giver of all?

2. The golden sunshine, vernal air.
Sweet flowers and fruits, thy love declare;
Where harvests ripen, thou art there
Giver of all!

3. For peaceful, homes, and healthful days.
For all the blessings earth displays.
We owe thee thankfulness and Praise.
Giver of all!

4. Thou didst not spare thine only
Son,
But gav'st him for a world undone,
And freely with that Blessed One
Thou givest all.

5. Thou giv'st the Spirit's blessed
dower,
Spirit of life, and love, and power,
And dost his sevenfold graces'
shower
Upon us all.

6. For souls redeemed, for sins
forgiven,
For means of grace and hopes of
heaven,
Father, what can to thee be given,
Who givest all?

7. We lose what on ourselves we
spend,
We have as treasure without end
Whatever, Lord, to thee we lend,
Who givest all;

8. To thee,.from whom we all derive
Our life, our gifts, our power to
give:
O may we ever with thee live,
Giver of all!
  -Bishop Christopher
    Wordsworth

820
Wonder of it all- Irregular Meter

1. There's the wonder of sunset at
evening,
The wonder as sunrise I see;
But the wonder of wonders that
thrills my soul
Is the wonder that God loves me.

Chorus
O, the wonder of it all! The wonder
of it all!
Just to think that God loves me.

O, the wonder of it all! The wonder
of it all!
Just to think that God loves me.

2. There's the wonder of spring time
and harvest
The sky, the stars, the sun;
But the wonder of wonders that
thrills my soul
Is a wonder that's only begun.
  -George Beverly Shea

821
Dominica-S.M.

1. Riches unsearchable
In Jesu's love we know;
And pleasures, springing from the
Well
Of life, our souls o'er flow.

2. The spirit we receive
Of wisdom, grace, and power;
And always sorrowful we live,
Rejoicing evermore.

3. Angels our servants are,
And keep in all our ways,
And in their watchful hands they bear
The sacred sons of grace:

4. Unto that heavenly bliss
They all our steps attend;
And God Himself our Father is,
And Jesus is our Friend.
  -Charles Wesley

822
Lynton -C. M.

1. Happy the heart where graces reign,
Where love inspires the breast;
Love is the brightest of the train,
And perfect all the rest.

2. Knowledge, alas, 'tis all in vain,
And all in vain our fear;

LOVE SHARING AND CARING

Our stubborn sins will fight and
reign. If love be absent there.

3. Tis love that makes our cheerful
feet
In swift obedience move:
The devils know, and tremble too;
But Satan cannot love.

4. This is the grace that lives and
sings
When faith and hope shall cease;
Strings
'Tis this shall strike our joyful
strings
In the sweet realm of bless.

5. Before we quite forsake our clay.
Or leave this dark abode.
The wings of love bear us away
To see our gracious God,
-Isaac Watts

823

Frogmore -6.4.6.4.

1. Beloved, let us love,
Love is of God;
In God alone hath love
Its true abode.

2. Beloved, let us love:
For they who love.
They only are His sons.
Born from above.

3. Beloved, let us, love:
For love is rest,
And he who loveth not.
Abide unblest

4. Beloved, let us love:
In love is light,
And he who loveth not,
Dwelleth in night.

5. Beloved, let us love:
For only thou
Shall we behold that God
Who loveth us.
-Horatius Bonar

824

Confidence L. M.

1. Jesus, Thy blood and righteousness
My beauty are, my glorious dress
·Midst flaming worlds, in these
·arrayed,
With joy shall I lift up my head.

2. Bold shall I stand in Thy great day;
For who aught to my charge shall
lay?
Fully absolved through these I am,
From sin and fear, from guilt and
shame.

3. The holy. meek, unspotted Lamb.
Who from the Father's bosom came
Who died for me, even me, to atone
Now for my Lord and God I own.

4. Lord, I believe Thy precious blood.
Which at the mercy-seat of God
For ever doth for sinners plead,
For me, even for my soul, was shed.

5. When from the dust of death I rise
To claim my mansion in the skies
Even then this shall be all my plea
Jesus hath lived, hath died for me

6. Jesus, be endless praise to Thee,
Whose boundless mercy hath for
me,
For me and all Thy hands have
made.
And everlasting ransom paid.

7. Lord, I believe, were sinners more
Than sands upon the ocean shore
Thou hast for all a ransom paid.
For all a full atonement made.

8. Ah! give to all Thy servants, Lard
With power to speak Thy gracious
· word,
That all who to Thy wounds Will flee
May find eternal life in Thee.

LOVE SHARING AND CARING

9. Thou God of power, Thou God of love,
Let the whole world Thy mercy prove'
Now let Thy word o'er all prevail;
Now take the spoils of death and hell,

10. O let the dead now hear Thy voice,
Now bid Thy banished ones rejoice,
Their beauty this. their glorious dress,
Jesus, Thy blood and righteous ness!

-Nicolaus Ludwig van Zinzendorf

825

St Bees -7.7.7.7.

1. Hark, my soul! it is the Lord;
Tis thy Saviour, hear His word;
Jesus speaks, and speaks to thee:
Say, poor sinner, lov'st thou Me?

2. I delivered thee when bound,
And, when bleeding, healed thy wound;
Sought thee wandering, set thee Right
Turned thy darkness into light.

3. Can a woman's tender care
Cease toward the child she bare?
Yes, she may forgetful be;
Yet will I remember thee.

4. Mine is an unchanging love,
Higher than the heights above,
Deeper than the depths beneath,
Free and faithful, strong as death.

5. Thou shall see My glory soon,
When the work of grace is done;
Partner of My throne shalt be;
Say, poor sinner, lov'st thou Me?

6. Lord, it is my chief complaint
That my love is weak and faint;
Yet I love Thee, and adore;
O for grace to love Thee more.
-William Cowper

826

Lunenburg - C. M.

1. Help us to help each other. Lord,
Each other's cross to bear
Let each his friendly aid afford,
And feel his brother's care.

2. Help us to build each other up,
Our little stock improve;
Increase our faith, confirm our hope,
And perfect us in love.

3. Up into Thee, our living Head,
Let us in all things grow,
Till Thou hast made us free indeed,
And spotless here below.

4. Then, when the mighty work is wrought,
Receive Thy ready bride:
Give us in heaven a happy lot
With all the sanctified.
-Charles Wesley

827

St. Godric -6.6.6.6.8.8.

1. Thou God of truth and love,
We seek Thy perfect way,
Ready Thy choice to approve, Thy providence to obey:
Enter into Thy wise design,
And sweetly lose our will in Thine.

2. Why hast Thou cast our lot
In the same age and place,
And why together brought
To see each other's face;
To join with loving sympathy,
And mix our friendly souls in Thee?

3. Didst Thou not make us one,
That we might one remain,
Together travel on,
And bear each other's pain;
Till all Thy utmost goodness prove,
And rise renewed in perfect love?

LOVE SHARING AND CARING

4. Then let us ever bear
   The blessed end in view,
   And join, with mutual care,
   To flight our passage through
   And kindly help each other on,
   Till all receive the starry crown.
   -Charles Wesley

828

The Love of God

1. The Love of God is greater far
   Than tongue or pen can ever tell;
   It goes beyond the highest star,
   And reaches to the lowest hell.
   The guilty pair, bowed down with care,
   God gave His Son to win;
   His erring child He reconciled,
   And pardoned from his sin.

   Chorus
   O love of God, how rich and pure!
   How measureless and strong!
   It shall forever more endure
   The saints' and angels' song.

2. When hoary time shall pass away,
   And earthly thrones and kingdoms fall,
   When men, who here refuse to pray,
   On rocks and hills and mountains call,
   God's love so sure, shall still endure,
   All measureless and strong;
   Redeeming grace to Adam's race
   The saints' and angels song.

3. Could we with ink the ocean fill,
   And were the skies of parchment made,
   Were ev'ry stalk on earth a quill,
   And ev'ry man a scribe by trade,
   To write the love of God above
   Would drain the ocean dry.

Nor could the scroll contain the whole,
Tho' stretched from sky to sky
   -F. M. Lahman

829

Stella -8.8.8.8.8.8,

1. What shall I do my God to love.
   My Saviour, and the world's, to praise?
   Whose tenderest compassions move
   To me and all the fallen race,
   Whose mercy is divinely free
   For all the fallen race and me.

2. I long to know, and to make know
   The heights and depths of love divine,
   The kindness Thou to me hast shown,
   Whose every sin was counted Thine:
   My God for me resigned His breath
   He died to save my soul from death.

3. How shall I thank Thee for the grace
   On me and all manl.ind bestowed?
   O that my every breath were praise!
   O that my heart were filled with God!
   My heart would then with love o'er flow,
   And all my life Thy glory show.
   -Charles Wesley

830

Elizabeth - Irregular meter

1. Jesus is all the world to me,
   My life, my joy, my all;
   He is my strength from day to day,
   Without Him I would fall.
   When I am sad to Him I go,
   No other one can cheer me so;
   When I am sad He makes me glad!
   He's my Friend.

LOVE SHARING AND CARING

2. Jesus is all the World to me.
   My Friend in trials sore:
   I go to Him for blessings, and
   He give them o'er and o'er.
   He sends the sunshine and the
   Rain.
   He sends the harvest's golden
   grain;
   Sunshine and rain, harvest of
   grain.
   He's my Friend.

3. Jesus is all the world to me.
   And true to Him I'll be;
   O, how could I this Friend deny,
   When He's so true to me?
   Following Him I know I'm right,
   He watches o'er me day and
   night;
   Following Him by day and night.
   He's my Friend.

4. Jesus is all the world to me,
   I want no better friends;
   I trust Him now. I'll trust Him when
   Life's fleeting days shall end.
   Beautiful life with such a Friend;
   Beautiful life that has no end;
   Eternal life, eternal joy, He's my
   Friend.
   　　　　　　-Will L. Thompson

831

Coine

1. Blest be the dear uniting love
   That will not let us part;
   Although our bodies far remove,
   We still are one in heart

2. "Joined one spirit to our Head.
   Where He appoints we go;
   And still in Jesus' steps we tread,
   And show His praise below.

3. Oh, may we ever walk in Him,
   And nothing know beside,
   Nothing desire or e'en esteem
   But Jesus crucified!

4. Closer and closer let us cleave
   To His beloved embrace,
   Expect His fulness to receive,
   And grace to answer grace.

5. Partakers of the Saviour's grace,
   The same in mind and heart
   Nor joy, nor grief, nor time, nor place
   Not life, nor death can part.

6. But we look forward to the day
   Which shall our flesh restore,
   When death shall all be done away.
   And we shall part no more.

832

The Bond of Love

1. We are one in the bond of love;
   We are one in the bond of love.
   We have joined our spirit with the
   Spirit of God;
   We are one in the bond of love.

2. Let us sing now. ev'ry one;
   Let us feel His love begun.
   Let us join our hands, that the world
   will know
   We are one in the bond of love.
   　　　　　　　　　O.Skillings

833

St Matthew - D. C. M.

1 We love Thee, Lord; yet not alone.
  because Thy bounteous hand
  Showers down its rich and
  ceaseless gifts on ocean and on
  land;
  We praise Thee, gracious Lord, for
  these, yet not for these alone
  The incense of Thy children's love
  arises to Thy throne.

LOVE SHARING AND CARING

2. We low Thee, Lord, because when
   we had err"d and gone astray,
   Thou didst recall our wandering
   souls Into the heavenward way,
   When helpless, hopeless, we were
   lost in sin and sorrow's night,
   A guiding ray was granted us from
   Thy pure fount of light.

3. Because, O Lord, Thou lovedst us
   with everlasting love,
   And sentest forth Thy Son to die
   that we might live above;
   Because, when we were heirs of
   wrath, Thou gavest hopes of
   heaven;
   We love because we much have
   sinn'd, and much have been
   forgiven.

   -W. Croft

834

St Matthlas - 8.8.8.8.8.8.

1. Jesus, my Lord, my God, my All,
   Hear me, blest Saviour, when I call;
   Hear me, and from Thy dwelling
   place
   Pour down the riches of Thy grace;
   Jesus, my Lord, I Thee adore,
   Oh make me love Thee more and
   more.

2. Jesus, too late I Thee have sought,
   How can I love Thee as I ought?
   And how extol Thy matchless fame,
   The glorious beauty of Thy name?
   Jesus, my Lord I Thee adore
   Oh make me love Thee more and
   more .

3. Jesus, what didst Thou find in me,
   That Thou hast dealt so lovingly?
   How great that joy that Thou hast
   brought
   So far exceeding hope or thought!
   Jesus, my Lord, I Thee adore,
   Oh make me love Thee more and
   more.

4. Jesus of thee shall be my song,
   To thee my heart and soul belong,
   All that I have or arm is Thine,
   And Thou, blest Saviour, Thou art
   mine.
   Jesus, my Lord, I Thee adore,
   Oh make me love thee more and
   more.

   -W.H. Monk

835

Hampstead- 5.5.8.8.5.5.

1. Jesus, still lead on,
   Till our rest be won;
   And, although the way be cheerless,
   We will follow calm and fearless:
   Guide us by Thy hand
   To our Fatherland.

2. If the way be drear,
   If the foe be near,
   Let not faithless fears o'er take us,
   Let not faith and hope forsake us;
   For through many a foe
   To our home we go.

3. When we seek relief
   From a long-felt grief,
   When oppress'd by new temptations,
   Lord, increase and perfect patience;
   Show us that bright shore
   Where we weep no more.

4. Jesus, still lead on,
   Till our rest be won:
   Heavenly Leader, still direct us,
   Still support, console, protect us,
   Till we safely stand
   In our Fatherland.

   -Charles Vincent

LOVE, SHARING AND CARING

836

Surrey-8.8.8.8.8.8.

1. Thee will I love, my strength, my
   tower.
   Thee will I love, my joy. my crown;
   Thee will I love with all my power,
   In all Thy works, and Thee alone;
   Thee will I love till sacred fire
   Fills my whole soul with pure
   desire.

2. I thank Thee. uncreated Sun,
   That Thy bright beams on me have
   shined;
   I thank Thee, who hast overthrown
   My foes, and heal'd my wounded
   mind;
   I thank Thee, whose enlivening
   voice
   Bids my freed heart in Thee rejoice.

3. Uphold me in the doubtful race,
   Nor suffer my feet again to stray;
   Strengthen my feet with heavenly
   grace
   Still to press forward in Thy way:
   That all my powers, with all their
   might,
   In Thy sole glory may unite.

4. Thee will I love, my joy, my crown;
   Thee will I love, my Lord, my God;
   Thee will I love, beneath Thy frown
   Or smile Thy sceptre or Thy rod;
   What though my flesh and heart
   decay,
   Thee shall I love in endless day.
   -H. Carey

837

Behold, What Love, What bound -less Love

1. Behold, what love, what boundless
   love,
   The Father hath bestowed
   On sinners lost, that we should be
   Now called the sons of God!

Chorus
Behold, what manner of love!
What manner of love the father
hath
Bestowed upon us,
That we, should be called
Should be called the sons of God.

2. No longer far from Him, but now
   By "precious blood" made nigh;
   Accepted in the "Well-beloved,
   Near to God's heart we lie.

3. What we in glory soon shall be,
   It doth not yet appear;
   But when our precious Lord we see,
   We shall His image bear.

4. With such a blessed hope in view,
   We would more holy be,
   More like our risen, glorious Lord,
   Whose face we soon shall see.

838

Give To The Winds Thy Fears - S.M.

1. Give to the winds thy fears;
   Hope. and be undismayed:
   God hears thy sighs, and counts thy
   tears,
   God shall lift up thy head.

2. Through waves, and clouds, and
   storms
   He gently clears thy way:
   Wait thou His time, so shall this
   night
   Soon end in joyous day.

3. Thou seest our weakness, Lord,
   Our hearts are known to Thee:
   lift Thou up the sinking hand,
   Confirm the feeble kneel

4. Let us in life, in death,
   Thy steadfast truth declare,
   And publish with our latest breath
   Thy love and guardian care.

LOVE, SHARING AND CARING

839

In Tenderness He sought me -
7.6.7.6.8.8. with Ref.

1. In tenderness He sought me,
   Weary and sick with sin,
   And on His shoulders brought me
   Back to His fold again
   While angels in His presence sang,
   Until the courts of heaven rang.

   Chorus
   Oh, the love that sought me!
   Oh, the blood that bought me!
   Oh, the grace that brought me to the fold.
   Wondrous grace that brought me to me the fold!

2. He washed the bleeding sin wounds,
   And poured in oil and wine;
   He whispered to assure me
   "I've found thee, thou art Mine,
   " I never heard a sweeter voice,
   It made my aching heart rejoice!

3. He pointed to the nail-prints,
   For me His blood was-shed
   A mocking crown so thorny,
   Was placed upon His head;
   I wondered what He saw in me,
   To suffer such deep agony.

4. I'm sitting in His presence
   The sunshine of His face,
   While with adoring wonder
   His bleeding I retrace.
   It seems as if eternal days
   Are far too short to sound His praise

5. So while the hours are passing,
   All now is perfect rest;

I'm waiting for the morning,
The brightest and the best
When He will call us to His side,
To be with Him. His spotless bride.

840

In Times Like These You Need A
Saviour- 7.6.7.6.

1. In times like these you need a Saviour
   In times like these you need an anchor.
   Be very sure Be very sure,
   Your anchor holds and grips the Solid Rock!

   Chorus
   This Rock is Jesus, Yes He's the One.
   This Rock is Jesus, the only One;
   Be very sure, be very sure,
   Your anchor holds and grips the Solid Rock!

3. In times like these you need the Bible.
   In times like these, O, be not idle
   Be very sure, be very sure,
   Your anchor holds and grips the Solid Rock!

3. In times like these I have a Saviour,
   In times like these, I have an anchor.
   I'm very sure, I'm very sure,
   My anchor holds and grips the Solid Rock!

   Chorus
   This Rock is Jesus, Yes. He's the One,
   This Rock is Jesus, the only One,
   I'm very sure, I'm very sure,
   My anchor holds and grips the Solid Rock!

LOVE, SHARING AND CARING

841

Jesus, Beloved Of My Heart -L.M.

1. Jesus, Beloved of my heart,
   Thy grace I earnestly implore;
   Oh, if Thou wilt the gift impart,
   I'll use it but to love Thee more.

2. The brightest forms of earthly love
   Are dull beside Thine own to me,
   With wistful eyes I look above,
   And wonder when Thy face I'll see.

3. Though Paradise has many joys,
   And flowers of beauty fair to see,
   Not gates of pearl nor angels voice
   Shall thrill my soul like love of Thee.

4. Without Thee no celestial light
   Shall shine to make my soul
   content;
   But with Thee this sad earth is
   bright.
   And glows with joy from heaven
   lent.

842

Love Divine, All Loves Excelling - 8.7.D.

1. Love divine, all loves excelling
   Joy of heaven, to earth come down;
   Fix in us Thy humble dwelling,
   All Thy faithful mercies crown;
   Jesus, Thou art all compassion,
   Pure, unbounded love Thou art;
   Visit us with Thy salvation,
   Enter every trembling heart

2. Come, almighty to deliver,
   Let us Thy grace receive;
   Suddenly return, and never,
   Never more Thy temples leave;
   Thee we would be always blessing,
   Serve Thee as Thy hosts above.
   Pray. and praise Thee, without
   ceasing
   Glory in Thy perfect love.

3. Finish then Thy new creation
   Pure and spotless let us be;
   Let us see Thy great salvation,
   Perfectly restored in Thee;
   Changed from glory into glory,
   Till in heaven we take our place,
   Till we cast our crowns before
   Thee,
   Lost in wonder, love, and praise.

843

Love Others As Thyself -S.M.

1. "Love other as thyself
   It is the Lord's command
   He made Himself an example
   By the way He loved us.

2. "Love him who's thy neighbour"
   Whether in peace or war
   He taught us to love all our foes,
   Repay evil with good.

3. "Love him who's thy neighbour
   The Lord's voice trumpets still
   So, all of us ought to prepare
   To love all our neighbours.

4. "Love him who's thy neighbours
   And those living next door
   Those that are in your
   neighbourhood
   And all your enemies

5. To love our neighbours as
   Jesus Himself loved us
   Jesus loved all His enemies
   And blessed and prayed for them.

844

Love Wonderful Love of God

1. Love, wonderful love of God,
   So boundless and so free;
   To think that Christ His only Son
   Should die on Calvary,
   Oh, Love so great, so vast, so high,
   That He should for the sinners die.

LOVE, SHARING AND CARING

Chorus
Love, wonderful love, the love of
God to me.
Love, wonderful love, so great, so
rich, so free:.
Wide. as wide as the ocean, deep,
as deep as the sea,
High, as high as the heav'ns above,
His love to me.

2. Love, wonderful love of God,
   To me has been made known,
   To me the Spirit freely gives.
   And claims me for His own,
   Oh, love so wondrous, so divine.
   That I am His and He is mine.

3. Love, wonderful love of God,
   With joy I now proclaim,
   To sinners lost that they may have
   Salvation through His name
   That they may now with others
   prove,
   "Christ's dying, and undying love".

845

Loved With Everlasting Love -
7.7.7.7.D.

1. Loved with .everlasting love,
   Led by grace that love to know,
   Spirit breathing from above,
   Thou hast taught me it is so,
   Oh this full and perfect peace!
   Oh this transport all divine!
   In a love which cannot cease,
   I am His and He is mine.

2. Heaven above is softer blue,
   Earth around is sweeter green;
   Something lives in every hue
   Christless eyes have never seen:
   Birds with gladder songs o'er flow,
   Flowers with deeper beauties
   shine,
   Since I know, as now I know,
   I am his and He is mine.

3. Things that once were wild alarms
   Cannot now disturb ,my rest,
   Closed in everlasting arms

Pillowed on the loving breast:
Oh, to lie forever here!
Doubt and care and self resign,
While He whispers in my ear
I am His and He is mine.

4. His forever, only His;
   Who the Lord and me shall part?
   Ah, with what a rest of bliss,
   Christ can fill the loving heart!
   .3 Heaven and earth may fade and flee;
   Firstborn light is gloom decline;
   But while God and I shall be,
   I am His and He is mine.

846

There is Joy In Serving Jesus
-8.7.8.7.

1. There is joy in serving Jesus,
   As I journey on my way,
   Joy that fills the heart with praises,
   Ev'ry hour and ev'ry day

Chorus
There is joy, joy,
Joy in serving Jesus,
Joy that throbs the heart:
Ev'ry moment, ev'ry hour,
As I draw upon His pow'r,
Joy that never shall depart

2. There is joy in serving Jesus,
   Joy that triumphs over pain;
   Fills my soul with heaven's music,
   Till I join the glad refrain.

3. There is joy in serving Jesus,
   As I walk alone with God;
   'Tis the joy of Christ, my Saviour,
   Who the path of suffering trod.

4. There is joy in serving Jesus,
   Joy amid the darkest night,
   For I've learned the wondrous
   Secret,
   And I'm walking in the light.

EVANGELISM

847

Lifeline-Irregular and Refrain

1. Throw out the lifeline across the
   dark wave,
   There is a brother whom someone
   Should save;
   Somebody's brother! oh, who then,
   will dare
   To throw out the lifeline, his peril to
   share?

   Chorus
   Throw out the lifeline!
   Throw out the lifeline!
   Someone is drifting away;
   Someone is sinking today.

2. Throw out the lifeline with hand
   quick and strong;
   Why do you tarry, why linger so
   longer?
   See! he is sinking; oh; hasten
   today.
   And out with the life-boat, away,
   then, away!

3. Throw out the lifeline to danger?
   fraught men,
   Sinking in anguish where you've
   Never been:
   Winds of temptation and billows of
   woe
   Will soon hurl them out where the
   dark waters flow.

4. Soon will the season of rescue be
   o'er,
   Soon will they drift to eternity's
   shore;
   Haste then, my brother, no time for
   delay,
   But throw out the lifeline and save
   them today.
   -Edward S. Ufford

848

Bremen (Munich) -7.6.7.6.D.

1. Lord of the living harvest
   That whitens o'er the plain,
   where angels soon shall gather
   Their sheaves of golden grain,
   Accept these hands to labour,
   These hearts to trust and love,
   And deign with them to hasten
   Thy kingdom from above.

2. As labourers in Thy vineyard
   Lord, send them out to be,
   Content to bear the burden
   Of weary days for Thee,
   Content to ask no wages
   When Thou shalt call them home,
   But to have shared the travail
   That makes Thy kingdom come.

3. Be with them, God the Father,
   Be with them, God the Son,
   Be with them, God the Spirit,
   Eternal Three in One!
   Make them a royal priesthood,
   Thee rightly to adore,
   And fill them with Thy fullness
   Now and for evermore.
   -John Samuel
   Bewley Monsel

849

Hyfrydol -8.7.8.7.D.

1. From the depths of sin and failure,
   From the despair as black as night,
   Lord, we hear our brothers calling
   For deliverance and for light.

   Chorus
   Use us, Lord, to speed Thy
   Kingdom;
   Through us may Thy will be done:
   Give us eyes to see the vision
   Of a world redeemed and won.

2. By the love that bore in silence
   Man's contempt and Satan's dart;
   By the longing for the lost ones
   That consumes the Saviour's
   heart;

3. By the Savoiur's blood that bought us
By the peace His merits bring,
By the spirit that constrains us
Now on earth to crown Him king;
-Timothy Rees

850

Cannock -L.M.

1. Send forth the gospel! Let it run
Southward and northward, east and west;
Tell all the earth Christ died and lives
Who' giveth pardon, life and rest?

2. Send forth Thy gospel, mighty Lord!
Out of this chaos bring to birth
Thine own creation's promised Hope;
The better days of heaven on earth.

3. Send forth Thy gospel, gracious Lord!
Thine was the blood for sinners shed;
Thy voice still pleads in human hearts;
To Thee Thine other sheep be led.

4. Send forth Thy gospel, holy Lord!
Kindle in us love's sacred flame;
Love giving all and grudging naught
For Jesus' sake, in Jesus' name.

5. Send forth the gospel! Tell it out!
Go, brothers, at the Master's call;
Prepare His way, who comes to reign,
The King of kings and Lord of all.
-H. E. Fox

851

Ring the Bells of Heaven

1. Ring the bells of Heaven! There is Joy today
For a soul returning from the wild!
See! The Father meets him out upon the way,
Welcoming His weary, wand'ring child.

Chorus
Glory! Glory! How the angels sing;
Glory! Glory! how the loud harps ring!
'Tis the ransomed army, like a Mighty sea,
Pealing forth the anthem of the free!

2. Ring the bells of Heaven! there is joy today.
For the wand'rer now is reconciled;
Yes, a soul is rescued from his Sinful way,
And is born a new, a ransomed child.

3. Ring the bells of Heaven! Spread the feast today!
Angels, swell the glad triumphant Strain!
Tell the joyful tidings, bear it far Away!
For a precious soul is born again.
-William O. Cushing

852

He Ransomed me

1. There's a sweet and blessed story
Of the Christ who came from glory,
Just to rescue me from sin and Misery;
He in loving kindness sought me,
And from sin and shame hath bro't
Hallelujah! Jesus ransomed me.

Chorus
Hallelujah, what a saviour!
Who can take a poor lost sinner,
Lift him from the miry clay and set Him free;
I will ever tell the story,
Shouting Glory, glory, glory,
Hallelujah! Jesus ransomed me.

EVANGELISM

2. From The depth of sin and sadness
   To the heights of joy and gladness
   Jesus lifted me, in mercy full and
   Free;
   With His precious blood He bo't
   me,
   When I knew Him not, He sought
   me,
   And in love divine He ransomed
   me.

3. From the throne of heavenly glory
   O, the sweet and blessed story!
   Jesus came to lift the lost in sin and
   woe
   Into liberty all glorious,
   Trophies of His grace victorious.
   Evermore rejoicing here below;

4. By and by with Joy increasing
   And with gratitude unceasing.
   Lifted up with Christ forever more
   to be;
   I will join the hosts there singing,
   In the anthem ever ringing,
   To the King of Love who ransomed
   me.

   -Julia H. Johnston

853

Stuttgart - 8.7.8.7.

1. Zions's King shall reign victorious;
   All the earth shall own His sway
   He will make His kingdom glorious
   He will reign through endless day.

2. Nations, new from God estranged.
   Then shall see a glorious light,
   Night to day shall then be changed,
   Heaven shall triumph in the sight.

3. Then shall Isreal, long dispersed.
   Mourning seek the Lord their God,
   Look on Him whom once they
   pierced.
   Own and kiss the chastening rod.

4. Mighty King, Thine arm revealing
   Now Thy glorious cause maintain;
   Bring the nations help and healing,
   Make them subject to Thy reign.

854

St. Cecilia -6.6,6.6.

1. Thy kingdom come, O God,
   Thy rule, O Christ. begin;
   Break with Thine iron rod
   The tyrannies of sin.

2. Where is Thy reign of peace,
   And purity, and love?
   When shall all hatred cease,
   As in the realm above?

3. When comes the promised time
   That war shall be no more,
   And lust, oppression, crime
   Shall flee Thy face before?

4. We pray Thee, Lord, arise,
   And come in Thy great might;
   Revive our longing eyes.
   Which languish for Thy sight.

5. Men scorn Thy sacred name
   And wolves devour Thy fold;
   By many deeds of shame
   We learn that love grows cold.

6. O'er heathen lands afar
   Thick darkness broodeth yet
   Arise, O morning Star,
   Arise, and never set

   -T. G.Hayne

855

Lischer. 6.6.6.6.8.8.

1. Rejoice, for Jesus reigns
   Enthroned in human hearts
   He breaks the prison chains
   And makes them free indeed;
   The devil might God's child
   oppose
   No fear of foe. God's word goes on.

EVANGELISM

2. The work of righteousness,
   Tidings of truth and peace;
   For comfort in our life
   Shall spread all round about
   Gentiles and Jews shall all bow down
   And will worship acceptably

3. There's pow'r with Thee for the
   Protection of Thine own;
   And to Thy high decree
   Shall millions take heed to
   The heav'ns rejoice to see Thy work
   The islands far hear Thy command.

4. This perfect heav'nly seed
   shall grow to a big trees;
   Like the blessed leaven
   Shall spread all o'er the earth;
   Till God the son comes back again
   It will go on, Amen, Amen.

856
Ring Out The Message

1. There's a message true and glad
   For the sinful and the sad,
   Ring it out, ring it out,
   It will give them courage new,
   It will help them to be true:
   Ring ft out, ring it out
   Chorus
   Merrily ring, Speed it away,
   Message divine, sent if today.
   Let it cheer the lost and those in
   doubt,
   darkness and doubt;
   Merrily ring, wonderful news,
   Making men free, happy and-free,
   Ring, ring, ring, ring,
   Ring the message out.

2. Tell the world of saving grace,
   Make it known in ev'ry place,
   Ring it out. ring it out;
   it win give them courage new,
   Him from whom all blessing flow;
   Ring it out, ring it out

3. Sin and doubt to sweep away,
   Till shall dawn the better day,
   Ring it out, ring it out,
   Till the sinful world be won .
   For Jehovah's mighty Son;
   Ring it out, ring it out.
   -James Rowe

857
The regions beyond

1. To the regions beyond I must go.
   I must go,
   Where the story has never been
   told;
   To the millions that never have
   heard of His love,
   I must tell the sweet story of old.

Chorus
To the regions beyond
I must go I must go,
Till the world, all the world,
His salvation shall know.

2. To the hardest of places He calls
   me to go,
   Not thinking of comfort or ease;
   The world may pronounce me a
   dreamer, a fool,
   Enough if the Master I please

3. Oh, ye that are spending your
   leisure and pow'rs
   In pleasures so foolish and fond;
   Awake from your selfishness,
   folly and sin,
   And go to the regions beyond.

4. There are other "lost sheep" that
   the Master must bring.
   And they must the message be
   told:
   He sends me to gather them out
   of all lands,
   And welcome them back to His
   fold
   -A. B. Simpson

EVANGELISM

858
The Wonderful Story

1. Oh, sweet is the story of Jesus,
   The wonderful Saviour of men,
   Who suffer'd and died for the
   sinner
   I'll tell it again and again!

   Chorus
   Oh, wonderful, wonderful story!
   The dearest that ever was told;
   I'll repeat it in glory. The wonderful
   story,
   Where I shall His beauty behold.

2. He came from the mansions of
   glory;
   His blood as a ransom He gave
   To purchase eternal redemption
   And oh, He is mighty to save!

3. His mercy flows on like a river,
   His love is unmeasured and free:
   His grace is for ever sufficent,
   It reaches and saves even me.
   -C. H Gabriel

859
Over the thorn and thistle

1. Over the thorn and thistle,
   Along the stony way.
   From the Shepherd's care to the
   desert
   There wander'd a sheep one day;
   And a voice fell sadly from far
   away:
   "My sheep, how long will thou
   love to stray!"
   "My sheep, how tong wilt thou
   love to stray?"

2. Over the thron and thistle.
   Along the stony way,
   With feet that bled, the Shepherd
   To where the wand'rer lay;
   He had heard It crying from far
   away:

"Lord, bring me home to Thy flock, I
pray!"
"Lord, bring me home to Thy flock, I
pray!"

3. "Over the thorn and thistle.
   Along the stony way,
   I have sought for thee, now trust Me:
   I'll bear the home today
   The wolf and lion flee far away
   When on My shoulder My sheep I lay,
   When on My shoulder My sheep I lay

4. Instead of the thorn and thistle.
   The myrtle bedecks the way
   Where the Shepherd feeds, and
   gently leads
   The sheep He found that day;
   And He leadeth others from far away
   To rest in fields of a cloudless day,
   To rest in fields of a cloudless day. .
   -H. W. G.

860
Come, Hear, His Word

1. Come, hear His Word God's
   servants now are speaking,
   Draw near to Him, and all dark cares
   dismiss,
   You shall be free. all those who
   comfort seeking,
   May have a taste of heav'nly joy and
   bliss.

   Chorus
   Have you in truth the love of Jesus
   known,
   Then tell the world you are His very
   own,
   Have you in truth the love of Jesus
   known,
   Then tell the world you are His very
   Own,

2. Believe in God and follow His
   anointed.
   Who guide us on the path to

heav'nly peace.
The leaders who the Lord Himself appointed,
To offer grace. God's love will never cease

3. If some there be who love not those who serve us,
How can they grasp the love of Christ aright.
Nor can they see how faith and pray'r preserve us,
And lead to Zion's mount of wondrous light

861

Jesus, The Saviour

1. Who is there able the heart to make Clean?
Jesus, Jesus!
Who is there able to free from all sin?
Jesus, the Saviour!

Chorus
Ring out the anthem o'er land and O'er wave.
He is the only One able to save:
Power He hath over death and the grave
Jesus, the Saviour!

2. Who is the Friend that is dearest of all
Jesus, Jesus!
Who standeth ready to answer each call?
Jesus, the Saviour!

3. Who hath prepared for His children a home?
Jesus, Jesus!
Who is it tenderly biddeth them come?
Jesus, the Saviour!
                        -Edgar Lewis

862

Will You Love My Saviour

1. Tell me, will you love my Saviour?
He would be your dearest Friend:
He would be your soul's Redeemer
And your guide till life shad end,

Chorus
Will you, will you love my Saviour?
Tis the prayer my spirit plead;
Willl you love my dear Redeemer?
He is all the sinner needs.

2. He win comfort in the sadness,
Ev'ry life must sometimes know,
And your heart will need the gladness
That His friendship can bestow.

3. Oh, you must not miss the blessing
That a life with Him will give;
Come to Him, your sin confessing,
He will make you glad to live.

4. Tell me, will you love my Saviour?
May I know it ere I die?
In the realms of joy and glory,
Will you meet me, by and bye?
                        -Mrs. Frank. .A Breck

863

Harwich -10.11.10.11:

1. All ye that pass by,
To Jesus draw nigh:
To you is it nothing that Jesus Should die?
Your ransom and peace,
Your surety He is:
Come, see if there ever was sorrow like His.

2. For what you have done .
His blood must atone:
The Father hath stricken for you

EVANGELISM

His dear Son,
The Lord, in the day
Of his anger, did lay
Your sins on the Lamb, and He bore
them away.

3. He answered for all:
O come at His call,
And low at His cross with astonish
ment fall!
But lift up your eyes
At Jesus's cries:
Impassive, He suffers; immortal. He
dies,

4. He dies to atone
For sins not His own;
Your debt He hath paid and your
work He hath done.
Ye all may receive
The peace He did leave,
Who made intercession "My Father,
Forgive!"

5. For you and for me
He prayed on the tree:
The prayer is accepted, the sinner
is free.
That sinner am I.
Who on Jesus rely,
And come for the pardon God will
not deny

6. My pardon I plea;
For a sinner I am,
A sinner believing in Jesus' name.
He purchased the grace Which now
I embrace:
O Father, Thou know'st He hath died
in my place;

7. His death is my plea;
My Advocate see,
And hear the blood speak that hath
answered for me
My ransom He was.

When He bled on the cross:
And by losing His life He hath
carried my cause.
-C. Wesley

864

Invitation - 9.9.9.6. and Refrain

1. Have you tried Jesus in all your
searching?
Have you tried Jesus fo peace
within
If you want answers to your life's
problems,
Have you tried Jesus to set you
free?

2. Have you tried Jesus as Lord and
saviour?
Have you tried Jesus to free you
within?
To find the answers to your life's
problems,
Have you tried Jesus to set you
free?

3. Have you tried Jesus as Lord and
Saviour?
Will you try Jesus to free you from
sin?
You'll find the answers to your life's
problems,
Will you try Jesus to set you free?
-Phil Perkins

865

Come with Me, Visit Calvary-
7.6.7.6.D. with Refrain

1. Come with me, visit Calvary,
Where our Redeemer died:
His blood, it fills the fountain.
Tis full, 'tis deep, tis wide.
He died from sin to sever,
Our hearts and live complete;
He saves and keeps for ever
Those lying at His feet

EVANGELISM

Chorus
To the uttermost He saves,
To the uttermost He saves,
Dare you now believe and His love receive,
To the uttermost Jesus saves.

2. I will surrender fully,
And do His blessed will;
His blood doth make me holy,
His presence me doth fill.
He's saving, I'm believing.
This blessed now I claim;
His Spirit rm receiving,
My heart is in a flame.

3. I've wondrous peace through trusting,
A well of joy within;
This rest is everlasting,
Each day I triumph win,
He gives me heavenly measure
Pressed down' and "running o'er.'.
Oh, what a priceless treasure,
Glory for evermore!

-J, Lawley

866

Come, let us all unite to sin

1. Come, let us all unite to sing
God is love!
While heav'n and earth their praises bring
God is love
Let ev'ry soul 'from sin awak,
Each in is heart sweet music make,
And sweetly sing for Jesus sake
God is love!

Chorus
God is love, God is love!
' Come, let us ail unite to sing:
God is love!

2. Oh, tell to earth's remotest bound,
God is love!
In Christ is full redemption found
God is love!
His blood can cleanse our sins away;
His Spirit turns our night to day,
And leads our souls with joy to say
God is love!

3. How happy is our portion here
God is love!
His promises our spirits cheer
God is love!
He is our Sun and Shield by day,
Our help, our hope, our strength, our stay,
He will be with us all the way
God is love!

4. What though my heart and flesh shall fail
God is love!
Through Christ I shall o'er death.
Prevail
God is love!
E'en Jordan's swell I will not fear.
For Jesus will be with me there.
My soul above the waves to bear
God is love!

-Howard Kingsbury

867

Lubeck-7.7.7,7.

1. Look to Jesus, and be saved,
See Him hanging on the tree;
Guilty art thou and enslaved.
But He bears thy guilt for thee.

2. Look, till thou canst see thy sin
In His body crucified;
All the lusts that lurked within.
All thy wilfulness and pride.

3. Look, and see the judgement fall
On that fault-less, guilt-bowed head;

EVANGELISM

He is made our sin for all
One hath died, and all are dead.

4. Look to Jesus, Look and live,
He has died thy death for thee;
Look, and trust, and love, and give
All thou art His prize to be.

5. Look with awe, till wondering love
Melts thy heart and dims thine eyes,
And, with prostrate saints above,
Rapt in praise thy spirit lies.
-W. Hay Aitken

868
Jesus Only is our Message - 8.7.8.7.D.

1. Jesus only is our Message,
Jesus all our theme shall be,
We will lift up Jesus ever,
Jesus only will we see.

Chorus
Jesus only, Jesus ever,
Jesus all In all we sing:
Saviour, Sanctifier, Healer,
Glorious Lord and coming King.

2. Jesus only is our Saviour.
All our guilt He bore away,
All our righteousness He gives us,
All our strength from day to day.

3. Jesus is our Sanctifier,
Cleansing us from self and sin,
And with all His Spirit's fulness,
Filling all our hearts within.

4. Jesus only is our Healer,
All our sicknesses He bare,
And His risen life and fulness.
All His members still may share.

5. Jesus only is our Power,
His the gift of Pentecost;

Jesus, breathe Thy power upon us.
Fill us with the Holy Ghost

6. And for Jesus we are waiting.
Listening for the Advent call,
But 'twill be Jesus only,
Jesus ever, all in all.
-A. B. Simpson

869
Simeon-L.M.

1. Come, sinners, to the gospel feast.
Let ev'ry soul be Jesus guest;
Ye need not one be left behind,
For God hath bidden alt mankind.

2. Sent by my Lord, on you I call;
The invitation is to all:
Come, all the world; come, sinner.
thou!
All things in Christ are ready now.

3. Come, all ye souls by sin op
pressed,
Ye restless wanderers after rest,
Ye poor, and maimed, and halt and
blind,
In Christ a hearty welcome find.

4. His love mighty to compel;
His conquering love consent to feel.
Yield to His love's resistless power.
And fight against your God no more.

5. This is the time; no more delay!
This is the Lord's accepted day;
Come in, this moment, at His call,
And live for Him who died for all. ,
C. Wesley

EVANGELISM

870

Jesus to Passing the Way

1. Is there a heart that is waiting,
   Longing for pardon today?
   Hear the glad message proclaiming
   Jesus Is passing this way.

   Chorus
   Jesus is passing this way.
   This way, today;
   Jesus is passing this way,
   Is passing this way today.

2. Is there a heart that has wandered
   Come with thy burden today;
   Mercy is tenderly pleading,
   Jesus is passing this way.

3. Is there a heart that is broken?
   Weary and sighing for rest?
   Come to the arms of thy Saviour,
   Pillow thy head on His breast.

4. Come to thy only Redeemer,
   Come to His infinite love:
   Come to the gate that is leading
   Homeward to mansions above.
                    -Annie L Jame

871

Enjoying a Full Salvation

1. If you want pardon, if you want
   peace,
   If you want sorrow or sighing to
   cease.
   Look up to Jesus who died on the
   tree,
   To purchase a full salvation.

   Chorus
   Living beneath the shade of the
   cross,
   Counting the jewels of earth but
   Dross;

Cleans'd in the blood that flows
from His side.
Enjoying a full salvation.

2. If you want Jesus to reign in your
   soul,
   Plunge in the fountain and you
   shall be whole;
   Washed in the blood of the
   Crucified One,
   Enjoying a full salvation.

3. If you want boldness, take part in
   the fight;
   If you want purity, walk in the light
   If you want liberty, shout and be
   free,
   Enjoying a full salvation.

4. If you want holiness, cling to the
   cross,
   Counting the riches of earth as
   dross;
   Down at His feet you'll be cleans'd
   and made free, Enjoying a full
   salvation.
                    -Unknown

872

I've a Saviour Kind and Tender

1. I've a Saviour, kind and tender,
   I've a Saviour full of grace,
   And a smile of winning sweetness
   Ever beams upon His face:
   In my heart's shrine of affection
   He shall hold the highest place.

   Chorus
   How I love Him! How I love Him!
   Since for me He bled and died
   How I love Him, Yes I love Him
   More than all the world beside.

2. For my sake He came from Heaven
   To this world of sin and shame;
   Bore my guilt, though He was
   guiltless,

EVANGELISM

And though blameless, took my
blame:
Can I ever cease to love Him,
And His goodness to proclaim.

3 Though I've often been unworthy,
He has constant been and true;
Though I wronged Him, He forgave
me
When I would my vows renew;
Though I spurned Him, He with
kindness
My rebellious heart did woo,

4. I've a Saviour, kind and tender,
He would be your Saviour too;
Will you not accept the pardon
Which He freely offers you?
Take Him now as your Redeemer,
Earth has not a friend so true.
-Chas. M. Fillmore

873
Hallelujah for the Cross

1. The cross it standeth fast:
Hallelujah, hallelujah!
Defying ev'ry blast:
Hallelujah, hallelujah!
The winds of hell have blown,
The world its hate hath shown,
Yet it is not overthrown;
Hallelujah for the Cross.

Chorus
Hallelujah, hallelujah,
Hallelujah, for the cross!
Hallelujah, hallelujah,
it shall never suffer loss!
Hallelujah, hallelujah,
Hallelujah, for the cross!
Hallelujah, hallelujah,
it shall never suffer loss!

2 It is. the old cross still:
Hallelujah, hallelujah!
Its triumph let us tell:
Hallelujah. Hallelujah!

The grace of God here shone
Thro' Christ the blessed Son,
Who did for sin atone:
Hallelujah for the cross!

3. 'Twas here the debt was paid:
Hallelujah, hallelujah!
Our sins on Jesus laid:
Hallelujah, hallelujah!
So round the cross we sing
Of Christ our offering,
Of Christ our living King:
Hallelujah for the Cross!
-Horatius Bonar

874
Mighty To Save

1. O bliss of the purified! bliss of the
free!
I plunge in the crimson tide open'd
for me;
O'er sin and uncleanness exulting I
stand,
And point to the print of the nails in
His hand.

Chorus
O sing of His mighty love; Sing of
His mighty love!
Sing of His mighty love, Mighty to
Save!

2. O bliss of the purified! Jesus is
mine.
No longer in dread condemnation I
pine;
In conscious salvation I'll sing of
His grace,
Who lifted upon me the light of His
face.

3. O bliss of the purified! bliss of the
the pure!
No wound hath the soul that His
blood cannot cure;

EVANGELISM

No sorrow bow'd head but may
sweetly find rest;
No tears, but may dry them on light
of His face.

4. O Jesus the crucified! Thee will I
sing!
My blessed Redeemer, my God,
and my King!
My soul, filled with rapture, shall
shout o'er the grave,
And triumph in death in the Mighty
to Save.

-E. Bottome

875
Moscow -6.6.4.6.6.6.4.

1. Thou whose almighty word
Chaos and darkness heard,
And took their flight,
Hear us, we humbly pray,
And where the gospel day
Sheds not its glorious ray,
Let there be light!

2. Thou who didst come to bring
On Thy redeeming wing
Healing and sight.
Health to the sick in mind,
Sight to the inly blind,
O now to all mankind
Let there be light!

3. Spirit of truth and love
Life giving, holy Dove,
Speed forth Thy flight:
Move on the water's face.
Spreading the beams of grace,
And in earth's darkest place
Let there be light!

4. Blessed and holy Three,
Glorious Trinity,
Wisdom, love, might;
Boundless as ocean's tide
Rolling in fullest pride,
Through the earth far and wide,
Let there be light!

-J. Marriott

876
Clarendon Street-11.11.11.11

1. O turn ye! O turn ye! for why will
ye die
When God in great mercy is
drawing so nigh?
Now Jesus invites you. the Spirit
says. Cornel
And angels are waiting to welcome
you home.

2. How vain the delusion that, white
you delay,
Your hearts may grow better by
staying away!
Come wretched, come thirsty,
come Just as you be,
While streams of salvation are
flowing so free.

3. In riches, in pleasures, what can
you obtain
To soothe your affliction or banish
your pain,
To bear up your spirits when
summon'd to die,
Or take you to Christ in the clouds
of the sky?

-Josiah Hopkins

877
Seeking for me

1. Jesus my Saviour, to Bethlehem
came,
Born in a manger to sorrow and
shame;
Oh, it was wonderful blest be His
name!
Seeking for me, for me! Seeking for
me!
Seeking for me! for me!
Seeking for me! for me!
Oh, it was wonderful blest be His
name!
Seeking for me! for me!

EVANGELISM

2. Jesus, my Saviour, on Calvary's tree,
Paid the great debt, and my soul He set free
Oh, it was wonderful how could it be?
Dying for me, for me for me!
Dying for me, for me!
Oh, it was wonderful how could it be?
Dying for me, for me!

3. Jesus, my Saviour, the same as of old,
While I was wand'ring afar from the fold,
Gently and long did He plead with my soul,
Calling for me, for me!
Calling for me, for me!
Gently and long did He plead with my soul
Calling for me, for me!

4. Jesus, my Saviour, shall come from on high
Sweet is the promise as weary years fly;
Oh, I shall see Him descend from the sky.
Coming for me, for me!
Coming for me, for me!
Oh, I shall see Him descend from the sky
Coming for me, for me!
-A. N

878
Thy crucified Him - 7.7.

1. From the Bethlehem manger home,
Walking His dear form beside.
We to Calv'rys mount have come,
Where our Lord was crucified.

Chorus
Sweet tones of love come down the ages through:
Father, forgive! they know not what they do"

2. Scornful words the soldiers fling.
Wicked rulers Him deride,
Saying, "if Thou be the King,
Save Thyself, Thou Crucified!"

3. Wondrous love for sinful men,
Of the sinless One that died!
May we wound Thee not again,
Thou, O Christ, the crucified!
-Mrs M. B. C. Stade

879
I will sing of Jesus -8.7.

1. I will sing the love of Jesus
Greater love was never known;
Yielding up His life for sinners,
Oh, what love to me was shown!

Chorus
I will praise my great Redeemer,
As my days are on the wing;
I will sing of Him who saves me,
I will magnify the Lord my King.

2 I will sing the words of Jesus
Words of life from lips Divine;
Full of comfort. Joy, and courage.
Precious to this soul of mine.

3. I will sing the grace of Jesus
Grace my heart may now receive;
He by faith will seal my pardon,
if His promise I believe.

4. I will sing the name of Jesus
Name of all most dear to me;
By the ransomed host in glory
Shall His name exalted be.
-E. A. Barnes

EVANGELISM

880

Tell the Glad Story Again

1, Tell the glad story of Jesus, who
came,
Full of compassion, the lost to
reclaim;
Tell of redemption thro' faith in His
name:
tell the glad story again!

Chorus
Tell it again, Tell it again? Tell the
glad story to suffering man;
Tell it, oh tell it, again!

2. Tell the glad story where, and
opprest,
Many in bondage are sighing for
rest;
Tell them in Jesus they all may be
blest:
Tell the glad story again!

3. Tell the glad story with patience and
love,
Urging the lost ones His mercy to
prove;
Tell them of mansions preparing
above:
Tell the glad story again!

4. Tell the glad story when Jordan's
dark wave
Calleth our loved ones its billows to
brave;
Tell them that Jesus is mighty to
save:
Tell the glad story again!
-Julia Sterling

881

Open wide the door - 7.7.7.5.

1. Jesus knocks: He calls to thee
"Weary one, oh come to Me!"

He can save, and only He:
Open wide the door!

Chorus
Open wide the door!
Open wide the door!
He can save, and only He:
Open wide the door!

2. Jesus knocks: He comes to save
Twas for thee His life He gave;
He hath triumph'd o'er the grave:
Open wide the door!

3. Jesus knocks, is knocking still:
Yield to Him at once thy wilt;
He with joy thy heart can fill:
Open wide the door!

4. Jesus knocks, the moments fly;
While salvation yet is nigh,
Ere the Saviour passeth by,
Open wide the door?
-W. Kitching

882

The story must be told - 8.7.D.

1. Oh, the precious gospel story,
How it tells of love to all!
How the Saviour in compassion
Died to save us from the Fall;
How He came to seek the lost
ones,
And to bring them to His fold;
Let us hasten to proclaim it,
For the story must be told.

Chorus
The story must be told,
The story must be told:
That Jesus died for sinners lost
The story must be told.

2. Oh, the blessed gospel story
Of His meek and lowly birth,
And the welcome of the angels
When they sang goodwill to earth

EVANGELISM

Of the cross on which He suffer'd,
As by prophets seen of old, of his
death and resurrection,
Let the story now be told.

3. Oh, the wondrous gospel story!
There is life in ev'ry word;
There is hope and consolation
Where the message sweet is
heard;
Let us tell it to the weary,
And its beauties all unfold;
'Tis the only guide to heaven,
And the story must be told.
                    -F. J. Crosby

883
Oh, precious words - C.M.

1. Oh, precious words that Jesus said!
"The soul that comes to Me,
I will in no wise cast him out,
Whoever he may be."
'Who ever he may be,
Whoever he may be;
I wilt in no wise cast him out,
Whoever he may be."

2 Oh, precious words that Jesus said!
"Behold, I am the Door,
And all that enter in by Me,
Have life for evermore."
"Have life forever more,
Have life for evermore;
And all that enter in by Me,
Have life for ever more."

3. Oh, precious words that Jesus said!
"Come, weary souls oppressed,
Come, take My yoke and learn of Me;
And I will give you rest."
"And I will give you rest.
And I will give you rest:
Come take My yoke and learn of Me;
And I will give you rest.

4. Oh, precious words that Jesus sad!
The world I overcame:
And they who follow where I lead,
Shall conquer in My name."
"Shall conquer in My name,
Shall conquer in My name;
And they who follow where I lead.
Shall conquer in My name.
                    -E J. Crosby

884
Gathering after tears

1. Steer our bark away to the Home
land,
Spread the sails of hope o'er the
sea;
Think of all the friends that await us.
When anchor'd safely there we
shall be.

Chorus
Gathering after tears into sunshine,
Gathering after labour into rest
Hear the ransome'd throng shouting
forth their joyful song,
Gathering to the mansions of the
blest.

2. Steer our bark away to the Home
land.
On without a fear let us go;
When the port of peace we are
Hearing,
The blessed harbour lights we shall
Know,

3. Bright and fair the hills of the
Homeland,
Clad in all the bloom of the spring:
There to Him who loved and
redeemed us,
Our joyful, Joyful praise we will sing.

4. Soft the winds that blow from the
Homeland,
Sweet the morn that breaks on the
Shore

EVANGELISM

Seen we'll meet again our beloved ones.
Where sorrow, pain, and death
Come no more.

F. J. Crosby

885

Come Unto Me

1. Hear the blessed Saviour calling the oppressed,
"O ye heavy laden, come to Me and rest;
Come, no longer tarry your load
Will bear,
Bring Me ev'ry bunden, bring me
Ev'ry care."

Chorus
Come unto Me; I will give you rest:
Take My yoke upon you. Hear Me
and be blest;
I am meek and lowly, Come and
trust My might;
Come, My yoke is easy. And My
burden's light

2. Are you disappointed, wand'ring here and there,
Dragging chains of doubt and.
loaded down with care?
Do unholy feelings struggle in your breast?
Bring your case to Jesus He was
give you rest

3. Stumbling on the mountains dark
with sin and shame,
Stumbling tow'rd the pit of hell's
consuming flame,
By the pow'rs of sin deluded and
oppressed.
Hear the tender Shepherd, "Come to
Me and rest,"

4. Have you by temptation often
conquered been,
Has a sense of weakness brought
distress within?
Christ will sanctify you, if you'll
Claim His best,
In the Holy Spirit, He will give you
rest

-Charles P. Jones

886

A Soul Winner for Jesus

1. I want to be a soul winner
For Jesus ev'ry day,
He does so much for me,
I want to aid the lost sinner
To leave his erring way,
And be from bondage free.

Chorus
A soul winner for Jesus,
A soul winner for Jesus,
O let me be each day
A soul winner for Jesus,
A soul winner for Jesus,
He's done so much for me.

2. I want to be a soul winner ;
And bring the lost to Christ,
That they His grace may know;
I want to live for Christ forever
And do His blessed will,
Because He loves me so.

3. I want to be a soul winner
Till Jesus calls for me,
To lay my burdens down;
I want to hear Him say, servant

EVANGELISM

887
No One Ever Cared for Me Like Jesus

1. I would love to tell you what I think
of Jesus since I found in Him a
friend so strong and true;
I would tell you how he changed my
life completely,
He did something that no other
friend could do.

Chorus
No one ever cared for me like
Jesus,
There's no other friend so kind as
He;
No one else could take the sin and
darkness from me,
O how much He cared for me,

2. All my life was full of sin when
Jesus found me,
All my heart was full of misery and
woe;
Jesus plac'd His strong and loving
arms about me,
And He led me in the way I ought to
go.

3. Everyday He comes to me with new
assurance,
More and more I understand His
words of love;
But I'll never know Just why He
came to save me,
Till some day I see His blessed face
above.
                                    -C. F. Weigle

888
I'll Be a Sunbeam

1. Jesus wants me for a sunbeam,
To shine for Him each day;

In ev'ry way try to please Him,
At home, at school, at play.

Chorus
A sunbeam, a sunbeam,
Jesus wants me for a sunbeam;
A sunbeam, a sunbeam,
I'll be a sunbeam for Him.

2. Jesus wants me to be loving.
And kind to all I see;
Showing how pleasant and happy
His little one can be.

3. I will ask Jesus to help me
To keep my heart from sin,
Ever reflecting His goodness,
And always shine for Him.

4. I'll be a sunbeam for Jesus;
I can if I but try;
Serving Him moment by moment,
Then live with Him on high.
                                    -Nellie Talbot

889
O Why Not To Night

1. O do not let the Word depart.
And close thine eyes against the
light;
Poor sinner, harden not your heart,
Be saved, O tonight.

Chorus
O why not tonight?
O why not tonight?
Wilt thou be saved?
Then why not to night?

2. Tomorrow's sun may never rise
To bless thy long deluded sight;
This is the time, O then be wise,
Be saved, O to night.

3. Our Lord in pity lingers still.
And wilt thou thus His love requite?
Renounce at once thy stubborn will,
Be saved, O to night?

EVANGELISM

4. Our blessed Lord refuses none
   Who would to Him their souls unite;
   Believe on Him, the work is done,
   Be Saved, O tonight
   -Elizabeth Reed

890
Come home

1. O soul in the far away county,
   Aweary, and famished, and sad,
   There's rest in the home of thy
   Father,
   His welcome will make thy heart
   glad.

Chorus
Come home, come home,
Oh, why will you longer roam?
Come home, come home,
O prodigal child, come home.

2. Arise and come back to thy Father,
   He'll meet thee while yet on the
   way;
   Assured of His tender compassion,
   Oh, why wilt thou longer delay?

3. Although thou hast sinned against
   heaven,
   And weak and unworthy may be,
   He offers thee full restoration.
   And pardon abundant and free.
   -Mabel Frost

891
The Light of the world is Jesus

1. The whole world was lost in
   darkness of sin,
   The light of the world is Jesus;
   Like sunshine at noon day His glory
   shone in,
   The light of the world is Jesus.

Chorus
Come to the Light.'tis shining for
thee;

Sweetly me Light has dawned upon
me;
Once I was blind, but now I can see
The Light of the world is Jesus.

2. No darkness have we who in Jesus
   Abide,
   The Light of the world is Jesus
   We walk in the Light when we
   follow our Guide,
   The Light of the world is Jesus.

3. Ye dwellers in darkness with sin-
   blinded eyes,
   The light of the world is Jesus;
   Go, wash, at His bidding, and light
   will arise.
   The Light of the world is Jesus.

4. No need of the sunlight in heaven
   we're told,
   The light of that world is Jesus
   The Lamb is the Light in the City of
   God
   The Light of that world is Jesus.
   -P. P. Bliss

892
Come, Inner, come

1. While Jesus whispers to you
   Come, sinner, come!
   White we are praying for you
   Come, sinner, come!
   Now is the time to own Him.
   Come. sinner, come!
   Now is the time to know Him.
   Come, sinner, come!

2. Are you too heavy laden!
   Come, sinner, come!
   Jesus with beer your burden
   Come, sinner, come!
   Jesus will not deceive you,
   Come, sinner, come!
   Jesus can now redeem you
   Come, sinner, come!

3. Oh, hear His tender pleading
   Come, sinner, come!
   Come and receive the blessing
   Come, sinner, come!

EVANGELISM

While Jesus whispers to you,
Come, sinner, come!
While we are praying far you,
Come, sinner, come!

-W. E. Witer

893

There to A Green Hill Far Away

1. There is a green hill far away,
   Without a city wall,
   Where the dear Lord was crucified,
   Who died to save us all.

   Chorus
   Oh, dearly, dearly has He loved,
   And we must love Him, too,
   And trust in His redeeming blood,
   And try His works to do.

2. We may not know, we cannot tell,
   What pains He had to bear.
   But we believe it was for us
   He hung and suffered there.

3. He died that we might be forgiven,
   He died to make us good,'
   That we might go at last to heaven,
   Saved by His precious blood.

4. There was no other good enough
   To pay the price of sin, He only
   could unlock the gate
   Of heaven and let us in.

   -Cecil F. Alexander

894

Wellesley

1. There's a wideness in God's mercy.
   Like the wideness of the sea;
   There's a kindness in His justice,
   Which is more than liberty.

2. There is welcome for the sinner,
   And more graces for the good;
   There is mercy with the Saviour,
   There is healing in His blood.

3. For the love of God is broader
   Than the measure of man's mind:
   And the heart of the Eternal
   Is most wonderfully kind.

4. If our love were but more simple;
   We should take Him at His word,
   And our lives would be all sunshine
   In the sweetness of our Lord.

   -Frederick W. Faber

895

Hankey 7.6.7.6.D. with Refrain

1. I love to tell the story Of unseen
   things above,
   Of Jesus and His glory, Of Jesus
   and His love.
   I love to tell the story, Because I
   know 'tis true
   It satisfied my longing as nothing
   else can do.

   Chorus
   I love to tell the story,
   Twin be my theme in glory
   To tell the old, old story
   Of Jesus and His love.

2. I love to tell the story, 'tis pleasant
   to repeat
   What seems, each time I tell it,
   More wonderfully sweet;
   I lcve to tell the story. For some
   have never heard
   The message of salvation From
   God's own holy Word.

3. I love to tell the story, for those who
   know it best
   Seem hungering and thirsting to
   hear it like the rest;
   And when in scenes of glory I sing
   the new, song.
   'Twill be the old, old story that I
   have loved so long.

   -Catherine Hankey

EVANGELISM

896

No One Understands -8.7.6.7. with Refrain

1. No one understands like Jesus
He's a friend beyond compare;
Meet Him at the throne of mercy,
He is waiting for you there.

Chorus
No one understands like Jesus,
When the days are dark and grim;
No one is so near, so dear as Jesus,
Cast your every care on Him.

2. No one understands like Jesus,
Every woe He sees and feels;
Tenderly He whispers comfort,
And the broken heart He heals.

3. No one understands like Jesus,
When the foes of life assail;
You should never be discouraged,
Jesus cares and will not fail.

4. No one understands like Jesus,
When you falter on the way,
Tho' you fail Him, sadly fail Him,
He will pardon you today.
-John W. Peterson

897

My Saviour's Love-8.7.8.7, with Refrain

1. stand amazed in the presence
Of Jesu the Nazarene,
And wonder how He could love me,
A sinner, condemned, unclean.

Chorus
How marvelous! how wonderful!
And my song shall ever be:
How marvelous is how wonderful!
Is my Saviour's love for me!

2. For me it was in the garden
He prayed, 'not My will but Thrine,"
He had not tears for His own griefs
But sweet drops of blood for mine.

3. In pity angels beheld Him.
And came from the world of light
To comfort Him in the Sorrows
He bore for my soul that night.

4. He took my sins and my Sorrows,
He made them His very own,
He bore the burden to Calv' ry.
And suffered and died alone.

5. When with the ransomed in glory
His face I at last shall see,
Twill be my joy thru the ages.
To sing of His love for me.
-Charles H-Gaberiel

898

Simeon L. M.

1. On all the earth Thy Spirit shower
the earth in righteousness renew;
Thy kingdom come, and hell's
O' erpower,
And to Thy sceptre all subdue.

2. Like mighty winds, or torrents fierce,
Let it opposers all o'errun;
And every law of sin reverse,
That faith and love may make all one.

3. Yes, let thy spirit in every place
Its richer energy declare;
While lovely temper, fruits of grace.
The kingdom of Thy Christ prepare.

4. Grant this, o holy God and true!
The ancient seer Thou didst Inspire;
To us perform the promise due;
Descend, and crown us now with fire.
-Henry More

EVANGELISM

899

Such Love

1. That God should love a sinner such
   as I,
   Should yearn to change my sorrow
   into bliss,
   Nor rest till He had planned to bring
   me nigh,
   How wonderful is love like this!

   Chorus
   Such love, such wondrous love,
   Such love, such wondrous love.
   That God should love a sinner such
   as I,
   How wonderful is love like this

2. That Christ should join so freely in
   the scheme,
   Although it meant His death on
   Calvary,
   Did ever human tongue find nobler
   theme
   Than love divine that ransomed me!

3. That for a willful outcast such as I,
   The Father planned, the Saviour
   bled and died;
   Redemption for a worthless slave to
   buy,
   Who long had law and grace defied.

4. And now He takes me to His heart
   a son,
   He asks not to fill a servant's place;
   The "Far off country" wand' rings ail
   are done.
   Wide open are His arms of grace.
   —C. Bishop

900

Tell the Good News

1. Christ was born in a distant land,
   Tell the good news, tell the good
   news;

Lived on earth for the good of man
Tell the good news, tell the good
news.

Chorus
Tell the good news. tell the good
news,
Tell the good news Christ has
come;
Tell the good news, tell the good
news,
Tell the good news to ev' ry one.

2. Christ became a man on earth,
   Tell the good news. tell the good
   news,
   Gave his life for man's re-birth,
   Tell the good news, tell the good
   news.

3. Christ arose and to heaven went,
   Tell the good news. tell the good
   news,
   All may follow who repent,
   Tell the good news, tell the good
   news,

4. Christ still lives in the word today,
   Tell the good news. tell the good
   news,
   Giving strength to all souls who
   pray.
   Tell the good news, tell the good
   news,
   —Gene Bartlett

901

I Love Him

1. Gone from my heart the world and all
   Gone are my sins and all that would
   alarm,
   Gone evermore, and by His grace I
   know
   The precious blood of Jesus
   Cleanses white as snow.

EVANGELISM

Chorus
I love him, I love Him,
Because He first loved me.
And purchased my salvation on
Calv'ry's tree.

2. Once I was lost upon the plains of
sin;
Once was a slave to doubts and
fears; within;
Once was afraid to trust a loving
God.
But now my guilt is washed away in
Jesus' blood.

3. Once I was bound, but now I am set
free;
Once I was blind, but now the light I
See;
Once I was dead, but now in Christ
I live
To tell the world the peace that He
alone can give.

            -S. C. Foster

902
A Passion for Souls

1. Give me a passion for soul, dear
Lord,
A passion to save the lost,
O that Thy love were by adored.
And welcomed at any cost.

Chorus
Jesus, I long, I long to be winning
Men who are lost, and constantly
sinning:
O may this hour be one or begin
ning
The story of pardon to tell

2. Though there are dangers untold
and stern
Confronting me in the way,
Willingly still would go,
nor turn, But trust Thee for grace
each day.

3. How shall this passion for souls be
mine
Lord, make Thou the answer clear,
Help me throw out the old Lifeline
To those who are struggling near.
            -Herbert G. Tovey

903
Calvary Covers It All

1. Far dearer than all that the world
can impart
Was the message that came to my
heart;
How that Jesus alone for my sin did
alone,
And Calvary covers it all.

Chorus
Calvary covers it all,
My past with its sin and stain;
My guilt and despair Jesus took on
Him there,
And Calvary covers it all.

2. The stripes that He bore and the
thorns that He wore
Told His mercy and love evermore;
And my heart bowed in shame, as I
called on His name,
And Calvary covers it all.

3. How matchless the grace, when I
looked in the face
Of this Jesus, my crucified Lord:
My redemption complete I then
found at His feet.
And Calvary covers it all.

4. How blessed the thought, that my
soul by Him bought.
Shall be His in the glory on high;
Where with gladness sand song I'll
be one of the throng,
And Calvary covers it all.
            -Mrs. Walter G- Taylor

EVANGELISM

904
Wonderful

1. Wonderful birth! To a marker He
   came
   Made in the likeness of man, to
   proclaim
   God's boundless love for a world
   sick with sin,
   Pleading with sinners to let Him
   come in.

   Chorus
   Wonderful name He bears,
   Wonderful crown He wears,
   Wonderful blessings His triumphs
   afford;
   Wonderful Calvary, Wonderful
   grace for me.
   Wonderful love of my wonderful
   Lord!

2. Wonderful life, full of service so free,
   Friend to the poor and the needy
   was He;
   Unfalling goodness on all He
   bestowed.
   Undying faith in the vilest He
   Showed.

3. Wonderful death, for it meant not
   defeat,
   Calvary made His great mission
   complete,
   Wrought our redemption, and when
   He arose.
   Banished forever the last of our
   Foes.

4. Wonderful hope! He is coming again
   Coming as King o'er the nations to
   reign;
   Glorious promise. His Word cannot
   fail,
   His righteous kingdom at last must
   prevail?

   -A. H. Ackley

905
Jesus to The Sweetest Name I Know

1. There have been names that I have
   Loved to hear,
   But never has there been a name
   So dear
   To this heart of mine, as the name
   divine,
   The precious, precious name of
   Jesus.

   Chorus
   Jesus is the sweetest name I know,
   And He's just the same as His
   lovely name,
   And that's the reason why I love
   Him so;
   Oh, Jesus is the sweetest name I
   know.

2. There is no name in earth or haav'n
   above.
   That we should give such honour
   and such love,
   As the blessed name, let us all
   Acclaim,
   That wondrous, glorious name of
   Jesus.

3. And some day I shall see Him face
   to face
   To thank and praise Him for His
   wondrous grace,
   Which He gave to me, when He
   made me free.
   The blessed Son of God called
   Jesus.

   -Lela Long

906
My Wonderful Lord

1. I have found a deep peace that I
   never had known
   And a joy this world could not
   afford Since

EVANGELISM

I yielded control of my body and soul
To my wonderful, wonderful Lord.

Chorus
My wonderful Lord, my wonderful Lord.
By angels and seraphs in heaven adored!
I bow at Thy shrine, my Saviour divine,
My wonderful, wonderful Lord.

2. I desire that my life shall be ordered by Thee,
That my will be in perfect accord with
Thine own sov'reign will, Thy desires to fulfill.
My wonderful, wonderful Lord.

3. All the talents I have, I have laid at Thy feet;
Thy approval shall be my reward.
Be my store great or small, I surrender it all
To my wonderful, wonderful Lord.

4. Thou art fairer to me than the fairest of earth,
Thou omnipotent, life giving Word,
O Thou Ancient of Days, Thou art worthy all praise,
My wonderful, wonderful Lord.

-Haldor Lillenas

907
I'm Gonna Keep on Singing

1. I'm gonna keep singing,
I'm gonna keep on shouting.
I'm gonna keep on lifting my voice
and let the world know Jesus saves.

2. I'm gonna keep on marching,
I'm gonna keep on fighting,
I'm gonna keep on lifting my voice
and let the world know Jesus Saves.

3. You trumpets keep on sounding.
You bells keep on ringing,
And ev'ry body keep lifting your voice
and let the world know Jesus saves.

-Andrae Crouch

908
Sweeter as The Years Go By

1. Of Jesus' love that sought me
When I was lost in sin;
Of wondrous grace that brought me
Back to His fold again;
Of heights and depths of mercy,
Far deeper than the sea.
And higher than the heavens,
My theme shall ever be.

Chorus
Sweeter as the years go by,
Sweeter as the years go by;
Richer, fuller, deeper, Jesus' love is sweeter,
Sweeter as the years go by.

2. He trod in old Judea
Life's pathway long ago;
The people thronged about Him,
His saving grace to know,
He healed the broken hearted,
And caused the blind to see:
And still His great heart yearneth
In love for even me.

3. Twas wondrous love which led Him
For us to suffer loss.
To bear without a murmur
The anguish of the Cross.
With saints redeemed in glory,
Let us our voices raise,
Till heav'n and earth reecho
With our Redeemer's praise.

Lelia N. Morris

EVANGELISM

909
He wore a crown of Thorns

1. 'Twas God's own Son who came to earth,
Who chose to know a low;y birth;
But, tho' King of matchless worth,
He wore a crown of thorns.

Chorus
He wore a crown of thorns that I
might wear a crown of glory!
He laid His heav'nly splendours by
to bring me love's sweet story.
In poverty He walked life's way,
In Olive's garden bowed to pray;
He wore a crown of thorns that
I might wear a crown of glory!

2. Wonderful Counsellor was He,
Matchless His grace; how could it be
That, at the last, He wore for me
That bitter crown of thorns?

3. Kind were the deeds that crowned each day,
Gracious the words His lips would say.
While He pursued the fateful way
To wear that crown of thorns

4. Never again His brow shall know
Piercings of agony and woe:
But twas for us that, here below.
He wore the crown of thorns.
                    -William M. Runyan

910
Try Jesus, He satisfies

1. Come unto Jesus all ye that labour,
All that are weary, worn and defiled.
Bring Him your burdens, seek now His favour,
Tell Him your sorrows, in Him Confide.

Chorus
He satisfies, He satisfies.
O will you let Him in your heart abide?
He'll keep your soul what ever betide.
Wont you try Jesus, He satisfies.

2. Come unto Jesus, don't waste a moment;
Your time so precious Is fleeting by,
All your transgressive, freely confessing,
He in His mercy, safely will hide.

3. Come unto Jesus. Saviour and brother,
Surely you need Him truest and best
Dearer than father, fonder than mother.
Come unto Jesus, He'll give you rest.
                    -Robert Martin

911
San Gabriel

1. My new life I owe to Thee,
Jesus, Lamb of Calvary;
Sin was canceled on the tree
Jesus, blessed Jesus!

2. Humbly at Thy cross I'd stay
Jesus, keep me there, I pray;
Teach me more of Thee each day,
Jesus, blessed Jesus!

3. Grant me wisdom, grace and pow'r
Lord, I need Thee ev'ry hour,
Let my will be lost in Thine,
Jesus, blessed Jesus!

4. I Saviour, Thou hast heard my plea
Thou art near, so near to me;
Now I feel Thy strength'ning pow'r,
Jesus, blessed Jesus!
                    -H. P. Blanchard

EVANGELISM

912
Just a Little talk with Jesus

1. I once was lost in sin but Jesus
took me in,
And then a little light from heaven
filled my soul;
It bathed my heart in love and wrote
my name above,
And just a little talk with Jesus
made me whole.

Chorus
Have a little talk with Jesus.
tell Him all about our troubles.
Hear our faintest cry, answer by an
by;
Feel a tittle pray'r wheel turning.
know a little fire is burning.
Find a little talk with Jesus makes it
right

2. Sometimes my path seems drear,
without a ray of cheer,
And then a cloud of doubt may hide
the light of day.
The mists of sin may rise and hide
the starry skies.
But just a little talk with Jesus clears
the way.

3. I may have doubts and fears, my
eyes be filled with tears,
But Jesus is a friend who watches
day and night;
I go to Him in pray'r. He knows my
ev'ry care,
And Just a little talk with Jesus
makes it right
-Cleavant Derricks

913
Galilee-8.7.8.7.

1. Jesus calls us: o'er the tumult
Of our life's wild, restless sea,
Day by day His sweet voice
soundeth,
Saying. 'Christian, follow Me."

2. Jesus calls us from the worship
Of the vain world's golden store.
From each idol that would keep us,
Saying, "Christian, love me more".

3. In our joys and in our sorrows,
Days of toil and hour's of ease.
Still He calls in cares and
pleasures,
"Christian, love me more" than
more"

4. Jesus call us; by Thy mercies
Saviour, may we hear Thy call.
Give our hearts to Thine obedience
Serve and love Thee best of all.
-Cecil F. Alexander

914
Don't Turn Him Away

1. Patiently, tenderly pleading,
Jesus is standing today.
At your heart s door He knocks as
before.
Oh, turn Him no longer away!

Chorus
Don't turn Him away, Don't turn
Him away.
He has come back to your heart
again
Altho' you've gone astray.
Oh, how you'll need Him to plead
you cause
On that eternal day!
Don't turn the Saviour away from
your heart;
Don't turn Him away.

2. Gracious, compassionate mercy
Bro't Him from mansions above;
Caused Him to wait Just out-side
your gate.
Oh, yield to His wonderful love!

3. Can you not now hear Him calling?
Do not ill treat such a Friend,
Give up your sin. Oh, let Him come in
Lo! He will be true to the end.

EVANGELISM

Now is the time to receive Him;
Grant Him admission today.
Grieve Him no more, But open your
door,
And turn Him no longer away.
                    -Haldor Lillenas

915
Blessed Redeemer

1. Up Catv'rys mountain, on dreadful
   mom,
   Walked Christ my Saviour, weary
   and worn;
   Facing for sinners death on the
   cross.
   That He might save them from
   endless loss.

   Chorus
   Blessed Redeemer, precious
   Redeemer!
   Seems now I see Him on Calvary's
   tree,
   Wounded and bleeding, for sinners
   pleading
   Blind and unheeding dying for me!

2. "Father, forgive them!" thus did He
   pray,
   E'en while His life blood flowed fast
   away;
   Praying for sinners while in such
   woe
   No one but Jesus ever loved so.

3. O how I love Him, Saviour and
   friend!
   How can my praises ever find end!
   Thru years unnumbered on
   heaven's shore.
   My tongue shall praise Him for
   evermore.
                    -Avis B. Christiansen

916
Jesus Saves

1. We have heard the joyful sound
   Jesus saves! Jesus saves!
   Spread the tidings all around
   Jesus saves! Jesus saves!
   Bear the news to ev'ry land,
   Climb the steeps and cross the
   waves;
   Onward! lis our Lord's command
   Jesus saves! Jesus saves!

2. Waft it on the rolling tide
   Jesus saves! Jesus saves!
   Tell to sinners far and wide
   Jesus saves! Jesus saves!
   Sing, ye fslands of the sea!
   Echo back, ye ocean waves!
   Earth shall keep her jubilee
   Jesus saves! Jesus saves!

3. Sing above the battle strife
   Jesus saves! Jesus saves!
   By His death and endless life
   Jesus saves! Jesus saves!
   Sing it softly thru the gloom,
   When the heart for mercy craves;
   Sing in triumph o'er the tomb
   Jesus saves! Jesus saves'

4. Give the winds a mighty voice
   Jesus saves! Jesus saves!
   Let the nations now rejoice
   Jesus saves! Jesus saves!
   Shout salvation fun and free,
   Highest hills and deepest caves;
   This our song of victory
   Jesus saves? Jesus saves!
                    -Priscilla J. Owens

917
Evington -L M.

1. Spirit of mercy, truth, and love,
   Oh shed Thine influence from
   above
   And still from age to age convey
   The wonders of this sacred day.

EVANGELISM

2. In every clime, by every tongue,
   Be God's surpassing glory sung:
   Let all the listening earth be taught
   The acts our great Redeemer wrought.

3. Unfalling Comfort, heavenly Guide,
   Still o'er Thy holy Church preside:
   Still let mankind Thy blessings prove;
   Spirit of mercy, truth, and love.
   -Henry Hiles

918

St George's, Windsor - 7.7.7.7.D.

I. Hark! the song of jubilee.
   Loud as mighty thunders roar.
   Or the fulness of the sea
   When it breaks upon the shore:
   Hallelujah! for the Lord
   God omnipotent shall reign:
   Hallelujah!" let the word
   Echo round the earth and man.

2. "Hallelujah!" Hark? the sound
   From the depths unto the skies,
   Wakes above, beneath, around,
   All creation's harmonies:
   See Jehovah's banner furled,
   Sheathed His sword; He speaks tis done,
   And the kingdoms of this world
   Are the kingdom of His Son.

3. He shall reign from pole to pole
   With illimitable sway;
   He shall reign when like a scroll
   Yonder heavens have passed away:
   Then the end; beneath His rod
   Man's last enemy shall fall;
   Hallelujah! Christ in God,
   God in Christ is All in all!
   -Sir G. J. Elvey

919

Greenland-7.6.7.6.D.

1. From Greenland's icy mountains,
   From India's coral strand,
   Where Africa's sunny fountains
   Roll down their golden sand;
   From many an ancient river,
   From many a palmy plain,
   They call us to deliver
   Their land from error's chain.

2. What though the spicy breezes
   Blow soft o'er Ceylon's isle
   Though every prospect pleases,
   And only man is vile:
   In vain with lavish kindness
   The gifts of God are strown,
   The heathen in his blindness
   Bows down to wood and stone.

3. Can we, whose souls are lighted
   With wisdom from on high.
   Can we to men benighted
   The lamp of life deny?
   Salvation. O salvation!
   The joyful sound proclaim,
   Till each remotest nation
   Has learnt Messiah's name.

4. Waft, waft, ye winds. His story.
   And you, ye waters, roll;
   Till like a sea of glory,
   It spreads from pole to pole;
   Till o'er our ransom'd nature,
   The Lamb for sinners slain,
   Redeemer, King Creator,
   In bliss returns to reign.
   -Sir G. J. Eivey

CHRISTIAN WARFARE

920

Crucis milites - 7.7.7.7.

1. Soldiers of the Cross, arise!
   Gird you with your armour bright:
   Mighty are your enemies,
   Hard the battle ye must fight

2. O'er a faithless fallen world
   Raise your banner in the sky;
   Let it float there wide unfurled;
   Gear it onward, lift it high.

3. 'Mid the homes of want and woe,
   Stangers to the living word,
   Let the Saviour's herald go,
   Let the voice of hope be heard,

4. Where the shadows deepest lie.
   Carry truth's unsullied ray;
   Where are crimes of blackest dye,
   There the saving sign display.

5. To the weary and the worn
   Tell of realms where sorrows cease;
   To the outcast and forlorn
   Speak of mercy and of peace.

6. Guard the helpless, seek the
   strayed;
   Comfort troubles, banish grief:
   In the might of God arrayed,
   Scatter sin and unbelief.

7. Be the banner still unfurled,
   Still unsheathed the Spirit's sword.
   Till the kingdoms of the world
   Are the Kingdom of the Lord.

   -Bishop W.
   Waisham How

921

Ein' feste Burg - 8.7.8.7.6.6.6.6.7.

1. A safe stronghold our God is still,
   A trusty shield and weapon;

He'll help us dear from all the ill
That hath us now o'er taken.
The ancient prince of hell
Hath risen with purpose fell;
Strong mail of craft and power
He weareth in this hour,
On earth is not his fellow.

2. With force of arms we nothing can,
   Full soon were we down-ridden;
   But for us fights the proper Man,
   Whom God Himself hath bidden
   Ask ye, Who is this same?
   Christ Jesus is His name,
   The Lord Sabaoth's Son:
   He, and no other one,
   Shall conquer in the battle.

3. And were this world all devils o'er
   And watching to devour us,
   We lay it not to heart so sore;
   Not they can overpower us,
   And let the prince of ill
   Look grim as e'er he will.
   He harms us not a whit;
   For why? his doom is writ;
   A word shall quickly slay him.

4. God's word, for an their craft and
   force,
   One moment will not finger,
   But, spite of hell, shall have its
   course;
   Tis written by His ringer
   And though they take our life,
   Goods, honour, children, wife,
   Yet is their profit small;
   These things shall vanish all,
   The city of God remaineth!

   -Martin Luther

922

Bunyan - 6.5.6.5.6.6.6.5.

1. Christian, unflinching stand,
   Satan defying!
   Outstreched is God's right hand,

All power supplying;
Valiant as saints of old,
Proudly the cross uphold,
Moved by His love untold
To live for Jesus.

2. Stern is your fight with wrong;
Christ stands beside you,
Hard grows the way and long;
His hand will guide you
Calmly each danger face,
Boldly His footsteps trace,
Seeking by God's good grace
To live for Jesus.

3. Friends by your side may fall:
Help and defend them,
Foes in distress may call:
Comfort and tend them,
Give ear to them that plead;
Bind up the hearts that bleed;
Learn by each kindly deed
To live for Jesus.
-E. W. Leachman

923

Grucis milites - 7.7.7.7.

1. Soldiers, who are Christ's below,
Strong in faith resist the foe;
Boundless is the pledged reward
Unto them who serve the Lord.

2. Tis no palm of fading leaves
That the conqueror's hand receives;
Joys are his, serene and pure,
Light that ever shall endure.

3. For the souls that overcome
Waits the beauteous heavenly home,
Where the blessed evermore
Tread on high the golden floor.

4. Passing soon and little worth
Are the things that tempt on earth;

Heavenward lift thy soul's regard;
God Himself is thy reward.

5. Father, who the crown dost give,
Saviour, by whose death we live,
Spirit, who our hearts doth raise,
Three in One, Thy name we praise
-Bourges Breviary

924

Truehearted -11.10,11.10. with Refrain

1. Truehearted whole hearted, faithful.
and loyal,
King of our lives, by Thy grace, we :
will be:
Under the standard, exalted and
royal,
Strong in Thy strength, we will battle
for Thee.

Chorus
Peal out the watch word! silence it
never!
Song of our spirits, rejoicing and
free,
Peal out the watch word! loyal
forever,
King of our lives, by Thy grace we
will be.

2. True hearted, whole hearted, fullest
allegiance
Yielding henceforth to our glorious
King;
Valiant endeavour and loving
obedience.
Freely and jealously now would we
bring.

3. True hearted, whole hearted,
Saviour all glorious!
Take Thy great power and reign
there alone

CHRISTIAN WARFARE

Over our wills and affections
victorious,
Freely surrendered and wholly
Thine own.

-Frances R. Havergal

925

Austrian Hymn -8.7.8.7.D.

1. We are living, we are dwelling
   In a grand and awful time,
   In an age on ages telling;
   To be living is sublime.
   Hark! the waking up of nations.
   Hosts advancing to the fray;
   Hand what soundeth is creation's
   Groaning for the latter day.

2. Will ye play, then? will ye dally
   Far behind the battle line?
   Up! it is Jehovah's rally;
   God's own arm hath need of thine.
   Worlds are charging, heaven
   beholding
   Thou hast but an hour to fight;
   Now, the blazoned cross unfolding.
   On, right onward for the right!

3. Sworn to yield, to waver, never.
   Consecrated, born again;
   Sworn to be Christ s soldiers ever,
   On! for Christ at least be men!
   On! let all the soul within you.
   For the truth's sake go abroad!
   Strike! let every nerve and sinew
   Tell on ages, tell for God.

A Cleveland Coxe

926

Arthur's st-6.6.6.6.8.8.

1. March on, O soul, with strength!
   Like those strong men of old.
   Who, against enthroned wrong,
   Stood confident and bold;
   . Who, thrust in pris'n or cast to
   Flame,
   Still made their glory in Thy name.

2. The sons of fathers we,
   By whom our faith is taught
   To fear no ill to fight
   The holy fight they fought
   Heroic warriors, ne'er from Christ.
   By any lure or guile, enticed.

3. March on, O soul, with strength.
   As strong the battle rolls!
   Gainst lies and lusts and wrongs,
   Let courage rule our souls:
   In keenest strife, Lord, may we
   stand,
   Upheld and strengthened by Thy
   hand.

4. Not tong the conflict soon ,
   The holy war shall cease.
   faith's warfare ended,
   won The home of endless peace!
   Look up! the victor's crown at
   length
   March on, O soul, march on, with
   Strength!

-Geoge T. Coster

927

**The Banner of the Cross-11.7.11.7.
with Refrain**

1. There's a royal banner given for
   display
   To the soldiers of the king;
   As an ensign fair we lift it up today,
   While as ransomed ones we sing.

   Chorus
   Marching on! on! on! Marching on!
   on! on!
   For Christ count ev'rything,
   And to crown Him king, toil and
   sing.
   Beneath the banner of the cross!

2. Though the foe may rage and
   gather as the flood,
   Let the standard be displayed'

And beneath its folds, as soldiers of
the Lord.
For the truth be not dismayed!

3. Over land and sea, wherever man
may dwell,
Make the glorious tidings known:
Of the crimson banner now the
story tell.
While the Lord shall claim his own!

4. When the glory dawns tis drawing
very near.
It is hastening day by day
Then before our King the foe shall
disappear
And the Cross the world shall
sway?

-Daniel W. Whittle

928

Redhead C. M.

1. In all ways chosen by the Lord
My journey will I go
Prevent me not ye Holy men
I will fellow thee there

2. If Jesus moves in the furnace
I will follow Him there
Prevent me not will be my word
If the world oppose me

3. In adoration, temptation
With thy Command I'll go
Prevent me not, for I will go
Unto Emmanuel.

4. And when my Saviour shall call me
And still my cry shall be
Prevent me not, death is coming
I will follow with joy.

-R Redhead

929

1. Awake, my soul, stretch every,
nerve.
And press with vigour on;
A heavenly race demands thy zeal
And an immortal awn.

2 A cloud of witnesses around Hold
thee in full survey:
Forget the steps already trod
And onward urge thy way.

3. Tis God's all animating voice
That calls thee from on high:
Tis His own hand presents the prize
To time aspiring eye.

4. That prize, with peerless glories
bright
Which shall new lustre boast.
Whrn victor's wreaths and
monarch gems
Shall end in common dust.

5. Blast Saviour, introduced by Thee
Have I my race begun:
And crowned with victory, at Thy
feet
I'll lay my honours down.
-Philip Doddridge

930

Colchester - 8.8.8:8.8.8.

2. Captain of Isreal's host, and guide
Of all who seek the land above.
Beneath Thy shadow we abide,
The cloud of Thy protecting love;
Our strength, Thy grace; our rule,
Thy word:

2. Our end, the glory of the Lord.
By Thine unerring Spirit led.
We shall not in the desert stray;
We shall not full direction need,
Nor miss our providential way,

CHRISTIAN WARFARE

As far from danger as from fear,
While love, almighty love, is near.

3. We've no abiding city here,
   But seek a city out of sight;
   Thither our steady Course we steer
   Aspiring to the plain of light
   Jerusalem, the saints' abode,
   Whose founder is the living God.

4. Through Thee, who all our sins hast Borne,
   Freely and graciously forgiven,
   With songs to Zion we return,
   Contending for our native heaven:
   That palace of our glorious King,
   We find it nearer while we sing.

5. Raised by the breath of love divine.
   We urge our way with strength renewed;
   The Church of the first-born to join,
   We travel to the mount of God;
   With joy upon our heads arise.
   And meet our Captain in the skies.
   —Charles Wesley

931

When the Battle's Over

1. Am I a soldier of the cross?
   A foll'wer of the Lamb?
   And shall I fear to own His cause
   Or blush to speak His name?

Chorus
And when the battle's over
we shall wear a crown!
Yes, we shall wear a crown!
Yes we shall wear a crown!
And when the battle's over
we shall wear a crown
In the new Jerusalem.
Wear a crown, wear a crown,
Wear a bright and shining crown;
And when the battle's over
We shall wear a crown
In the new Jerusalem.

2. Must I be carried to the skies
   On flow'ry beds of ease.
   White others fought to win the prize
   And sailed thru bloody seas?

3. Are there no foes for me to face?
   Must I not stem the flood?
   Is this vile world a friend to grace,
   To help me on to God?

4. Sure I must fight if I would reign
   Increase my courage, Lord!
   I'll bear the toil, endure the pain.
   Supported by Thy Word.
                        —Issac Watts. D.D.

932

The Army of the Living God.

1. Hand On the highway of life a sound,
   As crested waves of Ocean roar,
   Lash'd by the storm in its fury spent;
   As they beat upon the shore.

Chorus
Hand the tramp, tramp, tramp of
The army
as they march along the way of life,
They are weary of the toil and the travel,
of the bitterness of strife (of strife)
But they hope and trust looking ever
on the path the saints before have trod,
And as they march along their Faith grows
strong in the church of the living God.

2. Onward they march with a faith unmoved.
   By any change of time or creed;
   Their's to believe that the word of God
   Can supply the world's great need.

3. Step in the rank, you are needed there,
Cling to the church and God will Bless.
He is the hope of the whole wide world
For the cause of righteousness.
-C. Austin Miles

933

Foel Fras -L.M.

1. Fight the good fight with all thy might;
Christ is thy strength, and Christ thy right;
Lay hold on life, and it shall be
Thy joy and crown eternally;

2. Run the straight race through God's Good race
Lift up thine eyes, and seek His face;
Life with its way before us lies,
Christ is the path. and Christ the prize.

3. Cast care aside, lean on thy Guide;
His boundless mercy will provide;
Lean, and the trusting soul shall prove,
Christ is its life, and Christ its love.

4. Faint not, nor fear, His arms are near,
He changeth not, and thou art dear,
Only believe, and thou shall see
That Christ is all in all to thee.
-H. A. Harding

934

Birmingham-12.9.12.9.

1. We are soldiers of Christ, who is mighty to save,
And His banner the cross is unful'd;
We are pledged to be faithful and steadfast and brave
Against Satan, the flesh, and the world.

2. We are brothers and comrades, We stead side by side
And our faith and our hope are the same;
And we think of the cross on which Jesus has died,
When we bear the reproach of his name.

3. At the font we were mark'd with the cross on our brow
Of our grace and our calling the sign:
And the weakest is strong to be true to his vow
For the armour we wear is divine.

4. We will watch ready arm'd if the tempter draw near,
If he come with a frown or a smile:
We will heed not his threats, nor his flatteries hear,
Nor be taken by storm or by wile.

5. We will master the flesh, and its longings restrain.
We will not be the bond-slaves of sin,
The pure Spirit of God in our nature Shall reign,
And our spirits their freedom shall win.

6. For the world's love we live not hate we defy,
And we will not be led by the throng
We'll be true to ourselves, to our Father on high,
And the bright world to which we Belong.

7. Now let each cheer his comrade, let hearts beat as one,
While we follow where Christ leads the way;
'Twere dishonour to yield, or the Battle to shun,
We will fight, and will watch, and Will pray.

CHRISTIAN WARFARE

935

St. Osmund -8.7.8.7.8.7.

1. Why those fears? Behold, 'tis
   Jesus
   Holds the helm and guides the ship:
   Spread the sails, and catch the
   breezes
   Sent to waft us through the deep,
   To the regions
   Where the mourners cease to
   weep.

2. Though the shore we hope to land
   on
   Only by report is known,
   Yet we freely all abandon,
   Led by that report alone;
   And with Jesus
   Through the trackless deep move
   on.

3. Led by that, we brave the ocean;
   Led by that, the storms defy;
   Calm amidst tumultuous motion,
   Knowing that our Lord is nigh:
   Waves obey Him,
   And the storms before Him fly.

4. Oh, what pleasures there await us:
   There the tempests cease to roar
   There is that those who hate us
   Can molest our peace no more:
   Trouble ceases
   On that tranquil happy shore.
   -H.S. Irons

936

University College - 7.7.7.7.

1. Christian soldiers, onward go!
   Jesus' triumph you shall know;
   fight the fight, maintain the strife,
   strengthened with the bread of life.

2. Join the war and face the foe!
   Christian soldiers, onward go;
   boldly stand in danger's hour, ;
   trust your captain, prove his power.

3. Let your drooping hearts be glad,
   march in heavenly armour clad;
   fight, nor think the battle long
   soon shall victory be your song.

4. Sorrow must not dim your eye.
   soon shall every tear be dry;
   banish fear, you shall succeed:
   great your strength if great your
   need.

5. Onward, then in battle move!
   more than conquerors you shall
   prove;
   though opposed by many a foe
   Christian soldiers, onward go! ;
   -H.K. White

937

Ladywell- 8.6.8.6.D (C.M.)

1. The Son of God rides out to war
   The ancient foe to slay;
   his blood-red banner streams afar
   who follows him today?
   who bears his cross? Who shares
   his grief?
   who walk his narrow way?
   who faces rampant unbelief?
   who follows him today?

2. The martyr Stephen's eagle eye
   could pierce beyond the grave;
   he saw his master in the sky
   and called on him to save.
   By zealots he was stoned to death
   And, as he knelt to pray,
   he blessed them with his final
   breath,
   who follows him today?

CHRISTIAN WARFARE

3. The valiant twelve, the chosen few,
On them the Spirit fell;
and faithful to the Lord they knew
they faced the hosts of hell.
They died beneath the brandished steel.
became the tyrant's prey,
yet did not flinch at their ordeal
who follows them today?

4. A noble army young and old
From every nation came;
Some weak and frail, some strong and bold,
To win the martyr's fame.
Eternal joy to all is given
who trust you and obey:
O give us strength, great God of
To follow them today!

-R. Heber

938

Monks gate- 6.5.6.5.6.6.6.5.

1. Who honours courage here,
who fights the devil?
who boldly faces tear,
Who conquers evil?
We're not afraid to fight!
we'll scorn the devils spite:
Christ gives to us the right
to be his pilgrims.

2. Some may be terrified
by Satan's testing.
but faith is verified
when we're resisting.
There's no discouragement
shall cause us to relent
Our firm declared intent
to be his pilgrims.

3. Though evil powers intend
to break our spirit,
we know we at the end
shall life inherit.

So fantasies, away!
why fear what others say?
We'll labour night and day
to be his pilgrims

-Michael Saward

939

The Fight is On

1. The fight is on, the trumpet sound
Is ringing out,
The cry "To arms" is heard afar and near;
The Lord of hosts is marching victory,
The triumph of the Christ will soon appear.

Chorus
The fight is on, O Christian soldier,
And face to face in stern array,
with armor gleaming, and colors streaming,
The right and wrong engage today!
The fight is on, but be not weary;
Be strong, and in His might hold fast;
If God be for us, His banner o'er us,
We'll sing the victor's song at last!

2. The fight is on, arouse, ye soldiers
brave and true!
Jehovah leads, and vict'ry will assure;
Go, buckle on the armor God has given you,
And in His strength unto the end endure.

3. The Lord is leading on to certain victory;
The bow of promise spans the eastern sky;
His glorious name in ev'ry land shall honored be;
The morn will break, the dawn of peace is nigh.

-C.H. Morris

CHRISTIAN WARFARE

940

All Things Through Christ

1. Soldier, soldier, fighting in the
   world's great strife,
   On thyself relying,& battling for thy
   life,
   Trust thyself no longer.
   Trust to Christ, He's stronger,
   "I can all things, all things do
   Thru' Christ, which strength'neth
   me."

2. In your daily duty, standing up for
   right,
   Are your sometimes weary heart
   not always light?
   Doubt your Saviour never,
   This your motto ever.
   "I can all things, all things do
   Through Christ, which strength'neth
   me"

3. If your way be weary, He will help
   you through
   Help you in your troubles and your
   pleasures, too;
   Say, when Satan's by you,
   Say, when all things try you;
   "I can all things, all things do
   Through Christ, which strength'neth
   me."

4. In a world of trouble, tempted oft to
   stray
   You need never stumble; Satan
   cannot stay
   Will but tempt you vainly,
   If you tell him plainly
   "I can all things, all things do
   Through Christ, which strength'neth
   me."

5. Jesus' power is boundless as the
   sea;
   He is always able, able to keep me
   Power bring from my weakness,

Glory from my meekness
"I can all things, all things do
Through Christ, which strength'neth
me"

-R. Hudson Pope

941

Who Will Join Us

1. Behold the armies of the King
   Are marching forth in line;
   Their royal banners lifted high,
   In radiant splendour shine.

Chorus
Who will join us, who will join us,
Who will join us in the fray?
Who will join us, who will join us,
Who will join our ranks today?

2. And now among the foremost
   ranks,
   Where foe meets foe today,
   They stand erect with sword and
   shield.
   To brave the dread affray.

3. Behold, the King Himself is near.
   And while His own advance,
   The traitor legions backward fall
   Beneath their fearless glance.

4. Oh, glorious, glorious victory,
   With life's great battle done;
   The cross laid down, they wear the
   crown,
   Their faith in Christ hath won.

-M.G. Walker

942

The Song of the Soldier

1. Rise, ye children of salvation,
   All who cleave to Christ the Head;
   Wake, arise! O mighty nation,
   Ere the foe on Zion tread.

CHRISTIAN WARFARE

Chorus
Pour it forth a mighty anthem,
Like the thunders of the sea;
Thro' the blood of Christ our
ransom,
More than conquerors are we,
More than conquerors are we,
More than conquerors we are;
Thro' the blood of Christ our
ransom,
More than conquerors are we.

2. Saints and heroes long before us
Firmly on this ground have stood;
See their banners waving o'er us.
Conquerors through Jesus' blood.

3. Deathless, we are all unfearing,
Life laid up with Christ in God;
In the morn of His appearing
Floweth forth a glory flood.

4. Soon we shall all stand before Him,
See and know our glorious Lord;
Soon in joy and light adore Him,
Each receiving his reward.
                              -Falkner

943

New Yolk -7.6.7.6.D.

1. A life of overcoming,
A life of ceaseless praise,
Be this thy blessed portion
Throughout the coming days.
The victory was purchased
On Calv'y cross for thee,
Sin shall not have dominion.
The Son hath made thee free:

2. And would'st thou know the secret
Of constant victory?
Let in the Over Comer,
And He will conquer thee?
Thy broken spirit taken
In sweet captivity,
Shall glory in His triumph
And share His victory.

3. Though all the path before thee
The host of darkness fill,
Look to thy Father's promise,
And claim the victory still.
Faith sees the heavenly legions.
Where doubt sees naught but foes
And through the very conflict
Her life the stronger grows.

4. More stern will grow the conflict
As nears our King's return,
And they alone can face it
Who this great lesson learn:
That from them God asks nothing
But to unlatch the door
Admitting Him who through them
Will conquer evermore.
                    -Freda Hanbury Allen

944

Caersalem- 8.7.8.7.4.7.

1. Blessed Lord, in Thee is refuge,
Safety for my trembling soul.
Pow'r to lift my, head when dropping,
"Midst the angry billows' roll.
I will trust Thee,
All my life Thou shalt control.

2. In the past too unbelieving
"Midst the tempest I have been,
And my heart has slowly trusted
What my eyes have never seen.
Blessed Jesus,
Teach me on Thine arm to lean

3. Oh, for trust that brings me triumph,
When defeat seems strangely near!
Oh, for faith that changes fighting
Into victory's ringing cheer!
Faith triumphant!
Knowing not defeat or fear.

4. Faith triumphant blessed vict'ry!
Every barrier swept away!
Heaven descending, joy and fulness
Dawn of everlasting day!
Jesus only
Him to love and Him obey.
                              -H.H. Booth

CHRISTIAN WARFARE

945

Monks gate

1. He who would valiant be
   'Gainst all disaster,
   Let him in constancy
   Follow the Master.
   There's no discouragement
   Shall make him once relent
   His first avowed intent
   To be a pilgrim.

2. Who so beset him round
   With dismal stories,
   Do but themselves confound
   His strength the more is,
   No foes shall stay his might,
   Though he with giants flight;
   He will make good his right
   To be a pilgrim.

3. Since. Lord. thou dost defend
   Us with thy Spirit,
   We know we at the end
   Shall life inherit.
   Then fancies flee away!
   I'll fear not what men say,
   I'll labour night and day
   To be a pilgrim.

   -John Bunyan

946

Sound the Battle Cry

1. Sound the battle cry! See! the foe is
   nigh;
   Raise the standard high For the Lord;
   Gird your armour on. Stand firm,
   ev'ry one;
   Rest your cause upon His holy word.

   Chorus
   Rouse, then, soldiers! rally round
   the banner!
   Ready, steady, pass the word along;
   Onward, forward, shout aloud
   Hosannah!
   Christ is Captain of the mighty throng.

2. Strong to meet the foe, Marching on
   we go,
   While our cause we know Must
   prevail;
   Shield and banner bright Gleaming
   In the light;
   Battling for the right, We ne'er can
   fail.

3. Oh! Thou God of all Hear us when
   we call;
   Help us one and all, By Thy grace;
   When the battle's done, And the
   vict'ry won,
   May we wear the crown Before Thy
   face.

   -W.F. Sherwin

947

Si Mus Tibi - 6.5.

1. Forward! be our watch word,
   Steps and voices Joined;
   Seek the things before us,
   Not a look behind:
   Bums the fiery pillar
   At our army's head;
   Who shall dream of shrinking,
   By our Captain led?
   Forward thro' the desert,
   Thro' the toil and fight;
   Canaan lies before us,
   Zion beams with light.

2. Forward! flock of Jesus
   Salt of all the earth,
   Till each yearning purpose
   Spring to glorious birth:
   Sick, they ask for healing,
   Blind, they grope for day;
   Pour upon the nations
   Wisdom's loving ray!
   Forward, out of error,
   Leave behind the night;
   Forward through the darkness.
   Forward into light.

CHRISTIAN WARFARE

3. Glories upon glories
   Hath our God prepared,
   By the souls that love Him
   One day to be shared:
   Eye hath not beheld them;
   Ear hath never heard;
   Nor of these hath uttered
   Thought or speech a word;
   Forward, ever forward,
   Clad in armour bright;
   Till the veil be lifted,
   Till our faith be sight.

4. Far o'er your horizon
   Rise the city towers,
   Where our God abideth;
   That fair home is ours!
   Flash the gates with jasper,
   Shine the streets with gold;"
   Flows the gladdenning river,
   Shedding joys untold:
   Thither, onward, thither,
   In the Spirits might:
   Pilgrims, to your country,
   Forward into light!

   -H. Alford

948

Hold the fort

1. Ho, my comrades! see the signal
   Waving in the sky!
   Reinforcements now appearing,
   Victory is nigh!

   Chorus
   "Hold the fort, for I am coming."
   Jesus signals still;
   Wave the anser back to heaven,
   "By Thy grace we will."

2. See the mighty host advancing.
   Satan leading on:
   Mighty men around us falling,
   Courage almost gone!

3. See the glorious banner waving?
   Hear the trumpet blow!
   In our Leader's name we'll triumph
   Over ev'ry foe'

4. Fierce and long the battle rages
   But our help is near;
   Onward comes our great Com-
   mander,
   Cheer, my comrades, cheer!

   -P.P. Bliss

949

On the victory side

1. Our souls cry out, hallelujah!
   And our faith enraptured sings
   While we throw to the breeze the
   standard
   Of the mighty King of kings.

   Chorus
   On the vict'ry side. on the vict'ry
   side,
   In the ranks of the Lord are we;
   On the vict'ry side we will boldly
   stand.
   Till the glory land we see.

2. Our souls cry out, hallelujah! for
   the Lord himself comes near,
   And the shout of a royal army on
   the battle field we hear.

3. Our souls cry out, hallelujah!
   For the tempter flies apace,
   And the chains he has forged are
   breaking,
   Through the power of redeeming
   grace.

4. Our souls cry out, hallelujah!
   And our hearts beat high with "
   praise,
   Unto Him, in whose name we'll
   conquer,
   And our song of triumph raise.
   -James L. Black

950

Doncaster - S.M.

1. Quit you like men, be strong!
   Wax valiant in the fight;
   See! yonder Captain leads the
   throng,

CHRISTIAN WARFARE

2. Though battle's thunders roar,
   And hosts of darkness press,
   He is alive for evermore,
   And succours our distress.

3. List to the swelling strains
   Of those who fought and won,
   They laud the Lamb, the crimson stains
   His vesture are upon:

4. 'Twas through His precious blood,
   Confession to His name,
   And lives laid down, that they once stood
   And every foe o'er came.

5. Shall we, then. faint and fell
   When strength seems all but gone?
   Nay, rather, on your Captain call
   And look to Him alone;

6. "For I am strong when weak,"
   O count this saying true,
   The Lord doth strength and comfort
   As no one else can do.
   　　　　　　　　-Ernest T. Mellor

951

Forward

1. Christ, our mighty Captain, leads
   against the foe;
   We will never falter when He bids
   us go;
   Tho' His righteous purpose we may
   never know
   Yet we'll follow all the way.

Chorus.
Forward! forward! 'tis the Lord's command,
Forward! forward! to the promised land;
Forward! forward! let the chorus ring:
We are sure to win with Christ, our King!

2. Satan's fearful onslaughts cannot
   make us yield,
   While we trust in Christ, our
   Buckler and our Shield;
   Pressing ever on the Spirits sword
   we wield,
   And we follow all the way.

3. Let our glorious banner ever be
   unfurled
   From his mighty stronghold evil
   shall be hurled:
   Christ, our mighty Captain, over
   comes the world,
   And we follow all the way.

4. Fierce the battle rages, but twill not
   belong,
   Then triumphant shad we join the
   blessed throng,
   Joyfully uniting in the victor's song if
   we follow all the way.
   　　　　　　　　-Mrs. Frank A. Breck

952

Lifetime is Working Time

1. Lifetime is working time. Spend no
   idle days;
   Jesus is calling thee On the harvest
   ways.
   Working with a willing hand, Sing a
   song of praise;
   Work, ever work for Jesus!

Chorus
Swiftly the hours of labour fly,
Freighted with love let each pass by!
There is joy in labour for the
struggling neighbour,
Work, ever work for Jesus!

2. Lifetime is working time, Learn
   where duty lies;
   Grasp ev'ry passing day As a
   precious prize,

Glad to help the sorrowing, Glad to sympathize;
Work, ever work for Jesus!

3. Lifetime is working time, Do thy honest part;
Tho' in discouragements Bear a cheerful heart,
Trusting Jesus as thy Friend, Ne'er from Him depart,
Work, ever work for Jesus!
—Carrie E. Breck

953

St. Oswald- 8.7.8.7.

1. Courage, brother! do not stumble.
Though thy path be dark as night,
There's a star to guide the humble;
Trust in God, and do the right!

2. Let the road be rough and dreary,
And its end far out of sight;
Foot it' bravely! strong or weary;
Trust in God. and do the right!

3. Perish policy and cunning!
Perish all that fears the light!
Whether losing, whether winning,
Trust in God, and do the right!

4. Trust no party, sect, or faction;
Trust no leaders in the fight;
But in ev'ry word and action
Trust in God, and do the right!

5. Trust no lovely forms of passion,
Friends may look like angels bright;
Trust no custom, school, or flashing;
Trust in God, and do the right!

6. Simple rule, and safest guiding,
Inward peace, and inward might;
Star upon our path abiding;
Trust in God, and do the right?

7. Some will hate thee, some will love thee,
Some will flatter, some will slight;
Cease from man, and look above thee;
Trust in God, and do the right!
—Norman Macleod

954

Duke Street- L.M.

1. Go, labour on, spend, and be spent
Thy joy to do the Father's will;
It is the way the Master went,
Should not the servant tread it still?

2. Go, labour on: 'tis not for nought,
Thy earthly loss is heav'nly gain;
Men heed thee, love thee, praise thee not.
The Master praises what are men!

3. Men died in darkness at your side
Without a hope to cheer the tomb;
Take up the torch and wave it wide,
The torch that lights time's thickest gloom

4. Toil on, and in thy toil rejoice,
For toil comes rest, for exile home;
Soon shall thou hear the Bridegroom's voice,
The mid-night peal, Behold, I come!
—Horatius Bonar

955

Soldiers of Immanuel

1. Soldiers of Jesus! soldiers of the Cross!
Follow your Captain, counting all but loss;
If you fight the battle you shall gain Renown,
And if you are faithful you shall wear a crown.

CHRISTIAN WARFARE

Chorus(verses 1-4)
March on! March on! soldiers of
Immanuel
March on! March on! singing as we
go:
Glory! glory to the Lamb of Calvary!
In His might we conquer ev'ry foe.

2. Soldiers of Jesus! gird ye to the fray,
Stand in your armour in this evil day,
Where the battle rages there may
ye be found,
Where the need is greatest that is
holy ground.

3. Soldiers of Jesus! lift your standard
high;
Write on your banners: Jesus came
to die;
By the Cross of Jesus we the
vict'ry win,
For the blood of Jesus Cleanseth
from all sin.

4. Soldiers of Jesus! when the battle's
done.
Foes all are vanquish'd, and the
vict'ry won;
Then with shouts of triumph we
shall hail the King,
When the vaults of heaven with His
praises ring.

5. Soldiers of Jesus! of the Lamb once
slain,
Know ye that Jesus soon will
come to reign;
Lift your heads in gladness, victory is
nigh,
Send a shout of welcome through
the earth and sky.

Chorus (verse 5 only)
Come, Lord, Jesus! come and take
Thy people home;
Come, O come! we long Thy face
to see;

Come, Lord Jesus! claim the
kingdom and the pow'r,
Set the earth from all its bondage
free.

-J.J. Sims

956

On for Jesus!

1. On for Jesus! steady be your arm
and brave;
Onward, onward, take the shield
and sword;
On for Jesus! standard of your
Captain wave,
Pressing on ward, trusting in His
word.

Chorus
Marching, marching on,
We're marching onward still for
Jesus;
Marching, marching on,
Beneath the banner of the free;

2. On for Jesus! tiresome tho'the
conflict be,
Tho' the hosts of sin are pressing
hard;
On for Jesus! striving for the
victory.
Endless life will soon be your
reward.

3. On for Jesus! till the sound of strife
is o'er!
When the great Commander calls
for thee,
Thou shalt wear a crown of life
forever more,
And with Jesus reign eternally.
-J. Howard Entwisle

CHRISTIAN WARFARE

957

All the World for Jesus!

1. Take up the battle cry all along the
line,
Victory by and by, victory divine;
with your Commander nigh, foes in
vain combine,
Raise aloft the banner, let it bear the
sign:

Chorus
All the world for Jesus! Let the
chorus ring;
All the world for Jesus! crown Him
King:
All the world for Jesus! Let the
watchword be:
Forward go in Jesus' name to
victory,

2. Truth's armour you may claim, faith
will be your shield,
Fighting on in Jesus' Name, mighty
pow'r you wield;
Glory for God your aim, naught can
make you yield,
Shout aloud the triumph, sure to be
Reveal'd.

3. Soldiers, with courage go, go
forsaking all.
Onward, then, to meet the foe, soon
the foe shall fall;
Send mighty blow on blow, let no
fear appall,
In the Name of Jesus sound afar the
call.
                              -F.A. Breck

958

Awake! the Trumpet Is Sounding!

1. Awake! for the trumpet is sounding!
Awake to its call, and obey!
The voice of our Leader cries,
"Onward! " Oh, let us no longer
delay!

Chorus
No truce while the foe is
unconquer'd;
No laying the armour down!
No peace till the battle is ended.
And victory wins the crown!

2. Then gird on the sword of the Spirit
With helmet, and breast plate, and
shied;
And valiantly follow your Captain,
Detemin'd you never will yield!

3. Then forward! O army of Zion,
With hearts that are loyal and
brave!
Stand firm by the Cross and its
banner,
And trust in the "Mighty to save!
                              -F.J. Crosby

959

Victory Through Grace

1. Conquering now and still to
conquer,
Rideth a King in His might,
Leading the host of all the faithful
Into the midst of the fight:
See them with courage advancing,
Clad in their brilliant array,
Shouting the name of their
Leader, Hear them exultingly say:

Chorus
Not to the strong is the battle,
"Not to the swift is the race;
Yet to the true and the faithful
vict'ry is promised through grace."

2. Conquering now and still to
conquer:
Who is this wonderful King?
Whence all the armies which He
leadeth,

CHRISTIAN WARFARE

While of His glory they sing?"
He is our Lord and Redeemer,
Saviour Monarch Divine,
They are the stars that for ever
Bright in His kingdom will shine.

3. Conquering now and still to
conquer,
Jesus, Thou Ruler of all,
Thrones and their sceptres all shall
perish,
Crowns and their splendour shall
fall;
Yet shall the armies Thou leadest,
Faithful and true to the last,
Find in Thy mansions eternal
Rest, when their warfare is past.
                              -S. Martin

960

Faint, yet Pursuing

1. "Faint, yet pursuing," we press our
way
Up to the glorious gates of day;
Following Him who has gone
before,
Over the path to the brighter shore.

Chorus
"Faint, yet pursuing, "from day to
day,
Over the thorny and blood marked
way;
Strengthen and keep us, O Saviour
Friend,
Ever pursuing, unto life's end!

2. "Faint, yet pursuing, whate'er befal;
He who has died for us, died for all:
So should they come as a mighty
throng,
Bearing His banner aloft with song.

3. "Faint, yet pursuing," till eventide,
Under the cross of the Crucified;

Knowing, when darkly are skies
o'ercast,
Sorrow and sighing will end at last.

4. "Faint, yet pursuing:" the eye afar
Sees through the darkness the
Morning Star.
Shedding its ray for the weary feet,
Lighting the way to the golden
street.
                         -Mrs. W.R. Griswold

961

Gird on the Sword and Armour- 7.6.

1. Gird on the sword and armour!
Go raise the banner high!
The Captain of Salvation
To thee is ever nigh.

Chorus
Then wave the glorious banner!
Press forward in His name;
Fear not, for soon thy Captain
Will victory proclaim!

2. Gird on the sword and armour!
Let faith be thy strong shield;
His promise shall sustain then
On every battle field.

3. Gird on the sword and armour;
Press on, the foe to fight;
No enemy can harm thee.
For God sustains the right.
                              -C.H. Mann

962

The Ship of Temperance - 7.6.D.

1. Take courage, temp'rance workers!
You shall not suffer wreck,
While up to God the people's
pray'rs
Are ringing from your deck:
Wait cheerily, ye workers,

For daylight and for land.
The breath of God is in your sails,
Your rudder in His hand.

Chorus
Sail on!, O ship of hope!
Sail on for truth and right;
The breath of God is in your sails,
The heaven is in sight

2. Sail on!, sail on deep freighted
   With blessings and with hopes;
   The good old, with shadowy
   hands,
   Are putting at your ropes:
   Behind you, holy martyrs
   Uplift the palm and crown;
   Before you, unborn ages send
   Their benedictions down.

3. Speed on! your work is holy,
   God's errands never fail!
   Sweep on through storm and,
   darkness wild,
   The thunder and the hail:
   Toil on, the morning cometh,
   The port you yet shall win!
   And all the bells of God shall ring
   The "Ship of Temperance" in!
                    -John G. Whittier

963

Fall Into Line- 8.7.

1. Over hill and lofty mountain,
   Hear the gospel trumpet call;
   Listen to the strains inspiring,
   'Tis a message for us all.

Chorus
Fall into line for the conflict!
Fall into line for the conflict!
Rally at the trumpet's call, rally!
Rally, Christian soldiers all!

2. Girding on the royal armour,
   Wave the glorious banner high!

While for truth and right
contending,
Angels watch you from the sky.

3. Sound again the silver trumpet!
   Sound aloud the battle-cry!
   "All for Jesus, all for Jesus!
   We shall conquer though we die!
                    -Wm. H. Gardner

964

St Michael's- S.M.

1. What though th'accuser roar
   Of ills that I have done;
   I know them well, and thousands
   more:
   Jehovah findeth none.

2. His be the Victor's name
   Who fought our fight alone;
   Triumphant saints no honour claim
   Their conquest was His own.

3. By weakness and defeat
   He won the meed and crown;
   Trod all our foes beneath His feet,
   By being trodden down.

4. He hell in hell laid low;
   Made sin. He sin o'erthrew;
   Bowed to the grave, destroyed it so,
   And death, by dying, slew.

5. Bless, bless the Conqueror slain
   Slain by Divine decree
   Who lived, who died, who lives
   again,
   For thee, His saint, for thee!
                    -S.W. Gandy

965

Sentimental Songs

1. If you're in the battle for the Lord
   and right,
   Keep on the firing line,

CHRISTIAN WARFARE

If you win the vict'ry, brother, you
must fight,
Keep on the firing line;
There are many dangers which we
all must face,
If we die still fighting it is no
disgrace,
Cowards in the service should not
have a place,
Keep on the firing line.

Chorus
You must fight and be brave against
all evil,
Never run, tho foes combine;
If you would fight for God and right,
Keep on the firing line.

2. God will only use a soldier He can
trust.
Keep on the firing line,
If you wear the crown, then bear the
cross you must,
Keep on the firing line;
Life is but to labour for the Master
dear,
Help to banish darkness and to
spread good cheer,
We shall be rewarded for our
service here,
Keep on firing line.

3. When we get to heaven we shall be
so glad.
Keep on the firing line.
We shall praise the Saviour for the
Call we had,
Keep on the firing line:
'Twill be joy to see the souls we
helped to win.
Those we led to Jesus, from the
paths of sin.
Hear their welcome plaudit and go
marching in, Keep on firing line.
                        -J.R. Baxter, Jr

966

Mannheim- 8.7.8.7.8.7.

1. Lead us, heavenly Father, lead us
O'er the world's tempestuous sea;
Guard us, guide us, keep us, feed
us,
For we have no help but thee;
Yet possessing every blessing
If our God our Father be.

2. Saviour, breathe forgiveness o'er
us;
All our weakness thou dost know.
Thou didst tread this earth before
us,
Thou didst feel its keenest woe:
Lone and dreary, faint and weary.
Through the desert thou didst go.

3. Spirit of our God, descending,
Fill our hearts with heavenly joy,
Love with every passion blending,
Pleasure that can never cloy:
Thus provided, pardoned, guided,
Nothing can our peace destroy.
                        -James Edmeston

967

Liangoedmor. - 8.8.8.D.

1. O Lord of host, who didst upraise
Strong captains to defend the right,
In darker years and sterner days,
And armedst Israel for the fight;
Thou madest Joshua true and
strong.
And David framed the battle song.

2. And must we battle yet? Must we,
Who bear the tender name Divine,
Still barter life for victory sign?
The Crucified between us stands,
And lifts on high his wounded
Hands.

3. Lord, we are weak and wilful yet,
   The fault is in our clouded eyes;
   But thou, through anguish and regret,
   Dost make thy faithless children wise:
   Through wrong, through hate, thou dost approve
   The far off victories of love.

4. And so. from out of the heart of strife,
   Divine echoes peal and thrill;
   The scorned delights, the lavished life,
   The pain that serves a nation's will:
   Thy comfort stills the mourner's cries.
   And love is crowned by sacrifice.

5. As rains that sweep the clouds away,
   As winds that leave a calm in heaven,
   So let the slayer cease to slay:
   The passion healed, the wrath forgiven,
   Draw nearer, bid the tumult cease,
   Redeemer, Saviour, Prince of peace

   -A-C.Benson

968

University College- 7.7.7.7.

1. Much in sorrow, oft in woe,
   Onward, Christian, onward go!
   Fight the fight, maintain the strife.
   Strengthened with the bread of life.

2. Onward, Christians, onward go!
   Join the war, and face the foe;
   Faint not! much doth yet remain,
   Dreary is the long campaign.

3. Shrink not, Christians! Will ye yield?
   Will ye quit the painful field?

Will ye flee in danger's hour?
Know ye not your Captain's power?

4. Let your drooping hearts be glad;
   March, in heavenly armour clad
   Fight, nor think the battle long
   Victory soon shall tune your song

5. Let not sorrow dim your eye.
   Soon shall every tear be dry.
   Let not fears your course impede
   Great your strength, if great you need

6. Onward then to battle move;
   More than conquerors ye shall prove
   Though opposed by many a foe
   Christian soldiers, onward go!

   -Henry John Gauntlett

969

Lancashire-7.6.7.6.D.

1. Lead on, O King Eternal,
   The day or march has come;
   Hence-forth in field of conquest
   Your tents shall be our home.
   Through days of preparation
   Your grace has made us strong
   And now, O King Eternal,
   We lift our battle song.

2. Lead on, O King Eternal,
   Till sin's fierce war shall cease
   And holiness shall whisper
   The sweet Amen of peace;
   For not with swords loud clashing,
   Nor roll of stiring drums,
   With deeds of love and mercy
   The heav'nly kingdom comes.

3. Lead on, O King Eternal,
   We follow, not with fears;·
   For gladness breaks like morning
   Where'er Your face appears;
   Your cross is lifted o'er us;
   We journey in its light
   The crown awaits the conquest;
   Lead on, O God of might .

   -Ernest W. Shurtleff

CHRISTIAN WARFARE

970

Armageddon - 6.5.6.5.D. with

1. Who is on the Lord's side? Who sill
serve the King?
Who will be His helpers, Other lives
to bring?
Who will leave the world's side?
Who will face the foe?
Who is on the Lord's side?
Who for Him will go?
By Thy call of mercy, By Thy grace
divine,
We are on the Lord's side. Saviour.
we are Thine.

2. Not for weight of glory. Not for
crown and palm,
Enter we the army. Raise the
warrior palm;
But for love that claimeth Live for
whom He died;
He whom Jesus nameth Must be on
His side.
By Thy love constraining By Thy
Grace divine,
We are on the Lord's side, Saviour,
We are Thine.

3. Jesus, Thou hast bought us, Not
with gold or gem.
But with Thine own life-blood, For
Thy diadem.
With Thy blessing filling Each who
comes to Thee,
Thou hast made us willing, Thou
hast made us free. By Thy grand
redemption. By Thy grace divine,
We are on the Lord's side. Saviour.
we are Thine.

4. Fierce may be the conflict, Strong
may be the foe
But the King's own army None can
overthrow.

Round His standard ranging; Vict'ry
is secure;
For His truth unchanging Makes
the triumph sure.
Joyful enlisting By Thy grace divine.
We are on the Lord's side, Saviour,
we are Thine.
-Frances Ridley Havergal

971

Ebenezer - 8.7.8.7.D.

1. Once to every man and nation
Comes the moment to decide,
In the strife of truth with falsehood.
For the good or evil side;
Some great cause, some great
decision,
Off'ring each the bloom or blight,
And the choice goes by forever
Twixt that darkness and that light

2. Then to side with truth is noble,
When we share her wretched crust,
Ere her cause bring fame and profit,
And 'tis prosp'rous to be just
Then it is the brave man chooses
While the cowards stands aside.
Till the multitudes make virtue
Of the faith they had denied.

3. Though the cause of evil prosper.
Yet the truth alone is strong:
Though her portion be the scaffold,
And upon the throne be wrong,
Yet that scaffold sways the future,
And behind the dim unknown.
Standeth God within the shadow.
Keeping watch above his own.
-James Russel Lowell

972

Morning Light - 7.6.7.6.0.

1. Stand up! stand up for Jesus, Ye
soldiers of the Cross!
Lift high His royal banner: It must
not suffer loss.
From vict'ry unto vict'ry His army
Shall He lead.

Till ev'ry foe is vanquished, And
Christ is Lord indeed.

2. Stand up! stand up for Jesus! the
trumpet call obey;
Forth to the mighty conflict, In this
His glorious day:
Ye that are men now serve Him
Against unnumbered foes;
Let courage rise with danger, And
strength to strength oppose.

3. Stand up! stand up for Jesus
Stand in His strength alone:
The arm of flesh will fail you, Ye
dare not trust your own;
Put on the gospel amour, Each
piece put on with prayer;
Where duty calls, or danger, Be
never wanting there.

4. Stand up! stand up for Jesus! The
strife will not be long;
This day the noise of battle, The
next the victor's song:
To Him that over cometh. A crown
of life shall be;
He with the King of glory Shall reign
eternally.

-George Duffield

973

Diademata -S. M. D.

1. Soldiers of Christ, arise
And put your armor on,
Strong in the strength which God
supplies
Through His eternal Son;
Strong in the Lord of hosts,
And in His mighty pow'r,
Who in the strength of Jesus trusts
Is more than conqueror,

2. Stand then in His great might,
With all His strength endued,
And take, to arm you for the fight,
The panoply of God:

2. From strength to strength go on,
Wrestle and fight and pray;
Tread all the pow'rs of darkness
down,
And win the well fought day

3. Leave no unguarded place
No weakness of the soul
Take every virtue, ev'ry grace
And fortify the whole.
That having all things done
And all your conflict past
Ye may o'er come through Christ
alone,
And stand complete at last.

4. Leave no unguarded place
No weakness of the soul,
Take every virtue, every grace
And fortify the whole.
Indissolubly joined,
To battle all proceed;
But arm yourselves with all the
mind
That was in Christ, your Head
-Charles Wesley

974

St Gertrude-6.5.6.5.D with Refrain

1. Onward, Christian soldiers,
Marching as to war,
With the cross of Jesus going on
before?
Christ, the royal Master, Leads
against the foe;
Forward into battle See His banner
go!

2. At the sign or triumph Satan's host
doeth flee;
On, then, Christian soldiers, On to
victory!
Hell's foundations quiver At the
shout of praise;
Brothers, lift your voices, Loud your
anthems raise!

3. Like a mighty army Moves the
Church of God;
Brothers, we are treading Where
the saints have trod.
We are not divided, All one body we
One in hope and doctrine, One in
Charity.

4. Onward, then, ye people, Join our
happy throng:
Blend with ours your voices In the
triumph song.
Glory, laud and honour Unto Christ
the King
This thru countless ages Men and
angels sing.
                    -Sabine Baring Gould

975
Leoni -6.6.8.4.D.

1. The battle is the Lord's! The
harvest fields are white:
How few the reaping ands appear,
Their strength how slight!
Yet victory is sure We face a
vanquished foe;
Then forward with the risen Christ
To battle go!

2. The battle is the Lord's! Not ours in
strength or skill,
But His alone, in sovereign grace.
To work His will.
Ours, counting not the cost,
Unflinching, to obey;
And in His time His holy arm Shall
win the day.

3. The battle is the Lord's! The Victor
crucified
Must with the travail of His soul Be
satisfied.
The pow'rs of hell shall fail, And all
God's will be done,
Till every soul whom He has giv'n
To Christ be won.

4. The battle is the Lord's! Stand still,
my soul, and view
The great salvation God has
wrought Revealed for you.
Then, resting in His mighty, Lift high
His triumph song,
For pow'r, dominion, kingdom,
strength To Christ belong!
                    -Margaret Clarkson

976
Hotham -7.7.7.7.D.

1. Fainting soul, be bold, be strong.
Wait the leisure of thy Lord;
Though it seem to tarry long,
True and faithful is His word:
On His word my soul I cast
He cannot Himself deny,
It shall speak, and shall not lie,

2. Every one that seeks shall find,
Every one that asks shall have.
Christ, the Saviour of mankind.
Willing able all to save;
I shall His salvation see,
I in faith on Jesus call,
I from sin shall be set free,
Perfectly set free from all.

3. Lord, my time is in Thine hand;
Weak and helpless as I am,
Surely Thou canst make me stand,
I believe in Jesu's name:
Saviour in temptation Thou;
Thou hast saved me heretofore,
Thou' from sin dost save me now,
Thou shalt save me evermore.
                    -Charles Wesley

977
Victory-D.S.M.

1. Hark, how the watchmen cry!
Attend the trumpet's sound!
Stand to your arms. the foe is nigh.

CHRISTIAN WARFARE

The powers of hell surround:
Who bow to Christ's command,
Your arms and hearts prepare!
The day of battle is at hand!
Go forth to glorious war!

2. Go up with Christ your Head,
Your Captain's footsteps see,
Follow your Captain, and be led
To certain victory,
All power to Him is given,
He ever reigns the same;
Salvation, happiness, and heaven
Are all in Jesu's name.

3. Jesu's tremendous name
Puts all our foes to flight:
Jesus, the meek, the angry Lamb.
A Lion is in fight.
By all hell's host withstood,
We all hell's host o'erthrow,
And conquering them, through
Jesu's blood
We still to conquer go.

4. Our Captain leads us on;
He beckons from the skies,
And reaches out a starry crown,
And bids us take the prize:
Be faithful unto death,
Partake My victory;
And thou shall wear this glorious
wreath,
And thou shalt reign with Me!
-Charles Wesley

978

Clarion-6.4.6.4.6.7.6.4.

1. Hark, 'tis the watchman's cry:
Wake, brethren, wake!
Jesus Himself is nigh;
Wake, brethren, wake!
Sleep is for sons of night;
Ye are children of the light;
Yours is the glory bright;
Wake, brethren, wake!

2. Call to each wakening bank:
Watch, brethren, watch!
Clear is our Lord's command:
Watch, brethren, watch!
Be ye as men that wait
Always at their Master's gate,
E'en though He tarry late;
Watch, brethren, watch!

3. Heed we the Master's call:
Work, brethren, work!
There's room enough for all,
Work, brethren, work!
This vineyard of the Lord
Constant labour will afford;
He will your work reward:
Work, brethren, work!

4. Hear we the Saviour's voice:
Pray, brethren, pray!
Would ye His heart rejoice,
Pray, brethren, pray!
Sin calls for ceaseless fear,
Weakness needs the Strong One
near:
Long as ye struggle here,
Pray, brethren, pray!

5. Sound how the final chord,
Praise, brethren, praise!
Thrice holy is the Lord,
Praise, brethren, praise!
What more befits the tongues
Soon to join the angels' songs?
Whilst heaven the note prolongs,
Praise, brethren, praise!
-Anonymous

979

Justification L.M.

1. Arm of the Lord, awake, awake!
Thine own immortal strength put
on,
With terror clothed, hell's kingdom
shake,
And cast Thy foes with fury down.

2. As in the ancient days appear.
The sacred annals speak Thy fame
Be now omnipotently near,
To endless ages still the same.

3. Thy arm, Lord, is not shortened now,
It wants not now the power to save;
Still present with Thy people. Thou
Bear's! them through life's disparted
wave.

4. By death and hell pursued in vain,
To Thee the ransomed seed shall
come;
Shouting, their heavenly Zion gain,
And pass through death triumphant
home.

-Charles Wesley

980

As a Volunteer

1. A call for loyal soldiers Comes to
one and all;
Soldiers for the conflict, Will you
heed the call?
Will you answer quickly? With a
ready cheer?
Will you be enlisted as a volunteer?

Chorus
A volunteer for Jesus, A soldier
true!
Others have enlisted, Why not you?
Jesus is the Captain, We will never
fear;
Will you be enlisted As a volunteer?

2. Yes, Jesus calls for soldiers Who
are filled with pow'r,
Soldiers who will serve Him
Ev'ry day and hour;
He will not forsake you, He is ever
near;
Will you be enlisted as a volunteer?

3. He calls you, for he loves you With a
heart most kind, He whose heart
was broken.
Broken for mankind;
Now, just now He calls you. Calls in
accents clear.
Will you be enlisted as a volunteer?

4. And when the war is over, And the
vict'ry won,
When the true and faithful Gather
one by one,
He will crown with glory All who
there appear:
Will you be enlisted as a volunteer?
-W. S. Brown

981

Ring the bell, Watchman

1. Come, join our Army, to battle we
go;
Jesus will help us to conquer the foe.
Fighting for right and opposing the
wrong;
The Salvation Army is marching
along.

Chorus
Marching along, marching along,
The Salvation Army is marching along;
Soldiers of Jesus, be valiant and
strong;
The Salvation Army is marching along;

2. Come, join our Army, the foe must be
driven;
To Jesus, our Captain, the world shall
be given;
Foes may surround us, we'll press
through the throng;
The Salvation Army is marching along.

3. Come, join our Army, the foe we
Defy.
True to our Colours, we'll fight till
we die;

'Saved from all sin' is our war cry
and song;
The Salvation Army is marching
along.

4. Come, join our Army, and do not
delay,
The time for enlisting is passin
away;
Fierce is the battle, but victory will
come;
The Salvation Army is marching

982

Keep on believing

1. When you feel weakest, dangers
surround,
Subtle temptation, toubles abound,
Nothing seems hopeful, nothing
seems glad,
All is despairing, eventime sad:

Chorus
Keep on believing, Jesus is near,
Keep on believing, there's nothing
to fear!
Keep on believing, this is the way,
Faith in the night as well as the day.

2. If all were easy, if all were bright,
Where would the cross be? And
where the fight?
But in the hardness, God gives to
you
Chances of proving that you are
true.

3. God is your Wisdom, God is your
Might,
God's ever near you guiding you
right;
He understands you, knows all you
need.
Trusting in Him you'll surely
Succeed.

4. Let us press on then, never despair
Live above feeling, victory's there
Jesus can keep us so near to Him
That nevermore our faith shall grow
dim

983

Will you quit the filed

1. Will you quit the field?
Will you ever yield?
Will you boldly fight,
And defend the right?
Never, never, never!
Yes, for ever!

Chorus
Never quit the field till the foe is
slain,
Never quit the field, oh, never,
never yield;
Never quit the field till we vict'ry
gain,
Never, never, never!

2. When the foe is near
Will you have a fear?
Never, never, never!
Win you take your stand
With faith's sword in hand?
Yes, for ever!

3. Will you cease to sing
Praises to your King?
Never, never, never!
Bravely every day
Will you march away?
Yes for ever!

CHRISTIAN WARFARE

984
Gird on the armour

1. I have read of men of faith
   Who have bravely fought till death.
   Who now the crown of life are
   wearing:
   Then the thought comes back to
   me,
   Can I not a soldier be,
   Like to those martyrs bold and
   Daring?

   Chorus
   I'll gird on the armour and rush to the
   field,
   Determined to conquer, and never to
   yield;
   So the enemy shall know;
   Wheresoever I may go, That I am
   fighting for Jehovah.

2. I, like them, will take my stand
   With the sword of God in hand.
   Smiling amid opposing regions;
   I the victor's crown will gain,
   And at last go home to reign
   In Heaven's bright and sunny
   regions.

3. I will join at once the fight,
   Trusting in my Saviour's might,
   Who's strong and mighty to deliver;
   From my post I will not shrink,
   Though of death's cup I should drink;
   Hell to defeat is my endeavour.

4. Will you not enlist with me,
   And a valiant soldier be,
   Fighting to break Hell's ranks
   asunder?
   Jesus calls for men of war,
   Who will fight and ne'er give o'er,
   Routing the foe in fear and wonder.

985
Men of Harlech

1. Soldier, rouse thee! War is raging.
   God and fiends are battle waging;
   Ev'ry ransomed power engaging,
   Break the Tempter's spell.
   Dare ye still lie fondly dreaming,
   Wrapt in ease and worldly schem
   ing,
   While the multitude are streaming
   Downwards in Hell?

   Chorus
   Thro' the world resounding,
   Let the Gospel sounding,
   Summon all, at Jesus call,
   His glorious Cross surrounding.
   Sons of God, earth's trifles leaving,
   Be not faithless but believing;
   To your conquering Captain
   cleaving,
   Forward to the Fight!

2. Lord, we come. and from Thee
   never
   Self nor earth our hearts shall
   Sever.
   Thine entirety, Thine for ever,
   We will fight and die.
   To a world of rebels dying,
   Heaven and Hell and God defying,
   Everywhere we'll still be crying,
   Will ye perish why?

3. Hark! I hear the warriors shouting!
   Now the hosts of Hell we're
   routing:
   Courage! onward! never doubting,
   We shall win the day-See the foe
   before us falling, Sinners on the
   Saviour calling, Throwing off the
   bondage galling, Join our glad
   array.

CHRISTIAN WARFARE

986

I'll Stand for Christ

1. In The Army of Jesus we've taken
   our stand,
   To fight 'gainst the force of sin,
   To the rescue we go, Satan's power
   to o'er throw.
   And His captives to Jesus we'll win.

Chorus
I'll stand for Christ for Christ alone,
Amid the tempest, tempest and the
storm.
Where Jesus leads I'm follow on;
I'll stand, I'll stand for Christ alone.

2. We go forth not to fight "gainst the
   sinner, but sin:
   The lost and the outcast we love;
   While the claims of our King unto all
   we will bring,
   As we call them His mercy to
   prove.

3.' Yes, our warfare is great, and our
   many strong,
   Our aim he will ever oppose;
   But the battle's the Lord's, and to
   Him we belong.
   And with Him we shall conquer our
   Foes.

987

All Hail, I'm saved

1. Soldiers fighting round the Cross,
   Fight for your Lord;.
   Reckon all things else but loss,
   Fight for your Lord.

Chorus
All hail I'm saved
Oh, come and join our conquering
band.

All hail I'm saved
We'll conquer if we die.

2. Draw your word, on God rely,
   Fight for your Lord;
   And your ever foe defy,
   Fight for your Lord.

3. In the name of Christ your Friend,
   Fight for your Lord;
   With the powers of Hell contend.
   Fight for your Lord;

4. Fight the fight of faith with me,
   Fight for your Lord;
   Jesus gives the victory,
   Fight for your Lord.

5. Be thou faithful; hear Him cry;
   Fight for your Lord;
   In My service fight and die.
   Fight for your Lord.

6. See in Heaven the glorious prize
   Fight for your Lord;
   Glittering through the starry skies.
   Fight for your Lord.

7. Faithfully your weapons wield,
   Fight for your Lord;
   Stand your ground, and win the field
   Fight for your Lord.

988

Cossar

1. O Solider of Jesus, how blessed art
   Thou,
   For Jesus is waiting to strengthen
   thee now.
   Fear not to rely on the word of thy
   God.
   Step out on the promise Get
   washed in the Blood;
   Step out on the promise Get
   washed in the Blood.

2. Oh, ye that are hungry and thirsty, rejoice,
For ye shall be filled; oh. hear that sweet voice
Inviting you now to the banquet of God:
Step out on the promise get washed in the Blood.

3. Who sighs for a heart iniquity free?
O poor, troubled soul, there's a promise for thee!
There's rest, weary one, in the bosom of God:
Step out on the promise get washed in the Blood.

4. The promise cant save, though each promise is true;
Tis the Blood of the lamb-that does cleanse us right through;
It cleanses us now, oh. glory to God'
We rest on the promise we're washed in the Blood.

989

Stand like the brave

1. O soldier, awake! for the strife is at hand;
With helmet and shield, and a sword in thy hand,
To meet the bold Tempter, go, fearlessly go,
And stand like the brave, with thy face to the foe.
Stand like the brave, stand like the brave,
Stand like the brave, with thy face to the foe!

2. Whatever thy state, of the Tempter beware,
And turn not thy back, for no armour is there;
the legions of darkness if thou Wouldst o'erthrow,
Then stand like the brave. with thy face to the foe.

3. Doubt not, but press on for thy Captain is near
With grace to support, and with comfort to cheer;
His love like a stream in the desert will flow;
Then stand like the brave, with thy face to the foe.

990

Turn to the Lord

1. Onward! upward! Blood washed Soldier,
Turn not back, nor sheathe thy sword,
Let its blade be sharp for conquest
In the battle for the Lord.

2. From the great White Throne eternal God Himself is looking down;
He it is who now commands thee:
Take the cross and win the crown!

3. Onward! upward I doing, daring
All for Him who died for thee;
Face the foe, and meet with boldness
Danger, whatsoe'er it be.

4. From the battlements of Glory Holy ones are looking down;
Thou canst almost hear them shouting,
'On! let no one take thy crown?'

5. Onward! Till thy course is finished;
Like the ransomed ones before.
Keep the faith through persecution, Never give the battle o'er.

Onward! upward! till, victorious,
Thou shall lay thine armour down,
And thy loving Saviour bids thee
At His hand receive thy crown.

991

We're The Army

1. We're the Soldiers of The Army of
Salvation.
That God is raising now to save the
world;
And we won't lay down our arms till
ev'ry nation
Shall have seen the Flag of Blood
and Fire unfurled.

Chorus
We're The Army that shall conquer
As we go seek the lost,
And to bring them back to God;
And His Salvation to ev'ry nation
We will carry with the Fire and the
Blood.

2. Though the hosts of Hell and
darkness all surround us.
And by suffering and temptation we
are tried,
Well we know that not a foe can
e'er confound us,
While Jehovah's mighty power is on
our side.

3. So we'll put our trust in God, who
ne'er will fail us.
And we know that His Salvation we
shall see;
And through all the fighting, those
who shall assail us
Shall be conquered through the
Blood of Calvary.

992

Storm the forts

1. Soldiers of our God, arise!
The day is drawing nearer,
Shake the slumber from your eyes,
The light is growing clearer.
Sit no longer idly by,
While the heedless millions die.
Lift the Blood stained banner high.
And take the field for Jesus.

Chorus
Storm the forts of darkness,
Bring them down, bring them down!
Storm the forts of darkness,
Bring them down, bring them down!
Pull down the Devil's kingdom.
Where'er he holds dominion,
Storm the forts of darkness, bring
them down!
Glory, honour to the Lamb,
Praise and power to the Lamb:
Glory, honour, praise and power.
Before ever to the Lamb!

2. See the brazen hosts of Hell.
Art and power employing,
More than human tongue can tell.
Blood bought souls destroying.
Hark! from ruin's ghastly road,
Victims groan beneath their load:
Forward, O ye sons of God,
And dare or die for Jesus.

3. Warriors of the Bleeding Lamb,
Army of Salvation,
Spread the fame of Gilead's balm,
Conquer every nation.
Raise the glorious Standard higher.
Strike for victory never tire;
Forward march with Blood and Fire
And win the world for Jesus.

CHRISTIAN WARFARE

993
The Conquering Saviour

1. The conflict is over, the tempesst is past,
I'm resting in Jesus, I'm resting at last;
The billows that filled my poor soul with alarm
Are hushed at His word into stillness and calm.

Chorus
The conquering Saviour will break ev'ry chain,
And give us the vict'ry again and again;
The conquering Saviour will break ev'ry chain,
And give us the vict'ry again and again.

2. There's peace in believing, sweet peace to the soul,
To know that He maketh me perfectly whole;
There's joy everlasting to feel His Blood flow.
Tis life from the dead my Redeemer to know.

3. Oh, hinder me not while His love I proclaim:
My soul makes her boast in His wonderful name;
I stand with my foot on the neck of my foe.
Then, bounding with gladness. triumphant I go.

994
Strike for Victory

1. Strike, oh, strike for vict'ry,
Soldiers of the Lord,
Buckling on the amour,
Trusting in His word;
Lift His royal banner

High above the world;
Satan from his stronghold
Shall be hurled!

Chorus
Strike, strike for vict'ry,
warriors bold!
Strike till the vict'ry you behold!
Strike, strike for vict'ry,
Ne'er give o'er!
Jesus is our Captain, vict'ry's sure

2. Strike, oh, strike for victory.
Soldiers of the Cross,
Sacrificing pleasure,
Glorying in loss;
Bind the helmet stronger,
Tighter grasp the sword,
Conquering and to conquer,
Battling for the Lord!

3. Hand to hand united
Heart to heart as one,
Let us still keep marching.
Till the battle's won,
Ever pressing forward,
Mid the battle strife.
Till we gain the Kingdom,
Everlasting life.

995
We'll fight till Jesus comes

1. Summoned my labour to renew,
And glad to act my part,
Lord, in Thy name my work I do,
And with a single heart.

Chorus
We'll fight till Jesus comes,
We'll work till Jesus comes,
Well sing till Jesus comes.
And then we'll test at home.

2. End of my every action Thou,
In all things Thee I see;
Accept my offered labour now,
I do it unto Thee.

CHRISTIAN WARFARE

3. Servant of all, to toil for man
Thou didst not, Lord, refuse;
Thy majesty did not disdain
To be employed for us!

4. Thy bright example I pursue.
To Thee in all things rise;
And all I think, or speak, or do
Is one great sacrifice.

5. Careless through outward cares I go.
From all distraction free;
My hands are but engaged below.
My heart is still with Thee.

996

Salonica -4.10.10.10.4.

1. Come, labour on!
Who dare stand idle on the harvest plain,
While all around him waves the golden grain?
And to each-servant doth the Master say
"Go, work today!"

2. Come, labour on!
Claim the high calling angels cannot share,
To young and old the gospel gladness bear
Redeem the time; its hours too swiftly fly;
The night draws high.

3. Come, labour on!
Away with gloomy doubt and faithless fear!
No arm so weak but may do service here;
By hands the feeblest can our God fulfil
His righteous win.

4. Come, labour on!
No time for rest, till glows the western sky.
Till the long shadows o'er our pathway lie,
And a glad sound comes with the setting sun,
'Servant, well done!'

5. Come, labour on!
The toil is pleasant and the harvest sure;
Blessed art I those who to the end, endure
How full their joy, how deep their rest shall be,
O Lord, with Thee!
                    -Jane L. Borthwick

997

Murnich. 7.6.7.6.D.

1. My spirit, soul, and body
Jesus, I give to Thee,
A consecrated off'ring,
Thine evermore to be.
My all is on the attar,
Lord, I am all Thine own;
Oh, may my faith ne'er falter!
Lord, keep me Thine alone.

2. O Jesus, mighty Saviour!
I trust in Thy great name.
I look for Thy salvation,
Thy promise now I claim.
Now, Lord, I yield my members,
From sin's dominion free.
For warfare and for triumph.
As weapons unto Thee.

3. Oh, blissful seif-surrender,
To live, my Lord, by Thee!
Now, Son of God, my Saviour.
Live out Thy life in me. I'm Thine,
O blessed Jesus,
Washed in Thy precious blood.
Sealed by Thy Holy Spirit.
A sacrifice to God.
                    -Mrs James

CHRISTIAN WARFARE

998

Jesus, let Thy Splendour -6.5.6.5.D. and Refrain

1. Jesus, let Thy splendour
Like a mantle fall,
On this waiting spirit,
What I yield Thee all;
Clothe me with Thy beauty,
Bathe me in Thy will,
And with life triumphant
All my nature fill.

Chorus
Fellowship with Jesus,
This is victory,
They who own His Lordship
Know true liberty.

2. Give to me a vision
Reaching to the throne.
Let me see earth's problems
In that light alone;
Tis Thy Word assures me
All shall work for good,
Things that long have baffled
Soon be understood.

3. Blessed cross of Jesus,
I Thy power would prove,
Neath Thy shadow living.
Naught this soul shall move.
Sanctify me wholly,
Purge from every Stain,
All that makes for bondage,
Let it now be slain.

4. Fired with holy passion,
Moved by urge divine.
What shall henceforth hinder
Victory being mine?
Men may raise their war cry,
Lift their standards high,
But before love's challenge
Each vain thought shall fly.
                          -E. C. W. Bouton

999

Hatfield Hall -7.6.7.6.D.

1. I lay my sins on Jesus.
The spotless Lamb of God;
He bears them all, and frees us
From the accursed load.
I bring my guilt to Jesus
To wash my crimson stains
White in His blood most precious.
Till not a spot remains.

2. I lay my wants on Jesus;
All fulnes dwells in Him:
He heals all my diseases;
He doth my soul redeem.
I lay my griefs on Jesus.
My burdens and my cares;
He from them all releases;
He all my sorrows shares.

3. I rest my soul on Jesus,
This weary soul of mine;
His right hand me embraces;
I on His breast recline,
I love the name of Jesus.
Emmanuel, Christ the Lord;
Like fragrance on the breezes
His name abroad is pour'd.

4. I long to be like Jesus,
Meek, loving, lowly, mild:
I long to be like Jesus,
The Father's Holy Child;
I long to be with Jesus,
Amid the heavenly throng,
To sing with saints His praises,
And learn the angels' song.
                          -Charles Vincent

CHRISTIAN WARFARE

1000
Do You Fear The Foe

1. Do you fear the foe will in the
   conflict win?
   Is it dark without you, darker still
   within?
   Clear the darkened windows, open
   wide the door.
   Let the blessed sunshine in.

   Chorus
   Let the blessed sunshine in.
   Let the blessed sunshine in.
   Clear the darkened windows, open
   wide the door
   Let the blessed sunshine in.

2. Does your faith grow fainter in the
   cause you love?
   Are your prayers unanswered from
   the throne above?
   Clear the darkened windows, open
   wide the door
   Let the blessed sunshine in.

3. Would you go rejoicing on the
   upwind way,
   Knowing naught of darkness-
   dwelling in the day?
   Clear the darkened windows, open
   wide the door.
   Let the blessed sunshine in.

1001
Jesus Command That We Should Watch-C.M.

1. Jesus commands that we should
   watch
   Every hour of the day,
   He sends a revival to those
   Who pray for revival.

2. Jesus commands that we should
   pray
   To fight on and not faint,
   O Lord, make us to hear Thy call,
   Obedience is our life.

3. Jesus commands that we should
   watch
   The hour is near at hand
   That He shall call us from this world
   To, our home up in heav'n.

4. Jesus, we love to pray to Thee
   We love to hear Thy voice
   We love to walk in Thy precepts
   To where joy never ends.

1002
My Soul Be On Thy Guard-S.M.

1. My soul be on thy guard;
   Ten thousand foes arise,
   And hosts of sin are pressing hard
   To draw thee from the skies.

2. Oh, watch and fight and pray,
   The battle ne'er give o'er;
   Renew it boldly ev'ry day
   And help divine implore.

3. Ne'er think the vict'ry won
   Nor lay thine armour down;
   Thine arduous work will not be done;
   Till thou obtain thy crown.

4. Fight on, my soul, till death
   Shall bring thee to thy God;
   He'll take thee at thy parting breath
   To His divine abode.

CHRISTIAN WARFARE

1003

We Never Need Be Vanquished-
7.6.7.6.D.

1. We never need·be vanquished,
We never need give in,
Though waging war with Satan
And compassed round by sin.,
Temptations will beset us.
Allurements oft assail.
But in the name of Jesus.
We shall, we must prevail.

Chorus
Victory in Jesus' name,
victory our hearts proclaim.
Victory, glorious victory.

2. He leads us in triumph,
An overcoming band,
While vict'ry crowns His progress
"For none can stay His hand.
Our eyes are on our Leader.
His presence is our might;
He arms us for the conflict,
And trains our hands to fight.

3. God wills not that His people
By sin enthralled should be.
But their lives henceforward
Be lives of victory:,
And so at our disposal,
He places all His power,
That we from its resources
May draw in danger's hour.

4. Herein is hid the secret
Of an all-glorious life.
Whereby we conquer Satan,
And rise above sin's strife.
Abiding in the Saviour,
Self prostrate in the dust,
We live to do His bidding,
In glad perpetual trust.

5. We in ourselves are nothing,
A small and feeble host,
Nor have aught of prowess
Wherewith to make our boast,
Our stronghold is Christ Jesus,
His grace alone we plead,
His name our shield and banner.
Himself just all we need.

1004

With My Saviour Ever Near To
Guild Me - P.M.

I. With my Saviour ever near to guide
me,
I am safe, whatever may betide me;
From the storm and tempest He will
hide me.
In the hollow of His hands.

Chorus
In the hollow of His hand!
In the hollow of His hand!
I am safe whatever may be betide me,
In the hollow of His hand!

2. In His arms of love He doth enfold me;
Words of peace His voice divine
hath told me,
I am safe, for God Himself doth
hold me
In the hollow of His hand!

3.. He will guard my soul, and leave me
never.
From His love no power on earth
Shall sever.
And I know He'll keep me now and
ever,
In the hollow of His hand!

PILGRIMAGE

1005

Abridge-C.M.

1. Be thou my guardian and my guide,
   And hear me when I call;
   Let not my slippery footsteps slide,
   And hold me lest I fall.

2. The world, the flesh, and Satan dwell
   Around the path I tread;
   O save me from the snares of hell,
   Thou quickener of the dead.

3. And if I tempted am to sin,
   And outward things are strong,
   Do thou, O Lord, Keep watch Within,
   And save my soul from wrong.

4. Still let me ever watch and pray,
   And feel that I am frail;
   That if the tempter cross my way,
   Yet he may not prevail.
                                    -I. William

1006

Kocher -7.6.7.6.

1. O happy band of pilgrims,
   If onward ye will tread
   With Jesus as your fellow
   To Jesus as your Head!

2. O happy if ye labour
   As Jesus did for men!
   O happy if ye hunger
   As Jesus hungered then!

3. The Cross that Jesus carried
   He carried as your due:
   The Crown that Jesus weareth
   He weareth it for you.

4. The faith by which ye see him,
   The hope in which ye yearn

The love that through all troubles
To him alone will turn,

5. The trials that beset you,
   The sorrows ye endure,
   The manifold temptations
   That death alone can cure.

6. What are they but his jewels
   Of right celestial worth?
   What are they but the ladder
   Set up to heaven on earth?

7. O happy band of pilgrims.
   Look upward to the skies,
   Where such a fight affliction
   Shall win so great a prize.
                                    -J. M. Neale

1007

Martyrdom -C.M.

1. O God of Bethel, by whose hand
   Thy people still are fed,
   Who through this weary pilgrimage
   Hast all our fathers led:

2. Our vows, our prayers, we now present
   Before thy throne of grace;
   God of our fathers, be the God
   Of their succeeding race.

3. Through each perplexing path of life
   Our wandering footsteps guide;
   Give us each day our daily bread;
   And raiment fit provide.

4. O spread thy covering wings around.
   Till all our wanderings cease,
   And at our Father's love abode
   Our souls arrive on peace.
                                    -F. Doddridge 1008

PILGRIMAGE

1008

Ave virgo - 7.6.7.6.D.

1. Brothers, pining hand to hand
In one bond united,
Pressing onward to that land
Where all wrongs are righted:
Let your words and actions be
Worthy of your vocation;
Chosen of the Lord, and free,
Heirs of Christ's salvation.

2 Christ, the Way, the Truth, the Life,
Who hath gone before you
Through the turmoil and the strife,
Holds his banners o'er you:
All who see the sacred sign
Press towards heaven's portal,
Fired by hope that is divine.
Love that is immortal.

3. They who follow fear no foe,
Care not who assail them:
Where the Master leads they go,
He will never fail them.
Courage, brothers! we are one.
In the love that sought us;
Soon the warfare shall be done,
Through the grace he brought us.
                    -J. A. Warner

1009

Pater Omnium - 8.8.8.8.8.8.

1. Leader of faithful souls, and Guide
Of all that travel to the sky,
Come and with us, e'en us, abide,
Who would on Thee alone rely.
On Thee alone our spirits stay,
While held in life's uneven way.

2. We have no lasting city here,
But seek a city out of sight;
Thither our steady course we steer,
Aspiring to the plains of light,

Jerusalem, the saints' abode,
Whose founder is the living God.

3. Through Thee, who all our sins hast borne,
Freely and graciously forgiven,
With songs to Zion we return,
Contending for our native heaven;
That palace of pure glorious King,
We find it nearer while we sing.

4. Raised by the breath of love divine,
We urge our way with strength renewed;
The Church of Thy first born to join,
We travel to the mount of God.
With joy upon our heads arise.
And meet our Captain in the skies.
                    -Charles Wesley

1010

Norse air-D.C.M.

1. Our fathers were high minded men,
Who firmly kept the faith:
To freedom and to conscience true.
In danger and in death;
Great names had they but greater souls,
True heroes of their age,
Who, like a rock stormy seas,
Defied opposing rage.

2. For ail they suffered little cared
Those earnest men and wise:
Their zeal for Christ, their love of truth
Made them the shame despise:
Nor should their deeds be e'er forgot.
For noble men were they
Who struggled hard for sacred rights.
And bravely won the day.

3. As faithful as our fathers were
May we their children be:

PILGRIMAGE

And in our hearts their spirit live.
That gained our liberty.
God help us all to do and dare
Whatever can be done,
Till for the good old cause of truth
The victory shall be won.

-Henry Mayo Gunn

1011

St. Edmund-S.M.

1. Thou say'st, "Take up thy cross,
   O man, and follow Me"
   The night is black, the feet are slack. '
   Yet we would follow Thee.

2. But O, deer Lord, we cry,
   That we Thy face could see,
   Thy blessed face one moments
   space;
   Then might we follow Thee.

3. Comes faint and far Thy voice
   From vales to Galilee;
   The vision Cades in ancient shades:
   How should we follow Thee?

4. Ah, sense bound heart and blind!
   Is nought but what we see?
   Can time undo what once was true?
   Can we not follow Thee?

5. If not as once Thou cam'st
   In true humanity,
   Come yet as guest within the breast
   That bums to follow Thee.

6. Within our heart of hearts
   In nearest nearness be:
   Set up Thy throne within Thine own;
   Go, Lord: we follow Thee.

-Frauds Tumer Palgrave

1012

It's Not an Easy Road

1. It's not an easy road we are trav'ling
   to Heaven,
   For many are the thorns on the way;
   tis not an easy road but the Saviour
   is with us,
   His presence gives us joy ev'ry day.

Chorus
No, no, it's not an easy road,
No, no, it's snot an easy road;
But Jesus walks with me and
brighter my journey,
And lightens ev'ry heavy load.

2. tis not an easy road there are trail
   and troubles,
   And many are the dangers we meet;
   But Jesus guards and keeps so that
   nothing can harm us,
   And smooth the rugged path for our
   feet.

3. Though I am often footsore and
   weary from travel,
   Though I am often bowed down with
   care;
   A better day is coming when Home
   in the glory,
   Well rest in perfect peace over
   there.

-J. W. Peterson

1013

After the Sunrise

1. Sorrows surround us while treading
   life's road,   ;
   Troubles confound us, make heavy
   our load;
   Fetters that bound us. no longer will
   goad
   After the sunrise, how happy we'll be

PILGRIMAGE

Chorus
(After the sunrise),happy we'll be.
(We know after the sunrise,)
Jesus we'll see;
All will be glory, singing the story,
After the sunrise, how happy we'll be

2. Shadows will vanish when morning
shall come,
Love light will banish sin's vapors
like scum;
Even the clannish together will
hum,
After the sunrise, how happy we'll ·
Be.

3. Angels are waiting to carry the news,
Why stand debating, why longer
refuse?
Cease all your hating, be changing
your views,
After the sunrise, how happy we'll
be.

-J. R. Baxter. Jr.

1014

Heavenly Sunlight

1. Walking in sunlight all of my journey,
Over the mountains, thru the deep
vale:
Jesus has said, "I'll never forsake
thee."
Promise divine that never can fail.

Chorus
Heavenly sunlight, heavenly sunlight
Flooding my soul with glory divine;

2. Shadows around me, shadows
above me,
Never conceal my Saviour and
Guide;

He is the Light, in Him is no
darkness
Ever I'm walking close to His side.

3. In the bright sunlight, ever rejoicing,
Pressing my way to mansions
above;
Singing His praises, gladly I'm·
walking
Walking in sunlight, sunlight of love
-Henry J. Zelley

1015

Mainzer L.M.

1. We've no abiding city here:
This may distress the worldling's
mind
But should not cost the saint a tear.
Who hopes a better rest to find.

2. 'We've no abiding city here;
Sad truth, were this to be our home;
But let the thought our spirits cheer.
We seek a city yet to come.

3. We've no abiding city here:
We seek a city out of sight:
Zion its name: the Lord is there:
It shines with everlasting light.

4. Zion, Jehovah is her strength:
Secure, she smiles at all her foes;
And weary travellers at length
Within her sacred walls repose.

5. O sweet abode of peace and love,
Where pilgrims freed from toil are
bless'd,
Had I the pinions of a dove.
I'd fly ,to thee and be at rest.

6. But hush. my soul, nor dare repine;
The time my God appoints is best
While here, to do His will be mime;
And His, to fix my time of rest
-J. Mainzer

PILGRIMAGE

1016

The King's Business

1 I am a stranger here,
within a foreign land
My home is far away,
upon a golden strand;
Ambassador to be
Of realms beyond the sea,
I'm here on business for my King

Chorus

This is the message that I bring,
a message angels fain would sing;
"Oh, be ye reconciled,
Thus saith my Lord and King,
"Oh, be ye reconciled to God."

2 This is the King's command;
That all men, ev'ry where
Repent and turn away
from sin's seductive snare;
That all who will obey,
with Him shall reign for aye,
And that's my business for my King

3. My home is brighter far
Than Sharon's rosy plain,
Eternal life and joy thro'out
its vast domain;
My Sov'reign bids me tell
how mortals there may dwell,
And that's my business for my
King

-Flora H. Cassel

1017

All The Way

. Jesus, blessed Jesus, lead me All
along life's way.
With the Holy Manna feed me,
Ev'ry hour and day,
Keep me ever close beside Thee,
Lest my feet should roam,
And when this life is over,
Lead me safety home.

Chorus

All the way. All the way,
Saviour, lead me all the way,
To that land of endless day,
Saviour lead me all the way.

2. Jesus, blessed Jesus, lead me
Where e'er duty calls.
Tho' it be o'er lonely mountains
beside stone walls,
In the home of poor and lowly, I will
spread the light,
Point the sad and weary trave'ler To
the pathway bright

3. Jesus, blessed Jesus, lead me In
the gospel fight,
Help me battle ev'ry error, Stand for
truth and right,
With God's pow'r to go before me I
can conquer sin.
With Thy banner floating o'er me,
Life's hard battle win.

4. Jesus, blessed Jesus, lead me 'Till I
see God's face,
Till His smile shall rest upon me,
Filled with matchless grace,
Then when I have passed the portals
To that land above,
I shall praise Thee with immortal
For redeeming love.

-Carol Walls Hill

1018

The Saviour With Me

I. I must have the Saviour with me
For I dare not walk alone;
I must feel His presence near me
And His arm around me thrown.

Chorus

Then my soul shall fear no ill,
Let Him lead me where He will,
I will go without a murmur,
And His footsteps follow still.

PILGRIMAGE

2. I must have the Saviour with me,
   For my faith, at best, is weak;
   He can whisper words of comfort
   That no other voice can speak.

3. I must have the Saviour with me,
   In the onward march of life,
   Thro' the tempest and the sun shine,
   Thro' the battle and the strife,

4. I must have the Saviour with me,
   And His eye the way must guide;
   Till I reach the vale of Jordan,
   Till I cross the rolling tide.

   -Lizzie Edwards

1019
I will Guide Thee - 8.7.8.7. and Refrain

1. Precious promise God hath given
   To the weary passer by,
   On the way from earth to heaven.
   "I will guide thee with Mine eye."

2. When temptations almost win thee,
   And thy trusted watchers fly,
   Let this promise ring within thee:
   "I will guide thee with Mine eye."

3. When thy secret hopes have perished
   In the grave of years gone by,
   Let this promise still be cherised,
   "I will guide thee with Mine eye."

4. When the shades of life are falling,
   And the hour has come to die,
   Hear thy trusty Leader calling
   "I will guide thee with Mine eye."

   -N. Niles

1020
Hold Thou My Hand -11.10.11.10.

I. Hold Thou my hand! so weak I am and helpless;
   I dare not take one step without Thy aid!

Hold Thou my hand! for then, O loving Saviour,
No dread of ill shall make my soul afraid.

2. Hold Thou my hand! and closer, closer draw me
   To Thy dear self my hope. my joy, my all;
   Hold Thou my hand' lest haply I should wander,
   And missing Thee, my trembling feet should fall.

3. Hold Thou my hand! the way is dark before me
   Without the sunlight of Thy face divine;
   But when by faith I catch its radiant glory,
   What heights of joy, what rapturous songs are mine!

4. Hold Thou my hand! that, when I reach the margin
   Of that lone river Thou didst cross for me,
   A heavenly light may flash along its waters,
   And every wave like crystal bright shall be.

   -Grace J. Frances

1021
Lean on his Arms

1. Just lean upon the arms of Jesus.
   He'll help you along, help you along,
   If you will trust His love unfailing,
   He'll fill your heart with song.

Chorus
Lean on His arms, trusting in His love;
Lean on His arms, all His mercies prove;
Lean on His arms, looking home above,
Just lean on the Saviour's arms!

2. Just lean upon the arms of Jesus,
   He'll brighten the way, brighten the way:
   Just follow gladly where He leadeth,
   His gentle voice obey.

3. Just lean upon the arms of Jesus.
   Oh bring every care, bring every care
   The burden that has seemed so heavy,
   Take to the Lord in prayer.

4 Just lean upon the arms of Jesus,
   Then leave all to Him, leave all to Him
   His heart is full of love and mercy,
   His eye are never dim.

5. Just lean upon the arms of Jesus.
   He meets every need, meet every need.
   To all who take Him as a Saviour,
   He is a Friend Indeed.

                              -Edgar Lewis

1022

Jesus shall lead me - L.M. and Refrain

1. Where He may lead me I will go,
   For I have learn'd to trust Him so,
   And I remember twas for me.
   That He was slain on Calvary.

Chorus
Jesus shall lead me night and day.
Jesus shall lead me all the way:
He is the truest Friend to me,
For I remember Calvary.

2. O delight in His command,
   Love to be led by His dear hand,
   His divine will is sweet to me.
   Hallow'd by blood stain'd Calvary.

3. Onward I go, nor doubt nor fear,
   Happy with Christ, my Saviour near
   Trusting some day that I shall see,
   Jesus, my Friend of Calvary.

                              -W. C. Matin

1023

Franconia - S.M.

1. My time are in Thy hand
   My God, I wish them there;
   My life, my friend, my soul I leave
   Entirely to Thy calvary.

2. My time are in Thy hand.
   Whatever they may be,
   Pleasing or painful, dark or bright
   As best may seem to Thee.

3. My time are in Thy hand;
   Why should I doubt or fear?
   My Father's hand will never cause
   His child a needless tear.

4. My time are in Thy hand,
   Jesus, the crucified
   Those hands my cruel sins had pierced
   Are now my guard and guide.

5. My time are in Thy hard,
   I'll always trust in Thee;
   And, after death, at Thy right hand
   I shall for ever be.

                              -W. F. Lioyd

1024

Like Zion's Holy Mount -C.M. With Refrain

1. All they who put their trust in God
   Can never be removed;
   They stand secure like Zion's mount.
   By many ages proved

PILGRIMAGE

Chorus
Like the mount of God,
Like the mount of God;
They stand secure like Zion's
mount,
By many ages proved.
They can never be removed,
removed;
They stand secure like Zion's
mount.
They can never be removed.

2. As round about Jerusalem
The rugged mountains lie,
So round about His holy saints
Our God is ever nigh.

3. Tho' fierce the storm in fury beat
And awful thunders roar,
The children of the mighty God
Are safe for evermore.

4. Thus over shadowed by His love,
Where harm can ne'er betide,
Within this refuge safe and sure
I ever would abide.
                          -C. M. Seamans

1025
I have a Shepherd

1. I have a Shepherd, One I love so
well;
How He has bless'd me tongue can
never tell;
On the Cross He suffered, shed His
blood and died.
That I might ever in His love
Confidde.

Chorus
Following Jesus, ever day by day,
Nothing can harm me when He
leads the way;
Darkness or sunshine, what e'er
befall,
Jesus, the Shepherd, is my All in
All.

2. Pastures abundant doth His hand
provide,
Still waters flowing ever at my side.
Goodness and mercy follow on my
track.
With such a Shepherd nothing can I
lack.

3. When I would wander from the path
astray,
Then He will draw me back into the
way;
In the darkest valley I need fear no ill
For He, my Shepherd, will be with
me still.

4. When labour's ended and the
Journey done.
Then He will lead me safely to my
home;
There I shall dwell in rapture sure
and sweet.
With all the loved ones gathered
round His feet.
                          -Leonard Weavar

1026
Never Lose Sight of Jesus

1. O pilgrim bound for the heav'nly
land.
Never lose sight of Jesus!
He'll lead you gently with loving
hand:
Never lose sight of Jesus!

Chorus
Never lose sight of Jesus:
Never lose sight or Jesus
Day and night He will lead you right;
Never lose sight of Jesus!

2. When you are tempted to go astray,
Never lose sight of Jesus!
Press onward, upward, the narrow
way;
Never lose sight of Jesus!

PILGRIMAGE

3. Though dark the pathway may
    seem ahead.
    Never lose sight of Jesus!
    "I will be with you," His word hath
    said:
    Never lose sight of Jesus!

4. When death is knocking outside the
    door,
    Never lose sight of Jesus!
    Till safe with Him or the golden'
    shore
    Never lose sight of Jesus!

    J. Catma

1027

A Shelter in the Time Storm

1. The Lord's our Rock, in Him we
    hide:
    A shelter m the time of storm!
    Secure whatever ill betide:
    A shelter in the time of storm!

    Chorus
    Oh, Jesus is a Rock in a weary
    land!
    A weary land, A weary land; Oh,
    Jesus is a Rock in weary land,
    A shelter in the time of storm!

2. "^A shade by day; defence by night:
    A shelter in the time of storm!
    No fears alarm, no foes affright
    A shelter in the time of storm!

3. The raging storms may round us
    beat
    A shelter in the time of storm!
    We'll never leave our safe retreat,
    A shelter in the time of storm!

4. O Rock divine, O Refuge dear:
    A shelter tn the time of storm!
    Be Thou our helper evernear,
    A shelter in the time of storm!

    -V. J. C.

1028

Marching-8.7.8.7.

1. Through the night of doubt and
    sorrow
    Onward goes the pilgrim band
    Singing songs of expectation.
    Marching to the Promised Land.

2. Clear before us through the
    darkness,
    Gleams and burns the guiding light;
    Brother clasps the hand of brother
    Stepping fearless through night.

3. One the light of God's own pres-
    ence,
    O'er His ransomed people shed
    Chasing far the gloom and terror
    Brightening all the path we tread.

4. One the object of our journey;
    One the faith that never tires
    One the earnest looking forward
    One the hope our God inspire.

5. One the strain the lips of thousand
    Lift as from the heart of one
    One the conflict, one the peril,
    One the march in God begun.

6. One the gladness of rejoicing
    On the far, eternal shore,
    Where the One Almighty Father
    Reigns in love for evermore.

7. Onward, therefore, pilgrim battle
    Onward with the Cross our aids
    Bear its shame, and fight battle
    Till we rest beneath its shade.

8. Soon shall come the great awaking
    Soon the rending of the tomb
    Then the scattering of all shadows;
    And the end of toil and gloom.
    -S. Baring Gould

PILGRIMAGE

1029

Jesus, Hold my hand

1. As I travel thru this pilgrim land,
   There is a Friend who walks with me,
   Leads me safely thru the sinking sand,
   It is the Christ of Calvary;
   This would be my pray'r, dear Lord, each day
   To help me do the best I can,
   For I need Thy light to guide me day and night,
   Blessed Jesus, hold my hand.

2. Let me travel in the light divine
   That I may see the blessed way;
   Keep me that I may be wholly Thine
   And sing redemption's song some day;
   I will be a soldier brave and true
   And ever firmly take a stand,
   As I onward go and daily meet the foe,
   Blessed Jesus, hold my hand.

3. When I wander thru the valley dim
   Toward the setting of the sun,
   Lead me safety to a land of rest
   If I a crown of life have won;
   I have put my faith in Thee, dear Lord,
   That I may reach the golden-strand,
   There's no other friend on whom I can depend,
   Blessed Jesus, hold my hand.
   —Albert E. Brumley

1030

The love of Jesus - 7.6.

1. What a blessed hope is mine,
   Through the love of Jesus'
   I'm an heir of life Divine.
   Through the love of Jesus!

Chorus
He will my soul defend;
He, my unchanging Friend;
He will keep me to the end:
All glory be to Jesus!

2. I can sing without a fear,
   Praise the name of Jesus!
   He, my present help, is near.
   Praise the name of Jesus!

3. Pressing on my pilgrim way.
   Trusting only Jesus!
   Oh, 'tis joy from day to day.
   Trusting only Jesus'

4. Thus my journey I'll pursue,
   Looking unto Jesus'
   Till the land of rest I view,
   There to dwell with Jesus!
   —Robert Bruce

1031

Norris -8.8.8.9. with Refrain

1. I can hear my Saviour calling,
   I can hear my Saviour calling,
   I can hear my Saviour calling,
   Take thy cross and follow, follow Me"

Chorus
Where He leads me I will follow,
Where He leads me I will follow,
Where He leads me I will follow,
I'll go with Him, with Him all the way.

2. I'll go with Him thru the Judgement,
   I'll go with Him thru the judgement,
   I'll go with Him thru the judgement,
   I'll go with Him, with Him all the way.

3. He we give me grace and glory,
   He will give me grace and glory,
   He will give me grace and glory,
   And go with me, with me all the way.
   —E. W. Blandy

PILGRIMAGE

1032
Lead me, Saviour

1. Saviour, lead me, lest I stray,
   Gently lead me all the way;
   I am safe when by Thy side,
   I would in Thy love abide.

Chorus
Lead me, toad me,
Saviour, lead me, lest I stray,
Gently down the stream of time,
Lead me, Saviour, all the way.

2. Thou the refuge of my soul,
   When life's stormy billows roil,
   I am safe when Thou art nigh,
   All my hopes on Thee rely.

3. Saviour, lead me, then at last.
   When the storm of life is past,
   To the land of endless day,
   Where all tears are wiped away.
   -Frank M. Davis

1033
Our pilot

1. We sail along toward the harbour
   light,
   Over the great life sea;
   The breakers roar and the waves
   Dash light,
   Who will our pilot be?

Chorus
The Christ will our Pitot be.
A wonderful Guide is He;
So we'll sail, sail, sail!
Christ will our Pitot be.

2. We sail along in the morning bright,
   Happy and glad are we:
   But still we ask, as the rocks draw
   near,
   Who will our pilot be?   •

3. We sail along, there are shoals, they
   say.
   Dangers from which to flee;
   We face the storm with a heavy
   heart,
   Who will our pilot be
   -Lizzie Dearmond

1034
We have an anchor

1. Will your anchor hold in the storm
   of life,
   When the clouds unfold their wings
   of strife?
   When the strong tides lift, and the
   cables strain,
   Will your anchor drift, or firm
   remain?

Chorus
We have an anchor that keeps the
soul
Steadfast and sure while the billow
roil.
Fastened to the Rock which cannot
move,
Grounded firm and deep in the
Saviour's love.

2. His safely moored. twill the storm
   withstand.
   For 'tis wed secured by the
   Saviour's hand;
   Though the tempest rage and the
   winds blow.
   Not an angry wave shall our bark
   o'erflow.

3. When our eyes behold through the
   gathering night
   The city of gold, our harbour bright
   We shall anchor fast by the
   heavenly shore.
   With the storms all past forever
   more.
   -Priscillia J. Owens

PILGRIMAGE

1035

Brastod -7.7.7.7.

1. Children of the heav'nly King.
   As ye journey, sweetly sing;
   Sing your Saviour's worthly praise,
   Glorious in his works and ways.

2. We are trav'ling home to God,
   In the way the fathers trod:
   They are nappy now, and we Soon
   Their happiness shall see

3. Lift your eyes, sons of light,
   Zion's city is in sight:
   There our endless home shall be,
   There our Lord we soon shall see.

4. Fear not, brethren; joyful stand
   On the borders of your land;
   Jesus Christ, your Father's Son,
   Bids you undismayed go on.

5. Lord. obedient we go,
   Gladly leaving all below,
   Only thou our leader be,
   And we will still follow thee.
                        -John Cennik

1036

Moseley -6.6.6.6.

1. O love that casts' out fear,
   O love that casts out sin.
   Tarry no more without,
   But come and dwell within.

2. True sunlight of the soul,
   Surround us as we go;
   So shall our way be safe,
   Our feet no straying know.

3. Great love of God, come in!:
   Wellspring of heav'nly peace;
   Thou Living Water, come!
   Spring up, and never cease.

4. Love of the living God,
   Of Father and of Son;
   Love of the Holy Ghost,
   Fill thou each needy one.
                        -Horatius Bonar

1037

All The Way

1. All the way my Saviour leads me;
   What have I to ask beside?
   Can I doubt His tender mercy.
   Who thru life has been my guide?
   Heav'nly peace, divinest comfort,
   Here by faith in Him to dwell!
   For I know whate'er befall me,
   Jesus doeth all things well.

2. All the way my Saviour leads me;
   Cheers each winging path I tread.
   Gives me grace for ev'ry trial,
   Feeds me with the living bread:
   Tho' my weary steps may falter,
   And my soul athirst may be,
   Gushing from the Rock before,
   Lo! A spring of joy I see.

3. All the way my Saviour leads me;
   Oh, the fullness of His love!
   Perfect rest to me is promised
   In my Father's house above:
   When my spirit, cloth'd immortal,
   Wings its flight to realms of day,
   This my song thru endless ages:
   Jesus led me all the way.
                        -Fanny J. Crosby

1038

He Leadeth Me - L.M. with Refrain

1. He leadeth me! O blessed thought!
   O words with heav'nly comfort
   fraught!
   Whatever I do, wherever be,
   Still 'tis God's hand that leadeth
   me.

PILGRIMAGE

Chorus
He leadeth me, He leadeth me,
By His own hand He leedeth me;
His faithful follower I would be,
For by His hand He leadeth me.

2. Sometimes mid scenes of deepest
gloom,
Sometimes where Eden's
bowers bloom, By waters still, o'er
troubled sea,
Still 'tis His hand that leadeth me!

3. Lord, I would clasp Thy hand in
Mine,
Nor ever murmur nor repine;
Content, whoever lot I see,
Since 'tis my God that leadeth me!

4. And when my task on earth is done,
When by Thy grace the vict'rys won,
E'en death's cold wave I will not flee,
Since God thru Jordan leadeth me.
— Joseph H. Gilmore

1039
Close To Thee - 8.7.8.7.6.6.8.7.

1. Thou my everlasting portion,
More than friend or life to me;
All along my pilgrim journey,
Saviour, let me walk with Thee.
Close to Thee, close to Thee,
Close to Thee, close to Thee;
All along my pilgrim journey,
Saviour let me. walk with Thee.

2. Not for ease or worldly pleasure,
Nor for fame my prayer shall be;
Gladly will I toil and suffer,
Only let me walk with Thee.
Close to Thee, close to Thee.
Close to Thee, close to Thee;
Gladly will I toil and suffer,
Only let me walk with Thee.

3. Lead me through the vale of
shadows,
Bear me o'er life fitful sea;
Then the gate of life eternal
May I enter. Lord, with Thee.
Close to Thee. close to Thee,
Close to Thee, close to Thee;
Then the gate of life eternal
May I enter, Lord, with Thee.
— Fanny J. Crosby

1040
CWM Rhondda - 8.7.8.7.8.7.

1. Guide me, O Thou great Jehovah
Pligrim through this barren land;
I am weak, but Thou art mighty;
Hold me with Thy pow'rful hand
Bread of heaven, Bread of heaven
Feed me till I want no more,
Feed me till I want no more.

2. Open now the crystal fountain.
Whence the healing stream doth
flow;
Let the fire and cloudy pillar
Lead me all my Journey through
Strong Deliverer, strong Deliverer
Be Thou still my strength and .
shield,
Be Thou still my strength and
shield.

3. When I tread the verge of Jordan
Bid my anxious fears subside;
Bear me thro' the swelling current
Land me safe on Canaan's side;
Songs of praises, songs of praises
I will ever give to Thee,
I will ever give to Thee.
— William Williams

1041
St. Bartholomew L.M.

1. Where cross the crowded life,
Where sound the cries of race and
clan,
Above the noise of selfish strife,
We hear Thy voice, O Son of man.

PILGRIMAGE

2. In Haunts of wretchedness and
   need,
   On shadowed thresholds dark with
   fears.
   From paths where hide the lures of
   greed
   We catch the vision of Thy tears.

3. From tender childhood's
   helplessness,
   From woman's grief, man's
   burdened toil.
   From famished souls, from sorrow's
   stress,
   Thy heart has never known recoil.

4. The cup of water given for Thee
   Still holds the freshness of Thy
   grace;
   Yet long these multitudes to see
   The sweet compassion of Thy face.

5. O Master, from the mountain side,
   Make haste to heal these hearts of
   pain;
   Among these restless throngs
   abide,
   O tread the city's streets again:

6. Till sons of men shall learn Thy love,
   And follow where Thy feet have trod;
   Till glorious from Thy heaven above,
   Shall come the City of our God.
   -Frank Mason North

1042
O I want to see him

1. As I journey thro' the land singing
   as I go
   Pointing souls to Calvary, to the
   crimson flow,

Many arrows pierce my soul from.
without, within;
But my Lord leads me on. Thro
Him I must win.

Chorus
O I want to see Him, took upon His
face,
There to sing forever of His saving
grace;
On the streets of Glory let me lift
my voice;
cares an past, home at last, ever
to rejoice.

2. When in service for my Lord dark
   may be the night,
   But I'll cling more close to Him, He
   will give me light;
   Satan's snares may vex my soul,
   turn my tho'ts aside;
   By my Lord goes ahead, leads
   whate'er betide.

3. When in valleys low I look t'ward
   the mountain height,
   And behold my Saviour there.
   leading in the fight,
   With a tender hand out stretched
   t'ward the valley low.
   Guiding me, I can see, as I onward
   go.

4. When before me billows rise from
   the mighty deep.
   Then my Lord directs my bark; He
   doth safely keep,
   And He leads me gently on thro'
   this world below;
   He's real Friend to me, O I love
   Him so.
   -R. H. Cornelius

1043
Jesus, Saviour, Pilot Me

1. Jesus, Saviour pilot me
   Over life's tempestuous sea;
   Unknown waves before me roll,
   Hiding rocks and treach'rous
   shoal;

PILGRIMAGE

Chart and compass come from Thee.
Jesus, Saviour, pilot me!

2. As a mother stills her child,
   Thou canst hush the ocean wild;
   Boist'rous waves obey Thy will
   When Thou say'st to them,
   "Be still!" Wondrous Sov'reign of the
   sea, Jesus, Saviour, pilot me!

3. When at last I near the shore,
   And the fearful breakers roar
   Twixt me and the peaceful rest
   Then, while leaning on Thy breast,
   May I hear Thee say to me,
   Tear not, I will pilot thee!"
   -Edward Hooper

1044

Faithful guide

1. Holy Spirit, faithful Guide,
   Ever near the Christian's side;
   Gently lead us by the hand,
   Pilgrims in a desert land;
   Weary souls fore'er rejoice,
   While they hear that sweetest voice,
   Whispering softly, "Wanderer, come!
   Follow Me, I'll guide thee home."

2. Ever present, truest Friend,
   Ever near Thine aid to lend, leave us
   not to doubt and fear,
   Groping on in darkness drear,
   When the storms are raging sore,
   Hearts grow faint, and hopes
   give o'er,
   Whisper softly, "Wanderer, come!
   Follow Me, I'll guide thee home."

3. When our days of toil shall cease,
   Waiting still for sweet release,
   Looking up to heaven in prayer,
   Joyful that our names are there:
   Fearing not the dismal flood,
   Pleading naught but Jesus' blood,
   Whisper softly, "Wanderer, come!
   Follow Me, I'll guide thee home."
   -Marcus M. Weils

1045

Surely Goodness and Mercy

1. A pilgrim was I and a wand'ring,
   In the cold night of sin I did roam.
   When Jesus the kind Shepherd
   found me,
   And now I am on my way home.

Chorus
Surely goodness and mercy shall
follow me
All the days, all the days of my life
Surely goodness and mercy shall
follow me
All the days, all the days of my life.

2. He restoreth my soul when I'm
   weary,
   He giveth me strength day by day;
   He leads me beside the still waters
   He guards me each step of the way.

3. When I walk thru the dark lone
   some valley,
   My Saviour will walk with me there
   And safely His great hand will lead
   me
   To the mansions He's gone to
   prepare
   -John W. Peterson
   & Alfred B. Smith

1046

God Leads Us Along

1. In shady, green pastures, so rich
   and so sweet,
   God leads His dear children along
   Where the water's cool flow bathes
   the weary one's feet,
   God leads His dear children along

PILGRIMAGE

Chorus
Some thru the waters, some thru
the flood,
Some thru the fire, but all thru the
blood;
Some thru great sorrow, but God
gives a song,
In the night season and all the day
long.

2. Sometimes on the mount where the
sunshines so bright,
God leads His dear children along;
Sometimes in the valley, in darkest
of night,
God leads His dear children along.

3. Tho' sorrow befall us and Satan
oppose,
God leads His dear children along;
Thru grace we can conquer, defeat
all our foes,
God leads His dear children along.

4. Away from the mire and away from
the clay,
God leads His dear children along;
Away up in glory, eternity's day,
God leads His dear children along.
        -G. A. Young

1047
Jesus Will Be With You

1. Jesus will be with you wheresoe'er
you stray,
Jesus will be with you and will guide
your way;
Thro' the lonely deserts, over
mountains bare,
Jesus will be with you, brother, ev'ry
where.

Chorus
Jesus will be with you, Jesus will be
with you,
He will be your friend To comfort and
defend;
Jesus will be with you, Jesus will be
with you,
Jesus will be with you to the end.

2. Jesus will be with you wheresoe'er
you stray,
Jesus will be with you and will be
your stay;
Thro' the darksome valley with its
grief and care,
Jesus will be with you, brother,
don't despair.

3. Jesus will be with you wheresoe'er
you stray,
Jesus will be with you all along
life's way;
Thro' the chilly waters to the land
so fair.
Jesus will be with you. brother,
trust his care.
        -Rev. J. B. Mackay

1048
Brightly gleams our Banner

1. Brightly gleams our banner,
pointing to the sky.
Waving on Christ's soldiers to their
home on high!
Marching through the desert gladly
thus we pray,
Still with hearts united, singing on
our way

Chorus
Brightly gleams our banner, pointing
to the sky
Waving on Christ's soldiers to their
home on high.

2. Jesus, Lord and Master, at Thy
sacred feet.
Here with hearts rejoicing, see Thy
children meet,
Often have we left Thee, often gone
astray;
Keep us mighty Saviour in the
narrow way.

3. All our days direct us in the way we
go,
Lead us on victorious over every foe,
Bid Thine angels shield us when
the storm clouds
Pardon Lord, and save us in the
last dread hour.

PILGRIMAGE

4. Then with saints and angels may
we join above,
Offering prayers and praises at Thy
throne of love,
When the march is over, then
comes rest and peace
Jesus in His beauty, songs they
never cease.

1049
Sound The Gospel Of Grace Abroad-
P.M.L.

1. Sound the gospel of grace abroad.
There's life in the risen Lord,
Spread the news of the gift of God
There's life in the risen Lord,
God above desires it!
Sinful man requires it!

Chorus
Tell it around, let it abound
There's life in the risen Lord.

2. All by nature are doomed to die,
So saith the Holy Word,
Welcome therefore the joyful cry.
There's life in the risen Lord.
Welcome news of gladness
Antidote of sadness.

3. Saint, apostles and prophets, all
Published with one accord,
This deliverance from the fall
This life in the risen Lord
Glory be to Jesus,
Who from bondage frees us.

4. Pardon, power and perfect peace
The words of this life afford.
Never then let the tidings cease,
Of life in the risen Lord.
Open wide the portal,
Unto every mortal.

1050
Whither, Pilgrims, Are You Going
8.7.8.7.8.8.8.7.8.7.

1. Whither, pilgrims, are you going
Going each with staff in hand
We are going on a journey,
Going at our King's command,
Over hills and plains and valley
We are going to His palace.
We are going to His palace.
Going to the better land;
We are going to His palace,
Going to the better land.

2. Tell us, pilgrims, what you hope for
In that far-off, better land?
Spotless robes, and crowns of glory,
From a Saviour's loving hand;
We shall drink of life's clear river
We shall dwell with God for ever
We shall dwell with God for ever
In that bright, that better land,
We shall dwell with God for ever
In that bright, that better land

3. Doth ye not fear the way ye trod
O yet little pilgrim band
The Friend unseen goeth with us
Angels doth surround us still
Jesus Christ our Lord doth guide us
He shall watch us, He shall lead us
He shall watch us, He shall lead us
On this holy pilgrimage.
He shall watch us. He shall lead us
On this holy pilgrimage.

4. Pilgrims, may we travel with you
To that bright and better land
Come and welcome, come and
welcome
Welcome to our pilgrim band.
I Come, oh, come! and don't leave us
Christ is waiting to receive us
Christ is waiting to receive us
In that bright, that better land.
Christ is waiting to receive us
In that bright, that better land.

ENCOURAGEMENT

1051

Sweet Promise -11.11.11.11. an 'Refrain

1. Sweet is the promise,
I will not forget thee.
" Nothing can molest or
turn my soul away;
E'entho the night be
dark within the valley,
Just beyond is shining
one eternal day.

Chorus
"twill not forget thee or leave thee
In My hands I'll hold thee,
In My hands I'll hold thee,
In my arms I'll fold thee;
I will not forget thee or leave thee;
I am thy Redeemer, I will care for
thee."

2. Trusting the promise,
"I will not forget thee,"
Onward will I go with
songs of joy and love;
Tho' earth despise me.
tho' my friends forsake me,
I shall be remembered
in my home above.

3. When at the golden
portals I am standing,
All my tribulations,
all my sorrows past,
How sweet to hear the
blessed proclamation,
'Enter, faithful servant,
welcome home at last!"
-Charles H. Gabriel

1052

Sunshine - 9.6.8.6. with Refrain

1. There is sunshine in my soul today,
More glorious and bright
Than glows in any earthly sky.
For Jesus is my light

Chorus
Other's sunshine, blessed sunshine,
When the peaceful, happy moments roll:
When Jesus shows His smiling
Face,
There is sunshine in my soul.

2. There is music in my soul today,
A carol to my King. And Jesus, listening
can hear
The songs I cannot sing.

3. There is spring-time in my soul today,
For when the Lord is near
The dove of peace sings in my heart,
The flow'rs of grace appear.

4. There is gladness in my soul today,
And hope and love and praise,
For blessings which he gives me now,
For joys in future days.
-Eliza E-Hewitt

1053

Showers Of Blessing - 8.7.8.7. with Refrain

1. "There shall be showers of blessing
This is the promise of love;
There shall be seasons refreshing,
Sent from the Saviour above.

Chorus
Showers of blessing,
Showers of blessing we need;
Mercy drops round us are falling.
But for the showers we plead.

ENCOURAGEMENT

2. "There shall be showers of blessing
   Precious reviving again;
   Over the hills and the valleys,
   Sound of abundance of rain.

3. There shall be showers of Blessing"
   Send them upon us, O Lord;
   Grant to us now a refreshing,
   Come and now honour Your Word.

4. "There shall be showers of blessing"
   O that today they might fall,
   Now as to God we're confessing,
   Now as on Jesus we can!

   -Daniel W. Whittle

1054

Ville Du Havre-11.8.11.9. with Refrain

1. When peace like a river, attendeth my way,
   When sorrows like sea billows roll;
   Whatever my lot, Thou hast taught me to say,
   "It is well, it is well with my soul."

   Chorus
   It is well with my soul,
   It is well, it is well with my soul.

2. Though Satan should buffet, tho' trials should come,
   Let this blest assurance control,
   That Christ has regarded my helpless estate,
   And hath shed His own blood for my soul.

3. My sin O, the bliss of this glorious thought.
   My sin not in part but the whole,
   Is nailed to the cross and I bear it no more,

Praise the Lord, praise the Lord, O my soul!

4. And, Lord, haste the day when the faith shall be sight,
   The clouds be rolled back as a scroll,
   The trump shall resound and the Lord shall descend,
   "Even so" it is well with my soul

   -Horatio G. Spafford

1055

Tell It To Jesus

1. Are you weary, are you heavy' hearted?
   Tell it to Jesus, Tell it to Jesus;
   Are you grieving over joys departed?
   Tell it to Jesus alone.

   Chorus
   Tell it to Jesus, tell it to Jesus
   He is a friend that's well known:
   You have no other such a friend or brother.
   Tell it to Jesus alone.

2. Do the tears flow down your checks Unbidden?
   Tell it to Jesus, tell it to Jesus;
   Have you sins that to man's eye are hidden?
   Tell it to Jesus alone.

3. Do you fear the gath'ring clouds of sorrow?
   Tell it to Jesus, Tell it to Jesus;
   Are you anxious what shall be tomorrow?
   Tell it to Jesus alone.

4. Are you troubled with the thought of dying?
   Tell it to Jesus, Tell it to Jesus;
   For Christ's coming kingdom are you sighing?
   Tell it to Jesus alone.

   -J. E. Rankin

ENCOURAGEMENT

1056

Burdens Are Lifted At Calvary

1. Days are filled with sorrow and care,
   Hearts are lonely and drear;
   Burdens are lifted at Calvary,
   Jesus is very near.

   Chorus
   Burdens are lifted at Calvary,
   Calvary, Calvary;
   Burdens are lifted at Calvary
   Jesus is very near.

2. Cast your care on Jesus today,
   Leave your worry and fear;
   Burdens are lifted at Calvary
   Jesus is very near.

3. Troubled soul, the Saviour can see
   Ev'ry heart ache tear;
   Burdens, are lifted at Calvary
   Jesus is very near.

   -John M. Moore

1057

I Just Keep Trusting My Lord

1 I Just keep trusting my Lord as I
   walk along,
   I just keep trusting my Lord, and He
   gives a song;
   Tho' the storm clouds darken the
   sky O'er the heav'nly trail.
   I just keep trusting my Lord He will
   never fail!
   He's a faithful Friend, such a faithful
   Friend.
   I can count on Him to the very end;
   Tho' the storm clouds darken the sky
   O'er the heav'nly trail I just keep
   trusting my Lord He will
   Never fail!

2. I just keep trusting my Lord on the
   narrow way,
   I just keep trusting my Lord, as He
   Leads each day;
   Tho' the road is weary at times and
   I'm sad and blue,
   I just keep trusting my Lord He will
   see me through!
   He's a faith Guide, such a faithful
   Guide,
   He is always there walking by my
   side;
   Tho the road is weary at times and
   I'm sad and blue,
   I just keep trusting my Lord He will
   see me through!

   -John W. Peterson

1058

Touched By the Master's Love

1. I've been touched by the love of the
   Master today,
   I've been touched in a most unusual
   way.
   There's a joy in this heart that was
   filled with dismay.
   Since I've been touched by the
   Master's love.

   Chorus
   Yes, I've been touched by a love that
   is greater,
   I know Than all the love that a world
   full of heartache could show.
   And I sing with delight as through
   this world I go,
   Since I've been touched by the
   Master's love.

2. I've been touched by the love of the
   Master today,
   And it shows in the words I think and
   I say.'
   There's a longing with in that His
   will I obey,
   Since I've been touched by the
   Master's love.

   -J. E. P

ENCOURAGEMENT

1059
He Whispers Sweet Peace to Me

1. Sometime when misgivings darken
the day,
And faith's light I cannot see;
I ask my dear Lord to brighten the
way,
He whispers sweet peace to me.

Chorus
Yes, He whispers to me,
He whispers sweet peace to me,
When I am cast down in spirit and
soul,
He whispers sweet peace to me.

2. I could not go on without Him I know,
The world would o'er -whelm my
soul;
For I could not see the right way to
go,
When temptations o'er me roll.

3. I trust Him thru faith, by faith hold
His hand.
And sometimes my faith is weak,
And, then when I ask Him to take
command,
It seems that I hear Him speak.

4. He speaks in a still, small voice we
are told,
A voice that dispels all fear;
And when I'm in doubt or troubled
in soul.
That still small voice I can hear.

5. The trumpet will sound for our Lord's
return,
He's coming for you and me;
I praise His dear name, for this I now
yearn,
With Jesus to ever be.
                                    -W. M. Ramsey

1060
Someone To Care

1. When the world seems cold and
your friends seem few,
There is someone who cares for
you;
When you've tears in your eyes
your heart bleeds inside.
There is someone who cares for
you.

Chorus
Someone to care, Someone to share
all your troubles like no other can do;
He'll come down from the skies
and brush the tears from your eyes
You're His child and He cares for
you.

2. When your disappointments come
and you feel so blue,
There is someone who cares for
you;
When you need a friend, a friend till
the end,
There is someone who's a friend to
you.
                                    -J. Davis

1061
I Am Bound For Canaan

1. Storms do not alarm me,
they sometime must cease,
Trials cannot harm me,
for I have blessed peace;
All I've left behind me
I long for no more,
Better things shall find me
on Canaan's shore.

Chorus
Let those who will, stay in Egypt
land,
I am bound for Canaan,
Where milk and honey flowing.

shall ev'ry need supply;
All battles fought and the vict'ry won,
peace and joy my portion,
My soul shall rest,
on its shore by and by.

2. Troubles do not fret me,
they cannot abide,
Tho' they may beset me,
In Jesus I will hide;
All the world's commotion
about me may roar,
There's no stormy ocean
on Canaan's shore.

3. I in grace abiding
and trying to stay
In the shadow hiding,
of Canaan's perfect day;
All I trust may fail me,
t'will matter no more,
Nothing can assail me
on Canaan's shore.

-C. Austin Miles

1062

Jesus, Blessed Jesus

1. There's One who can comfort when
all else fails,
Jesus, blessed Jesus,
A Saviour who saves tho' the foe
assails,
Jesus, blessed Jesus;
Once He traveled the way we go,
Felt the pangs of deceit and woe;
Who more perfectly then can know
Than Jesus, blessed Jesus'.

2. He heareth the cry of the soul
distressed,
Jesus, blessed Jesus;
He healeth the wounded, He giveth
rest,
Jesus, blessed Jesus;
When from loved ones we're called
to part,
When the tears in our anguish
Start,

None can comfort the breaking heart
Like Jesus, blessed Jesus.

3. He never forsakes in the darkest hour,
Jesus, blessed Jesus;
His arm is around us with keeping
pow'r,
Jesus, blessed Jesus;
When we enter the Shadow land,
When at Jordan we trembling stand,
He will meet us with outstretched
hand,
This Jesus, blessed Jesus.

4. What joy it will be when we see His
face,
Jesus, blessed Jesus;
Forever to sing of His love and grace,
Jesus, blessed Jesus:
There at home on that shining shore,
With the loved ones gone on before,
We will praise Him forevermore.
Our Jesus, blessed Jesus.

-Chas. H. Gabriel

1063

His Grace Is Enough For Me

1. Just when I am disheartened,
Just when with cares oppressed,
Just when my way is darkest,
Just when I am distressed
Then is my Saviour near me,
He knows my ev'ry care;
Jesus will never leave me,
He helps my burdens bear.

Chorus
His grace is enough for me, for me,
His grace is enough for me;
Thro' sorrow and pain, Thro" loss or
gain,
His grace is enough for me.

2. Just when my hopes have vanished,
Just when my friends forsake,
Just when the fight is thickest,

ENCOURAGEMENT

Just when with fear I shake
Then comes a still small whisper
"Fear not, my child, I'm near."
Jesus brings peace and comfort,
I love His voice to hear.

3. Just when my tears are flowing,
Just when with anguish bent,
Just when temptation's hardest,
Just when with sadness rent
Then comes a tho't of comfort:
"I know my Father knows,"
Jesus has grace sufficient
To conquer all my foes.
　　　　　　　　-J. Bruce Evans

1064

O Thou, In Whose Presence

1. O Thou, in whose presence my
soul takes delight,
On whom in affliction I call,
My comfort by day and my song in
the night.
My hope, my salvation my all!

2. Where dost Thou, dear Shepherd,
resort with thy sheep,
To feed them in pastures of love;
Say, why in the valley of death
should I weep.
Or alone in this wilderness rove?

3. Oh, why should I wander, an allien
from Thee,
Or cry in the desert for bread?
Thy foes will rejoice when my
sorrows they see.
And smile at the tears I have shed.

4. He looks! and the thousands of
angels rejoice,
And myriads wait for His word;
He speaks! and eternity filled with
His voice,
Re-echoes the praise of the Lord.

5. Dear Shepherd! I hear, and will
follow Thy call;
I know the sweet sound of Thy voice
Restore and defend me, for Thou art
my all,
And in Thee I will ever rejoice;
　　　　　　　　-Joseph Swain

1065

O Crown Of Rejoicing

1. O crown of rejoicing that's waiting
for me,
When finished my course, and when
Jesus I see.
And when from my Lord come the
sweet sounding word,
Receive faithful servant, the joy of
the Lord.

Chorus
O crown of rejoicing, O wonderful
song;
O joy everlasting, O glorified throng
O beautiful home, my home can it
be?
O glory reserved for me.

2. O wonderful song that in glory I'll
sing,
To Him who redeemed me to Jesus
my King;
All glory and honour to Him shall be
giv'n,
And praises unceasing forever in
Heav'n.

3. O joy everlasting when heaven is
won,
Forever in glory to shine as the sun
No sorrow nor sighing these all flee
away,
No night there, no shadows 'tis one
endless day.

4. O wonderful name which the
glorified bear,
The new name which Jesus

ENCOURAGEMENT

bestows on us there;
To him that o'er cometh "twill only
be giv'n,
Blest sign of approval, our welcome
to heav'n.

1066
The Lord Has Cleansed Me

1. The Lord has cleansed and washed
   me free.
   even from sins unknown to me.
   Great joy and gladness fill my soul,
   for soon I'll reach the heav'nly goal,
   There to behold glorious King,
   and songs of praise I'll ever sing.

2. A love. this world cannot perceive,
   from Christ my Lord I did receive.
   His spirit filled my thirsting soul,
   and brought me nearer to my goal,
   With overwhelming joy I sing,
   a hymn to my eternal King.

1067
There Is A Wondrous Ringing

1. There is a wondrous ringing
   as from a silver bell
   And in my heart it's singing.

   Chorus
   Tis well with me, yes it is well. Oh,
   melody from heaven thy sound
   forever may swell
   Sweet comfort hast Thou given;
   'Tis well with me, yes it is well.

2. It weaves a soft enchantment
   and casts a magic spell
   it fills me with contentment.

3. I feel the strong protection,
   It's more than words can tell
   If I stay in connection.

1068
El Nathan-C.M. with Refrain
ᐟ

1. I know not why God's wondrous
   grace
   To me He hath made known,
   Nor why, unworthy, Christ in love
   Redeemed me for His own.

   Chorus
   But "I know whom I have believed,
   And am persuaded that He is
   able
   To keep that which I've committed
   Unto Him against that day."

2. I know not how this saving faith
   To me He did impart,
   Nor how believing in His Word
   Wrought peace within my heart.

3. I know not how the Spirit moves,
   Convincing men of sin,
   Revealing Jesus through the Word,
   Creating faith in Him.

4. I know not what of good or ill
   May be reserved for me,
   Of weary ways or golden days
   Before His face I see.

5. I know not when my Lord may
   come,
   At night or noon day fair,
   Nor if I'll walk the vale with Him,
   Or "meet Him in the air."
                       -Daniel W. Whittle

1069
Through The Love Of God Our
Saviour - 8.4.8.4.8.8.8.4.

1. Through the love of God our
   Saviour,
   All wilt be well;
   Free and changeless is His favour,
   All, all is well:
   Precious is the blood that healed
   us;

ENCOURAGEMENT

Perfect is the grace that sealed us;
Strong the hand stretched forth to
shield us,
All must be well.

2 Though we pass through tribulation
All will be well;
Ours is such a full salvation,
All, all is well;
Happy still in God confiding;
Fruitful if in Christ abiding;
Holy through the Spirit's guiding;
All must be well.

3. We expect a bright tomorrow;
All will be well;
Faith can sing through days of
sorrow,
All, all is well:
On our Father's love relying,
Jesus every need supplying,
Or in living or in dying,
All must be well.

              -Mary Peters

1070

I Need Jesus

1. I need Jesus, my need I now
confess;
No one like Him in times of deep
distress;
I need Jesus, the need I gladly own:
Tho' some may bear their load
alone,
Yet I need Jesus.

Chorus
I need Jesus, I need Jesus,
I need Jesus ev'ry day!
Need Him in the sunshine hour,
Need Him when the storm clouds
low'r;
Ev'ry day along my way,
Yes, I need Jesus.

2. I need Jesus, I need a Friend like
Him,
A Friend to guide when paths of life
are dim,
I need Jesus, when foes my soul
assail:
Alone I know I can but fall,
So I need Jesus.

3. I need Jesus, I need Him to the end;
No one like Him He is the sinners'
Friend;
I need Jesus, no other friend will do;
So constant, kind, so strong, and
true,
Yes, I need Jesus.
              -G. O. Webster

1071

Beauty Por Ashes

1. I sing the love of God, my Father,
Whose Spirit abides within;
Who changes all my grief to
gladness,
And pardon me all my sin.
Tho' clouds may lower, dark and
dreary,
Yet He has promised to be near;
He gives me sunshine for my
shadow,
And "beauty for ashes," here.

Chorus
He gives me joy in place of sorrow;
He give free love that casts out
few,
He gives me sunshine for my
shadow,"
And beauty for ashes," here.

2. I sing the love of Christ, my
Saviour
Who suffered upon the tree;
That, in the secret of His presence,
My bondage might freedom be.

ENCOURAGEMENT

He comes "to bind the broken hearted;"
He comes the fainting soul to cheer;
He gives me "oil of joy" for mourning.
And "beauty for ashes." Here.

3. I sing the beauty of the Gospel
That carters not thorns, but flow'rs;
That bids me scatter smiles and sunbeams
Wherever are lonely hours.
The "garment of His praise" it offers
For "heaviness of spirit," dear;
It gives me sunshine for my shadow,
: And "beauty for ashes . here,
-J. G. Crabbe

1072
Master, the tempest is raging

1. Master, the tempest is raging!
The billows are tossing high!
The sky is o'er shadowed with blackness,
Nor shelter or help is nigh:
"Carest Thou not that we perish
How canst Thou lie asleep,
When each moment so madly is threat'ning
A grave in the angry deep?

Chorus
The winds and the waves shall obey My will,
Peace be still!
Whether the wrath of the storm toss'd sea,
Or demons, or men, or whatever it be,
No waters can swallow the ship where lies
The Master of ocean, and earth.
and skies,
They ail shall sweetly obey My will:
Peace be still! Peace be still!

They all shall sweetly obey My will:
Peace! peace be still!"

2. Master, with anguish of spirit I bow
in my grief today;
The depths of my sad heart are troubled;
Oh, waken and save. I pray!
Torrents of sin and of anguish
Sweep o'er my sinking soul;
And I perish! I perish! dear Master:
Oh hasten, and take control.

3. Master, the terror is over,
The elements sweetly rest;'
Earth's sun in the calm lake is mirrored
And heaven's within my breast;
Linger, O blessed Redeemer,
Leave me alone no more;
And with joy I shall make the blest harbour,
And rest on the blissful shore.
-Mary A. Baker

1073
Euphony - 8.8.8.8.8.8.

1. Now I have found the ground wherein
Surely my soul's anchor may remain.
The wounds of Jesus, for my sin
Before the world's foundation slain;
Whose mercy shall unshaken stay,
When heav'n and earth are fled
Away.

2. Father, Thine everlasting grace
Our scanty thought surpasses far,
Thy heart still melts with tenderness.
Thy arms of love still open are.
Returning sinners to receive.
That mercy they may taste and live.

3. O love, thou bottomless abyss,
My sins are swallowed up in Thee!
Covered is my unrighteousness,

ENCOURAGEMENT

Nor spot of guilt remains on me,
While Jesu's blood through earth
and skies
Mercy, free, boundless mercy,
cries.

4. With faith I plunge me in this sea,
Here is my hope, my joy, my rest;
Hither, when hell assails, I flee,
I look into my Saviour's breast;
Away, sad doubt, and anxious fear!
Mercy is all that's written there.

5. Though waves and storms go o'er
my head,
Though strength and health be
gone
Though joys be withered all and
dead
Though every comfort be with
drawn,
On this my steadfast soul relies,
Father, Thy mercy never dies.

6. Fixed on this ground will I remain,
Though my heart fail, and flesh
decay;
This anchor shall my soul sustain,
When earth's foundations melt
away;
Mercy's full power I then shall
prove,
Loved with an everlasting love.
                              -J. Wesley

1074

If God Be For Us -11.8.11.8. With Refrain

1. Rejoice in the Lord oh, tell His
mercy cheer;
He sunders the bands that enthrall;
Redeem'd by His blood why should
we ever fear
Since Jesus is our "all in all"?

Chorus
"If God be for us, if God be for us,
If God be for us,
Who can be against us? who?
Who? who?
Who can be against us, against
us?"

2. Be strong in the Lord' rejoicing in
His might,
Be loyal and true day by day;
When evils assail, be valiant for the
right,
And He will be our strength and
stay.

3. Confide in His word His promises
so sure;
In Christ they are "yea and amen";
Though earth pass away, they ever
shall endure,
'Tis written o'er and o'er again.

4. Abide in the Lord: secure in His
control,
'Tis life everlasting begun:
To pluck from His hand the
Weakest, trembling soul
It never, never cad be done!
                    -James McGranahan

1075

Hallelujah! tis done

1. Tis the promise of
God full salvation to give
Unto him who on Jesus,
His Son, will believe.

Chorus
Hallelujah! 'tis done, I believe on
the Son;
I am saved by the blood of the
Crucified One.
Hallelujah tis done. I believe on
the Son;
I am saved by the Blood of the
Crucified One.

2. Tho' the pathway be lonely and
dangerous too,
Surely Jesus is able
to carry me thro'.

ENCOURAGEMENT

3. Many loved ones have
I in yon heavenly throng,
They are safe now in glory,
and this is their song.

4. There are prophets and
kings in that throng I behold,
And they sing while they march
through
the streets of pure gold.

5. There's a part in that
chorus for you and for me,
And the theme of our praises
for ever will be:

-P. P. Bliss

1076

Jesus only-8.7.8.7.D.

1. What tho' clouds are hov'ring o'er
me,
And I seem to walk alone,
Longing,'mid my cares and
crosses,
For the joys that now are flown!
If I've Jesus,"Jesus only"
Then my sky will have a gem;
He's the Sun of brightest splendour,
And the star of Bethlehem.

2. What tho' all my earthly journey
Bringeth naught but weary hours;
And, in grasping for life's roses,
Thorns I find instead of flow'rs!
I've Jesus, "Jesus only,"
I possess a cluster rare;
He's the "Lily of the Valley,"
And the "Rose of Sharon" fair.

3. What though all my heart is yearning
For the loved of long agon
Bitter lessons sadly learning
From the shadowy page of woe!
If I've Jesus, "Jesus only,"
He'll be with me to the end;
And, unseen by mortal vision,
Angel bands will o'er me bend.

4. When I soar to realms of glory,
And an entrance I await,
If I whisper," Jesus only!"
Wide will open the pearly gate;
When I join the heavenly chorus,
And the angel hosts I see
Precious Jesus, "Jesus only,"
Will my theme of rapture be.
-Hattie M. Conrey

1077

Tryphena -8.8.8.

1. Why should I fear the darkest hour,
Or tremble at the tempter's power?
Jesus vouchsafes to be my Tower.

2. Though hot the flight, why quit the
field?
Why must I either flee or yield?
Since Jesus is my mighty Shield?

3. When creature comforts fade and
die,
Worldlings may weep, but why
should!?
Jesus still lives and stilt is nigh.

4. Though all the flocks and herds
were dead,
My soul a famine need not dread,
For Jesus is my living Bread.

5. I know not what may soon betide,
Or how my wants shall be supplied;
But Jesus knows and will provide.

6. Though sin would fill me with
distress,
The throne of grace I dare address,
For Jesus is my Righteousness.

7. Though faint my prayers and cold
my love,
My steadfast hope shall not remove
While Jesus intercedes above.

ENCOURAGEMENT

8. Against me earth and hell combine;
   But on my side is power Divine:
   Jesus is all, and He is mine.
   -J. Newton

1078

No, Never Alone

1. 'Fear not, I am with thee",
   I Blessed golden ray.
   Like a star of glory
   Lighting up my way!
   Thro' the clouds of midnight
   This bright promise shone;
   I will never leave thee,
   Never will leave thee alone.'

   Chorus
   No, never alone No, never alone;
   He promised never to leave me,
   Never to leave me alone No, never
   alone.
   No, never alone; He promised never
   to leave me
   Never to leave me alone.

2. Roses fade around me,
   Lilies bloom and die,
   Earthly sun beams vanish.
   Radiant still the sky! Jesus,
   Rose of Sharon,
   Blooming for His own,
   Jesus, heaven's sunshine.
   Never will leave me alone.

3. Steps unseen before me,
   Hidden dangers near;
   Nearer still my Saviour,
   Whispering; 'Be of cheer;
   Joys, like birds of spring time,
   To my heart have flown,
   Singing all so sweetly,
   'He will not leave me alone.'
   -E. E. Hewitt

1079

Casting all your Care upon Him -C.M.

1. How sweet, my Saviour, to repose
   On Thine almighty power!

To feel Thy strength upholding me,
Thro' ev'ry trying hour.

Chorus
"Casting all your cares upon Him,
Casting all your cares upon Him;
Casting all your cares upon Him
for He careth, He careth for you"

2. It is Thy will that I should cast
   My ev'ry care on Thee;
   To Thee refer each rising grief,
   Each new perplexity;

3. That I should trust Thy loving care
   And look to Thee alone,
   To calm each troubled thought to
   rest,
   In prayer before Thy throne.

4. Why should my heart then be
   distrest.
   By dread of future ill?
   Or why should unbelieving fear
   My trembling spirit fill?
   -Caesar Malan, D. D.

1080

I Know that Jesus ever Lives -L.M.

1. I know that Jesus ever lives,
   And has prepared a place for me;
   And crowns of victory He gives
   To those who would His children be!

   Chorus
   Then ask me not to linger long,
   Amid the gay and thoughtless
   throng;
   For I am only waiting here
   To hear the summons: "Child, come
   home!"

2. I'm trusting Jesus Christ for all,
   I know His blood now speaks for me
   I'm listening for the welcome call.
   To say:" The Master waiteth thee!"

ENCOURAGEMENT

3. I'm now enraptured with the thought
   I stand and wonder at His love
   That He from heaven to earth was
   brought
   To die, that I might live above.

4. I know that Jesus soon will come;
   I know the time will not be long,
   Till I shall reach my heavenly home,
   And join the everlasting song.
   -Ira D. Sankey

1081

O Brother, Life's Journey Beginning

1. O brother, life's journey beginning,
   With courage and firmness arise!
   Look well to the course thou art
   choosing;
   Be earnest, be watchful, and wise!
   Remember two paths are before
   thee,
   And both thy attention invite;
   But one leadeth on to destruction.
   The other to joy and delight.

   Chorus
   God help you to follow His banner,
   And serve Him wherever you go;
   And when you are tempted, my
   brother,
   God give you the grace to say "No!"

2. O brother, yield not to the tempter,
   No matter what others may do:
   Stand firm in the strength of the
   Master.
   Be loyal, be faithful, and true?
   Each trial will make you the
   stronger.
   If you, in the name of the Lord.
   Fight manfully under your Leader,
   Obeying the voice of His word.

3. O brother, the Saviour is calling!
   Beware of the danger of sin:

Resist not the voice of the Spirit,
That whispers so gently within.
God calls you to enter His service
To live for Him here. day to day;
And share by and by in the glory
That never shall vanish away.
-I. D. Sankey

1082

Able to Deliver

1. O troubled heart,, be thou not afraid.
   In the Lord thy God let thy hope be
   stay'd;
   He will hear thy cry and will give
   thee aid,
   Whate'er thy cross may be.

   Chorus
   He is able still to deliver thee.
   And His own right hand thy defence
   shall be.
   He is able still to deliver thee,
   Then be thou not afraid.

2. O troubled heart, tho' thy foes unite
   Let thy faith be strong and thy
   armour bright:
   Thou shalt over come thro' His
   power and might,
   And more than conq'ror be.

3. O troubled heart, when thy way is
   drear,
   He will rescue thee and dispel thy
   fear:
   In thy greatest need He is always
   near
   To Him all glory be!
   -F. J. Crosby

1083

Joy Cometh in the Morning

1. Oh, weary pilgrim, lift your head:
   For joy cometh in the morning'

ENCOURAGEMENT

For God in His own Word hath said
That joy cometh in the morning!

Chorus
Joy cometh in the morning!
Joy cometh m the morning!
Weeping may endure for a night;
But joy cometh in the morning!

2. Ye trembling saints, dismiss your
fears;
For joy cometh in the morning!
Oh, weary mourner, dry your tears:
For joy cometh in the morning!

3. Rejoice! the night will soon be gone:
For joy cometh in the morning!
And then shall come the glorious
dawn:
For joy cometh in the morning!

4. Oh, may we all be glad today!
For joy cometh in the morning!
Our God shall wipe all tears away:
For joy cometh in the morning!
-M. M. Wienland

1084

Rest In the Lord

1. Rest in the Lord, O weary, heavy
laden'
Look unto Him your ever present
Guide;
Rest in the Lord, whose Word is
truth eternal;
Leave all to Him, whatever may
betide.

2. Rest in the Lord, and tell Him all
your sorrow;
Trust in His love, so boundless, full,
and free;
He will not leave, nor will He e'er
for sake you;
Rest in the Lord, and sweet your
rest shall be.

3 Rest in the Lord, and when your toil
is over
When ev'ry storm and danger, you
have pass'd
Lo! He has said whose Word
abideth ever,
You shall receive His welcome
home at last
-F. J. Crosby

1085

Redhead-4.7.7.7.

1. When our heads are bowed with
woe;
When our bitter tears o'er flow,
When we mourn the lost, the dear
Jesus, Son of David, hear!

2. Thou our feeble flesh hast worn;
Thou our mortal griefs hast borne;
Thou hast shed the human tear;
Jesus, Son of David, hear!

3. When the heart is sad within,
With the thought of all its sin;
When the spirit shrinks with fear,
Jesus, son of David, hear!

4. Thou the shame, the grief, hast
Known;
Though the sins were not Thine own
Thou hast designed their load to
hear;
Jesus, Son of David, hear!

5. When our eyes grow dim in death
When we have the parting breath
When our solemn doom is near
Jesus, Son of David, hear!

6. Thou hast bowed the dying head;
Thou the blood of life hast shed;
Thou hast filled a mortal bier;
Jesus, Son of David, hear!
-H. H. Milman D. D.

ENCOURAGEMENT

1086
Jesus Understands

1. Bow'd beneath your burden, is
there none to share?
Weary with the journey, is there
none to care?
Courage, way worn trav'ler, heed
your Lord's commands,
There's to cheer you, Jesus
understand.

Chorus
Yes, he understands, All his ways are
best.
Hear. he calls to you, "Come to me
and rest,"
Leave the unknown future in the
Master hand,
Whether sad or joyful, Jesus
understands,

2. Ev'ry heavy burden he will gladly
share,
Are you sad and weary?" Jesus
has a care;
Well he knows the path way o'er
life's burning sands,
Courage, fainting pilgrim, Jesus
understands.

3. Tho' temptation meet you, Jesus
can sustain,
Life has vexing problem which He
can explain;
Serve him where he sends you
though in distant lands,
Do not doubt or question, Jesus
understands.   .

4. Weary heart, he calls you, "Come
to me and rest,"
Does the path grow rugged? yet his
way is best;
Leave the unknown future in the
Master's hands,
Whether sad or joyful, Jesus
understands.
                           -Birdle Bell

1087
Trust

1. All that our Saviour hath spoken
Came from the heart of God;
Surely it cannot be broken,
Seal'd with His precious blood.

Chorus
Tempests may rage and thunder,
Mountains be rent asunder,
Nations may fear and wonder .
Trust, and be undismay'd.

2. As unto Abram was given
God's cov'nant word of peace,
"Counting the stars" of the even
So shall thy faith increase.

3. Trust when the light warm and
tender
Seemeth to thee withdrawn.
Wait a few hours, and in splendour
Morning again will dawn!

4. When in the fires of affliction;
Fully in Him confide;
Jesus will speak benediction,
Walking His saint beside

|5. Trust! tho all others forsake thee,
Yet there remains one Friend;
Mercy and truth shall o'er take thee
Down to thy journey's end;

6. Trust under ev'ry condition
Till thou shalt reach thy home;
Trust, till in perfection
That which is real hath come.
                           -Thoro Harris

1088
His Promise to me

1. Darkness may o'er take me and my
song forsake me,

But alone I never shall be:
For the friend beside me promised
He would guild me
And will keep His promise to me.

Chorus
He will keep His promise to me.
All the way with me He will go;
He has never broken any promise spoken;
He will keep His promise, I know.

2. Should misfortune meet me, friends may fail to greet me,
But if true to Jesus I stay
He will still uphold me. let His love enfold me
Ev'ry dreary mile of the way.

3. How the tho't enthralls me, that whate'er befalls me
One will always love me the same;
Not a trial ever causes Him to sever
From the ones who honour His name.

- James Rowe

1089
The Sheltering rock

1. There is a Rock in a weary land,
Its shadow fails on the burning sand,
Inviting pilgrims as they pass,
To seek a shade in the wilderness.

Chorus
Then why will ye die?
O why will ye die?
When the Shelt'ring Rock is so near by,
O why will ye die?

2. There is a Well in a desert plain,
Its waters call with entreating strain,
"Ho, ev'ry thirsting, sin sick soul.
Come, freely drink, and thou shalt be whole."

3. A great fold stands with its portals wide,
The sheep astray on the mountain side;
The Shepherd climbs o'er Mountains steep;
He's searching now for His wandr'ing sheep.

4. There is a cross where the saviour died
His blood flowed out in a crimson tide
A sacrifice for sins of men,
And free to all who will enter in
-Rev. W. E. Penn

1090
Jesus answers prayer

1. Plead the precious promises of Jesus,
Cast upon Him all your anxious care,
Call upon Him and He will deliver
For Jesus answers prayer.

Chorus
Jesus answers prayer, Jesus , answers prayer,
Cast on Him your burden, roll on Him your care:
Plead His word of love and His promise prove,
For Jesus answers prayer.

2. When the storm and stress of life surround you,
And the load seems more than you can bear,
Go to Him for aid and He will help 'you,
For Jesus answers prayer.

3. When perplexing problems you are facing.
And the path seems rugged ev'rywhere,
Look to Jesus, he will safely guide you
For Jesus answers prayer.

ENCOURAGEMENT

4. Matters not what sorrows may
enfold you,
There is One who can your heart
aches share;
Go to Him whatever may befall you,
For Jesus answers prayer.
-Richard Hainsworth

1091
The Peace That Jesus Gives

1. Like the sunshine after rain,
Like a rest that follows pain;
Like a hope returned again,
Is the peace that Jesus gives.

Chorus
Oh, the peace that Jesus gives
Never dies, it always lives;
Like the music of a psalm,
Like a glad, eternal calm
Is the peace that Jesus gives,
Is the peace that Jesus gives.

2. Like the soft, refreshing dew,
Like a rosy daybreak new,
Like a friendship tender, true,
Is the peace that Jesus gives.

3. Like a river deep and long,
With its current, ceaseless, strong,
Like the cadence of a song,
Is the peace that Jesus gives
-Haldor Lillenas

1092
Breslau-LM.

1. Take up thy cross, the Saviour
said,
If thou wouldst my disciple be;
Deny thyself, the world forsake.
And humbly follow after me.

2. Take up thy cross; let not its weight
Fill thy week spirit with alarm;
His strength shall bear thy spirit up,
And brace thy heart, and nerve thine
Arm.

3. Take up thy cross, nor heed the
shame,
Nor let thy foolish pride rebel;
The Lord for thee the Cross
endured.
To save thy soul from death and hell.

4. Take up thy cross then in his
strength.
And calmly every danger brave;
Twill guide thee to a better home.
And lead to victory o'er the grave.

5. Take up thy cross, and follow Christ
Nor think till death to lay it down;
For only he who bear the cross
May hope to wear the glorious
crown.

6. To thee, great Lord, the One in
Three,
All praise for evermore ascend;
O grant us in our Home to see
The heavenly life that knows no end
-C. W. Everest

1093
Morgenglanz der Ewigkeit - 7.7.7.3.

1. 'Christian, seek not yet repose,'
Hear thy guardian Angel say;
Thou art in the midst of foes:
Watch and pray!"

2. Principalities and powers.
Mustering their unseen array,
Wait for thy unguarded hours:
Watch and pray!

3. Gird thy heavenly armour on,
Wear it ever, night and day;
Ambushed lies the evil one:
Watch and pray!

4. Hear the victors who o'er come;
   Still they mark each warrior's way,
   All with one sweet voice exclaim:
   Watch and pray!'

5. Hear, above all, hear thy Lord,
   Him thou lovest to obey;
   Hide within thy heart his word:
   Watch and pray!'

6. Watch as if on that alone
   Hung the issue of the day;
   Pray, that help may be sent down:
   Watch and pray!'
   -Charlotte Elliott

1094

Surrey-8.8.8.8.8.8.

1. The Lord my pasture shall prepare,
   And feed me with a shepherd's care;
   His presence shall my wants supply,
   And guard me with a watchful eye;
   My noonday walks he shall attend,
   And all my midnight hours defend.

2. When to the sultry globe I faint,
   Or on the thirsty mountain pant,
   To fertile vales and dewy meads
   My weary wandering steps he leads,
   Where peaceful rivers, soft and slow,
   Amid the verdant landscape flow,

3. Though in a bare and rugged way
   Through devious lonely wilds I stray,
   Thy bounty shall my pains beguile;
   The barren wilderness shall smile
   With sudden greens and herbage crowned,
   And streams shall murmur all Around.

4. Trough in the paths of death I tread,
   With gloomy horrors overspread
   My steadfast heart shall fear no ill,
   For thou, O Lord, art with me still:
   Thy friendly crook shall give me aid
   And guide me through the dreadful shade.
   -J. Abdison

1095

He Giveth More Grace - Irregular meter

1. He giveth more grace when the burden grows greater;
   He sendeth more strength when the labor increase.
   To added affliction He addeth His mercy;
   To multiplied trials, His multiplies peace.

Chorus
His love has no limit; His grace has no measure;
His pow'r has no boundary known unto men.
For out of His infinite riches in Jesus,
He giveth, and giveth, and giveth again!

2. When we have exhausted our store of endurance.
   When our strength has failed ere the day is half done,
   When we reach the end of our hoarded resources,
   Our Father's full giving is only begun.
   -Annie Johnson Flint

ENCOURAGEMENT

1096
Consolator -11.10.11.10.

1. Come, ye disconsolate, where'er ye
   languish;
   Come to the mercy seat, fervently
   kneel;
   Here bring your wounded hearts,
   here tell your anguish;
   Earth has no sorrow that heav'n can
   not heal.

2. Joy of the desolate, Light of the
   straying,
   Hope of the penitent, fadeless and
   pure,
   Here speaks the comforter, tenderly
   saying.
   "Earth has no sorrow that heav'n
   cannot cure."

3. Here see the Bread of Life; see
   waters flowing,
   Forth from the throne of God, pure
   from above;
   Come to the feast of love; come,
   ever knowing
   Earth has no sorrow but heav'n can
   remove.
   -Thomas Moore

1097
All Your Anxiety - Irregular

1. Is there a heart o'er bound by
   sorrow?
   Is there a life weighed down by
   care?
   Come to the cross each burden
   bearing,
   All your anxiety leave it there.

Chorus
All your anxiety, all your care,
Bring to the mercy seat leave it
There;

Never a burden He cannot bear.
Never a friend like Jesus!

2. No other friend so keen to help you,
   No other friend so quick to hear,
   No other place to leave your
   burden,
   No other one to hear your power.

3. Come then at once delay no longer!
   Heed His entreaty kind and sweet:
   You need not fear a disappointment
   You shall find peace at the mercy
   seat.
   -Edward Henry Joy

1098
St. Anne-C.M.

1. O God. our help in ages past,
   Our hope for years to come,
   Our shelter from the stormy blast,
   And our eternal home!

2. Under the shadow of Thy throne
   Thy saints have dwelt secure;
   Sufficient is Thine arm alone,
   And our defense is sure.

3. Before the hills in order stood,
   Or earth received her frame,
   From everlasting Thou art God,
   To endless years the same.

4. A thousand ages in Thy sight
   Are like an evening gone;
   Short as the watch that ends the
   night
   Before the rising sun.

5. Time, like an ever rolling stream,
   Bears all its sons away;
   They fly, forgotten, as a dream
   Dies at the op'ning day.

6. O God, our help in ages past,
   Our hope for years to come.
   Be Thou our guard while life shall
   last,
   And our eternal home.
   -Isaac Watts

ENCOURAGEMENT

1099
Balm in Gilead - Irregular

Chorus
There is a balm in Gilead
to make the wounded whole;
There is balm in Gilead
to heal the sin sick soul.

1. Sometimes I feel discouraged,
And think my work's in vain.
But then the Holy Spirit
Revives my soul again.

2. If you cannot preach like Peter,
If you cannot pray like Paul,
You can tell the love of Jesus,
And say; "He died for all."
-Traditional Spiritual

1100
God cares - C.M. with Refrain

1. Be not dismayed whate'er betide,
God will take care of you;
Beneath His wings of love abide,
God will take care of you.

Chorus
God will take care of you,
Thro' every day, o'er all the way;
He will take care of you,
God will take care of you,

2. Thro' days of toil when heart doth fail.
God will take care of you;
When dangers fierce your path assail,
God will take care of you.

3. All you may need He will provide,
God will take care of you;
Nothing you ask will be denied,
God will take care of you.

No matter what may be the test,
God will take care of you;
Lean, weary one, upon His breast,
God will take care of you.
-Civilla D. Martin

1101
Dwelling In Beulah land

1. Far away the noise of strife upon
my ear is falling,
Then I know the sins of earth beset
on ev'ry hand:
Doubt and fear and things of earth
in vain to me are calling,
None of these shall move me from
Beulah Land.

Chorus
I'm living on the mountain,
underneath a cloudless sky,
I'm drinking at the fountain that
never shall run dry;
Oh, yes? I'm feasting
on the manna from a bountiful
supply.
For I am dwelling in Beulah Land.

2. Far below the storm of doubt upon
the world is beating,
Sons of men in battle long the
enemy withstand:
Safe am I within the castle of God's
Word retreating,
Nothing then can reach me, 'tis
Beulah Land.

3. Let the stormy breezes blow, their
cry cannot alarm me;
I am safely sheltered here,
protected by God's hand:
Here the sun is always shining,
here there's naught can harm me,
I am safe forever in Beulah Land.

ENCOURAGEMENT

4. Viewing here the works of God, I
   sink in contemplation
   Hearing now His blessed voice, I
   see the way He planned:
   Dwelling in the Spirit here I learn of
   full salvation,
   Gladly will I tarry in Beulah Land.
   -C. Austin Mites

1102

I'm Living In His Love

1. He did not come to spare all the
   woes of life,
   Or bear me upon flow'ry of ease,
   He does not shield my ears from
   cries of pain and strife,
   Nor hide my eyes from scenes that
   may displease,
   But sure am I His pow'r has form'd
   this world I see,
   And stronger still His mighty love for
   me;
   So without fear I'm living in that love
   each day;
   My God will take me thru the
   storms, let come what may.

2. I cannot tell what lies beyond the
   towring range.
   Or what the distant valley holds for
   me,
   My path ways lead throgh lands
   ·and waters cold and strange,
   Tomorrow comes, but has no
   guarantee.
   But sure am I His pow'r has fom'd
   this world I see,
   And stronger still His saving grace
   for me;
   So without fear Im living in God's
   love each day.
   My God will take me thru the
   storms, let come what may.
   -Ralph Carmichael

1103

If Your Heart Keeps Right

1. If the dark shadows gather As you
   go along,
   Do not grieve for their coming, Sing
   a cheery song,
   There is joy for the taking, it will
   soon be light.
   Ev'ry cloud wears a rainbow If your
   heart keeps right.

Chorus
If your heart keeps right, If your
heart keeps right.
There's a song of gladness in the
darkest night;
If your heart keeps right, If your
heart keeps right,
Ev'ry cloud will wear a rainbow.
If your heart keeps right.

2. Is your life just a tangle Full of toil
   and care?
   Smile a bit as you Journey, Others'
   burdens share;
   You'll forget all your troubles,
   Making their lives bright,
   Skies will grow blue and sunny
   If your heart keeps right.

3. There are blosoms of gladness
   'Neath the winter's snow,
   From the gloom and the darkness
   Comes the morning's glow;
   Never give up the battle, You will
   win the fight,
   Gain the rest of the Victor If your
   heart keeps right.
   -Lizzie De Armond

1104

Turn Your Eyes Upon Jesus

1. O soul, are you weary and,
   troubled?

No light in the darkness you see?
There's light for a look at the
Saviour,
And life more abundant and free!

Chorus
Turn your eyes upon Jesus,
Look full in His wonderful face;
And the things of earth will grow
strangely dim
In the light of His glory and grace.

2. Through death into life everlasting
He passed, and we follow Him there;
Over us sin no more hath dominion,
For more than conqu'rors we are!

3. His word shall not fail you He
promised;
Believe Him and all will be well:
Then go to a world that is dying,
His perfect salvation to tell!
-Helen H. Lemmel

1105

No Not One 10.6.10.6. with Refrain

1. There's not a friend like the lowly
Jesus,
No, not one! No, not one!
None else could heal all our soul's
disease,
No, not one! No, not one!

Chorus
Jesus knows all about our
struggles.
He will guide till the day is done;
There's not a friend like the lowly
Jesus
No, not one! No, not one!

2. No friend like Him is so high and
holy:
No, not one! No, not one!
And yet no friend is so meek and
lowly,
No, not one! No, not one!

3. There's not an hour that He is not
near us,
No, not one! No, not one!
No night so dark but His love can
cheer us,
No, not one! No, not one!

4. Did ever saint find this Friend
forsake him?
No, not one! No, not one!
Or sinner find that He would not
take him?
No, not one! No, not one!

5. Was e'er a gift like the Saviour
given?
No, not one! No, not one!
Will He refuse us a home in
heaven?
No, not one! No, not one!
-Johnson Oatman, Jr.

1106

Maitland

I. Must Jesus bear the cross alone,
And all the world go free?
No, there's a cross for ev'ry one,
And there's a cross for me.

2. The consecrated cross I'll bear,
Till death shall set me free,
And then go home my crown to
wear,
For there's a crown for me.

3. Upon the crystal pavement, down
At Jesus pierced feet,
Joyful, I'll cast my golden crown,
And His dear name repeat.

4. Oh! precious cross! Oh! glorious
crown! '
Oh! resurrection day!
Ye angels, from the stars come
down,
And bear my soul away.
-Thomas Shepherd

ENCOURAGEMENT

1107

His Eye Is On The Sparrow

1. Why should I feel discouraged,
Why should the shadows come,
Why should my heart be lonely
And long for Heav'n and home
When Jesus is my portion?
My constant friend is He:
His eye is on the sparrow,
And I know He watches me;
His eye is on the sparrow,
And I know He watches me.

Chorus
I sing because I'm happy,
I sing because I'm free,
For His eye is on the sparrow,
And I know He watches me.

2. "Let not your heart be troubled,"
His tender word I hear,
And resting on His goodness
I lose my doubt and fears;
Tho' by the path He leadeth
But one step I may see:
His eye is on the sparrow,
And I know He watches me;
His eye is on the sparrow,
And I know He watches me.

3. Whenever I am tempted,
Whenever clouds arise,
When songs give place to sighing
When hope within me dies,
I draw the closer to Him,
From care He sets, me free;
His eye is on the sparrow,
And I know He cares for me;
His eye is on the sparrow,
And I know He cares for me.
                    -Mrs. L. D. Martins

1108

Austrian hymn 8.7.8.7.D.

1. Glorious things of thee are spoken,
'Zion, city of our God;
He whose word can not be broken

Formed thee for His own abode
On the Rock of Ages founded,
What can shake thy sure repose?
With salvation's walls surrounded,
Thou mayst smile at all thy foes.

2. See, the streams of living waters,
Springing from eternal Love,
Well supply thy sons and daughters,
And all fear of want remove.
Who can faint while such a river
Ever flows their thirst to assuage?
Grace which, like the Lord, the Giver,
Never fails from age to age!

3. Round each habitation hovering,
See the cloud and fire appear
For a glory and a covering,
Showing that the Lord is near!
Thus deriving from their banner
Light by night and shade by day,
Safe they feed upon the manna
Which He gives them when they pray.
                    -John Newton

1109

Never Alone

1. I've seen the lightning flashing
And heard the thunder roll,
I've fell sin's breakers dashing,
Which tried to conquer my soul;
I've heard the voice of my Saviour,
He bid me still fight on
He promised never to leave me,
Never to leave me alone.

Chorus
No, never alone, No, never alone
He promised never to leave me,
Never to leave me alone;
No, never alone. No, never alone
He promised never to leave me,
Never to leave me alone.,

ENCOURAGEMENT

2. The world's fierce winds are blowing
   Temptation's sharp and keen;
   I have a peace in knowing
   My Saviour stands between;
   He stands to shield me from danger
   When all my friends are gone
   He promised never to leave me.
   Never to leave me alone.

3. When in affliction's valley
   I tread the road of care.
   My Saviour helps me carry
   The cross so heavy to bear;
   Tho all around me is darkness
   And earthly joys are flown,
   My Saviour whispers His promise
   Never to leave me alone.

4. He died on Calv'ry mountain,
   For me they pierced His side.
   For me He opened that fountain,
   The crimson, cleansing tide;
   For me He's waiting in glory
   Upon His heav'nly throne
   He promised never to leave me,
   Never to leave me alone,

   -Uknown

1110
Is My Name Written There

1. Lord, I care not for riches,
   neither silver nor gold
   I would make sure of heaven,
   I would enter the fold,
   In the book of Thy kingdom
   with its pages so fair,
   Tell me Jesus, my Saviour,
   is my name written there?

Chorus
Is my name written there
On the page white and fair?
In the book of Thy kingdom,
Is my name written there?

2. Lord, my sins they are many,
   like the sands of the sea,
   But Thy blood, O my Saviour,
   is sufficient for me;
   For Thy promise is written
   in bright letters that glow,
   "Tho your sins be as scarlet,
   I will make them like snow."

3. O that beautiful city ;
   with its mansions of light,
   With its glorified beings
   in pure garments of white;
   Where no evil thing cometh
   to despoil what is fair,
   Where the angels are watching
   yes, my name's written there.

v. 3 Chorus
Yes, my name's written there
On the page white and fair;
In the book of Thy kingdom,
Yes, my name's written there!

   -Mary A. Kidder

1111
Just When I Need Him Most

1. Just when I need Him Jesus is
   near.
   Just when I fatter, just when I fear;
   Ready to help me, ready to cheer,
   Just when I need Him most.

Chorus
Just when I need Him most,
Just when I need Him most,
Jesus is near to comfort and cheer,
Just when I need Him most.

2. Just when I need Him Jesus is true.
   Never forsaking all the way through;
   Giving for burdens Pleasures anew,
   Just when I need Him most

3. Just when I need Him Jesus is
strong,
Bearing my burdens all the day
long;
For all my sorrow giving a song,
Just when I need Him most.

4. Just when I need Him He is my all,
Answering when upon Him I call;
Tenderly watching lest I should fall,
Just when I need Him most.
                    -William C. Poole

1112

Let us Hear you Tell it

1. O brother, have you told how the
Lord forgave?"
Let us hear you tell it over once again
Thy coming to the cross where He
died to save,
Let us hear you tell it over once again
Are you walking now in His blessed
light?
Are you cleansed from ev'ry guilty
stain? ,
Is He your joy by day and your
song by night?
Let us hear you tell it over once again.

Chorus .
Let us hear you tell it over,
tell it over once again;
Tell the sweet and blessed story,
It will help you on to glory
Let us hear you tell it over once again.

2.When toiling up the way was the
Saviour there?
Let us hear you tell it over once again;
Did Jesus bear you up in His tender
care?
Let us hear you tell it over once again.
Never have you found such a friend
as He,
Who can help you 'midst the toil
and pain;
Oh all the world should hear what
He's done for thee;
Let us hear you tell it over once again.

3. Was ever on your tongue such a
blessed theme?
Let us hear you tell it over once again;
Tis ever sweeter far than the sweetest
dream
Let us hear you tell it over once again.
There are aching hearts in the
world's great throng,
Who have sought for rest, and all in
vain;
Hold Jesus up to them by your word
and song;
Let us hear you tell it over once again.

4. The battles you have fought and the
victories won.
Let us hear you tell it over once again;
'Twill help them on the way who
have just begun
Let us hear you tell it over once again.
We are striving now with the hosts of
sin,
Soon with Christ our Saviour we
shall reigns
Ye ransomed of the Lord, try a soul
to win;
Let us hear you tell it over once again.
                    -J. M. Whyte

1113

As pants the hart for cooling Streams
- C.M.

1. As pants the hart for cooling streams,
When heated in the chase,
So longs my souls, O God, for
Thee,
And Thy refresing grace.

2. For Thee, my God, the living God,
My thirsty soul doth pine;
O when shall I behold Thy face,
Thou Majesty divine!

3. Why restless, why cast down, my
soul!
Trust God, who will employ,

His aid for thee and change these sighs
To thankful hymns of joy.

4. God of my strength, how long shall
Like one forgotten, mourn!
Forlorn, forsaken, and exposed
To my oppressor's scorn.

5. Why restless, why cast down, my soul!
Hope still, and thou shalt sing
The praise of Him who is thy God,
Thy health's eternal spring;

1114

Lord, Shall Thy Children Come To Thee - 8.8.8.8.8.8.

1. Lord; shall Thy children come to Thee!
A boon of love divine we seek:
Brought to Thine arms in infancy,
Ere heart could feel, or tongue could speak,
Thy children pray for grace, that they
May come themselves to Thee to-day.

2. Lord, shall we come? and come again,
Oft as we see your table spread,
And, tokens of thy dying pain,
The wine pour'd out, the broken bread?
Bless, bless, O Lord, Thy children's prayer,
That they may come and find Thee there.

3. Lord, shall we come? not thus alone
At holy time, or solemn rite,
But every hour till life be flown,
Through weal or woe, in gloom or light,
Come to Thy throne of grace, that we
In faith, hope, love, confirm'd may Be

4. Lord, shall we come? Come yet again?
Thy children ask one blessing more;.
To come, not now alone; - but then
When life, and death, and time are o'er,
Then, then to come, O Lord, and be
Confirm'd in heaven, confirm'd by Thee.

1115

My Stubborn Will At Last Hath yielded

1. My stubborn will at last hath yielded
I would be Thine and Thine alone;
And this the prayer my lips are bringing
Lord, let in me Thy will be done.

Chorus
Sweet will of God, still fold me closer,
Till I am wholly lost in Thee:
Sweet will of God, still fold me closer,
Till I am wholly lost in Thee.

2. I'm tired of sin, footsore and weary,
The darksome path hath dreary grown,
But now a light has ris'n to cheer me!
I find in Thee my Star, my Sun.

3. Thy precious will, O conqu'ring Saviour
Doth now embrace and compass me;
All discords hushed, my peace a river,
My soul, a prisoned bird set free.

4. Shut in with Thee, O Lord, for ever,
My wayward feet no more to roam;
What power from Thee my soul can sever?
The centre of God's will my home.

ENCOURAGEMENT

1116

O Jesus Shepherd Thou Art
8.7.8.7.

1. O Jesus Shepherd Thou art
Then, fear and distrust remove
From the lion and the wild bear
And from wild and evil beasts
Jesus will guard His lonely sheep
Jesus will care for His own.

2. Satan nearly over powered me
Jesus said "this is my sheep"
He died in order to save me
Jesus what great love is this?
With Jesus, victory is sure
There's nought Him can overcome.

3. He lead me in the way of Life,
Near the gently flowing stream,
He makes me rest in green
pastures
Where poisonous weeds do not
grow
There I hear the voice of Jesus
There he makes my heart rejoice.

4. When I walk the valley of death
And there's fear along my way
I shall not fear any evil
For my Shepherd is so near,
His rod and staff they comfort me
For they make His sheep rejoice.

1117

The Lord Hath Declared And The
Will Perform

1. The Lord hath declared and the
Lord will perform;
"Behold! I am near to deliver
A refuge and fortress, a covert in
storm
He keepth His promise forever,

Chorus
For ever! for ever! Oh, not for a
day!
He keepeth His promise for ever!
To all who believe, to all who obey,
He keepeth His promise for ever!

2. Who seek Him shall find Him, shall
find Him today,
The word is to all. "whosoever"!
No soul that entreateth He turneth
away;
He keepeth His promise for ever.

3. Though often my toil seems but
labour in vain.
I leave with The Lord my
endeavour!
I patiently wait for the sunshine
and rain.
He keepeth His promise forever.

4. The bonds that unite us in earth's
dearest ties.
The rude hand of Time will dissever
But we shall renew them again in
the skies,
He keepeth His promise for ever.

1118

Thou Hast Snapped My Fetters -
11.11.11,11.

1. Thou hast snapped my fetters;
Thou hast made me
Liberty and gladness, I have found
in Thee;
Liberty from bondage, from my
weary load, free,
Satan's slave no longer now a child
of God.

Chorus
I am Thine, Lord Jesus, Ever Thine,
Thine I am,
And my heart is singing, Glory to
the Lamb,

2. Living in the sunshine, shining in
Thy light,
Fighting as Thy soldier, mighty in
Thy might;

ENCOURAGEMENT

Going on Thy mission, pointing men to Thee,
Telling of the Saviour who can set them free.

3. Such the life, Lord Jesus, I would ever live.
Such the grateful tribute I would ever give;
Witnessing for Thee, Lord, everywhere I go.
Of the Blood that cleanseth, washing white as snow.

4. And when life is ended, when the vict'ry's won,
When I hear from Thee, Lord the glad words. "Well done."
With what joy and rapture shall I sing of Thee.
Who from sin's dark chains didst set my spirit free!

1119
Thine. Thine For Ever Blessed Bond-C.M.

1. Thine-thine for ever" blessed bond
That knits, us, Lord, to Thee;
May voice, and heart, and soul respond
Amen, so let it be.

2. When this world strikes its dulcet harp,
And earth our heaven appears,
Be Thine for ever, "clear and sharp,
God's trumpet in our ears.

3. When sin in pleasure's soft disguise
Would work us deadliest harm,
May Thine for ever" from the skies
Steal down and break the charm.

4. When Satan flings his fiery darts
Against our weary shield,
May Thine for ever" in our hearts
Forbid us faint or yield.

5. Thine all along the flowery Spring,
Along the summer prime,

Till autumn fades in welcoming
The silver frost of time.

6. "Thine, Thine for every, "body, soul
Henceforth devote to Thee,
While everlasting ages roll;
Amen, so let it be.

1120
There's A Peace In My Heart That The World Never Gave

1. There's a peace in my heart that the world never gave
A peace it can not take away:
Though the trial of life may Surround like a cloud.
I've a peace that has come there to Stay.

Chorus
Constantly abiding Jesus is mine:
Constantly abiding rapture divine:
He never leaves me lonely whispers, O so kind:
"I will never leave thee, Jesus is mine.

2. All the world seemed to sing of a Saviour and King
When peace sweetly came to my heart:
Troubles all fled away and my night turned to day
Blessed Jesus, how glorious Thou art!

3. This treasure I have in a temple of clay.
While here on His footstool I roam;
But He's coming to take me some glorious day,
Over there to my heavenly home!

OVERCOMING TRIALS AND TEMPTATION

1121

What Though Clouds Are Novering O'er Me - 8.7.8.7.D.

1. What though clouds are novering
   o'er me.
   And I seem to walk alone,
   Longing, 'mid my cares and crosses,
   For the joys that now are flown!
   If I've Jesus, "Jesus only,"
   Then my sky will have a gem;
   He's the Sun of brightest splendour
   And the star of Bethlehem.

2. What though all my earthly journey
   Bringeth naught but weary hours;
   And, in grasping for life's roses,
   Thorns I find instead of flow'rs!
   If I've Jesus, "Jesus only,"
   I possess a cluster rare;
   He's the "Lily of the Valley,"
   And the "Rose of Sharon" fair.

3. What though all my heart is
   yearning
   For the loved of long ago,
   Bitter lessons sadly learning
   From the shadowy page of woe!
   If I've Jesus, "Jesus only,"
   He'll be with me to the end;
   And, unseen by mortal vision,
   Angel bands will o'er me bend.

4. When I soar to realms of glory,
   And an entrance I await,
   If I whisper, "Jesus only!"
   Wide will open the pearly gate;
   When I join the heavenly chorus,
   And the angel hosts I see,
   Precious Jesus, "Jesus only.'
   Will my theme of rapture be

1122

Why Should I Charge My Soul With Care

1. Why should I charge my soul with
   care?
   The wealth in every mine.
   Belongs to Christ, God's Son and
   Heir,
   And He's a Friend of mine.

Chorus
Yes, He's a Friend of mine,
And He with me doth all things
sharer
Since all is Christ's and Christ is
mine,
Why should I have a care?
For Jesus is a Friend of mine.

2. The silver moon, the golden sun,
   And all the stars that shine,
   Are His alone, yes, every one,
   And He's a Friend of mine.

3. He daily spread a glorious feast,
   And at His table dine,
   The whole creation, man and
   beast,
   And He's a Friend of mine.

4. And when He comes in bright
   array,
   And leads the conquering line,
   It will be glory then to say,
   That He's a Friend of mine.

1123

St. Bernard -C. M.

1. All ye who seek for sure relief
In trouble and distress,
Whatever sorrow vex the mind.
Or guilt the soul oppress.

2. Jesus, who gave Himself for you
Upon the cross to die,
Opens to you His sacred heart;
O to that heart draw nigh.

3. Ye hear how kindly He invites;
Ye hear His words so blest;
'All ye that labour come to Me,
And I will give you rest.'

4. O Jesus, joy of saints on high,
Thou hope of sinners here,
Attracted by those loving words
To Thee we lift our prayer.

5. Wash Thou our wounds in that dear blood
Which from Thy heart doth flow;
A new and contrite heart on all
Who cry to Thee bestow.
-E. Caswall

1124

Bourton -L. M.

1. God is the refuge of His saints,
When storms of sharp distress invade;
Ere we can offer our complaints,
Behold Him present with His aid!

2. Let mountains from their seats be hurled
Down to the deep, and buried there,
Convulsions shake the solid world,
Our faith shall never yield to fear.

3. Loud may the troubled ocean roar;
In sacred peace our souls abide;
While every nation, every shore,
Trembles, and dreads the swelling tide.

4. There is a stream, whose gentle flow
Makes glad the city of our God,
Life, love, and joy still gliding through,
And watering our divine abode.

5. This sacred stream', Thy vital word,
Thus all our raging fear control;
Sweet peace Thy promises afford,
And give new strength to fainting souls.

6. Zion enjoys her Monarch's love,
Secure against the threatening hour;
Nor can her firm foundation move,
Built on His faithfulness and power.
-Isaac Watts

1125

After

1. After the toil and the neat of the day,
After my troubles are past,
After the sorrows are taken away,
I shall see Jesus at last.

Chorus
He will be waiting for me
Jesus, so Kind and true;
On His beautiful throne,
He will welcome me home
After the day is through.

2. After the heart aches and sighing shall cease,
After the cold winter's blast.
After the conflicts comes glorious peace, I shall see Jesus at last.

3. After the shadows of evening shall
   fall,
   After my anchor is cast,
   After I list to my Savior's last call,
   I shall see Jesus at last.
   -N. B. Vandall

1126

Albert Tindley- Leave It There

1. If the world from you withhold of its
   silver and its gold,
   And you have to get along with
   meager fare,
   Jesus remember in His word,
   how He feeds the little bird;
   Take your burden to the Lord and
   leave it there.

Chorus
Leave it there, leave it there,
Take your burden to the Lord and
leave it there;
If you trust and never doubt,
He will surely bring you out
Take your burden to the Lord and
leave it there.

2. If your body suffers pain
   and your health you can't regain,
   And your soul is almost sinking in
   despair,
   Jesus knows the pain you feel
   He can save and He can heal;
   Take your burden to the Lord and
   leave it there.

3. When your enemies assail
   and your heart begins to fail,
   Don't forget that God in Heaven
   answers pray'r,
   he will make a way for you
   and will lead you safely thru;
   Take your burden to the Lord and
   leave it there.

4. When your youthful days are gone
   and old age is stealing on,
   And your body bends beneath the
   weight of care:

He will never leave you then
He'll go with you to the end;
Take your burden to the Lord and
leave it there.
                              -Albert Tindley

1127

Conquerors through the blood

1. Conquerors and overcomers now
   are we,
   Thro' the precious blood of Christ
   we've victory,
   If the Lord be for us, we can never
   fail:
   Nothing "gainst his mighty pow'r can
   e'er prevail:

Chorus
Conquerors are we,
thro' the blood, thro' the blood;
God will give us victory
thro' the blood, thro' the blood,
Thro' the Lamb for sinners slain,
Yet who lives and reigns again,
More than conquerors are we.
More than conquerors are we.

2. In the name of Israel's God we'll
   onward press,
   Overcoming sin and all
   unrighteousness;
   Not to us but unto Him the praise
   shall be
   For salvation and for blood bought
   victory.

3. Unto Him that over cometh shall be
   giv'n
   Here to eat of hidden manna sent
   from heav'n
   Over yonder he the victor s psalm
   Shall bear
   And a robe of white, and golden
   crown shall wear.
                              -Mrs. C. H. Morris

OVERCOMING TRIALS AND TEMPTATION

1128

I've a friend

1. Tho' the world allure with its gilded charm,
I'm a child of God whom it cannot harm;
He will me uphold by his mighty arm
Ev'ry moment of my day.

Chorus
I've a friend who will ev'ry need supply
I've a home far beyond the starry sky,
And you know, that is just the reason why
I am singing Hallelujah!

2. I can ne'er forget how upon the tree
Laid the Son of God, there to die for me;
Yet to save my soul, thus it had to be,
There could be no other way.

3. I would e'er be true to my Lord and King,
Ev'ry waking hour praises to him sing,
Knowing that at last he my soul shall bring
Evermore with him to stay.
                                    -C. Austin Miles

1129

St. Agatha-7.7.5.

1. Thou who didst on calvary bleed,
Thou who dost for sinners plead,
Help me in my time of need;
Jesus, hear my cry.

2. In my darkness and my grief,
With my heart of unbelief,
I, who am of sinners chief,
Lift to Thee mine eye.

3. Foes without and fears within,
With no plea Thy, grace to win.
But that Thou canst save from sin,
To Thy cross I fly.

4. Others, long in fetters bound,
There deliverance sought and found,
Heard the voice of mercy sound,
Surely so may I.

5. There on Thee I cast my care,
There to Thee I raise my prayer,
Jesus, save me from despair,
Save me, or I die,

6. When the storms of trial lower,
When I feel temptation's power,
In the last and darkest hour.
Jesus, be Thou nigh
                                    -F. Southgate

1130

Eln" Feste Burg-8.7.8.7.6.6.6.6.7.

1. God Is our fortress and our rock,
our mighty help in danger;
he shields us from the battle's shock
and thwarts the devil's anger
for still the prince of night
prolongs his evil fight;
he uses every skill
to work his wicked will
no earthly force is like him.

2. Our hope is fixed on Christ alone, the
Man, of God's own choosing;
without Him nothing can be won and
fighting must be losing:
so let the powers accursed
come on and do their worst,
the Son of God shall ride
to battle at our side,
and he shall have the victory.

OVERCOMING TRIALS AND TEMPTATION

3. The word of God will not be slow
while demon hordes surround us,
though evil strike its cruellest blow
and death and hell confound us:
for even if distress should take all
we possess, and those who mean
us ill should ravage, wreck, or kill,
God's kingdom is immortal!

-Martin Luther

1131
Southwell-8.6.8.6.

1. He lives in us, the Christ of God,
his Spirit joins with ours;
he brings to us Father's grace
with power beyond our powers.
And if enticing sin grows strong.
when human nature fails, God's
Spirit in our inner self fights with us,
and prevails.

2. Our pangs of guilt and fears of
death
are Satan's stratagems
by Jesus Christ who died for us
God pardons; who condemns?
And when we cannot feel our faith
nor bring ourselves to pray,
the Spirit pleads with God for us
in words we could not say.

3. God gave his Son to save us all
no other love like this!
then shall he ever turn away
from those he marks as his?
And God has raised him from the
grave,
in this we stand assured;
so none can tear us from his love in
Jesus Christ our Lord.

-Michael Perry

1132
St. Matthias -8.8.8.8.8.8.

1. Still near me, O my Saviour, stand
and guard me in temptation's hour,
within the hollow of your hand
uphold me by your saving power:
no force in earth or hell shall move
or ever tear me from your love.

2. Still let your love point out my way
what gifts of grace your love has
brought!
still counsel me from day to day,
direct my work, inspire my thought:
and if I fall, soon let me hear your
voice, and know that love is near.

3. In suffering, let your love be peace,
in weakness let your love be
power;
and when the storms of life shall
cease,
Jesus, in that tremendous hour,
through death to life still be my
guide and save me then, for whom
you died!

-Charles Wesley

1133
Bow Brickhill -8.8.8.8.

1. O Christ of all the ages, come!
we fear to journey on our own;
without you near we cannot face
the future months, the years
unknown.

2. Afflicted, tempted, tried like us,
you match our moments of
despair;
with us you watch the desert
hours, and in our sorrows you are
there.

3. O Saviour, fastened to a cross by
tearing nails our selfish ways;
the grieving, caring Lord of love,
you bear the sins all our days.

4. Triumphant from the grave you rise
the morning breaks upon our sight;
and with its dawning, future years
will shine with your unending light.

5. O Christ of all the ages, come!
the days and months and years go by;
accept our praise, redeem our lives:
our strength for all eternity.
                              -Micheal Perry

1134

Countless Mercies

1. Are you heavy laden and with
sorrow tried?
Stop and took to Jesus Helper,
Friend, and Guide;
Think of all His mercies such a
boundless store!
Tears will change to praises as you
count them o'er.

Chorus
Countless mercies' such a
boundless store!
Countless mercies ? Press 'd and
running o'er!
Countless mercies? try to count
them o'er,
Till you gaze in wonder at your
boundless store.

2. Think of hidden dangers He hath
brought you thro';
Think of all the burdens He hath
borne for you:
Count His words of comfort in your
deepest need;
Count the times when Jesus proved
a Friend indeed.

3. Does your pathway darken 'neath a
cloud of fear?
Count your many mercies, dry each
bitter tear;

Even 'mid the shadows trust Him
without fear;
"Home will be the sweeter for the
dark down here."

4. As He looks from heaven now on
you and me,
Don't you know He chooseth what
each day shall be?
Trust Him loving wisdom, tho' the
host tears start
Give to Him the incense of
a grateful heart.
                              -Flora Kirkland

1135

The God to whom I pray

1. The God who fed His people thro' the
parted sea,
And from Egyptian bondage, set His
children free,
Who rain'd down bread from heaven
all the orlgrim way,
Is the God to whom I pray.

Chorus
Just the same today, just the same
today,
As when He led His people thru' the
sea;
His trustful child I'll be, For In His
word I see,
The God who doeth wonders Is just
the same today.

The God who rescued Daniel from
the lions's den,
And from the fiery furnance, sav'd
the three young men,
Who speaks, and constellations will
His voice obey,
Is the God to whom I pray,

3. The God who stills the tempest with
a word divine,
And on the clouds of sorrow, makes
His rainbows shine

who from the tomb of Jesus rolled
the stone away.
Is the God to whom I pray.

4. The God who clothes the lily in its
robe of snow,
Who in the barren desert makes tis
rivers flow;
The God who lifts the sinner from
the miry clay.
Is the God to whom I pray.
-L. E. Hewitt

1136

Grace sufficient for thee

1. They that trust in the Lord are
secure.
Tho' the storm rages dark o'er-the
sea;
for this anchor of promise is sure
My grace is sufficient for thee."

Chorus
My grace is sufficient for thee."
My grace is sufficient for thee"
Oh, matchless, boundless grace of
God,
My grace is sufficient for thee!".

2. What a boon to the pilgrim opprest,
What a balm such a promise must
be
To the laden ones seeking for rest.
"My grace is sufficient for thee."

3. In the race for the prize, fainting
soul,
Though aweary you bow down the
knee,
Rise again, and press on the goal:
My grace is sufficient for thee."

4. Neither trial nor doubt brings
dismay,
Nor from danger that comes will I
flee
For I stand on this promise today
My grace is sufficient for thee."
-C. M. Robinson

1137

He Never Forgets His Own

1. When shadows darken my earthly
way,
And long and dreary seems the day,
This promise sweet comes my soul
to greet,
He never forgets his own.

Chorus
He never forgets his own.
He never forgets his own;
Tho' friends deny, there is
One so nigh Who never forgets his
own.

2. When cherish'd plans all here seem
to fail,
And doubt and fear my soul assail,
'Tis then I rest on his loving breast
Who never forgets his own.

3. O no, he never forgets his own,
And dearer he has daily grown,
Since that glad day when he came
to stay,
And made my poor heart his home.
-Lida Shivers Leech

1138

Solid Rock - 8.8.8.8.8.8.8.

1. My hope is build on nothing less
Than Jesus blood and righteousness;
I dare not trust the sweetest frame,
But wholly lean on Jesus' name.

Chorus
On Christ, the solid rock. I stand;
All other ground is sinking sand,
All other ground is sinking sand.

2. When darkness seems to veil His
face
I rest on His unchanging grace;
In ev'ry high and stormy gale
My anchor holds within the veil.

3. His oath, His covenant, and blood,
Support me in the "whelming flood;
When all around my soul gives way
He then is all my hope and stay.

4. When He shall come with trumpet sound,
Oh, may I then in Him be found;
Dressed in His righteousness alone,
Faultless to stand before the throne.
-Edward Mote

1139

Count Your Blessings

1. When upon life's billows you are tempest toss'd,
When you are discouraged, thinking all is lost.
Count your many blessing, name them one by one,
And it will surprise you what the Lord hath done.

Chorus

Count your blessings, name them one by one,
Count your blessings, see what God hath done;
Count your blessings, name them one by one,
And it will surprise you what the Lord hath done.

2. Are you ever burden'd with a load of care?
Does the cross seem heavy you are called to bear?
Count your many blessings, ev'ry doubt will fly,
And you will be singing as the days go by.

3. When you look at others with their lands and gold,

Think that Christ has promised you His wealth untold,
Count your many blessings, money cannot buy
Your reward in heaven, nor your home on high.

4. So amid the conflict, whether great or small,
Do not be discouraged, God is over all,
Count your many blessings, angels will attend,
Help and comfort give you to your journey's end.
-Johnson Oatman, Jnr.

1140

University College - 7.7.7.7.

1. Oft in danger, oft in woe,
Onward, Christians, onward go;
Fight the fight, maintain the strife,
Strengthen'd with the Bread of Life,

2. Shrink not, Christians: will ye yield?
Will ye quit the painful field?
Will ye flee in danger's hour?
Know ye not your Captain's power?

3. Let your drooping hearts be glad;
March in heavenly armour clad:
Fight, nor think the battle long;
Soon shall victory tune your song.

4. Let not sorrow dim your eye,
Soon shall every tear be dry;
Let not fears your course impede,
Great your strength if great your need.

5. Onward then to glory move,
More than conquerors ye shall prove;
Though opposed by many foe,
Christian soldiers, onward go.
-H. K. White

OVERCOMING TRIALS AND TEMPTATION

1141
The Sure Foundation

1. There stands a Rock on shores of
   time
   That rears to heav'n its head
   sublime;
   That rock is cleft, and they are blest
   Who find within this cleft a rest.

   Chorus
   Some build their hopes on the ever
   drifting sand,
   Some on their fame, or their
   treasure, or their land;
   Mine's on a Rock that forever will
   stand,
   Jesus, the "Rock of Ages."

2. Rock's a cross, its arms
   outspread,
   Celestial glory bathes its head;
   To its firm base my all I bring,
   And to the rock of ages cling.

3. That Rock's a tower, whose lofty
   height.
   Illum'd with heav'n unclouded light,
   Opens wide its gate beneath the
   dome
   Where saints find rest with Christ
   at home.
   -T. C. O'kane

1142
Wait and Murmur Not - LM.

1. O weary heart, there is a Home,
   Beyond the reach of toil and care;
   A home where changes never come
   Who would not fain be resting there?

Chorus
Oh wait, meekly wait, and murmur
not!
Oh wait, meekly wait, and murmur
not!
Oh wait, Oh wait Oh wait, and
murmur not!

2. Yet when bow'd down beneath the
   load
   By heav'n allow'd, thine earthly lot;
   Look up! thou it reach that blest
   abode:
   Wait, meekly wait, and murmur
   not!

3. If in thy path some thorns are found,
   Oh, think who bore them on His
   brow;
   If grief thy sorrowing heart has
   found,
   It reached a holier than thou.

4. Toil on! nor deem, though sore it be,
   One sigh unheard, one prayer
   forgot;
   The day rest will dawn for thee:
   Wait, meekly wait and murmur not!
   -W. H. Bellamy

1143
Be Still, O Heart

1. Be still, O heart; why fear and
   tremble?
   What evil can thy steps betide?
   Tho' foes, a mighty host. assemble,
   Fear not, for God is on thy side.

   Chorus
   Be still, O heart!
   What evil can betide thee?
   Fear not, fear not,
   With God to walk beside thee.

2. Be still, O heart! the Lord of glory
   Was once a man acquaint with
   grief;

He stoops to hear tell all thy story
He loves, He cares. Hell send relief.

3. Be still, O heart! cease fearing, fretting
About the future all unknown;
Ne'er think the Master is forgetting
About His child His loved and own.

4. Be still; O heart! thy Lord will send thee
The clouds or sunshine as is best;
His own right hand shall e'er defend thee;
Then trust His love, and be at rest
                              -J. H. Watson

1144

Hope On-8.7.

1. Hope on, hope on, O troubled heart!
If doubts and fears o'er take thee,
Remember this the Lord hath said,
He never will forsake thee.'
Then murmur not, still bear thy lot,
Nor yield to care or sorrow;
Be sure the clouds that frown today
Will break In smiles tomorrow.

2. Hope on, hope on! tho' dark and deep
The shadows gather o'er thee;
Be not dismay'd: thy Saviour holds
The Lamp of Life before thee.
And if He will that thou today
Shouldst tread the vale of sorrow,
Be not afraid; but trust and wait
The sun will shine tomorrow.

3. Hope on, hope on! go bravely forth,
Thro' trial and temptation;
Directed by the Word of truth.
So full of consolation.
There is a calm for ev'ry storm;

A joy for ev'ry sorrow;
A night from which the soul shall wake
To hail an endless morrow.
                              -R. Bruck

1145

Thy Saviour Knows them All - D. C. M.

1. O troubled heart, there is a balm
To heal thy ev'ry wound!
In Thy Redeemer's blessing side
That balm alone is found.
The hidden anguish of the soul.
The burning tears the fall,
. The sigh that rends thy arching breast
Thy Saviour knows them all.

2. Go where no ear but His can hear.
No eye but His can see;
Has He not said that as thy day
E'en so thy strength shall be?
Though heaven and earth should pass away.
His word can never fail,
If thou by faith approach His throne,
By faith thou shalt prevail.

3. Then why cast down? these passing ills,
Thy path that sometimes dim,
Will work together for thy good
If thou but trust in Him:
The many blessings of the past
With gratitude recall;
Then tell thy sorrows at the feet
Of Him who knows them all.
                              -F. J. Crosby

1146

Thy Will be Done - 8.8.8.4.

1. My God my Father, while I stray
Far from my home, on life's rough way,

Oh, teach me from my heart to say,
Thy will be done!"

Chorus
Thy will be done!
Thy will be done!
Oh, teach me from my heart to say,
Thy will be done!

2. What tho' in lonely grief I sigh
For friends beloved, no longer nigh.
Submissive we still would I reply
Thy will be done!

3. Let but my fainting heart be blest
sweet with Thy sweet Spirit for its
guest,
My God, to Thee I leave the rest
Thy will be done!

4. Renew my will from day to day:
Blend it with Thine; and take away
All now that makes it hard to say,
Thy will be done!

5. Then when on earth I breathe no
More
The prayer oft mixed with tears
before
I'll sing upon a happier shore,
Thy will be done!
                    -Charlotte Elliott

1147

Trust On-7.6.

1. Trust on, trust on, believer!
Tho' long the conflict be,
Thou yet shall prove victorious;
Thy God shall fight for thee.

Chorus
Trust on! trust on!
Tho' dark the night and drear
Trust on! trust on!
The morning dawn is near.

2. Trust on! The danger presses,
Temptation strong is near,

Over life's dang'rous rapids
He shall thy passage steer.

3. The Lord is strong to save us,
He is a faithful Friend:
Trust on, trust on, believer
Oh, trust Him to the end!
                    -Eliza A. Walker

1148

Victory

1. Hallelujah, what a thought!
Jesus full salvation brought,
Victory, victory.
Let the pow'rs of sin assail,
Heaven's grace can never fall,
Victory, victory.

Chorus
Victory yes, victory;
Hallelujah I I'm free,
Jesus gives me victory,
Glory, glory, hallelujah!
He is all in all to me, hallelujah.

2. I am trusting in the Lord,
I am standing on his word,
Victory, victory.
I have peace and joy within,
Since my life is free from sin;
Victory, victory.

3. Shout your freedom ev'rywhere,
His eternal peace declare,
Victory, victory.
Let us sing it here below,
In the face of ev'ry foe,
Victory, victory.

4. We will sing it on that shore,
When this fleeting life is o'er,
Victory, victory.
Sing it here, ye ransomed throng,
Start the everlasting song:
Victory, victory.
                    -B. E. Warren

OVERCOMING TRIALS AND TEMPTATION

1149
Life's railway to Heaven

1. Life is like a mountain rail road,
With an engineer that's brave;
We must make the run successful,
From the cradle to the grave;
Watch the curves, the fills, the tunnels.'
Never after, never quail;
Keep your hand upon the throttle,
And your eye upon the rail.

Chorus
Blessed Saviour, Thou wilt guide us
Till we reach that blissful shore;
When the angels wait to join us
In Thy praise for evermore.

2. You will roll up grades of trial;
You will cross the bridge of strife;
See that Christ is your conductor
On this ligntning train of life;
Always mindful of obstruction.
Do your duty, never fail;
Keep your hand upon the throttle.
And your eye upon the rail.

3. You will often find obstructions;
Look for storms of wind and rain;
On a fill, or curve, or trestle,
They will almost ditch your train;
Put your trust alone In Jesus;
Never falter, never fail;
Keep your hand upon the throttle,
And your eye upon the rail.

4. As you roll across the trestle,
Spanning Jordan's swelling tide;
You behold the Union Depot
Into which your train will glide;
There you'll meet the Superintendant,
God the Father, God the Son,
With the hearty joyous plaudit,
"Weary pilgrim, welcome home."
-M. E. Abbey

1150
Victory In my soul

1. The blood of the Lamb covers
every sin.
And His will doth how control,
My life is filled with His pow'r
divine,
There's victory in my soul.

Chorus
There's victory in my soul,
There's victory in my soul,
The conquering pow'r o'er the life of
sin
Gives victory in my soul.

2. By faith in His name, I shall
overcome sin,
And His glories I'll behold.
'Gainst ev'ry foe I'll the conflict win,
There's victory in my soul.

3. By the power of life in our
conquering King,
I His face shall soon behold,
And with Him dwell and His glory
sing,
There's victory in my soul.

4. O the joy and sweet peace from
our Father above,
When His pow'r doth take control.
When His Spirit fills soul and heart
with love,
There's victory in my soul.
-R. E. Winsett

1151
Lift me up above the Shadows

1. Lift me up above the shadows,
Plant my feet on higher ground.
Lift me up above the clouds Lord.
Where the pure sunshine Is found;
Lift me up above my weakness,
lift me up Into Thy strength,
Lift me up above the shadows,
Till I stand with Thee at length.

Chorus
Lift me up above the shadows,
Lift me up and let me stand
on the mountain tops of glory,
Let me dwell in Beulah land.

2. Lift me up above the shadows,
For the storms are raging high,
Let me up, my blessed Saviour,
Let me to Thy bossom fly,
There no evil thing can touch me,
Over on the shining side,
Lift me up above the shadows,
Let me evermore abide.

3. Lift me up above the shadows,
Out of sorrow into joy,
Lift me up above my grief,
Lord give me gold for my alloy;
Then, when death must claim my
Spirit and the storms of life are past.
Lift me up above the shadows.
Till in heav'n I stand at last.

4. Lift us up above the shadows,
When to earth You come again.
Let us be in the assembly,
As Thy Bride to ever reign;
In Thy kingdom, full of glory,
with our friends we'll ever be,
Lift us up above the shadows.
There to dwell eternally.
-Herbert Buffum

1152

The Lily of the Valley

1. I have found a friend in Jesus, He's
everything to me,
He's the fairest of ten thousand to
my soul
The Lily the Valley, in Him alone I
see
All I need to cleanse and make me
fully whole.
In sorrow He's my comfort, in
Trouble He's my stay,

He tells me every care on Him to roll:
He's the Lily of the Valley, the Bright
and Morning Star,
He's the fairest of ten thousand to
my soul.

2. He all my griefs has taken, and all
my sorrows borne;
In temptation He's my strong and
mighty tower;
I have all for Him forsaken, and all my
idols torn
From my heart, and now He keeps
me by His power,
Though all the world forsake me, and
Satan tempt me sore,
Through Jesus I shall safely reach
the goal;
He's the Lily of the Valley, the Bright
and Morning Star.
He's the fairest of ten thousand to
my soul.

3. He will never, never leave me, nor yet
forsake me here,
While I live by faith and do His
blessed will;
A wall of fire about me, I've nothing
now to fear,
With His manna He my hungry soul
shall fill.
Then sweeping up to glory to see His
blessed face,
Where rivers of delight shad ever roll:
He's the Lily of the Valley, the Bright
and Morning Star,
He's the fairest often thousand to
my soul.
-English Melody

1153

Wait, and Murmur Not

1. O troubled heart, there is a home,
Beyond the reach of toil and care;
A home where changes never come:
Who would not fain be resting there?

OVERCOMING TRIALS AND TEMPTATION

Chorus
O wait, meekly wait, and murmur not.
O wait, meekly waft, and murmur not,
O wait, O wait, O wait, and murmur Not.

2. Yet when bowed down beneath the load.
By heaven allowed, thine earthly lot.
Look up! thou' It reach that blest abode;
Wait, meekly wait, and murmur not

3. Toil on, nor deem, tho' sore it be,
One sigh unheard, one prayer forgot;
The day of rest will dawn for thee;
Wait, meekly wait, and murmur not.
-W. H. Ballamy

1154
Nellein- 7.7.7.7.

1, Forty days and forty nights you were fasting in the wild;
forty days and forty nights tempted and yet undefiled.

2 Burning heat throughout the day,
bitter cold when light had fled;
prowling beasts around your way,
stones your pillow, earth your bed

3. Shall not we your trials share.
learn your discipline of will;
and with you by fast and power
wrestle with powers of hell?

4. So if Satan, pressing hard, soul and body would' destroy:
Christ who conquered, be our guard;
Give to us the victor's joy.

5. Saviour, may we hear your voice
keep us constant at your side;
and with you we shall rejoice at the eternal Eastertide.
-G. H. Smyttan

1155
St. Mary Magdalene - 6.5.6.5.D.

1. In the hour of trial,
Jesus, pray for me,
Lest by base denial
I depart from Thee;
When Thou seest me waver.
With a look recall,
Nor for fear or favour
Suffer me to fall.

2. With its witching pleasures
Would this vain world charm,
Or its soldier treasure
Spread to work me harm,
Bring to my remembrance
Sad Gethsemane,
Or, in darker semblance,
Cross-crowned Calvary.

3. If with sore affliction
Thou in love chastise,
Pour Thy benediction
On the sacrifice;
Then, upon Thine altar
Freely offered up,
Though the flesh may falter,
Faith shall drink the cup.

4. When in dust and ashes'
To the grave I sink,
While heaven's glory flashes .
O'er the shelving brink,
On Thy truth relying
Through that mortal strife,
Lord, receive me, dying,
To eternal life.
-James Montgomery

OVERCOMING TRIALS AND TEMPTATION

1156
Bremen - 7.6.7.6.

1. God is my strong salvation;
   What foe have I to fear?
   In darkness and temptation
   My light, my help is near.

2. Though hosts encamp around me,
   Firm to the fight I stand;
   What terror can confound me.
   With God at my right hand?

3. Place on the Lord reliance;
   My soul, with courage wait;
   His truth be thine affiance.
   When faint and desolate.

4. His might thine heart shall strong
   then
   His love thy joy increase;
   Mercy thy days shall lengthen;
   The Lord will give thee peace.
   > -James Montgorney

1157
Filitz -6.5.6.5.

1. O Let whose sorrow
   No relief can find,
   Trust in God, and borrow
   Ease for heart and mind.

2. Where the mourner, weeping,
   Sheds the secret tear,
   God His watch is keeping,
   Though none else be near.

3. God will never leave thee;
   All thy wants He knows,
   Feels, the pains that grieve thee,
   Sees thy cares and woes.

4. If in grief thou languish,
   He will dry the tear,
   Who His children's anguish
   Soothes with succour near.

5. All thy woe and sadness,
   In this world below.
   Balance not the gladness
   Thou in heaven shalt know.

6. When thy gracious Saviour.
   In the realms above.
   Crowns thee with His favour,
   Fills thee with His love.
   > -Heinrich
   > Siegmund Oswald

1158
Christchurch - 6.6.6.6.8.8.

1. March on, my soul, with strength,
   March forward, void of fear
   He who hath led will lead,
   While year succeedeth year
   And as thou goest on thy way.
   His hand shall hold thee day by day.

2. March on, my soul; with strength,
   In ease thou dar'st not dwell:
   High duty calls thee forth.
   Then up, and quit thee well!
   Take up thy cross, take up thy
   sword.
   And fight the battles of thy Lord!

3. March on, my soul with strength,
   With strength, but not thine own;
   The conquest thou shalt gain,
   Though Christ thy Lord alone;
   His grace shall nerve thy feeble
   arm,
   His love preserve thee save from
   harm.

4. March on, my soul. with strength,
   From strength to strength march on;
   Warfare shall end at length.
   All foes be overthrown,
   Then, O my soul, if faithful now,
   The crown of life awaits thy brow.
   > -William Wright

OVERCOMING TRIALS AND TEMPTATION

1159

Blott En Dag - Irregular

1. Day by day and with each passing
   moment,
   Strength I find to meet my trials
   here;
   Trusting in my Father's wise
   bestowment,
   I've no cause for worry or for fear.
   He whose heart is kind beyond all
   measure
   Gives unto each day what He
   deems best
   Lovingly, its part of pain and
   pleasure,
   Mingling toid with peace and rest.

2. Ev'ry day the Lord Himself is near
   me,
   With a special mercy for each hour;
   All my cares He fain would bear,
   and cheer me,
   He whose name is Counsellor and
   Pow'r.
   The protection of His child and
   treasure
   Is a charge that on Himself He laid;
   "As your days, your strength shall
   be in measure,"
   This the pledge to me He made.

3. Help me then in ev'ry tribulation
   So to trust Your promises, O Lord,
   That I lose not faith's sweet
   consolation
   Offered me within Your holy Word.
   Help me, Lord, when toil and
   trouble meeting,
   E'er to take, as from a father's
   hand,
   One by one, the days, the moments
   fleeting,
   Till I reach the promised land.
   -Carolina Sandell Berg

1160

Orwigsburg -10.9.10.9. with Refrain

1. I must tell Jesus all of my trials,
   I cannot bear these burdens alone;
   In my distress He kindly will help me,
   He ever loves and cares for His own.

Chorus
I must tell Jesus! I must tell Jesus!
I cannot bear my burdens alone;
I must tell Jesus! must tell Jesus!
Jesus can help me, Jesus alone.

2. I must tell Jesus all of my troubles,
   He is a kind, compassionate friend;
   If I but ask Him, He will deliver.
   Make of my troubles quickly an end.

3. O how the world to evil allures me!
   O how my heart, is tempted to sin!
   I must tell Jesus, and He will help me
   Over the world the vict'ry to win.
   -Elisha A. Hoffman

1161

Duncannon -C.M. with Refrain

1. King of my life, I crown Thee now,
   Thine shall the glory be;
   Lest I forget Thy thorn crowned brow,
   Lead me to Calvary.

Chorus
Lest I forget Gethsemane;
Lest I forget Thine agony;
Lest I forget Thy love for me,
Lead me to Calvary.

2. Show me the tomb where Thou
   wast laid,
   Tenderly mourned and wept,
   Angels in robes of light arrayed
   Guarded Thee whilst Thou slept.

3. Let me like Mary, through the gloom,
   Come with a gift to Thee;
   Show to me now the empty tomb,
   Lead me to Calvary.

4. May I be willing, Lord, to bear ,
   Daily my cross for Thee;
   Even Thy cup of grief to share,
   Thou hast borne all for me.

            –Jennie Evelyn Hussey

1162

Praise -8.8.6.D.

1. Come on, my partners in distress.
   My comrands through the wilderness
   Who still your bodies feel,
   Awhile forget your griefs and fears
   And look beyond this vale of tears
   To that celestial hill.

2. Beyond the bounds of time and
   space
   Look forward to that heavenly
   place
   The saints secure abode
   On faith's strong eagle-pinions rise,
   And force your passage to the
   skies
   And scale the mount of God.

3. Who suffer with our Master here,
   we shall before His face appear,
   And by His side sit down,
   To patient faith the prize is sure,
   And all that to the end endure
   The cross, shall wear the crown.

4. Thrice blessed, bliss-inspiring hope!
   It lifts the fainting spirits up, to life the
   it brings to life the dead;
   Our conflicts here shall soon be
   past
   You and I ascend at last,
   Triumphant with our Head.

5. That mysterious Deity
   We soon with open face shall see:
   The beatific sight

Shall fill heaven's sounding courts
with praise,
And wide diffuse the golden blaze
Of everlasting light

6. The Father shining on His throne,
   The glorious co-eternal Son,
   The Spirit, one and seven,
   Conspire our rapture to complete;
   And lo! we fall before His feet,
   And silence heightens heaven.

7. In hope of that ecstatic pause,
   Jesus, we now sustain the cross,
   And at Thy footstool fall,
   Till Thou our hidden life reveal.
   Till Thou our ravished spirits fill,
   And God is all in all.

            –Charles Wesley

1163

Grainger -C. M.

1. Workman of God! O lose not heart,
   But learn what God is like,
   And in the darkest battle-field
   Thou shalt know where to strike.

2. Thrice blest is he to whom is given
   The instinct that can tell
   That God is on the field when He
   Is most invisible.

3. For God is other than we think;
   His ways are far above,
   Far beyond reason's height, and
   reached
   Only children love.

4. Then learn to scorn the praise of
   man,
   And learn to lose with God;
   For Jesus won the world through
   shame,
   And beckon thee His road.

5. For right is right, since God is God
   And right the day must win;
   To doubt would be disloyalty
   To falter would be sin.

            –Frederick Williams Faber

OVERCOMING TRIALS AND TEMPTATION

1164

Greenland-7.6.7.6.D.

1. From trials unexampled
Thy dearest children are;
But let us not be tempted
Above what we can bear;
Exposed to no temptation
That may our souls o'er power,
Be Thou our strong salvation
Through ever fiery hour.

2. Ah! leave us not to venture
Within the verge of sin;
Or if the snare we enter,
Thy timely help bring in;
And if Thy wisdom try us,
Till pain and woe are past,
Almighty Love, stand by us,
And save from first to last.

3. Fain would we cease from sinning
In thought, and word, and deed;
From sin in it's beginning we
languish to be freed;
Our fallen nature's shame
Jesus, we dare require
Deliverance in thy name.

4. For every sinful action
Thou hast atonement made,
The perfect satisfaction
Thy precious blood has paid:
But take entire possession.
To make an end of sin,
To finish the transgression.
Most holy God, come in!
                    -Charles Wesley

1165

Angel's Song L. M.

1. Jesus, my Saviour Brother Friend,
On whom I cast my every care,

On, whom for all things I depend,
Inspire, and then accept, my prayer.

2. If I have tasted of Thy grace,
The grace that sure salvation
brings;
If with me now Thy Spirit stays.
And hovering hides me in His
wings:

3. Still tet Him with my weakness stay,
Nor for a moment's space depart
Evil and danger turn away,
And keep till He renews my heart.

4. When to the right or left I stray,
His voice behind me may I hear,
Return, and walk in Christ thy way;
Fly back to Christ, for sin is near;

5. His sacred unction from above,
Be still my Comforter and Guide;
Till all the hardness He remove,
And in my loving heart reside.

6. Jesus, I fain would walk in Thee,
From nature's every path retreat;
Thou art my Way, my leader be,
And set upon the rock my feet.

7. Uphold me, Savour, or I fall,
O reach me out Thy gracious hand!
Only on Thee for help I call,
Only by faith in Thee I stand.
                    -Charles Wesley;

1166

Azmol -C.M.

1. I'm not ashamed to own my Lord,
Or to defend His cause.
Maintain the honour of His word,
The glory of His Cross.

2. Jesus, my God I know His name
His name is all my trust;
Nor will He put my soul to shame,
Not let my hope be lost.

3. Firm as His throne His promise stands,
   And He can well secure
   What I've committed to His hands
   Till the decisive hour.

4. Then will He own my worthless name
   Before His Father's face,
   And in the new Jerusalem
   Appoint my soul a place.
   —Isaac Watts

1167

Each step I take

1. Each step I take my Saviour goes before me,
   And with loving hand He leads the way
   And with each breath I whisper "I adore Thee,"
   Oh, what joy to walk with Him each day.

Chorus
Each step I take I know that He will guide me,
To higher ground He ever leads me on
Until some day the last step will be taken,
Each step I take just leads me closer home.

2. At times I feel my faith begin to waver
   When up ahead I see a chasm wide
   It's then I turn and look up to my saviour,
   I am strong when He is by my side.

3. I trust in God, no matter come what may,
   For life eternal in His hand,
   He holds the key that opens up the Way,
   That will lead me to the promised land.
   —W. Elmo Mercer

1168

Vox Dilecti- C.M.D.

1. I heard the voice of Jesus say,
   "Come unto Me and rest;
   Lay down, thou weary one, lay down Thy head upon My breast"
   I came to Jesus as I was,
   Weary, and worn, and sad;
   I found in Him a resting place,
   And He has made me glad.

2. I heard the voice of Jesus say,
   "Behold, I freely give
   The living water, thirsty one, Stoop down, and drink, and live."
   I came to Jesus, and drank Of that life giving stream;
   My thirst was quenched, my soul revived, And now I live in Him.

3. I heard the voice of Jesus say,
   "I am this dark world's Light:
   Look unto Me, thy mom shall rise,
   And all the day be bright."
   I looked to Jesus, and I found In Him my Star, my Sun;
   And in that Light of life I'll walk, Till trav'ling days are done.
   —Horatius

1169

Yield not to temptation

1. Yield not to temptation, For yielding is sin;
   Each vict'ry will help you Some other to win;
   Fight manfully onward, Dark passions subdue;
   Look over to Jesus, He'll carry you through.

Chorus
Ask the Saviour to help you,
Comfort, strengthen and keep you;
He is willing to aid you,
He will carry you through.

2. Shun evil companions, Bad
language disdain;
God's name hold in reverence, Nor
take it in vain;
Be thoughtful and earnest, Kind-
hearted and true;
Look ever to Jesus, He'll carry you
through.

3. To him that o'er cometh, God giveth
a crown;
Thro' faith we will conquer, Tho'
often cast down;
He who is our Saviour, Our strength
will renew;
Look ever to Jesus, He'll carry you
through.

-Horatio R-Palmer

1170

The Best Friend Is Jesus

1. Oh, the best Friend to have is
Jesus,
When the cares of life upon you
roll;
He will heal the wounded heart,
He will strength and grace impart:
Oh, the best Friend to have is
Jesus!

Chorus
The best Friend to have is Jesus!
The best Friend to have is Jesus!
He will help you when you fall,
He will hear you when you call:
Oh, the best Friend to have is
Jesus!

2. What a Friend I have found in
Jesus!
Peace and comfort to my soul He
brings;
Leaning on His mighty arm,
I will fear no ill nor arm,
Oh, the best Friend to have is
Jesus!

3. Though I pass thro' the night of
sorrow,
And the chilly waves of Jordan roll,
Never need I shrink nor fear,
For my Saviour is so near:
Oh, the best Friend to have is
Jesus!

4. When at last to our home we
gather
With the loved ones who have gone
before,
We will sing upon the shore,
Praising Him for evermore:
Oh, the best Friend to have is
Jesus!

-P. Bilhorn

1171

Victory in My Soul

1. There is vict'ry within my soul;
For the Spirit with me abides
Let the waves of temptation roll,
Jesus keeps me whate'er betides.

Chorus
Victory! Victory! Vict'ry! in my soul;
I have glorious victory since Jesus
took control,
Victory! Victory! Sweeping like a
flood;
I have glorious victory thro' Jesus
blood.

2. Tho' the conflict be fierce and long,
Tho' the tempter my heart assail;
In my weakness I yet am strong,
For with Jesus I'll e'er prevail.

3. I have victory over sin,
I have victory o'er the grave;
Even death now has; lost its sting,
Hallelujah! I know I'm sav'd.

-Haldor Lillena

OVERCOMING TRIALS AND TEMPTATION

1172

I am Alpha and Omega

1. My trust I place now and ever
   In One my soul can deliver,
   A Refuge strong, failing never,
   For His word is sure.

   Chorus
   I am Alpha and Omega,
   The beginning and the ending
   Which is and which was,
   And which is to come.
   I am Alpha and Omega,
   The Beginning and the ending,
   The Almighty, the Almighty,
   saith the Lord.

2. My heart with joy now is telling
   Of Him who finds there a dwelling,
   Whose love is gently compelling
   On His word to rest.

3. Jehovah, God! Still attend me,
   From doubt and fear still defend me,
   Faith to sustain ever send me,
   That my soul fail not.
   -C. Austin Miles

1173

Saffron Walden-8.8.8.6.

1. Oft when I seem to tread alone
   Some barren waste with thorns o'er grown,.
   A Voice of love in gentlest tone
   Whispers, "Still cling to Me."

2. Though faith and hope a while to tried.
   I ask not, need not, aught beside;
   How safe. now calm, how satisfied,
   The souls that cling to Thee!

3. They fear not life's rough storms to brave,
   Since Thou art near and strong to save;
   Nor shudder e'en at death's dark wave,
   Because they cling to Thee.

4. Blest is my lot, whate'er befall:
   What can disturb me, who appal,
   While, as my strength, my rock, my all, Saviour, I cling to Thee?
   -A. H. Brown

1174

Toss'd With Rough Winds, And Faint With Fear-8.6.8.6.

1. Toss'd with rough winds, and faint with fear,
   Above the tempest, soft and dear,
   What still small accents greet mine ear?
   'Tis I, be not afraid.

2. 'Tis I, who washed thy spirit white;
   'Tis I, who gave thy blind eyes sight;
   'Tis I, thy Lord, thy life, thy light;
   'Tis I, be not afraid.

3. These raging winds this surging sea,
   Have spent their deadly force on Me;
   They bear no breath of wrath to thee;
   'Tis I; be not afraid.

4. This bitter cup, I drank it first;
   To thee it is no draught accurst;
   The hand that gives it thee is pierced;
   'Tis I, be not afraid

5. When on the other side thy feet
   Shall rest mid thousand thy head,
   My blessing is around thee shed:
   'Tis I, be not afraid.

6. When on the other side thy feet
   Shall rest mid thousand welcomes sweet,
   On well-known voice thy heart shall greet,
   'Tis I, be not afraid.

1175

**There's A Place I Love To Tarry -
8.7.8.7.with Ref.**

1. There's a place I love to tarry
   When my soul is sad, oppressed,
   'Tis alone with Christ my Saviour
   Where He bids me "Come and rest"

Chorus
Just to be alone with Jesus Just to
hear Him softly say:
"Fear not, though the world forsake you,
"Lo I'm with you always."

2. When the cares of life heavy,
   And beneath my cross I bend;
   Then I go alone with Jesus,
   For He is my dearest Friend.

3. When the tempter would assail me,
   Jesus bids me to Him flee:
   He's my Refuge, Friend and Saviour,
   He is all in all to me.

WATER BAPTISM

1176

St. Michel's-11.11.11.11.

1. O Thou who in Jordan
   didst bow Thy meek head,
   And, 'whelmed in our sorrows,
   didst sink to the dead,
   Then rose from the darkness
   to glory above,
   And claimed for Thy chosen the
   kingdom of love.

2. Thy footsteps we follow,
   to bow in the tide,
   And are buried with Thee in
   the death Thou hast died;
   Then wake in Thy likeness
   to walk in the way That brightens
   and brightens to shadowless day.

3. O Jesus, our Saviour,
   O Jesus, our Lord,
   By the life of Thy passion,
   the grace of Thy word,
   Accept us, redeem us,
   dwell ever within.
   To keep, by Thy Spirit,
   our spirits from sin.

4. Till, crown'd with Thy glory,
   and waving the palm,
   Our garments all white from
   the blood of the Lamb,
   We join the bright millions
   of saints gone before,
   And bless Thee, and wonder,
   and praise evermore.
   -George W. Bethune

1177

McComb- 8.7.8.7.

1. This rite our blest Redeemer gave
   To all in Him believing;
   He leads us through this hallowed
   wave,
   To His example cleaving.

2. I'll follow then my glorious Lord,
   Whate'er the ties I sever;
   He saved my soul. and left His Word
   To guide me now and ever.

3. Jesus, to Thee I yield my all;
   In Thy kind arms enfold me;
   My heart is fixed, no fears appall,
   Thy gracious power shall hold me.

4. How sweet the way divine to take,
   So clear in Jordan's story,
   On souls that follow Christ shall
   break
   The Spirit's beam of glory.
   -Sylvanus D. Phelps

1178

Greenville-8.7.8.7.8.7.

1. Thou has said, exalted Jesus,
   "Take thy cross and follow me";
   Shall the word with terror seize us?
   Shall we from the burden flee?
   Lord, I'll take it, Lord, I'll take it,
   And rejoicing, follow Thee.

2. While this liquid tomb surveying,
   Emblem of my Saviour's grave,
   Shall I shun its brink, betraying
   Feelings worthy of a slave?
   No, I'll enter. No. I'll enter,
   Jesus entered Jordan's wave.

3. Blest the sign which thus reminds
   me,
   Saviour, of Thy love for me;
   But more blest the love that binds
   me
   In its deathless bonds to Thee;
   Oh, what pleasure, Oh, what
   pleasure,
   Buried with my Lord to be!

4. Fellowship with Him possessing,
   Let me die to earth end sin;

WATER BAPTISM

Let me rise t'enjoy the blessing
Which the faithful soul shall win;
May I ever, May I ever
Follow where my Lord has been.
-John E. Giles

1179

Pass field- 5.5.7.D.

1. Born of the water,
   born of the Spirit
   sons of the wind and the fire;
   sealed with his promise.
   we shall inherit
   more than the most we desire.

2. One through redemption,
   one with the Father
   children of grace and of heaven;
   joyfully sharing
   faith with each other,
   sinners whose sins are forgiven.

3. Glory, all glory,
   glory to Jesus
   die we in him and we live!
   friends for his service,
   heirs to the treasures
   God, and God only, can give.
   -Michael Perry

1180

L.M. and Refrain

1. O happy day, that fixed my choice,
   On Thee, my Saviour and my God!
   Well may this glowing heart rejoice,
   And tell its raptures all abroad.

Chorus
Happy day, happy day.
When Jesus wash'd my sins away!
He taught me how to watch and
pray.
And live rejoicing ev'ry day.

2. 'Tis done, the great transaction's
   done!
   I am my Lord's and He is mine:
   He drew me and I followed on,
   Charmed to confess the voice divine.

3. Now rest, my long-divided heart,
   Fixed on this blissful centre, rest:
   Nor ever from thy Lord depart,
   With Him of every good possessed.

4. High heaven, that heard the solemn
   vow,
   That vow renewed shall daily hear,
   Till in life's latest hour I bow,
   And bless in death a bond so dear.
   -P. Doddridge

1181

Philippine-L.M.

1. O Lord, thy people gathered here
   Uplift their joyful hearts as one,
   And praise thee, with no thought of
   fear,
   For his bright gift, a life begun,

2. For thou art seen in every place,
   Through all the world thy beauties
   shine;
   But only man may win the grace
   To know the inward light of thine,

3. And so we trace the tender brow,
   And pray these eyes may learn to
   gaze
   Through all this world of here and
   now
   To find thee and to see thy ways.

4. Praise, Lord, for this sweet world
   we know
   With all the joys thy children share,
   And that unknown to which we go,
   Both now and ever 'neath thy care!
   -Mrs. K.E. Roberts

WATER BAPTISM

1182

Warsaw - 6.6.6.6.8.8.

1. Father of all, to thee
   With loving hearts we pray,
   Through him. in mercy given,
   The life, the truth, the way:
   From heaven, thy throne, in mercy shed
   Thy blessings on each bended head.

2. Father of all, to thee
   Our contrite hearts we raise,
   Unstrung by sin and pain,
   Long voiceless in thy praise:
   Breathe thou the silent chords along,
   Until they tremble into song.

3. Father of all, to thee
   We breath unuttered fears,
   Deep-hidden in our souls,
   That have no voice but tears:
   Take thou our hand, and through the wild
   Lead gently on each trustful child.

4. Father of all. may we
   In praise our tongue employ,
   When gladness fills the soul
   With deep and hallowed joy:
   In storm and calm give us to see
   The path of peace which leads to thee.
                                    -J. Julian

1183

Stand, Soldier Of The Cross- SM.

1. Stand, soldier of the cross,
   Thy high allegiance claim,
   And vow to hold the world but loss
   For Thy Redeemer's name.

2. Arise, and be baptized
   And wash thy sins away;
   Thy league with God be solemnized,
   Thy faith avouched today.

3. Our heavenly country now,
   Our Lord and master, thine,
   Receive imprinted on thy brow
   His passion's awful sin.

4. No more thine own but Christ's
   With all the saint of old,
   Apostles, seers, evangelists,
   And martyr throngs enrolled.

5. In God's whole armour strong,
   From hell's embattled pow'rs;
   The warfare may be sharp and long
   The victory must be ours.

6. Oh, bright the conqueror's crown,
   The song of triumph sweet,
   When faith casts every trophy down
   At our great Captain's feet

1184

We Are Baptised Unto His Death - C.M.

1. We are baptised unto His death
   By water baptism
   And we go down Into the grave
   Buried with Jesus Christ.

2. Buried with Christ to sin no more
   That we may rise with Him
   Him That we may partake of new grace
   That fits us for the skies.

3. O Holy Ghost, come unto us
   That all our words may be
   The hope of His soon appearing
   And Christ's revelation.

4. Lord, let our faith be glorified,
   Our joy and crown fulfil;
   To live a life of heav'n on earth.
   On high to reign with Thee.

HOLY COMMUNION

1185

Elberton- 10.10.

1. Draw nigh and take the Body of the
   Lord,
   And drink the holy Blood for you
   outpoured.

2. Saved by that Body and that holy
   Blood,
   With souls refreshed, we render
   thanks to God.

3. Salvation's giver, Christ the only
   Son,
   By his dear Cross and Blood the
   victory won.

4. Offered was he for greatest and for
   least,
   Himself the Victim, and himself the
   Priest.

5. Victims were offered by the law of
   old,
   Which in a type this heavenly
   mystery told.

6. He, Lord of life, and Saviour of our
   race,
   Hath given the safeguard of
   salvation here.

7. Approach ye then with faithful hearts
   sincere,
   And take the safeguard of salvation
   here.

8. He that his saints in this world rules
   and shields
   To all believers life eternal yields;

9. He feeds the hungry with the Bread
   of heaven,
   And living streams to those who
   thirst are given.

10. Alpha and Omega, to whom shall
    bow
    All nations at the Doom, is with us
    now.
                                -J.M. Neale

1186

Leamington -10.10.10.10.

1. Thee we adore, O hidden Saviour thee,
   Who in thy Sacrament dost deign to
   be;
   Both flesh and spirit at thy Presence
   fail,
   Yet here thy Presence we devoutly
   Hail.

2. O blest memorial of our dying Lord,
   Who living Bread to men doth here
   afford!
   O may our souls for ever feed on thee,
   And thou, O Christ, for ever precious
   be.

3. Fountain of goodness. Jesus, Lord
   and God,
   Cleanse us, unclean, with thy most
   cleansing Blood;
   Increase our faith and love, that we
   may know
   The hope and peace which from thy
   Presence flow

4. O Christ, whom now beneath a veil
   we see,
   May what we thirst for soon our
   portion be:
   To gaze on thee unveiled, and see
   thy face,
   The vision of thy glory and thy grace.
                            -St. Thomas Aquinas

1187

Das walt Gott- L.M.

1. The heavenly Word. Proceeding
   forth
   Yet leaving not the Father's side,
   Accomplishing his work on earth
   Had reached at length life's
   Eventide.

HOLY COMMUNION

2. By false disciple to be given
   To foemen for his life athirst,
   Himself, the very Bread of heaven,
   He gave to his disciples first,

3. He gave himself in either kind,
   His precious Flesh, his precious
   Blood;
   In love's own fulness thus designed
   Of the whole man to be the food.

4. By birth their fellow man was he,
   Their meat, when sitting at the
   board;
   He died, their ransome to be;
   He ever reigns, their great reward.

5. O saving Victim, opening wide
   The gate of heaven to man below,
   Our foes press on from every side:
   Thine aid supply, thy strength
   bestow.

6. All praise and thanks to thee
   ascend
   For evermore, blest One in Three;
   O grant us life that shall not end
   In our true native land with thee.
       -St. Thomas Aquinas

Jesus, with the law complying,
Keeps the feast its rites demand:
Then, more precious food supplying,
Gives himself with his own hand.

4. Word made flesh, true bread he
   maketh
   By his word his Flesh to be,
   Wine his Blood; which whoso taketh
   Must from carnal thoughts be free:
   Faith alone, though sight forsaketh,
   Shows true hearts the mystery

5. Therefore we. before him bending,
   This great Sacrament revere:
   Types and shadows have their
   ending,
   For the newer rite is here;
   Faith, our outward sense befriending,
   Makes our inward vision clear.

6. Glory let us give and blessing
   To the Father and the Son,
   Honour, might, and praise, address
   ing,
   While eternal ages run;
   Ever too his love confessing,
   Who, from Both, with Both is One.
       -St. Thomas Aquinas

1188

Tantum ergo - 8.7.8.7.8.7.

1. Now. my tongue, the mystery telling
   Of the glorious Body sing,
   And the Blood, all price excelling,
   Which the Gentiles' Lord and King.
   In a Virgin's womb once dwelling,
   Shed for this world's ransoming.

2. Given for us, and condescending
   To be born for us below,
   He, with men in converse blending,
   Dwelt the seed of truth to sow,
   Till he closed with wondrous ending
   His most patient life of woe.

3. The last night, at supper lying,
   Mid the Twelve, his chosen band,

1189

Adoro Te- 10.10.10.10.

1. Here, O my Lord, I see Thee face to
   face;
   Here would I touch and handle
   things unseen,
   Here grasp with firmer hand the
   eternal grace.
   And all my weariness upon Thee
   lean.

2. Here would I feed upon the bread of
   God,
   Here drink with Thee the royal wine
   of heaven:
   Here would I lay aside each earthly
   load,
   Here taste afresh the calm of sin
   Forgiven.

HOLY COMMUNION

3. I have no help but Thine; nor do I
   need
   Another arm save Thine to lean
   upon:
   It is enough, my Lord, enough
   indeed;
   My strength is in Thy might, Thy
   might alone.

4. Mine is the sin, but Thine the
   righteousness;   :
   Mine is the guilt, but Thine the
   cleansing blood;
   Here is my robe, my refuge, and my
   peace
   Thy blood, Thy righteousness, O
   Lord my God.

5. Feast after feast thus comes and
   passes by.
   Yet, passing, points to the glad
   feast above,
   Giving sweet foretaste of the festal
   joy.
   The Lamb's great bridal feast of
   bliss and love.

   -Horatius Bonar

1190
Come for the Feast is Spread

1. Come for the feast is spread:
   Hark to the call!
   Come to the Living Bread,
   Broken for all:
   Come to his "house of win,"
   Low on His breast recline,
   All that He hath make thine;
   Come sinner, come.

2. Come where the fountain flows -
   River of life
   Healing for all thy woes,
   Doubting and strife;
   Millions have been supplied,
   No one was e'er denied;
   Come to the crimson tide,
   Come, sinner come.

3. Come to the throne of grace,
   Boldly draw near;
   He who would win the race;

Must tarry here;
Whate'er thy want may be
Here is the grace for thee.
Jesus Thy only plea:
Come, Christian, Come.

4. Jesus, we come to Thee,
   Oh, take us in!
   Set Thou our spirits free;
   Cleanse us from sin!
   Then, in your land of light,
   All clothed in robes of white,
   Resting not day nor night,
   Thee will we sing.

1191

Heirapolis- L.M.

1. Jesus, Thou Joy of loving hearts,
   Thou Fount of life, Thou Light of
   men!
   From the best bliss that earth
   imparts
   We turn unfill'd to Thee again.

2. Thy truth unchang'd hath ever
   stood;
   Thou savest those that on Thee
   call;
   To them that seek Thee Thou art
   good,
   To them that find Thee, all in all

3. We taste Thee, O Thou living
   Bread!
   And long to feast upon Thee still
   We drink of Thee, the Fountain
   head,
   And thirst our souls from Thee to
   fill.

4. Our restless spirits yearn for Thee
   Where'er our changeful lot is cast,
   Glad when Thy-gracious smile we
   see,
   Blest when our faith can hold Thee
   fast.

5. O Jesus, ever with us stay!
   Make all moments calm and bright;
   'Chase the dark night of sin away;
   Shed o'er the world Thy holy light.

   -Bernard of Clairvaux

HOLY COMMUNION

1192

Moseley- 6.6.6.6.

1. I hunger and I thirst;
   Jesus, my manna be:
   Ye living waters, burst
   Out of the rock for me;

2. Thou bruised and broken Bread,
   My life-long wants supply;
   As living souls are fed,
   Oh feed me, or I die.

3. Thou true life-giving Vine, Let me
   Thy sweetness prove;
   Renew my life with Thine,
   Refresh my soul with love.

4. Rough paths my feet have trod,
   Since first their course began;
   Feed me, Thou Bread of God;
   Help me. Thou Son of Man.

5. For still the desert lies
   My thirsting soul before;
   O living waters, rise
   Within me evermore.

   -Henry Smart

1193

Baca - 6.6.6.6.6.6.

1. I Gave My life for thee,
   My precious blood I shed,
   That thou might'st ransom'd be,
   And quicken'd from the dead.
   I gave My life for thee;
   What hast thou given for Me?

2. I spent long years for thee,
   In weariness and woe,
   That an eternity
   Of joy thou mightest know,
   I spent long years for thee,
   Has thou spent one for Me?

3. My Father's home of light,
   My rainbow-circled throne,
   I left for earthly night,
   For wanderings sad and lone.
   I left it all for thee;
   Hast thou left aught for Me?

4. I suffer'd much for thee,
   More than thy tongue can tell,
   Of bitterest agony,
   To rescue thee from hell.
   I suffer'd much for thee;
   What canst thou bear for Me?

5. And I have brought to thee,
   Down from My home above,
   Salvation full and free,
   My pardon and My love,
   Great gifts I brought to thee;
   What hast thou brought to Me?

6. Oh, let thy life be given,
   Thy years for Me be spent,
   World-fetters all be riven,
   And joy with suffering blent.
   I gave Myself for thee;
   Give thou thyself to Me.
   -W.H. Havergal

1194

Schmucke Dich -8.8.8.8.D.

1. Deck yourself, my soul, with
   gladness,
   leave the gloomy haunts of
   sadness.
   Come into the daylight's splendour,
   there with joy your praises render
   to the Lord whose grace unbounded
   has this royal banquet founded;
   though all other powers excelling,
   with my soul he makes his dwelling.

2. Lord; I bow before you lowly,
   filled with joy most deep and holy,
   as with trembling awe and wonder
   all your mighty works I ponder
   how, by mystery surrounded,
   depth no man has ever sounded,
   none may dare to pierce unbidden
   secrets that in you are hidden.

3. Shining sun, my life you brighten,
radiance, you my soul enlighten;
joy, the best of all man's knowing,
fountain, swiftly in me flowing:
at your feet I kneel, my Maker
let me be a fit partaker
of this sacred food from heaven,
for our good, your glory, given.

4. Jesus, Bread of life, I pray you,
let me gladly here obey you;
never to my hurt invited,
always by your love delighted:
from this banquet let me measure,
Lord, how vast and deep its treasure;
through the gifts your hands have given
let me be your guest in heaven.
-J. Franck

1195
Bread of Heaven - 7.7.7.7.7.7.

1. Bread of heaven, on you we feed,
for your flesh is food indeed;
always may our souls be fed
with this true and living bread,
day by day our strength supplied
through your life, O Christ, who
died.

2. Vine of heaven, your precious blood
seals today our peace with God;
Lord, your wounds our healing give,
to your cross we look and live:
Jesus, with your power renew those
who live by faith in you!
-J. Conder

1196
Saltfleetby All Saints -8.6.8.6.

1. In memory of the Saviour's love
we keep the sacred feast,
where every humble contrite heart
Is made a welcome guest.

2. By faith we take the bread of life
by which our souls are fed,
and drink the token of his blood
that was for sinners shed.

3. Around his table here we sing
the wonders of his love,
and so anticipate by faith
the heavenly feast above.
-T. Cotterill

1197
St. Columba-8.7.8.7.

1. Here, Lord, we take the broken
bread
and drink the wine, believing
that by your life our souls are fed,
your parting gifts receiving.

2. As you have given, so we would give
ourselves for others' healing;
as you have lived, so we would live
the Father's love revealing.
-C. V. Richer

1198
Ach. Gott Und Herr - 8.7.8.7.

1. Strengthen for service, Lord, the
hands
that holy things have taken;
let ears that now have heard your
songs
to clamour never waken.

2. Lord, may the tongues which 'Holy'
sang
keep free from all deceiving:
the eyes which saw your love be
bright,
the glorious hope perceiving:

3. The feet that tread your holy courts
from light be never banished;
the bodies by your Body fed,
be with new life replenished.
-Syriac Liturgy

HOLY COMMUNION

1199
Rockingham - 8.8.8.8.

1. My God, now is your table spread,
your cup with love still overflows:
so may your children here be fed
as Christ to us his goodness shows.

2. This holy feast, which Jesus makes
a banquet of his flesh and blood
how glad is he who comes and takes
this sacred drink, this royal food!

3. His gifts that richly satisfy
are yet to some in vain displayed:
did not for them the Saviour die
may they not share the children's bread?

4. My God. here let your table be
a place of joy for all your guests,
and may each one salvation see
who now its sacred pledges taste.
-P. Doddridge

1200
Killibegs -8.8.8.8.

1. Now let us from this table rise
renewed in body, mind and soul;
with Christ we die and live again,
his selfless love has made us whole.

2. With minds alert, upheld by grace,
to spread the word in speech and deed,
we follow in the steps of Christ
at one with man in hope and need.

3. To fill each human house with love,
it is the sacrament of care:
the work that Christ began to do
we humbly pledge ourselves to share;

4. Then give us courage, Father God.
to choose again the pligrim way,
and help us to accept with joy
the challenge of tomorrow's day!
-Fred Kaan

1201
I know He's mine

1. There's One above all earthly friends
Whose love all earthly love transcenda
It is my Lord and Christ divine,
My Lord because I know he's mine.

Chorus
I know he's mine, this friend so dear,
He lives with me. he's ever near,
Ten thousand charms around him shine,
And best of all I know he's mine.

2. He's mine because he died for me,
He saved my soul he set me free;
With joy I worship at his shrine And cry,
"Praise God, I know he's mine."

3. He's mine because he's in my heart,
And never, never will we part:
Jesus the branch is to the vine I'm joined to Christ;
I know he's mine.

4. Some day upon the streets of gold
Mine eyes his glory shall behold,
Then, while his arms around me twine.
I'll cry for joy, "I know he's mine."
-Johnson Oatman

1202
Belmont-C.M.

1. According to Thy gracious word,
In meek humility,
This will do, my dying Lord:
I will remember Thee.

HOLY COMMUNION

2. Thy body, broken for my sake,
   My bread from heaven shall be;
   Thy testamental cup I take,
   And thus remember Thee.

3. Gethsemane can I forget?
   Or there Thy conflict see,
   Thine agony and bloody sweat,
   And not remember Thee?

4. When to the cross I turn mine eyes,
   And rest on Calvary,
   O Lamb of God, my sacrifice,
   I must remember Thee:

5. Remember Thee, and all Thy pains,
   And all Thy love to me;
   Yea, while a breath, a pulse
   remains,
   Will I remember Thee.

6. And when these failing lips grow
   dumb,
   And mind and memory flee,
   When Thou shalt in Thy kingdom
   come
   Then Lord, remember me.
   　　　　　　　　　-J. Montgomery

1203

Let us break bread together

1. Let us break bread together on our
   knees;
   Let us break bread together on our
   knees.
   When I fall on my knees; With my
   face to the rising sun,
   O Lord have mercy on me.

2. Let us drink the cup together on our
   knees;
   Let us drink the cup together on our
   knees;
   When I fall on my knees; With my
   face to the rising sun,
   O Lord have mercy on me.

3. Let us praise God together on our
   knees;
   Let us praise God together on our
   knees.

When I fall on my knees; With my
face to the rising sun,
O Lord have mercy on me.

1204

Martyrdom. - C. M.

1. For ever here my rest shall be,
   Close to Thy bleeding side;
   This all my hope, and all my plea.
   For me the Saviour died.

2. My dying Saviour, and my God,
   Fountain for guilt and sin,
   Sprinkle me ever with Thy blood,
   And cleanse, and keep me clean.

3. Wash me, and make me thus Thine
   own,
   Wash me, and mine Thou art,
   Wash me, but not my feet alone,
   My hands, my head, my heart.

4. The atonement of Thy blood supply
   Till faith to sight improve,
   Till hope in full fruition die,
   And all my soul be love.
   　　　　　　　　　-Charles Wesley

1205

Bread Of Life

1. Here at Thy table, Lord, This
   sacred hour,
   O let us feel Thee near, In loving
   power;
   Calling our thoughts away from self
   and sin,
   As to Thy banquet hall We enter in.

2. Sit at the feast, dear Lord, Break
   Thou the bread;
   Fill Thou the cup that brings Life to
   the dead:
   That we may find in Thee, Comfort
   and peace;
   And from all sorrow win A full
   release.

HOLY COMMUNION

3. So shall our life of faith Be full, be sweet;
   And we shall find our strength For each day meet:
   Fed by Thy living bread, All hungry past,
   We shall be satisfied, And saved at last.

4. Come then, O holy Christ, Feed us, we pray;
   Touch with Thy pierced hand Each common day;
   Making this earthly life Full of Thy grace,
   Till in the home of heav'n We find our place,

                                   -Mary P. Hoty

1206
Before Thy Mercy Seat O Lord

1. Before Thy mercy seat O Lord
   Saiviour before Thee we gather
   To penitently beg for forgiveness
   For all the covenants broken.

2. We humbly renew our pledge
   By Thy great strength do uphold us
   To train our children religiously
   To serve and do your perfect will.

3. Grant us Thy grace to seek always
   Salvation for acquaintances
   Trying to be, faithful in deportment
   Walk circumspectly in the world.

4. Grant us to faithfully keep pledge
   And to be just in all dealings
   Set worthy sample of Christian
   In all we say and think and do.

5. Help us to shun and to avoid
   All forms of tattling, backbiting ,
   Excessive anger to abhor
   But quickly seek to reconcile.

6. Grant us to watch over ourselves
   In brotherly love affection
   Cultivate Christian sympathy
   Give aid in sickness and distress.

7. We humbly plead Saviour Divine
   Make us perfect in all good works
   To do that which will please your will
   As the saints in heaven comply.

1207
I Know There Is Power In Jesus' Blood

1. I know there is power in Jesus' blood
   For He washed my sins away,
   And I know there is joy in serving Him For He turned my night to day,

Chorus
There is power, power wonder working power
There is power, power, purifying power,
There is power in Jesus blood.

2. I know there is power in Jesus' blood.
   From my guilt He set me free;
   When f came unto Him with all my sins
   And His blood availed for me.

3. I know there is power in Jesus' blood,
   For all things have been made new;
   Since His own precious blood has been applied
   And has cleansed me through and through.

1208
The Day Is Come, The Feast to Nigh
C.M.

1. The day is come, the feast is high
   I give Myself to you
   Behold I give my blood to you
   Shed for your redemption.

HOLY COMMUNION

2. Till my Father's kingdom above
Before I drink again
By then, no more shall tears be
shed
It shall be joy for aye.

3. This supper shall e'er continue
Until his kingdom come
All o'er the world shall many souls
Eat this supper and drink.

4. God's blessing shall be poured from
heav'n
Upon all those who eat
And from my Father's throne on
high
I'll prepare them a place.

5. But now, for the present I'll drink
The bitter cup for you
And for your sakes, I'll drink the
cup
Of sore anguish of death.

6. Ye cannot know my deep sorrow
Nor yet, my glory seen
But this, continue ye to do
And thus, remember me.

1209

The Holy Communion - P.M.

1. The Holy Communion
The grace of God it is
To eat the bread and drink the wine
In remembrance of Thee.

Chorus
In remembrance of that feast
We are gathered today
To show the Lord's coming back
again.
Until He will come back again.
Until My
(Until my Father's kingdom on high)

Before I.
(Before I drink with you once again)
This is our type of passover feast
Time of deliverance is
When, I by faith, cling to that shed
blood.
I shall freedom receive
Sickness and need shall flee,
Satan's army may rise
We shall conquer them all.

2. The blood that flowed for sin
We see, in this, the type
It is a witness in our heart
That Thou really loves us.

3. This little type of feast,
If it is here so sweet
How sweeter still in heav'n above
When we shall see Thy face.

1210

Till He Come Oh Let The Words
7.7.7.D.

1: Till He come!" Oh let the words
Linger on the trembling chords;
Let the "little white" between
In their golden light be seen;
Let us think how heaven and home
Lie beyond that "Till He come!"

2. When the weary ones we love
Enter on their rest above
Seems the earth so poor and vast?
All our life-joy overcast?
Death and darkness and the tomb
Only whisper "Till He come!"

3. See the feast of love is spread,
Drink the wine and break the bread
Sweet memorials - till the Lord
Call us around His heavenly board
Some from earth, from glory some
Severed only "Till Me come!"

CHRISTIAN MARRIAGE

1211

Melcombe -L.M.

1. O thou who gavest power to love
That we might fix our hearts on Thee,
Preparing us for joys above
By that which here on earth we See;

2. Thy Spirit trains our souls to know
The growing purpose of thy will,
And gives to love the power to show
That purpose growing larger still:

3. Larger, as love to reverent eyes
Makes manifest another soul,
And shows to life a richer prize,
A clearer course, a nobler goal.

4. Lord, grant thy servants who implore
Thy blessing on the hearts they blend,
That from that union evermore
New joys may blossom to the end.

5. Make what is best in each combine
To purge all earthly dross away,
To strengthen, purify, refine,
To beautify each coming day.

6. So may they hand in hand advance
Along life's paths from troubles free;
Brave to meet adverse circumstance
Because their love points up to thee.
                    -Bishop Mandell Creighton

1212

Christus der ist Mein Leben -7.6.7.6.

1. We lift our hearts, O Father,
To Thee our voices raise,

For these Thy suppliant servants,
In mingled prayer and praise:

2. Praise for the joy of loving,
All other joys above,
Praise for the priceless blessing
Of love's response to love.

3. Prayer that the glad surrender
Of self may perfect be,
That each be one with other,
And both be one in Thee;

4. Prayer that Thou wilt accomplish
The promise of today,
And crown the years with blessing
That shall not pass away;

5. Praise for the hope most glorious
That looks beyond the veil
Where faith and hope shall vanish,
But love shall never fail.
                    -E. A. Welch

1213

Alverstoke -11.10.11.10.

1. O happy home where Thou art loved the dearest,
Thou loving friend, and Saviour of our race,
And where among the guests there never cometh
One who can hold such high and honored place.

2. O happy home where each one serves Thee, lowly,
Whatever his appointed work may be,
Till every common task seems great and holy,
When it is done, O Lord, as unto Thee.

3. O happy home where Thou art not forgotten
When joy is overflowing, full, and free;

CHRISTIAN MARRIAGE

O happy home where every wounded spirit
Is brought, Physician, Comforter, to Thee.

4. Until at last, when earthly work is ended,
All meet Thee in the blessed home above
From whence Thou camest; where Thou hast ascended,
Thy everlasting home of peace and love.

-Carl J. P. Spitta

1214

St. Agnes-C.M.

1. Happy the home when God is there
And love fills every one,
When with united work and prayer
The Master's will is done.

2. Happy the home where God's strong love
Is starting to appear,
Where all the children hear His Fame
And parents hold Him dear;

3. Happy the home where prayer is heard
And praise is everywhere,
Where parents love the sacred word
And its true wisdom share.

4. Lord, let us in our homes agree
This blessed peace to gain;
Unite our hearts In love to Thee,
And love to all will reign.

-Henry Ware. Jr.

1215

Christian Home- Irregular

1. God, give us Christian homes!
Homes where the Bible is loved and taught.
Homes where the Master's will is sought,
Homes crowned with beauty Thy love hath wrought:
God, give us Christian homes;
God, give as Christian homes!

2. God, give us Christian homes!
Homes where the father is true and strong.
Homes that are free from blight of wrong,
Homes that are joyous with low song
God, give us Christian homes;
God, give us Christian homes!

3. God. give us Christian homes!
Homes where the mother, in queenly quest.
Strives to show others Thy way is best.
Homes where the Lord is an honored guest;
God, give us Christian homes;
God, give us Christian homes!

4. God give us Christian homes!
Homes where the children are led to know
Christ in H»s beauty Who loves them so,
Homes where the alter fires burn and glow;
God, give us Christian homes;
God, give us Christian homes!

-B. B. McKinney

CHRISTIAN MARRIAGE

1216

St. George S. M.

1. How welcome was the call,
   And sweet the festal lay,
   When Jesus deigned in Cana's hall
   To bless the marriage day.

2. And happy was the bride,
   And glad the bridegroom's heart;
   For He who tamed at their side
   Bade grief and ill depart.

3. His gracious power divine
   The water vessels knew;
   And plenteous was the mystic wine
   The wondering servants drew.

4. O Lord of life and love,
   Come Thou again today,
   And bring a blessing from above
   That ne'er shall pass away.
   -Henry Williams Baker

1217

Irene 8.6.8.4.

1. Rest in the Lord from harps above
   The music seems to thrill
   Rest in His everlasting love,
   Rest and be still.

2. Rest thou, who claimest for thine
   own
   Thy chosen bride today,
   Affianced in His faith alone.
   Thy bride for aye.

3. And thou, whose trustful hand is
   given
   Avouching here thy spouse,
   Rest, for a Father seals in heaven
   His children's vows.

4. Rest ye, who cluster round them
   both
   To mingle praise and prayers;
   Your God affirms the plighted troth,
   Your God and theirs.

5. Rest, for the Heavenly Bridgeroom
   here
   Is standing by your side,
   And in this union draws more near
   His mystic bride.

6. Rest in the Lord thrice Holy Dove,
   In us Thy word fulfil
   Rest in His everlasting love,
   Rest and be still.
   -J. B. Dykes

1218

Perfect Love -11.10.11.10.

1. O Perfect Love, all human thought
   transcending,
   Lowly we kneel in prayer before
   Thy throne,
   That theirs may be the love which
   knows no ending,
   Whom Thou for evermore dost join
   is one.

2. O perfect Life, be Thou their full
   assurance
   Of tender charily and steadfast faith.
   Of patient hope, and quiet brave
   endurance,
   With childlike trust that fears nor
   pain nor death.

3. Grant them the joy which brightens
   earthly sorrow,
   Grant them the peace which calms
   all earthly strife
   And to life's day the glorious
   unknown morrow
   That dawns upon eternal love and
   life.
   -J. Bamby

CHRISTIAN MARRIAGE

1219

Maryton -8.8.8.8. (L.M.)

1. Jesus the Lord of love and life,
   draw near to bless this man and
   wife;
   as they are now in love made one,
   let your good will for them be done.

2. Give them each day your peace and
   joy.
   let no dark clouds these gifts
   destroy;
   in growing trust may love endure,
   to keep their marriage bond secure.

3. As they have vowed to have and
   hold,
   each by the other be consoled;
   in wealth or want, in health or pain,
   till death shall part, let love remain.

4. Deepen, O Lord, their love for you,
   and in that love, their own renew;
   each in the other find delight, as lives
   and interests now unite.

5. Be to them both a guide and friend,
   through all the years their home
   defend:
   Jesus the Lord of love and life,
   stay near and bless this man and
   wife.
                         -James E. Seddon

1220

St Matthias - 8.8.8.8.8.8.

1. Father on high to whom we pray,
   and lift our thankful heart above
   for all your mercies day by day,
   for gifts of heart and home and love:
   protect them still beneath your care

Lord, in your mercy, hear our prayer.

2. O Christ who came as man to earth,
   and chose in Egypt's land to be
   a homeless child of alien birth,
   an exile and a refugee:
   for homeless people everywhere
   Lord, in your mercy, hear our prayer.

3. Spirit divine, whose work is done
   in souls renewed and lives restored
   strive in our hearts to make us one
   one faith, one family, one Lord till at
   the last one home we share
   Lord, in your mercy, hear our prayer
                       -Timothy Dudley Smith

1221

Cornwall - 8.8.6.8.8.6.

1. Great God, we praise the mighty love
   which urges us to rise above
   constructing doubts and fears:
   whose purpose is to set us free
   to live our lives creatively
   Throughout the coming years.

2. We praise you far the love we see
   in man and wife and family,
   in friends and neighbours too;
   the love which nurtured us from birth,
   the love which teaches human worth
   and leads our minds to you.

3. We praise you most for love supreme
   which breaks through pain and death
   to stream
   in unrestricted light;
   which from Christ's resurrection
   dawn
   has shone, and never been with
   drawn,
   to make our future bright.

4. For by your perfect love refined
   our own will not be undermined
   by futile guilt and shame;
   but through disaster, grief or trife

CHRISTIAN MARRIAGE

by futile guilt and shame;
but through disaster, grief or strife
we'll re-affirm the joy of life and
glorify your name.

-A. Gaunt

1222

St. Alphege -7.6.7.6.

1. A The voice that breathed o'er Eden,
That earliest wedding day,
The primal marriage blessing,
It hath not passed away.

2. Still in the pure espousal
Of Christian man and maid
The Holy Three are with us,
The threefold grace is said,

3. For dower of blessed children,
For love and faith's sweet sake,
For high mysterious union
Which nought on earth may break.

4. Be present, heavenly Father,
To give away this bride,
As Eve Thou gav'st to Adam
Out of his own pierced side.

5. Be present, gracious Saviour,
To join their loving hands,
As Thou didst bind two natures
In Thine eternal bands.

6. Be present. Holy Spirit,
To bless them as they kneel,
As Thou for Christ the Bridgeroom
The heavenly spouse dost seal.

7. O spread Thy pure wings o'er them!
Let no ill power find place,
When onward through life's journey
The hallowed path they trace.

8 To cast their crowns before Thee,
In perfect sacrifice,

Till to the home of gladness
With Christ's own bride they rise.

-John. Keble

1223

Melcombe -L.M.

1. O Father, Thou who givest all
The bounty of Thy perfect love,
We thank Thee that upon us fall
Such tender blessings from above.

2. We thank Thee for the grace of
home,
For mother's love and father's care;
For friends and teachers, all who
come
Our joys and hopes and fears to
Share;

3. For eyes to see and ears to hear,
For hands to serve and arms to lift,
For shoulders broad and strong to
bear.
For feet to run on errands swift.

4. For faith to conquer doubt and fear,
For love to answer every call,
For strength to do and will to dare.
We thank Thee, O Thou Lord of all.

-John Haynes Holmes

1224

Illsley -LM.

1. O Father, by whose sovereign sway
The sun and stars in order move,
Yet who hast made us bold to say
Thy nature and thy name is love:

2. O royal Son. whose every deed
Showed love and love's divinity.
Yet didst not scorn the humblest need
At Cana's feast in Galilee:

3. O Holy Spirit, who dost speak
In saint and sage since time began.

CHRISTIAN MARRIAGE

Yet givest courage to the weak
And teachest love to selfish man:

4. Be present in our hearts today,
   All powerful to bless, and give
   To these thy children grace that they
   May love, and through their loving
   live.

   -Cyril Argentine Alington

1225

Rhosyemeddre -6.6.6.6.8.8.8.

1. Our Fattier, by whose Name
   All fatherhood is known,
   Who dost in love proclaim
   Each family thine own,
   Bless thou all parents, guarding well,
   With constant love as sentinel,
   The homes in which thy people
   dwell.

2. O Christ, thyself a child
   Within an earthly home,
   With heart still undefiled,
   Thou didst to manhood come;
   Our children bless, ev'ry place,
   That they may all behold thy face,
   And knowing thee may grow in
   grace.

3. O Spirit, who dost bind
   Our hearts in unity,
   Who teachest us to find
   The love from self set free,
   In all our hearts such love increase
   That ev'ry home, by this release,
   May be the dwelling place of peace
   -F. Bland Tucker

1226

Day of Rest-7.6.7.6 D.

1. O Father, all creating,
   Whose wisdom, love, and power

First bound two lives together
In Eden's primal hour
Today to these Thy children
Thine earliest gifts renew:
A home by Thee made happy,
A love by Thee kept true.

2. O Saviour, Guest most bounteous
   Of old in Galilee.
   Vouchsafe today Thy presence
   With those who call on Thee:
   Their store of earthly gladness
   Transform to heavenly wine,
   And teach them in the tasting
   To know the gift is Thine.

3. O Spirit of the Father.
   Breathe on them from above,
   So mighty Thy pureness,
   So tender in Thy love,
   That, guarded by Thy presence,
   From sin and strife kept free,
   Their lives may own Thy guidance
   Their hearts be ruled by Thee.

4. Except Thou build it, Father,
   The house is built in vain;
   Except Thou, Saviour, bless it,
   The joy will turn to pain:
   But nought can break the union
   Of hearts in Thee made one:
   And love Thy Spirit hallows
   Is endless love begun.
   -John Ellerton

1227

Saffron Walden - 8.8.8.6.

1. O God of Love, to Thee we bow
   And pray for these before Thee now,
   That, closely knit in holy vow,
   They may in Thee be one.

2. When days are filled with pure
   When paths are plain and skies
   bright,
   Walking by faith and not by sight
   May they in Thee be one.

3. Then stormy winds fulfill Thy will,
And all their good seems turned to ill,
Then, trusting Thee completely, still
may they in Thee be one.

4. Whate'er in life shall be their share
Of quickening joy or burdening care,
In power to do and grace to bear,
May they in Thee be one.

5. Eternal Love, with them abide;
In Thee for ever may they hide,
For even death cannot divide
Those whom Thou makest one.
-William Vaughan Jenkins

1228

Our house

1. Our house is the place I love best,
Our house isn't like all the rest;
For our love makes something special
out of our house our house,
At our house we are taught to obey,
And our house is a church when we pray;
For God's love makes something special
out of our house ev'ry day.
-Flo Price

1229

Finlandia

1. O give us homes built firm upon the Saviour,
Where Christ is Head and Counselor and Guide;
Where ev'ry child is taught His love and favor
And gives his heart to Christ, the crucified:
How sweet to know that tho his footsteps waver

His faithful Lord is walking by his side!

2. O give us homes with godly fathers, mothers,
Who always place their hope and trust in Him;
Whose tender patience turmoil never bothers,
Whose calm and courage trouble cannot dim;
A home where each finds joy in serving others,
And love still shines, tho' days be dark and grim.

3. O give us homes where Christ is Lord and Master,
The Bible read, the precious hymns still sung;
Where prayer comes first in peace or in disaster,
And praise is natural speech to every tongue;
Where mountains move before a faith that's vaster,
And Christ sufficient is for old and young.

4. O Lord, our God, our homes are Thine forever!
We trust to Thee their problems, toil, and care;
Their bonds of love no enemy can sever
If Thou art always Lord and Master there:
Be Thou the centre of our least endeavor;
Be Thou our Guest, our hearts and homes to share.
-Barbara B. Hart

1230

Let It ring

1. I'll praise the Lord in my house,
Will you praise the Lord in yours?

CHRISTIAN MARRIAGE

If we praise the Lord in this state,
Soon this whole great country will
know that
Jesus Christ our Saviour has
conquered ev'ry foe.

Chorus
It's ringing here, its ringing there,
The joy of the Lord is ev'rywhere.
It's ringing loud, It's ringing clear.
The joy of the Lord is here!

2. I'll thank the Lord in my house,
Will you thank the Lord in yours?
If we thank the Lord in our town,
Will you thank the Lord in yours?
If we thank the Lord in this state.
Soon this whole great country will
know that
Jesus Christ our Saviour has
conquered ev'ry foe.

3. I'll serve the Lord in my house,
Will you serve the Lord in yours?
If we serve the Lord in our town,
Will you serve the Lord in yours?
If we serve the Lord in this state,
Soon this whole great country will
know that
Jesus Christ our Saviour has
conquered ev'ry foe.

-Kurt Kaiser

1231

O Lord, Put Thy Seal Upon
7.7.7.7.7.7.

1. O Lord, put Thy seal upon
This wedlock that we witness
In Thy honour, meet with us
Bless their promises of love
Make this fellowship holy
For them and also with Thee.

2. Thou wert present in Cana
In a marriage. Just as this
Meet with us while we are here
Thou, the fountain of blessings

Adorn this marriage with joy
Such as the world cannot give.

3. Not for miracle we ask
Such as water be made wine
But all of our heart desire
Is that we taste of Thy love
May Thy power divine, we pray
Make holy our natural love.

4. O Lord, from today onward
Husband and wife let us be
How ever long it may be
To the very end with Thee
In the land of rest above
In Thy home high up in heav'n.

1232

Ye Little Ones Keep Close To God
L.M.

1. Ye little ones keep close to God
In trembling and humility
Knees bow down before Him,
Our Lord and Saviour and our
Friend.

2. O Saviour, let Thy great mercy
Fill us with gratitude to Thee
And in our pilgrimage on earth
May we receive more of Thy grace.

3. O Saviour, may all evil thoughts
Be far away flung from our hearts,
And each day, give us Thy wisdom
To choose to walk the narrow way.

4. In times of sickness and good
health,
In times of plenty or in need,
And when the hour of death shall
come
Deliver us with Thy great pow'r.

CHILDREN AND YOUTH

1233

David-D.C.M.

1. O, David was a shepherd lad,
And guarded well the sheep;
By night and day, good times or
bad,
His watch he used to keep,
But David's less than David's Son,
Though a Shepherd too is he;
Through all the world his pastures
run,
And of his flock are we.

2. O, David was a shepherd lad,
And more he dared to do:
Goliath all in armour clad
With sling and stone he slew,
But David's Son, more daring yet,
Put weapons all away;
All evil things with goodness met,
And stronger was than they.

3. O, David was a shepherd lad,
And a kingdom he attained;
And gold and glory great he had,
And forty years he reigned.
But David's Son is rich in love,
And reigns eternally;
For King he is in heaven above,
And on the earth shall be.
                          -E. Erskine Clark

1234

Quem pastores - 8.8.8.7.

1. Jesus, kind above all other,
Gentle Child of gentle Mother,
In the stable born our Brother,
Whom the angel hosts adore:

2. Jesus, cradled in a manger,
Keep us free from sin and danger,
And to all, both friend and stranger
Give thy blessing evermore.
                          -J. M. Neale

1235

Dayspring-CM.

1. We have a King who came to earth
To win the world for God,
And we, the children of the King,
Must follow were he trod.

2. The banner that our King unfurled
Was love to every man,
So we must try to show that love
In all the ways we can.

3. The enemies he came to fight
Are selfishness and sin:
Then who would be a traitor now
And let this foemen in?

4. He bids us keep our bodies pure,
For 'tis the pure and clean
Can see the glory of the King,
And tell what they have seen.

5. We are a little company,
But we are pledged to bring
Pure holy lives, kind joyful hearts,
And bring them to the King.
                          -Margaret Cropper

1236

Jesus Loves Me - 7.7.7.7. with Refrain

1. Jesus loves me, this I know,
For the Bible tells me so;
Little ones to Him belong,
They are weak, but He is strong.

Chorus
Yes, Jesus loves me,
Yes, Jesus loves me,
Yes, Jesus loves me,
The Bible tells me so.

CHILDREN AND YOUTH

Chorus
Arise, arise, The Master calls for thee;
Arise, arise, O youth of God.
March on to victory!

2. Arise, O youth of God
His kingdom tarries long;
Bring in the day of joy and peace,
And end the night of wrong,

3. Arise, O youth of God!
The church for you doth wait;
Her strength shall make your spirit strong;
Her service make you great.

4. Lift high the cross of Christ!
Tread where His feet have trod;
Be loyal to the King of kings;
March on, O youth of God!
-William P, Memil

1239

Berthold - 7.6.7.6.D.

1. With happy voices ringing,
Thy children, Lord, appear;
Their joyous praises bringing
In anthems full and clear,
For skies of golden splendor,
For azure rolling sea,
For blossoms sweet and tender,
O Lord, we worship Thee.

2. For though no eye beholds Thee.
No hand thy touch may feel.
Thy universe unfolds Thee,
Thy starry heav'ns reveal;
The earth and all its glory,
Our homes and all we love
Tell forth the wondrous story
Of One who reigns above.

3. And shall we not adore Thee,
With more than joyous song,
And live in truth before Thee.
All beautiful and strong?

2. Jesus loves me! He who died
Heaven's gate to open wide;
He will wash away my sin,
Let His little child come in.

3. Jesus loves me! He will stay
Close beside me alt the way,
Then His little child will take
Up to heaven, for His dear sake.
-Anna B. Warre

1237

In Memoriam - 8.6.7.6.7.6.7.6.

1. There's a Friend for little children
Above the bright blue sky;
A friend who never changeth,
Whose love can never die,
Unlike our friends by nature,
Who change with changing years,
This Friend is always worthy
The precious name He bears.

2. There's a home for little children
Above the bright blue sky.
Where Jesus reigns in glory,
A home of peace and joy;
No home on earth is like it
Nor can with it compare,
For every one is happy,
Nor can be happier there.

3. There's a robe for little children
Above the bright blue sky,
A harp of sweetest music,
A palm of victory,
All, all above is treasured,
And found in Christ alone;
Lord, grant thy tittle children
To know Thee as their own
-A. Midlane

1238

Leavell S.M. with Refrain

1. Arise, O youth of God!
Have done with lesser things;
Give heart and soul and mind and strength
To serve the King of kings.

CHILDREN AND YOUTH

Lord, bless our souls' endeavor
Thy servants true to be,
And through alt life, forever,
To live our praise to Thee.
                    -William G. Tarrant

1240

Battshill -7.7.7.7.

Thank you for the world so sweet;
Thank you for the food we eat;
Thank you for the birds that sing:
Thank you. God, for everything
                    -Jonathan Battishill

1241

Priase Him -10.6.10.6.

1. Praise Him, praise Him,
   all His children praise Him!
   He is love, He is love.

2. Thank Him, thank Him,
   all His children thank Him!
   He is love, He is love.

3. Love Him, love Him,
   all His children love Him!
   He is love, He is love.

4. Crown Him, crown Him,
   all His children crown Him!
   He is love. He is love.

5. Serve Him, serve Him,
   all His children serve Him!
   He is love, He is love.
                    -Percy Deamer

1242

Hmerton -6.5.6.5.

1. Waken! Christian children,
   Up and let us sing,
   With glad voice, the praises
   Of our new born King.

2. Come, nor fear to seek Him,
   Children though we be,
   Once He said of children,
   "Let them come to Me."

3. In a manger lowly,
   Sleeps the heavenly Child;
   O'er Him fondly bendeth
   Mary, mother mild.

4. Far above that stable,
   Up in heaven so high.
   One bright star out-shineth,
   Watching silently.

5. Fear not then to enter,
   Though we cannot bring
   Gold, or myrrh, or incense
   Fitting for a King,

6. Gifts He asketh richer,
   Offerings costlier still,
   Yet may Christian children
   Bring them if they will.

7. Brighter than all jewels
   Shines the modest eye;
   Best of gifts He loveth
   Childlike purity.

8. Haste we then to welcome
   With a joyous lay
   Christ the King of Glory,
   Born for us today.
                    -S. C. Hamerton

1243

All Things Bright And Beautiful - 7.6.7.6. and Refrain

Chorus
All things bright and beautiful,
all creatures great and small,
all things wise and wonderful
the Lord God made them all.

1. Each little flower that opens,
   each little bird that sings
   he made their glowing colours,
   he made their tiny wings.
                    All things bright.

2. The purple headed mountain,
   the river running by,
   the sunset, and the morning
   that brightens up the sky:
   > All things bright....

3. The cold wind in the winter,
   the pleasant summer sun,
   the ripe fruits in the garden
   he made them every one.
   > All things bright....

4. He gave us eyes to see them,
   and lips that we might tell
   how great is God almighty,
   who has made all things well!
   > All things bright...
   > -Cecil F. Alexander

1244

Kum Ba Yah -8.8.8.5.

1. Father God in heaven,
   Lord most high:
   hear your children's prayer,
   Lord most high:
   hallowed be your name,
   Lord most high
   O Lord, hear our prayer,

2. May your kingdom come
   here on earth;
   may your will be done
   here on earth,
   as it is in heaven
   so on earth
   O Lord, hear our prayer.

3. Give us daily bread
   day by day,
   and forgive our sins
   'day by day,
   as we too forgive
   day by day
   O Lord, hear our prayer.

4. Lead us in your way,
   make us strong;
   when temptations come
   make us strong;
   save us from all sin,
   keep us strong
   O Lord, hear our prayer.

5. All things come from you,
   all are yours
   kingdom, glory, power,
   all are yours;
   take our lives and gifts,
   all are yours
   O Lord, hear our prayer.
   > -James E. Seddon

1245

In Memoriam - 8.6.7.6.7.6.7.6.

1. There's a song for all the children
   that makes the heavens ring,
   a song that even angels can
   never, never sing;
   they praise him as their maker
   and see him glorified,
   but we can call him Saviour
   because for us he died.

2. There's a place for all the children
   where Jesus reigns in love,
   a place of joy and freedom
   that nothing can remove;
   a home that is more friendly
   than any home we know,
   where Jesus makes us welcome
   because he loves us so.

3. There's a friend for all the children
   to guide us every day,
   whose care is always faithful and
   never fades away;
   there's no one else so loyal
   his friendship stays the same;
   he knows us and he loves us,
   and Jesus is his name.
   > -A. midlane

CHILDREN AND YOUTH

1246
If I Come To Jesus

1. If I come to Jesus;
   He will make me glad;
   He will give me pleasure
   When my heart is sad.

   Chorus
   If I come to Jesus,
   Happy shall be,
   He is gently calling
   Little ones like me.

2. if I come to Jesus,
   He will hear my pray'r,
   For He loves me dearly,
   And my sins did bear.

3. if I come to Jesus,
   He will take my hand;
   He will kindly lead me
   To a better land.

4. There with happy children,
   Robed in snowy white,
   I shall see my Saviour,
   In that world so bright.
      -Fanny J. Crosby

1247
Do You Know What Makes Us Happy

1. Do you know what makes us happy
   When so many hearts are sad?
   We are little friends of Jesus,
   That is why we are so glad;

   Chorus
   We are little friends, we are loving friend
   We are happy, happy little friends of Jesus
   We are little friends, we are loving friends,
   We are happy all day along.

2. Jesus loves the children clearly,
   In His word He tells them so;
   Once He took them up and bless'd them,
   Many, many years ago.

3. We are little lambs of Jesus;
   He, our Shepherd kind and dear,
   Speaks, and though we do not see Him,
   In our hearts His voice we hear.
      -S. Martin

1248
Trinity Chapel

1. I am so glad that our Father in Heav'n
   Tells of His love in the Book He has g'v'n,
   Wonderful things in the Bible I see;
   This is the dearest, that Jesus loves me,

   Chorus
   I am so glad that Jesus loves me,
   Jesus loves me, Jesus loves me:
   I am so glad that Jesus loves me,
   Jesus loves even me.

2. Tho' I forget Him and wander away,
   Still He doth love wherever I stray;
   Back to His dear loving arms would flee,
   When I remember that Jesus loves me,

3. Oh, if there's only one song I can sing,
   When in His beauty I see the great King,
   This shall my song in eternity be:
   "Oh, what a wonder that Jesus loves me."
      -Philip P. Bliss

CHILDREN AND YOUTH

1249

Rickmansworth - 8.3.8.3.

1. Jesus, the children are calling;
   O draw near!
   Fold the young lambs inThy
   bosom,
   Shepherd dear.

2. Slow are our footsteps and fading,
   Oft we fall;
   Jesus the children are calling;
   Hear their call!

3. Cold is our love, Lord, and narrow;
   Large is Thine,
   Faithful, and strong and tender:
   So be mine.

4. Gently, Lord. lead Thou our mothers;
   Weary they;
   Bless all our sisters and brothers
   Night and day.

5. Fathers themselves are God's
   children;
   Teach them still;
   Let the good Spirit show all men
   God's wise will.

   -Annie Matheson

1250

Herongate - L.M.

1. It is a thing most wonderful,
   Almost too wonderful to be,
   That God's own Son should come
   from heav'n
   And die to save a child like me.

2. And yet I know that it is true;
   He came to this poor world below,
   And wept and toiled and mourned
   and died,
   Only because He loved us so.

3. I cannot tell how He could love
   A child so weak and full of sin;
   His love must be most wonderful,
   If He could die my love to win.

4. It is most wonderful to know
   His love for me so free and sure;
   But 'tis more wonderful to see
   My love for Him so faint and poor.

5. And yet I want to love Thee, Lord;
   Oh, light the flame within my heart,
   And I will love Thee more and more
   until I see Thee as Thou art
   -W. W. How

1251

North Coates -6.5.6.5.

1. Jesus, high in glory,
   Lend a list'ning ear;
   When we bow before Thee,
   Children's praises hear.

2. Tho' Thou art so holy,
   Heav'ns almighty King,
   Thou wilt stoop to listen
   While Thy praise we sing.

3. We are little children,
   Weak and apt to stray:
   Saviour, guide and keep us
   In the heavenly way.

4. Save us, Lord, from sinning,
   Watch us day by day:
   Help us now to love Thee,
   Take our sins away.

5. Then when Thou shalt call us
   To our heavenly home.
   We will gladly answer,
   "Saviour, Lord, we come."

6. In the many mansions,
   From all sin set free,
   Loud shall be our praises,
   When Thy face we see.
   -Harriet B. McKeever

CHILDREN AND YOUTH

1252

Goshew -6-5.6.5.0

1. Jesus is our Shepherd,
   Wiping ev'ry tear;
   Folded in His bosom,
   What have we to fear?
   Only let us follow
   Whither He doth lead,
   To the thirsty desert
   Or the dewy mead.

2. Jesus is our Shepherd;
   Well we know His voice;
   How its gentle whisper
   Makes our heart rejoice!
   Even when He chideth,
   Tender His life tone;
   None but He shall guide us;
   We are His alone.

3. Jesus is our Shepherd:
   For the sheep He bled;
   Every lamb is sprinkled
   With the blood He shed:
   Then on each He setteth
   His own secret sign;
   They that have My Spirit,
   These, 'saith He, 'are Mine.'

4. Jesus is our Shepherd;
   Guarded by His arm,
   Though the wolves may raven,
   None can do us harm:
   When we tread death's valley,
   Dark with fearful gloom,
   We will fear no evil,
   Victors o'er the tomb.
                    -Hugh Stowell

1253

Glory-8.6.8.6.8.8.

1. Around the throne of God in heav'n
   Thousands of children stand,

Children whose sins are all forgiv'n,
A holy, happy band

Chorus
Singing: Glory, glory, glory!
Singing: Glory, glory, glory!

2. What brought them to that world
   above?
   That heav'n so bright and fair.
   Where all is peace, and joy, and love;
   How came those children there?

3. Because the Saviour shed His blood
   To wash away their sin;
   Berthed in that pure and precious
   flood.
   Behold them white and clean

4. On earth they sought the Saviour's
   grace,
   On earth they loved His name:
   So now they see life blessed face.
   And stand before the Lamb
                    -Anne Shepherd

1254

Portrush -11.11.11.12.

1. We are little children,
   very young indeed,
   But the Saviour's promise
   each of us may plead.

Chorus
If we seek Him early,
if we come today,
We can be His little friends,
He, has said we may.

2. Little friends of Jesus,
   what a happy thought!
   What a precious promise
   in the Bible taught;

3. Little friends of Jesus,
   walking by His side,
   With His arm around us
   Ev'ry step to guide.

We must love Him dearly
with a constant love,
Then we'll go and see Him
in our home above.

　　　　　　　　-Fanny J. Crosby

1255

Gleniffer 5.5.6.5.6.4.6.4.

1. Jesus bids us shine With a clear,
pure light,
Like a little candle burning in the
night;
In this world is darkness, So we
must shine,
You in your small corner, And I in
mine.

2. Jesus bids us shine. First of all for
Him;
Well He sees and knows it If our
light is dim;
He looks down from heaven To see
us shine,
You in your small corner, And I in
mine.

3. Jesus bids us shine, Then for all
around,
Many kinds of darkness In this world
abound
Sin and want and sorrow So we must
shine.
You in your small corner, And I in
mine.

　　　　　　　　-Susan Warner

1256

Shining for Jesus

1. Shining for Jesus ev'rywhere I go;
Shining for Jesus in this world of
woe;
Shining for Jesus, more like Him I
grow;
Shining all the time for Jesus.

Chorus
Shining all the time, shining all the
time
Shining for Jesus, beams of love
divine;
Glorifying Him ev'ryday and hour,
Shining all the time for Jesus.

2. Shining for Jesus when the way is
bright;
Shining for Jesus in the darkest
night;
Shining for Jesus, making burdens
light;
Shining all the time for Jesus.

3. Shining for Jesus in a world of sin;
Shining for Jesus bringing lost
ones in;
Shining for Jesus, glorifying Him;
Shining all the time for Jesus.

4. Shining for Jesus while He gives
me grace;
Shining for Jesus while I run the
race;
Shining for Jesus till I see His face;
Shining all the time for Jesus.
　　　　　　　　-Charles Inglis

1257

Happy-6.4.6.4.6.7.6.4.

1. There is a happy land, Far, far
away,
Where saints in glory stand, Bright,
bright as day:
O how they sweetly sing, 'Worthy is
our Saviour King"
Loud let His praises ring, Praise,
praise for aye.

2. Come to this happy land, Come,
come away
Why will ye doubting stand? Why
still delay:
O we shall happy be When, from sin
and sorrow free, Lord, we shad live
with Thee, Blest, blest for aye.

CHILDREN AND YOUTH

3. Bright in that happy land Beams
    ev'ry eye:
    Kept by a Father's hand, Love
    cannot die:
    In then to glory run; Be a crown
    and kingdom won;
    And, bright above the sun, Reign,
    reign for aye.

    -Andrew Young

1258
Strassburg - C.M.

1. Dear Father, keep me through this
    day
    Obedient, kind and true:
    That, always loving thee, I may
    Seek all thy will to do.

    -G. W. Briggs

1259
Haslemere - 5.5.5.5.

1. God whose name is Love,
    Happy children we:
    Listen to the hymn
    That we sing to thee.

2. Help us to be good,
    Always kind and true,
    In the games we play
    Or the work we do.

3. Bless us every one
    Singing here to thee.
    God whose name is Love.
    Loving may we be!

    -Florence Hoatson

1260
Camber-6.5.6.5.

1. Little drops of water,
    Little grains of sand,
    Make the mighty ocean
    And the beauteous land.

2. Little deeds of kindness,
    Little words of love,
    Make our earth an Eden,
    Like the heavens above.

3. Little seeds of mercy
    Sown by youthful hands,
    Grow to bless the nations
    Far in other lands.

4. Glory then for ever
    Be to God on high,
    Beautiful and loving,
    To eternity.

    -Mrs. J. A. Camey

1261
Jesus Christ Our Saviour

1. Who came down from heav'n to
    earth?
    Jesus Christ our Saviour!
    Came a child of lowly birth?
    Jesus Christ our Saviour!

Chorus
Sound the chorus loud and clear
He hath brought salvation near.
None so precious, none so dear:
Jesus Christ our Saviour!

2. Who was lifted on the tree?
    Jesus Christ our Saviour!
    There to ransom you and me?
    Jesus Christ our Saviour!

3. Who hath promised to forgive?
    Jesus Christ our Saviour!
    Who hath said, "Believe and live"?
    Jesus Christ our Saviour!

4. Who is now enthroned above?
    Jesus Christ our Saviour!
    Whom should we obey and love?
    Jesus Christ our Saviour!

5. Who again from heaven shall
come?
Jesus Christ our Saviour!
Take to glory all His own?
Jesus Christ our Saviour!

-El Nathan

1262

Beatitude-C.M.

1 The Word of God shall be my guide
And teach me every day;
Its truth will keep me near His side
And help me go His way.

2. There is a Life for me to live,
And God would be therein,
That by His presence He may give
The power to strive and win.

-Calvin W. Laufer

1263

StBuudwater C.M.

1. When Jesus enter'd the Temple
The shout of praise, we heard
The children acknowledged His right
And they rejoic'd in Him

2. Hosannah raise the Temple high
And mixed with divers tongues
Hosannah to the King of heav'n
Unto the David's seed

3. Renew our days, O Lord in Thee
O when children praise Thee
Great is Thy strength and goodness
Lord As in the days of Old

-John Hopkins

1264

I Was Glad When They Said

1. I was glad when they said unto me,
Let us go into the house of the Lord;
I was glad when they said unto me,
Let us go into the house of the Lord.

-B. B. McKinney

1265

Glenfinlas -6.5.6.5.

1. Do no sinful action;
Speak no angry word;
Ye belong to Jesus,
Children of the Lord.

2. Christ is kind and gentle,
Christ is pure and true,
And His little children
Must be holy too.

3. There's a wicked spirit
Watching round you still,
And he tries to tempt you
To all harm and ill.

4. But ye must not hear him,
Though 'tis hard for you
To resist the evil,
And the good to do.

5. Christ is your own master;
He is good and true,
And His little children
Must be holy too.

-Cecil Frances Alexander

1266

Tryggare Kan Ingen Vara - L.M.

1. Children of the heav'nly Father
Safely in His bosom gather;
Nestling bird nor star in heaven
Such a refuge was given

2. God His own doth tend and nourish,
   In His holy courts they flourish;
   From all evil things He spares them,
   In His mighty arms He bears them.

3. Neither life nor death shall ever
   From the Lord His children sever,
   Unto them His grace He showeth,
   And their sorrows all He knoweth.

4. Praise the Lord in joyful numbers,
   Your Protector never slumbers;
   At the will of your Defender
   Ev'ry foe-man must surrender.

5. Though, he giveth or He taketh,
   God His children ne'er forsaketh;
   His the loving purpose solely
   To preserve them pure and holy.
   -Carolina Sandell Berg

1267
Holy, Holy-Irregular

1. Holy, holy, holy, holy,
   Holy, holy, Lord God Almighty;
   And we lift our hearts before
   You as a token of our love,
   Holy, holy, holy, holy.

2. Gracious Father, gracious Father.
   We're so blest to be Your children,
   gracious Father,
   And we lift our hearts before
   You as a token of our love,
   Gracious Father, gracious Father.

3. Gracious Jesus, precious Jesus,
   We're so glad that You've redeemed
   us, precious Jesus;
   And we lift our hearts before
   You as a token of our love,
   Precious Jesus, precious Jesus.

4. Holy Spirit, Holy Spirit,

Come and fill our hearts anew.
Holy Spirit;
And we lift our hearts before
You as a token of our love,
Holy Spirit, Holy Spirit

5. Holy, holy, holy, holy.
   Holy, holy, Lord God Almighty;
   And we lift our hearts before
   You as a token of our love,
   Holy, holy, holy, holy.

6. Hallelujah, hallelujah,
   Hallelujah, hallelujah;
   And we lift our hearts before
   You as a token of our love,
   Hallelujah, hallelujah.
   -Jimmy Owens

1268
Be Glorified - Irregular

1. In my life, Lord, be glorified, be glorified,
   In my life. Lord. be glorified, today.

2. In my song. Lord, be glorified, be glorified,
   In my song, Lord, be glorified, today.

3. In Your Church. Lord, be glorified, be glorified,
   In Your Church, Lord, be glorified, today.
   -Bob Kilpatrick

1269
Children-8.7.7.7.11.

1. Jesus loves the tittle children,
   All the children of the world.
   Red and yellow, black and white
   They are precious in His sight
   Jesus loves the little children,
   All the children of the world.
   -Reverend C. H. Woolston

CHILDREN AND YOUTH

1270

Yesterday, Today and Tomorrow - Irregular

1. Yesterday He died for me, yesterday, yesterday,
Yesterday He died for me, yesterday,
Yesterday He died for me, died for me This is history.

Today He lives for me, today, today,
Today He lives for me, today,
Today He lives for me, lives for me This is victory.

Tomorrow He comes for me, He comes, He comes,
Tomorrow He comes for me, He comes.
Tomorrow He comes for me, comes for me This is mystery;

O friend, do you know Him? know Him? know Him?
O friend, do you know Him? know Him?
O friend, do you know Him? do you know Him?
Jesus Christ the Lord. Jesus Christ the Lord,
Jesus Christ the Lord.

-Jack Wyrtzen

1271

Away in a manger -11.11.11.11.

1. Away in a manger, no crib for a bed,
The little Lord Jesus laid down His sweet head;
The stars in the sky looked down where He lay,
The little Lord Jesus, asleep on the hay.

2. The cattle are rowing, the Baby awakes,
But little Lord Jesus no crying He makes,

I love Thee, Lord Jesus, look down from the sky,
And stay by my cradle till morning is nigh.

3. Be near me. Lord Jesus. I ask Thee to stay
Close by me for ever, and love me, I pray.
Bless all the dear children in Thy tender care,
And fit us for heaven, to live with Thee there.

-Source unknown

1272

Innocents - 7.7.7.7.

1. Gentle Jesus, meek and mild,
Look upon a little child,
Pity my simplicity,
Suffer me to come to Thee.

2. Fain I would to Thee be brought
Gracious Lord, forbid it not;
In the kingdom of Thy grace
Give a little child a place.

3. Fain I would be as Thou art;
Give me Thy obedient heart;
Thou art pitiful and kind;
Let me have Thy loving mind.

4. Let me above all fulfil God my heavenly Father's will;
Never His good Spirit grieve,
Only to His glory live.

5. Lamb of God, I look to Thee:
Thou shall my example be;
Thou art gentle, meek, and mild:
Thou wast once a little child.

6. Thou didst live to God alone;
Thou didst never seek Thine own;
Thou Thyself didst never please:
God was all Thy happiness.

7. Loving Jesus, gentle Lamb,
In Thy gracious hands I am:
Make me, Saviour, what Thou art:
Live Thyself within my heart.

8. I shall then show forth Thy praise,
   Serve Thee all my happy days;
   Then the world shall always see
   Christ, the holy Child, in me.
       -Charles Wesley

1273

Newbury - C.M.

1. I love to think, though I am young,
   My Saviour was a child;
   That Jesus walked this earth along,
   With feet all undefiled.

2. He kept His Father's word of truth,
   As I am taught to do;
   And while He walked the paths of
   youth,
   He walked in wisdom too.

3. I love to think that he who spake
   And made the blind to see,
   And called the sleeping dead to
   wake,
   Was once a child like me.

4. That He who wore the thorny
   crown,
   And tasted death's despair, Had a
   kind mother like my own,
   And knew her love and care.

5. I know 'twas all for love of me
   That he became a child,
   And left the heavens, so fair to see,
   And trod earth's pathway wild.

6. Then, Saviour, who wast once a
   child,
   A chilled may come to Thee;
   And O in all Thy mercy mild,
   Dear Saviour, come to me!
       -Edwin Paxton Hood

1274

Irby- 8.7.8.7. .7.

1. Once in royal David's city
   Stood a lowly cattle shed,
   Where a mother laid her baby
   In a manger for His bed.

Mary was that mother-mild,
Jesus Christ her little child.

2. He came down to earth from heaven
   Who is God and Lord of all,
   And His shelter was a stable,
   And His cradle was a stall,
   With the poor, and meek, and lowly
   Lived on earth our Saviour holy.

3. And through all His wondrous
   childhood.
   He would honour and obey,
   Love, and watch the lowly maiden
   Christian children all must be
   Mild, obedient, good as He.

4. For He is our childhood's pattern;
   Day by day like us He grew;
   He was little, weak, and helpless;
   Tears and smiles like us He knew,
   And He feeleth for our sadness,
   And He shareth in our gladness.

5. And our eyes at last shall see Him,
   Through His own redeeming love;
   For that child so dear and gentle
   Is our Lord in heaven above;
   And He leads His children on
   To the place where He is gone.
       -Cecil France Alexander

1275

Tours-7.6.7.6.D.

1. When, His salvation bringing,
   To Zion Jesus came,
   The children all stood singing
   Hosanna to His name;
   Nor did their zeal offend Him,
   But, as He rode along,
   He let them still attend Him,
   And smiled to hear their song.

2. And, since the Lord retaineth
   His love for children still,
   Though now as King He reigneth
   On Zion's heavenly hill,
   We'll flock around His banner

Who site upon the throne,
And cry aloud: Hosanna,
To David's royal Son!

3. For, should we fail proclaiming
Our great Redeemer's praise,
The stones, our silence shaming,
Would their hosannas raise.
But shall we only render
The tribute of our words ?
No' while our hearts are tender,
They too shall be the Lord's.
-John King

1276

1. We thank You for your kindness,
We thank You for your love.
We've been In heav'nly places,
Felt blessings from above
We've been sharing all the good things,
the fam'ly can afford,
Let's just turn our praise t'ward heaven;
And praise the Lord.

Chorus
Let's just praise the Lord?
Praise the Lord!
Let's just lift our hands t'ward heaven
and praise the Lord;
Let's just praise the Lord,
praise the Lord,
Let's just lift our hands t'ward heaven
and praise the Lord.

2. Just the precious name of Jesus is
worthy of our praise,
Let us bow our knee before Him,
Our hands to heaven raise;
When He comes in clouds of
Glory with Him to ever reign,
Let's lift our happy voices,
and praise His dear Name.
-Gloria Gaither

1277
I Would Be Like Jesus

1. Earthly pleasures vainly call me;
I would be like Jesus;
Nothing worldly shall enthrall me;
I would be like Jesus.

Chorus
Be like Jesus, this my song,
In the home and in the throng;
Be like Jesus, all day long!
I would be like Jesus.

2. He has broken ev'ry fetter,
I would be like Jesus;
That my soul may serve Him better,
I would be like Jesus.

3. All the way from earth to Glory
I would be like Jesus,
Telling o'er and o'er the story,
I would be like Jesus.

4. That in heaven He may meet me,
I would be like Jesus;
That His words "Well done" may greet me,
I would be like Jesus.
-James Rowe

1278
Happiness Is the Lord

1. Happiness is to know the Saviour,
Living a life within His favour,
Having a change m my behaviour,
Happiness is the Lord;

2. Happiness is a new creation.
"Jesus and me" in close relation,
Having a part In His salvation,
Happiness is the Lord
Real joy is mine, no matter if tear
drops start;

I've found the secret,
it's Jesus in my heart!

3. Happiness is to be forgiven,
Living a life that's worth the livin'
Taking a trip that leads to heaven,
Happiness is the Lord,
Happiness is the Lord,
Happiness is the Lord!
-Ira F. Stanphill

1279

Love, Love

1. I know the sweetest little word,
'Tis Love, love;
The sweetest word man ever heard.
is Love, love.

Chorus
God's Love, love. Is wider than the sea;
It reaches all, yes, even me; God's Love, love.

2. It keeps me happy ev'ry day. His Love, love;
It makes me sing along the way, Love, love.

3. It guides these little feet of mine, His Love, love;
It keeps them in the path divine. His Love, love.
-C. L. Dorris

1280

Serve the Lord in Youth

1. Serve the Lord in the days of youth,
Learn His law and accept His truth;
Sing His praise with a ready tongue,
While the heart is young,
While yet the heart is young.

Chorus
Serve the Lord in youthful days,
Do His will and walk His ways,
Wait not for what the years may bring.
But serve Him. O serve Him;

2. Give to Him what He gave to you,
Buoyant strength and a courage true;
Ringing voices and eyes alight,
Souls all pure and white,
Unstained and pure and white.

3. Serve Him then, ev'ry youthful day.
Choose His guidance without delay;
Waste no part of these precious years,
Youth soon disappears,
Too soon It disappear.
-Edith Sanford Tillotson

1281

BattleHyffln15.15.15.with Refrain

1. Mine eyes have seen the glory of the coming of the Lord,
He is trampling out the vintage where the grapes of wrath are stored:
He hath loosed the fateful lightning of His terrible swift sword;
His truth is marching on.

Chorus
Glory! glory. Hallelujah!
Glory! glory, hallelujah!
Glory! glory, hallelujah!
His truth is marching on.

2. I have seen Him in the watch-fires of a hundred circling camps,
They have builded Him an altar in the evening dews and damps;
I can read His righteous sentence

by the dim and flaring lamps
His day is marching on.

3. He has sounded forth the trumpet
that shall never sound retreat,
He is sifting out the hearts of men
before His judgement seat;
O be swift, my soul, to answer
Him! be jubilant, my feet!
Our God s marching on.

4. In the beauty of the lilies Christ
was born across the sea,
With a glory in His bosom that
transfigures you and me;
As He died to make men holy, let
us live to make men free.
While God is marching on.

-Julia Ward Howe

1282

Oh, Be Careful

1. Oh, be careful, little eyes, what you
see,
Oh, be careful, little eyes, what you
see.
For the Father up above Is looking
down in love,
So be careful, little eyes, what you
see.

2. Oh, be careful, little ears, what you
hear,
Oh, be careful, little ears, what you
hear,
For the Father up above Is looking
down in love,
So be careful, little ears, what you
hear.

3. Oh, be careful, little tongue, what
you say,
Oh, be careful, little tongue, what
you say,
For the Father up above is looking
down in love.
So be careful, little tongue, what
You say.

4. Oh, be careful, little hands, what
you do.
Oh, be careful, little hands, what
you do,
For the Father up above is looking
down in love,
So be careful, little hands, what
you do.

5. Oh, be careful, little feet, where
you go,
Oh, be careful, little feet, where
you go,
For the Father up above is looking
down in love,
So be careful, little feet, where
you go.

1283

St. Lambert-6.5.6.5.

1. Jesus, meek and gentle,
Son of God most High;
Pitying, loving Saviour,
Hear Thy children's cry.

2. Pardon our offences,
Loose our captive chains,
Break down every idol
Which our soul detains.

3. Give us holy freedom,
Fill our hearts with love;
Draw us, holy Jesus,
To the realms above.

4. Lead us on our journey,
Be Thyself the way
Through terrestrial darkness
To celestial day.

5. Jesus, meek and gentle,
Son of God most High;
Pitying, loving Saviour;
Hear Thy children's cry.

-R. R. Chope

CHILDREN AND YOUTH

1284

Tallis -7.6.8.6.

1. I want to be like Jesus
   So lowly and so meek;
   For no one mark'd an angry word,
   That ever heard Him speak.

2. I want to be like Jesus,
   So frequently in prayer;
   Alone upon the mountain top,
   He met His Father there.

3. I want to be like Jesus:
   I never, never find
   That He, though persecuted, was
   To any one unkind.

4. I want to be like Jesus,
   Engaged in doing good;
   So that of me it may be said,
   "She hath done what she could."

5. I want to be like Jesus,
   Who sweetly said to all,
   ":Let little children come to Me:"
   I would obey the call.

6. But oh, I'm not tike Jesus,
   As any one may see;
   O gentle Saviour, send Thy grace,
   And make me like to Thee.
   —T. Tallis

1285

Old Hundredth-L.M.

1. Be present at our table, Lord,
   Be here and everywhere adored;
   Bless these Thy gifts and grant that we
   May feast in Paradise with Thee.

2. We thank Thee, Lord, for this our food,
   For life, and health, and every good:
   May manna to our souls be given,
   The bread of life sent down from heaven.

1286

Winchester Old-C.M.

1. O Lord, our hearts would give Thee praise,
   Ere now our school we end;
   For this Thy day, the best of days,
   Jesus, the children's Friend.

2. Lord, grant Thy word in every heart,
   Our souls from sin defend,
   That we from Thee may ne'er depart,
   Jesus, the children's Friend.

3. Lord, bless our homes and give us grace,
   Thy Sabbaths so to spend,
   That we in heaven may find a place,
   With Thee, the Children's Friend.

1287

Caritas - 8.4.8.4.8.8.8.4.

1. One there is above all others,
   Oh, how He loves!
   His is love beyond a brother's.
   Oh, how He loves!
   Earthly friends may fail or leave us,
   One day soothe, the next day grieve us,
   But this Friend will ne'er deceive us,
   Oh, how He loves!

2. 'Tis eternal life to know Him,
   Oh, how He loves!
   Think, O think how much we owe Him.
   Oh, how He loves!

HEALING AND DELIVERANCE

With His precious blood Me bought
us,
In the wilderness He sought us,
To His fold He safely brought us,
Oh, how He loves'

3. We have found a friend in Jesus,
Oh, how He loves!
Tis His great delight to bless us,
Oh, how He loves!
How our hearts delight to hear Him,
Bid us dwell in safety near Him:
Why should we distrust or fear Him?
Oh, how He loves!

4. Through His name we are forgiven,
Oh, how He loves!
Backward shall our foes be driven,
Oh, how? He loves'
Best of blessings He'll provide us,
Nought but good shall e'er betide us,
Safe to glory He will guide us,
Oh, how He loves!

-R. W. Beafy

1288

Dublin-C.M.

1. See Isreal's gentle Shepherd stand
With all engaging charms;
Hark! how He calls the tender
lambs,
And folds them in His arms.

2. Permit them to approach. He cries,
Nor scorn their humble name'
For twas to bless such souls as
these The Lord of angels came.

.3. We bring them, Lord, in thankful
hands,
And yield them up to Thee;
Joyful that we ourselves are Thine,
Thine let bur children be.

Philip Doddridge

1289

There Is A Path That Leads To God -
C.M.

1. There is a path that leads to God,
All other go astray;
Narrow but pleasant is the road
And Christians love the way

2. It leads straight through this world of
sin,
And dangers must be passed;
But those who boldly walk therein,
Will get to heaven at last.

3. How shall an intent pilgrim dare
This dangerous path to tread?
For on the way is many a snare
For youthful travellers spread.

4. While the broad road, where
thousand go.
Lies near and opens fair;
And many turn aside, I know.
To walk with sinners there.

5. But lest feeble steps should slide,
Or wander from Thy way, Lord,
condescend to be my guide,
And I shall never stray.

6. Then I may go without alarm
And trust His word of old,
The lambs. He'll gather with His arm,
And lead them to the fold."

7. Thus I may safely venture through
Beneath my Shepherd's care,
And keep the gate of heaven in view.
Till I shall enter there.

HEALING AND DELIVERANCE

1290
Requiem-8.7.8.7.7.7.

1. Thou to whom the sick and dying
   Ever came, nor came in vain,
   Still with healing word replying
   To the wearied cry of pain,
   Hear us, Jesus, as we meet
   Suppliants at thy mercy-seat.

2. Still the weary, sick, and dying
   Need a brother's, sister's, care,
   On thy higher help relying
   May we now their burden share,
   -Bringing all our offerings-meet
   suppliants at thy mercy-seat.

3. May each child of thine be willing,
   Willing both in hand and heart,
   All the law of love fulfilling,
   Ever comfort to impart;
   Ever bringing offerings meet,
   Suppliant to thy mercy seat.

4. So may sickness, sin. and sadness
   To thy healing virtue yield,
   Till the sick and sad, in gladness,
   Rescued, ransomed, cleansed, healed,
   One in thee together meet,
   Pardoned at thy judgement seat.
   -G. Thring

1291
Tallis' canon - L.M.

1. God moves in a mysterious way
   His glorious wonders to perform;
   He plants His foot-steps in the sea,
   And rides upon the raging storm.

2. Deep in unfathomable mines
   Of never-failing skill,
   He treasures up His bright designs,
   And works His sovereign will.

3. Ye fearful saints, fresh courage sake;
   The clouds ye so much dread
   Are big with mercy, and shall break
   In blessings on your head.

4. Judge not the Lord by feeble sense,
   But trust Him for His grace:
   Behind a frowning providence
   He hides a smilling face.

5. His purpose with ripen fast,
   Unfolding every hour;
   The bud may have a bitter taste,
   But sweet will be the flower.
   -William Cowper

1292
Herongate - L.M.

1. O Thou through suffering perfect made,
   On whom the bitter cross was laid,
   In hours of sickness, grief and pain,
   No sufferer turns to Thee in vain,

2. Oh loving Saviour, Thou canst cure
   The pains and woes Thou didst endure;
   For all who need, Physician great,
   Thy healing balm we supplicate.

3. But O far more, let each keen pain
   And hour of woe be heavenly gain,
   Each stroke of Thy chastising rod
   Bring back the wanderer nearer God.

4. O heal the bruised heart within;
   O save our souls all sick with sin;
   Give life and health in bounteous store
   That we may praise Thee evermore.
   -W. Watsham

HEALING AND DELIVERANCE

1293

Deliverance -10.10.10.10. with Refrain

1. 'Tis the grandest theme thro' the ages rung;
   'Tis the grandest theme for a mortal tongue;
   'Tis the grandest theme that world e'er sung:
   Our God is able to deliver thee.

   Chorus
   He is able to deliver thee, He is able to deliver thee;
   Tho' by sin opprest, Go to Him for rest;
   Our God is able to deliver thee,

2. 'Tis the grandest theme in the earth or main;
   'Tis the grandest theme for a mortal strain;
   'Tis the grandest theme, tell the world again:
   Our God is able to deliver thee.

3. 'Tis the grandest theme, let the tidings roll To the guilty heart, to the sinful soul;
   Look to God in faith, He will make thee whole:
   Our God is able to deliver thee.

   -William A. Ogden

1294

Sutton common - 6.6.8.6.

1. Heal me, hands of Jesus and search out all my pain;
   restore my hope, remove my fear and bring me peace again.

2. Cleanse me, blood of Jesus,
   Take bitterness away;

   let me forgive as one forgiven and bring me peace today.

3. Know me, mind of Jesus, and show me all my sin;
   dispel the memories of guilt and bring me peace within.

4. Fill me, joy of Jesus:
   anxiety shall cease and heaven's serenity be mine, for Jesus brings me, peace!

   -Michael Perry

1295

The Cleansing Wave

1. Oh, now I see the crimson wave,
   The fountain deep and wide;
   Jesus, my Lord. mighty to save,
   Points to His wounded side.

   Chorus
   The cleansing stream I see!
   I plunge, and oh, it cleanseth me;
   Oh, praise the Lord, it cleanseth me.
   It cleanseth me, yes. cleanseth me.

2. I see the new creation rise,
   I hear the speaking blood;
   It speaks! polluted nature dies
   Sinks 'neath the crimson flood.

3. I rise to walk in heav'n own tight,
   Above the world and sin;
   with hearts made pure and garments white,
   And Christ enthroned within.

4. Amazing grace! 'tis heav'n below,
   To feel the blood applied;
   And Jesus, only Jesus know,
   My Jesus calcified.

   -Mrs. Phoebe Palmer

HEALING AND DELIVERANCE

1296

Penlan - 7.6.7.6.D.

1. His eyes will guide my footsteps
When faltering age is near;
his light will lift my darkness
and help my ears to hear:
in faith I claim the promise
of Jesus love for me;
the Lord of hope and healing
who made the blind to see.

2. When others fail or leave me,
he comes to me in prayer;
when life no longer needs me
I find my comfort here:
his promises are faithful
he lives, my closest friend;
I know that he will keep me
until my days shall end.

3. He comes when I am weary,
in pain or in distress;
with patient understanding
and perfect gentleness:
he was far more forsaken
than I shall ever be;
the presence of my Saviour
is everything to me.
-C. Porteous

1297

Hawkhurst -8.8.8.8. (L.M.)

1. See, Christ was wounded for our
sake,
and bruised and beaten for our sin,
so by sufferings we are healed,
for God has laid our guilt on him.

2. Look on his face, come close to him
see you will find no beauty there:
despised, rejected, who can tell
the grief and sorrow he must bear?

3. Like sheep that stray we leave
God's path.
to choose our own and not his will;
like sheep to slaughter he has gone,
obedient to his Father's will.

4. Cast out to die by those he loved,
reviled by those he died to save,
see how sin's pride has sought his
death,
see how sin's hate has made his
Grave.

5. For on his shoulders God has laid
the weight of sin that we should bear;
so by his passion we have peace,
through his obedience and his
prayer.
-Brian Foley

1298

Melcombe - 8.8.8.8.(L.M.)

1. We give God thanks for those who
knew
the touch of Jesus's healing love;
they trusted him to make them
whole,
to give them peace, their guilt
remove.

2. We offer prayer for all who go
relying on his grace and power,
to help the anxious and the ill,
to heal their wounds, their fives
restore.

3. We dedicate our skills and time
to those who suffer where we live,
to bring such comfort as we can
to meet their need, their pain relieve.

4. So Jesus' touch of healing grace
lives on within our willing care;
by thought and prayer and gift we
prove his mercy still, his love we
share.
-Michael Perry

HEALING AND DELIVERANCE

1299

He Headeth Me - L.M. with Refrain

1. He Healeth me, O blessed truth,
   His mighty Word renews my youth,
   By His own pow'r from sickness
   free.
   My precious Saviour healeth me.

Chorus
He healeth me, He healeth me,
By His own Word He healeth me;
His faithful witness I would be,
For by His Word He healeth me.

2. Sometimes thro' testin times I go,
   Dark seems the way, and full of
   woe;
   But in the furnace tho' I be,
   My great Physician healeth me.

3. Lord, I would spread this truth
   abroad, The mighty power of
   Thy word;
   It's just the same. the blind now
   see,
   And demons at Thy presence flee.

4. For sin and sickness doth depart,
   When thou dost reign within the
   heart;
   And I from all the curse am free,
   Since Christ, my Saviour, healeth
   me.
   -Anonymous

1300

The Hem of His Garment

1. She only touched the hem of His
   garment
   As to His side she stole,
   Amid the crowd that gather'd
   around Him.
   And straightway she was whole.

Chorus
Oh, touch the hem of His garment,
And thou, too, shalt be free;
His saving pow'r this very hour
Shall give new life to thee.

2. She camp in fear and trembling
   before Him,
   She knew her Lord had come;
   She felt that from Him virtue had
   healed her,
   The mighty deed was done.

3. He fumed with, "Daughter, be of
   good comfort,
   Thy faith hath made, thee whole;"
   And peace that passeth all under
   standing
   With gladness filled her soul.
   -Goe. F. Root

1301

Angelus-L.M.

1. At even, ere the sun was set,
   The sick, O Lord, around Thee lay;
   O in what divers pains they met!
   O with what joy they went away!

2. Once more 'tis eventide and we,
   Oppressed with various ills, draw
   near;
   What if Thy form we cannot see,
   We know and feel that Thou art
   here.

3. O Saviour Christ, our woes dispel:
   For some are sick, and some are sad
   And some have never loved Thee
   well,
   And some have lost the love they had.

4. And some are pressed with worldly
   care,
   And some are tried with sinful doubt,
   And some such grievous passion
   tear,
   That only Thou canst cast them out.

5. And some have found the world is
vain
Yet from the world they break not
them pain,
And some have friends who give
them pain
Yet have not sought a friend in Thee

6. O saviour Christ Thou too art Man;
Thou hast been troubled, tempted,
tried
Thy kind but searching glance can
scan
The very wounds that shame would
hide!

7. Thy touch has still its ancient
power,
No word from Thee can fruitless fall;
Hear in this solemn evening hour,
And in Thy mercy heal us all.
-H. Twells

Or is it that our faith is growing
feeble,
And Christian energy is waxing cold?

4. Why do we not with equal expectat
ion,
Now bring our sick ones to the Lord
in prayer
Right through the throng of
unbelieving scruples
Up to His very side and leave them
there?

5. He never health refused in bygone
ages,
Nor feared to take the
"chastisement" away;
Then why not ask it now. instead of
praying
For "patience" to endure from day to
day?
-A. H. Lewis

1302

Lagos-11.10.11.10.

1. He healed them all the blind, the
lame, the palsied,
The sick in body and the weak in
mind
Whoever came, no matter how
afflicted,
Were sure a sovereign remedy to find.

2. His word gave health, His touch
restored the vigour
To every weary pain exhausted frame,
And all He asked before He gave the
blessing
Was simple faith in Him from those
who came

3. And is our Lord, the kind, the good, the
tender
Less loving now than in those days
Of old?

1303

Bethesda-8.6.8.8.6.

1. O Saviour Christ, at Thy behest
We gather in Thy Name
As humble suppliants, to be blest,
That in our need so full confessed
Thy healing pow'r may claim.

2. Behold the sick, the blind the lame!
To whom else can we go?
Oh, show to us Thou art the same
As when Thy touch healed all who
came
Thy freedom full to know.

3. For Thou didst share in days of
yore
Our sorrow and our woe;
Oh, who can tell Thine anguish sore,
That from Thy stripes and wounds
may pour
A cleansing, healing flow

4. Thou didst the perfect work
complete:
Our all is found in Thee!
The scars so deep in hands and
feet
Are pledge of our redemption
sweet,
Deliverance full and free.

5. Our dear High Priest, on Thee we
wait,
Thou sympathising Friend.
Thyself dost feel our weak estate;
Do Thou, in Thy compassion great,
Thy grace to each extend.

6. Thy wondrous virtue now impart:
Thy healing power display!
Bid doubt and anxious fear depart.
Inspiring faith in every heart
Thy gift to claim this day.

7. O touch our, eyes: so shall we see
That Thou art by our side.
Restored and quickened shall we
be,
And blessed with perfect liberty.
Shall in Thy life abide.
-L. F. W. Woodford

1304

St. Agnes-10.10.10.10.

1. Our blessed Lord, in this Thy
presence sweet,
Behold us lowly bending at Thy
feet.
Fain would we meet Thee on this
hallowed ground
Where ev'ry Blood bought blessing
may be found; ╲

2. Drawn by the strength of Thine
own mighty love,
Gladly we come Thy healing touch
to prove,
All power is Thine we echo back
Thy word
In heaven and earth, Thou never
changing Lord.

3. We grasp Thy promises so sure, so
free,
To all who in their weakness call on
Thee.
Th' effectual fervent prayer Thou
dost receive,
With strength renewing all who dare
believe.

4. Thy servants bless who now before
Thee stand,
Who here fulfill the word of Thy
command;
And as the anointing oil shall gently
flow.
Thy heavenly unction on each life
bestow.

5. As holy hands now minister, with
prayer,
May we discern Thy wondrous
hands that bear
The marks of Thine affliction for our
And thus in humble faith Thy
heating take.

6. If to Thine eye that pierces deep.
within
There stands revealed the hidden
stain of sin
Still unconfessed, Oh, grant us
grace that we
May purge our lives afresh and
purer be.

7. Thus joined to Thee our living Head'
above,
Thy life we share, and in Thy
triumph move:
Knit with our fellow members here
below,
From strength to strength we shall
Thy fulness know.
-L. F. W. Woodford

HEALING AND DELIVERANCE

1305
Seraph - D.C.M.

1. Thine arm, O Lord, in days of old
Was strong to heal and save;
It triumphed o'er disease and death,
O'er darkness and the grave.
To Thee they went, the blind, the
dumb,
The palsied and the lame, the leper
with his tainted life,
The sick with fever'd frame;

2. And lo! Thy touch brought life and
health
Gave speech, and strength, and
sight;
And youth renewed, and frenzy
Calmed,
owned Thee the Lord of light.
And now, O Lord, be near to bless,
Almighty as of yore,
In crowded street, by restless couch
As by Gennesaret's shore.

3. Be Thou our great Deliverer still,
Thou Lord of life and death;
Restored and quicken, soothe and
bless
With Thine Almighty breath.
To hands that work, and eyes that
see,
Give wisdom's heavenly lore,
That whole and sick and weak and
strong
May praise Thee evermore.
-E. H. Piumptre

1306
Austria-8.7.8.7.D.

1. Jesus is the same for ever,
as of old, so now today;
All the hosts of hell endeavour
Vainly to obstruct His sway.

In His people's hearts He reigneth.
Finishes what He begins;
Jesus still "all power" retaineth,
Saves His people from their sins.

2. Jesus is the same for ever,
Yes, He heals the sick today,
As of old, so now, He ever
Turns one suffering child away;
He can cure the worst diseases.
For He understands our frame;
Bore our griefs, and so releases
All who dare their rights to claim.

3. Jesus is the same for ever,
Still He says "In Me abide."
From His love no power can sever
Those who in their Lord confide.
Sweetly from all care He frees us,
Ours the comfort His the shame.
Blessed Saviour, precious Jesus!
There's no music like Thy name.
-T. Price

1307
Petition -7.6.7.6.D.

1. Sometimes a light surprises
The Christian while he sings;
It is the Lord Who rises
With healing in His wings:
When comforts are declining,
He grants the soul again
A season of clear shining,
To cheer it after rain.

2. In holy contemplation,
We sweetly then
The theme of God's salvation,
And find it ever new.
Set free from present sorrow,
We cheerfully can say,
E'en let th' unknown tomorrow
Bring with it what it may:

3. It can bring with it nothing
But He will bear us through;
Who gives the lilies clothing

HEALING AND DELIVERANCE

Will clothe His people too:
Beneath the spreading heavens
And He who feeds the ravens
Will give His children bread.

4. Though vine or fig-tree neither
Their wonted fruit should bear,
Though all the field should wither,
Nor flocks nor herds be there,
Yet, God the same abiding,
His praise shall tune my voice;
For, while in Him confiding,
I cannot but rejoice.

-W. Cowper

1308
The Great Physician Now Is Near

1. The great Physician now is near.
Thy sympathising Jesus;
He speaks the drooping hear to
Cheer
Oh hear the voice of Jesus.

Chorus
Sweetest note in seraph song,
Sweetest name on mortal tongue
Sweetest carol ever sung, Jesus,
blessed Jesus.

2. Your many sins are all forgiv'n,
Oh, hear the voice of Jesus;
Go on your way in peace to heav'n,
And wear a crown with Jesus.

3. All glory to the dying Lamb!
I now believe in Jesus:
I love the blessed Saviour's name,
I love the name of Jesus.

4. His name dispels my guilt and fear,
No other name but Jesus,
Oh! how my soul delights to hear
The precious name of Jesus.

-Wm. Hunter

1309
Jesus Knows Thy Sorrow - 6.5.

1. Jesus knows thy sorrow,
Knows thine ev'ry care;
Know^thy deep contrition,
Hears thy feeblest prayer.
Do not fear to trust Him
Tell Him all thy grief,
Cast on Him thy burden,
He will bring relief.

2. Trust the heart of Jesus,
Thou art precious there;
Surely he would shield thee
From the tempter's snare;
Safely He would lead thee.
By His own sweet way,
Out into the glory
Of a brighter day.

3. Jesus knows thy conflict,
Hears thy burdened sigh;
When thy heart is wounded,
Hears thy plainative cry:
He thy soul will strengthen,
Overcome thy fears;
He will send thee comfort,
Wipe away thy tears.

-Rev. W. O.Cushing

1310
Come, Great Deliverer, Come

1. Oh, hear my cry, be gracious now
to me,
Come, Great Deliv'rer, come!
My soul bowed down is longing now
for Thee.
Come, Great Deliv'rer come!

Chorus
I've wandered far away o'er
mountains cold,
I've wandered far away from home:
Oh, take me now, and bring me to
Thy fold!
Come, Great Deliv'rer, come!

2. I have no place, no shelter from the night,
Come Great Deliv'er, come!
One look from Thee would give me life and light,
Come, Great Deliver'rer, come!

3. My path is lone, and weary are my feet;
Come, Great Deliverer, come!
Mine eyes look up Thy loving smile to meet,
Come, Great Deliverer, come!

4. Thou wilt not spurn contrition's broken sigh,
Come, Great Deliverer, come!
Regard my prayer, and hear my humble cry,
Come, Great Deliverer, come!
-F. J. Crosby

1311
My Great physician - 7.6.

1. Thou art my great "Physician."
My savior and my All;
I look to Thee for blessing,
And on Thy mercy call.
With tend' rest care Thou watchest
Beside the couch of pain,
And givest health and healing,
When human help is vain;

2. When in the midnight watches,
With anxious care oppress'd,
I often hear Thee whisper,
"come unto Me and rest."
Thou carest for the weary.
Dost mark the sparrow's fall:
Then surely I can trust Thee,
Thou art my "All in All";

3. Thou art my "Tower of Refuge,"
My "strength" upon the way;
My "Hope" of endless glory,
When end life's fleeting day!
Thou art the only "Healer"

For body, mind, and soul,
And when all others fail me,
Thy touch can make me whole.

4. Thou art my "Resurrection"
To life that never dies,
Where Thou art now preparing
A mansion in the skies:
Then hasten Thine appearing,
To take Thy people home,
Where sickness, pain, and sorrow,
Shall never, never come.
-F. J. Crosby

1312
The Son Hath Made Me Free

1. I was once in Egypt's bondage,
But deliv'rance came to me;
And I'm living now in Canaan.
For the Son hath made me free.

Chorus
I am dwelling now in Canaan, now in Canaan,
Jesus' blood avails for me, yes, for me;
I am free from condemnation, condemnation,
For the Son hath made me free.

2. I was once a slave to Satan.
And he worked his will in me:
But I'm bound by sin no longer.
For the Son hath made me free.

3. Ere I entered in to Canaan.
Inbred sin remained in me;
But from it I've found a cleansing.
For the Son hath made me free.

4. All my fear, all condemnation,
All that stood 'twixt God and me;
Praise His name! are left behind me.
For the Son hath made me free.
-Mirian E. Oatman

HEALING AND DELIVERANCE

1313

The Healing Waters

1. Oh, the joy of sins forgiv'n,
   Oh, the bliss the blood washed
   know,
   Oh, the peace akin to heav'n,
   Where the healing waters flow.

Chorus
Where the healing waters flow,
Where the joys celestial glow.
Oh, there's peace and rest and love
Where the healing waters flow!

2. Now with Jesus crucified,
   At His feet I'm resting low;
   Let me evermore abide
   Where the healing waters flow.

3. Oh, this precious perfect love!
   How it keeps the heart aglow,
   Streaming from the fount above,
   Where the healing waters flow.

4. Oh, to lean on Jesus breast,
   While the tempests come and go!
   Here is blessed peace and rest,
   Where the healing waters flow.

5. Cleansed from ev'ry sin and stain,
   Whiter than the driven snow,
   Now I sing my sweet refrain,
   Where the healing waters flow.
   -H. H. Heimar

1314

Stoerl -C.M.

1. Father whose will is life and good
   For all of mortal breath, Bind
   strong the bond of brotherhood
   Of those who fight with death.

2. Empower the hands and hearts and
   wills
   Of friends both near and far.
   Who battle with the body's ills,
   And wage thy holy war.

3. Where'er they heal the maimed and
   blind,
   Let love of Christ attend:
   Proclaim the Good Physician's mind.
   And prove the Saviour friend.

4. O Father, look from heav'n and
   bless,
   Where'er thy servants be,
   Their works of pure unselfishness,
   Made consecrate to thee.
   -Hardwicke
   Drummond Rawnsley

1315

Wiltehire-C.M.

1. I know not what the future hath
   Of marvel or surprise,
   Assured alone that life and death
   God's mercy underlies.

2. And if my heart and flesh are weak
   To bear an untried pain,
   The bruised reed he wilt not break,
   But strengthen and sustain.

3. No off'ring of my own I have,
   Nor works my faith to prove;
   I can but give the gifts he gave,
   And plead his love for love.

4. And so beside the silent sea
   I wait the muffled oar;
   No harm from him can come to me
   On ocean or on shore.

5. I know not where his islands lift
   Their fronded palms in air;
   I only know I cannot drift
   Beyond his love and care.
   -John Greenleaf Whittier

1316

St. Peter - C.M.

1. How sweet the name of Jesus
   sounds
   In a believer's ear!
   It soothes his sorrows, heals his
   wounds,
   And drives away his fear.

2. It makes the wounded spirit whole
   And calms the troubled breast;
   Tis manna to the hungry soul
   And to the weary, rest.

3. Dear name! the rock on which
   I build,
   My shield and hiding place;
   My never failing treasury, filled
   With boundless stores of grace!

4. Jesus, my Shepherd, Brother
   Friend,
   My Prophet, Priest and King,
   My Lord, my Life, my Way, my
   End, Accept the praise I bring.

5. Till then I would Thy love proclaim
   With ev'ry fleeting breath;
   And may the music of Thy name
   Refresh my soul in death.
   -John Newton

1317

Pass Me Not 8.5.8.5. with Refrain

1. Pass me not, O gentle Saviour
   Hear my humble cry!
   While on others Thou art calling,
   Do not pass me by.

Chorus
Saviour, Saviour, Hear my humble
cry!
While on others Thou art calling,
Do not pass me by.

2. Let me at a throne of mercy
   Find a sweet relief;
   Kneeling there in deep contrition
   Help my unbelief.

3. Trusting only in Thy merit,
   Would I seek Thy face;
   Heat my wounded, broken spirit,
   Save me by Thy grace.

4. Thou the spring of all my comfort,
   More than life to me!
   Whom have I on earth beside Thee?
   Whom in heav'n but Thee?
   -Fanny J. Crosby

1318

He Touched Me - Irregular meter

1. Shackled by a heavy burden,
   'Neath a load of guilt and shame;
   Then the hand of Jesus touched me,
   And now I am no longer the same.

Chorus
He touched me, O, He touched me.
And O, the joy that floods my soul;
Something happened, and now I
know,
He touched me and made me whole.

2. Since I met this blessed Saviour,
   Since He cleansed and made me
   whole;
   I will never cease to praise Him,
   I'll shout it while eternity rolls.
   -William J. Gather

HEALING AND DELIVERANCE

1319

Does Jesus Care

1. Does Jesus care when my heart is
   pained
   Too deeply for mirth and song;
   As you burdens press, and the
   cares distress,
   And the way grows weary and
   Long?

Chorus
O yes, He cares I know He cares
His heart is touched with my grief;
When the days are weary, the long
nights dreary,
I know my Saviour cares.

2. Does Jesus care when my way is
   dark
   With a name - less dread and fear?
   As the day - light fades into deep
   night shades.
   Does He care enough to be near?

3. Does Jesus care when I've tried and
   failed
   To resist some temptation strong;
   When for my deep grief I find no
   relief.
   Tho my tears flow all the night long?

4. Does Jesus care when I've said
   goodbye
   To the dearest on earth to me,
   And my sad heart aches till it nearly
   breaks Is it aught to Him?
   does He see?
   -Frank E. Graeff

1320

The Healer

1. On the Cross crucified,
   In great sorrow He died;
   The Giver of life was He.

Yet my Lord was despised and
rejected of men,
This Jesus of Calvary

Chorus
He was wounded for our
trangressions,
He was bruis'd for our iniquities;
Surely He bore our sorrows,
And by His stripes we are healed.

2. Price for healing was paid,
   As those cruel stripes we made,
   Within Pilate's judgement hall.
   Now His suff'ring affords perfect
   healing for all.
   This wonderful Healer's mine.

3. Came the leper to Christ,
   Saying "Surely I know,
   That Thou, Lord, canst make me
   whole."
   When His great faith was seen
   Jesus said "Yes. I will."
   And touch'd him and made him
   clean.

4. He has healed my sick soul.
   Made me ev'ry whit whole,
   And He'll do the same for you.
   He's the same yesterday and today
   and for aye,
   This Healer of men today.
   -Lois Irwin

1321

Christ For The World We Sing

1. Christ for the world we sing;
   The world to Christ we bring.
   With loving zeal;
   The poor and them that mourn.
   The faint and over borne,
   Sin sick and sorrow worn.
   Whom Christ doth heal.

2. Christ for the world we sing;
   The world to Christ we bring,
   With fervent pray'r;
   The wayward and the lost,
   By restless passions tossed,
   Redeemed at countless cost
   From dark despair.

3. Christ for the world we sing;
   The world to Christ we bring,
   With one accord,
   With us the work to share,
   With us reproach to dare,
   With us the cross to bear,
   For Christ our Lord.
                     -Samuel Wolcott

1322

Jesus Has Lifted Me

1. Out of the depths to the glory
   above,
   I have been lifted in wonderful love;
   From ev'ry fetter my spirit is free,
   For Jesus has lifted me!

   Chorus
   Jesus has lifted me! Jesus has
   lifted me!
   Out of the night into glorious light,
   Yes, Jesus has lifted me!

2. Out of the world into heavenly rest,
   into the land of the ransomed and
   blest;
   There in the glory with Him I shall be
   For Jesus has lifted me!

Out of myself into Him I adore;
There to abide in His love evermore,
Thro' endless ages His glory to see,
My Jesus has lited me!
                     -Avis B. Chnstiansen

1323

Dolgelly-6.6.6.6.8.8.

1. Thou, Lord, hast power to heal,
   And thou wilt quickly aid,
   For thou dost deeply feel
   The stripes upon us laid:
   Thou who wast wounded by the rod
   Uplifted in the hand of God.

2. Send speedy help, we pray.
   To him who ailing lies,
   That from his couch he may
   With thankful heart arise;
   Through prayers which all availing
   find
   Thine ear, O Lover of mankind.

3. O blinded are our eyes,
   And all are held in night;
   But like the blind who cries,
   We cry to thee for tight;
   In penitence, O Christ, we pray,
   Give us the radiant light of day.
                     -J. B.

1324

National Hymn -10.10.10.10.

1. Heralds of Christ, who bear the
King's commands,
Immortal tidings in your mortal
hands,
Pass on and carry swift the news
ye bring,
Make straight, make straight the
highway of the King.

2. Thro' desert ways, dark fen and
deep morass,
Thro' jungles, sluggish seas, and
mountain pass,
Build ye the road, and falter not, nor
stay,
Prepare across the earth the King's
highway.

3. Where once the twisting trail in
darkness wound,
Let marching feet and joyous song
resound,
Where burn the fun'ral pyres, and
censers swing,
Make straight, make straight the
highway of the King.

4. Lord, give us faith and strength the
road to build,
To see the promise of the day
fulfilled,
When war shall be no more and
strife shall cease
Upon the highway of the Prince of
peace.

-Laura S. Copenhaver

1325

Toiling On - 12.12.12.12. with Refrain

1. To the work! to the work! we are
servants of God,

Let us follow the path that our
Master has trod;
With the balm of His counsel our
strength to renew,
Let us do with our might what our
hands find to do.

Chorus
Toiling on, toiling on, Toiling on,
toiling on;
Let us hope, let us watch,
And labour till the Master comes.

2. To the work! to the work? let the
hungry be fed,
To the fountain of life let the weary
be led;
In the cross and its banner our glory
shall be,
While we herald the tidings,
"Salvation is free!"

3. To the work! to the work! there is
labour for all.
For the kingdom of darkness and
error shall fall;
And the name of Jehovah exalted
shall be
In the loud swelling chorus,
"Salvation is free!"

4. To the work! to the work! in the
strength to the Lord,
And a robe and a crown shall our
labour reward
When the home of the faithful our
dwelling shall be,
And we shout with the ransomed,
"Salvation is free!"

-Fanny J. Crosby

1326

Amesbury-C.M.D.

1. O Master Workman of the race,
Thou Man of Galilee,
Who, with the eyes of early youth,
Eternal things didst see;

We thank Thee for Thy boyhood faith
That shone Thy whole life through:
"Did ye not know it is My work
My Father's work to do?"

2. O carpenter of Nazareth.
Builder of life divine,
Who shapest man to God's own law.
Thyself the fair design.
Build us a tow'r of Christ-like height,
That we the land may view,
And see, like Thee, our noblest work,
Our Father's work to do.

3. O Thou who dost the vision send.
And givest each his task,
And with the task sufficient strength:
Show us Thy will, we ask;
Give us a conscience bold and gold;
Give us a purpose true,
That it may be our highest Joy
Our Father's work to do.

-Jay T. Stocking

1327

Ash Grove-12.11.12.11.D.

1. The Master hath come, and He calls us to follow
The track of the footprints He leaves on our way;
Far over the mountain and through the deep hollow,
Tha path lead us on to the mansions of day:
The Master hath called us, the children who fear Him,
Who march 'neath Christ's banner, His own little band;
We love Him and seek Him, we long to be near Him,
And rest in the tight of His beautiful Land.

2. The Master hath called us; the road may be dreary,
And dangers and sorrows are strewn on the track;
But God's Holy Spirit shall comfort the weary;
We follow the Saviour and cannot turn back;
The Master hath called us: though doubt and temptation
May compass our journey, we cheerfully sing:
"Press onward, look upward," thro' much tribulation;
The children of Zion must follow their King.

3. The Master hath called us, in life's early morning.
With spirits as fresh as the dew on the sod:
We turn from the world, with its smiles and its scorning,
To cast in our lot with the people of God:
The Master hath called us. His sons and His daughters,
We plead for His blessing and trust in His love;
And through the green pastures. beside the still waters.
He'll lead us at last to His kingdom above.

-Sarah Doudney

1328

Shere-S.M.

1. Put thou thy trust in God,
In duty's path go on;
Walk in His strength with faith and hope,
So shall thy work be done.

2. Commit thy ways to Him,
Thy works into His hands,

And rest on His unchanging word,
Who heaven and earth commands.

3. Though years on years roll on,
His covenant shall endure;
Though clouds and darkness hide
His path,
The promised grace is sure.

4. Give to the winds thy fears;
Hope, and be undismayed;
God hears thy sighs and counts
thy tears;
God shall lift up thy head.

5. Through waves, and clouds, and
storms His power will clear thy way;
Wait thou His time; the darkest
night
Shall end in brightest day.

6. Leave to His sovereign sway
To choose and to command;
So shalt thou, wondering, own
His way How wise, how strong His
hand.

-Paul Gerhardt

1329

St. Agnes (Langran) - 10.10.10.10.

1 Come ye yourselves apart and rest
awhile,
Weary, I know it, of the press and
throng,
Wipe from your brow the sweet
and dust of toil,
And in My quiet strength again be
strong.

2. Come ye aside from all the world
holds dear,
For converse which the world has
never known,
Alone with Me and with My Father
here.

With Me and with My Father not
alone.

3. Come, tell Me all that ye have said
and done,
Your victories and failures, hopes and
fears.
I know how hardly souls are wooed
and won:
My choicest wreaths are always wet
with tears.

4. Come ye and rest: the journey is too
great.
And ye will faint beside the way and
sink:
The bread of life is here for you to
eat,
And here for you the wine of love to
drink.

5. Then, fresh from converse with your
Lord, return
And work till daylight softens into
even:
The brief hours are not lost in which
ye learn
More of your Master and His rest in
heaven.

-J. Langran

1330

Everton -8.7.8.7.D

1. Lord, your church on earth is
seeking
power and wisdom from above:
teach us all the art of speaking
with the accents of your love.
We wilt heed your great commission
sending us to every place
'Go, baptize, fulfil my mission;
serve with love and share my grace!'

2. You release us from our bondage,
lift the burdens caused by sin;
give new hope, new strength and
courage.

grant release from fears within,
Light for darkness, joy for sorrow,
love for hatred, peace for strife
these and countless blessings
follow
as the Spirit gives new life.

3. In the streets of every city
where the bruised and lonely live,
we will show the Saviour's pity
and his longing to forgive.
In all lands and with all races
we will serve, and seek to bring
all mankind to render praises
Christ, to you, redeemer king.
-H. Sherlock

1331

Gonfalon Royal - 8.8:8.8.

1. O Spirit of the living God,
in all the fluffiness of your grace,
wherever human feet have trod,
descend upon our fallen race:

2. Give tongues of fire and hearts of
love
to preach the reconciling word;
anoint with power from heaven
above
whenever gospel truth is heard:

3. Let darkness turn to radiant light,
confusion vanish from your path;
those who are weak inspire with
might
let mercy triumph over wrath!

4. O Spirit of our God, prepare
the whole wide world the Lord to
meet;
breathe out new life, like morning
air,
till hearts of stone begin to beat:

5. Baptize the nations; far and near
the triumphs of the cross record;
till Christ in glory shall appear
and every race declare him Lord!
-J. Montgomery

1332

Old Clarendonian -8.8.8.8.

1. Send out the gospel! Let it sound
northward and southward, east and
west;
tell all the world Christ died and lives
he gives us pardon, life and rest.

2. Send out the gospel, mighty Lord!
Out of this chaos bring to birth
your own creation's promised hope:
the coming days of heaven on earth.

3. Send out your gospel, gracious Lord!
Yours was the blood for sinners
shed;
your voice still pleads in human
hearts
may all mankind to you be led.

4. Send out your gospel, holy Lord!
Kindle in us love's sacred flame;
love giving all with heart and mind,
for Jesus' sake, in Jesus' name.

5. Send out the gospel! Make it
known!
Christians, obey your master's call;
sing out his praise! he comes to
reign.
the King of kings and Lord of all.
-H. E. Fox

1333

Fulda-8.8.8.8.

1. We have a gospel to proclaim,
good news for men in all the earth;
the gospel of a Saviour's name:
we sing his glory, tell his worth.

2. Tell of his birth of Bethlehem,
not in a royal house or hall
but in a stable dark and dim:
the Word made flesh, a light for all.

3. Tell of his death at Calvary,
   hated by those he came to save;
   in lonely suffering on the cross
   for all he loved, his life he gave.

4. Tell of that glorious Easter morn:
   empty the tomb. for he was free;
   he broke the power of death and
   hell,
   that we might share his victory.

5. Tell of his reign at God's right hand,
   by ad creation glorified;
   he sends his Spirit on his church
   to live for him the lamb who died.

6. Now we rejoice to name him king:
   Jesus is Lord of all the earth;
   this gospel message we proclaim:
   we sing his glory, tell his worth.
   -E. J. Bums

1334

Call For Workers

1. In the vineyard of the Lord,
   There is work for all to do;
   Will you go and work today,
   With a purpose strong and true?

   Chorus
   Heed the call, brother dear,
   For workers today;
   Let your eyes see the need
   Of workers, today.

2. Brother, sister, hear the call!
   All along, your aid afford;
   Let us strive to save the lost
   Strive to save by work and word.

3. Mark the spirit's direful fate,
   Wheresoever sin is found;
   Come, and lend a helping hand,
   Let the shackles be unbound.

4. Oh, for workers strong and brave.
   Who will lift the banner high;

So the lost can see the way,
To the mansions in the sky.
                          -J. H. Sheppard

1335

A Watchman on Zion's Wall

1. Will you be a watch on Zion's wall?
   Warn the helpless nations far and
   wide;
   Sound the prophet's message long
   foretold;
   Man's one hope is Christ, the
   crucified.

   Chorus
   Go and shout it from the city wall;
   Herald upward, outward, far and
   wide:
   Truth and love, the victory will win-
   Build your nope in Christ the
   crucified.

2. All have sinn'd and judgment day
   must come;
   Love has paid the debt to set men
   free:
   Lest you warn the lost. they'll surely
   die.
   And their blood may be requir'd of
   Thee.

3. Save yourselves, proclaim the
   gospel way,
   Free salvation thru the Christ alone;
   Let God's mighty, saving word
   prevail,
   Soon He'll send His Son to claim His
   own.
                          -T. J. Finley

1336

Bring Them In

1. Hark! 'tis the Shepherd's voice I
   hear,
   Out in the desert dark and drear,
   Calling the sheep who've gone
   astray,
   Far from the Shepherd's fold away.

Chorus
Bring them in Bring them in,
Bring them in from the fields of sin;
Bring them in, Bring them in,
Bring the wand'ring ones to Jesus.

2 Who'll go and help the Shepherd kind,
Help Him the wand'ring ones to find?
Who'll bring the lost ones to the fold.
Where they'll be shetter'd from the cold?

3. Out in the desert hear their cry,
Out on the mountain wild and nigh,
Hark Itis the Master speaks to thee,
"Go, find my sheep where'er they be."

-Alexcenah Thomas

1337

Holley -L.M.

1. Lord, speak to me, that I may speak
In living echoes of Thy tone;
As Thou hast sought, so let me seek
Thy erring children lost and lone.

2. Oh, lead me, Lord, that I may lead
The wand'ring and the erring feet;
Oh, feed me, Lord, that I may feed
Thy hungry ones with manna sweet

3 Oh, stengthen me, that while I stand
Firm on the rock, and strong in Thee,
I may stretch out a loving hand
To wrestlers with the troubled sea.

4. Oh, teach me. Lord, that I may teach
The precious things Thou dost
Impart; '

And wing my words, that they may reach
The hidden depths of many a heart.

5. Oh, give Thine own sweet rest to me,
That I may speak, with soothing power,
A word in season, as from Thee,
To weary ones, in needful hour.

6. Oh, fill me with Thy fulness, Lord,
Until my very heart o'erflow
In kindling thougt and glowing word,
Thy love to tell, Thy praise to show.

7. Oh, use me, Lord, use even me,
Just as Thou wilt, and when, and where
Until Thy blessed face I see,
Thy rest, Thy joy, Thy glory share.

-France R. Havergal

1338

Work, While 'tis Day

1. Work, time is passing, the hours quickly fly;
Work while the sunlight is beaming on high;
Waste not the moments, for night draweth nigh,
Soon you shall labour no more.

Chorus
Work, toiler, work, there is labour for you!
Work, toiler, work, to His service be true!
Work while 'tis day, Work while you may
Work, toiler, work for Jesus!

2. Faithfully labour with head and with hand,
Ever obeying the Master's, command;

Though you the purpose may not understand,
Work, for the day's flying fast.

3. Work, for beside thee he standeth
to bless;
He will direct thee thro' earth's
wilderness;
God will protect thee, no foes shall
oppress;
Work for Him, then. while you may.

4. Jesus, thy Master, has gone to
prepare
In His blest kingdom a home bright
and fair;
Rest there awaits you. His joy thou
shalt share:
Work, then, the day soon is gone.
-Laura E. Newell

1339

Blshopgarth-8.7.8.7.D.

1. "For My sake and the Gospel's,
go And tell Redemption's story;"
His heralds answer. "Be it so,
And Thine, Lord, all the glory!" .
They preach His birth, His life.
His cross,
The love of His atonement,
For whom they count the world but
loss.
His Easter, His enthronement.

2. Hark, hark, the trump of Jubilee
Proclaims to every nation,
From pole to pole, by land and sea,
Glad tidings of salvation:
As nearer draws the day of doom,
While still the baffle rages,
The heavenly Dayspring, through
the gloom
Breaks on the night of ages.

3. Still on and on the anthems spread
Of Hallelujah voices,
In concert with the holy dead

The warrior-Church rejoices;
Their snow-white robes are washed
on blood;
Their golden harps are ringing;
Earth, and the Paradise of God,
One triumph-song are singing.

4. He comes, whose Advent Trumpet
drowns
The last of Time's evangels
Emmanuel crowned with many
crowns,
The Lord of saints and angels:
O Life, Light, Love, the great I AM,
Triune, who changest never:
The throne of God and of the Lamb
Is Thine, and Thine for even
-E. H. Bickersteth

1340

**Tell The Whole Wide World -8.7.8.7.
and Refrain**

1. Tell the whole wide world of Jesus,
Bear the news from shore to shore;
Telling sinners of the Saviour,
Let the light spread more and more.

Chorus
Tell the world, the whole wide world;
Bear the news from shore to shore;
Tell the whole wide world of Jesus,
Praise His name for evermore!

2. Send abroad the gospel heralds,
Let them take the blessed light
Into every land of darkness,
Piercing through the shades of
night

3. Yes, we'll send the joyful message
Over mountain, over wave,
Telling everywhere of Jesus,
And His mighty power to save.

4. While we pray for other nations,
Send them help with willing hand,

MISSIONARIES AND FIELD WORKERS

Let us not forget the home fields
Jesus for our native land!

-E. E. Hewitt

1341

If Jesus Goes with Me

1. It may be in the valley, where
   countless dangers hide;
   It may be in the sunshine, that I in
   peace abide;
   But this one thing I know if it be dark
   or fair,
   If Jesus is with me, I'll go any
   where!

Chorus
If Jesus goes with me, I'll go
anywhere!
'Tis heaven to me, Where'er I may
be.
If He is there! I count it a privilege
here
His cross to bear; if Jesus goes
with me,
I'll go anywhere.

2 It may be I must carry the blessed
   word of life
   Across the burning deserts to those
   in sinful strife;
   And though it be my lot to bear my
   colours there,
   If Jesus goes with me, I'll go
   anywhere!

3 But if it be my portion to bear my
   cross at home,
   While others bear their burdens
   beyond the billow's foam,
   I'll prove my faith in Him confess
   His judgments fair,
   And if He stays with me, I'll stay
   anywhere!

4. It is not mine to question the
   judgments of my Lord,

It is but mine to follow the leadings of
His Word;
But if I go or stay, or whether here or
there. I'll be with my Saviour, content
anywhere!

-C. Austin Miles

1342

Onward and upward - 6.5,6.5-D. and Refrain

1. Onward, still, and upwards, Follow'
   ever more
   where our mighty Leader Goes in
   love before;
   "Looking unto Jesus," Reach a
   helping hand,
   To a struggling neighbour, Helping
   him to stand.

Chorus
Marching onward, upward,
Marching steadily onward, Jesus
leads the way,
Marching onward, upward,
Onward unto glory to the perfect day.

2. Onward, ever onward, Thro' the
   pastures green,
   Where the streams flow softly Under
   skies serene;
   Or, if need be, upward, O'er the
   rocky steep,
   Trusting Him to guide us, Strong to
   save and keep.

3. Upward, ever upward, T'ward the
   radiant glow,
   Far above the valley, Where the mist
   hangs tow;
   On, with songs of gladness, Till the
   march shall end,
   Where ten thousand thousand
   Hallelujahs blend.

-E. E. Hewitt

1343
Seeking The Lost

1. Seeking the lost, yes, kindly
   entreating
   Wanderers on the mountain astray;
   'Come to Me,'His message
   repeating,
   Words of the Master speaking
   today.

Chorus
Going afar Upon the mountain.
Bringing the wand'rer back again,
back again,
Into the fold Of my Redeemer.
Jesus the Lamb for sinners slain,
for sinners slain.

2. Seeking the lost, and pointing to
   Jesus,
   Souls that are weak and hearts that
   are sore;
   Leading them forth in ways of
   salvation,
   Showing the path to life ever more.

3. Thus I would go on missions of
   mercy,
   Following Christ from day unto day;
   Cheering the faint, and raising the
   fallen:
   Pointing the lost to Jesus the way.
   -W. A. Ogden

1344
Lenox -6.6.6.6.8.8.8.

1. Blow ye the trumpet, blow
   The gladly solemn sound;
   let all the nations know,
   To earth's remotest bound;
   The year of jubilee is come,
   The year of Jubilee is come,
   Return, ye ransom'd sinners,
   Home.

2. Jesus, our great high priest,
   Has full atonement made,
   Ye weary spirits rest,
   Ye mourning souls be glad;
   The year of jubilee is come,
   The year of jubilee is come,
   Return, ye ransom'd sinners,
   home

3. Exalt the Lamb of God,
   The sin atoning Lamb,
   Redemption by His blood
   Through all the world proclaim;
   The year of jubilee is come
   The year of jubilee is come.
   Return ye ransom'd sinners,
   home.
   -Charles Wesley

1345
Harvest Home P.M.

1. O where are the reapers that
   garner in
   The sheaves of the good from the
   fields of sin
   With sickles of truth must the work
   be done,
   And no one may rest till the
   harvest's home.

Chorus
Where are the reapers? O who will
come
And share in the glory of the harvest
home?
O who will help us to garner in
The sheaves, good from the fields
of sin!

2. Go out in the bye ways and search
   them all;
   The wheat may be there, though the
   weeds are tall;
   Then search in the highway and
   pass none by,
   But gather from all for the home on
   High.

3. The fields are all rip'ning and far and wide
The world is awaiting the harvest tide;
But reapers are few and the work is great,
And much will be lost should the harvest wait.

4. So come with your sickles, ye sons of men,
And gather together the golden grain;
Toil on till the Lord of the harvest come,
Then share in the joy of the harvest home.

-Ebenezer E. Rexford

1346

The Straying Sheep

1. How many sheep are straying,
Lost from the Saviour's fold!
Upon the lonely mountain
They shiver with the cold;
Within the tangled thickets,
Where poison vines do creep,
And over rocky ledges
Wander the poor, lost sheep;

Chorus
O come, let us go and find them!
In the paths of death they roam.
At the close of the day 'twill be sweet to say:
'I have brought some lost one home.'

2. O who will go to find them?
Who, for the Saviour's sake,
will search with tireless patience
Thro' brier and thro' brake?
Unheeding thirst or hunger,
Who still, Who still, from day to
Day,

Will seek, as for a treasure,
The sheep that go astray?

3. Say, will you seek to find them?
From pleasant bow'rs of ease
Will you go forth determin'd
To find the least of these?
For still the Saviour calls them,
And looks across the world,
And still He holds wide open
The door into His fold.

4. How sweet 'twould be at evening
If you and I could say, 'Good
Shepherd, we've been seeking
The sheep that went astray!
Heart sore and faint with hunger,
We heard them making moan,
And lo! we come at night fall,
And bear them safely home.'

-E. M. H. Gates

1347

Harvest Fields

1. Harvest fields are waiting,
While the waving grain;
Christ the Master calleth,
Soon the day will wane:
Hasten at His bidding,
Join the reaper band;
Help them at their labour,
Work with willing hand.

Chorus
Harvest fields are waiting,
Labour while you may;
Time is swiftly flying,
Come and work today.

2. Harvest fields are waiting,
Do not linger long;
Borne upon the breezes
Comes the reaper's song:
Patiently, O toiler,
Pluck the golden grain
Ere the shades of ev'ning
Fall o'er hill and plain.

MISSIONARIES AND FIELD WORKERS

3. Harvest fields are waiting,
Who will come today,
Join the band of reapers,
Bear the sheaves away?
Soon the day of toiling
Win be ever past;
May the Master's greeting Be,
Well done! at last.

-Birdie Bell

1348

Tell It out

1. Tell it out among the heathen that
the Lord is King!
Tell it out! Tell it out!
Tell it out among the nations, bid
them shout and sing!
Tell it out! Tell it out!
Tell it out with adoration that He
shall increase,
That the mighty King of Glory is the
King of Peace;
Tell it out with jubilation, tho' the
waves may roar,
That He sitteth on the water floods,
our King for evermore!

Chorus
Tell it out among the heathen that
the Lord is King!
Tell it out! Tell it out!
Tell it out among the nations, bid
them shout and sing!
Tell it out

2 Tell it out among the heathen that
the Saviour reigns!
Tell it out! Tell it out!
Tell it out among the nations, bid
them burst their chains!
Tell it out! Tell it out!
Tell it out among the weeping ones
that Jesus lives;
Tell it out among the weary ones
what rest He gives;
Tell it out among the sinners that He
came to save;
Tell it out among the dying that He
triumph'd o'er the grave!

3. Tell it out among the heathen,
Jesus reigns above! Tell it out!
Tell it out'
Tell it out among the nations that
He reigns in love! Tell it out!
Tell it out!
Tell it out among the high ways and
the lanes at home;
Let it ring across the mountains and
the ocean foam!
Like the sound of many waters let
our glad shout be,
Till it echo and re-echo from the
islands of the sea!

-F. R. Havergal

1349

They that Wait upon the Lord

1. Ho, reapers in the whitened harvest!
Oft feeble, faint, and few;
Come, wait upon the blessed Master
Our strength He will renew.

Chorus
For "they that wait upon the Lord
shall renew their strength,
they shall mount up with wings,
they shall mount up with wings as
eagles:
They shall run and not be weary;
they shall walk and not faint;
They shall run and not be weary;
they shall walk and not faint;
They shall run and not be weary,
shall walk and not faint."

2. Too oft aweary and discouraged,
We pour a sad complaint;
Believing in a living Saviour,
Why should we ever faint?

3. Rejoice! for He is with us always,
Lo, even to the end!
Look up! take courage and go
forward
All needed grace He'll send!

-J. McGranahan

1350

Brunswick - 8.6.8.6.8.6.

1. Dismiss me not from thy service,
Lord,
But train me for thy will;
For even I, in field so broad, Some
duties may fulfil;
And I will ask for no reward,
Except to serve thee still.

2. All works are good, and each is best
As most it pleases thee;
Each worker pleases, when the
rest
He serves in charity;
And neither man nor work unblest
Wilt thou permit to be.

3. Our Master all the work hath done
He asks of us today;
Sharing his service, every one
Share too his sonship may:
Lord, I would serve and be a son;
Dismiss me not, I pray.
-G. F, Bradby

1351

Saved to Serve

1. Going forth at Christ's command,
Going forth to ev'ry land;
Full salvation making known,
Thro' the blood of God's dear Son.

Chorus
"Saved to serve!" the watchword
ring,
Saved to serve our glorious King;
Tell the story o'er and o'er,
Saved to serve for evermore.

2. Serving God thro' all our days,
Toiling not for purse or praise;

But to magnify His name,
While the gospel we proclaim.

3. Seeking only souls to win
From the deadly power of sin;
We would guide their steps aright,
Out of darkness into light.
-El Nathan

1352

When Jesus reigns Within

1. There is gladness in my soul
There is joy beyond control
Since Jesus reigns within
For He drives all sins away
and He brings the perfect day
Since Jesus reigns within

Chorus
Since Jesus reigns within
Since Jesus reigns within
There is peace that fills the soul
There is joy beyond control
Since Jesus reigns within

2. There is rapture, there is peace
That for ever will increase
Since Jesus reigns within
There are blessings waiting me
There is glorious victory
Since Jesus reigns within

3. I am never left alone
When I am the Lord's alone
Since Jesus reigns within
And it makes my soul rejoice
When by faith I hear His voice
Since Jesus reigns within

4. I have heaven in my soul
Tho" the billows round me roll
Since Jesus reigns within
As I press my onward way
To the land of perfect day
Since Jesus reigns within
-R. D. Achely.

1353

Send The Gospel Light

1. Send the Light, oh, send it quickly
Far across the heaving main;
Speed the news of full salvation
Thro' a dear Redeemer's name.

Chorus
Send the Light, oh, send rt quickly
To the isles beyond the sea;
Let them hear the wondrous story
Love is boundless, grace is free!

2. Send the Light, where souls are dying
In their darkness, gloom, and night;
Haste, oh, haste! the days are fleeting,
And the hours how swift their flight

3. Send the Light the Lord commands it;
To His Holy Word attend:
"Go ye forth and preach My gospel;
Lo! I'm with you to the end."

-F. J. Crosby

1354

Missionary Hymn

1. Far, far away in heathen darkness dwelling,
Millions of souls for ever may be lost;
Who, who will go Salvation's story telling
Looking to Jesus, counting not the cost?

Chorus
"All power is given unto Me!
All power is given unto Me!
Go ye into all the world and preach the gospel;
And lo, I am with you alway."

2. See o'er the world wide open doors inviting:
Soldiers of Christ, arise and enter in!
Christian, awake! your forces all uniting,
Send forth the gospel, break the chains of sin!

3. "Why will ye die?" the voice of God is calling;
"Why will ye die?" re-echo in His Name:
Jesus hath died to save from death appalling;
Life and salvation therefore go proclaim.

4. God speed the day when those of every nation,
"Glory of God" triumphantly shall sing;
Ransomed, redeemed, rejoicing in salvation, Shout "Hallelujah, for the Lord is King!"

-James McGranahan

1355

Brighten the Corner Where You Are

1. Do not wait until some deed of greatness you may do,
Do not wait to shed your light afar;
To the many duties ever near you now be true,
Brighten the corner where you are.

Chorus
Brighten the corner where you are!
Brighten the corner where you are!
Someone far from harbor you may guide across the bar,
Brighten the corner where you are.

2. Just above are clouded skies that
   you may help to clear,
   Let not narrow self your way debar;
   Tho into one heart alone may fall
   your song of cheer,
   Brighten the corner where you are.

3 Here for all your talent you will ,
   surely find a need,
   Here reflect the Bright and Morning
   Star;
   Even from your humble hand the
   bread of life may feed,
   Brighten the corner where you are.
   -Ina Duley Ogdon

1356
Have I done My best for Jesus

1. I wonder, have I giv'n my best to
   Jesus
   Who died upon the cruel tree?
   To think of His great sacrifice at
   Calv'ry,
   I know my Lord expects the best
   from me.

Chorus
How many are the lost that I have
lifted?
How many are the chained I've
helped to free?
I wonder, have I done my best for
Jesus,
When He has done so much for
me?

2. The hours that I have wasted are so
   many,
   The hours I've spent for Christ so
   few.
   Because of all my lack of love for
   Jesus,
   I wonder if His heart is breaking,
   too?

3. I wonder have I cared enough for
   others,
   Or have I let them die atone?

I might have helped a wand'rer to
the Savour;
The seed of precious Life I might
have sown.

4. No longer will I stay within the valley,
   I'll climb to mountain heights above;
   The world is dying now for want of
   someone
   To tell them of the Savior's match
   less love.
   -Ensign Edwin Young

1357

Win Them for Him

1. Just to tell the Savior's story,
   Just to witness for His glory,
   There are many waiting in their
   doubt and blindness, Win them for Him!
   Speak a word to friend or neighbor,
   Joyous for the Master is labour,
   Telling of His joy divine, His
   love and kindness. Win them for Him!

Chorus
Serve Him, labour for His glory,
and your witness He will bless,
Serve Him, tell the wondrous stroy,
and His love divine confess, and
gladly
Serve Him, pointing those around
you
to the Light that ne'er can dim,
Haste, for days are winging, souls
to
Jesus bringing, Win them for Him!

2. Just a word, the King confessing,
   Just to point the path to blessing,
   Some have never, never heard the
   call so tender, Win them for Him!
   There is work that wait your doing,
   Eager haste, your strength
   renewing,
   Service for the Master you can
   Daily render, Win them for Him!

3. Just to live a life so lowly,
Witness for the King so holy;
Let your light so shine that those
around may know Him, Win them
for Him!
Just a word. His voice obeying,
Just a word to help the straying,
Tell them of a Saviour blest,
how much we owe Him. Win them
for Him!

-Elsie Duncan Yale

1358

Can He Depend On You

1. Jesus the Saviour came down from
above,
Came to bring mercy and love;
"Crucify him" the mob scornfully
cried,
So He on Calvary died.
While on the cross He prayed:
Father, forgive,
For us He died that for Him we
might live,
Can He depend on you?

Chorus
Can He depend on you,
His blessed will to do?
Will you be crowned with faithful
and true,
Can He depend on you?

2. He from the grave on the third day
arose,
Missions of man to disclose;
Go preach the gospel, all who will
may hear,
Thru Him be free from all fear;
Bid them believe, to repent and
obey,
Walk in the newness of life;
Keep the light glowing to show
them the way
Leading from sin and strife..

3. Jesus the the Savour is coming
again,
With His own ever to reign,
Are you preparing to stand by His
side.
Or in that day be dented?
Have you told others the story of
love,
Showing them what they should do?
These are the precepts that come
from above,
Can He depend on you?

1359

Reapers Are Needed

1. Standing in the market places all
the season thro',
Idly saying, Lord, is there no work
that I can do?
O how many loiter, while the Master
Calls anew,
"Reapers! reapers! Who will work
today?"

Chorus
Lift thine eyes and look upon the
fields that stand
Ripe and ready for the willing
gleaner's hand,
Rouse ye, O sleepers! Ye are
needed as reapers!
Who will be the first to answer,"
Master, here am I"?
Far and wide the ripened grain is
bending low,
In the breezes gently waving to and
fro,
Rouse ye, O sleepers, Ye are
needed as reapers,
And the golden harvest days are
swiftly passing by.

2. Ev'ry sheaf you gather will become a
jewel bright
In the crown you hope to wear in
yonder world of light;

Seek the gems immortal that are
precious in his sight!
"Reapers! reapers! Who will work
today!

3. Morning hours are passing and the
evening follows fast;
Soon the time of reaping will forever
more be past;
Empty handed to the Master will
you go at last?
"Reapers! reapers! Who will work
today?"

-C. H. Gabriel

1360

Angel's song - L.M.

1. Lord, pour thy Spirit from on high,
And thine ordained servants bless;
Graces and gifts to each supply,
And clothe thy priests with
righteousness.

2. Within thy temple when they stand,
To teach the truth as taught by
thee,
Saviour, like stars in thy right hand,
Let all thy Church's pastors be.

3. Wisdom and zeal and faith impart,
Firmness with meekness, from
above,
To bear thy people in their heart,
And love the souls whom thou dost
love;

4. To watch and pray and never faint,
By day and night their guard to
keep,
To warn the sinner, cheer the saint,
To feed thy lambs, and tend thy
Sheep.

5. Then, when their work is finished
here.
May they in hope their charge
resign;
When the chief Shepherd shall
appear,
O God, may they and we be thine.

-James Montgomery

1361

Scales -11.11.11.11. with Refrain

1. Set my soul afire, Lord, for Thy holy
Word.
Burn it deep within me, let Thy
voice be heard:
Millions grope in darkness in this
day and hour.
I will be a witness, fill me with Thy
pow'r.

Chorus
Set my soul afire, Lord, set my soul
afire,
Make my life a witness of Thy
saving pow'r.
Millions grope in darkness, waiting
for Thy Word.
Set my soul afire, Lord, Set my soul
afire.

2. Set my soul afire, Lord, for the lost
in sin,
Give to me a passion as I seek to win;
Help me not to falter, never let
me fail.
Fill me with Thy Spirit, let Thy will
prevail.

3. Set my soul afire, Lord, in my daily life,
Far too long I've wandered in this
day of strife:
Nothing else will matter but to live
for Thee.
I will be a witness, for Christ lives
in me.

-Gene Bartlett

MISSIONARIES AND FIELD WORKERS

1362
Christ For The Whole Wide World

1. Christ for the whole wide world'
Our task has just begun,
For millions wait in every land
The message of God's Son.
Shall they be left in sin,
To die without His word,
Without the Saviour Jesus Christ,
Because they never heard?

Chorus
We will give, we will pray,
We will witness every day,
That the millions of the whole wide
world
May know our Saviour's love.

2. Christ for the whole wide world!
His message must be sent
To millions dying in their sin
To call them to repent.
Christ Jesus died to save,
But they can never know
Until we bring our gifts of love
And bid His heralds go!

3. Christ for the whole wide world!
His heralds will proclaim
Salvation for men everywhere
In Jesus blessed name,
And we who cannot go
To bear His tidings far
Will pray for those who take the
Word and witness where we are.
                    -Hattie Bell Allen

1363
It Pays To Serve Jesus

1. The service of Jesus true pleasure
affords,
In Him there is joy without an alloy;
'Tis heaven to trust Him and rest on
His words; it pays to serve Jesus
each day.

Chorus
It pays to serve Jesus, it pays every
day,
It pays every step of the way;
Tho' the pathway to glory may
sometimes be drear,
You'll be happy each step of the
way.

2. It pays to serve Jesus whatever
may betide,
It pays to be true whate'er you may
do;
'Tis riches of mercy in Him to abide;
it pays to serve Jesus each day.

3. Tho' sometimes the shadows may
hang o'er the way,
And sorrows may come to beckon
us home,
Our precious Redeemer each toil
will repay:
It pays to serve Jesus each day.
                    -Frank C. Huston

1364
Ellesdie

1. Hark, the voice of Jesus calling,
"Who will go and work today?
Fields are white, and harvest waiting,
Who will bear the sheaves away?"
Loud and long the Master calleth,
Rich reward He offers free;
Who will answer, gladly saying,
"Here am I. send me. send me?"

2. If you cannot cross the ocean
And the heathen lands explore,
You can find the needy nearer,
You can help those at your door;
If you cannot give the thousands,

You can give the widow's mite;
And the least you do for Jesus
Will be precious in His sight.

3. If you cannot sing like angels,
   If you cannot preach like Paul,
   You can tell the love of Jesus,
   You can say He died for all;
   If you cannot rouse the wicked,
   With the judgment's dread alarms,
   you can lead the little children
   To the Saviour's waiting arms;

4. Let none hear you idly saying.
   "There is nothing I can do,"
   While the souls of men are dying,
   And the Master calls for you,
   Take the task He gives you gladly,
   Let His work your pleasure be,
   Answer quickly while He calleth,
   Here am I, send me, send me."
   -Daniel March

1365

Bringing In The Sheaves

1. Sowing in the morning, sowing
   seeds of kindness,
   Sowing in the noon tide and the
   dewy eve;
   Waiting for the harvest, and the time
   of reaping,
   We shall come rejoicing, bringing in
   the sheaves.

   Chorus
   Bringing in the sheaves, bringing in
   the sheaves,
   We shall come rejoicing, bringing in
   the sheaves;
   Bringing in the sheaves, bringing in
   the sheaves,
   We shall come rejoicing, bringing in
   the sheaves.

2. Sowing in the sunshine, sowing in
   The shadows,

Fearing neither clouds nor winter's
chilling breeze;
By and by the harvest and the labour
ended,
We shall come rejoicing, bringing in
the sheaves.

3. Going forth with weeping, sowing for
   the Master.
   Tho' the loss sustained our spirit of
   ten grieves;
   When our weeping's over, He will bid
   us welcome,
   We shall come rejoicing, bringing in
   the sheaves.
   -Knowies Shaw

1366

Must I Go, And Empty Handed

1. "Must I go, and empty handed,"
   Thus my dear Redeemer meet?
   Not one day of service give Him,
   Lay no trophy at His feet?

   Chorus
   "Must I go, and empty handed?"
   Must I meet my Saviour so?
   Not one soul with which to greet
   Him
   Must I empty handed go?

2. Not at death 1 shrink nor falter,
   For my Saviour saves me now;
   But to meet Him empty handed,
   Thought of that now clouds my brow,

3. O the years in sinning wasted,
   Could I but recall them now,
   I would give them to my Saviour,
   To His will I'd gladly bow.

4. O ye saints, arouse, be earnest,
   Up and working while yet 'tis day;
   Ere the night of death o'er take thee.
   Strive for souls while still you may.
   -C. C. Luther

MISSIONARIES AND FIELD WORKERS

1367

Boylston -S.M.

1 A charge to keep I have, God to
glorify.
A never dying soul to save, And fit it
for the sky.

2. To serve the present age, My calling
to fulfill;
O may it all my pow'rs engage To
do my Master's will.

3 Arm me with watchful care As in
Thy sight to live, And
now Thy servant, Lord, prepare A
strict account to give!

4. Help me to watch and pray, And still
on Thee rely, O
let me not my trust betray, But press
to realms on high.

-Charles Wesley

1368

I Can Safely Go-11.11.11.11.With Refrain

1. Any where with Jesus I can safely
go;
Anywhere He leads me in this world
below;
Anywhere without Him dearest joys
would fade;
Anywhere with Jesus I am not afraid.

Chorus
Anywhere! anywhere! Fear I
cannot know;
Anywhere with Jesus I can safely
go.

2. Anywhere with Jesus I am not
alone,
Other friends may fail me, He is still
my own;
Though His hand may lead me over
dreary ways,
Any were with Jesus is a house of
Praise.

3. Anywhere with Jesus over land
and sea,
Telling souls in darkness of
salvation free;
Ready as He summons me to go
or stay.
Anywhere with Jesus He points the
way.

-Jessie Pounds

1369

Footsteps - 9.4.9.4. with Refrain

1. Sweetly, Lord, have we heard
Thee calling,
"Come, follow Me"
And we see where Thy foot prints
falling,
Lead us to Thee.

Chorus
Foot prints of Jesus
that make the pathway glow:
We will follow the steps of Jesus
where'er they go.

2. Tho they lead o'er the cold, dark
mountains, Seeking His sheep,
Or along by Siloam's fountains,
Helping the weak.

3. If they lead thro' the temple holy,
Preaching the Word,
Or in homes of the poor and lowly,
Serving the Lord.

4. Then at last, when on high He
sees us.
Our journey done, We will rest
where the steps of Jesus
End at His throne.

-Mary B. C. Siade

MISSIONARIES AND FIELD WORKERS

1370

Toronto -11.10.11.10. with Coda

1. So send I you to labour
   unrewarded,
   To serve unpaid, unloved, unsought.
   unknown.
   To bear rebuke, to suffer scorn and
   scoffing
   So send I you. to toil for Me alone.

2 So send I you to bind the bruised and
   broken.
   O'er wand'ring souls to work, to
   weep, to wake.
   To bear the burdens of a world
   aweary
   So send I you, to suffer for My
   sake.

3 So send I you to loneliness and
   longing.
   With heart ahung'ring for the loved
   and known,
   Forsaking home and kindred, friend
   and dear one
   So send I you, to know My love
   alone.

4. So send I you to leave your life's
   ambition,
   To die to dear desire, self will resign.
   To labour long, and love where men
   revile you
   So send I you. to lose your life in
   Mine.

5 So send I you to hearts made hard
   by hatred.
   To eyes made blind because they
   will not see,
   To spend, tho it be blood, to spend
   and spare not
   So send I you, to taste of Calvary.
            -Margaret Clarkson

1371

Rescue .11.10.11.10. with Refrain

1. Rescue the perishing, care for the
   Dying.
   Snatch them in pity from sin and
   grave;
   Weep o'er the erring one, lift up the
   Fallen.
   Tell them of Jesus, the mighty to
   save.

   Chorus
   Rescue the perishing. Care for the
   dying.
   Jesus is merciful. Jesus will save.

2. Tho they are slighting Him, still He
   is waiting,
   Waiting the penitent child to
   receive;
   Plead with them earnestly, plead
   with them gently.
   He will forgive if they only believe.

3. Down in the human heart, crushed
   by the tempter,
   Feelings lie buried that grace can
   restore;
   Touched by a loving heart, wakened
   by kindness,
   Cords that are broken will vibrate
   once more.

4. Rescue the perishing, duty demands
   It
   Strength for your labour the Lord will
   provide;
   Back to the narrow way patiently
   win them,
   Tell the poor wand'rer a Savour had
   died.
           -Fanny J. Crosby

MISSIONARIES AND FIELD WORKERS

1372

Bardbury -8.7.8.7.D.

1. Saviour, like a shepherd lead us,
   Much we need Thy tender care;
   In Thy pleasant pastures feed us,
   For our use Thy folds prepare:
   Blessed Jesus, blessed Jesus.
   Thou hast bought us, Thine we are;
   Blessed Jesus, blessed Jesus,
   Thou hast bought us, Thine we are.

2. We are Thine; do Thou befriend us,
   Be the Guardian of our way;
   Keep Thy flock, from sin defend us,
   Seek us when we go astray:
   Blessed Jesus, blessed Jesus,
   Hear,
   O hear us when we pray;
   Blessed Jesus, blessed Jesus,
   Hear,
   O hear us when we pray.

3. Thou hast promised to receive us,
   Poor and sinful though we be;
   Thou hast mercy to relieve us,
   Grace to cleanse, and pow'r to free:
   Blessed Jesus, blessed Jesus,
   Early let us turn to Thee;
   Blessed Jesus, blessed Jesus,
   Early let us turn to Thee.

4. Early let us seek Thy favor;
   Early let us do Thy will;
   Blessed Lord and only Savour,
   With Thy love our bosoms fill:
   Blessed Jesus, blessed Jesus,
   Thou hast loved us, love us still,
   Blessed Jesus, blessed Jesus,
   Thou hast loved us, love us still.
   -Hymns for the Young

1373

Swabia - S.M.

1. Sow in the morn thy seed,
   At eve hold out thine hand;
   To doubt and fear give thou no
   heed,
   Broadcast it o'er the land.

2. Beside all waters sow,
   The highway furrows stock,
   Drop it where thorns and thistles
   grow,
   Scatter it on the rock.

3 The good, the fruitful ground,
   Expect not here nor there;
   O'er hill and vale, by plots 'tis
   found:
   Go forth, then everywhere.

4. And duty shall appear,
   In verdure, beauty, strength,
   the tender blade, the stalk, the ear,
   And the full corn at length.

5. Thou canst not toil in vain;
   Cold, heat, and moist, and dry,
   Shall foster and mature the grain
   For gamers in the sky.

6. Thence, when the glorious end,
   The day of God is come,
   The angel reapers shall descend,
   And heaven cry: Harvest home!
   -James Montgomery

1374

Watchman - S.M.

1. Rise up, O men of God!
   Have done with lesser things;
   Give heart and soul and mind and
   strength
   To serve the King of kings.

2. Rise up O men of God! His
   kingdom tarries long;
   Bring in the day of brotherhood;
   And end the night of wrong.

3. Rise up, O men of God!
   The Church for you doth wait,
   Her strength unequal to her task;
   Rise up and make her great.

4. Lift high the Cross of Christ!
   Tread where His feet have trod;
   As brothers of the Son of Man
   Rise up, O men of God!
   —William Pierson Merrill

1375

Wir Pflugen' 7.6.7.6.D. and Refrain

1. We plough the fields, and scatter
   The good seed on the land,
   But it is fed and watered
   By God's almighty hand;
   He sends the snow in winter,
   The warmth to swell the grain,
   The breezes, and the sunshine,
   And soft refreshing rain.

Chorus
All good gifts around us
Are sent from heaven above
Then thank the Lord, O thank the
Lord,
For all His love.

2. He only is the Maker
   Of all things near and far:
   He paints the wayside flower,
   He lights the evening star;
   The winds and waves obey Him,
   By Him the birds are fed;
   Much more to us. His children,
   He gives our daily bread.

3. We thank Thee then, O Father
   For all things bright and good. .
   The seed-time and the harvest.
   Our life, our health, our food;
   Accept the gifts we offer
   For alt Thy love imparts,
   And, what Thou most desirest,
   Our humble, thankful hearts.
   —Matthias Claudius

1376

Birstal - L.M.

1. Shall I, for tear of feeble man;
   The Spirit's course in me restrain?

Or, dismayed, in deed and word
Be a true witness for my Lord?

2. Saviour of men, Thy searching eye
   Doth all my inmost thoughts descry,
   Doth aught oh earth my wishes
   raise,
   " Or the world's pleasures or its
   praise?

3. The love of Christ doth me constrain
   To seek the wandering souls of men;
   With cries, entreaties; tears, to
   save,
   To snatch them from the gaping
   grave.

4. My life, my blood, I here present,
   If for Thy truth they may be spent:
   Fulfill Thy sovereign counsel, Lord;
   Thy will be done, Thy name adored.

5. Give me Thy strength, O God of
   power:
   Then, let winds blow or thunders
   roar;
   Thy faithful witness will I be:
   'Tis fixed; I can do all through Thee!
   —Johann Joseph Winckler

1377

Let the lower lights be burning

1. Brightly beams our Father's mercy
   From His light house ever more,
   But to us He gives the keeping
   Of the lights along the shore.

Chorus
Let the lower lights be burning!
Send a gleam across the wave
Some poor fainting, struggling sea
man
You may rescue, you may save.

2. Dark the night of sin has settled,
   Loud the angry billows roar;
   Eager eyes are watching, longing,
   For the lights along the shore.

3. Trim your feeble lamp, my brother,
   Some poor sailor tempest tossed,
   Trying now to make the harbor,
   In the darkness may be lost.
   -P. P. Bliss

1378

Tidings

1. O Zion, haste, Thy mission high
   fulfilling,
   To tell to all the world that God is
   light
   That He who made all nations is not
   willing
   One soul should perish, lost in
   shades of night.

Chorus
Tidings of peace, Tidings of Jesus,
Redemption and release.

2. Behold how many thousands still
   are lying
   Bound in the darksome prison
   house in sin.
   With none to tell them of the
   Saviour's dying,
   Or of the Me He died for them to win.

3. Proclaim to ev'ry people, tongue
   and nation
   That God in whom they live and
   move is love:
   Tell how He stooped to save His lost
   creation,
   And died on earth that man might
   live above.

4. Give of Thy sons to bear the
   message glorious;
   Give of thy wealth to speed them on
   their way;
   Pour out thy soul for them in pray'r
   victorious;
   And all thou spendest Jesus will
   repay.

5. He comes again; O Zion, ere thou
   meet Him
   Make known to ev'ry heart His
   saving grace;
   Let none whom He hath ransomed
   fail to greet Him,
   Thro' thy neglect, unfit to see His
   face.
   -Mary A. Thompson

1379

Speak, my Lord

1. Hear the Lord of harvest sweetly
   calling,
   "Who will go and work for Me
   today?
   Who will bring to Me the lost and
   dying?
   Who will point them to the narrow
   way?"

Chorus
Speak, my Lord, speak, my Lord,
Speak, and I'll be quick to answer
Thee;
Speak, my Lord, speak, my Lord.
Speak, and I will answer, "Lord,
send me."

2. When the coal of fire touched the
   prophet,
   Making him as pure, as pure can
   be.
   When the voice of God said,
   "Who'll go for us?"
   Then he answered, "Here I am,
   send me."

3. Millions now in sin and shame are
   dying.
   Listen to their sad and bitter cry;
   Hasten, brother, hasten to the
   rescue;
   Quickly answer, "Master, here am I"

Soon the time for reaping will be over;
Soon we'll gather for the harvest home:
May the Lord of harvest smile upon us,
May we hear His blessed, "Child, well done."

-George Bennard

1380

Lift Him Up

1. How to reach the masses, men of ev'ry birth,
For an answer Jesus gave the key:
"And I, if I be lifted up from the earth.
Will draw all men unto Me."

Chorus
Lift Him up, Lift Him up,
Still He speaks from eternal:
And I, if I be lifted up from the earth,
Will draw all men unto Me."

2. Oh! the world is hungry for the living Bread,
Lift the Savour up for them to see;
Trust Him, and do not doubt the words that He said,
I'll draw all men unto Me."

3. Don't exalt the preacher, don't exalt the pew,
Preach the Gospel simple, full and free;
Prove Him and you will find that promise is true,
I'll draw all men unto Me."

4, Lift Him up by living as a Christian ought,
Let the world in you the Savour see;
Then men will gladly follow Him who once taught,
I'll draw all men unto Me."

-Johnson Oatman, Jr

1381

We've a Story to Tell

1. We've a story to tell to the nations
That shall turn their hearts to the right,
A story of truth and mercy,
A story of peace and light.

Chorus
For the darkness shall turn to dawning,
And the dawning to noonday bright,
And Christ's great kingdom shall come to earth,
The kingdom of love and light

2. We've a song to be sung to the nations
That shall lift their hearts to the Lord,
A song thsat shall conquer evil
And shatter the spear and sword.

3. We've a message to give to the nations
That the Lord who reigneth above
Hath sent us His Son to save us
And show us that God is love,

4. We've a Savour to show to the nations
Who the path of sorrow hath trod,
That all of the world's great peoples
Might come to the truth of God.

-H. Ernest Nichol

1382

This Little Light of Mine

1. This little of mine,
I'm going to let it shine,
Oh, this little light of mine,
I'm going to let it shine, Hallelujah,
This little light of mine,
I'm going to let it shine,
Let it shine, let it shine, let it shine.

MISSIONARIES AND FIELD WORKERS

2. Ev'ry where I go,
   I'm going to let it shine,
   Oh, ev'ry where I go.
   I'm going to let it shine. Hallelujah,
   Ev'ry where I go,
   I'm going to let it shine,
   let it shine, let it shine, let it shine.

3. All in my house,
   I'm going to let it shine,
   Oh, all in my house,
   I'm going to let it shine, Hallelujah,
   All in my house,
   I'm going to let it shine,
   let it shine, let it shine, let it shine.

4. I'm not going to make it shine,
   I'm just going to let it shine,
   I'm not going to make it shine,
   I'm just going to let it shine,
   Hallelujah,
   I'm not going to make it shine,
   I'm just going to let it shine,
   let it shine, let it shine, let it shine.

5. Out in the dark,
   I'm going to let it shine,
   Oh, out in the dark.
   I'm going to let it shine. Hallelujah.
   Out in the dark,
   I'm going to let it shine,
   let it shine, let it shine, let it shine.
   -Lilian M. Bowie

1383
Work, for the Night Is Coming

1. Work, for the night is coming,
   Work thru the morning hours;
   Work while the dew is sparkling,
   Work 'mid springing flow'rs.
   Work when the day grows brighter
   Work in the glowing sun;
   Work, for the night is coming,
   When man's work is done.

2. Work, for the night is coming,
   Work thru the sunny noon;
   Fill brightest hours with labour
   Rest comes sure and soon.
   Give ev'ry flying minute
   Something to keep in store;
   Work, for the night is coming,
   When man works no more.

3. Work, for the night is coming,
   Under the sunset skies:
   While their tints are glowing,
   Work, for daylight flies;
   Work till the last beam fadeth.
   Fadeth to shine no more;
   Work, while the night is dark'ning.
   When man's work is o'er.
   -Annie L Coghill

1384

Llangloffan -7.6.7.6.D.

1. Facing a task unfinished,
   That drives us to our knees,
   A need that, undiminished,
   Rebukes our slothful ease.
   We, who rejoice to know Thee,
   Renew before Thy throne
   The solemn pledge we owe Thee
   To go and make Thee known.

2. Where other lords beside Thee
   Hold their unhindered sway.
   Where forces that defied Thee
   Defy Thee still to-day
   With none to heed their crying
   For life and love and light
   Unnumbered souls are dying,
   And pass into the night.

3. We bear the torch that flaming
   Fell from the hands of those
   Who gave their lives proclaiming
   That Jesus died and rose.
   Ours is the same commission,
   The same glad message ours,
   Fired by the same ambition.
   To Thee we yield our powers.

4. O Father who sustained them,
   O Spirit who inspired.

MISSIONARIES AND FIELD WORKERS

Saviour, whose love sustained them,
To toil with zeal untired,
From cowardice defend us,
From lethargy awake!
Forth on Thine errands send us
To labour for Thy sake.

F. Houghton

5. There to reap in joy for ever
Fruit that grow from seed here sown,
There to be with Him who never
Ceases to perserve His own,
And with gladness, And with gladness
Give the praise to Him alone.

1385

Speed Thy Servants, Saviour, Speed Them-8.7.8.7.8.7.

1. Speed thy servants. Saviour, speed them;
Thou art Lord of winds and waves:
They were bound, but Thou hast freed them;
Now they go to free the slaves.
Be Thou with them, Be Thou with them;
'Tis Thine arm alone that saves.

2. Friends, and home, and all forsaking
Lord, they go at Thy command;
As their stay Thy promise taking,
While they traverse sea and land:
O be with them! O be with them!
Lead them safely by the hand.

3. Where no fruit appears to cheer them,
And they seem to toil in vain,
Then in mercy. Lord, draw near them,
Then their sinking hopes sustain;
Thus supported. Thus supported,
Let their zeal revive again.

4. In the midst of opposition,
Let them trust, O Lord, in Thee;
When success attends their mission,
Let Thy servants humbler be;
Never leave them, Never leave them,
Till thy face in heaven they see.

1386

Those Who Make Their Labour Druggery-8.8.8.D.

1. Those who make their labour druggery
Do the Lord's work with idleness,
Those who make religion a cloak
Do not understand work and faith;
They separate what God has so joined;
Diligence with devotedness.

2. The work we do are established
When it's done with the Spirit's zeal
God, who created days and nights
Decreed to rest on the seventh
As we work to redeem the time
Pleases our God whom we worship.

3. We will rejoice if God gives us
Such labour with enthusiasm,
Because such work that He commands
Shall be offering for His glory;
Like saints above as we worship,
It swells our fellowship of love.

1387

There's a Call Comes Ringing o'er The Restless Wave - P.M.

1. There's a call comes ringing o'er the restless wave,
Send the light! Send the light!
There are souls to rescue, there are souls to save,
Send the light! Send the light!

MISSIONARIES AND FIELD WORKERS

Chorus
Send the light the blessed gospel
Light,
Let us shine from shore to shore!
Send the light! And let its radiant
beams
Light the world for evermore.

2. We have heard the Macedonian call
today,
Send the light! Send the light!
And a golden off'ring at the cross
we lay,
Send the light! Send the light!

3. Let us pray that grace may
everywhere abound,
Send the light! Send the light!
And a Christ like spirit everywhere
be found,
Send the light! Send the light!

4. Let us not grow weary in the work
of love,
Send the light! Send the light!
Let us gather jewels for a crown
above,
Send the light! Send the light!

1388

We Are Marching On - P.M.

1. We are marching on, with shield
and banner bright;
We will praise His name, rejoicing
in His might.
Arid we'll work till Jesus calls.
From the youthful ranks our army
we prepare,
As we rally round our blessed
standard here;
And the Saviour's cross we early
learn to bear,
While we work till Jesus calls.

Chorus
Then awake, then awake
Happy song, happy song
Shout for joy, shout for joy
As we gladly march along.
We are marching onward, singing
as we go,

To the promised land where living
waters flow:
Come and join our ranks as pilgrims
here below,
Come and work till Jesus calls.

2. We are marching on: our Captain.
ever near,
Will protect us still, His gentle voice
we hear;
Let the foe advance, we'll never,
never fear,
For we'll work till Jesus calls,
Then awake, awake, our happy,
happy song;
We will shout for joy, and gladly
march along;
In the Lord of hosts let ev'ry heart be
strong,
While we work till Jesus calls.

3. We are marching on the strait and
narrow way,
That will lead to life and everlasting
day
To the smiling fields, that never will
decay:
But we'll work till Jesus calls,
We are marching on, and pressing
t'wards the prize.
To a glorious crown beyond the
glowing skies.
To the radiant fields where pleasure
never dies
And we'll work till Jesus calls.

1389

With Joyfulness -10.9.10.9.with Ref.

1. With joyfulness we shall work
the Master
Go we forth with willing hands to
do,
Whatsoever to us He hath
Appointed
Faithfully our mission we'll pursue

THE CHURCH TRIUMPHANT

Chorus
Toiling for Jesus
Joyfully we go, yes, joyfully we go,
Toiling for Jesus,
In His vineyard here below.

2. Sweetly, sweetly, we will tell the
story
Of His love to mortals here below;
Christ, the brightness of the
Father's glory
Freely here His blessings will
bestow.

3. Meekly, meekly, toiling for the
Master,
Walking, faithfully the path He trod;
Leading wanderers to the dear
Redeemer
Pointing sinners to the Lamb of
God.

1390
Ye Servants Of The Lord - S.M.

1. Ye servants of the Lord
Hear ye the Masters call';
Follow where ever He leads you
He calls you to His way.

2. The Father you worship
Has the power to bestow;
With complete trust in His promise
Fight manfully like men.

3. Go, manifest the Lord
Also His great mercy
Among the miserable sinners
Of Adam's fallen race.

4. In the name of our Lord
We will wish you "God speed"
We pray Him who has sent you out'
To prosper all your work

THE CHURCH TRIUMPHANT

1391
St. Thomas - S.M.

1. I love Thy kingdom, Lord,
   The house of Thine abode,
   The Church our blest Redeemer
   saved
   With His own precious blood.

2. I love Thy Church, O God!
   Her walls before Thee stand,
   Dear as the apple of Thine eye,
   And graven on Thy hand.

3. For her my tears shall fall;
   For her my prayers ascend;
   To her my cares and toils be giver
   Till toils and cares shall end.

4. Beyond my highest joy
   I prize her heavenly ways,
   Her sweet communion, solemn
   vows,
   Her hymns of love and praise.

5. Sure as Thy truth shall last,
   To Zion shall be given
   The brightest glories earth can yield,
   And brighter bliss of heaven.
   -Timothy dwight

1392
Benediction-8.7.8.7.8.7.

1. Alleluia! Song of gladness,
   Voice of everlasting joy:
   Alleluia! Sound the sweetest
   Heard among the choirs on high.
   Hymning in God's blissful mansion
   Day and night incessantly.

2. Alleluia! Church victorious,
   Thou mayst lift the joyful strain.
   Alleluia! Songs of triumph

Well befit the ransom'd train.
Faint and feeble are our praises
While in exile we remain.

3. Alleluia! Songs of gladness
   Suit not always souls forlorn.
   Alleluia! Sounds of sadness
   'Midst our joyful strains are borne;
   For in this dark world of sorrow
   We with tears our sins must mourn.

4. Praises with our prayers uniting,
   Hear us, blessed Trinity;
   Bring us to Thy blissful presence,
   There the Paschal Lamb to see,
   There to Thee our Alleluia
   Singing everlasting.

1393
Lostwithiel - 7.7.8.7.7.7.8.7.

1. Head of the church triumphant,
   We joyfully adore Thee;
   Till Thou appear, Thy members
   here
   Shall sing like those in glory:
   We lift our hearts and voices,
   With bless'ed anticipation,
   And cry aloud, and give to God
   The praise of our salvation.

2. While in affliction's fumance,
   And passing through the fire,
   Thy love we praise in grateful lays
   Which ever brings us nigher:
   We clap our hands, exulting
   In Thine almighty favour:
   The love divine, that made us
   Thine,
   Shall keep us Thine for ever.

3. Thou dost conduct Thy people
   Through torrents of temptation:
   Nor will we fear, while Thou art near
   The fire of tribulation;
   The world, with sin and Satan,
   In vain our march opposes,
   By Thee we shall break through
   Them all,
   And sing the song of Moses,

4. By faith we see the glory
To which Thou shalt restore us,
The world despise, for that high prize
Which Thou hast set before us:
And, if Thou count us worthy,
We each, with dying Stephen,
Shall see Thee stand at God's right hand
To call us up to heaven.

-J. Turle

1394

Victory all the time

1. They who know the Saviour shall in Him be strong,
Mighty in the conflict of the right "gainst wrong.
This the blessed promise given in God's word,
Doing wondrous exploits, they who know the Lord.

Chorus
Victory! Victory! blessed blood bought victory,
Victory! victory! vict'ry all the time,
As Jehovah liveth, Strength divine He giveth,
Unto those who know Him vict'ry all the time.

2. In the midst of battle be not thou dismayed,
Though the powers of darkness 'gainst thee are arrayed;
God, thy strength, is with thee, causing thee to stand, Heaven's allied armies wait at thy command.

3. Brave to bear life's testing, strong the foe to meet,
Walking like a hero midst the furnace heat,
Doing wondrous exploits with the Spirit's sword
Winning souls for Jesus, praise, O praise the Lord.

-Mrs. C. H. Morris

1395

Duke Street-L.M.

1. O God, above the drifting years
The shrines our fathers founded stand,
And where the higher gain appears,
We trace the working of Thy hand.

2. From out their tireless prayer and toil
Emerge the gifts that time has proved,
And seed laid deep in sacred soil
Yields harvests rich in lasting good.

3. The torch to their devotion lent
Lightens the dark that round us lies;
Help us to pass it on unspent,
Until the dawn lights up the skies.

4. Fill Thou our hearts with faith like theirs,
Who served the days they could not see;
And give us grace, through ampler years,
To build the kingdom yet to be.

-John Wright Buckham

1396

All Saints New

1. The Son of God goes forth to war,
A kingly crown to gain;
His blood red banner streams afar
Who follows in His train?
Who best can drink his cup of woe,
Triumphant over pain,
Who patient bears his cross below,
He follows in His train.

2. The martyr first, whose eagle eye
Could pierce beyond the grave,
Who saw his Master in the sky,
And called on Him to save:

THE CHURCH TRIUMPHANT

Like Him, with pardon on His
tongue
In midst of mortal pain,
He prayed for them that did the
wrong:
Who follows in his train?

3. A glorious band, the chosen few
On whom the Spirit came,
Twelve valiant saints, their hope
they knew,
And mocked the cross and flame:
They met the tyrant's brandished
steel,
The lion's gory mane;
They bowed their necks the death
to feel:
Who follows in their train?

4. A noble army, men and boys,
The matron and the maid,
Around the Saviour's throne rejoice,
In robes of light arrayed:
They climbed the steep ascent of
heaven Thro' peril, toil, and pain:
O God, to us may grace be given
To follow in their train.
                        -Reginald Heber

1397

Eatington-C.M.

1. The Church triumphant in thy love,
Their mighty joys we know;
They sing the Lamb in hymns
above,
And we in hymns below.

2. Thee in thy glorious realm they
praise,
And bow before thy throne;
We in the kingdom of thy grace:
The kingdom are but one.

3. The holy to the holiest leads,
From hence our spirits rise,
And he that thy statues treads
Shall meet thee in the skies.
                        -Charles Wesley

1398

Aurelia-7.6.7.6.D.

1. The Church's one foundation
Is Jesus Christ her Lord;
She is His new creation
By water and the Word:
From heav'n came and sought her
To be His holy bride;
With His own blood He bought her,
And for her life He died.

2. Elect from ev'ry nation. Yet one o'er
all the earth,
Her charter of salvation One Lord,
one faith, one birth;
One holy name she blesses,
Partakes one holy food,
And to one hope she presses,
With ev'ry grace endued.

3. Mid toil and tribulation And tumult
of her war,
She waits the consummation
Of peace for evermore;
Till with the vision glorious Her
longing eyes are blest.
And the great Church victorious
Shall be the Church at rest.

4. Yet she on earth hath union With
God the Three in One,
And mystic sweet communion With
those whose rest is won:
O happy ones and holy! Lord, give
us grace that we,
Like them, the meek and lowly,
On high may dwell with Thee.
                        -Samuel J. Stone

THE CHURCH TRIUMPHANT

1399
St. Catherine-8.8.8.8.8.8.

1. Faith of our fathers! living still
   in spite of dungeon, fire and sword:
   O how our hearts beat high with joy
   Whene'er we hear that glorious
   word!
   Faith of our fathers, holy faith!
   We will be true to thee till death!

2. Our fathers, chained in prisons dark,
   Were still in heart and conscience
   free:
   How sweet would be their children's
   fate?
   If they like them could die for thee!
   Faith of our fathers, holy faith!
   We will be true to thee till death!

3. Faith of our fathers! we will strive
   To win all nations unto thee,
   And thro' the truth come from God,
   Mankind shall then be truly free.
   Faith of our fathers, holy faith!
   We will be true to thee till death!

4. Faith of our fathers! we will love
   Both friend and foe in all our strife:
   And preach thee too as love knows
   how,
   By kindly words and virtuous life:
   Faith of our fathers, holy faith!
   We will be true to thee till death!
   -Frederick W. Faber

1400
Jericho Tune D.S.M.

1. Forth rode the knights of old
   With armour gleaming bright,
   By noble deeds and actions bold
   To fight for God and right.

To lay the tyrant low,
To set the captive free,
The hosts of evil to o'er throw
By might of purity.

2. A vision flamed above,
   A voice within spoke clear,
   Thy symbol of Christ's mighty love
   Shone radiant and near.
   Then, burning with desire,
   By zeal and love possessed,
   The knights of old with heart afire
   Rode out upon the quest.

3. In every age the same,
   From hut and princely hall,
   The pilgrim knights who bear His
   name
   Have followed at His call.
   Now each with glory crowned,
   And waiting on His will,
   They stand His splendid throne
   around
   And serve more nobly still.

4. Still, still the vision glows
   Still calls the voice divine;
   Still sink the weak, oppressed by
   foes,
   And still the captives pine;
   Still loyal to their Lord,
   With zeal and patience shod,
   With shield of faith and mystic
   sword, Go forth the knights of God.
   -Vera Evaline Walker

1401
Frogmore - 6.4.6.4.

1. Their names are names of kings
   Of heavenly line;
   The bliss of earthly things
   They did resign.

2. Chieftains they were, who warred
   With sword and shield;
   Victors for God the Lord
   On foughten field.

3. Sad were their days on earth,
   Mid hate and scorn,
   A life of pleasure's dearth,
   A death forlorn;

4. Yet blest that end in woe,
   And those sad days;
   Only man's blame below;
   Above God's praise.

5. A city of great name
   Is built for them,
   Of glorious golden fame
   Jerusalem!

6. Redeemed with precious blood
   From death and sin,
   Sons of the Triune God,
   They enter in.

7. So doth the life of pain
   In glory close;
   Lord God, may we attain
   Their grand repose.
                    -Samuel John Stone

4. They have conquered death and
   Satan
   By the might of Christ the Lord.

3. Marching with Thy Cross their
   banner.
   They have triumphed, following
   Thee, the Captain of salvation,
   Thee, their Saviour and their king.
   Gladly, Lord, with Thee they
   suffered;
   Gladly, Lord, with Thee they died:
   And by death, to life immortal
   They were born ana glorified.

4. God of God. the One-bogotten,
   Light of Light, Immanuel.
   In whose body joined together
   All the saints for ever dwell.
   Pour upon us of Thy fullness.
   That we may for evermore
   God the Father. God the Son, and
   God the Holy Ghost adore.
                    -Christopher Wordsworth

1402

Deerhurst - 8.7.8.7.D.

1. Hark! The sound of holy voices,
   Chanting at the crystal sea:
   Hallelujah! Hallelujah!
   Hallelujah' Lord, to Thee:
   Multitude, which none can number,
   Like the stars in glory stand,
   Clothed in white apparel, holding
   Palms of victory in their hand.

2. They have come from tribulation,
   And have washed their robes in
   blood,
   Washed them in the blood of Jesus
   Tried they were, and firm they stood
   Mocked, imprisoned, stoned,
   tormented,
   Sawn asunder, slain with sword,

1403

Mylon-C.M.

1. Give me the wings of faith to rise
   Within the veil, and see
   The saints above, how great their
   joys,
   How bright their glories be.

2. Once they were mourners here
   below,
   And poured out cries and tears;
   They wrestled hard. as we do now,
   With sins, and doubts, and fears.

3. I ask them whence their victory
   came:
   They, with united breath.
   Ascribe their conquest to the Lamb.
   Their triumph to His death.

THE CHURCH TRIUMPHANT

4. They marked the footsteps that He trod,
His zeal inspired their breast;
And, following their incarnate God,
Possess the promised rest.

5. Our glorious Leader claims our praise
For His own pattern given;
While the long cloud of witnessess
Show the same path to heaven.
              -Isaac Watts

1404

St. Lawrence - C.M.

1. Our life is hid with Christ in God;
Our Life shall soon appear,
And shed His glory all abroad
In all His members here.

2. Our souls are in His mighty hand,
And He shall keep them still;
And you and I shall surely stand
With Him on Zion's hill.

3. O what a joyful meeting there!
In robes of white arrayed,
Palms in our hands we all shall bear,
And crowns upon our head.

4. Then let us lawfully contend,
And fight our passage through:
Bear in our faithful minds the end,
And keep the prize in view.
              -Charles Wesley

1405

Rest-8.8.8.8.8.8.

1. The saints of God, their conflict past,
And life's long battle won at last,
No more they need the shield or sword;

They cast them down before their Lord
O happy saints' For ever blest,
At Jesus feet how safe their rest.

2. The saints of God, their wanderings done,
No more their weary course they run,
No more they faint, no more they fall,
No foes oppress, no fears appal:
O happy saints! For ever blest,
In that dear home, how sweet their rest.

3. The saints of God, life's voyage o'er,
Safe landed on that blissful shore,
No stormy tempests now they dread,
No roaring billows lift their head:
O happy saints! For ever blest,
In that calm haven of their rest.

4. O God of saints, to Thee we cry;
O Saviour, plead for us on high;
O Holy Ghost, our Guide and Friend,
Grant us Thy grace till life shall end:
That with all saints our rest may be
In that bright paradise with Thee.
              -William Dalrymple
                   Maclagan

1406

St. Justin-8.8.6.D.

1. O God, to whom the faithful dead
Still live, united to their Head,
Their Lord and ours the same;
For all Thy saints, to memory dear,
Departed in Thy faith and fear,
We bless Thy holy name.

2. By the same grace upheld, may we
So follow those who followed Thee,

As with them to partake
The full reward of heavenly bliss:
Merciful Father, grant us this
For our Redeemer's sake.

-Josiah Conder

1407

Church Triumphant L.M.

1. We sing praise of Him who died,
Of Him who died upon the Cross:
The sinner's hope let men deride:
For this we count the world but loss.

2. Inscribed upon the Cross we see
In shining letters God is love,
He bears our sins upon the tree:
He brings us mercy from above.

3. The Cross it takes our guilt away
It holds the fainting spirit up;
It cheers with hope the gloomy day,
And sweetens every bitter cup.

4. It makes the coward spirit brave,
And nerves the feeble arm for fight;
It takes its terror from the grave,
And gilds the bed of death with light.

5. The balm of life, the cure of woe,
The measure and the pledge of love,
The sinner's refuge here below,
The angels' theme in heaven above.

-Thomas Kelly

1408

After A Few More Years - 7.7.D

1. After a few more years
After a few more times
We shall be gathered with all those
Who are slept in the tomb '

Chorus
Jesus my Lord and God
Help me prepare for Thee,
Wash Thou me in Thy precious blood
And take my sins away.

2. After a few more days
Spent in this wicked world
We'll reach the land where there's no sun
A land of fadeless day,

3. After a few more storms
On this wave bitten shore
We'll leave the stormy seas and reach
A shore that's ever calm

4. After a few troubles
After partings are done,
After our sad and bitter tears,
There will be no more tears,

5. A few more days of rest,
Is all we have on earth
We shall get to a place of rest
Where it shall never end.

6. A few more days to wait,
And He, Christ shall return
The One who died that we may live
And reign with Him forever.

1409

Called Unto Holiness

1. Called unto holiness," Church of our God,
Purchase of Jesus, redeemed by His blood;
Called from the world and its idol to flee,
Called from the bondage of sin to be free.

Chorus
"Holiness unto the Lord," is our watchword and song,

THE CHURCH TRIUMPHANT

"Holiness unto the Lord," as we're matching along:
Sing it, shout it. Loud and long
"Holiness unto the Lord," now and for ever.

2. "Called unto holiness," children of light,
Walking with Jesus in garment of white;
Raiment unsullied, nor tarnished with sin,
God's Holy Spirit abiding within.

3. "Called unto holiness," praise His dear name,
This blessed secret to faith now made plain.
Not our own righteousness, but Christ within,
Living and reigning, and saving from sin.

4. "Called unto holiness," glorious thuoght!
Up from the wilderness wandering brought
Out from the shadows and darkness of night
Into the Canaan of perfect delight.

5. "Called unto holiness," Bride of the Lamb,
Waiting the Bridegroom's returning again;
Lift up your heads, for the day draweth near
When in his beauty the King shall appear.

1410
Lord Jesus, Thou Thy Church Hast Graced - 6.8.8.8.8.8.

1. Lord Jesus, Thou Thy Church hast graced
With gifts supernal and divine;

Gift of Thy Spirit, pure and chaste
With heavenly lustre here to shine.
Ascending to Thy Father's throne,
Thou hast bestowed them on thine own.

2. In Thee, our living head, are stored
Treasures of wisdom, light and love;
On us, Thy member, Thou hast poured
This wealth of blessing from above.
Oh, may we prove, this very hour,
The nine-fold splendour of Thy Power!

3. Speak, Lord! By word of Wisdom pure,
Thy will reveal Thy mind impart;
By word of knowledge, swift and sure
Illume, instruct, and guide each heart
So shall we trace. Thy way divine,
Line upon line, in clear design,

4. Thy mighty faith on us bestow,
Beyond our measure or our thought;
Let gifts of healing from Thee flow,
And wonders in Thy name be wrought.
Make bare Thine arm, confirm Thy word,
That all may own Thee Christ and Lord!

5. Through our lip! We would aspire
To speak the praises of Thy love,
Gifted with pure prophetic fire
And holy unction from above;
Whilst, through Thy searching Spirit taught
The secret springs of life and Thought

6. With tongues of men or seraph strain,
Speak, forth Thy word in praise in Prayer;

MFM Ministries Hymnbook

545

Then make each heaven-sent
message plain,
That we thy glories may declare
Grace every gift with love's high
theme:
Yea, reign o'er all, O Love supreme!

1411

O Lord Our God, Stretch Out Thy Hand-C.M.

1. O Lord our God, stretch out Thy
hand
Let us Thy glory see
That all of us may see Thy sign
To melt the heart of stone.

2. In Thy mercy, forgive our sins,
Deliver us from guilt
That the new year we have started
May come to end with Thee.

3. Send Thy Holy Ghost from above
That we may love Thee most   ;
That the sinner who has no love
May learn to love others.

4. And when we come before Thee,
Lord in our eternal home
That many may join with us here
To give our praise to Thee.

1412

We Lay Down This Foundation, Today - L.M.

1. We lay down this foundation, today
In Thy name, Lord our God
We beseech Thee our dear Saviour
Keep this holy place in Thy care.

2. And when these Thy people seek
Thee
And sinners seek Thee in this house

Hear, Almighty from heav'n above
O Lord our God, forgive their sin.

3. When Thy ministers preach the
Word
The gospel of Jesus Thy Son,
Almighty God, in Thy great name
Wrought our wonderful miracles

4. And when the little children sing;
Their hymns praise unto their king
Let angels join them in His praise
And earth and heav'n lend their
chorus.

5. Jehovah will Thou dwell with us
In this our wicked, sinful world?
Jesus Christ will Thou be our King?
Holy Ghost will Thou find rest here?

6. May Thy glory never depart
From This house that we are building
Make Thy kingdom within our hearts
And establish Thy throne within

HEAVEN

1413

Alford -7.6.8.6.D.

1. Ten thousand times ten thousand,
   In sparkling raiment bright,
   The armies of the ransomed saints
   Throng up the steeps of light'
   'Tis finished, all is finished,
   Their fight with death and sin:
   Fling open wide the golden gates,
   And let the victors in,

2. What rush of alleluias
   Fills all the earth and sky;
   What ringing of a thousand harps
   Be speaks the triumph nigh!
   O day, for which creation
   And all its tribes were made,
   O joy, for all its former woes
   A thousand fold repaid!

3. O then what raptured greetings
   On Canaan's happy shore,
   What knitting severed friendships up
   Where partings are no more!
   Then eyes with joy shall sparkle
   That brimmed with tears of late;
   Orphans no longer fatherless,
   Nor widows desolate.

4. Bring near Thy great salvation,
   Thou Lamb for sinners slain,
   Fill up the roll of Thine elect,
   Then take Thy power and reign:
   Appear, Desire of nations,
   Thine exiles long for home;
   Show in the heavens Thy promised sign,
   Thou Prince and Saviour, come.
   -H. Alford

1414

Stars In My Crown 12.9.12.9. with Refrain

1 I am thinking today of that beautiful land
   I shall reach when the sun goeth down;
   When thro' wonderful grace by my Saviour I stand.
   Will there be any stare in my crown?

Chorus
   Will there be any stare, any stare in my crown
   When at evening the sun goeth down?
   When I wake with the blest In the mansions of rest,
   Will there be any stare in my Crown?

2. In the strength of the Lord let me labour and pray.
   Let me watch as a winner of souls,
   That bright stars may be mine in the glorious day,
   When His praise like the sea billow rolls.

3. Oh, what joy it will be when His face I behold.
   Living gems at His feet to lay down;
   It would sweeten my bliss in the city of gold,
   Should there be any stars in my crown?
   -Eliza E. Hewit

1415

Mansions Over The Hilltop

1. I'm satisfied with just a cottage below.
   A little silver and a little gold;
   But in that city where the ransomed will shine.
   I want a gold one that's silver lined.

HEAVEN

Chorus
I've got a mansion just over the hiltop,
In that bright land where we'll never grow old,
And someday yonder we will never more wander
But walk on streets that are purest gold.

2. Tho often tempted, tormented and tested
And like the prophet, my pillow a stone;
And tho I find here no permanent dwelling,
I know He'll give me a mansion my own.

3. Don't think me poor or deserted or lonely,
I'm not discouraged, I'm Heaven bound;
I'm just a pilgrim in search of a city,
I want a mansion, a harp and a crown.

-Ira Stanphill

1416

No Tears In Heaven

1. No tears in Heaven, no sorrows given,
All will be glory in that land;
There'll be no sadness, all will be gladness,
When we shall join that happy band.

Chorus
No tears no tears, no tears up there,
Sorrow and pain will all have flown;
No tears no tears, no" tears up there,
No tears in Heaven will be known.

2. Glory is waiting, waiting up yonder
Where we shall spend an endless day;
There with our Saviour, we'll be forever,
Where no more sorrow can dismay

3. Some morning yonder, we'll cease to ponder,
O'er things this life has bro't to view;
All will be clearer, loved ones be dearer,
In Heav'n where all will be made new.

-Robert S. Arnold

1417

Heaven's Jubilee

1. Some glad morning we shall see Jesus in the air,
Coming after you and me, joy is ours to share;
What rejoicing there will be when the saints shall rise,
Headed for that jubilee, yonder in the Skies.

Chorus
Oh, what singing, Oh, what shouting,
On that happy morning when we all shall rise;
Oh, what glory. Hallelujah!
When we meet our blessed Saviour in the skies.

2. Seems that now I almost see all the sainted dead,
Rising for that jubilee, that is just ahead;
In the twinkling of an eye, changed with them to be,
All the living saints to fly to that Jubilee.

HEAVEN

3. When with all that heav'nly host we
   begin to sing,
   Singing in the Holy Ghost, how the
   heav'ns will ring;
   Millions there will join the song, with
   them we shall be
   Praising Christ thru ages long,
   heaven's jubilee.
   -Adger M. Pace

1418
Heaven Will Surely Be Worth It All

1. Often I'm hindered on my way,
   Burdened so heavy I almost fall;
   Then I hear Jesus sweetly say:
   "Heaven will surely be worth it all."

   Chorus
   Heaven will surely be worth it all,
   Worth all the sorrows that here befall;
   After this life with all its strife,
   Heaven will surely be worth it all.

2. Many the trials, toils, and tears,
   Many a heartache may here appall;
   But the dear Lord so truly says:
   "Heaven will surely be worth it all."

3. Toiling and pain I will endure,
   Till I shall hear the death angel call;
   Jesus has promised and I'm sure
   "Heaven will surely be worth it all."
   -W. Oliver Cooper

1419
Christchurch - 6.6.8.8.

1. Jerusalem on high
   My song and city is,
   My home whene'er I die,
   The centre of my bliss:

   Chorus
   Oh happy place, when shall I be,
   My God, with Thee, to see Thy face

2. There dwells my Lord, my King,
   Judged here unfit to live;
   There angels to Him sing,
   And lowly homage give;

3. The patriarchs of old
   There from their travels cease;
   The prophets there behold
   Their long'd for Prince of Peace:

4. The Lamb's apostles there
   I might with joy behold,
   The harpers I might hear
   Harping on harps of gold:

5. The bleeding martyrs, they
   Within those courts are found,
   Clothed in pure array,
   Their scars with glory crown'd:

6. Ah, woe is me, that I
   In Kedar's tents here stay!
   No place like that on high;
   Lord thither guide my way:
   -Charles Steggall

1420
All Saints-8.7.8.7.7.7.

1. Who are these like stars appearing,
   These, before God's throne who
   stand?
   Each a golden crown is Wearing,
   Who are all this glorious hand?
   Hallelujah! hark, they sing,
   Praising loud their heavenly King.

2. Who are these in dazzling brightness,
   Clothed in God's own righteousness:
   These, whose robes of purest
   whiteness
   Shall their lustre still possess,
   Still untouch'd by time's rude hand?
   Whence come all this glorious
   Band?

HEAVEN

3. These are they who have contended
For their Saviour's honour long,
Wrestling on till life was ended,
Following not the sinful throng;
These, who well the fight sustain'd,
Triumph by the Lamb have gain'd.

4. These are they whose hearts were riven,
Sore with woe and anguish tried,
Who in prayer full oft have striven
With the God they glorified;
Now, their painful conflict o'er
God has bid them weep no more.

5 These are they who watch'd and waited
Offering up to Christ their will,
Soul and body consecrated,
Day and night to serve Him still;
Now in God's most holy place
Blest they stand before His face.

1421

Sine Nomine 10.10.10. with Alleluias

1. For all the saints who from their labors rest,
Who Thee by faith Before the world confessed,
your name, O Jesus, be for ever blessed
Alleluia, alleluia!

2. You were their rock, their fortress, and their might,
You, Lord, their captain in the well fought fight;
and in the darkness their unfailing Light:
Alleluia, alleluia'

3. So may your soldiers, faithful, true, and bold,
Fight as the saints who nobly fougth of old,
And win with them the victor s crew of gold:
Alleluia, alleluia!

4. One holy people, fellowship divine!
We feebly struggle, they in glory shine;
in earth and heaven the saints in praise combine:
Alleluia, alleluia!

5. And when the fight Is fierce, the warfare long,
far off we hear the distant triumph song;
and hearts are brave again, and arms are strong,
Alleluia, alleluia!

6. The golden evening brightens in the west:
soon, soon to faithful warriors comes their rest,
the peaceful calm of paradise the . blessed.
Alleluia, alleluia!

7. But look! there breaks a yet more glorious day:
saints all triumphant rise in bright array;
The King of glory passes on His way:
Alleluia, alleluia!

8. From earth's wide bounds, from dawn to setting sun,
Through heaven's gates to God the Three-in-One
they come, to sing the song on earth begun:
Alleluia, alleluia!

-William W. How

HEAVEN

1422

arching To Zion - 6.6.8.8.6.6. with Refrain.

1. Come, we that love the Lord,
   And let our joys be known,
   Join in a song with sweet accord,
   Join in a song with sweet accord
   And thus surround the throne,
   And thus surround the throne.

   Chorus
   We're marching to Zion,
   Beautifully, beautiful Zion;
   We're marching upward to Zion,
   The beautiful city of God.

2. Let those refuse to sing
   Who never knew our God,
   But children of the heav'nly King,
   But children of the heav'nly King
   May speak their joys abroad,
   May speak their joys abroad.

3. The hill of Zion yields
   A thousand sacred sweets
   Before we reach the heav'nly fields,
   Before we reach the heav'nly fields
   Or walk the golden streets,
   Or walk the golden streets.

4. Then let our songs abound
   And every tear be dry;
   We're marching thro' Immanuel's ground,
   We're marching thro' Immanuel's ground
   To fairer worlds on high,
   To fairer worlds on high.

   -Isaac Watts

1423

I'll Never Be Lonely Again

1. Here I walk a rocky road,
   And I tote a heavy load,
   And so often I get weary and complain;
   But when I get up there,
   I will never have a care
   And I'll never be lonely again.

   Chorus
   No, I'll never be lonely again,
   No, I'll never be lonely again,
   For I'll be so free from the things that worry me,
   And I'll never be lonely again.

2. Here sometimes I feel alone,
   And I miss the ones who've gone,
   As down here for just a while I still remain;
   But sometimes after a while
   I'll look back and only smile,
   And I'll never be lonely again.

3. In that country over there,
   I will never know a care,
   And no one shall there grow hungry or be cold;
   There'll be no briny tears,
   and they'll count not time by years,
   And no one there shall ever grow old.

   -M. Lynwood Smith

1424

Hilltops of Glory

1. Onward rejoicing I tread life's way,
   Higher I'm climbing each passing day;
   Hilltops of glory now rise in view,
   where all shall be made new.

HEAVEN

Chorus
Hilltops of glory I now can see
O brother won't you come go with me?
Safe on the mountain I soon shall Hiltops of glory land.

2. Way down in Egypt mid burning,
Moses had started for Canaan's land;
Never turn backward always ascend
On to the journey's end.

3. Footsteps of Jesus before us lead,
We tread life's journey His warnings heed;
Evil allurements cannot-prevail,
I'm on the upward trail.

-Roy Harris

1425
The Last Mile Of The Way

1. If I walk in the pathway of duty,
If I work till the close of the day;
I shall see the great King in His beauty,
When I've gone the last mile of the way.

Chorus
When I've gone the last mile of the way,
I will rest at the close of the day,
And I know there are joys that await me,
When I've gone the last mile of the Way.

2. If for Christ I proclaim the glad story,
If I seek for His sheep gone astray,
I am sure He will show me His glory,
When I've gone the last mile of the way.

3. Here the dearest of ties we must sever,
Tears of sorrow are seen ev'ry day:
But no sickness, no sighing for ever
When I've gone the last mile of the way.

4. And if here I have earnestly striven.
And have tried all His will to obey,
Twill enhance all the rapture of heaven,
When I've gone the last mile of the way.

-Rev. Johnson Oatman, Jr

1426
Beulah Land

1. I've reached the land of corn and wine,
And all its riches freely mine;
Here shines undimmed one blissful day,
For all my night has passed away.

Chorus
O Beulah land, sweet Beulah land,
As on thy highest mount I stand,
I look away across the sea,
Where mansions are prepared for me,
And view the shining glory shore,
My Heav'n, my home forever more!

2. My Saviour comes and walks with me,
And sweet communion here have we;
He gently leads me by His hand,
For this is Heaven's borderland.

3. A sweet perfume upon the breeze
Is borne from eververnal trees,
And flow'rs, that never fading grow,
Where streams of life forever flow.

4. The zephyrs seem to float to me.
Sweet sounds of Heaven's melody,
As angels with the white robed throng
Join in the sweet Redemption song.

-Edgar Page

HEAVEN

1427

Saved By Grace

1. Some day the silver cord will break,
   And I no more as now shall sing;
   But O the joy when I shall wake
   Within the palace of the King!

   Chorus
   And I shall see Him face to face,
   And tell the story Saved by grace;
   And I shall see Him face to face,
   And tell the story Saved by grace.

2. Someday my earthly house will fall,
   I cannot tell how soon 'twill be,
   But this i know my All in All
   Has now a place in Heav'n for me.

3. Some day, when fades the golden
   sun
   Beneath the rosy tinted west,
   My blessed Lord will say,
   "Well done!" And I shall enter into
   rest.

4. Some day: till then I'll watch and wait,
   My lamp all trimmed and burning
   bright,
   That when my Saviour opens the
   gate,
   My souls to Him may take its flight.
   　　　　　　　　　-Fanny J. Crosby

1428

Nearer Home - D.S.M.

1. For ever with the Lord!
   Amen, so let it be!
   Life from the dead is in that word:
   'Tis immortality,
   Here in the body bent,
   Absent from Him I roam;
   Yet nightly pitch my moving tent
   A day's march nearer home.

2. My Father's house on high,
   Home of my soul. how near
   At times to faith's foreseeing eye
   Thy golden gates appear!
   My thirsty spirit faints
   To reach the land I love,
   The bright inheritance of saints
   Jerusalem above.

3. For ever with the Lord!
   Father, if 'tis Thy will,
   The promise of that faithful word,
   E'en here to me fulfil.
   Be Thou at my right hand,
   Then can I never fail;
   Uphold Thou me, so I shall stand,
   Fight, and I must prevail.

4. So when my latest breath.
   Shall rend the veil in twain,
   By death I shall escape from death,
   And fife eternal gain.
   Knowing as I am known;
   How shall I love that word!
   And oft repeat before the throne,
   For ever with the Lord!
   　　　　　　　　　-James Montgomery

1429

Sweet By And By -9.9.9.9. with Refrain

1. There's a land that is fairer than
   day,
   And by faith we can see it afar.
   For the Father waits over the way
   To prepare us a dwelling place
   there.

   Chorus
   In the sweet by and by,
   We shad meet on that beautiful
   shore;
   In the sweet by and by,
   We shall meet on that beautiful
   Shore.

2. We shall sing on that beautiful shore
The melodious songs of the blest;
And our spirits shall sorrow no more
Not a sigh for the blessing of rest.

3. To our bountiful Father above
We will offer our tribute of praise,
For the glorious gift of His love
And the blessings that hallow our days.

-Sanford F. Bennet

1430

Beulah -D.C.M.

1. Jerusalem, my happy home,
Name ever dear to me!
When shall my labours have an end,
In joy, and peace, and thee?
When shall these eyes thy heav'n built walls
And pearly gates behold,
Thy bulwarks with salvation strong,
And streets of shining gold?

2. There happier bowers then Eden's bloom,
Nor sin nor sorrow know:
Blest seats, through rude and stormy scenes
I onward press to you.
Why should I shrink at pain and woe,
Or feel, at death, dismay?
I've Canaan's goodly land in view,
And realms of endless day.

3. Apostles, prophets, martyrs there
Around my Saviour stand;
And soon my friends in Christ below
Will join the glorious band.
Jerusalem, my happy home,
My soul still pants for thee!
Then shall my labours have an end,
When I thy joys shall see.

-Joseph Bromohead

1431

Never Thirst Again - C.M. and Refrain

1. There is a land of pure delight
Where saints immortal reign,
Infinite day excludes the night,
And pleasures banish pain.

Chorus
We're feeding on the living Bread,
We're drinking at the fountain head:
And who so drinketh, Jesus said,
Shall never, never thirst again.
What! never thirst again?
No, never thirst again!
What! never thirst again?
No, never thirst again!
And who so drinketh, Jesus said,
Shall never, never thirst again!

2. There everlasting spring abides,
And never withering flowers:
Death, like a narrow sea divides
This heavenly land from ours.

3. O could we make our doubts remove
Those gloomy thoughts that rise,
And see the Canaan that we love
With unbeclouded eyes.

4. Could we but climb where Moses stood
And view that landscape o'er,
Not Jordan's stream, nor death's cold flood,
Should fright us from the shore.

-Isaac Watts

1432

No Stranger There

1. When the pearly gates are open'd
To a sinner sav'd be grace,

HEAVEN

When thro' everlasting mercy,
I behold my Saviour's face,
When I enter in the mansions
Of the city bright and fair,
I shall' have a royal welcome,
For I'm be no stranger there.

Chorus
I shall be no stranger there,
Jesus will my place prepare;
He will meet me. He will greet me,
I shall be no stranger there.

2. Thro' time's everchanging seasons,
I am pressing t'ward the goal;
'Tis my heart's sweet native
country,
'Tis the homeland of my soul;
Many lov'd ones, cloth'd with
beauty,
In those wondrous glories share;
When I rise, redeemed, forgiven,
I shall be no stranger there.

3. There my dear Redeemer liveth,
Blessed Lamb upon the throne;
By the crimson marks upon them,
He will surely claim His own.
So, whenever sad or lonely,
Look beyond the earthly care;
Weary child of God, remember,
You will be no stranger there.
-E. E. Hewitt

1433

Altogether Lovely

1. Beautiful the fields beyond the river!
Glorious the thousands gathered
there!
But who in heav'n, so full of grace
and glory
Who with Him, our Saviour, can
compare?

Chorus
Oh, He is the chief among ten,
thousand!
Roll His praise in joyful waves
along!
For "altogether, altogether lovely!"
Shall for ever be our happy song!

2. Altogether, altogether lovely!
He is calling tenderly to thee;
My soul, why not accept His great
salvation,
Offered now so rich, so full, so
tree?

3. Altogether, altogether lovely,
Hear His voice how tender still the
call:
"Come, come, ye weary ones and
heavy laden,
Come to Me, and let your burdens
fall! your burdens fall!"
-G. F. Root

1434

No Night There

1. In the land of fadeless day
Lies the "city foursquare,"
It shall never pass away,
And there is "no night there."

Chorus
God shall "wipe away all tears,"
There's no death, no pain, nor
fears;
And they count not time by years,
For there is "no night there."

2. All the gates of pearl are made,
In the "city foursquare,"
All the streets with gold are laid,
And there is "no night there,"

3. And the gates shall never close
To the "city foursquare,"
There life's crystal river flows,
And there is "no night there.

HEAVEN

4. There they need no sunshine
   bright,
   In the "city foursquare,"
   For the Lamb is all the light,
   And there is "no night there."
   —John R. Clements

1435

Sin Can Never Enter There.

1. Heaven is a holy place,
   Filled with glory and with grace,
   Sin can never enter there;
   All within its gates are pure,
   From defilement kept secure,
   Sin can never enter there.

   Chorus
   Sin can never enter there,
   Sin can never enter there;
   So, if at the judgement here,
   Sinful spots your soul shall mar,
   You can never enter there.

2. If you hope to dwell at last,
   When your life on earth is past,
   In that home so bright and fair,
   You must here be clean'd from sin,
   Have the life of Christ within,
   Sin can never enter there."

3. You may live in sin below,
   Heaven's grace refuse to know,
   But you cannot enter there;
   It will stop you at the door,
   Bar you out for evermore,
   Sin can never enter there.

4. If you cling to sin till death,
   When you draw your latest breath,
   You will sink in dark despair,
   To the regions of the lost,
   Thus to prove at awful cost,
   Sin can never enter there.
   —C. W. Naylor

1436

Where Shall I Be

1. When judgement day is drawing nigh,
   Where shall I be?
   When God the works of men shall try,
   Where shall I be?
   When east and west the fire shall roll,
   Where shall I be?
   How will it be with my poor soul?
   Where shall I be?

   Chorus
   O where shall I be when the first
   trumpet sounds,
   O where shall I be when it sounds so
   loud?
   When it sounds so loud as to wake
   up the dead?
   O where shall I be when it sounds?

2. When wicked men his wrath shall see,
   Where shall I be?
   And to the rocks and mountains flee,
   Where shall I be?
   When hills and mountains flee away,
   Where shall I be?
   When all the works of men decay,
   Where shall I be?

3. When heav'n and earth as some
   great scroll,
   Where shall I be?
   Shall from God's angry presence roll,
   Where shall I be?
   When all the saints redeem'd shall
   stand,
   Where shall I be?
   For ever blest at God's right hand,
   Where shall I be?

4. All trouble done, all conflict past,
   Where shall I be?
   And old A poll you slain at last,
   Where shall I be?
   When Christ shall reign from shore
   To shore,

HEAVEN

Where shall I be?
And peace abide forevermore,
Where shall I be?
-C. P. Jones

1437
Gettin' Ready to Leave This World

1. Laying up my treasures in that home
above,
Trusting, fully trusting in the Savior's
love;
Doing what I can for heaven's Holy
Dove,
I'm a gettin' ready to leave this
"world.

Chorus
Gettin' ready to leave this world,
Gettin' ready for the gates of pearl;
Keeping, watching, both
Gettin" ready to leave this world.

2. 'Trusting in the riches of His saving
grace,
In each earthly trial I His love can
trace;
Sure that up in heaven I shall find a
place,
I'm a gettin' ready to leave this
world.

3. To prepare a mansion, Jesus said,
"I'll go, If it were not true I would
have told you so;"
Just a little while to linger here
below,
I'm a gettin' ready to leave this world.
-Luther G. Presley

1438
The Great Reaping Day

1. There is coming a day when to
judgement we'll go,
There to reap as in life we've sown,

Death eternal we'll reap if we sow to
the flesh,
Heaven's joys then will never be
known.

Chorus
May we sow righteous seed for the
reaping
Which is coming to ev'ry one,
O the joy on that day when we hear
Jesus say,
Come, ye blessed, a crown you
have won.

2. Ev'ry day passing by are sowing the
seed
Fruits of life or of death will bear,
When you reap what you sow to that
land may you go,
To that bright, happy home ever
there.

3. If you'd win life eternal there's no
time to lose,
Look around you, the fields are white,
Go ye forth to the field, sow and reap
golden grain,
Soon will fall the dark shadows of
night.

4. Ev'ry act you perform is as seed to
some one,
For the influence will ne'er die,
Then be careful each day what you
do, what you say,
For you'll meet it again by and by.
-R. E. Winsett

1439
In The City Where the Lamb Is Light

1. There's a country far beyond the
starry sky,
There's a city where there never
comes a night;
If we're faithful we shall go there by
and by,
Tis the city where the Lamb is the
light.

HEAVEN

1440

Ev'rybody Will Be Happy Over There

Chorus

In that city where the Lamb is the light,
The city where there cometh no night;
I've a mansion over there,
And when free from toil and care,
I am going where the Lamb is the light.

2. Here we have our days of sunshine, but we know
That the sun which shines upon us now so bright
Will be changed to clouds and rain until we go
To the city where the Lamb is the light.

3. There the flowers bloom forever and the day
Shall be an eternal day without a night;
" And our tears shall be forever wiped away,
In that city where the Lamb is the light.

4. Here we have our disappointments all the while,
And our fondest hopes but meet with bitter blight;
Tho' by night we weep, the morning brings smile,
In that city where the Lamb is the light.

5. Then let sunlight fade, let the twilight bring its gloom,
Not a shadow can my blissful soul affright;
For I know that up in heaven there is room,
In that city where the Lamb is the light.

-Herbert Buffum

1. There's a happy land of promise over in the great beyond,
Where the saved of earth shall soon the glory share;
Where the souls of men shall enter and live on forever more,
Ev'rybody will be happy over there.

Chorus

Ev'rybody will be happy,
Will be happy over there;
We will shout and Sing His praise,
Ev'rybody will be happy over there.

2. Mothers, fathers, sisters, brothers will be singing 'round the throne,
In that land where no one ever knows a care;
And the Christians of all ages Will join in the triumph song,
Ev'rybody will be happy over there.

3. We will hear no body praying and no mourning in that land,
For no burdens there will be for us to bear;
All the people will be singing "Glory, glory to the Lamb,"
Ev'rybody will be happy over there.

4. There we'll meet the One who saved us and kept us by His grace,
And who brought us to that land so bright and fair;
We will praise His name forever as we look upon His face,
Ev'rybody will be happy over there.
-E. M. Bartiett

HEAVEN

1441
My Name's Written There

1. I am bought not with riches,
   Neither silver nor gold;
   But Christ hath redeemed me,
   I am safe in His fold;
   In the Book of His kingdom,
   With its pages so fair,
   Through Jesus my Saviour,
   My name's written there.

   Chorus
   My name's written there,
   On the page white and fair;
   In the Book of God's kingdom,
   My name's written there.

2. My sins, they were many,
   Like the sands of the sea,
   But the blood of my Saviour
   Is sufficient for me;
   For His promise is written,
   In bright letters that glow,
   Tho' your sins be as scarlet,
   I will make them like snow.

3. Oh! that beautiful city,
   With its mansions of light,
   With its glorified beings,
   In pure garments of white;
   Where no evil thing cometh
   To despoil what is fair;
   Where the angels are watching,
   My name's written there.
                    -B. B. McKinney

1442
The Home Over There

1. O think of the home over there,
   By the side of the river of light,
   Where the saints, all immortal and
   fair,
   Are robed in their garments of,
   while.

Chorus
Over there, over there,
O think of the home over there,
Over there, over there, over there,
O think of the home over there.

2. O think of the friends over there,
   Who before us the journey have
   trod,
   Of the songs that they breathe on
   the air,
   In their home in the palace of God.

3. My Saviour is now over there,
   There my kindreds and friends are
   at rest,
   Then away from my sorrow and care,
   Let me fly to the land of the blest.

4. I'll soon be at home over there,
   For the end of my journey I see;
   Many dear to my heart, over there,
   Are watching and waiting for me.
                    -D. W. Huntington

1443
Shall We Gather At The River

1. Shall we gather at the river,
   Where bright angel feet have trod;
   With its crystal tide forever
   Flowing by the throne of God?

Chorus
Yes, we'll gather at the river,
The beautiful the beautiful river;
Gather with the saints at the river
That flows by the throne of God.

2. On the margin of the river,
   Washing up its silver spray,
   We will walk and worship ever,
   All the happy golden day.

3. Ere we reach the shining river,
   Lay we every burden down;

HEAVEN

Grace our spirits will deliver,
And provide a robe and crown.

4. Soon we'll reach the shining river,
Soon our pilgrimage will cease,
Soon our happy hearts will quiver
With the melody of peace.
-Rev. Robert Lowry

1444

We'll Understand It Better

1. We are often tossed and driv'n
on the restless sea of time,
Somber skies and howling tempests
oft succeed a bright sunshine,
In that land of perfect day,
When the mists have rolled away,
We will understand it better
by and by.

Chorus
By and by, when the morning comes,
When the saints of God are
gathered home,
We'll tell the story How we've over
come;
For we'll understand it better
by and by.

2. We are often destitute
of the things that life demands,
Want of food and want of shelter,
thirsty hills and barren lands,
We are trusting in the Lord,
and according to His Word,
We will understand it better
by and by.

3. Trials dark on ev'ry hand,
and we cannot understand,
All the ways that God would lead us
to that blessed Promised Land;
But He guides us with His eye,
and we'll follow till we die;
For we'll understand it better
By and by.

4. Temptations, hidden snares often
take us unawares,
And our hearts are made to bleed
for many a thoughtless word or deed,
And we wonder why the test
when we try to do our best,
But we'll understand it better
by and by.
-C. A. Tindley

1445

When They Ring The Golden Bells

1. There's a land beyond the river,
That we call the sweet forever,
And we only reach that shore by
faith's decree;
One by one we'll gain the portals,
There to dwell with the immortals,
When they ring the golden bells for
you and me.

Chorus
Don't you hear the bells now ringing?
Don't you hear the angels singing?
Tis the glory hallelujah Jubilee.
In that far-off sweet forever,
Just beyond the shining river,
When they ring the golden bells for
you and me.

2. We shall know no sin or sorrow,
in that haven of tomorrow,
When our barque shall sail beyond
the silver sea;
We shall only know the blessing
Of our Father's sweet caressing,
When they ring the golden bells
for you and me.

3. When our days shall know their
number,
And in death we sweetly slumber,
When the King commands the spirit
to be free;
Never more with anguish laden,

HEAVEN

We shall, reach that lovely Eden,
When they ring the golden bells
for you and me.

-Dion De Marbelle

1446
Glory Song -10.10.10.10. with Refrain

1. When all my labours and trials are
   o'er,
   And I am safe on that beautiful
   shore,
   Just to be near the dear Lord I
   adore
   Will through the ages be glory for
   me.

Chorus
O that will be glory for me,
Glory for me, glory for me:
When by His grace I shall look on
His face,
That will be glory, be glory for me.

2. When by the gift of His infinite
   grace,
   I am accorded in heaven a place,
   Just to be there and to look on His
   face
   Will through the ages be glory for
   me

3. Friends will be there I have loved
   long ago;
   Joy like a river around me will flow;
   Yet, just a smile from my Saviour, I
   know,
   Will through the ages be glory for
   me.

-Charles H. Gabriel

1447
Pearly Gates - 8.7.8.7. with Refrain

1. Love divine, so great and wondrous,
   Deep and mighty, pure, sub-lime;

Coming front the heart of Jesus
Just the same thru tests of time.

Chorus
He the pearly gates will open,
So that I may enter in;
For He purchased my redemption,
And forgave me all my sin.

2. Like a dove when hunted, fright
   ened,
   As a wounded fawn was I,
   Broken hearted, yet He healed me
   He will heed the sinner's cry.

3. Love divine, so great and wondrous
   All my sins He then forgave,
   I will sing His praise for ever,
   For His blood. His pow'r to save.

4. In life's eventide, at twi-light,
   At His door I'll knock and wait;
   By the precious love of Jesus,
   I shall enter heaven's gate.

-Frederick A. Blom

1448
Heaven - 8.7.8.7. with Refrain

1. Sing the wondrous love of Jesus,
   Sing His mercy and His grace;
   In the mansions bright and blessed
   He'll prepare for us a place.

Chorus
When we all get to heaven,
What a day of rejoicing that will be!
When we all see Jesus,
We'll sing and shout the victory.

2. While we walk the pilgrim path-way
   Clouds will over spread the sky;
   But when trav'ling days are over,
   Not a shadow, not a sigh.

3. Let us then be true and faithful,
   Trusting, serving every day;
   Just one glimpse of Him in glory
   Will the toils of life repay.

HEAVEN

4. Onward to the prize before us!
Soon His beauty we'll behold;
Soon the pearly gates will open,
We shall tread the streets of gold.
-Eliza E. Hewit

1449
Promised Land - C.M. and Refrain

1. On Jordan's stormy banks I stand,
And cast a wishful eye
To Canaan's fair and happy land,
Where my possessions lie.

Chorus
I am bound for the promised land,
I am bound for the promised land;
O who will come and go with me?
I am bound for the promised land.

2. All o'er those wide extended plains
Shines one eternal day;
There God the Son forever reigns
And scatters night away.

3. No chilling winds nor pois'nous breath
Can reach that healthful shore;
Sickness and sorrow, pain and death
Are felt and feared no more.

4. When shall I reach that happy place,
And be forever blest? When shall
I see my Father's face,
And in His bosom rest?
-Samuel Stennett

1450
Home Beautiful Home

1. There is a Home eternal
Beautiful and bright
where sweet joys supernal
Never are dimm'd by night
Ever around the bright throne;
When, oh, when shall I see thee,
Beautiful, beautiful! Home?

Chorus
Home! Beautiful Home!
Bright, beautiful Home!
Bright, Home of our Saviour
Bright, beautiful Home!

2. Flowers are ever springing
In that Home so fair,
Little children singing
Praises to Jesus there.
How they swell the glad anthem,
Ever around the bright throne!
when, oh, when shall I see thee,
Beautiful, beautiful Home?

3. Soon shall I join the ransomed,
far beyond the sky;
Christ is my salvation,
Why should I fear to die?
soon my eyes shall behold Him
Seated upon the bright throne;
Then, oh, then shall I see thee,
Beautiful, beautiful Home!
-H. R. Palmes

1451
Hark, Hark, My Soul

1. Hark, hark, my soul!
Angelic songs are swelling
O'er earth's green fields and
ocean's wave beat shore;
How sweet the truth those blessed
strains are telling
Of that new life when sin shall be
no more!

Chorus
Angels of Jesus, angels of light,
Singing to welcome the pilgrims
of the night!

2. Far, far away, like bells at evening pealing,
The voice of Jesus sounds o'er
land and sea,

HEAVEN

And laden soul by thousands
meekly stealing,
Kind Shepherd, turn their weary
steps to Thee.

3. Onward we go, for still we hear
them singing,
Come, weary souls, for Jesus bids
you come;
And thro' the dark, its echoes
sweetly ringing,
The music of the gospel leads us
home.

4. Angels, sing on! Your faithful
watches keeping;
Sing us sweet fragments of the
songs above;
Till morning's joy shall end the night
of weeping,
And life's long shadows break in
cloudless love.

-Frederick W. Faber

1452

I Belong to the King

1. I belong to the King, I'm a child of
His love
I shall dwell in His palace so fair;
For He tells of its bliss in yon
heaven above,
And His children its splendors shall
share.

Chorus
I belong to the King, I'm a child of
His love,
And He never forsaketh His own;
He will call me some day to His
palace above,
I shall dwell by His glorified throne.

2. I belong to the King, and He loves
me, I know,
For His mercy and kindness; so free,
Are unceasingly mine wheresoever I
go,
And my refuge unfailing is He.

3. I belong to the King, and His
promise is sure,
That we all shall be gathered at last
In His kingdom above, by life's
waters so pure,
When this life with its trials is past

-Ida R Smith

1453

When We See Christ

1. Ofttimes the day seems long, our
trials hard to bear,
We're tempted to complain, to
murmur and despair;
But Christ will soon appear to catch
His Bride away,
All tears forever over in God's eternal
day.

Chorus
It will be worth it all When we see
Jesus,
Life's trials will seem so small when
we see Christ;
One glimpse of His dear face all
sorrow will erase,
So bravely run the race till we see
Christ.

2. Sometimes the sky looks dark with
not a ray of light,
We're tossed and driven on, no
human help in sight;
But there is One in heav'n who
knows our deepest care,
Let Jesus solve your problem just go
to Him in pray'r.

3. Life's day will soon be o'er all storms
forever past,
We'll cross the great divide to glory,
safe at last;
We'll share the joys of heav'n a harp,
a home, a crown,
The tempter will be banished,
we'll lay our burden down

-Esther Kerr Rusthoi

HEAVEN

1454
Some Golden Daybreak

1. Some glorious morning sorrow will cease,
Some glorious morning all will be peace;
Heartaches all ended, Labour all done,
Heaven will open Jesus will come.

Chorus
Some golden day break Jesus will come;
Some golden day break, battles all won,
He'll shout the vict'ry, break thro" the blue,
Some golden day break, for me, for you.

2. Sad hearts will gladden, all shall be bright,
Goodbye forever to earth's dark night;
Changed in a moment, like Him to be,
Oh, glorious daybreak, Jesus I'll see.

3. Oh, what a meeting, there in the skies,
No tears nor crying shall dim our eyes;
Loved ones united eternally,
Oh, what a day break that morn will be.

-C. A. Blackmore

1455
My Saviour First Of All

1. When my life work is ended, and I cross the swelling tide,
When the bright and glorious morning I shall see;
I shall know my Redeemer when I reach the other side,
And His smile will be the first to welcome me.

Chorus
I shall know Him, I shall know Him,
As redeemed by His side I shall stand;
I shall know Him, I shall know Him,
by the print of the nails in His hand.

2. Oh, the soul thrilling rapture when I view His blessed face,
And the luster of His kindly beaming eye;
How my full heart will praise Him for the mercy, love and grace,
That prepares for me a mansion in the sky.

3. Oh, the dear ones in glory, how they beckon me to come,
And our parting at the river I recall;
To the sweet vales of Eden they will sing my welcome home,
But I long to meet my Saviour first of all.

4. Thro" the gates to the city in a robe of spotless white,
He will lead me where no tears shall ever fall;
In the glad song of ages I shall mingle with delight;
But I long to meet my Saviour first of all.

-Fanny J. Crosby

1456
A Glorious Church

1. Do you hear them coming, brother?
Thronging up the steeps of light,
Clad inglorious shining garments,
Blood washed garments pure and white.

Chorus
"Tis a glorious church without spot or wrinkle,

HEAVEN

Washed in the blood of the Lamb;
'Tis a glorious church without spot
or wrinkle,
Washed in the blood of the Lamb.

2. Do you hear the stirring anthems
Filling all the earth and sky?
'Tis a grand, victorious army
Lift its banner up on high!

3. Never fear the clouds of sorrow.
Never fear the storms of sin;
We shall triumph on the morrow
Even now our joys begin.

4. Wave the banner, shout His praises,
For our victory is nigh!
We shall join our conq'ring Saviour,
We shall reign with Him on high!
-Ralph E. Hudson

1457
Where We'll Never Grow Old

1. I have heard of a land on the
faraway strand,
'Tis a beautiful home of the soul;
Built by Jesus on high, there we
never shall die,
'Tis a land where we never grow
old.

Chorus
Never grow old, never grow old,
In a land where we'll never grow
old;
Never grow old, never grow.
In a land where we'll never grow
old

2. In that beautiful home where we'll
never more roam,
We shall be the sweet by and by;
Happy praise to the King thru
eternity sing,
Tis a land where we never shall
Die.

3. When our work here is done and
the life crown is won,
And our troubles and trials are o'er,
All our sorrow will end. and our
voices will blend
With the loved ones who've gone
on before.
-Jas. C. Moore

1458
Holy, Holy, is What The Angels Sing

1. There is singing up in heaven
such as we have never known
Where the angels sing the praises
of the Lamb upon the throne
Their sweet harps are ever tuneful
and their voices always clear
Oh, that we might be more like
them while we serve the Master
here.

Chorus
Holy, holy, is what the angels sing,
And I expect to help them make
the courts of heaven ring;
But when I sing redemption's story
they will fold their wings,
For angels never felt the joys that
our salvation brings.

2. But I hear another anthem,
blending voices clear and strong
"Unto him who hath redeem'd us
and hath brought us," is the song
We have come thro' tribulations to
this land so fair and bright
In the fountain freely flowing he
hath made our garments white.

3. Then the angels stand and listen,
for they cannot join that song
Like the sound of many waters,
by that happy, blood wash'd throng
For they sing about great trials,
battles fought and vict'ries won.
And they praise their great
Redeemer who hath said to them,
"well done"

HEAVEN

4. So, although I'm not an angel,
   yet I know that over there
   I will join a blessed chorus
   that the angels cannot snare.
   I will sing about my Savour
   who upon dark Calvary
   Freely pardon'd my transgressions,
   died to set a sinner free.
                    -Johnson Oatman, Jr

1459

Come Over

1 There's a land of peace and plenty,
   And its gates are open wide,
   And the pure in heart and holy
   In its shelter may abide;
   It is not thro' gates of glory
   That a soul must enter in;
   But all who would find entrance there
   Must leave the ways of sin.

   Chorus
   Come over, come over,
   To the land of corn and wine;
   There's nothing can compare
   With the many holy pleasures there;
   Come over, come over,
   Leave the desert plain below
   And come away, away, come over.

2. There is bread of heaven growing,
   In its fair and fertile fields,
   And the wine of love its vineyard
   To the thirsting mortal yields:
   There are mountain heights of glory
   That await the trav'ler's rod,
   And blest retreats where empty souls
   Draw nearer unto God.

3. Who would stay without its borders,
   In the desert dart and drear,
   When the luscious grapes of Eschol
   Are so very, very near?
   Enter in then with rejoicing,
   For the Lord is on your side,
   And in his glorious presence
   Ever more you shall abide.

1460

Ashbrooke-6.6.

1. There is a blessed home
   Beyond this land of woe,
   Where trials never come,
   Nor tears of sorrow flow;
   Where faith is lost in sight.
   And patient hope is crown'd,
   And everlasting light
   Its glory throws around.

2. There is a land of peace,
   Good angels know it well;
   Glad songs that never cease
   Within its portals swell;
   Around its glorious throne
   Ten thousand saints adore
   Christ, with the Father One,
   And Spirit evermore,

3. Oh joy all joys beyond,
   To see the Lamb who died.
   For ever there enthroned,
   For ever glorified;
   To give to Him the praise
   Of every triumph won,
   And sing through endless days
   The great things He hath done.

4. Look up, ye saints of God.
   Nor fear to tread below
   The path your Saviour trod
   Of daily toil and woe;
   Wait but a little while
   In uncomplaining love,
   His own most gracious smile
   Shall welcome you above.
                    -George, F. Vincent

HEAVEN

1461

Cum Christo - L.M.

1. Let me be with Thee we where Thou art,
   My Saviour, my eternal rest;
   Then only will this longing heart
   Be fully and for ever blest.

2. Let me be with Thee where Thou art,
   Thy unveil'd glory to behold;
   Then only will this wandering heart
   Cease to be treacherous, faithless,
   cold.

3. Let me be with Thee where Thou art,
   Where spotless saints Thy name
   adore:
   Then only will this sinful heart
   Be evil and defiled no more.

4. Let me be with Thee where Thou art,
   Where none can die. where none
   remove
   There neither death nor life will part
   Me from Thy presence and Thy love.
   —Arthur Page

1462

Regent Square-8.7.8.7.8.7.

1. Light's abode, celestial Salem,
   Vision whence true peace doth spring,
   Brighter than the heart can fancy,
   Mansion of the highest King;
   O how glorious are the praises
   Which of thee the prophets sing!

2. There for ever and for ever
   Alleluia is out-poured;
   For unending, for unbroken
   Is the feast-day of the Lord;
   All is pure and all is holy
   That within thy walls is stored.

3. There no cloud nor passing vapour
   Dims the brightness of the air,
   Endless noon-day, glorious noon-day
   From the Sun of suns is there;
   There no night brings rest from
   labour
   For unknown are toil and care.

4. O how glorious and resplendent,
   Fragile body, shall thou be,
   When endued with so much beauty,
   Full of health, and strong and free,
   Full of vigour, full of pleasure
   That shall last eternally!

5. Now with gladness, now with courage
   Bear the burden on thee laid,
   That hereafter these thy labours
   May with endless gifts be paid;
   And in everlasting glory
   Thou with brightness be arrayed.
   —Thomas a Kempis

1463

O Paradise - Irregular

1. Oh, Paradise, oh Paradise,
   Who doth not crave for rest?
   Who would not seek the happy land,
   The mansions of the blest;
   Where loyal hearts, and true,
   Stand ever in the light,
   All rapture, through and through
   In God's most holy sight?

2. Oh Paradise, oh Paradise,
   The world is growing old;
   Who would not be at rest and free
   Where love is never cold?
   Where loyal hearts, and true.
   Stand ever in the light.
   All rapture, through and through
   In God's most holy sight?

3. Oh Paradise, oh Paradise,
   I want to sin no more,
   I want to be where Jesus is
   Upon thy spotless shore;
   Where loyal hearts, and true,
   Stand ever in the light,
   All rapture, through and through
   In God's most holy sight?

4. Oh Paradise, oh Paradise,
   I shall not wait for long;
   E'en now the loving ear may catch
   Faint fragments of thy song;
   Where loyal hearts, and true,
   Stand ever in the light,
   All rapture, through and through
   In God's most holy sight?

5. Lord Jesus, King of Paradise
   Oh keep me in Thy love,
   And guide me to that happy land
   Of perfect rest above;
   Where loyal hearts, and true,
   Stand ever in the light,
   All rapture, through and through
   In God's most holy sight.

   -J. T. Cooper

1464

Church Militant - 7.7.7.6.

1. Jesus, with Thy church abide.
   Be her Saviour, Lord, and Guide,
   While on earth her faith is tried:
   We beseech Thee, hear us.

2. Arms of love around her throw,
   Shield her safe from every foe,
   Calm her in the time of woe:
   We beseech Thee, hear us.

3. Keep her life and doctrine pure,
   Help her, patient to endure,
   Trusting in Thy promise sure:
   We beseech Thee, hear us.

4. Be Thou with her all the days,
   May she safe from error's ways,
   Toil for Thine eternal praise:
   We beseech Thee, hear us.

5. May her voice he ever clear,
   Warning of a judgement near,
   Telling of a Saviour dear
   We beseech Thee, hear us.

6. All her ruin'd works repair,
   Build again Thy temple fair,
   Manifest Thy presence there:
   We beseech Thee, hear us.

7. All her fetter'd powers release,
   Bid our strife and envy cease,
   Grant the heavenly gift of peace:
   We beseech Thee, hear us.

8. All her questions reconcile,
   Let not Satan's touch defile,
   Let not worldly snares beguile;
   We beseech Thee, hear us.

9. May she one in doctrine be,
   One in truth and charity,
   Winning all to faith in Thee:
   We beseech Thee, hear us.

10. May she guide the poor and blind
    Seek the lost until she find,
    And broken hearted bind:
    We beseech Thee, hear us.

11. Save her love from growing cole
    Make her watchmen strong and
    bold,
    Fence her round Thy peaceful fold
    We beseech Thee, hear us.

12. May her priests Thy people fee:
    Shepherds of the flock indeed
    Ready, where they call to lead
    We beseech Thee, hear us.

13. May they live the truths they know,
And a holy pattern show,
As before Thy flock they go:
We beseech Thee, hear us.

14. May the grace of Him who died,
And the Father's love abide,
And the Spirit ever guide:
We beseech Thee, hear us.

15. All her evil purge away,
All her doubts and fears allay,
Hasten, Lord, her triumph day:
We beseech Thee, hear us.

16. Help her in her time of fast,
Till her toil and woe are past.
And the Bridegroom come at last:
We beseech Thee, hear us.

17. May she then all glorious be,
Spotless and from wrinkle free,
Pure and bright and worthy Thee:
We beseech Thee, hear us.

18. Fit her all Thy joy to share,
In the home Thou dost prepare,
And be ever blessed there:
We beseech Thee, hear us.
                        -C. R. Cuff

1465

After This Dismal And Dark Worh - C.M.

1. After this dismal and dark world
Eternal glory waits
A country of eternal joy
No mortal eye hath seen.

2. Our eyes long to see half Thy joy
Beautiful city, bright,
How our hearts would have wished
to leave
This world, the vale of tears.

3. No sickness nor pain will be there
No sorrow will be there,
It's health and joy e'en all day long.

4. No night in those fair cities bright
It is perpetual day
For sin, the source of all the curse
Will not enter therein.

5. May this cherished hope of heaven
Set all our hearts aflame
Grant to us that this faith and love
Lift high our thoughts to God.

6. O Lord, in mercy, make us meet
For Thy bright courts above,
And grant that our hearts may
prepare
To join the heavenly throng.

1466

Asleep in Jesus! Blessed sleep - L.M

1. Asleep in Jesus'. Blessed sleep!
From which none ever wake to
weep;
A calm and undisturbed repose,
Unbroken by the last of foes.

2. Asleep in Jesus! Oh, how sweet
To be for such a slumber meet!
With holy confidence to sing
That death hath lost its venomed
sting

3. Asleep in Jesus! Peaceful rest!
Whose waking is supremely blest;
No fear - no woe - shall dim the
hour
That manifests the Saviours's
Power.

HEAVEN

1467
Sleep On, Beloved, Sleep And Take Thy Rest-P.M.

1. Sleep on, beloved, sleep and take
thy rest,
Lay down thy head upon thy
Saviour's Breast;
We love thee well. but Jesus loves
thee best;
Good night, good night, good night!

2. Calm is thy slumber as an infant's
sleep;
But thou shall wake no more to toil
and weep,
Thine is a perfect rest, secure and
deep:
Good night, good night, good night!

3. Until the shadows from this earth are
cast,
Until He gathers in His sheaves at
last,
Until the twilight gloom is over
passed, Good night, good night,
good night!

4. Until the Lord's new glory flood the
skies
Until the loved in Jesus shall arise,
And He shall come, but not in lowly
guise,
Good night, good night, good night!

5. Until, made beautiful by Love Divine
Thou in the likeness of thy Lord shall
shine,
And He shall bring that golden
crown of thine Good night, good
night, good night!

6. Only "Good night!" beloved not
"Farewell!"
A little while and all His Saints shall
dwell

In hallowed union, indivisible:
Good night, good night, good night!

7. Until we meet and all his before His
Throne,
Clothed in the spotless robe He
gives His own.
Until we know, even as we are
known, Good night, good night,
good night!

1468
There Is No Night In Heaven - S.M

1. There is no night in heaven;
In that blest world above
Work never can bring weariness
For work itself is love.

2. There is no grief in heaven;
For life is one glad day;
And tears are of those former
things
Which all have pass'd away,

3. There is no sin in heaven;
Behold that blessed throng
All holy is their spotless robe,
All holy is their song.

4. There is no death in heaven;
For they who gain that shore
Have won their immortality,
And they can die no more,

5. Lord Jesus, be our guide;
Oh lead us safely on,
Till night and grief and sin and
death
Are past, and heaven is won

HEAVEN

1469
What Are These Arrayed In White -
7.7.7.7.D.

1. What are these arrayed in white
   Brighter than the noonday sun?
   Foremost of the sons of light,
   Nearest the eternal throne?
   These are they that bore the cross
   Nobly of their Master stood;
   Sufferers in His righteous cause,
   Followers of the dying God.

2. Out of great distress they came,
   Washed their robes by faith below
   In the blood of yonder Lamb
   Blood that washes white as snow.
   Therefore are they next the throne,
   Serve their Maker day and night:
   God resides among His own,
   God doth in His saints delight.

3. More than conquerors at last,
   There they find trials o'er;
   They have all their sufferings past,
   Hunger now and thirst no more;
   No excessive heat they feel
   From the sun's direct ray,
   In a milder clime they dwell,
   Region of eternal day.

4. that on the throne doth reign,
   Them the Lamb shall always feed
   With the tree of life sustain,
   To the living fountains lead;
   He shall all their sorrows chase,
   All their wants at once remove,
   Wipe the tears from every face,
   Fill up every soul with love.

1470
When This Passing World Is Done -
7.7.7.7.7.6.

1. When this passing world is done,
   When has sunk you glaring sun,
   When we stand with Christ in glory,
   Looking o'er life's finish'd story,
   The Lord, shall I fully know
   Not till then, how much I owe.

2. When I stand before the throne.
   Dress'd in beauty not my own;
   When I see Thee as Thou art,
   Love Thee with unsinning heart;
   Then, Lord, shall I fully know.
   Not till then, how much I owe.

3. When the praise of heaven I hear,
   Loud as thunders to the ear
   Loud as many waters' noise,
   Sweet as harp's melodious voice;
   Then, Lord, shall I fully know,
   Not till then, how much I owe.

4. Even on earth, as through a glass,
   Darkly, let Thy glory pass;
   Make forgiveness feet so sweet,
   Make Thy spirit's help so meet;
   Even on earth, Lord, make me know
   Something of how much I owe.

5. Chosen not for good in me,
   Waken'd up form wrath to flee,
   Hidden in the Saviour's side.
   By the Spirit sanctified.
   Teach me, Lord, on earth to show
   By my love how much I owe,

HEAVEN

1471

**When You Start For The Land Of
Heavenly Rest -11.8.11.8. with Ref.**

1. When you start for the land of
   heavenly rest,
   Keep close to Jesus all the way;
   For He is the Guide, and He knows
   the way best;
   Keep close to Jesus all the way

   Chorus
   Keep close to Jesus, keep close to
   Jesus,
   Keep close to Jesus all the way;
   By day or by night never turn from
   The right,
   Keep close to Jesus all the way.

2. Never mind the storms of trials as
   you go.
   Keep dose to Jesus all the way;
   'Tis a comfort and joy His favour to
   know,
   Keep dose to Jesus all the way.

3. To be safe from the dark of the evil
   one,
   Keep close to Jesus all the way;
   Take the shield of faith till the victory
   is won,
   Keep close to Jesus all the way.

4. We shall each our home in heaven
   by and by,
   Keep close to Jesus all the way;
   Where to those we love well never
   say good bye,
   Keep dose to Jesus all the way.

GENERAL

1472

Song 46-10.10.

1. Peace, perfect peace, in this dark
world of sin?
The Blood of Jesus whispers peace
within.

2. Peace, perfect peace, by thronging
duties pressed?
To do the will of Jesus, this is rest.

3. Peace, perfect peace, with sorrows
surging round?
On Jesus' bosom naught but calm
is found.

4. Peace, perfect peace, with loved
ones far away?
In Jesus' keeping we are safe and
they.

5. Peace, perfect peace, our future all
unknown?
Jesus we know, and he is on the
throne,

6. Peace, perfect peace, death
shadowing us and ours?
Jesus has vanquished death and all
its powers.

7. It is enough: earth's struggles soon
shall cease.
And Jesus call us to heaven's
perfect peace.
                    -Bishop E. H. Bickersteth

1473

Wiltshire-C.M.

1. Through all the changing scenes of
life,
In trouble and in joy,
The praises of my God shall still
My heart and tongue employ.

2. O magnify the Lord me,
With me exalt his name;
When in ditress to him called,
He to my rescue came.

3. The hosts of God encamp around
The dwellings of the Just;
Deliverance he affords to all
Who on his succour trust.

4. O make but trial of his love:
Experience will decide
How blest are they, and only they,
Who in his truth confide.

5. Fear him, ye saints, and you will
then
Have nothing else to fear;
Make you his service your delight,
Your wants shall be his care.

6. To Father, Son, and Holy Ghost,
The God whom we adore
Be glory, as it was; is now,
And shall be evermore:
                    -N. Tate arid N. Brandy

1474

Lydia-8.6.8.6.

1. Jesus! the name high over all
In hell or earth or sky;
angels and men before that and
devils fear and fly.

2. Jesus' the name to sinners dear,
the name to sinners given;
it scatters all their guilty fear,
it turns their hells to heaven.

3. Jesus the prisoner's fetters breaks
and bruises Satan's head;
power into strength less souls he
speaks
and life into the dead.

4. O that the world might taste and
see
The riches of his grace!
the arms of love that welcome me
would all mankind embrace.

5. His righteousness alone I show,
his saving grace proclaim;
this is my work on earth below,
to cry 'Behold the Lamb!'

6. Happy if with my final breath
I may but gasp his name,
preach him to all, and cry in death,
'Christ Jesus is the Lamb!
-C. Wesley

1475

Wondrous Story - 8.7.8.7. with Refrain

1. I will sing the wondrous story
Of the Christ who died for me
How He left His home in glory
For the cross of Calvary.

Chorus
Yes, I'll sing the wondrous is story
Of the Christ who died for me,
Sing it with the saints in glory,
Gathered by the crystal sea.

2. I was lost but Jesus found me
Found the sheep that went astray,
Threw His loving arms around me,
Drew me back into His way.

3. Days of darkness still come o'er
me,
Sorrow's paths I often tread;
But the Saviour still is with me
By His hand fm safely led.

4. He will keep me till the river
Rolls its waters at my feet;
Where the loved ones I shall meet.
-Francis H. Rowley

1476

Wonderful grace -Irregular meter

1. Wonderful grace of Jesus, Greater
than all my sin.
How shall my tongue describe it,
Where shall its praise begin?
Taking away my burden, Setting my
spirit free,
For the wonderful grace of Jesus
reaches me.

Chorus
Wonderful the matchless grace of
Jesus,
Deeper than the mighty rolling sea;
Wonderful grace, all sufficient for
me, for even me;
Broader than the scope of my
transgression
Greater far than all my sin and
shame;
O magnify the precious name of
Jesus, Praise His name!

2. Wonderful grace of Jesus,
Reaching to all the lost,
By it I have been pardoned, saved
to the uttermost,
Chains have been torn asunder,
Giving me liberty,
For the wonderful grace of Jesus
reaches me.

3. Wonderful grace of Jesus,
Reaching the most defiled,
By its transforming power Making
him God's dear child,
Purchasing peace and heaven
For all eternity;
For the Wonderful grace of Jesus
reaches me.

GENERAL

1477
Wonderful is my Redeemer

1. Wonderful is my Redeemer,
   wonderful is He,
   Saying me from sin and sorrow,
   washed at Calvary;
   Wonderful the Prince or glory,
   mighty God is He,
   Wonderful is my Redeemer,
   wonderful to me.

Chorus
Wonderful, wonderful,
Jesus is to me, Gave Himself for
my shame there at,
Calvary; marvelous saving grace
set my spirit free,
Wonderful is He.

2. He gave Him self to die a ransom
   there on yonder tree,
   His saving grace my soul to save,
   Could it ever be?
   Salvation's plan for ev'ry man He
   purchased pardon free,
   Wonderful is my Redeemer,
   wonderful to me.

3. Redeeming love sent from above,
   He died for you and me,
   Go tell the message of His love
   Salvation now is free;
   No longer wart, the fields are white
   the call o'er distant sea,
   Wonderful is my Redeemer,
   wonderful to me.
                            -Alton Howard

1478
I am Ready for Service

1. Listen to me Master's pleading,
   There is urgently with for all;
   Heed the Spirits interceding,
   Give this answer to the call:

Chorus
I am ready for service for
Thee, dear. Lord, Here am I, send
me,
I am willing to be what you'd have
me be,
I will go where you want me to go.
I am ready for service for Thee.
dear Lord, Here am I, send me.

2. There's a voice to you now calling,
   Will you heed the earnest word?
   On the ear 'tis gently falling.
   Give this answer to your Lord:

3. Many souls in sin are dying;
   Haste to help them while you may.
   For the time is swiftly flying,
   Will you now to Jesus say?
                            -J. Lincoln Hall

1479
Hidden Peace

1. I cannot tell thee whence it came,
   This peace within my breast;
   But this I know. there fills my soul
   A strange and tranquil rest.

Chorus
There's a deep, settled peace in
my soul,
There's a deep. settled peace in
my soul
Though the billows of sin hear me
roll,
He abides, Christ abides.

2. Beneath the toil and care of life,
   This hidden stream flows on;
   My weary soul no longer thirsts,
   Nor am I sad and lone.

3. I cannot tell the half of love,
   Unfeigned, supreme, divine,

That caused my darkest in most
self
With beams of hope to shine.

4. I cannot ten thee why He chose
To suffer and to die;
But if I suffer here with Him.
I'll reign with Him for aye.
-J. S. Brown

1480
Revive they work, O Lord

1. Revive Thy work, O Lord!
Thy mighty arm make bare;
Speak with the voice that wakes
the dead,
And make Thy people hear?

Chorus
Revive Thy work, O Lord,
While here to Thee we bow
Descend, O gracious Lord,
descend, Oh, come and Bless us now.

2. Revive Thy work O Lord!
Disturb this sleep of death;
Quicken the smould'ring embers
now
By Thine Almighty breath.

3. Revive Thy work, O Lord!
Create soul thirst for Thee;
And hung' ring for the bread of
"life.
Oh, may our spirits be!

4. Revive Thy work, O Lord!
Exalt Thy precious name:
And by the Holy Ghost, our love
For Thee and Thine inflame.
-Albert Midlane

1481
Give Him the Glory
1. It was down at the feet of Jesus,
O the happy, happy day!

That my soul found peace in
believing,
And my Sins were wash'd away.

Chorus
Let me tell the old, old, story
Of His grace so full and free,
For I feel like giving Him the glory
For His wondrous love to me.

2. It was down at the feet of Jesus,
Where I found such perfect rest,
Where the light first dawn'd on my
spirit,
And my soul was truly blest.

3. It was down at the feet of Jesus,
Where I bro't my guilt and sin,
That He canced'd all my transgres
sions,
And Salvation enter'd in.
-Elisha A. Hoffman

1482
I Know I Love Thee Better, Lord

1. I know love Thee better, Lord,
Than any earthly joy;
For Thou hast given me the peace
Which nothing can destroy.

Chorus
The half has never yet been told,
Of love so full and free!
The half has never been told.
The blood it cleanseth me'

2. I know that Thou art nearer still
Than any earthly throng;
And sweeter is the thought of Thee
Than any lovely song!

3 Thou hast put gladness in my
heart
Then may I well be glad!
Without the secret of Thy love
I could not but be sad.

GENERAL

4. O Saviour, precious Saviour mine!
   What will Thy presence be,
   If such a life of joy can crown
   Our walk on earth with Thee?
   -Frances R. Havergal

1483
The name of Jesus

1. The name of Jesus is so sweet,
   I love its music to repeat;
   It makes my joys full and complete,
   The precious name of Jesus.

   Chorus
   "Jesus," O how sweet the name?
   "Jesus," every day the same;
   "Jesus," let all saints proclaim
   Its worthy praise forever.

2. I Jove the name of Him whose heart
   Knows all my griefs,
   and bears a part;
   Who bids all anxious fears depart
   I love the name of Jesus.

3 That name I fondly love to hear,
   It never fails my heart to cheer;
   Its music dries the fallen tear.
   Exalt the name of Jesus.

4 No word of man can ever tell
   How sweet the name I love so well;
   Oh, let its praises ever swell,
   Oh, praise the name of Jesus.
   -Rev. W. C. Martin

1484
McDaniel -12.8.12.8. with Refrain

1. What a wonderful change in my I
   ife has been wrought
   Since Jesus came into my heart?
   I have light in my soul for which
   long I have sought,
   Since Jesus came into my heart!

Chorus
Since Jesus came into my heart,
Since Jesus came into my heart,
Floods of joy o'er my soul like sea
billows roll,
Since Jesus came into my heart.

2. I have ceased from my wand'ring
   and going astray,
   Since Jesus came into my heart!
   And my sins, which were many, are
   all washed away,
   Since Jesus came into my heart!

3. I shall go there to dwell in that City I
   know,
   Since Jesus came into my heart!
   And rm happy, so happy, as
   onward I go,
   Since Jesus came into my heart!
   -Rufus K. McDaniel

1485
Satisfied-8.7.8.7. with Refrain

1. All my life long I had panted
   For a drink, from some clear
   spring,
   That I hoped would quench the
   burning
   Of the thirst I felt within,

   Chorus
   Hallelujah! I have found Him
   Whom my soul so long has craved!
   Jesus satisfies my longings
   Thru His blood I now am saved.

2. Feeding on the husks around me,
   Till my strength was almost gone.
   Longed my soul for something
   better,
   Only still to hunger on.

3. Well of water ever springing,
   Bread of life so rich and free,

Untold wealth that never faiteth,
My Redeemer is to me.
                    -Clara T. Williams

1486
Lenox 6.6.6.6.8.8. with Repeat

1. Arise, my soul, arise,
    Shake off thy guilty fear's.
    The bleeding Sacrifice
    In my behalf appears.
    Before the throne my Surety stands,
    Before the throne my Surely stands;
    My name is written on His hands.

2. He ever fives above
    For me to intercede,
    His all redeeming love,
    His precious blood to plead.
    His blood atoned for all our race,
    His blood atoned for all our race,
    And sprinkles now the throne of grace.

3. Five bleeding wounds He bears,
    Received on Calvary.
    They pour effectual prayers;
    They strongly plead for me.
    "Forgive him, oh, forgive they cry,
    "Forgive him, oh, forgive they cry,
    "Nor let that ransomed sinner die."

4. The Father hears Him pray,
    His dear Anointed One;
    He cannot turn away
    The presence of His Son.
    His Spirit answers to the blood,
    His Spirit answers to the blood,
    And tells me I am born of God.

5. My God is reconciled;
    His pard'ning voice I near.
    He owns me for His child;
    I can no longer fear.
    With confidence I now draw nigh,
    With confidence I now draw nigh,
    And Father, Abba, Father," cry.
                    -Charles Wesley

1487
Hyfrydol-8.7.8.7.D.

1. Jesus! what a Friend sinners!
    Jesus! Lover of my soul;
    Friends may fad me, foes assail me,
    He, my Saviour, makes me whole.

2. Jesus! what a Strength in weakness!
    Let me hide myself in Him;
    Tempted, fried, and sometimes falling.
    He, my Strength; my vic'try wins.

3. Jesus! what a Help in sorrow!
    While the billows o'er me roll,
    Even when my heart is breaking,
    He, my Comfort, helps my soul.

4. Jesus! what a Guide and Keeper!
    While the tempest still is high,
    Storms about me, night overtakes me,
    He, my Pilot, hear a my cry.

5. Jesus! I do now receive Him,
    More than all in Him I find,
    He hath granted me forgiveness,
    I am His, and He is mine.
                    -J. Wilbur Chapman

1488
Harris-8.7.3.7.D.

1. Who can cheer the heart like Jesus.
    By His presence all divine?
    True and tender, pure and precious.
    O how blest to call Him mine!

Chorus
All that thrills my soul is Jesus,
he is more than life to me;
And the fairest of ten thousand
In my blessed Lord I see.

2. Love of Christ so freely given,
   Grace of God beyond degree,
   Mercy higher than the heaven,
   Deeper than the deepest sea!

3. What a wonderful redemption!
   Never can a mortal know
   How my sin, tho red like crimson,
   Can be whiter than the snow.

4. Ev'ry need His hand supplying,
   Ev'ry good in Him I see;
   On His strength divine relying,
   He is all in aft to me.

5. By the crystal flowing river
   With the ransomed I will sing,
   And forever and forever
   Praise and glorify the King

   -Thoro Harris

1489
In My Heart There Rings a Melody

1. I have a song that Jesus gave me,
   It was sent from heav'n above;
   There never was a sweeter
   melody,
   'Tis a melody of love.

Chorus
In my heart there rings a melody,
There rings a melody with
heaven's harmony.
In my heart heart there rings a
melody;
There rings a melody of love.

2. I love the Christ who died on
   Calv'ry,
   For He washed my sins away;
   He put within my heart a melody,
   And I know Hi's there to stay.

3. 'Twill be my endless theme in glory,
   With the angels I will sing;
   'Twill be a song with glorious
   harmony,
   When the courts of heaven ring.

   -Eton M. Roth

1490
Still Sweeter Every Day

1. To Jesus ev'ry day I find my heart
   is closer drawn,
   He's fairer than the glory of the
   gold and purple dawn;
   He's all my fancy pictures in its
   fairest dreams; and more,
   Each day He grows still sweeter
   than He was the day before.

Chorus
The half cannot be fancied this
side the golden shore:
O there He'll be still sweeter than
He ever was before.

2. His glory broke upon me when I
   saw Him from afar,
   He's fairer than the lily, brighter
   than the morning star,
   He fills and satisfies my longing
   spirit o'er and o'er,
   Each day He grows still sweeter
   than He was the day before

3. My heart is sometimes heavy but
   He comes with sweet relief;
   He folds me to His bossom when I
   droop with blighting grief
   I love the Christ who all my
   burdens in His body bore,
   Each day He grows still sweeter
   than He was the day before.

   -W. C. Martin.

GENERAL

1491
It Is Glory Just to Walk with Him

1. It is glory just to walk with Him
whose blood ransomed me,
It is rapture for my soul each day;
It is joy divine to feel Him
near where e'er my path may be,
Bless the Lord. it's glory all the way!

Chorus
It is glory just to walk with Him,
It is glory just to walk with Him;
He will guide my steps aright
Thru the vale and o'er the height;
It's glory just to walk with Him.

2. It is glory when the shadows fall to
know that He is near,
O what joy to simply trust and
pray!
his glory to abide in Him
when skies above are dear,
Yes, with Him it's glory all the way!

3. Twill be glory when I walk with Him
on heaven's golden shore.
Never from His side again stray;
Twill be glory, wondrous glory
with Saviour evermore,
Everlasting glory all the way!
-Avis B. Christiansen

1492
Crusaders' hymn 5.6.8.5.5.8.

1. Fairest Lord Jesus, Ruler of all
nature,
O Thou of God and man the Son:
Thee will I cherish, Thee will I
honour,
Thou my souls glory, joy, and crown.

i2. Far are tie meadows, Fairer still
the wood-lands,
Robed in the blooming garb of
spring
Jesus is fairer, Jesus is purer,
Who makes the woeful heart to
sing,

3. Fair is the sunshine. Fairer still the
moonlight,
And all the twinkling starry host:
Jesus shines brighter, Jesus shines
purer
Than all the angels heaven can
boast.

4. Beautiful Saviouri Lord of the
nations!
Son of God and Son of Man!
Glory and honour, Praise, adora
tion
Now and forever more be Thine!
-From Munster Gesangbuch

1493
Be Ye Strong in the Lord and
The Power of His Might

1. Be ye strong in the Lord and the
power of His might
Firmly Standing for the truth of His
word;
He shall lead you safety through
the thickest of the fight.
You shall conquer in the through
the Lord!

Chorus
Firmly stand for the right
On to victory at the king's command
For the honour of the Lord,
And the triumphant of His word,
In the strength of the Lord firmly
stand

2. "Be ye strong in the Lord and
the power of His mighty!"
Never turning from the face of the
foe,
He will surely by you stand, as you
battle for the right:
In the power of His might onward
go!
3. "Be ye strong in the Lord and
power of His might!"
For His promises shall never,
never fail,
He will hold thy right hand, while
battling for the right,
Trusting Him thou shall for ever
more prevail.

1494

God Of Our Fathers, Known Of Old - 8.8.8.8.8.8.

1. God of our fathers, known of fold,
Lord of our far-flung battle line,
Beneath whose awful hand we
hold
Dominion over palm and pine
Lord God of hosts, be with us yet,
Lest we forget - lest we forget!

2. The tumult and the shouting dies,
The captains and the rings depart;
Still stands Thine ancient sacrifice,
A humble and a contrite heart,
Lord God of hosts, be with us yet,
Lest we forget-lest we forget!

3. Far-called, our naives melt away,
Oh dune and headland s inks the
fire;
Lo, all our pomp of yesterday
Is one with Nineveh and Tyre!
Judge of the nations, spare us yet,
Lest we forget - test we forget!

4. If, drunk with sight of power, we
Loose

Wild tongues that have not Thee in
awe,
Such boasting as the Gentiles use
Or lesser breeds without the law
Lord God of Hosts, be with-us yet,
Lest we forget - lest we forget!

5. For heathen heart that puts her trust
In reeking tube and iron shard,
All valiant dust that builds on dust,
And guarding, calls not Thee to
guard:
For frantic boast and foolish word
Thy mercy on Thy people, Lord!

1495

God's Peace Be Unto This House - 7.7.7.7.D.

1. God's peace be unto this house
And all those dwelling therein
May God's peace from heav'n above
Dwell on earth with men of peace;
Let the Holy-Ghost descend
That the blessing may come down,
Prince of peace, receive Thy crown
And the fulness of Thy grace.

2. Christ. Thou art my Lord and God
Let me Thy good herald be:
Remember Thy word, we pray;
Visit them and visit me;
Let salvation enter in
This house and att that dwell there,
Deliver our hearts from sin
Make us Thy holy abode.

3. Do not let us grow weary
Till the promise is fulfilled,
Until we shall be Thine own
By our being sanctified;
Grant that our love be renewed
That we find our lost blessing
And may we be the temple of
Father, Son and Holy Ghost.

GENERAL

1496

I Shall Wear A Golden Crown - 7.4.7.4.6.8.t.4. With Ref.

1. I shall wear a golden crown,
When I get home;
I shall lay my burdens down,
When I get home;
Glad in robes of glory,
I shall sing the story,
Of the Lord who brought me,
When I get home.

Chorus
When I get home when I get home
All sorrow will be over when I get
home
When I get home when I get home
All sorrow will be Over when I get
home.

2. All the darkness will be past,
When I get home;
I shall see the light at last,
When I get home;
Light from heaven streaming,
O'er my pathway beaming,
Ever guides me onward
Till I get home.

3. I shall see my Saviour's face.
When I get home;
Sing again of saving grace,
When I get home;
I shall stand before Him;
Gladly I'll adore Him
Ever to be with Hire,
When I get home.

1497

Some Day, But When I Cannot Tell - 8.8.8.6. with Ref.

1. Some day, but when I cannot tell,
To toil and tears I'll bid farewell;

For I shall with the angels dwell,
Some day, some blessed day.

Chorus
Some day, some day
I'll be at home with Christ to stay,
Some day, some blessed day.

2. Some day within the gates so fair
A golden harp my hands shall bear
And glistening robes of white I'll
wear,
Some day some blessed day.

3. Some day I'll see my Saviour's
face,
And, welcomed to His blest
embrace,
Shall with His people find a place,
Some day, some blessed day.

4. Some day, some blessed day, I
know
I'll find the loved of long ago,
And learn how much to Christ I
owe,
Some day, some blessed day.

1498

Standing At The Rortal, Of The Op'ning Year-11.11.11.11

1. Standing at the portal, of the
op'ning year,
Words of comfort meet us, hushing
ev'ry fear.
Spoken through the silence, by our
Father's voice.
Tender, strong and faithful, making
us rejoice.

Chorus
Onward, then and fear not,
children of the day!
For His Word shall never, never
pass away!

2. I the Lord, am with thee, be thou
   not afraid!
   I will help and strengthen, be thou
   not dismayed?
   Yea, I will uphold thee, with My
   own right hand;
   Thou art called and chosen, in My
   sight to stand.

3. For the year before us, O what rich
   supplies
   For the poor and needy, living
   streams shall rise;
   For the sad and sinful, shall His
   grace abound,
   For the faint and feeble, perfect
   strength be found.

4. He will never fail us, He will not
   forsake;
   His eternal covenant, He will never
   break!
   Resting on His promise, what
   have we to fear?
   God is all sufficient, for the coming
   year.

1499
We Speak Of The Land Of The Blest
- 8.9.8.8.

1. We speak of the land of the Blest,
   Of that country so bright so fair;
   And oft are its glories confessed;
   But what must it be to be there?
2. We speak of its pathways of Blest,
   Of its watts decked with Jewels
   most rare. .
   Its wonders and pleasures untold;
   But what must it be to be there?

3. We speak of its freedom from sin,
   From sorrow, temptation, and care,
   From trials without and within;
   But what must it be to be there.

4. We speak of its Anthems of praise,
   With which we can never compare,
   The sweetest oh earth we can
   raise,
   But what must it be to be there.

5. We speak of its service of love
   Of the robes which the glorified
   wear,
   The Church of the First-bonrabove;
   But what must it be to be there.

6. Do Thou. Lord, 'midst pleasure of
   woe,
   Still for Heaven our spirits prepare;
   And shortly we also shall know,
   And feel what it is to be there.

1500
Mighty Is The Lord

1. Mighty is the Lord, our God give
   praise to His great name,
   Saints of earth, and hosts of heav'n
   proclaim abroad His fame;
   Come rejoicing. shout "Hosanna"
   that all men might see;
   Mighty is the Lord who lives
   eternally.

Chorus
Mighty is the lord, the Lord who
dwells in the heavens
Mighty is the gracious Lord who
rules o'er the sea;
Mighty is the Lord of Hosts who
doth never slumber,
Mighty is the Lord who lives
eternally.

2. Holy is the Lord of Hosts, whose
   reign shall never cease,
   He can save the fallen race and
   give His servants peace;
   All the earth should sing His
   praises, for He makes us free;
   Mighty is the Lord who lives
   eternally.

3. Mighty is our God, Jehovah,
   wondrous is His grace'
   He is building now in heav'n, that
   we might have a place;
   How He makes us want to serve
   Him, His own people be;
   Mighty is the Lord who fives

GENERAL

1501
Hallowed Day and Holy

1. Hallowed Day and Holy
   thou holy day of rest
   We ought to give one full day
   to God, the good and kind
   Other days bring the tear drops
   thou wipes the tears away
   Thou art a day of gladness
   I love thy happy morn.

2. Hallowed day and Holy
   there is no work today
   we will suspend our labour
   Until tomorrow's day
   How beautiful and how bright
   Thou blessed day of rest
   Other days speak of troubles
   But thou give hope of rest

3. Hallowed Day and Holy
   Here how the Church bell says
   Give one day to thy Maker
   who gave t6 you six days.
   We shall take leave of labour
   To go and worship there
   Both we and all our dear friends
   On to the house of pray'r

4. Hallowed Day and Holy
   thy hour delights me so
   A taste of heav'n you give us
   Like that eternal rest
   Lord, let me be partaker
   Of rest beyond the grave
   To sing and serve Thee ever
   With all Thy saints above.
   - Unknown

1502
Where There Are No Years

1. In this world there are burdens we
   must bear.
   and our eyes are made wet and
   dim with tears
   There's no grief neither sorrow
   over there
   In that land where there are no
   Days nor years.

Chorus.
In that land where there are no
days nor years
Neither sorrow nor anguish or tears
we shall dwell there in peace and
our joys ne'er shall cease
In that land where there are no
days nor years

2. Tho' we toil oft our labor seems in
   vain
   we have faith tho' no fruit our vision
   cheers
   but the Lord will ail mystery make
   plain
   In that land where there are no
   days nor years

3. so we smile as we labour day by
   day ,and forget all our sorrows,
   griefs
   For when all earthly things have
   passed away
   We shall dwell where there ane.np
   days nor years

1503
IRISH C.M.

1. For mercies, countless as the
   sands
   Which daily I receive.
   From Jesus, my Redeemer's hands
   My soul, what canst thou give?

2. Alas, from such a heart as mine
   what can I bring Him forth?
   My best is stain'd and dyed with sin
   My all is nothing worth.

3. Yet this acknowledgment I'll make
   for all Ho has bestow'd
   salvation's sacred cup I'll take
   I'll call upon my God

4 The best return for one like me,
   So wretched and so poor,
   Is from His gifts to draw a plea,
   And ask Him still for more.

5. I cannot serve Him as I ought
No works have I to boast
Yet would I glory in the thought
That I shall owe Him most.

1504

IRISH C.M.

1. To Thee, O comforter divine
for all thy grace and pow'r be nigh
Sing we Alleluia!

2. To Thee, whose faithful love had place
In God's great covenant of grace
Sing we Alleluia!

3. To Thee. whose faithful pow'r doth heal
enlighten, sanctify and seal
Sing we Alleluia!

4. To the, our teacher and our friend
Our faithful leader to the end
Sing we Alleluia!

5. To Thee, by Jesus Christ sent down
Of all his gifts the sun and crown
Sing we Alleluia!

1505

Who-so-ever.

1. Who can find salvation free?
Whosoever will, whosoever will
Who can live eternally
Whosoever will may come

Chorus
Whosoever will may come
Whosoever will may come
Ev'ry one may have salvation free
whosoever will may come

2. So the Lord hath loved us all
Whosoever will whosoever will
So that if we heed His call
Whosoever will may come

3. Ever He is calling still
Whosoever will, whosoever will
Ever this, His holy will
Whosoever will may come.

THEMATIC INDEX

Holy Trinity

Worship And Adoration

Praise And Thanksgiving

THEMATIC INDEX

THEMATIC INDEX

THEMATIC INDEX

Acceptance And Repentance

Decision And Devotion

THEMATIC INDEX

THEMATIC INDEX

THEMATIC INDEX

Second Comming Of Christ

Faith

THEMATIC INDEX

Prayer

THEMATIC INDEX

THEMATIC INDEX

THEMATIC INDEX

Pilgrimage

THEMATIC INDEX

THEMATIC INDEX

THEMATIC INDEX

THEMATIC INDEX

THEMATIC INDEX

THEMATIC INDEX

ALPHABETIC INDEX OF FIRST LINE

ALPHABETIC INDEX OF FIRST LINE

ALPHABETIC INDEX OF FIRST LINE

ALPHABETIC INDEX OF FIRST LINE

ALPHABETIC INDEX OF FIRST LINE

ALPHABETIC INDEX OF FIRST LINE

ALPHABETIC INDEX OF FIRST LINE

ALPHABETIC INDEX OF FIRST LINE

ALPHABETIC INDEX OF FIRST LINE

ALPHABETIC INDEX OF FIRST LINE

ALPHABETIC INDEX OF FIRST LINE

ALPHABETIC INDEX OF FIRST LINE

ALPHABETIC INDEX OF FIRST LINE

ALPHABETIC INDEX OF FIRST LINE

Printed in Great Britain
by Amazon

41037872R00344